May 26 th 1896

congratulate you upon
outh. A telegram from
ormed us of difficulty
ll is on. During the
ff Sabine Pass, we pre-
en, and with considerable
The collier lay at
or tide. The Seminole,
chor on the (say, starboard)
t, by veering a long

Letters and Papers
of
Alfred Thayer Mahan

OTHER TITLES IN THE NAVAL LETTERS SERIES

Aboard the USS Monitor: 1862
Aboard the USS Florida: 1863–65
From the Fresh-Water Navy: 1861–64

Captain Alfred Thayer Mahan sketched aboard the USS *Chicago* in 1893
Courtesy of Naval History Division

NAVAL LETTERS SERIES

LETTERS AND PAPERS
OF

ALFRED THAYER
MAHAN

VOLUME II

1890-1901

Edited by
Robert Seager II
and
Doris D. Maguire

NAVAL INSTITUTE PRESS
ANNAPOLIS, MARYLAND

Library of Congress Catalogue Card No. 73–91863
Complete Set ISBN 0–87021–339–3
Volume I ISBN 0–87021–341–5
Volume II ISBN 0–87021–343–1
Volume III ISBN 0–87021–344–x

Printed in the United States of America

Contents

KEY TO REPOSITORIES
OF LETTERS AND PAPERS

APS	American Philosophical Society, Philadelphia, Pa.
BPL	Boston Public Library
CHS	Church (Episcopal) Historical Society, Austin, Tex.
CIW	Carnegie Institution, Washington, D.C.
CorUL	Cornell University Library
	Andrew D. White Collection
CROCS	County Record Office, Chichester, Sussex, England
CUL	Columbia University Library
	Frederick William Holls Papers
	Seth Low Collection
	Brander Matthews Papers
	Edmund C. Stedman Collection
	General Manuscript Collection
	Special Manuscript Collection
DCL	Dartmouth College Library
DUL	Duke University Library
	Samuel A'Court Ashe Letters
FRCS	Federal Records Center, Suitland, Md.
	(Transcripts of courts-martial in which Mahan participated)
HSD	Historical Society of Delaware, Wilmington, Del.
HSP	Historical Society of Pennsylvania, Philadelphia, Pa.
	Dreer Collection
	Gratz Collection
HUL	Harvard University Library
	A.T. Mahan Collection
	W.H. Page Collection
JHU	Johns Hopkins University Library
	Daniel C. Gilman Collection
LC	Library of Congress
	American Historical Association Collection
	Nelson W. Aldrich Collection
	Joseph H. Choate Collection
	Grover Cleveland Collection
	William Conant Church Collection
	John A. Dahlgren Collection
	Josephus Daniels Collection
	George Dewey Collection
	George Dewey Collection (Naval Historical Foundation—NHF)

LC (continued)	Felix Frankfurter Collection (W.H. Moody Letters)
	John Hay Collection
	J. Franklin Jameson Collection
	Library of Congress Archives
	Stephen B. Luce Collection (NHF)
	Alfred Thayer Mahan Collection (includes letters collected from various persons and places by the late Captain William D. Puleston, USN)
	William McKinley Collection
	William H. Moody Collection
	John Bassett Moore Collection
	Richard Olney Collection
	Charles O'Neil Collection
	Horace Porter Collection
	Mary Edith Powel Collection
	Joseph Pulitzer Collection
	Herbert Putnam Collection
	Whitelaw Reid Collection
	Theodore Roosevelt Collection
	Elihu Root Collection
	William Sims Collection
	Charles Sperry Collection
	Benjamin F. Tracy Collection
	U.S. Naval War College Collection (NHF)
	Henry White Collection
MCGUA	McGill University Library Archives
MHS	Massachusetts Historical Society, Boston, Mass.
	William C. Endicott Collection
	Henry Cabot Lodge Collection
	John D. Long Collection
	James F. Rhodes Collection
NA	National Archives
	Record Groups 19, 23, 24, 26, 37, 38, 45, 57, 59, 74, 78, 79, 80, 84, 153, 156, 217, 313, and 405.
NDL	Navy Department Library
NHS	Newport (R.I.) Historical Society
NMM	National Maritime Museum, Greenwich, England
	C.A.G. Bridge Collection
	William H. Henderson Collection
NWC	Naval War College Library, Newport, R.I.
	Alfred Thayer Mahan Collection (includes Mahan Family Papers)
	Naval War College Archives

NYHS	New-York Historical Society, New York, N.Y.
	Charles S. Fairchild Collection
	Naval History Society Collection
NYPL	New York Public Library, New York, N.Y. (Astor, Lenox, and Tilden Foundations)
	Anthony Collection
	John S. Billings Collection
	Century Collection
	Alfred Bushnell Hart Collection
OANHD	Operational Archives, Division of Naval History, Navy Yard, Washington, D.C.
	General Board File
	Z.B. File, Alfred T. Mahan
PAC	Public Archives of Canada
PUL	Princeton University Library
	Robert Mountsier Collection
	Charles Scribner's Sons Archives
RL	Redwood Library, Newport, R.I.
SCI	Seamen's Church Institute Archives, New York, N.Y.
SHSW	State Historical Society of Wisconsin, Madison, Wis.
UML	University of Michigan Library
UNC	University of North Carolina Library
	Silas McBee Collection
USNAM	U.S. Naval Academy Museum (includes correspondence of the U.S. Naval Institute)
UVL	University of Virginia Library, Charlottesville, Va.
UWL	University of Wisconsin Library
YUL	Yale University Library
	Knollenberg Collection
	Penniman Collection
	Pruden Family Collection
Letters in Private Collections	Identified, cited, and acknowledged at point of entry.
Letters to Editors	Identified and cited at point of entry.
Printed Letters and Excerpts	Identified, cited, and acknowledged at point of entry.

Note: All letters, manuscripts, notes, materials, clippings, photocopies, and other Mahan and Mahan-related data collected during the preparation of these volumes have been presented by the editors to the Naval War College Foundation for deposit in the U.S. Naval War College Naval Historical Collection in Newport, Rhode Island.

Letters and Papers
of
Alfred Thayer Mahan

To Stephen B. Luce

Elizabeth, New Jersey, April 4, 1890 [LC]

My dear Admiral: I have been trying for some time latterly to gather information as to the effect upon commerce of the wars between 1793 and 1805; not only in the matter of prizes taken and state papers in the shape of decrees, orders in council, and so forth but also as regards the modifications in the routes followed by trade in consequence of the ebb and flow of military control, especially upon the sea.

So far I have had little success. I do not mean to imply that I have not met hints and straws of information—clues in following up which I might find great pleasure, if I had abundant time; but what I want is to find the work, to some extent at least, done to my hand, the information garnered and systematized, and I thought I would ask you, if convenient to enquire at the Redwood Library[1] whether among old magazines or State documents, like parliamentary enquiries some such facts might be found.

I have started now to go through the *Naval Chronicle*[2] systematically— but I feel in view of the large task I have undertaken of writing up the naval history of those active years, from the strategic and tactical point of view, that it would be a waste of effort, considering my time, to undertake the tabulation of prize lists.

In 1794, Howe convoyed the West and East Indian fleets through the Channel with his whole force, and sent eight ships of the line with them across the Bay of Biscay. In 1799 the "very rich" convoys for the same quarters, for the Medn., for the Baltic, for Newfoundland, *all* sail with one or two frigates as their protection. In 1799, a large sale of prize vessels which bring "extravagant" prices, the victory of the Nile having secured the control of the Medn., the merchants are buying every ship fitted for that trade that they can lay hold of. From 1796–1798 hardly an English ship of war in that sea. What a pity the *Chronicle* only started in 1798.

There is another question on which your knowledge of naval archaeology may help me. When was the use of the half-hour glass superseded by time pieces? The tangle of the times in the various logs and other accounts of

---

1. In Newport, Rhode Island.
2. A British publication "Containing a General and Biographical History of the Royal Navy of the United Kingdom, with a Variety of Original Papers on Nautical Subjects." Volumes 1–40. January 1799–December 1818. London: J. Gold.

Howe's actions in 1794, seems partly due to the sentry forgetting to turn the glass.

I have been hard at work all the winter, reading and studying but have as yet written nothing except the account of Howe's campaign and the battles attending it. That of June 1st, 1794 is the only melee I have ever tried to represent by a plan, and a very troublesome job I found it. As yet, while I have, I think, accumulated a good deal of information, I have not succeeded in reaching any generalizations upon the course and mutual bearing of events—but hope light will break through the obscurity after a while.

The proof reading and plans of my book have retarded me somewhat, though I have tried to make up by working double times. All was completed, however, three weeks or more ago and I should think it would be upon the market some time this month. I am now afraid the McCalla[3] court-martial, if there come one, may catch me, as I am dangerously handy.

Please make our kind regards to Mrs. Luce and Mrs. Noyes. Both Mrs. Mahan and myself have constantly regretted Newport, which we would not have left could we have secured the music for our eldest daughter.

To Stephen B. Luce

Elizabeth, New Jersey, April 9, 1890 [LC]

My dear Admiral: I have received your letter and wish to express our sympathy with yourself and Mrs. Luce in her recent illness. Rumors that she had been in bad health had reached us, but nothing definite. I congratulate you both on her recovery.

I found in the *Pictorial History of England*[1] some account of English commerce at the period named and was by it guided to Macpherson's *Annals of Commerce*,[2] published in 1805, a copy of which is in the Astor Library. There are interesting and suggestive figures and a number of important isolated facts; but no systematic presentation from my point of view. A list of prizes made by the French, year by year, from 1793 to 1805 would be invaluable, and files of French papers of that date particularly

---

3. Bowman Hendry McCalla, class of 1864, was commanding officer of the *Enterprise* during her 1887–1890 cruise. Eleven members of his crew accused him of cruel treatment and unusual punishment, and a Board of Inquiry established to look into the charges led to a court-martial.

1. George Lillie Craik and C. MacFarlane, *Pictorial History of England*. 4 vols. London: Charles Knight, 1838–1841. In 1847 an 8-volume edition was published.

2. David Macpherson, *Annals of Commerce, Fisheries, and Navigation . . . from the Earliest Accounts to the Meeting of the Union Parliament in 1801. . . .* 4 vols. London: Nichols & Son, 1805.

useful. I fancy I shall nowhere find just what I want, which emphasizes the necessity of its being done by me; it is not strategy nor tactics, yet from my point of view essential to a full presentation of the maritime history of any epoch.

I thank you for your offer of speaking to Ramsay, but I think it will not be necessary. The day after I wrote you, I received a letter from Meigs, telling me about the appropriation and asking for my views about the location and details of the building. I seized the opportunity of suggesting my fears about the McCalla trial and a second letter from M. [Meigs] tells me I will not be ordered. This assurance may be modified by unexpected developments, but is probably the most that can reasonably be asked.

I regret with you the saddling of the torpedo course upon the College. It may, however, prove to be a benefit to the former instead of the injury I have feared to the latter. You know my general conviction that the admission of questions of manufacture and material is most dangerous; not so much in themselves necessarily, perhaps, but because the whole drift of the navy is to put its trust in material development, rather than in strategic sagacity and tactical superiority. For this reason I shall favor, as far as I can, assigning to Annapolis or Washington Yard all questions of advanced instruction in ordnance and mechanics or machinery of any kind; and with Ramsay's antecedents I am hopeful we may thus preserve the College in the main from what would be to me a most dangerous leaven.

To Francis M. Ramsay

Elizabeth, New Jersey, April 15, 1890 [NA]

Commodore: Your kind request to me to give my opinions as to the place and character of the building for the Naval War College, in case the appropriation recommended by the Naval Committee becomes a law, found me unprepared with any formulated views. During the time I was connected with the College, very small annual appropriations and a very gradual development were the most at which we dared to aim; and the design to give $100,000 was immediately followed by my own detachment, and the probability that I should have no further connection with the institution. You will, therefore, I trust, make allowance for any immatureness or incompleteness which may appear to you in the following suggestions.

As regards the site, the building formerly used for the College, and now by the Training Station, has the very best position on the island. It is partly sheltered, by the hill behind, from the North and North-West wind of winter, while it faces, and is fully open-to, the prevailing South-West breezes of the summer. The height above high water mark is not less than thirty feet, and the slope down is gradual, yet sufficient for satisfactory sewerage.

The building is too substantial, and has received too recent repair—is in short too useful—to be removed. It faces nearly due south; the front, which is much longer than the sides, follows therefore nearly an east and west line. I think that on the prolongation of this east and west front, or a little to the rear (i.e. north) of such prolongation, would be the best situation for the new College building. It would then share the advantages which I have already named, as belonging to the old building.

The space to the west is, upon the whole, decidedly better than that to the east. In the latter direction the ground falls away rapidly toward the shallow passage which separates Coaster's Harbor Island from the Island of Rhode Island. Built under this hill, there would be more shelter from the north and west winds, but the far greater advantage of the summer sea-breeze would be lost. The sewerage would have to go farther to reach Narragansett Bay, while to carry it into the shallow passage between the two islands would be suicidal.

To the west of the existing building the ground is of uniform grade till the shore line is reached, when there are bluffs. To the north it rises gradually, and slopes gradually to the south. There is, if my memory serve me, considerably more room than to the east, and that without encroaching upon the present drill ground of the Training Station. As regards the relations of a possible building to its surroundings, which should always be considered, a handsome building will show well there, and harmonize with the scene. On the east side of the island it will be hidden. The decisive features in favor of the west side, however, are more space, better sewerage, and the exposure to the sea-breeze.

I have not said anything about the situations north and south of the existing building. The ground south is now used for a drill ground, for which it is well adapted; while to the north, the crest of the island is soon reached. Beyond it the sea-breeze is cut off and the north wind has full sweep.

In my opinion, somewhere due west or nearly so, of the existing building will be the best location. If it is found that it comes too near the space now used for a ball ground by the apprentices, the lay of the ground will permit the building to be put a few yards further north, without inconvenience or the sacrifice of much shelter, if the ball ground itself cannot be shifted.

With regard to the character of the building to be erected, general suggestions only will be expected from me; the details of the plan will of course be settled by the Bureau and the architect, if one be employed.

My experience of two years and more, living in the former College building, led me to appreciate keenly the well known advantages of thick walls and comparatively small window space, in so isolated and exposed a situation. After the repairs that were at first in progress were finished, we never knew what it was to suffer from cold in winter, nor from heat in summer. The advantages in the matter of plumbing and water arrangements are also obvious; the pipes were never frozen, except possibly on one occasion in the attic before steam heat was carried there. Even then I doubt what was the cause of the break, which was not discovered for a long time. There will be real economy in very thick walls.

The rooms most used in the day time should, when possible, be on the south side, as generally warmer in winter and more airy in summer, from the prevailing winds. This is a matter of experience. The south rooms were at times a little difficult to warm thoroughly in winter, with violent south winds, without unduly heating the rest of the building. The wind seemed to force the outer temperature inside. Such winds are exceptional in winter, and with the prevailing north winds, even in the coldest weather, the south rooms were always comfortable. There were few days in which I did not have my office window (south) well open.

I assume that quarters will be provided for a certain number of officers attached to the College Staff. These I estimate as four in number, exclusive of the officer in charge, who used to be called President. I do not know exactly whether this officer will be attached to the College alone, or be in general charge of Coaster's Harbor Island, or of the Station at Newport. I append my reasons for requiring four officers, stating the general scope of the departments at the head of which they would stand.

I do not think it desirable that these officers should have permanent assistants in their respective departments. Considering the character of the institution and probable shortness of the course of instruction, it appears to me that they should alone be nearly sufficient for their work, and should seek such assistance as they need, in supplementary lectures, from officers on other duty. By this combination, of a permanent head devoted to the development of his department with voluntary assistance from other officers throughout the navy, the College will be kept in more living contact with the general service, be saved from too close routine methods, and, what is yet more valuable, will promote the mental professional activity of the service by such a diffusion of effort. If the Chief of the Bureau of Navigation approve, the Office of Naval Intelligence should be required to supplement to some extent the College course. The functions of the two are essentially and very closely related.

Besides the four heads of departments, a young officer should be attached as aid or executive to the Officer in charge. Preferably he should be a bachelor, for reasons which will be given; if married, quarters for his family should not be assigned. For medical and pay officers the College can depend upon the Training Station.

There will then be quarters for one officer in charge of the College, for four heads of departments, and for one aid to the Officer in charge. To these must be added accommodation for officers temporarily resident as lecturers, as has heretofore happened for periods varying from one to four weeks, and the arrangements for lecture room, library, and other necessary conveniences for the work of the College and for the officers in attendance upon the course. Incidentally, I will say that I do not think provision of quarters can be made for the latter. The majority will always be married men, and will prefer usually to have their families with them; while the presence of a number of women and children at that distance from Newport would, even if otherwise feasible, be a source of jarring and trouble.

My idea would be to have one set of quarters assigned to the aid to the Commandant *and* for temporary lecturers. During my presidency I arranged to receive the lecturers at my own table, and rooms in the College part of the building were assigned to them; but it cannot be expected that future presidents will always be willing to do the former, and it is not desirable that sleeping rooms should be in the College proper. A set of quarters, having bed-rooms large enough to be used for writing also, with dining room and parlor, would meet a need of the College, something in short like the Board House at Annapolis. It will very probably be found at the end of a course that there are officers who would like to follow up some line of professional enquiry at the College, and such quarters might for the time be available for individuals among them.

The College proper needs 1: a Lecture Room; 2: a Library; 3: a storing room for maps, plans, charts &c. not in immediate use; 4: offices for each of the permanent officers, one for the clerical work of the College, and at least one spare office, in all eight offices. The room for maps might be so arranged as to serve for a Board Room. There should also be, 5: a large apartment where officers attending the course can congregate for conversation and special purposes, when at any time detained on the island for an hour or two; as between lectures, or when practical exercises are going on. This room should be capable of use as a dining room when, as will sometimes happen, a class remains on the island during a day and needs lunch. For such a purpose, for the occasional lecturers, and for the additional cleaning entailed by the presence of increased numbers, a small force of servants should be employed during the session. If this room be adjacent to the quarters for the aid, the kitchen belonging to the latter could probably serve all occasional purposes.

The Lecture Room at the former building was large enough superficially, but had not sufficient height. It should be lofty enough to admit the display of maps at least eighteen feet high. The light should come from above. Inconvenience was experienced from the light striking in the eyes of either speaker or listeners, and if it had not been for the windows on the third side, the trouble might have been serious.

The Library in the former building was large enough for the books then on hand and for some time to come, but not to meet future wants. The Library should also have table or desk accommodation for officers of the class who wish to write, or to use the books in getting up any subject. In short, it should be a quiet study room for officers not provided with offices.

It appears to me probably a good arrangement for the Library and Lecture Room to have the height of two floors, that of each of these being determined by the necessities of the offices &c. distributed upon them.

A suitable number of Water Closets and Urinals are of course required for the College Building.

Two floors, with basement and attic, will probably be enough for the College proper. Heating apparatus, coal and other storage and the various wants of a building in the way of closets &c. may, I suppose, be left to the future architect.

The question of the distribution of the quarters of permanent officers and of the College proper belongs also to the architect. I am writing under the impression that the terms of the act will allow only one building. In that case the natural arrangement seems to put the private quarters at the two ends and the College building in the middle.

Accommodation will also be needed for a certain number of men employed on the grounds. The heating and lighting apparatus for instance needs tending during the night, and night watchmen may be thought expedient. Judging from my experience the men, even though residing in Newport and having families, often prefer to sleep on the premises rather than come out in the early morning. Shall such accommodation be provided in the building proper, or in an adjunct to it? These men will need also water closets and washing and messing place. There was an outbuilding, but in very bad condition, used for this purpose.

There is another question, viz: stabling. The College should not depend solely upon communication by boat with Newport. If a stable were put up with four stalls for the government, and four for the heads of departments, and with wagon space, it would be found a very great convenience. In the country a horse and wagon is almost a necessity. It would be understood of course that the government furnished only the stabling room and care of the building and horses; the horses would belong to the individuals and be fed by them. I presume that the commandant of the station would, like other commandants, be allowed his carriage and horses, and there should certainly be two horses for general use.

Hoping that these suggestions, which spring mainly from my own experience during three sessions of the College, may be of assistance to you, I have the honor to be [etc.].

To Francis M. Ramsay

Elizabeth, New Jersey, April 28, 1890 [NA]

My dear Commodore: I have received your letter of the 25th, and will with pleasure take charge of the correspondence you desire.

In the present state of things I presume the first thing will be to write to Jewell,[1] to explain why this step, though informal, is being taken. He is the head of the War College, under his Bureau, at present; and although I know he wishes to be free from the charge, he might not altogether like being ignored, if my correspondence come to his ears, as it can hardly fail to do. Would it not also, perhaps, be better if there were some understanding between yourself and Folger[2] before I begin?

The matter is not in any sense a delicate one, if I understand the present status. The Secretary of the Navy desires the change which the House has made, and there is little reason to think that the Senate will object.[3] Ordnance has never really taken hold of the College, and can have no feeling about its returning where it belongs. It is necessary that steps be taken by some one *now*, without waiting the Senate's action, which may be deferred for months. All this is too plain to allow of any sensitiveness being offended, but I should be better satisfied to begin by writing to Jewell.

I should like to hear from you whether you would like Soley's lectures on International Law continued. The series as given heretofore was excellent, having been constructed with special reference to questions likely to come before naval officers, and was greatly appreciated by the officers who attended, as well as by myself. My own opinion is much in favor of maintaining a course on this subject, which will receive attention nowhere else; but as the College is about to take a new, and we hope a permanent departure, it may be well for you to decide before this session whether you will give a place to International Law.

I shall assume, unless otherwise directed, that I may ask any of the lecturers of 1888, and I shall not exceed a two months course without your sanction. I do not, however think that we can do more than that. I shall keep the Bureau informed of my action, by official letters.

---

1. Theodore Frelinghuysen Jewell, class of 1864, who at this time was Inspector of Ordnance in the Bureau of Ordnance, which had charge of the Torpedo Station.
2. William Mayhew Folger, class of 1864, Chief of the Bureau of Ordnance.
3. On June 30, 1890, Congress approved the appropriation that transferred the Naval War College and the Torpedo School from Goat Island back to Coaster's Harbor Island.

To William H. Henderson

Elizabeth, New Jersey, May 5, 1890 [NMM]

My dear Captain Henderson: Our past correspondence, and your interest in the study of the military (and most important) side of our profession, leads me to ask your acceptance of a book just published by me, under the title of *The Influence of Sea-Power upon History*; a copy of which I have requested the publisher to send you with my compliments.

When I was first asked to lecture on Naval History at our War College, I proposed to myself at once the question, "How shall I make the experience of wooden sailing ships, with their pop-guns useful in the naval present?" The first reply was: "By showing the tremendous influence Naval Power, under whatever form, has exerted upon the Course of History"; the second, as I went on with my studies was: "By showing that the leading principles of war received illustration in the old naval experience, just as they did in land warfare under all its various phases during the past twenty-five centuries."

The present work is the outcome. The former motive, as probably the more popular and taking, is set forth in the preface; but the latter has been always kept in view while writing.

My wish is to continue the work through Trafalgar and possibly beyond but my power to do so will depend upon the content of the publishers with the pecuniary results. If, therefore, the book should commend itself to you as filling a gap, I hope you will give it a send among your people. I have ordered a copy sent to Sir G. T. Phipps Hornby[1] and to Admiral Colomb.

You will perhaps be interested to know, that, under our new administration, there is every promise of our Naval War College getting fairly on its legs again. I have great hopes that it will in a short time make some substantial contribution to naval thought, and perhaps persuade our people that naval matériel is not all the battle; that first-rate men in second rate ships are better than second-rate men in first-rate ships.

To Stephen B. Luce

Haverford College Post Office, Pennsylvania, May 7, 1890 [LC]

My dear Admiral: Before this can reach [you], you will, I hope, have received a copy of my book, which I have asked the publishers to send you.

1. Sir Geoffrey Thomas Phipps Hornby had been commander-in-chief of the Mediterranean Fleet, 1877–1880, president of the Royal Naval College, 1881–1882, and commander of the first evolutionary squadron in 1885. He was an authority on naval tactics and strategy.

It is not necessary to bespeak your indulgent criticism of either the aims or the execution of the work. You will remember that my principal aim has been to write a critical *military* history of the naval past, not a chronicle of naval events. If on calmer and more leisurely perusal, the work shall be found in any degree to deserve the favorable opinion expressed by some who heard the lectures, I hope you will consider what can be done to further the circulation, for the sake of the publishers and for the further continuance of the undertaking as well as for my own benefit. It is not necessarily, nor on the face, an attractive subject to the public; they must be led to the water ere they will drink.

Whatever usefulness the book may be found to have, the merit is ultimately due to yourself, but for whose initiation it would never have been undertaken. But for the impulse you gave, I should still have been contented to drift on, smitten with the indifference to the higher military considerations, which is too common in the service. It is, therefore, in every way fitting that you should receive this acknowledgment at my hands, and I wish at the same time to thank you for the start you gave me.

I am in this part of the country for a few days, but my address continues at Elizabeth.

To Benjamin F. Tracy

Elizabeth, New Jersey, May 10, 1890 [LC]

Sir: I beg your acceptance of a copy of a work published by me, called the *Influence of Sea Power upon History* which I have forwarded to your address.

The book had its origin in a series of lectures, delivered by me at the Naval War College, during the past four years, upon Naval History. The object kept in view throughout the series, additional to that which is implied in the title and expressed in the preface, was to lay a broad foundation for the study of naval warfare, under modern conditions, by a systematic presentation and analysis of the naval strategy and tactical methods of the past. A preparation of this character is uniformly assumed by military writers, and has the emphatic approval of the greatest modern soldiers; but there exists such a strong impression, that all investigation of the naval past is a mere groping among the dead, that I have felt the advisability of explaining and defending, even to a person of your broad and liberal views, the attempt which is embodied in these pages.

To Henry Cabot Lodge[1]

Elizabeth, New Jersey, May 19, 1890 [MHS]

Sir: Your interest in both historical and naval matters, as well as your position on the Naval Committee, leads me to ask your acceptance of a copy of a book published by me, *The Influence of Sea Power upon History* which I have forwarded to you at the House.

The work aims at being a *military*, and somewhat critical, history of naval events during the period covered by it. My object has been to follow, as far as I could, in the footsteps of military historians endeavouring to make the experience of the past influence the opinions and shape the policy of the future.

There is a very common impression that naval conditions are so changed, that they are practically obsolete for present usefulness. I believe that this feeling, which I once shared, is very erroneous. My own opinions have undergone much modification through careful study of the past. I find the same effect upon very intelligent officers of our own service, and the importance of such study is being increasingly recognized by foreign officers of distinction.

Nevertheless, so strong is the prevailing opinion in America, that I feel compelled, even to a gentleman of your literary habits, to advance an explanation for the length of which I beg to apologize.

To Francis M. Ramsay

Elizabeth, New Jersey, June 3, 1890 [NA]

Commodore: The War College being amalgamated with the Torpedo Station last year, it was commonly, and doubtless accurately, believed that an addition was made to the appropriation for the combined institution, intended for the additional expenditures that would have to be made at Goat Island.

There are certain drawings and maps lacking that are highly desirable for the College in its course of instruction; and if, as I confidently think, but little expenditure has been made during the current fiscal year for College purposes, the small amount necessary to make them might well be drawn from the supposed additional appropriation, by the approval of the Bureau of Ordnance, and thus spare the demands upon the appropriation for the

---

1. At this time Republican congressman from Massachusetts.

coming year; which may prove heavier than usual, being the first of a new departure.

The drawings alluded to are: 1. A Map of the North and South Atlantic Oceans, showing the principal routes followed by Commerce, and indicating graphically, by the use of colors or other suitable devices, the amounts of trade passing over different parts of the sea at different seasons of the year. The object of such a map will be to show in what parts of the sea commercial shipping centres, and accumulates, at particular seasons; and its use, for the objects of the War College, will be to illustrate the theory of the Destruction and Protection of Commerce, carried on in a systematic manner, as a well-concerted operation of war. It is evidently one of the College's aims to familiarize the minds of naval officers with the methods, and to set before them well-devised plans, for protecting our own commerce, when we have one, and for harassing that of an enemy in the most efficient manner. It will be desirable, if the data are at hand in the Intelligence Office, to extend such a map to the entire sea-surface of the world, within the latitudes used by Commerce; and it is evident also that the data for its construction, and the best ability to supervise it, should be found in the Intelligence Office. I estimate that its cost, on a scale suitable for the lecture-room will be in the neighborhood of $500, rather more than less.

2. Plans of the principal types of fighting-ships now afloat, or building, of our own or foreign navies, made especially with a view to illustrate their tactical powers or weaknesses. Lieut. J. F. Meigs made some such drawings, and is much more familiar with the details of the required plans than myself; and if you should approve my suggestion, I would ask you to call upon him for more particular information.

So also as to the map of Commercial routes—the subject is not one that engaged my own particular attention; but I heard the lectures of Lieut. C.C. Rogers on that subject, as those of Mr. Meigs on the tactical features of ships. I am entirely convinced of the value of the lectures, and of the necessity of the drawings; and if I am not mistaken as to the current appropriation, it is quite right that it should be called upon in order to spare the next one.

To Francis M. Ramsay

Elizabeth, New Jersey, June 22, 1890 [NA]

Commodore: I respectfully request permission to change my residence and address to Newport R. I.

To Francis M. Ramsay

Newport, Rhode Island, July 3, 1890 [NA]

Commodore: I have the honor to report my arrival in this place in accordance with the Bureau's permission to change my residence. My particular address is "Hall Cottage, Merton Road."

I beg to say also that I am very short of official stationery; and if it should please the Bureau, I would be glad to receive a couple of packages of official penalty stamped envelopes and half a ream of official paper, letter size, half sheets. I have from time to time a good deal of miscellaneous correspondence to carry on under the Bureau's semi-official instructions.

To Helen Evans Mahan

Newport, Rhode Island, July 9, 1890 [NWC]

Do not read this till you are quiet *in your own room.*

My dear Helen: Mamma has told me that you had asked her how you could make yourself care for persons whom you do not naturally love. The question shows a recognition, on your part, of a feature of your disposition which we have noticed for some time, and concerning which you need some advice.

In the first place, my dear child, you must not allow yourself to be worried about this trait of your character, which renders you indifferent to most persons, as though it were a *fault*, or a sin, for which you are originally responsible. It was born in you, without your will. But while it is not a fault, it is a very serious *defect*, against which you are bound as a Christian to strive, as earnestly as you would against any other natural defect, or weakness.

You will notice that indifference to other people, the failure to be moved by their happiness or sorrow, though not as bad as hatred, or ill-will, to them, is nevertheless as much opposed to that charity, or love, which our Lord and His apostles dwell upon as the great distinctive grace of the Christian character. It is well to note this. Like yourself, I am naturally indifferent to others; and for many years I thought it almost something to be proud of. I did not meddle with other people's business, which is undoubtedly a good thing; unfortunately, in me it was due to the fact that I did not care anything about their business, whether it went well or ill. It is only very lately that I have realized that it is not enough to refrain from, and keep under, bad or unkind feelings towards others; charity demands

[13]

that we have toward them feelings of kindly interest; of sympathy; even of affection, in accordance with the relationship which they bear to us, as relatives, as friends, or as neighbors.

You have in your Aunt Rosie[1] a very good example of what this charity should be—in her affection for her mother. You know how devoted it is. I have heard her say that it is no merit in her to do all she does for her mother *because she loves her so*; and in that she is quite right, it is no *merit* in her any more than your indifference is a *fault* in you; it is a natural trait. But do you not see what a lovely trait it is, and how far better we all would be if we by nature loved others as Rosie loves her mother; not so much, of course, in every case, but having for every one a degree of interest and love proportioned to their relationship to us. That we have not, is because our nature is fallen.

Now as to the means of gaining this better nature, it is necessary to distinguish between your part and God's part. Your part is to give care and thought as to your loving duty to others, and then to try earnestly and carry it out. First of all in your home; next among your other relatives, then extending to others about you. For instance, at Bar Harbor, there is Grannie and Marraine. The former can go about but little, and though she has many friends who either from natural affection, or Christian kindness, go to see her, yet every little visit is an incident and a pleasure in her day. I know that she has shown such a very marked partiality for Lyle, that it is not to be wondered at she has lost the affection of her other grandchildren; but the evidence of her love for you is not the measure of your duty of kindness to her. Go to see her frequently, and not grudgingly or of necessity; remembering that God loves a *cheerful* giver. This is less hard than you may think; a moment of prayer and effort of the will will scatter all sense of inconvenience and reluctance.

But doing this, and such like things, though necessary, will not of themselves give you the spirit of love which you desire. They are external acts, though good acts; and are of the nature of those "works," of which St. Paul says they cannot save us. They are done against our nature, which seeks its own welfare or pleasure rather than that of another person; whereas that which we are to desire is that change of heart, or change of nature, through which we will naturally and without effort do right and kind things. By our present nature we seek self; by our new nature we shall seek the good of others. Here you may see the value of that instance which I have used, of Rosie's love to her mother. Rosie doubtless dislikes some people, and is indifferent to many; but in one particular she affords a very beautiful example of what our redeemed and new nature will be. She does her kindnesses to her mother, not because she ought to, but because she loves her

---

1. Rosalie Evans.

by nature; her acts of kindness therefore are not "works," but "fruits"; they spring naturally from what she is, and therefore, though not meritorious, they are evidence of a character that in this particular is lovely.

Such a change of nature, from indifference to love like this, is beyond a man's power. Works we can do, but change our nature we cannot. This is God's part. He requires of us our will and wish, which if we have we will doubtless do works of love; but do what we will, He only can change the heart.

Therefore, to become what you wish, to have kindly interest in and sympathy with others, you must: 1st do works of kindness; and 2d pray continually to God to change your nature in this respect and give you a loving heart. It will take time, but never despair of it. I believe you do try not to have unkind feelings towards others, but dont stop content with that; aim at having kind interest in them.

Both your mother and I think of you, my dear child, among your present surroundings. Your friends seem to be very kind and fond of you; but we cannot be without some apprehension, believing that they are in their aims and principles entirely worldly—living that is for this world, and not for the next. It is not for me to judge them in this respect, but only to caution you to be careful, and not allow yourself to attach undue importance to, and care too much for, the comforts and pleasures of this world. We are all too apt to do this, but particularly when surrounded by them, as you now are. The "deceits of the world," as the Litany calls them, are very pleasant, particularly in youth; but the deceit is there, for they are found on experience to be unsatisfying in the end. Yet the strange thing is that even those who have by experience found this hollowness, and even talk of their emptiness, still cling to them by force of habit. I trust you may escape their taking such hold upon you. Remember that life is not only uncertain, but that it is *short*. You may or may not have a life of average length; but even if you live long—at the longest, life is short; and long before its end pleasure ceases to please. At the end, but one thing gives pleasure; and that is a nature which, having been renewed by God, brings forth those fruits which are pleasant here, love, joy, peace, and which endure beyond the grave.

To Helen Evans Mahan

Newport, Rhode Island, July 20, 1890 [NWC]

My darling Helen: I am going to write to you on a subject which may seem somewhat strange, particularly at your present age; but it is one upon which you are sure to hear, probably already have heard, a good deal of light nonsense talked. Nonsense is not always a bad thing; but it is a bad thing, a great misfortune, when correct and serious ideas are never even so much as named, in connection with a matter of the utmost importance; when false and ruinous views pass current as true and reasonable. I am going to write to you about marriage.

It is often said that marriage is the most important incident in a woman's life; and yet, in the same breath almost, it will be asserted that marriage is a lottery. What a desperate view of life is this! that its most important event is to be decided by chance. But, on the other hand, what a faithless, what a wicked thing for a Christian to say; only to be excused on the ground of a thoughtlessness almost as culpable as unbelief. Can the same person believe that God will hear and answer prayer, and at the same time believe that He will not overrule and provide the marriage most suitable, to those who ask His guidance. Here, however, is the real root of the evil. Most of those who call themselves Christians, form their plans and their opinions of life, and go on from day to day, without asking God's guidance; and they are governed in their views of marriage by the views of the world, by the light foolish remarks of those with whom they associate. Money, good looks, a dozen other qualities desirable enough in themselves, are dwelt upon as the serious reasons for entering upon so serious a step. You will even hear some say that a man who leaves them alone, to go their own way, is the husband they would have—a married life apart from one another. Truly, when one hears such absurdities, one begins to see why, in the Bible, Folly and Wickedness are used as synonymous.

In one sense, my dear child, you are over young to think about marriage; I hope several ripening years, of growth in grace and wisdom, may pass over your head before that time comes to you. But you have reached the age when, whether I like it or not, you will be hearing and talking and thinking about this and such things. Now let me say to you: "Be not a child in understanding, in evil be a child, but in understanding a woman." Since marriage and relations with men must needs be in your thoughts, let all your thoughts in such matters be referred to God. Put yourself under His care. Dont, if you can avoid it, think or perplex yourself about your future; but do not be ashamed, at your early age, to ask Him that this may be His care. Ask Him that if He wishes you to marry He may guide you to the man to whose care He will entrust you, and whose happiness and home it may be your privilege to make. To be dwelling on and looking to marriage continually is morbid; but to be daily commending yourself to Him is but prudent; for, if you do not thus seek His protection, the momentous decision may come upon you unawares, and you may add another to the long list of unhappy souls, of whom it is written: "Lo, this is one who took not God for his strength, but trusted in himself."

And so also be careful as to opinions you may form. "Prove all things; hold fast that which is good." I have not set out to frame a set of opinions for you, and I shall not advance any here. My one thought now is to induce you now to begin and take a Christian view of marriage, which "is not to be entered into unadvisably or lightly; but soberly, reverently, advisedly discreetly and in the fear of God." To think that, with these words of the marriage service before them, there should be communicants found who enter on that holy state without ever asking God's guidance, and for low motives of mere money, or the attraction of love which regards not God's will. Truly to such, marriage *is* a lottery, and worse than a lottery. Were not God's mercy far beyond our shortcomings, marriage for most would be a lottery without prizes.

If you thus commend your future to God, He will surely direct it. You may not find all the happiness you would have, but you will have kept the course which shall bring you, yes and yours also, peace at the last. If you are to marry hereafter, the happiness of your future home, the well being of your husband and children, may depend upon the prayers you are saying and the thoughts you are thinking now.

July 21st. We shall be looking eagerly for your return, my dear child, for your absence already begins to seem long. You will find a very pleasant home and surroundings here, though very little society I fear—but after so much fun you will be able to subside for a while. Your mother sends you much love. I am sorry to write you only solemn letters, but I am very busy trying to get on with my work in hand.

To Charles H. Davis[1]

Newport, Rhode Island, August 23, 1890 [NA]

Sir: I beg to acknowledge the receipt of your letter of the 20th and, yesterday afternoon, of the sample maps alluded to.

I have examined the latter and they seem to me to be perfectly satisfactory in almost every respect. The few changes that I would suggest are confined in the enclosed memorandum, which I will ask you to submit to the officer in immediate charge of the work for his consideration.

[Enclosure]

---

1. Commander Davis, class of 1864, had been Chief Intelligence Officer since September 1, 1889. He was a brother-in-law of Henry Cabot Lodge.

Aug. 23d. 1890

1 May not confusion arise from the use of black to indicate *both* German and sailing routes, especially as the German is at times so narrow as easily to be taken for a line and not a band. The same objection is avoided as regards steamers (red), British being pink.

2 It would be a desirable addition to have the areas of the several colonies indicated by their respective colors. There is no object in distinguishing between contiguous colonies of the same nation, as Canada or Australia, but when bounded by foreign possessions, yes—as in case of Guiana or Cape of Good Hope or New Guinea.

In this connection I would suggest dividing Africa according to recent treaties, if they seem to be generally accepted while the map is making.

3 I would suggest showing the coasting trade of the United States by striking color, so as to show vividly its relative tonnage, and to impress at a glance our extreme vulnerability here, if without a powerful navy, whatever the harbor defenses.

4 The small area of the British isles, compared with the enormous tonnage that reaches them, suggests breaking the two bands off before reaching the coast, carrying them however far enough to indicate their point of approach. The map as sent me seems to fulfill this condition quite satisfactorily.

5 I will submit later a list of naval battles and their position, which I should like marked with crossed flags and perhaps with dates.

6 No other comment occurs to me now. Let me repeat my warning to be sparing of names when they crowd together, or otherwise tend to confusion.

I will retain the maps, unless their return be asked for.

To Benjamin F. Tracy

Hall Cottage, Newport, Rhode Island, September 6, 1890 [LC]

Dear Sir: Can you without inconvenience have orders of some kind issued to me? Those under which I am now acting expire shortly, and in writing to the Detail Office, I am fettered by your directions not to speak on the subject of which you spoke to me.[1]

The vague term Special Duty covers everything. I beg to submit to you

---

1. The Secretary had asked Mahan to undertake the preparation of secret contingency plans for naval war with Great Britain and other nations.

again my wish to be allowed to choose my residence, within reasonable limits, on account of my means, as I can expect no quarters.

I wrote to Ramsay on the matter of residence on the 1st, but I see in the papers that he has left Washington. I should not trouble you, but that I have to decide immediately whether to keep this house or not.

To Stephen B. Luce

Newport, Rhode Island, September 16, 1890 [LC]

My dear Admiral: I was summoned to Washington on Friday last, and had rather satisfactory interviews with the Secy. and Ramsay. They have decided to begin now with the College building, and Mr. Mackay,[1] the last appointed Civil Engineer, is to come here and consult with me as to the site and general plan. I shall be glad to have any suggestions you would like to make, for consideration. Mr. Mackay thought $100,000 would be rather scant.

Ramsay also told me that he wanted me to go ahead and take steps for next year's course. I fancy there is no expectation of any this year. The great difficulty now hovering in the future is to find scholars, from among the number of men now qualifying as experts in steel and the mechanical arts, who will care about such trifles as the conduct of war. Can you solve that conundrum?

[P.S.]   The plan we suggest will go to the Dept. and an architect for technical elaboration and adjustment. It will express the needs not the absolute final arrangements.

To Stephen B. Luce

Newport, Rhode Island, September 17, 1890 [LC]

My dear Admiral: I send you, under another cover, an article I have prepared for the *Atlantic*,[1] on which I would be glad to have your opinion. My doubts are mainly as to my exordium, on the first three pages; as regards its policy for my personal interest, in the implicit dissent from the dominant

1. George Mackay, a Civil Engineer with relative rank of lieutenant, had entered the service in April, 1890, and was assigned to the Bureau of Yards and Docks.
1. "The United States Looking Outward," *Atlantic Monthly*, (December 1890).

policy, and yet more as to the general question of naval officers dealing with questions which enter into present politics. On the other hand, there seems no reason why an officer, being also a citizen, should not express opinions on matters which are not merely politics, but affect the national interests. The connection between expansion of trade and other foreign policy seems to me natural and fitting.

My head has been tired and thick the last three weeks, so that I equally distrust my own judgment and shrink from the labor of re-writing. While my principal concern is about the pages named, I shall be glad of any criticism on the others.

To Francis M. Ramsay

Newport, Rhode Island, September 17, 1890 [NA]

Commodore: I beg to acknowledge the receipt of the Department's order of Septr. 15th, 1890, continuing me on my present duty until Sept. 30th, 1891.

I respectfully ask the Department's permission to change my residence, *on Oct. 1st*, 1890, to 75 East 54th, New York City.

To Stephen B. Luce

Newport, Rhode Island, September 21, 1890 [LC]

My dear Admiral: Mr. Mackay turned up day before yesterday, and has been hard at work expressing my ideas in a drawing, to which of course he will contribute the details of arrangement and distribution which I have no aptitude for.

As regard the demands of the College proper I find your views much the same as my own. But as to the Torpedo Department I have grave doubts. I do not see any reason why the College should undertake instruction in chemistry and electricity because charged with a Torpedo Department. Torpedo School is a very vague term. Moreover, there already exists a mile off the necessary plant; with what color can it be reproduced at Coaster's? I have been to see Jewell, and he says they will need their chemical and electrical apparatus equally, after giving up their formal courses, as now. I grant you the absurdity, of having the two plants, seems involved in the absurdity of tacking the Torpedo School to the College, for which Whitney is primarily responsible. Mr. Tracy has not had time to think over the matter.

My own opinion is that the first necessity is to supply, along with the College apartments, quarters for the instructors. The presence, and mutual association of those men, fitly chosen, will constitute the College, far more really than even the Library, Lecture and other rooms. You, like myself, realize that those instructors have first to instruct themselves, then develop their course, and next, together with the president, co-ordinate the different branches into a whole. Till then, you have no College.

In my letter to Ramsay, in April last, I based my scheme of building on the presence of four instructors, one of whom [would be] in charge of the Torpedo Course. These, with the president and an aid, would make six. I purposed one of the six sets of quarters to serve as the board-house at Annapolis for transient guests, lecturers &c, and for the aid. The dining room [to be] a lunch room [in] an emergency. The smoking room in the body of the College building.

Mr. Mackay thinks not more than four quarters, with the College building, can be put up with the money. The provision for Chemical and Electrical Instruction cannot be made without sacrificing any idea of quarters. I have looked over the two appropriations, for 90 and 91. The latter refers to the former, which in turn applies to an establishment where quarters, electric and chemical establishments already existed. My own opinion is that the latter should not be in the College building proper; but, however that be, we are confronted with the fact that the appropriation was framed for an entirely different state of things from that to which it now has to be applied. The only thing therefore is to make the best use, within the vague terms of the appropriation, to carry out its general purpose. To my mind, that is to be done by providing, substantially, the same we found in the admirably arranged old building with such additions as experience showed necessary, and to bring together around the Library and Lecture room, in terms of constant intercourse, the brains of the institution. In the Torpedo Officer the Torpedo School receives its recognition. There is no provision for the paraphernalia of the Torpedo—that is to say for boats for Torpedoes &c &c;—as for the preliminary instruction in chemistry and electricity, let the men come prepared in that. In fact, if they cannot obtain that at Annapolis or Goat Island they will not profit by any instruction in Torpedoes.

I daresay [illegible] would like to make a change. I shall not probably be in a position to have any say in the matter, but he should never with my consent come to any institution over which I preside.

With kind remembrances to Mrs. Luce [etc.].

To Horace E. Scudder[1]

Newport, Rhode Island, September 23, 1890 [HUL]

My dear Sir: I enclose the article which I undertook, at your suggestion, to write for the *Atlantic*. It has been delayed longer than I had expected by a kind of mental lethargy from which all, I suppose, suffer at times, and to which the climate of this place seems particularly conducive. I was also very tired by previous work when your letter was received.

I have submitted the article to my friend Adml. Luce, who, after approving it, says: "If I can have an advanced copy or two for a N.Y. paper, it is just possible they will review it at length, and thus call attention to it"; a suggestion which I leave in your hands.

[P.S.] After Oct. 1. my address will be "75 East 54th St, N.Y."

To Francis M. Ramsay

Newport, Rhode Island, September 24, 1890 [NA]

My dear Commodore: If the *Swatara*'s officers are coming home, permit me to remind you of a previous suggestion concerning Lieut. Rooney.[1] He is the very man for superintending the work on the College building, conscientious, attentive, painstaking; what he dont know, he will take pains to learn. He is also, as I before said, the officer I would choose for aid. His constitution, I think, is not strong; wherefore a station with outdoor work, not too heavy, and a healthy climate is desirable for him.

To Francis M. Ramsay

Newport, Rhode Island, September 24, 1890 [NA]

Commodore: Civil Engineer Mackay having reported to me on the 19th inst., we made two visits to Coasters Harbor Island to determine the proper site for the intended War College building, in accordance with your verbal order to me of September 12th. We both think that by far the best site is that mentioned in my semi-official letter to you of last May, (or April), viz: one hundred and fifty feet west of the building formerly occupied by

---

1. Editor of the *Atlantic Monthly*.
1. W. R. A. Rooney, class of 1874, had been at the War College in 1887.

the College. I beg to say that this does not represent a compromise of opinion, but was reached by Mr. Mackay uninfluenced by me.

As regards the plan of the building, I beg to remark that the Appropriation limiting us was originally framed to meet the requirements of the Torpedo Station, where quarters and a variety of other buildings already exist. The last Appropriation Act transferred the lump sum to another locality, where no such conditions exist, but without modifying the terms, by which the money was to cover "all expenses of designing, erecting, and furnishing."

In my semi-official letter before mentioned, I sketched out the various subjects to be handled by the College, and concluded that there should be resident a president and four other officers, (including the Torpedo Officer), constituting the faculty; and that it was desirable that there should be a sixth set of quarters, constituting a "Board House" for such purposes as that at Annapolis. The College will call largely on outside lecturers. There should be a place to put them, and this sixth house would also serve to house a junior officer, detailed as aid for executive work.

Mr. Mackay and myself agreed that the building should be planned to cost no more than $85.000, leaving $15.000 for margin and furnishing. For this sum he thinks that not more than four sets of quarters can be put up, additional to the College building. I have directed him, therefore, to prepare a plan for *one* large building, having all the College accommodations in the middle, and two wings, each of which will contain two houses for quarters. The requirements of the College and quarters have been given him, and he is to work out the details, in a plan to be submitted to you.

It has also been suggested to me by Admiral Luce that the Torpedo course will require electrical and chemical apparatus, and building for instruction. Remarking again that the appropriation was made for Goat Island, where these already existed, I beg to present a short argument. The electrical and chemical plant necessary are, and will always be required, at the Torpedo Station, as well as at the Naval Academy. It is impossible that government can intend to duplicate at Coaster's, what is to be found a mile away; and any strictly "post-graduate" scientific course should be taken at Annapolis, where ample facilities of plant and able instructors are found. The College is therefore entitled to expect in those who come to it, not students of chemistry and electricity, but men already qualified by their knowledge to go on with the study of the use of the torpedo in war, which alone properly belongs to it. The apparatus required for this will be rather of boats, torpedoes of different kinds, and other out door material, not to be included under a "War College *building*."

On the other hand, the essence of the War College is in the association of several qualified men for the study and development of the Art of Naval War, to be imparted afterwards to others. Each will have his specialty; but the harmonious development of the whole can only be had by close and frequent personal intercourse and discussion. For this end it is essential to bring them living together, by means of quarters, and close to the Library, already well stocked with works they will need. I think, too, it will be found in time that such a body will be most serviceable to the Department, by examining and reporting on questions of naval warfare for which their studies should give them special fitness. However that be, there can be no question that the development and systematizing of the Conduct of Naval War is the special object of the College, and that this can be best achieved by bringing together the men whom the Bureau shall choose for the task. Whatever might be done with an abundant appropriation, I myself have no doubt that quarters, as described, are the first necessity, for the reasons I have assigned.

To complete the organization I have suggested, two more houses are needed, which might be added to the wings; or a house for the president might be put up separate from the others. If an objection be made to the expense, the reply is apt: that one hundred thousand dollars was given by two Congresses for a station already in an advanced state of development; here it is voted for one that has nothing. With the two additional houses, the College will have everything in the shape of building that I can foresee for years to come; except perhaps a stable, which, if wanted, could be a cheap structure of wood.

On the other hand, if the Training Station go afloat again, the building now occupied by it, and formerly by the College, would amply fulfil all the needs of the latter for additional quarters.

To Stephen B. Luce

Newport, Rhode Island, September 25, 1890 [LC]

My dear Admiral: Mr. Mackay has come and gone; and I have reported to Ramsay that it is our unanimous judgment that the proper site, by far, the new building is due west of the old, about 150 feet from it, facing south. I have also recommended apartments for the College resembling the former, but the lecture room to have the height of two floors; and rather more offices, which can on occasion be used as bed-rooms for occasional visitors. There will be one bed room and water closet especially designed as such.

On either wing there will be a block of two houses, giving quarters for four instructors, including the Torpedo officer. The outside dimensions of the whole building: 200 x 48 feet.

I added that my calculations for the needs of the College has been—one president, four principal heads of departments, and one aid *resident*. The house to be used by the latter to be considered a board house, for the reception of occasional lecturers, upon whom the College will, and should, largely call.

Mr. Mackay considers the above the utmost that can be done now using $85,000 for building, and reserving $15,000 for margin and furnishing. I recommended that quarters for president and aid should be asked for; but added that, if the Training Station went afloat again, the old building would fully answer all demands for that purpose and board house.

In this connection, it is an interesting coincidence that Hogg has just written that the officers of the Training Station are to go on shore pay from Sept. 1889, thus incurring large forfeiture. This I had from Davy Jones,[1] while visiting the Station yesterday.

The above are the leading features of what is perhaps only a first approximation. I broached the subject of Electrical and Chemical apparatus, and argued that, with the two full plants at Annapolis and Goat Id., the College was entitled to expect of the men who came to it sufficient knowledge to go on with the use of the torpedo in war; that any apparatus for that purpose would be mainly of boats, torpedoes of various kinds, and other outdoor material, not to be included under the head of a "building." I now always interpose when the College is spoken of as scientific; claiming that war may pre-suppose science, but that in itself it is an Art.

Stanton[2] finds that the site will interfere with his drills. Are not men odd? Mackay and I measured the drill ground left, six acres; and the meadow behind where the hospital now is, ten acres. But they "always fire blank cartridges from the howitzers westward over the bay" & I suppose earth will leave her orbit if they fire them south west, from the sea-wall.

I recd. and am much obliged for your comments on my article. I cant honestly with myself, call Blaine a statesman; so I compromised on "public man." The railroad I was talking of was the Canada Pacific, not the Isthmian, but your misunderstanding led me to clear up the passage. It has been forwarded.

We leave here the night of Sept. 30 for N.Y.; where our address for the winter will be 75 East 54th St.

[P.S.] In my argument for quarters I urged that the essence of the College was in the association of capable instructors, with each other and a good library, in order to develop harmoniously the treatment of the Art of War, and then to impart it. This can only be done by providing quarters. The College building is accessory to the living staff and provides them the most favorable conditions for their work.

---

1. David P. Jones, Chief Engineer, who was attached to the training ship *Richmond*.
2. Oscar F. Stanton, class of 1855.

To Horace E. Scudder

Newport, Rhode Island, September 26, 1890 [HUL]

Dear Sir: I am glad to know that my article met your wishes and shall be pleased to accept any change in the title that may seem for the better. If you should wish at any time a fuller treatment of the political and commercial aspects of the Pacific and Central America, I venture to recommend to you my friend, Lieut.-Comd. C. H. Stockton, who has paid particular attention to that subject.[1] His present address is "U.S.S. *Thetis*, Navy Pay Officer, San Francisco."

I wish on my own part to submit a proposition to you. I am preparing a continuation of my work on *Sea Power*.[2] In connection with it I hope to treat two subjects, separately, in chapters. The first is the true relation of England to the wars of the French Revolution, and her consequent function in the general European struggle, with a discussion of the conduct of the war by her ministry. I am led to traverse, though not polemically, the positions of the Whig School of historians and politicians, represented by Goldwin Smith,[3] Gladstone, Earl Russell[4] etc, as to the "two Mr. Pitts," the justifiableness of the war, its policy etc.[5] Without claiming any original matter, I think I have here some originality in the point of view.

The second subject is the War on Commerce that marked that great struggle. For this I have collated a good many odd facts from obscure corners, and I think I can produce from the grouping of those facts a paper of somewhat novel interest, but I have not yet begun it. The former subject is tolerably well under way.

Would you care to have either of these for the *Atlantic*? I dont think I could undertake that either would cover much less than 30 pages of the *Atlantic*, occupying therefore two or three numbers, at your discretion; nor do I feel confident of having either ready before January 1st, because my time is much engaged otherwise.

It will be understood that while *offering* these for your acceptance, I do so at your usual rates, for I cannot afford, with the other demands upon me, to do any purely volunteer work.

There will be no *battles* in either paper.

---

1. Mahan probably based his recommendation of Stockton on the latter's lectures at the Naval War College. At this time, Stockton's only publication was a pamphlet on the U.S. Naval Asylum.
2. *The Influence of Sea Power upon the French Revolution and Empire, 1793–1812.*
3. A prolific writer on political and moral questions. He taught constitutional history at Cornell from 1868 to 1871.
4. British Prime Minister from 1846 to 1852 and from 1865 to 1866.
5. "Pitt's War Policy" was finally published in *The Quarterly Review* (July 1892).

To Horace E. Scudder

75 East 54th Street, New York, October 8, 1890 [HUL]

My dear Sir: I am quite satisfied with your proposition of the 3d inst. It is no more than just that you should see the papers before accepting them, and I myself shall work more freely than under the sense of a positive engagement to deliver by a fixed time. I shall not waste time, but pressure is distasteful to me and I cannot quite foresee how far, in words, my proposed papers will lead me.

[P.S.] On second thought I enclose a letter from a commander in the Navy[1] which you will perhaps be good enough to return me. The latter part refers to a subject in which I know many Germans are interested, though I do not know how far it comes in the range of practical politics, as yet, viz: the annexation of Holland *with its vast colonial empire* to the German Empire. Curaçao would be included. Will the U.S. stand this? However that be, as a possible, and important, subject for discussion by Americans, I take pleasure in dropping the germ into an editorial mind.

To Francis M. Ramsay

75 East 54th Street, New York, October 8, 1890 [NA]

Commodore: I shall have a good deal of writing, and probably also of drawing, to do this winter in connection with my work for the Naval War College. I would, therefore, respectfully ask that a desk be purchased for me out of the appropriation for "building and furnishing" the College. I have enquired in New York, and find that one of the kind and size I require can be had for $25.00, possibly less. It will cost but little to send it afterwards to the College, when the latter is established.[1]

To Francis M. Ramsay

75 East 54th Street, New York, October 8, 1890 [NA]

Commodore: I have been notified by Civil Engineer Mackay that he has ready preliminary plans for the proposed War College building, which

---

1. Albert S. Barker, class of 1863, who at this time was assigned to the Bureau of Navigation. *See* Mahan to Scudder, October 11, 1890.

1. Ramsay replied: "The Bu does not feel authorized to purchase furniture to be used in private homes."

it is desirable we should discuss together. I respectfully request, therefore, that he may be ordered here for that purpose.

I beg also to say that I have received a letter from a friend in Newport, who has some knowledge of building, to the effect that there is, in his opinion, a sufficient quantity of stone in the island, in the existing stone walls and in the old quarry, to erect a building such as proposed. In view of the narrowness of the appropriation to carry out its purpose, for the reasons given in my letter of Sept 25th, it would be well if Mr. Mackay were directed before returning to investigate the possibilities of the island in this respect. I will put before him, in that case, the views of the gentleman mentioned. If a large saving in material can thus be effected, it will certainly be worth while.

To Horace E. Scudder

75 East 54th Street, New York, October 11, 1890 [HUL]

My dear Sir: I return the proofs[1] today—corrected. From my point of view the title you have given is not very fortunate, for the United States seems to me, and to most military men, very far indeed from being on guard. "The United States Asleep" would, according to us, more accurately describe the real state of the case, nor do I think the title summarizes the gist of my paper. I know, however, that the question of titles has its own peculiar aspects of which you are a better judge than myself; and with the above comment I am content to leave the matter in your hands.

I know nothing of Barker's[2] aptitudes as a writer; indeed he himself is almost a stranger to me. There is no telling what a man can do till he is tried, and I think you will find a keener sensibility to the bearing of external events upon the interests of the United States among naval officers than among the same number of men in any other profession. I feel pretty sure that Barker could produce a sensible, readable paper on the subject, if he has given more than passing attention to it.

If my belief, that the United States is about to be forced out of her policy of isolation, is well founded, the age needs prophets to arouse the people. It is from gentlemen of your profession that they would naturally arise.

1. Of "The United States Looking Outward."
2. *See* Mahan to Scudder, October 8, 1890.

To Horace E. Scudder

75 East 54th Street, New York, October 13, 1890 [HUL]

My dear Sir: What would you think of the title "The United States Awaking," or "The Awaking of the United States," for my article? I would prefer the former as less sharply definite; the time may come, so clearly marked, that the future historian will adopt the latter as a chapter heading (like Sumter).

Dont trouble yourself to reply to this mere suggestion.

To Stephen B. Luce

75 East 54th Street, October 27, 1890 [LC]

My dear Admiral: You kindly offered quite a while ago to write to Laughton about some information I wanted. I dont like to trouble you; nor is there immediate hurry, but if you happen to be writing the following is what I want. Is there in any available form, tabulated or otherwise, the amount of tonnage entering and clearing from British ports during the years 1803–1815: showing how much was native and how much foreign; the values of the exports and imports &c. Perhaps the shortest way to put it would be: "Are there in accessible form returns of British commerce similar to that given by Macpherson's *Annals of British Commerce*?" The latter only come to 1802.

I want also any information about the losses of British vessels by capture, not merely number but tonnage; the numbers of privateers in given years the numbers of them taken, and the like information with regard to the chief maritime enemies of Great Britain during those eventful years. Macpherson gives none of this.

I dont of course wish any one to attempt to collect such data for me but only to know what books exist from which I might gather them myself, in whole or in part.

In the recent discussion in the *U.S. Magazine*, in which Ad. Tryon led off on the subject of National insurance,[1] there have been statements made which seem to me only half-truths as to the prosperity of Great Britain during the Napoleonic Wars; and as far as my own imperfect information goes I think many of the speakers had but a partial knowledge of the matter, and overlooked many factors of importance. There was also one very

---

1. Sir George Tryon, "National Insurance," *United Service Magazine* (July 1890).

definite statement by Mr. Hubert Haines, a lawyer, that Gr. Britain lost 10,281 vessels by capture 1793–1815. Such precision implies data; where are they?

I hope you have recd. the *Life of Lord Torrington,*[2] which was accidentally packed with our books. I returned it by mail. The numbers of the *Illustrated Naval and Military Magazine*[3] I left with Mrs. Evans to return you when you came back to Newport. Many thanks for both.

Mr. Mackay has about completed the plans for the College building, which will provide, though on a more ample scale, the same accommodations as the old building, and have four sets of quarters two on each wing. I hope to submit them to Ramsay by the end of this week.

To Francis M. Ramsay

75 East 54th Street, New York, October 31; November 12, 1890 [NA]

Commodore: Acting under your orders to us, Civil Engineer Mackay has prepared plans for the intended Naval War College Building, according to the data furnished by me as to the requirements. The plan provides a simple building, having the College rooms of all sorts in the middle, and on each wing two sets of quarters for the officers attached as instructors—making four in all. I have before explained to you my ideas of the general character of the course, and that there would be required quarters for a president, or superintendent, four principal instuctors, and a sixth house to serve, like the Board House at Annapolis, for casual official visitors and outside lecturers, and also for the aid to the president. The appropriation, however, will only allow four houses.

I examined the plans of Mr. Mackay when he visited me here ten days ago, and approved the principal features. There remained only some minor changes of details, not sufficient to require my seeing them again, which Mr. Mackay tells me he has introduced. His estimate for the building, including boilers and other steam-heating apparatus, is $90.000. I have made a list of the necessary furniture and find, by prices given either here or in Newport, that the furnishing can be done inside of $9000. As most of the prices are retail there would probably be a reduction on this sum, which includes both College and quarters.

There was a certain amount of furniture turned over to the Torpedo Station, at the amalgamation of January 1889, of which I presume a schedule

---

2. Probably, a printed version of the manuscript *Life of Lord Torrington* (George Byng) found in the Hardwicke Collection in the British Museum. It was written from Byng's own journals and papers.
3. *Illustrated Naval and Military Magazine,* a British publication.

exists. I was not then at the College. This embraced chairs for lecture room, a large library table, desks and other office furniture; as well as six or eight sets of bed-room furniture, including mattresses and springs &c. These would materially help our estimates; but, as the quarters furniture has been put in use at the houses of the Torpedo Station, it might be well not to inconvenience the officers there, if the present appropriation will suffice. I must add that there are also book-cases for the library.

Nov. 12. 1890

I found only today a letter from Mr. Mackay dated Oct 29th, which, having reached here while I was out of the house, was mislaid. I enclose it for your information, and wish to say that my estimate for furniture included only two mantels for each house, *downstairs*, and one for the reception room of the College. I do not think that with steam heat, fires ought to be needed in the bed-rooms; and, in the narrowness of the appropriation, it is not safe to count on being able to put in as many as Mr. Mackay has planned.

I take the liberty of remarking again, as I did in a former letter, that the appropriation $100.000 was originally made for Goat Island, where there already existed much more than is to be found on Coaster's Harbor.

To Francis M. Ramsay

75 East 54th Street, New York, November 5, 1890 [NA]

My dear Commodore: I am only waiting to hear from Mackay to make an official report upon the site and plan for the College Building. We have agreed upon the plans, and I desired him, ten days ago, to let me know when he would be ready to put them before you. He estimates the building at $90.000. I find that the furnishing, College proper and quarters, can be brought within $9.000. This provides only for four resident officers, in my judgment not quite enough. Six is the number I set, *including* superintendent.

Can you have sent me a package of large, official envelopes, and two of semi-official letter size? I have much writing to do.

To Francis M. Ramsay

75 East 54th Street, New York, November 7, 1890 [NA]

My dear Commodore: I wrote some weeks ago, to ask you to let me have a letter which I sent you last April or May, in which I sketched my ideas of the College Course. I hate to trouble so busy a man, but it will give me so much labor to grind it all out again for my present guidance, that I am impelled to ask once more. If it has been mislaid, then I will have to get it otherwise.

To Stephen B. Luce

75 East 54th Street, New York, November 15, 1890 [LC]

My dear Admiral: The status of the College building is this. The plans have been in Ramsay's hands for about a week. There was an accidental delay of a week, owing to a letter from Mackay coming while I was out, and being put where I failed to see it. Supposing he was not ready, I wrote Ramsay unofficially about the delay—and he *telegraphed* to Mackay at the Washn. yard. So I suppose he was in a hurry. A few days later I wrote myself to Mackay to know why the waiting, and his reply led to a search and discovery of the mislaid letter. There was otherwise, I think, no time lost that could be saved. What Ramsay is doing now I dont know. I saw Soley something over a month ago here, and he told me he intended pressing the College business, but what he may have actually done I have no knowledge.

As regards the Torpedo Course, I have written to Newell[1] asking him if he would like to take charge of that in its entirety—and expressing to him the same view I already have to you. I have also written to Stockton, and he has replied he would be very glad to take orders to the College. Newell has not yet answered, and of course no arrangements can be complete until confirmed by Ramsay. A similar invitation has been sent to Hanford[2] but he cannot be heard from before January. His term on board the *Pensacola* expires in the spring. If these all accept, they, with the president, would form the "faculty"; all for whom quarters can be provided, *unless* the old College building is turned over to us again. That would solve all difficulties. The election of an adverse House makes it improbable that we can get any further appropriations for building, at present; though I do hope Herbert will be promoted to a more important Committee.

I am much obliged to you for writing to Laughton. I have just learned how to use the Journals of the House of Commons, and am finding some very useful and I think interesting data on the points I named. But the

---

1. John Stark Newell, class of 1865.
2. Franklin Hanford, class of 1866, who wrote pamphlets on historical subjects and owned an excellent library on naval history, later given to the New York Public Library.

period 1793–1815, compared to the century and a quarter of my first course of lectures, is as "a year of Europe to a cycle of Cathay"[3]—and not only full of incident but complicated like a tangled skein of worsted. I think I am farther along than I seem, though it is much like pushing through a thicket; a little more light is the only sign of a clearing.

To Stephen B. Luce

75 East 54th Street, New York, December 20, 1890 [LC]

My dear Admiral: Thank you very much for Laughton's letter, which I return. I have hold of Porter's Book, which I got a clue to in my other reading, and will send for Norman[1] to the Navy Dept.

Will you enquire for me at the Redwood whether they have a book, by an author named Walsh, entitled *Letter on the Genius of the French Government*[2], and published in this country in 1810. Also, if they have any work on the Continental System, or Continental Blockade of Napoleon. I have collected a great many facts, and have had to study the subject very carefully, for want of any systematic treatise. There is only one pamphlet on it in the Astor Library—and that is of a most partial and inadequate character. I propose to bring it in, in a chapter (or lecture) on Commerce Destroying, to which it belongs; but the subject demands a book, and I am surprised if none has been produced, except that, as one man said, every one connected with or affected by it would be glad to forget that it ever existed. In its far reaching ramifications, its multiplicity of incidents, its effects on the populations, and on the course of events, it affords a field for a powerful and interesting work. But to produce it requires time and opportunities out of my reach. Of course, if found in the Redwood, I could not expect to profit by it until I come to Newport.

I wrote to Ramsay about the Lyceum Library[3] two days after I met you, but have never recd. any reply. He is a desperate man to do duty with, and all the more because you feel that he is not indolent but unable to catch up. He is in possession of all I can say about the buildings, &, I believe at my suggestion, has showed the plans to Meigs, who brought Bradford also into the consultation. Both of them have strongly advocated my views in

3. A reference to "Better fifty years of Europe than a cycle of Cathay," from Tennyson's *Locksley Hall*, line 184.

1. Charles Boswell Norman, *The Corsairs of France* . . . With portraits and a map. London: S. Low, Marston, Searle & Rivington, 1887.
2. Robert Walsh, *A Letter on the Genius of the French Government*. Baltimore: P. H. Nicklin & Co., 1810. The *Letter*, 253 pages in length, concerned taxation.
3. Probably, the New York Lyceum.

the main, c.f. as to quarters; nor have they intimated any divergence of consequence from the plans.

I have been thinking a great deal about the presidency of the College. Ramsay being what he is, I incline to think a more pushing & driving person than myself is desirable. His inertia appalls me. Writing is of no use, and I cant afford to go on and tackle him, even if he were a man easily moved. I will say to you also, in strict confidence, that I am unwilling to break up the arrangements of my family and go back to Newport for what may be, and should be, a short time. To break up and move, to give up an apartment which suits us and we might not be able to recover, to remain but a year or so, is out of the question for me. Next fall I shall be six years on shore and half way up the captains' list. Besides, the education of my children would just now be very unfavorably affected by my taking them away from N.Y., which I need not do, if I go to sea. Within the last day or two I have thought of Chadwick. He has not the rank we have often thought desirable but I believe he has everything else. He is highly thought of by the Secy., is a friend of Soley, and is generally looked upon as a very able man throughout the service. I understand he is likely to leave the *Yorktown*[4] in April, and if he took this duty, he could not only have it from the beginning of the new departure, but could look to a length of tenure which has an inevitable influence upon the elasticity of a man's action. I want to be allowed time "on other duty" to complete my present undertaking and would gladly, in order to do so, as well as from my interest in the College, cooperate as a lecturer to any extent he might wish. I have been rather disappointed not to recognize Soley's interest in the College by any evident manifestation. It certainly exists; perhaps now that the Reports and Estimates are in, and, as I see, the appn. Bill framed, he may turn to it.

I read with much gratification the reviews you mention, and had attributed the *Edinburgh* to Laughton,[5] from his correspondence with you and the exordium that I "was lecturer at the Naval War College." He mentioned several slight errors in my diagrams, but said, very justly, that I could not have access to the numerous sources of information attainable in England. I had exhausted all I could get, and considered myself fortunate to come off so easy at his hands, for he probably knows more naval history than any English speaking man living. Pity he dont produce a great work instead of piddling about in the byways of naval history. If he had, I need not have fallen into my mistakes and yet all that is best in my book would still have been worth writing.

---

4. A 1,700-ton, 230-foot, twin-screw, armored gunboat. Launched in 1888, she mounted 10 guns of various calibres and was capable of 17.5 knots.
5. The unsigned review of Mahan's first *Influence* book by John Knox Laughton is in the *Edinburgh Review* for October 1890, pp. 420–453, titled "Captain Mahan on Naval Power."

I hope very soon now to be able to begin writing on the new series of lectures, to become in turn, I hope, a new book. It is vastly more complicated a subject than the former and I feel will task my abilities for a clear presentation. I wish you were now president and I had but the one thing to do.

To Charles H. Davis

75 East 54th Street, New York, December 23, 1890 [OANHD]

My dear Davis: I send back your paper[1] because I think it, as well as my own, had best be in Washington for the present. Our differences are, as you say, of detail only. You have added to my paper, at the least, the special information as to the grain routes of Great Britain, and as to the vessels available for torpedo boats; besides other suggestions, either as criticism or of endorsement, which should cause the two to be read together. I do not feel convinced as to your arrangement of the 18 ships outside New York. By day light and clear weather, it would be perfectly conclusive; but even of an ordinary night, and much more in an obscure one, the flank ships would be unjustifiably exposed. If we had twelve ships inside, the only secure arrangement for *them*, would be to have an equal number in supporting distance before each entrance. Even so we, assuming the offensive, would have an advantage. Eighteen ships gives 17 intervals, or over six miles from ship to ship. The three ships on either flank would be over forty miles from the ninth and tenth, (i.e. center) of the line; i.e. nearly two hours steaming, if they close upon each other. But will the second and third ship *dare* to close upon the center, that is run away, till they have first ascertained the extent of the danger indicated by the firing.

As regards our influencing the grain routes through the Mediterranean, I feel also skeptical; but this admits of calculation, and I think should be gone into.

Meantime, I feel something more ought to be doing. I cannot press Folger. His duties are too important, his character for energy too well known, to admit a doubt that he will take the matter up as soon as he can properly. It is also evident that, in our present condition, the development of the material, ordnance among the rest, is a more urgent necessity than these plans as to what to do when we have anything to do it with.

While waiting for Folger, I think we might elaborate our suggestions to

---

1. A critique of Mahan's "Plan of Operations in Case of War with Great Britain." *See* Paper, "Contingency Plan of Operations in Case of War with Great Britain," December 1890.

[35]

the Secretary. One, I think, would be to form and classify a list of merchant steamers and naval vessels available for cruisers. The classification I would make depend, firstly, upon draft of water; though, upon second thoughts, it is probable most of them could enter any of our ports. My idea is, accepting *"dissemination"* as the proper theory for the commerce destroyers, to present a table, allotting them to the ports which should ordinarily be their rendezvous, and in which at any rate they would assemble at the outbreak of hostilities. Wilmington N. C., and the Delaware, will both be more easily used by vessels of moderate draft; and the former, from the dangers of the approaches, will always have advantages for those who have local knowledge.

A similar table, prescribing the number and names of vessels, on the lakes, that should be retained on L. Ontario, as soon as matters become threatening. This should be accompanied by a statement of the guns and fittings for them that are immediately available, and with a concise statement of steps to be taken at once to equip this force.

I would also suggest that a capable intelligence officer be directed to acquaint himself with the hydrography of L. Ontario, and be sent in the spring to make a personal examination of the ground about Sacket's Harbor and Chaumont Bay, and recommend the spots where batteries could be placed with a view, (1) to protecting the entrance, (2) to keeping a hostile fleet beyond bombarding distance of the anchorage chosen for these vessels. Other things being equal, points that require least artificial preparation should be chosen. I think the Navy will have to take care of the lakes by itself, though we might properly borrow an engineer officer. The question of hiring and organizing labor from the surrounding district might well be gone into; for we shall not need *experienced* diggers.

I think also, besides the list of *our* merchant vessels available for commerce destroying, a list of those Great Britain could spare for the same purpose is desirable. This list need not be by name, nor as precise as our own, but it would serve to determine whether Great Britain having coaling stations in Ireland, Gibraltar and Malta could so patrol the ground on either side of the straits, and from them to the Channel, as to make it impossible for our cruisers, having no coal stations, to remain there. In other words it is important to decide whether Great Britain could so control that part of the sea as to enable her grain ships to dispense with convoy. My *impression* is she could, but impressions should be subjected to the test of facts; and the necessary facts are: the number of cruisers that *each* party can put on the ground and the coal supply. On this side the ocean we have the advantage as to coal.

I fancy most of the above can be supplied from the files of your office; but I hope you will improve upon them. Meanwhile, I wish you would consult with Folger, showing him this letter if necessary, as to whether it would not be well, in the coming holidays, to notify the Secretary of the progress so far made. Folger could, for instance, refer to your letter and mine; and if the Secy. wished to enter into the matter, he could read them and Folger could add in verbal comment his own ideas.

Lastly, as I know the Secy wishes us to consider the cases of other foreign nations, I would submit to you and Folger, the advisability of our taking up *next*, and at once, Germany and Spain. I recommend them rather than France, because more nearly equal to ourselves, and because, with both, the ground of meeting would probably be the Gulf and Caribbean. France, in fact, would differ from England only in having to secure a base of operations near our own coast. In the existing inequality of naval strength we could not attempt Martinique nor hold Guadeloupe. Talk this over with him, and if you agree with me I will send for charts at once and start this matter.

[P.S.]   Did I, or did I not recommend you to read Adams's History of the Administrations of Jefferson and Madison.[2] If not, I do, and especially note how a state of unpreparedness, no greater than the present caused us to fill our belly with dirt. Recommend it to every purblind Congressman you meet, and to every naval officer.

Also can you have me sent a half ream of paper like this, and a package of letter envelopes (not official size).

To Stephen B. Luce

75 East 54th Street, New York, December 31, 1890 [LC]

My dear Admiral: I should like to see the book—Walsh on the *Genius of the French Govt.*—if, as I understand you to intimate, it might be sent to me. I would suggest that it would perhaps be safer, and no more expensive to send it by express, to collect here. Would you, in that case be kind enough to insert a memorandum of the time when it must be returned. I would also be glad to have Laughton's address. I have found among my notes—and forgotten—a list of British losses of merchantmen 1793–1800, taken from *Naval Chronicle*; and it differs so much from Norman's that I would like to know which to trust. I have now begun to write the chapter on the Commerce Destroying of the Wars 1793–1815; on which I have, as it seems to me, notes for a volume.

Among possible men for the presidency of the College, I have thought

---

2. Henry Adams, *History of the United States of America.* New York: C. Scribner's Sons, 1889–1891.

of two others—Joe Miller[1] and Bunce.[2] The latter I dont know much about as an unprejudiced administrator, but we have had some correspondence off and on, and I know him to be impressed with the fact that no attention is being paid to the question of how to fight our ships &c &c—and an undue amount, *comparatively*, to material. If Chadwick would take the Torpedo under one of these, it would be a good combination; but with Jewell where he is, I doubt his accepting a second place.

To Benjamin F. Tracy

75 East 54th Street, New York, January 2, 1891 [LC]

Dear Sir: I have received to day a letter from Adm. Walker,[1] asking me whether I would accept command of the *Boston*,[2] which her present captain is shortly to leave.

If, as I understand, the *Boston* is to remain on the North Atlantic, I should be disposed to say yes; but the confidential duty you have given me prevents my doing so, without knowing your wishes beforehand. The progress of that duty is as follows: I drew up a paper containing my views in the case of England,[3] and sent it over six weeks ago to Folger. He and Davis have considered it, and the latter has also put down his opinions. Folger is very heavily occupied, and has not yet intimated his readiness for a meeting; so none has been held. I anticipate very little divergence of opinion between us. Seeing Folger's necessary delay, I wrote yesterday to Davis to send me data, needed to take up the cases of Spain and Germany, and the West Indies generally; so as to get matters further forward by the time F. has more leisure.

Walker expressed a doubt as to whether I ought to have the College; but my own judgment is that, as I should go to sea in any event, in a year or less, it is better that the building and organization should now pass into the hands of a person who will look forward to a term of years. I should recommend Chadwick.

I have been sedulously engaged preparing a set of lectures upon Naval

1. Joseph N. Miller, class of 1854.
2. Francis M. Bunce, class of 1857, at this time president of a commission to select a suitable site for a dry dock on the Gulf of Mexico.

1. John G. Walker, the former Chief of the Bureau of Navigation, was at this time commanding the South Atlantic Station.
2. A 3,189-ton, steel protected cruiser commissioned in 1887. The captain who was leaving her was James O'Kane. The *Boston* and the *Atlanta* were the smaller of the ABC cruisers, the *Chicago* being the largest.
3. *See* Paper, "Contingency Plan of Operations in Case of War with Great Britain," December 1890.

Warfare, in continuation of my former course on the same subject, since published. The very flattering opinion expressed, both here and in England, on the latter, have caused me to hope that I might make another substantial addition to the scanty miliary literature of our profession; but the prospect of sea duty that would keep me mainly on our own coast is an advantage I dont care to forego. If the *Boston* were leaving the country for two years, I should not want her.

As Admiral Walker requests a *speedy* reply, may I ask you to instruct me whether to accept or decline.

To Stephen B. Luce

75 East 54th Street, New York, January 6, 1891 [LC]

My dear Admiral: I am very much obliged to you for the book[1] which was received yesterday. I have nearly read it through, and will return it within the fortnight, having made a few extracts, to add to the already voluminous material I have gathered.

To Stephen B. Luce

75 East 54th Street, New York, January 14, 1891 [LC]

My dear Admiral: I have written to-day a letter to the Secretary through Mr. Raymond,[1] suggesting that the president of the College, like the Supt. of the Academy, should have the sea pay of his grade. On my own part I have rested my wishes on the fact that to leave New York will entail an extra expense, not to say hindrance, in the education of my children which I cannot willingly incur. I did not enlarge upon the fact that this education is not a matter of accomplishments, but of preparation for my girls which, in part at least, is likely to come upon them.

I added that I apprehend that there will be difficulty in getting *suitable* men willing to take the place, if it has no advantages over others open to them. This will be especially true if they are of a rank to aspire to the Academy or a Navy Yard.

Will you think over this, and if the Secretary approve, decide whether you could forward the attainment of this, or in any way help it.

1. Walsh, *Letter on the Genius of the French Government.*

1. Henry Warren Raymond, a newspaperman, was private secretary to Secretary of the Navy Tracy.

To Stephen B. Luce

New York, January 16, 1891 [LC]

My dear Admiral: I returned to day by express the Redwood[1] book you were good enough to lend me. It will contribute a few items to my next series of lectures and I venture to recommend it to yourself, as a somewhat unique contemporary account from a point of view we have little other knowledge of. I enclose the express receipt, and thank you for the loan.

Your letter was received this morning. I heard from Meigs a week ago that Ramsay does not want me to go to sea for a year, and I understand the Secretary feels the same; but there are some things that it is neither for a man's interest nor reputation to urge. I will not personally urge anything that looks to my remaining ashore for any considerable time; nor will I press the sea pay business myself, beyond the suggestion made to the Secretary.

I dont know what Ramsay is doing about the new building. I hear he still disapproves my plan, but has not yet any of his own; yet the advertisements for contract ought to be out now. What a pity that so upright, industrious and in a way able, a man should have so little power of covering ground; so little of the general's faculty.[2]

With kind regards to Mrs Luce and yourself from us both I am [etc.].

To Benjamin F. Tracy

75 East 54th Street, New York, March 14, 1891 [LC]

Dear Sir: I regretted exceedingly not having the opportunity of speaking to you about the War College while in Washington, as well as attending to the other business for which I was needed there.

Ramsay and myself are in accord as to the general aims and conduct of the College, but there is between us a radical difference as to the character of the building. He tells me he intends to submit the matter to you at once, and he impresses me as so far doubting his own ground as to be very willing easily to accept your judgment, if it should accord with mine. I cannot but

---

1. Redwood Library. The book was Walsh, *Letter on the Genius of the French Government.*
2. Secretary Tracy had held the rank of brevet brigadier general in the Union Army from 1864–1865.

[40]

think, seeing that four months have passed since my plans were submitted to him, that it is greatly to be desired that you should fix a day, summon me and, in consultation with him, settle the matter. Building could begin this month, but nothing is ready—the contracts have to be advertised and assigned; and prior even to that I think the *details* will need an architect's revision, resulting probably in considerable modifications, in particulars, while retaining the fundamental ideas.

The subordination in which I stand to Ramsay has kept me silent during this long delay; but the wish he himself expressed, that I should see you, justifies me in writing this.

In my plans I have allowed for all the needs of the lecture system, as I can see it in the light of my experience, and also for four sets of quarters for instructors. Ramsay says this will be open to criticism as being too much quarters and too little college. My reply is: There is all the college that can be required; but moreover the life and utility, the brains of the institution, will be in the faculty. The number four is not a guess. It is based on a curriculum which I have submitted to him. To properly develop the college course, the instructors must be brought together on the spot, for mutual consultation as well as for individual labor, as is the case in all educational institutions.

I shall not take up your time by a long argument. An hour of undisturbed talk can put you in possession of all the considerations. May I be permitted to urge upon you the great potential utility of the College to the service, and beg you to identify its start with your administration. The professional success my own book has had, in England and here, is due less to its own merit than to the utter barrenness of naval literature bearing on the Art of Naval War. Such as it is, it is due wholly to my assignment as instructor to the College. That you have thought to find in me a man suitable for the special work you have assigned me, is attributable to the same sole cause. In five or ten years, if the College be put in operation, you will have a dozen men as good and better. If it fail, you will still have able officers; but you will not know where to lay your hand on one from whom you can certainly expect, beyond the ordinary acquirements of a naval officer, a sound and well-digested knowledge of the principles of war. This acquirement requires the fostering care of the government, for which the College will furnish a channel.

If you decide upon such consultation as I suggest, a further subject for consideration at it should be the length of my tenure as president, which ought to be short, and the choice of my successor. I have on this suggestions to offer, both as to the man and the manner. It is a very important matter. I hope also you may give me an opportunity for fifteen minutes private conversation.

To Horace E. Scudder

75 East 54th Street, New York, March 25, 1891 [HUL]

My dear Sir: I send you today, by express prepaid, duplicate copy (manifold) of part of my intended book.[1] I estimate the matter to be equivalent to about sixty pages of the *Atlantic*.

I have prefixed a quotation from Fyffe's *Modern Europe*,[2] which in this book will close the preceding chapter; and which sums up the argument of which my paper is a development.

I believe I have brought together here, in a monograph, and placed in their relation to one another and in part to history, a series of events nowhere else similarly treated; and consequently lost to sight in the mass of other more dazzling, but really less influential incidents.

Mr. Henry Adams[3] has necessarily dwelt upon part of my subject, but from a different standpoint as affecting the U.S. rather than Europe. He begins in 1801, I in 1793; and it does not fall within his scope to trace the parallelism in action of the Republic and the Empire. I differ also from him and most Americans, in my view of the policy of Great Britain; so that upon the whole I think my treatment and subject rather gain, in interest, from the fact of his preceding me. There is besides a great deal of matter foreign to his work.

The manuscript is ready for the printer; and I have indicated where it can be broken into six parts, if that arrangement please you.

In conclusion I hope it is clearly understood that the copyright remains with me, for future publication in book form, as part of my work to which it is essential.

To Richardson Clover[1]

75 East 54th Street, New York, March 28, 1891 [NA]

My dear Mr. Clover: Can you spare me one of your printed Catalogues of Charts issued to European squadron? I want from it to ask some charts from you for my present work.

---

1. *The Influence of Sea Power upon the French Revolution and Empire, 1793–1812.*
2. Charles Alan Fyffe, *A History of Modern Europe.* 3 Vols. New York: H. Holt and Company, 1887–1891.
3. *History of the United States of America.*

1. Hydrographer, Bureau of Navigation, class of 1867. From 1887 to 1888 he had been in attendance at the War College, and from 1894 to 1895 he was Mahan's Executive Officer in the *Chicago*.

I mentioned to you in Washington my intention of writing you with reference to Meigs' suggestion that we might have a few lectures on the subject of winds and ocean currents connected with the next summer's course. The idea seems to me a good one, and I should be very glad if you think anything can be done in the Hydrographic Office to carry it out; but I should like to have the treatment keep in view the bearing of such facts upon possible military operations. I cannot do more than indicate the idea; but I feel very strongly that anything permanently adapted into our course there must justify its connection with the main idea of the College—the conduct of war. Such limitations are not narrow. The subject can be treated as fully as its importance demands, on its own account, and the military bearing of the facts given can be indicated either passingly, as they are brought forward; or else, more formally, by a systematic exposition at the end. That winds and currents affect the length of a voyage indicates at once that they have strategic bearing.

You know the uncertainties that surround me, and which have made me backward in asking this, or other favors; but if you can have this done, I shall feel much indebted.

To Stephen B. Luce

75 East 54th Street, New York, April 20, 1891 [LC]

My dear Admiral: You will be pleased to learn that I have a letter from Ramsay, that the Sec'y and himself are very anxious to get the building commenced; and the Secretary authorizes me to consult an architect. Ramsay thinks that if a suitable man can be found in Newport it would be better to employ him as being on the spot. I don't find these instructions quite clear, perhaps because of my inexperience with architects and I am rather chary about consulting a man whom I may not be able to employ. I have written him therefore to suggest that the best plan would be to advertise at once for plans and estimates, according to the usual contract system; basing upon the plans exhibited in department, but allowing any arrangements that will meet the same and with more economical or convenient dispositions.

Meanwhile I thought I would write you, both for the gratification I think you will feel in knowing a start is to be made, and also to ask you if you can make any suggestions that will expedite, and especially name men whom you have reason to believe would be among the best.

To Horace E. Scudder

75 East 54th Street, New York, April 21, 1891 [HUL]

My dear Sir: I received the packet of manuscript[1] and your letter on Saturday.[2] Your understanding was quite correct as to what I expected the length of the paper to be; but I found it impossible to bring the facts within the compass I had hoped. If my occupations permitted and anyone willing to publish I could write a book on the subject.

I have not in my mind at this moment any subject for an article, but in case any occurs to you as falling in my line of thought I shall be very glad to hear of it.

To Francis M. Ramsay

Telegram Newport, Rhode Island, April 28, 1891 [NA]

My address is care of Jewell Torpedo Station.

To Richardson Clover

75 East 54th Street, New York, May 8, 1891 [NA]

Dear Mr. Clover: Your letter of the 23d ult. ought to have been answered sooner; but I was away from home, and I have to do all my own clerking, so, with my other writing, my correspondence is always behind.

I would propose for Hayden[1] not more than five lectures—three would be better—of an hour and a quarter duration. They would be delivered on successive days, as far as depended on me, Saturdays and Sundays being excepted, and I think certainly not more than one trip to Newport. I have usually succeeded in running men straight along in the shortest possible time. As regards the stenographic work, if you will give me an estimate of the amount, I will submit the question to Ramsay. There is money, but I dont know if he will give it.

I am much obliged to you for your kindness about the maps. I shall want some but am not quite ready to say which. I should like now sailing directions for the Mediterranean; an *old* and worn copy preferred not to be returned (date immaterial).

---

1. "Pitt's War Policy" which Scudder declined to publish in the *Atlantic Monthly*. It was subsequently placed in *Quarterly Review* (July 1892).
2. *See* Mahan to Scudder, March 25, 1891.

1. Edward Everett Hayden, class of 1879, marine meteorologist in the Hydrographic Office and editor of pilot charts from 1886 to 1892.

To Francis M. Ramsay

75 East 54th Street, New York, May 11, 1891 [NA]

Commodore: I have to day received a visit from Mr. George C. Mason Jr., who has submitted to me the enclosed paper, giving the views of their firm concerning the construction of the intended War College building, and opinions as to cost; together with their own charges, which I know to be somewhat within the customary fees of architects. I will add that Mr. Mason says close personal supervision will be given to the work throughout by his father, who is resident in Newport; as well as by himself who is a frequent visitor there.

Under another cover I send you the elevation of the building, which is based upon the plans submitted by Mr. Mackay and myself; with the modification of two lecture rooms instead of one. Mr. Mason observed that the principal entrance stairway was more expensive and less convenient than one he could introduce; but that he had in this elevation conformed to the plans of the Bureau. I told him, subject to your approval, that his modification would doubtless be accepted, if less expensive.

I ask your especial attention to the closing paragraph, relative to using the stone of the island, now being freely taken by the City of Newport, without charge, for its streets and roads. There being a crushing machine, as well as the material, on the spot, will make an economy in the estimates of contractors.

The enclosed paper is simply a preliminary and outline, to serve as a base for the specifications; which Messrs. Mason will not of course enter upon until engaged. Mr. Mason desired me to represent to the Bureau the lateness of the season, and the advisability of beginning work as soon as possible; both on account of the weather, and of the better work put in by men in the long days. If no time is lost he thinks he can certainly get covered in by winter; but he will need ten days to prepare the specifications for advertising. I believe the appropriation does not expire with this fiscal year, but do not know.

The Bureau knows that I am absolutely without experience, public or private, in building matters, and I would therefore suggest that both the enclosed paper, as a basis for specifications, and the specifications themselves, should undergo further scrutiny than my own. Since seeing Mr. Mason, I notice in Par. 13, that it is not clear (though I think implied) that the steam boiler and piping are included in the estimate; and I should think it desirable that the steam pipes should enter the attic, which story, I may observe, is really an addition to the Bureau's plan.

With this possible exception, concerning which I will write to Mr. Mason, the enclosed propositions seem to me satisfactory.

I beg to submit to the Bureau's consideration that Mr. Mason Jr. resides in Philadelphia and will be ready at any moment to go to Washington for consultation in reply to letter or telegram. His address is "Drexel Building."

I also send by express a specimen of the Fall River granite, from Mr. Mason.

To Benjamin F. Tracy

75 East 54th Street, New York, May 12, 1891 [LC]

Dear Sir: I have been asked by Appleton's to prepare a *Life of Admiral Farragut*, to be ready this year; and I have consented, understanding from you and Ramsay that it was not the Department's wish I should go to sea in that time. I think I may also thus find room to say something for the Navy. If you disapprove, will you let me know shortly?

The architect yesterday sent me plans and estimate for the College building, and urged as rapid dispatch as possible, that he might get covered in by winter. I forwarded them at once, after examination, to Ramsay.

To Francis M. Ramsay

New York, May 12, 1891 [NA]

Commodore: I write only a line to catch the mail, and say that I have this evening received from Mr. Mason a letter in reference to Par. 13 of their estimate, to the effect that the apparatus for steam heating and all fittings connected therewith are included in the estimate, as presented.

To Francis M. Ramsay

New York, May 19, 1891 [NA]

Commodore: I beg to acknowledge the receipt of your letter of yesterday, enclosing one to Messrs. Geo. C. Mason and Son, of Newport. The latter has been forwarded according to your directions.

To Bouverie F. Clark[1]

New York, May 22, 1891 [LC]

My dear Clark: I was delighted to hear from you again and of course very much pleased at the kind things you said about my book. It has met with a very gratifying reception in England much more so than in our country—which I rather anticipated if it had any success at all. Our people are interested in other matters and unless one can tickle the national vanity, army and navy affairs are little regarded.

I congratulate you upon getting in so much sea-service. It is rather unusual, I think, to get afloat so soon after promotion as you did. I have been on shore ever since I came back from the old station—not idling, far from it—busier than I ever was before in my life; but it is a nuisance, and I think worse, a mistake, for a man to go to sea again at fifty, after five years on terra firma. I talk about retiring when our law allows, five years hence—the decision, however, will turn upon family interests which have yet to take shape.

The Chilians have disappointed every one. I only have a compensation. I ventured some predictions as to the result of the Latin-American incapacity for governing themselves; and just as I was about to publish the beggars settled down and behaved with remarkable decency for some time. However, as the book was in press, they broke out again from Guatemala down to Buenos Ayres; and when Chili joined in the riot the case was made, for it is always open to say during my life, why look at Chili; after thirty years quiet the blood was too strong etc. I *am* sorry for them however; such doings are bad for all hands.

I dont see any likelihood of my coming your way. A man with a family and small means is pretty well anchored and that is my fix. Unless my next ship takes me across I am not likely to go. The line of study I took up after my return and which found shape in my book has rather inclined our present government to keep me at hand, but the change two years hence will likely enough leave me out in the cold.

I suppose you may have heard that Cook[2] has been losing one wife and getting another, a reasonable interval passing between the two events, which I put in rather sharp proximity. I have not seen number two, but hear she is neither young nor fair, but has a modicum of substantial merits that are worthy of consideration in middle life.

You may possibly hear of me again as an author in the coming twelve-

---

1. Captain Clark, RN, whom Mahan knew from his tour in the *Wachusett* on the Pacific Station.
2. Probably, Augustus Paul Cooke, who commanded the *Lackawanna* on the Pacific Station during Mahan's tour.

month, as I am pretty well on with a continuation to Trafalgar. The period thence to 1812 I run over hastily, and when this book is done I shall want a rest; the former is nothing to it in point of work.

Wishing you all sorts of good luck I am [etc.].

To Richardson Clover

75 East 54th Street, New York, May 24, 1891 [NA]

Dear Mr. Clover: I wrote you nearly a fortnight ago about Hayden's proposed lectures,[1] asking you to let me know just what was wanted (as near as may be) in clerical assistance that I might submit it to Ramsay. Did you get the letter?

To Richardson Clover

75 East 54th Street, New York, May 25, 1891 [NA]

Sir: May I ask of you the favor to send me, in connection with my work for the Naval War College, sailing directions for the Mediterranean, giving wind and weather; and also the following Charts viz: B.A. 790; 2115; 2630; 2681.

It will greatly convenience me if the charts could be mailed at once.

To Richardson Clover

New York, May 27, 1891 [NA]

My dear Mr. Clover: I have written today to Ramsay, recommending the employment of the stenographer and asking him to send for you in the matter. If you happen in his office the day this comes, or the next, he may think to speak.

The charts I asked for came this morning. Many thanks.

---

1. *See* Mahan to Clover, May 8, 1891.

To Endicott Peabody[1]

75 East 54th Street, New York, May 31, 1891 [HUL]

My dear Sir: Mrs. Mahan tells me she has heard, that you find boys coming from the tuition of Mr. Lyon, in this city, to compare favorably with those from other schools here. I trust that our hope of sending our boy[2] to you in time, may be my excuse for asking if you could advise me in this matter in favor of Mr. Lyon, or any other. Do you know anything of a Mr. F. G. Ireland, a graduate of Harvard?

It is perhaps well to say I shall regard any opinion you express, as entirely ex officio and confidential.

To Francis M. Ramsay

New York, June 6, 1891 [NA]

My dear Commodore: I have received today from the Masons[1] an appointment to meet them in this city on Tuesday, when they will submit the plans and specifications, after discussing which I shall forward them to you. I hope therefore you may receive them on Wednesday.

The enclosed was received three days ago. I did not think necessary to make a letter of it, and its contents will be embodied in the plans.

To Richardson Clover

75 East 54th Street, New York, June 9, 1891 [NA]

Dear Mr. Clover: Can you send me Sailing Directions with the wind and weather of the Mediterranean? I need it very much, and can return if desired.

Has Ramsay said anything about Hayden's amanuensis? I have not heard from him.

[P.S.] I congratulate you that the question of being Hydrographer is settled.

---

1. Rector of Groton School, Groton, Massachusetts.
2. Lyle Evans Mahan.

1. *See* Mahan to Ramsay, May 11, 1891.

To Francis M. Ramsay

Commodore: I forward to you to day, by mail, the specification, accompanied by eight plans, for the proposed Naval War College Building, submitted by the Architects.

Having examined them, I see nothing to which it appears necessary especially to draw the Bureau's attention, except the following:

On pages 3 and 4, permission is conceded to the contractor to use stone from the island quarries for certain purposes, and also water from a specified source. This water supply is *not* from the reservoir, but from a well, little used, which stands near the south-east corner of the present principal building. The quarries are those now being freely used by the city of Newport. I see no objections whatever to the concessions, but draw the Bureau's attention to them.

The architects request me to ask the Bureau's consideration of the following points:

1. On the plan showing drawings for windows, there is sketched *in pencil*, on the pediment of the Dormer Windows, an ornamental device. The architects wish to know if the Bureau approves either of those there sketched, or will prefer some other. This is merely a question of taste.

2. The architects recommend that, when the plans and specifications have been approved, with such alterations as the Bureau prescribes, that copies be on exhibition at their offices in Philadelphia and Newport, and such other place, or places, as the Bureau may direct. They recommend that copies to be taken away be not furnished to persons thinking of bidding; as in such cases they are often taken idly, with no serious purpose, therefore necessitating an indefinite number of copies.

3. The third point does not concern the building in itself, but does concern the effect upon it produced by the character of the site. Owing to the rapid slope from rear to front, even with the corrected grade, in certain portions of the rear basement, the windows will be half below the ground outside. This will not obtain in all windows but in some. To correct this by raising the basement, would necessitate a considerable increase of wall; and make the front basement, when the windows are fully clear of the ground, disproportionately high. I may observe that this inconvenience exists in the present building, and is not very serious. The architects, however, suggest to the Bureau that it would be perfectly feasible, at the cost of a few hundred dollars, certainly not a thousand to remove the soil for some distance in the rear, so as to obviate this trouble. While thus removing, it would be well, they say, to incline the ground immediately in rear, so

that it should fall *away* from the building; so that, when meeting the slope of the hill, the two would form a gutter. This gutter would carry the water, running down the hill toward the building, to one side. This was done, (the gutter) while I occupied the present building, because the water thus descending found its way through the old masonry.

The Architects mention this, not because it immediately or greatly affects the building, but that the Bureau may be warned as to the fact. I would respectfully suggest to the Bureau, that the appropriation for current expenses would be available for this expenditure, which concerns not the building but the grounds connected with it. Mr. Mason, Senior, said he could in a very short time obtain for the Bureau an estimate from a responsible party for doing this work.

I have omitted to notice that the partial screening of the rear windows in the existing building has been less troublesome, because the basements there extend clear through from front to rear. In the plan now to be executed, the basements of the two quarters to the rear will suffer.

[P.S.] The detail Drawing for excavations and footings helps to illustrate the effect of the grade.

To Francis M. Ramsay

New York, June 12, 1891 [NA]

Commodore: I enclose herewith a letter and drawing from the architects of the War College Building, showing the excavations that would be necessary to the north (rear) of the building, in order entirely to free the basement windows, and provide gutter, as explained in my letter to you of the 10th inst.

Messrs. Mason now estimate the cost of such excavation at $1400 to $1500. As regards their suggestion of embodying it in the specifications, I have only to submit that to the Bureau; expressing the opinion that, as it is entirely exterior to the building, and not in any way essential to its construction, the cost is not properly chargeable to the building appropriation. The appropriation for current expenses, either this financial year or next, seems the proper one to bear the cost of changes in the grounds.

A contract might be made for the excavation, specifying that the ground removed should be deposited in such place as the government might direct. It could there be utilized for the grading necessary in the site.

To Francis M. Ramsay

New York, June 13, 1891 [NA]

My dear Commodore: It occurred to me to-day, thinking over the question of the grade in rear of the College building, that there will have to be a roadway around the building. Why would it not be a good idea to have such road, together with the necessary excavation as suggested by the Messrs. Mason, thrown into our contract?

I should think there could be no difficulty about the road-making going on at the same time as the building. A track for carts, bringing materials, will have to be marked out in any event; and the materials for macadamizing are on the island, and constantly used by the city.

Bunce ought, I presume, to have some say as to where and how the road should branch off from the existing road. Beyond that, its course will be dictated by the walls and doors of the building. The gutter should of course be beyond the road.

It seems to me that such contract for road and excavation not only can, but ought, to come out of appropriation for current expenses. Whether this year's can be saved, you can judge better than I.

To Francis M. Ramsay

New York, June 15, 1891 [NA]

My dear Commodore: I send by usual official channel to day a requisition for some stationery for the College. May I suggest that the most convenient ordering would be by Newport Purchasing Paymaster; to be sent to Stockton there.

The heat here is awful; so I fear you are having a bad time in Washington.

To Francis M. Ramsay

Elizabeth, New Jersey, June 22, 1891 [NA]

Commodore: I respectfully request permission to change my residence during the summer months, from July 1 to September 30, to Richfield Springs, New York. The work I now have in hand will be benefited by the change; and I shall be equally available, if the Department wish me for any other duty during that period.

To Francis M. Ramsay

Navy Department, Washington, D.C., June 27, 1891 [NA]

Commodore: Having reported to Captain R. L. Phythian, in obedience to the Department's order of June 25, as a Member of a Board[1], I beg respectfully to submit to the Department that the duty to which I am thus assigned is one for which I have, by previous study, no special aptitude; while it will materially interfere, from the complicated nature of the question before the Board, with my present work, for which I have made extensive preparation, and which, so far as I know, no other officer is at present ready to undertake.

Under these circumstances I respectfully submit to the Department whether it will not be well to substitute for me, as Member of the Board, some other officer.

To Francis M. Ramsay

Richfield Springs, New York, July 2, 1891 [NA]

Commodore: I have to report that agreeably to the Department's permission, dated June 24, 1891, I have changed my residence to Richfield Springs, New York; and that my particular address here is "Care of J. E. Ackerman."

To Francis M. Ramsay

Richfield Springs, New York, July 12, 1891 [NA]

Commodore: I have to acknowledge receipt of Bureau's order to proceed to Annapolis and report on July 15th to Captain Phythian for board duty, and will proceed accordingly.

To Francis M. Ramsay

Richfield Springs, New York, August 12, 1891 [NA]

Commodore: I have the honor to acknowledge the Department's order of August 10, directing me to report at Annapolis, on the 18th inst, on Board duty, and will proceed accordingly.

---

1. The Board on Line Officers.

To Richardson Clover

Naval Academy, August 24, 1891 [NA]

Sir: I have the honor to acknowledge receipt of several charts, this day, and have returned to your office, by this mail, such of them as I have no need of.

To Francis M. Ramsay

Richfield Springs, New York, September 4, 1891 [NA]

My dear Commodore: I write earlier than the time suggested by you about the renewal of my orders, which expire on the 30th. inst., because it is urgently necessary for me now to make my arrangements about house and schooling for my family, which depend on them.

As you know, I have been continuously employed since my last cruise upon subjects connected with the War College, except the time occupied by the N.W. Navy Yard Commission. Since that expired, I have been occupied in preparing for and writing a series of lectures on Naval History, consecutive with those formerly delivered by me, and since published in book form. The material for the second set is now all in hand, and four-fifths, I estimate, are written. They will form a body of about twenty-five lectures—certainly not less.

My hope has been that, considering my long connection with this work, and the probably not far distant end of my shore duty, I should be permitted to continue on the same duty until wanted for sea service, whatever the decision of the Department about relieving me as head of the College.

Hoping this may meet your views and that my orders may be issued as soon as possible, for I must at once decide whether to renew my lease in New York, I am [etc.].

To Benjamin F. Tracy

Richfield Springs, New York, September 9, 1891 [LC]

Dear Sir: I wrote to Commodore Ramsay last week, asking for the renewal of my orders, which expire on the 30th. He replies he can give me no definite answer because I *may* be ordered to sea.

I am prepared to go to sea, when wanted; but it is important for me to know definitely whether I can settle my family in New York for this winter.

If I go to sea, I can do so. If the orders under which I acted last year are renewed, I can likewise do so. Will it be possible for you to notify me that I can count on one or the other contingency? I wont ask which. All I am anxious about is the settlement of my family, which presses.

My hope has been that I should be allowed to finish a course on Naval History I have been writing for the War College—for which about six months more will be needed—but beyond stating the fact, I have no wish to influence the Department.

I have written Ramsay to the same effect.

To Francis M. Ramsay

Naval Academy, September 24, 1891 [NA]

Commodore: Referring to my present orders, dated September 4, to proceed to Annapolis, as member of the Board on Line Officers, I respectfully request that when directed to return to my station, I may be permitted to change my official residence from Richfield Springs, N.Y., to New York City.

To Richardson Clover

75 East 54th Street, New York, November 3, 1891 [NA]

My dear Mr. Clover: Some time ago I wrote the Hydrographic Office for a copy of B.A. Chart 2630, and was answered that there was then none on hand.

Can you send me a copy now, and with it also B.A. 2842a, which I think will answer my purpose in the Baltic.

To James G. Wilson[1]

New York, November 17, 1891 [HSP]

My dear Sir: In looking over the plates in Farragut's *Life of the Admiral*,[2] and in my own *Gulf and Inland Waters* in Scribner's Series, I have

---

1. The editor of *Appleton's Cyclopedia of American Biography*, *The Memorial History of the City of New York*, and *The Great Commanders Series*, published by D. Appleton, in which Mahan's *Admiral Farragut* appeared in 1892.
2. Loyall Farragut, *The Life of David Glasgow Farragut, First Admiral of the United States Navy, Embodying His Journals and Letters*. New York: D. Appleton & Co., 1879.

concluded that upon the whole for the purpose of this book it would be better to take the plans of the battle of New Orleans and of Mobile Bay from the former work than from my own. It is not necessary to give the reasons at length for this opinion.

The map of the greater part of Farragut's command at page 52 of my book would be a desirable addition. If there be any trouble on account of copyright it can be obtained from the ante bellum report of the Mississippi River Commr., barring some entirely unimportant additions made by me.

Personally I think it would be better also to give the plans of Vicksburg and Port Hudson found in Farragut's *Life*.

To Stephen B. Luce

75 East 54th Street, New York, November 24, 1891[1]

My dear Admiral: I have just received your letter and must dictate my reply as I am in bed with a bad cold.

I quite agree with you that the head of the College ought to be appointed, but the great difficulty for him, as well as for me, is to get the Department to certainly pledge a class; everything connected with the Art of War is subordinated to the question of material. Navy Yard duty, Steel Inspection, Branch Hydrographic Offices &c. are vastly more important in the apprehension of the Department than the question of fighting ships in battle. In connection with the Stagnation Board I counted up the number of Officers on Shore duty, below the grade of Commander, and found it to be over 190. Neither these nor the Captains of Receiving Ships, nor any other Captains or Commanders, can be spared for so trifling a matter as that dealing with the Art of War. There is no question, however, that a man, whose special business it was, might keep the Department more stirred up in the matter; as it is, the real difficulty in inviting Mr. Ropes, or any body else, civil or military, to prepare lectures, is the uncertainty whether there will be any class to hear them. If a class were *assured*, I would myself ask Ropes. I, myself, personally should be prepared with an extensive course of lectures not only on the Naval Campaigns, but upon the Military as well, of the French Revolution from 1793 to 1805. Stockton will also, I hope, have some historical studies and I think among us we can get up a course.

Chadwick, I understand, is certainly designated for my successor but he told me yesterday that there was some hesitation to order him at once as there are certain Board duties which they wish him to attend to. I expect to see him in two or three days and will speak to him. I own to believing

---

1. This letter was made available to the editors through the courtesy of Rear Admiral John D. Hayes.

myself that if he is to have the College it is more important for him to be at the work now than to be on Boards. As for my going to sea, my position on the Roster in the last two years has been such as to make it a matter of probability and I have therefore been unwilling to take my family from educational advantages they have here on such an uncertainty. I will not apply *not to go to sea*, but I have said to the Secretary and to Ramsay that I should be glad to remain ashore until I have completed the course of lectures above alluded to; in which case if not delivered they could be published.

I have just finished a brief life of Farragut and I hope when published, that it will show as a military biography a value which I shall owe wholly to my College work.

I shall always be glad, Admiral, to receive any suggestions from you and hope you will feel that at any time you are at liberty to write to me about matters pertaining to the College or anything else. With kind regards for Mrs. Luce, Mrs. Noyes and yourself, in which Mrs. Mahan joins I am [etc.].

To Stephen B. Luce

75 East 54th Street, New York, December 11, 1891 [LC]

My dear Admiral: I have heard with profound regret of the great affliction which has befallen your family in Mr. Walter's[1] death. I had not the privilege of knowing him well, but have heard him most highly spoken of. Mrs. Mahan and myself beg to assure you and Mrs. Luce of our great sympathy and hope that you will at a fitting time say the same on our behalf to Mrs. Walter.

I enclose you a copy of a letter I addressed to Ramsay a few days ago, as to which I will ask your entire secrecy, except to Stockton who has already seen it. I think it for several reasons best that Ramsay should not know I have spoken of the matter to any other.

This morning I had letter from him, or rather from Barker[2] written at his request, saying he would give the recommendation careful consideration. At the same time he sent me word that I was on the detail to relieve Remey on board the *Charleston*.[3] Whether this has been fixed by the Secretary, or means only that he intends to name me I dont know. It will be something of a disappointment as I had hoped to complete my lectures and if not delivered at least have them ready for publication; but I shall make no demur.

---

1. The first husband of Luce's oldest daughter, Caroline.
2. Albert S. Barker.
3. Launched in 1888, this armored cruiser of 3,730 tons mounted eighteen 6- and 8-inch guns of the latest design. At 320 feet, and with twin screws capable of driving her at 18.5 knots, she was attached to the Squadron of Evolution from 1889 to 1892.

To Stephen B. Luce

75 East 54th Street, New York, December 14, 1891 [LC]

My dear Admiral: I received your letter this morning. My opinion concerning Ramsay and the dangers of the College entirely coincides now with your own. As regards him, my expression has always been that he overlays it like a young baby. I have however recently been reaching the conviction that Soley has not unnaturally become so absorbed in his own particular line of work as to smother *his* interest in the College. Of this a sufficient indication is that he wishes Chadwick not to be ordered at present, in order to be available for certain Board duties connected with his own sphere. Chadwick's interest I fear is somewhat perfunctory, and he inclines to refer everything to Soley. From the way he speaks, while always asserting his interest—and truthfully of course—I yet think he would easily abandon it at the slightest suggestion from the department of other duty.

The condition being critical, in my judgment the best and almost the only available step is for Senator Aldrich to go direct to the Secretary, representing the condition of the building as approaching readiness—and say to him that unless something is done at once there will be no course this year and if there is no course this year then the last chance under this administration is gone. The step to be taken (by the Secy) is to order a president at once, whose *sole* duty shall be prescribed in his orders viz: to arrange for and in a general way supervise a course for next autumn. If Chadwick is wanted for other duty and prefers to take it then let him step aside for the time at least.

As regards myself, *if* Chadwick prefers not to take hold at once I would be willing to do so—only I cannot for money reasons come to live in Newport before next summer. But Chadwick's rights must be carefully preserved, for I myself suggested him, and the thing has gone too far for him to be cut under. On the other hand he should either be ordered at once or give it up.

The Secretary I think is a real believer in the College and if Aldrich could see him and make the simple point that the president must be ordered *now* if the College is to live, I think likely he would do it; but Aldrich had better get from him that the orders will be issued at once, not next week.

As regards myself I think you will appreciate that I cannot move now without risk of being misunderstood—both on account of my advocacy of Chadwick and the imminence of my orders for sea. Besides, the recency of my letter to Ramsay makes it rather indelicate for me to write yet to the Secretary. If you think it would do any good for you to write to Aldrich, I see no other step now open—only he must go to Tracy not to Soley. The latter would be useless.

Will you before very long return my letter to Ramsay. It is the only copy I have. No hurry—only when you have finished.

[P.S.]   Please regard the fact of this letter as confidential except towards Stockton with whom I have no secrets as regards the College. Of course you are at liberty to say that you know, or have reason to believe, I would accept the presidency in case of Chadwick's not wishing to go.

To Benjamin F. Tracy

Telegram   New York, December 17, 1891 [NA]

Will report tomorrow before ten A.M.[1]

To Stephen B. Luce

New York, December 17, 1891 [LC]

My dear Admiral: It is needless to say how very proud I am of your compliments to me in your memorandum for Senator Aldrich. I beg, however, to thank you for them and to admit fully that it is to my association with the War College I owe whatever of the acquirements may with any justice be attributed to me. I do not see anything more that can now be done, in the uncertainty of Chadwick's movements &c. I have just had a telegram ordering me to Washington. What it is about I do not of course know; but I shall probably have an opportunity of talking over the College affairs, and I go with the purpose of getting something done, if it is possible to effect it. I shall endeavour to see both the Secretary and Mr. Aldrich about the College. The former I know has an appreciation of its value but he has been swept away by the urgent call for the development of the material. I hope yet it may be possible to make him see that the manner of using the material can be studied at the same time with the development.

I enclose the memorandum.[1]

---

1. Mahan was ordered to Washington in conjunction with the American-Chilean crisis of 1891–1892.

1. Enclosure not found.

To Stephen B. Luce

Navy Department, Washington, D.C., December 19, 1891 [LC]

My dear Admiral: I find the Secretary is away not to return for a week which I suppose means not till after Xmas. Aldrich is also gone home, I am told for the holidays. I write more especially on the latter account, to warn you that a possibility of seeing him may arise.

I have not as yet had any conversation with Ramsay; nor have I hopes from any that may arise because it is so difficult to bring him to a decision. I question also the advisability of talking to Soley. An order from the Secretary himself to appoint the president by a formal order, and as such and immediately is the first thing now to be done.

To Stephen B. Luce

75 East 54th Street, New York, December 26, 1891 [LC]

My dear Admiral: I ran on home night before last for Xmas, and am to return to Washington to-morrow night to complete the work on which I am engaged. Chadwick came on in the same train and I opened a conversation with him about the College, telling him among other things of my letter to Ramsay. I did not mention your name; but spoke of Stockton's restlessness and letter, and of the absolute necessity of a president being immediately ordered. He said that he felt himself to be drifting away from the work (which in fact he has never taken up) and that he believed the only (or the best) present solution would be for me to take it up.

This difficulty being removed there remains no difficulty to *me* in accepting the position if the Department offers it to me. But, whosoever takes it will have an immense difficulty to encounter in Ramsay. It is really painful to see a high-toned, honorable, industrious man of considerable ability whose greatest faculty is that of getting himself and every one else into irons; whose chief contribution to any movement not originating with himself is to tie its legs and add weight after weight till the back is broken.

I shall doubtless have opportunities of seeing the Secretary, and I shall seek the chance of speaking to him very plainly as to the unrecognized utility of the College. There has a disposition grown up to consider my opinion of importance (a kind of special knowledge) due to the reputation the book gained me. I remark frequently to those who make such allusion that, if

[60]

any aptitude exist, it is due wholly to my association with the College; that I recognize constantly the influence, upon my perceptions and upon the strength of my convictions, of my historical and strategic reading. I add that I also recognize the denseness of my ignorance prior to my joining the college; and that now, in studying problems of a certain character (notably the attack of a fortified port), chiefly *tactical*, I have to admit disadvantages owing to no opportunity for studying such questions. I bring to them no special knowledge of details, only a few general principles, & I have laboriously to apply these, and under pressure of time seek to solve difficulties, whose solution to a man who had studied before would be rapid. This amounts to saying that a single expert (if such exist) cannot now meet the wants of the government. Had Whitney's ignorant stupidity not stopped us three years ago, we should by this time have had some one who could take up a fortified harbor, discern the strong & weak points at a glance; and out of many methods of attack have in his mind the relative advantages and disadvantages of each—in short a man capable of sound and rapid decision, which in the particular case I am not. In a general way I purpose saying these things to the Secretary, for if I dont see him I shall make a point of getting this before him. I intend to insist upon two things—first the immediate appointment of a president and next a positive order that a class of at least *fifteen* for two months must be forthcoming for next September. Ramsay will say it is impossible to find them. To that I shall say to the contrary that the knowledge which it is proposed to impart is more important than the branch hydrographic offices, than the naval observatory, than the inspection of steel, or than the special duty of ordnance instruction in Washington; that captains of receiving ships have no duty which for two months their Executives could not do, &c.

Quoting instances of people not going to sea, did you know that Farragut did not go to sea from 1848 to 1858; and that the cruise ending in the former year was only a twelve-month? Consequently from 1843 to 1858 he spent but one year at sea. His is still a name to conjure with. It is true he had a genius for war & was also an improving man.

I would suggest that in speaking of my reputation, which seems at present the most obvious work of the College, it would be well to add how keenly I feel deficiencies in certain directions, not having had time to cover all points—which shows the necessity of gathering a *group* of officers who may cover the whole ground. Also, granting I have such important attainments as some think, they are due to the College; and how absurd that with so many able men in the Navy there are not dozens who possess the same. Excuse my appearance of egotism, for I really am not vainglorious.

To Stephen B. Luce

75 East 54th Street, New York, January 5, 1892 [LC]

My dear Admiral: I came home last night, having asked the Secy's permission because my expenses were far outrunning my mileage. It is probable I may soon be called back—but yesterday I spoke to him about the College, saying I had refrained from doing so before, knowing how much he must be occupied with the various aspects of the Chilian affair. He was in a very happy humor at the moment. I said the two absolutely essential things were the immediate ordering of a president, and the assurance of him that a class, of no more than ten, should be ordered this year. If this administration goes out, I added, without putting the College on its legs then there was no telling if it ever would get on them. He said, the two things *shall be done*. He forgets, however; and it is desirable, if Aldrich move at all, that he ask for the *immediate* issue of orders. Neither Ramsay nor Soley can be relied upon. I hear from many quarters that the latter is trying to scoop in almost all the business of the Bureaus, and in so doing irritates Ramsay's habit of detailed enquiry, swamps himself with business details, fears responsibility and postpones action. How far all this is true I dont know, but am convinced that he is too busy for any sustained interest in the College. Moreover, I think he has cooled very much toward me personally—yet, Chadwick having failed, I dont myself see just who, except myself, is temporarily available. The Secretary is the only reliance, and if I were Aldrich I should go straight to him ignoring the others. I said to the Secretary I shall take the liberty of reminding you of this as soon as the Chilian business takes certain shape. Of course I could not speak of myself in the connection. I did not see Aldrich who I dont think was in Washington. On Herbert I called, but purposely refrained from making it a business visit.

[P.S.] If you meet Stockton, will you tell him the substance of this. Naturally, it is best not talked about as it antagonizes Ramsay and probably Soley also.

To Francis M. Ramsay

75 East 54th Street, New York, January 9, 1892 [NA]

Commodore: I respectfully request that the following work may be ordered for the War College Library:
Strategic Geography, The Theatres of War of the Rhine and the Danube —Published by Edwd. Stanford, London.

The book, of 78 pages, is not only valuable in itself but will materially assist in the preparation of a needed map for the course of instruction. I would request it might be ordered immediately.

To Stephen B. Luce

75 East 54th Street, New York, January 10, 1892 [LC]

My dear Admiral: Your letter of the 6th reached me a day or two before that of the 4th which was forwarded from Washington. I shall very gladly take a hand in the conference you propose. Folger is a man who fully appreciates the value of the College aims, although he himself has taken up as a speciality one part of the material development of the service.

I wait impatiently and somewhat anxiously the outcome of the Chilian trouble. That their rulers are aware of the impolicy of forcing us to war, I am sure; but I doubt they may too much fear their mob. It is astounding that our government should allow matters to drag so, when there is a question of so formidable a vessel as the *Prat*[1] thus getting time to escape. We are so confident in our bigness and so little realize the great extra load entailed by the distance of Chili, in case of war. The ultimate result, I suppose can be little doubtful, but we may first get some eye openers.

I am liable to be called back to Washington at any moment. If I am, I will see Aldrich, if at all possible; but I a little hesitate to write under present conditions.

With kind remembrances to your family from us both.

To James G. Wilson

Navy Department, Washington, D.C., January 26, 1892 [UML]

My dear Sir: There has been a slight delay in the first proofs[1] sent me, owing to Mrs. Mahan's uncertainty in forwarding and to Sunday intervening. They will now I hope come straight along. I hope, if any expense to me attend alterations in the galley poofs, you will let me know; as I have had an unpleasant experience in consequence of such alterations in one of my works, and which the very slight improvement in the text did not at all compensate. My stay here depends in part on the turn the Chilean

---

1. The *Captain Prat* was a veritable monster launched by Chile in 1890; a barbette ship, steel-sheathed and coppered, 6,900 tons, 380 feet, with a steel belt 12 inches thick. She could generate 12,000 h.p. and cruise at 19 knots.

1. Of his *Admiral Farragut*.

business takes; but the New York address is best. Not feeling quite sure where to send the proof, I return to you. If it should go elsewhere, pray notify me.

To Stephen B. Luce

Washington, D.C., January 28, 1892 [LC]

My dear Admiral: I have just returned from a visit to the Capitol to see Mr. Aldrich, the first time I have felt at liberty to leave the Department for a long period; and found that he had started for home yesterday noon. He will not probably return before Monday, if then. It is less important as I could only say to him what I have already said to the Secy, and mean to say again—that it is vitally important to order at once a president to the College and engage to him that a class shall present itself next summer or fall. As regards myself I can not say more than that I will be willing to take the position if desired by the Department. It will, however, be pecuniarily impossible for me to go to Newport to live before next July 1. I have rented my apartment in N.Y. to Oct 1, and cannot possibly afford to take quarters elsewhere except for the summer months. I shall hope, however, that the Dept. will cover my going there occasionally by orders, as well as bring me on to Washn. once or twice to look after the appropriations. All this assumes that the Dept. will order me to the presidency, concerning which I know nothing. As I wrote you before, the Secretary said to me positively that the president should be ordered when the Chilian business was off, and that a class should be forthcoming. What will be wanted will be for Aldrich to support this decision by his own personal urgency. This is Mr. Tracy's last opportunity; and if it go unimproved there can be no telling what we will get from another administration. The prevalent opinion here seems to be that the war is now wholly off and I intend to ask Mr. Tracy to let me go home, having been here now a fortnight.

4 P.M.

I have just come from the Secretary. He asked me what I wanted to do—I replied I had my work on the continuation of my former book to finish. He then said, "Why dont you finish it?" and added, "Do you want to go as Prest. of the War College?" I said I did, for as far as I could see there was no one else to do it, at present. He said he would have me ordered; and when I explained the impossibility of my leaving N.Y. at present, he said: "We will give you orders to go to Newport as necessary." To this nothing can be added, except to see that, if it slips his mind, he is reminded.

He said also that the war is over; and I think will be at leisure, as much as a Secretary ever is, to hear any propositions you wish to make. He feels, and I think justly, that the energy with which he has pushed naval preparations has had much to do with the final pacific outcome. I believe myself that Chile simply temporized to see how much we would stand, and had our naval effort been less vigorous and sustained there would have been a collision.

I shall leave for home tomorrow.

With kind remembrances to Mrs. Luce and the other ladies of your family [etc.].

To Francis M. Ramsay

75 East 54th Street, New York, February 24, 1892 [NA]

Commodore: I respectfully acknowledge the receipt of the Department's order of February 23, assigning me to duty as President of the Naval War College.

To Francis M. Ramsay

75 East 54th Street, New York, February 26, 1892 [NA]

Commodore: Referring to the Department's order of February 23, assigning me to duty as president of the Naval War College, I beg to be informed whether it is the intention of the Department to order a class there this year, and if so at about what time. I think that without serious difficulty a course of six weeks, independent of any cooperative work by the squadron, can be secured.

I also ask for instructions whether I shall now proceed, by personal correspondence, to obtain if possible officers to take charge of the various divisions of the course. There being four sets of quarters, will allow three such officers besides the president. These will be enough to begin the work of building up a well considered course of instruction in Naval Warfare; although, as I showed in the plan submitted to you some time ago, the subject divides into at least four heads, each of which will fully occupy the time of a competent man. It is to be desired that the president should not continue to be, as he in the past was, charged with one of these branches. It narrows his interest too much.

Having leased my present apartment until September 30 next, it is pecuniarily impossible for me to move to Newport until quarters are ready. I should like, however, to go there next week to see the condition of the work, and to consult with Lieut-Com. Stockton concerning the course and other matters connected with the College. I therefore respectfully ask for orders to go there for that purpose and to return upon completion.

To Benjamin F. Tracy

New York, March 1, 1892 [NA]

Sir: I have the honor to acknowledge receipt of Department's order of February 27, to proceed to Newport on temporary duty and will proceed accordingly.

To Francis M. Ramsay

75 East 54th Street, New York, March 12, 1892 [NA]

Commodore: I understand that advertisement is shortly to be made for proposals to increase the water supply of Coaster's Harbor Island, so as to provide for the additional consumption due to the War College. I venture to suggest the desirability that stipulation in some way be made by which the water piping of the building be as soon as possible connected with the source of supply. The consumption must at first be small, yet until it is provided for the building cannot be occupied, although it is likely to be ready in June.

If there is to be a course in August or September, it is desirable that myself and Lieut. Commander Stockton be on the spot and in residence by July 1st.

To Richardson Clover

75 East 54th Street, New York, March 15, 1892 [NA]

Dear Mr. Clover: I am writing up the Trafalgar campaign and among other particulars I find that the Spaniards accuse Villeneuve[1] of bad manage-

---

1. Pierre Charles de Villeneuve, who fought in the battles of Cap Finisterre and Trafalgar, where he was taken prisoner on October 21, 1805. Freed, he killed himself at Rennes in 1806, rather than face the rage of Napoleon.

ment in this: that being bound from the Windward Ids. to Ferrol he sighted the Azores instead of crossing their meridian five degrees north of them. In consequence of this mistake, they say, he made the approach to the Portuguese coast south of the point he should, and there met the N.E. winds which at that season (July) prevail off Cape Finisterre.

A glance at the map of Atlantic makes this seem likely to me; but my knowledge is not precise enough. Nor does it seem worth while to ask for sailing Directions simply to work up this one point, so I thought I would ask you to send me answers to these three questions, either by yourself or an asst.

1. Do the sailing directions from West Indies to Vigo, Ferrol or Bay of Biscay (Bordeaux) recommend any latitude to follow at that season (July)?

2. Do north-west winds prevail over south-west in North Atlantic generally at that season?

3. Do north-*east* winds occur frequently and last long off Spanish & Portuguese coasts at that season?

By answering these you will greatly oblige me.

Villeneuve was fifty days from West Indies to Ferrol with a fleet. Nelson same month (also sighting Azores) 35 days to Cape Spartel.

To Richardson Clover

75 East 54th Street, New York, March 21, 1892 [NA]

Dear Mr. Clover: Will you let me know whether there is in the Canaries, or in the Cape Verde islands, a bay of any size called Santiago Bay; or whether there be such in both?[1]

My reason is that Napoleon in appointing a very important rendezvous in a Santiago Bay in one place speaks of it as in Canaries, at another in Cape Verde. It is scarcely worthwhile to ask for a chart; but ordinary atlases do not give the information.

To Francis M. Ramsay

New York, March 23, 1892 [NA]

Commodore: I have to acknowledge the receipt of the Department's order to report as member of a General Court Martial at Richmond, Va, on the 28 inst. and will report accordingly.

---

1. Clover replied that "Santiago" is a common name in the Cape de Verde Islands, but uncommon in the Canaries and Madeiras, U.S. sailing directions showing only the one at Funchal, Madeira.

To Francis M. Ramsay

New York, March 23, 1892 [NA]

Commodore: Referring to my orders to report in Richmond as member of a General Court Martial, I would ask the Department to consider that the work upon which I am engaged is one that I can devolve on no one else, and which must therefore stop entirely during the continuance of a trial that will probably be long. From the particular position of the War College this work must be the main dependence in the coming season; and I am particularly anxious to bring it to a conclusion, so as to devote myself to the general work of the College, with which it to some extent will interfere, until ended.

It is needless to enlarge upon either the difficulty of the work or its importance to the College, if well done. The Department will, I hope, accept my estimate for that. A consecutive and sustained attention is a large element, not only of success, but of rapidity. Breaks lose not only their own length of time, but that which is necessary to gather up again the dropped threads. The Board on Promotions, and the special duty on which I was called to Washington this winter have both thrown me back, though unavoidably.

Not on account of the importance of my work in comparison with that of others, but because I cannot, as most can, turn it over to another, I ask the Department's consideration as to whether I may not be relieved from this duty.[1]

To Francis M. Ramsay

75 East 54th Street, New York, April 29, 1892 [NA]

My dear Commodore: I hear from Davis, who has kindly been supervising for me the draughtsman at work for the War College, that the map in hand has reached a point at which it is desirable for me to examine it—that he himself does not like to decide certain details without my seeing them. I myself also wish to get a better impression of the work than my imagination can give, to see how much more detail it can bear without confusion. I write therefore to ask you to give me orders to go to Washington and return for that purpose.[1]

1. Ramsay wrote in the margin, "No."

1. Ramsay granted this request.

To Francis M. Ramsay

New York, June 7, 1892 [NA]

My dear Commodore: Davis, who has been superintending the map under construction for the College, writes me (having investigated the matter at my request) that forty days work about will be required to finish it after the end of this fiscal year. A somewhat closer estimate can doubtless be made a fortnight hence.

Both Davis and myself consider Mr. Calvert to have worked diligently, as well as with at least average rapidity—no fault is to be imputed to him. The map I look upon as important to be completed according to the details laid down by me, and that the forty days' work should be done. I take this opportunity to say that having done my best, with the cordial support of the Bureau, to forestall the College wants in both books and maps, I see no reason why any expenditures beyond this one, for those objects, should be incurred during the next fiscal year.

I bring the matter before you now in order that, if there be any preference on the part of the Bureau to charge this work against the balance of this year's appropriation, you may be able so to order.

There frequently is a small unexpended balance that has to be turned in. If such be the case this year, I wish to recommend that it be used to purchase copies of my work *The Influence of Sea Power upon History*, in number not exceeding a dozen. There is no copy of it in the library (I think) although it is a direct outcome of the College, and it constitutes a really useful book of reference for the College purposes.

As a matter of necessary economical policy, I venture here to recommend that, at least until the spring of 1893, no book or map be bought or ordered for the College unless on the statement of the president that it is needed for immediate use. I know something about the Collection and am confident few will be needed under such conditions. By next spring we shall see our way clearer.

To D. Appleton and Company

75 East 54th Street, New York, June 8, 1892 [CUL]

Gentlemen: I return the map of the "Scene of Farragut's Operations." It is correct, except in one trifling particular. The highland at Vicksburg touches the river, whereas the map is there shaded. I have drawn two ink lines by taking which as limiting shading on either side, a correct impression will be given.

Would it not be an improvement to take upper right hand corner (within dotted line) for title, thus:

Scene of Farragut's operations
1862–1864
The shaded portions indicate alluvial land

That part of the map is unimportant. This is merely a suggestion.

To Francis M. Ramsay

75 East 54th Street, New York, June 11, 1892 [NA]

Commodore: I respectfully recommend that the periodicals named in the enclosed list be ordered for the Naval War College, by annual subscription, to begin July 1, 1892.

[Enclosure]
Revue Maritime et Coloniale.
1. *Le Yacht.*[1]
2. *Journal* of the Royal United Service Institution of Great Britain.[2]
3. *Naval and Military Magazine.*[3]
4. The London *Engineer.*[4]
5. *Engineering*—London.[5]
6. *La Lumière Électrique.*[6]

To Francis M. Ramsay

75 East 54th Street, New York, June 13, 1892 [NA]

My dear Commodore: I have asked Stockton to present a request for repairs to the old College furniture, which he writes me a thoroughly reliable firm in Newport (known to me) will do for $75. In view of the probable contractor for the furniture, I fear many delays. If this can be repaired at once I will still be able to move to Newport early in July.

As I go there, I cannot meanwhile take my family elsewhere, and I do not wish to keep them long in New York in this heat. With the old furniture repaired we can make out till the new arrives—after a sufficient fashion.

---

1. *Journal de la marine: Le yacht.* Paris, 1878– .
2. Royal United Service Institution *Journal.* London, 1857– .
3. *Naval and Military Magazine* (London, 1827–1828) became the *United Service Journal and Naval and Military Magazine*, and later the *United Service Magazine.*
4. *Engineer.* London, 1856– .
5. *Engineering; An Illustrated Weekly Journal.* London, 1866– .
6. *La lumière électrique.* Paris, 1879–1894; 1908–1916.

To Francis M. Ramsay

75 East 54th Street, June 13, 1892 [NA]

My dear Commodore: Stockton writes me that the lowest bidder for the College furniture is W. B. Moses and Son, of Washington. I venture to suggest that Stockton, having for some months past made a special study of this furniture business, as well as having a special interest that the best articles be furnished, it would in any event be desirable that he should be the senior member of a *special* Board of Inspection to inspect it. Considering also that so very much of it is Cabinet work, and so much depends upon the quality of the wood employed, it would, it seems to me, be well to provide that a naval carpenter who has special knowledge of cabinet wood, if such there be, should be a junior member, even if one had to be ordered from a neighboring station for the special service.

As regards Stockton it seems to me so eminently proper that he should be on the board that I can hardly imagine Bunce hesitating—but Stockton seems to think he may. If the carpenter meets your approval, you would have to act.

In any event, as I said, much fitness would be needed in a Board receiving articles for so trying a climate as Newport. It may be doubly necessary in a case where the struggle is likely to arise with a contractor trying to make us take the cheapest he can put off on us. They have neither personally nor by representative examined the samples.

[P.S.] Would failure to examine the samples be a reason for rejecting a bid, if not materially lower than the next above it by a more responsible firm?

To Francis M. Ramsay

75 East 54th Street, New York, June 17, 1892 [NA]

Commodore: I beg respectfully to recommend that Lieut-Comdr. Stockton be authorized to employ from and after July 1, 1892, for the service of the War College, the building and the grounds, the following men at the monthly wages named:

1 Janitor and Clerk	at $65.
1 Stableman	at $45.
1 Laborer	at $35.

and that the College horses be put at the disposal of the College at that date, or as soon thereafter as the stableman can be procured.

To Francis M. Ramsay

Telegram   Elizabeth, New Jersey, June 20, 1892 [NA]

Immediate total interruption of causeway will be most inconvenient to college Could not Chief of Engineers postpone till furniture grading & water contracts completed.

To Francis M. Ramsay

Elizabeth, New Jersey, June 20, 1892 [NA]

My dear Commodore: Stockton writes me that the Enginr. officer in Newport expects the Causeway to be cut off for teams from June 22 to July 15. The shortness of the notice compelled me to telegraph you. This will, he represents, interfere with the delivery of furniture at the College door as the contract provides—also with the grading and with the water supply contract. The two former are due July 1, the latter August 1.

I am not sufficiently familiar with the work to know what can be done—but it seems evident that, in a climate like Newport's, a three weeks job, at this season of the year, can easily have the required postponement without any fatal loss of time.

The contractors can easily allege that the interruption of the only road materially alters the terms upon which they contracted, and so impose much additional loss of time and possibly make claims for compensation.

I forbear criticism, because ignorant—but it at first blush looks as though there had not been due consideration on the part of one branch of the government of the difficulties of another.

To Francis M. Ramsay

Elizabeth, New Jersey, June 24, 1892 [NA]

Commodore: Some time ago I said to you that it was important, if a class, whencesoever drawn, come to the College this year, that Lt. Commdr. Stockton and myself should be in residence by July 1; and in any event, if the College is to develop, no unnecessary delay should occur.

It is now a week from that date and the quarters will be ready for occupancy upon the arrival of the furniture, required to be delivered by

July 1. I therefore request that orders may be issued to me to proceed there; but as travel is very heavy at that time, I would also ask to be allowed a few days scope, to make the necessary arrangements for my family to go with me.

It is permissible to remind you that it is most desirable the relations between the Training Station and the College should be clearly defined when I report. My own views on this matter are already before you, as well as my recommendation for a force of three men to be employed from July 1.

In this connection, as emphasizing the distinction between the general character of the two institutions, as well as for other reasons, I suggest that, as was formerly the practice, officers connected with the College be not required to wear uniform within its limits, except on special occasions. As you know, this has always been the case at the Torpedo School.

To Francis M. Ramsay

Elizabeth, New Jersey, July 4, 1892 [NA]

Commodore: Day before yesterday I called at the factory which is to furnish the parlor furniture contracted for by Mr. Moses, and was there told that the pieces cannot be ready before the end of this month; possibly not before August 10.

This particular part of the furnishing is, of course, not absolutely essential —we can move in without it; but if like delay is to occur with regard to articles absolutely necessary to ordinary house-living, or if inspection cannot be made before the whole contract is completed, a very bad effect will be produced upon our preparations. I think best therefore to mention the fact to you.

Within a week, two years will have elapsed since the appropriation became available, and I had hoped that before that time we should be in occupancy and busied with the arrangements to meet a class. However extensive and accurate a man's knowledge of his subject, certain facilities and a considerable amount of preparation for each days work is needed, and the installment of conveniences for illustration, by maps and otherwise, will demand time and study. To have a class, however constituted, coming close on the heels of our ocupying an entirely new building, will much complicate our work. It will be done; but in a hurry and scramble that will impair its thoroughness.

I hope that in some way the Bureau may be able to expedite the occupancy of the building.

To Benjamin F. Tracy

Elizabeth, New Jersey, July 8, 1892 [LC]

Dear Sir: I greatly hope that the status of the War College may receive
your early attention.

I am so completely in the dark that I know not what to think, but I much
fear that, unless the Department soon takes some decisive action, my
position will become untenable. Personally, I am quite willing to step aside—
but in the interests of the College it will be necessary so to define the position of its head as will ensure his self-respect—as such.

My views have been communicated a month ago to Commodore Ramsay,
in a semi-official letter.

To Benjamin F. Tracy

Naval War College, July 16, 1892 [NA]

Sir: Having been informed that Lieut. Tasker H. Bliss, U.S.A., of the
First Artillery, and now Aide-de-Camp to General Schofield, is an ap-
plicant for the position of Professor of Modern Languages at the Military
Academy, I wish to place on record at the Department that Lieut. Bliss was
on duty with me at the Naval War College, 1886 and 1887, as lecturer on
Military Science; and that I was particularly struck with his grasp of his
subjects, with his clear and forcible manner of imparting information, and
his untiring capacity for work. I am not able to speak from personal knowledge of his acquaintance with Modern Languages.

I should be pleased if a copy of this letter could be sent to Lieut. Bliss
through the customary channels.

To Francis M. Ramsay

Elizabeth, New Jersey, July 18, 1892 [NA]

Commodore: I have the honor to acknowledge the receipt of the Department's order of July 16, directing me to proceed to Newport, report
to Captain F. M. Bunce, and relieve him of the charge of the War College
and Torpedo School. I will proceed accordingly, and report July 21.

I also beg to acknowledge receipt of Department's Order, enclosed with
the above, defining the relations of the War College and Naval Training
Station.

To Francis M. Ramsay

Naval War College, July 21, 1892 [NA]

Commodore: I have the honor to report that, in obedience to the Department's order of July 16, I have today reported to Captain F. M. Bunce, and relieved him of the charge of the War College and Torpedo School.

To Washington I. Chambers[1]

Naval War College, July 27, 1892 [NWC]

My dear Mr. Chambers: Notwithstanding my partial and hurried reply of last week your letter of the 16th has remained in my mind as unanswered, though acknowledged.

I wish very much to meet the objections you raise, for I am sincerely desirous of so far arousing your interest and convincing your mind as to lead you to accept orders here. I am so, partly from personal reasons, wishing to secure the success of an undertaking largely committed to me; and also because I believe the College represents a side of naval interest to which little attention—systematic attention, at any rate—is being paid.

It was not my purpose to ignore, much less to deny the navy's share in the responsibility for its material development. It is the tendency of all subordinates to shrug their shoulders, thank God it is none of their business, and disclaim responsibility; and the Navy is so thoroughly drilled into the theory of subordination, both by its military constitution and by the much-insisted-on truth of the subordination of the military to the Civil authority, that it is especially prone to this fault. I concede freely that we should be on our guard against this besetting weakness, and that we may do much. Nevertheless, responsibility ultimately is inseparable from power; and in the last analysis the *power* to remedy our deficiences rests with the taxpayers and their representatives. I fancy the difference between our views, here, is not radical.

Nor do I believe it is in the matter of Naval Architecture. The latter is one—and the only one you cite in your letter—of those technical specialties, with whose methods my address said the College has little *direct* concern. I have not a copy of the address with me and so must depend upon my

---

1. Chambers, class of 1876, was an early designer of gun turrets, armored cruisers, and the "dreadnought" type of battleship. He also devised techniques for the firing and control of torpedoes. Known as "The Father of Naval Aviation," he was the first to use a launching catapult. He accepted Mahan's invitation, and lectured on the Nicaraguan Canal.

recollection of its words. I must also recur to the fact that in a short address, meant to make a clear sharp impression upon hearers, it is easy to fall into a seeming exaggeration of expression. To correct this on every point involves not only loss of time, but wearies the hearer and blurs the impression essential to be conveyed.

To my statement about methods and details you oppose such a correction: *1* One of the chief points in the study of Naval Strategy should be to shape a course of Naval Construction Policy. This I have, as a lecturer on naval strategy, enlarged on from time to time. Enforcing my views by illustrations, though my aim at affecting our policy has been not by direct action, but by the indirect influence of spreading sound ideas (as I consider them) *2* (You say) Such important affairs cannot be wisely directed without some attention to methods and details. But have I said such attention should not be given? I have said that the College, existing for a certain purpose, should concentrate its effort on that purpose and matters akin to it, but I certainly never meant to imply that it should look disdainfully or carelessly on the processes which underly its own investigations. In the specialization which is so marked a feature of modern life, each specialty has to accept the work of the others that exist alongside of it. It neither rejects nor ignores their conclusions, which are often essential to its own work; but it takes them at second hand. If it insists upon independent investigation of matters outside its own field, it loses the concentration essential to success, and in fact ceases to be a specialty.

Viewed thus, the question of the amount of detail, or "methods," that enters into the work of the College, or of any particular lectures at the College, becomes one of more or less, and I am far from affecting to consider that my own particular definition of the quantum is conclusive. It is not given to one man to define accurately the length, breadth and height, to which a new institution is to attain. Personally, I believe rather in growth along general lines, accepting day by day the influences that legitimately commend themselves, than in a hard and fast 'a priori' systematization. Such general lines I sought to lay down in my address.

You say truly this is a mechanical age; and it is useless to kick against the pricks. We must take the age as we find it; but if convinced, as I am, that the trust in machinery has been pushed beyond reason, that the living human factor is more and more relegated to a position hopelessly inferior, one must try, not to force the current back, but to deflect it somewhat. If you had had to listen to all the propositions made to me, or will read the original report of Luce's board recommending the institution of the College, you can scarcely fail to realize that there was danger of the art of war disappearing under a deluge of machinery. The College would become a simple (or complex) School of Technology; and as such, in view of the many already existing, would have no excuse for continuance.

[76]

What the upshot will be, I know not. Of one thing I am certain—survive or perish—that the leading idea of the College carries with it an opportunity for original work that will live or die with it. Of this the success of my own work, abroad and at home, is a proof—for the success is not due to me (at least primarily) but to the College thought.

I do not think that there is between us any such divergence of thought as necessitates our remaining apart, or would invalidate your usefulness here. Certainly I should deprecate the using of much of your time (as a teacher) in the explanation of the *processes* of naval architecture, of gun building, or steam-engineering; but I should with equal certainty not object to your dwelling upon the *principles* that govern methods of construction, showing the bearing of them upon this or that point of the handling of ships, or upon their efficiency in action. The usefulness of the College in the long run will result not from the predominance of my views, or your views, but from the fair collision of opinion among men connected with it, who are willing to accept the fact that excellence is a plan of gradual growth and gradual evolution, and are not impatient of waiting as well as striving.

Let me hear from you again before very long. There is no haste about your coming here, but there should also be no *needless* delay in reaching conclusions, for if not you, (as I hope), then I must be looking out else-where. I think I have number three—with yourself our staff will be, for the time, complete.

To James R. Soley[1]

Naval War College, August 4, 1892 [NA]

Sir: I respectfully request that the two maps constructed this year in the Department, for the War College, may be forwarded here as soon as possible.

They are: 1. The North West Coast of the United States, and 2. A Strategic Map of Central Europe. The latter, if not quite ready, is very nearly so; the other is completed. Both are wanted for this year's course and it is desirable to have them very shortly.

To James R. Soley

Telegram   Newport, Rhode Island, August 19, 1892 [NA]

I suggest four consecutively[1] between Oct 15 & 30.

---

1. At this time, Assistant Secretary of the Navy.
1. Lectures on steam engineering. In 1892, they were delivered by Passed Assistant Engineer I. N. Hollis.

To James R. Soley

Naval War College, August 20, 1892 [NA]

Sir: I respectfully request authority to employ an additional laborer at $35—per month—from September 1 to the end of the approaching session of the College.

To Francis M. Ramsay

Naval War College, August 21, 1892 [NA]

The thirteen pillows are, as their length indicates, bolsters—needed, 9 for the double beds, including guest chamber in College proper, and 4 for the three-quarter beds. They were forgotten in the furniture contract.[1]

To James R. Soley

Naval War College, August 30, 1892 [NA]

Sir: I respectfully request that the Naval War College may be supplied with a complete set of General Orders and Circulars of the Navy Department, issued since the publication of the book of "General Orders and Circulars from 1863 to 1887."

To Francis M. Ramsay

Naval War College, August 31, 1892 [NA]

Commodore: With reference to the enclosed requisition I desire to state, that, owing to the prolonged drought and unusual heat of this summer,

---

1. This letter was written in response to:

14849—Endorsement. Bureau of Navigation, Navy Department.

August 19, 1892.

Respectfully returned to the President, Naval War College, Newport, R.I., for information regarding the 13 pillows asked for. For what purposes are they required?

F. M. Ramsay, Chief of Bureau

Mahan's reply elicited from the Bureau:

24 to W. Col.—Bedding not allowed except guest chamber. Be governed by "Allowance of Furniture" Y & D '88—36: 224

the grass sown upon the slope of the College terrace has entirely failed, and almost wholly in rear of the building; and I am informed by an experienced person that the amount of seed asked for will be needed for a proper sowing, which should be done in September.

To James R. Soley

Telegram   Newport, Rhode Island, September 2, 1892 [NA]

Secretary cannot be present at College opening.

To Francis M. Ramsay

Naval War College, September 5, 1892 [NA]

Sir: In addition to the periodicals ordered by the Bureau for the War College, the following annuals are also needed.
Hasell's Cyclopedia—1892[1]
Naval Annual—Brassey—1892[2]
Colonial Office List—1892[3]
These are all published in London and can be secured through Mr. B. F. Stevens.

To Horatio R. Storer

Naval War College, September 17, 1892 [NWC]

My dear Sir: I am ashamed to have so long delayed acknowledging your letter of the 4th with its enclosures[1]. The neglect has been due to my putting

---

1. E. D. Price, ed., *Hazell's Annual Cyclopedia*, 1891–1895. New York: C. Scribner's Sons, 1891–1895.
2. *Brassey's Naval Annual*. Portsmouth, England: J. Griffin & Co., and New York: Van Nostrand, 18?–1913; London: W. Clowes & Sons Ltd., 1914– .
3. *The Dominions Office and Colonial Office List . . . Comprising Historical and Statistical Information Respecting the Overseas Dominions and Colonial Dependencies of Great Britain*. London: Waterlow & Sons Ltd., 1862– . Various titles; in 1892 it was called *The Colonial Office List*.
1. Storer had sent Mahan three naval commemorative medals, viz: the destruction of the Dutch fleet by the British in 1677; Admiral Lord Howe's occupation of Narragansett Bay in 1778; and the victory of HMS *Shannon* over USS *Chesapeake* in 1814. Storer to Mahan, September 4, 1892, at the Naval War College.

it carefully away out of sight—so that, with my preoccupations, it has been constantly forgotten. The medals are most valuable, and will, I hope, prove the beginning of a collection that in the future will possess both value and interest. I beg to thank you most sincerely for your thought of the College.

To Francis M. Ramsay

Naval War College, October 5, 1892 [NA]

Commodore: In view of the increasing storminess of the weather and the insufficient boat accommodation for transporting the officers attending the course of lectures, I have to day submitted a requisition to be allowed to employ an omnibus to carry a part of the class when, in my opinion, the weather demands. Although the estimate is for $100, the probability is that not over $50 will be required, in the short remaining period. May I ask the Bureau, if it approve, to telegraph me in advance of the return of the requisition.[1]

It may be prudent for me to add that, in making these contingent requisitions, I keep constantly in view the Bureau's limitation of expenses, prescribed in its letter 15076.

To Benjamin F. Tracy

Naval War College, October 10, 1892 [LC]

Dear Mr. Tracy: I send you to day by mail a copy of my *Life of Farragut*, just published.

If I have at all succeeded in my aim to write a competent military biography of our great admiral, I owe the power to do so to my studies of the past few years, and to my prolonged connection with the College. For both I have to thank you; and it is at once fitting and a pleasure to make this acknowledgment of my indebtedness to you.

To James R. Soley

Naval War College, October 29, 1892 [NWC]

Sir: I have to submit the following report of the operations of the Naval War College and Torpedo School during the current year.

---

1. The Bureau did approve.

The new College building having been accepted May 28, 1892 by the Department, by the orders of the latter I took charge on the 22nd. of July, and preparations were at once made for a course to begin in September.

The College opened on the 6th. of September and the course embraced the subjects named in enclosure A, annexed to this report.

It will be seen that, with the exception of the very few officers who have in former years been directly associated with the College, the lectures given by any one person have been few. It is, however, to be remarked that the variety and character of the subjects themselves have illustrated one most important and interesting office of the College, viz: to afford specialists in the different departments of naval activity an opportunity, and encouragement, to communicate the results of their experience to the general service, by a means—the lecture system—which has commended itself so largely to the intelligence of our age and country.

It is, on the other hand, evident that such subjects, not having always between themselves a direct and immediate connection, will gain both in interest and value by being grouped round a central course of study; their relations to which will illustrate and enhance their individual importance, and at the same time bring them into closer working union with each other.

It is proposed to accomplish this further object by means of a permanent staff, attached to the College during service tours of duty, whose office will be to develop in a systematic and orderly manner a treatment of the Art of Naval War, upon the outlines of the "Programme"* annexed to this report B. Concerning this programme it may safely be said that, though doubtless as yet defective, it on the one hand contains nothing which is not important to naval officers to understand and know, and on the other hand no one of the topics there named for treatment can be claimed as having received in any shape, here or abroad, the consideration it needs. If cavil be made at the modest attention proposed to be given to commercial interests, the reply is apt—that commercial interests underlie and give rise to the creation of navies, and largely dictate their employment, in war as in peace.

As this programme is developed, the results will be imparted also by lectures; but to ensure something more than mere passive reception, it is intended that cases involving questions of Naval Strategy and of Naval Tactics in their various branches, shall be propounded early in each course, to which written solutions will be required before detachment. As before said there is almost total want, here and abroad, of any systematic treatment of these subjects, and consequently of text books; the scanty material that does exist has, however, been collected, and will be at the disposition of students. By means of this and of lectures, sufficient matter should be supplied to stimulate the working of their own minds, which is the important consideration.

* Programme of Depts forwarded you sometime ago.

The requisite staff has just been secured. Henceforth the course will develop steadily, and, it may be hoped, rapidly.

Having now given seven years to the study of these subjects, with my whole attention engaged upon them, and in view of the opposition the College has had hitherto to encounter, I feel warranted and compelled to say that no sustained work has been done, nor is any now being done upon them, except by and through the College. Its claim upon the favor of the Government and Congress depends upon the importance of the subjects, with which it alone, among the organizations of the Navy, undertakes to deal.

Annex A

List of Lectures delivered at the U.S. Naval War College and Torpedo School during the Session of 1892.

Lecturer	Subject	Number of Lectures
*Capt. A. T. Mahan	Naval History with strategic & tactical discussions of the events	
do	narrated. Naval strategy with applications to the Caribbean Sea.	15 6
Comdr. P. F. Harrington	The Ram and its Tactics.	6
Lieut. J. F. Meigs	The Gun and its Tactics.	5
Comdr. T. F. Jewell	The Torpedo in Naval Warfare.	1
*Lieut. F. J. Drake	The Howell Torpedo.	3
Lieut. T. C. McLean	The Whitehead Torpedo.	2
Comdr. C. H. Stockton	The Commercial & Political conditions existing in the regions to be affected by the Inter-Oceanic Canal, and the probable changes resulting therefrom.	6
do	The Strategic features of the Pacific.	3
do	Preparations for War.	1
Lt. Comdr. A. R. Couden	Armor for War-Ships.	1
Lieut. J. C. Soley	The Naval Militia.	1
Lieut. J. B. Murdock	Applications of Electricity in Naval Warfare.	3
*Lieut. S. W. B. Diehl	Compass errors and Compensations.	2
*Lieut. J. H. Sears	Naval Lessons in the recent Civil War in Chile.	3
Lieut. W. I. Chambers	The Nicaragua Canal.	2
*Ensign A. P. Niblack	Naval Signalling.	2

Lecturer	Subject	Number of Lectures
Med. Director R. C. Dean	Naval Hygiene as affected by food supplies.	5
Surgeon C. A. Siegfried	Naval Hygiene. Morbific Influences affecting seamen, their causes and prevention.	4
*P. A. Eng. I. N. Hollis	Engines, speed and coal endurance of Modern Ships of War.	4
Nav. Constr. J. J. Woodward	The designing of War-Ships and the effect of injuries upon their tactical qualities.	3
*Navy Constr. D. W. Taylor	Speed Trials of Ships of War.	2
Capt. F. A. Mahan U. S. Engineers	Coast Defences.	5

Those lectures with note attached were printed *after* delivery giving announcement that they had been delivered at War College as a rule.[1] The rule of the College was that once printed the lecture was not to be again delivered.

To James R. Soley

Naval War College, October 30, 1892 [NA]

Sir: The extra laborer authorized by the Department's telegram of September 5, will now be discharged.

The remaining laborer, besides his general employments, has now also to attend to the steam heating apparatus, involving a good deal of night work, and will also have additional duties to perform because the men will henceforth have to mess within the building. Having now for some time had him and his work under consideration, I recommend that his pay be increased from $35 to $45 per month.

To George Sydenham Clarke[1]

Newport, Rhode Island, November 5, 1892 [LC]

My dear Major Clarke: Your letter of August 20 has remained long unanswered, but my want of time and the pressure upon me has amounted

---

1. The note reads "Since Printed" and the lectures concerned are herein identified by an asterisk.

1. Later, 1st Baron Sydenham of Combe, Clarke was a British Army officer who wrote

not merely to an excuse but to sheer inability; for your letters demand not the chit-chat of the day but some attention of mind.

My next book in continuation of the one issued two years ago, will soon be out;[2] and if you have time to read it consecutively you will find, I think, that my views on ports and particularly on colonial ports, of which you have so many, is radically the same as your own. My utterances are generally made passively; I have not written a systematic treatise on coast defence—of which I am not a master—but in several places I say, by the way, that ports like Malta and Gibraltar are even more dependent upon the Fleet than the Fleet upon them. The time element too I clearly recognize both in my thought and word. Of course, a person who is writing with a particular object is frequently neglectful to guard his meaning when speaking of matters other than the principal one. My idea of a naval port upon which a fleet can rest is, generally, that it should be able to hold out independent of the Fleet, for a length of time dependent upon its importance, both to the general defence system and in its intrinsic value.

Upon the subject of the relations of our two countries, if you have access to the *Atlantic Monthly*—an American magazine—and care to look it up, you will find in September or October, 1890, an article by myself in which I express a feeling somewhat similar to your own.[3] I fear, however, that the time is not yet full ripe. The exigencies of politics and very particularly the Irish vote in our country, prevents clear reason from making itself felt. For it is upon a reasonable perception of our mutual interests that I would like to see policy of the two nations conjoined. Equally with yourself I am impressed with the feeling that to work together for our mutual good and if necessary against the rest of the world, would be the highest statesmanship—for in political traditions as well as by blood we are kin, the rest alien. To reach this happy state then is needed first, an appeal to reason, or, as they say now, "enlightened self interest." I trust that upon the recognition of the facts, sentiments of affection may follow.

Goodrich is now on your side of the water, somewhere in the Mediterranean, commanding the *Constellation*, a sailing ship which has gone to bring here some exhibits from somewhere.[4] I am sorry to be so vague but the particular port of destination has clean gone out of my head. Upon returning, he will be in our training system for boys, with which he has been associated for over a year past. I doubt if he will have any time to get to

---

extensively on military affiairs. At this time, he was Secretary of the Colonial Defence Committee. Among other offices he held, he was Secretary to the Committee of Imperial Defence, 1904–1907.

2. *The Influence of Sea Power upon the French Revolution and Empire, 1793–1812.*

3. "The United States Looking Outward," *Atlantic Monthly* (December 1890).

4. The Naval Academy training ship *Constellation* went to Naples, where she took aboard the Vatican exhibits for the World's Fair, and thence to Le Havre for the French exhibits.

England. If you wish to write him, a letter through B. F. Stevens, 4 Trafalgar Square would certainly find him. The ship's arrival at Gibraltar was cabled a few days ago. I *think* she is bound to Genoa.

I shall look with interest and some anxiety to the reception of my coming book on your side. Although I attempt no controversy, I have felt the necessity of supporting my case all through, and consequently a certain amount of argument underlies the current of my story—though it does not, I hope, rise too obtrusively to the surface. It has been intensely interesting to me, but thank God! it is done. I don't think I shall ever again tackle such a task. The proofs being all read, and nothing but the binding to do, it should be out this month.

To Horace E. Scudder

New York, November 18, 1892 [HUL]

Dear Sir: Presuming on your kind expressions of two years ago, I send you today by express an article on Admiral Earl St. Vincent, of, I calculate, about 8000 words.[1] If it approve itself to you I would suggest that I could furnish four other of similar character, of British admirals standing high in the second order of merit. Their lives are full of incident, touching the U.S. history in almost every case; and my expectation would be to make a short anecdotal sketch of each one, not exceeding in length the one now sent. There is also one French admiral who would lend himself to the same treatment.

All these are men with whose biographies I have had to familiarize myself for my forthcoming book;[2] but the treatment will be so far different as not to infringe in interest. Rather, those who read the book may like to hear something more of them, and to others it will be all brand new.[3]

To Horace E. Scudder

Newport, Rhode Island, November 22, 1892 [HUL]

My dear Sir: I was much gratified upon my arrival yesterday to find your letter, and to know that the sketch of St. Vincent was acceptable.[1]

With regard to the other class of subjects to which you allude, it has been

---

1. "Admiral the Earl of St. Vincent," *Atlantic Monthly* (March 1893).
2. *The Influence of Sea Power upon the French Revolution and Empire, 1793–1812.*
3. Under his signature Mahan wrote: "Author of *Influence of Sea Power, etc.*"

1. "Admiral the Earl of St. Vincent (Jervis)," *Atlantic Monthly* (March 1893).

my wish to take them up as a pursuit, and, if circumstances would permit my withdrawal from active service, I should gladly and by preference undertake to make a specialty of them. I am persuaded that the navy—and I may even say the country—needs a voice to speak constantly of our external interests in matters touching the navy, and perhaps also maritime matters generally. Except myself, I know no one in the navy disposed to identify himself with such a career—and in the lack of a better I should greatly like to do it. Were the present administration to remain in power, I might hope for such indulgence until the time, three or four years hence, when I can retire; but with the impending change no one can foresee what can be done. I certainly believe I could be more useful in this way than by simple sea-going.

With the preoccupations of the past two years over my book, I felt the impossibility of diverting time to writing for magazines. If the book prove a decided success, I shall have done my last in that line; and shall confine myself to shorter, and I hope more lucrative efforts.

I am at present bound up with an engagement of six months' standing to contribute an article on the N.Y. Navy Yard to a History of N.Y. City being published.[2] I hope to finish it by January & continue my biographies.

To Francis M. Ramsay

Naval War College, November 30, 1892 [NA]

Commodore: Replying to the Bureau's endorsement on the enclosed Requisition No. 22, I have to say that the carpenters services required are in addition to the $100 allowed on requisition No. 13.

There have been and are constantly occurring small items of repairs, due partly to imperfections only betrayed by weather in a new building, partly to the effects of extreme damp—a characteristic of this climate—and extreme dryness from steam heat.

These, with certain new fittings and trivial accidents, have required the frequent services of a carpenter. It has been a question in my mind whether it would not be more profitable to the College to employ a carpenter as an addition of the permanent force as was formerly done—but the more prudent course appears to me to test the matter by the experience of this year on the present plan.

---

2. *The Memorial History of the City of New York, from its First Settlement to the Year 1892.* James Grant Wilson, ed. 4 vols. New York: New-York History Company, 1892–1893. For some reason, Mahan's article was not used. The chapter on the Navy Yard, in Volume IV, was contributed by T. F. Rodebough.

To Francis M. Ramsay

Naval War College, November 30, 1892 [NA]

Sir: I have the honor to acknowledge the receipt of the Department's order of the 28th November to report in person at the Department for special temporary duty, and will proceed accordingly.

To Francis M. Ramsay

Naval War College, December 1, 1892 [NA]

Commodore: Referring to Requisition No. 21 for books approved by the Bureau, I find that there is a probable error in the estimated cost, which should be $100 instead of $50; $100 being probably somewhat outside the real cost. The two expensive items are the bound copies of the *Revue Maritime*, and of the *Journal of the Royal United Service Institution*. The question of value of back numbers is always uncertain, but there seems no safe basis on which to estimate, except that of publication price.

If it please the Bureau, I recommend that the requisition stand with this explanation, as no accession to the library is more essential than the completion of these files. I return the first and second requisition, as the Bureau may possibly wish them.

To Francis M. Ramsay

Naval War College, December 2, 1892 [NA]

Commodore: I beg to return herewith B. F. Stevens' letter of November 19, concerning Book Catalogues, which has been noted.

To Francis M. Ramsay

Naval War College, December 2, 1892 [NA]

Commodore: Replying to Bureau's letter 16558b, I beg to submit the following statement of probable payments that will have to be made between November 25, and July 1, from the appropriation for the fiscal year. From these I omit $177.50, Requisition 63, Training Station, Oats and

Grain, as this purchase has not been made; and, as the horses were not restored to the College, they will not, I presume, be fed from its appropriation.

Memorandum of Probable Payments to be Made from
Appropriation for Naval War College & Torpedo School from
November 25, 1892 and July 1, 1893.

Ice	12.19
Work of Carpenter	200.00
Work of Machinist	150.00
Transportation of class in bad weather	30.00
Miscellaneous tools, utensils &c.	169.40
Work of Mason	50.00
Coal	3015.00
Stationery	426.96
Telephone	45.00
Miscellaneous repairs	100.00
Proportional cost of lighting and water supply	1000.00
Work upon grounds, material and labor	300.00
Labor roll	805.00
Maps and Plans	600.00
Library and books	400.00
Washing	12.75
Total	$7316.30

To Francis M. Ramsay

Navy Department, Washington, D.C., December 5, 1892 [NA]

Commodore: I beg to call your attention to the item of six hundred tons of coal to be furnished to the Naval War College, under contract for the fiscal year of 1893. Two hundred tons of this amount, I am informed by Commander Stockton, were estimated to be furnished in kind to the Naval Training Station, as fuel, to defray the increased consumption, at the pumping stations and the electric light dynamo, due to supplying the College with light and water. If the expense for this increased consumption is paid in money, by transfer requisitions, the College will be left with two hundred tons of coal that it does not need, and at the same time will lose a thousand dollars, rather more than less, which can ill be spared from the scanty appropriation. Its work will be seriously crippled.

The estimate on which the existing contract for 600 tons is based was submitted last May, before I had official connection with the matter. I asked

Captain Bunce before leaving Newport on the 2nd instant, whether he would be willing to receive in kind the additional coal burned on account of the College, and he told me he would.

To Francis M. Ramsay

New York, December 7, 1892 [NA]

The Bureau is informed that I have this day received the Department's order of December 3d, 1892, to proceed to Navy Yard Mare Island and report on the 14th inst to Rear Admiral Irwin[1] as member of a General Court Martial.

To Benjamin F. Tracy

75 East 54th Street, New York, December 7, 1892 [LC]

Dear Mr. Tracy: My enforced absence on the Johnson Court-martial[1] necessitates my asking the publishers to send you a copy of my forthcoming work, which I would have liked to send myself, and suitably inscribed. It deals with the French Revolutionary period, and analyzes critically all the most celebrated naval operations, including the whole of Nelson's.

The work is the one upon which my own reputation must rest, as well as my claims upon the future consideration of the Department, in determining my employments. That I have been able to complete it is due wholly to your support—I may say even to your protection.

I hope, and I believe, it will command the interest and approval of the Navy. If so, I shall owe the success to you, and it gives me great pleasure thus explicitly to acknowledge my obligation of gratitude.

To John Irwin

Telegram   Ogden, Utah, December 13, 1892 [FRCS]

Train eight hours late accident will telegraph again cannot be on time.

---

1. John Irwin, class of 1853, commanding Navy Yard, Mare Island.

1. Commander Henry L. Johnson, class of 1863, was charged with careless navigation while commanding the *Mohican*, found guilty, and dismissed from the service.

To John Irwin

Telegram   Blue Canal, California, December 14, 1892 [FRCS]

Unless accident will reach Vallejo Junction by four P M.

To Francis M. Ramsay

Navy Yard, Mare Island, December 14, 1892 [NA]

Sir: I have the honor to inform the Bureau that I have, in obedience to the Department's order of the 3d December reported to Rear Admiral John Irwin for duty as member of a General Court Martial.

To Benjamin F. Tracy

San Francisco, California, December 27, 1892 [NA]

Sir: Referring to the Department's order of December 3, directing me, after the conclusion of Court Martial, to resume duties at Newport, I respectfully ask permission to defer my return there to January 31, 1893, which will be about one month after reaching the East.[1]

I also request that the reply to this letter may be sent me to 75 East 54th St, New York.

To Benjamin F. Tracy

75 East 5th Street, New York, January 6, 1893 [NA]

Sir: Referring to the Department's order of December 3, 1892, directing me, after service on Court Martial, to resume duties at Newport—and being desirous of a month's leave at this season—I respectfully ask permission to delay my return to Newport until January 31st 1893.

A request to the same effect was mailed by me in San Francisco, after the order dissolving the Court was received. I expected that it would reach the Department on the 4th inst.

---

1. Leave was granted until January 31, 1893.

To Francis M. Ramsay

75 East 54th Street, New York, January 9, 1893 [NA]

Commodore: I beg to acknowledge the receipt of the Department's letter of January 7, granting me leave of absence till January 31.
My address will be as above.

To Benjamin F. Tracy

75 East 54th Street, New York, January 23, 1893 [LC]

Dear Mr. Tracy: As the time of your leaving office is approaching, I submit to you the following, in case you should see fit to transmit it to your successor with a favorable endorsement.

If the law remains as now, I purpose to retire at the end of my forty years—in 1896. I so intend, believing that I can achieve greater success, personally, with my pen, than by continuing on the active list; and also that I can do better work for the navy, by developing further the line of professional thought upon which I have been for seven years engaged.

With retirement only three years off, I do not wish to go to sea, as that would necessarily interrupt my present studies, and break threads which, at my age, I may not be able again to unite. In fact, my whole aim may be frustrated. I wish, therefore to continue employed as I have been through your administration.

I shall not try to compass my end by indirect means. If the new Secretary is not persuaded that the service will gain by thus using me, I shall not gainsay his decision. You know, however, what my aptitudes are; and can tell him, if you so think, that it would be well to keep me pursuing this study of the Conduct of War, parallel to the development of the Material of War, which is now advancing so rapidly.

In conclusion, my employment in this way does not necessarily imply my continuance as President of the College, nor am I aiming at that.

To Horace E. Scudder

75 East 54th Street, New York, January 25, 1893 [HUL]

Dear Sir: I send you today, by express prepaid, manuscript sketch of Admiral Saumarez, one of the most distinguished British officers of the Nelsonic period.[1]

---

1. "Admiral Saumarez," *Atlantic Monthly* (May 1893).

Saumarez was essentially the line-of-battle-ship captain; and his career presents such an epitome of the action of the British Navy, during its most momentous period, that I think it will possess both interest and instruction for readers of the class to which the *Atlantic* is addressed.

I have held the manuscript ten days, thinking to send with it the sketch of Lord Exmouth[2]—the frigate captain—afterwards the hero of Algiers. He accompanied Burgoyne's expedition, was among those surrendered at Saratoga, and was also the British officer who so nearly nabbed Benedict Arnold on Lake Champlain. I shall not be able to complete this for some weeks.

To these I thought to add Lord Howe,[3] whose connection with the American Revolution is well known, and with whom much anecdote is associated—and finally Suffren and Tourville—the two most renowned of French admirals.[4]

I see in the morning paper that the House Naval Committee recommends a bill allowing us to retire after thirty years. If this take effect, I propose to master the questions of our general external policy, in matters relating to the navy—according to your kind suggestions—and follow up the line of my former article. Until things settle, it would be wasting time to attempt this.

To the Editor of The New York Times

New York, January 30, 1893[1]

There is one aspect of the recent revolution in Hawaii which seems to have been kept out of sight, and that is the relation of the islands not merely to our own and to European countries, but to China. How vitally important they may become in the future is evident from the great number of Chinese, relatively to the whole population, now settled in the islands.

It is a question for the whole civilized world, and not for the United States only, whether the Sandwich Islands, with their geographical and military importance unrivaled by that of any other position in the North Pacific, shall in the future be an outpost of European civilization or of the comparative barbarism of China. It is sufficiently known, but not, perhaps, generally noted in our country that many military men abroad, familiar with Eastern conditions and character—notably Sir Garnet Wolseley[2]—look with

---

2. "Admiral Lord Exmouth (Pellew)," *Atlantic Monthly*, (July 1893).
3. "Admiral Earl Howe," *Atlantic Monthly* (January 1894).
4. The articles on Admirals Suffren and Tourville were not written.

1. From *The New York Times*, February 1, 1893.
2. Wolseley served in the Sepoy Mutiny, 1857–1858, and accompanied the Anglo-French expedition into China in 1860.

apprehension toward the day when the vast mass of China—now inert—may yield to one of those impulses which have in past ages buried civilization under a wave of barbaric invasion. The great armies of Europe, whose existence is so frequently deplored, may be providentially intended as a barrier to that great movement, if it come. Certainly, while China remains as she is, nothing more disastrous for the future can be imagined than that general disarmament of Europe which is the Utopian dream of some philanthropists.

China, however, may burst her barriers eastward as well as westward—toward the Pacific as well as toward the European Continent. In such a movement it would be impossible to exaggerate the momentous issues dependent upon a firm hold of the Sandwich Islands by a great, civilized, maritime power. By its nearness to the scene, and by the determined animosity to the Chinese movement which close contact seems to inspire, our own country, with its Pacific coast, is naturally indicated as the proper guardian for this most important position. To hold it, however, whether in the supposed case or in war with a European State, implies a great extension of our naval power. Are we ready to undertake this?

To Roy B. Marston[1]

N.P., N.D. Probably, New York, January 1893[2]

Such a tunnel would be a bridge between France and Great Britain. . . .

Historically, every bridge is an element of danger. . . . It may safely be predicted that once built it will not be destroyed, but that throughout any war reliance will be placed upon its defences. History teaches us again and again the dangers of surprise—the dangers of over-confidence. You will have continually in your midst an open gap, absorbing a large part of your available force for its protection. As to the effect upon the sea power of Great Britain, it is obvious that your Navy, were it tenfold its present strength, can neither protect the tunnel nor remedy the evils incurred by its passing into the hands of an enemy. . . . It is an odd kind of thing—making one lay down the pen and muse—to think of an open passage to Great Britain in the hands of a foe, and British ships, like toothless dogs, prowling vainly round the shores of the island.

---

1. A director of Sampson Low, Marston & Company, the English publishers of Mahan's books on the influence of sea power.
2. This incomplete letter, reprinted by permission, was in response to a letter dated January 6, 1893, from Marston asking Mahan's views on the wisdom of a "submarine tunnel between England and France." Mahan's letter is in R. B. Marston, "Captain Mahan and Our Navy," *The Sphere* (June 11, 1904), p. 250.

To Horace E. Scudder

Washington, D.C., February 3, 1893 [HUL]

My dear Sir: I received your letter accepting my article on Saumarez shortly before leaving N.Y. for here. As the administration has but four weeks to go, and I dont know what may next happen, I will suggest for your consideration whether it would not be advisable to send the proofs—as with St. Vincent[1]—some time this month to the Naval War College, Newport. I expect to return there next week.

I entirely adopt your views as to the direction of my future efforts; and, were I assured of freedom of course, would ask your suggestions now as [to] more particular details of reading and thought upon public matters connected with my own line of thought. Meanwhile, the sketches of the British admirals were taken up, as matters with which I had a present familiarity which must soon pass from me. I thought they could be made readable—and would prove novel.

The Forum asked me yesterday for an article on the Hawaii question, which, although the notice was short—a week only—I consented to attempt.[2] They intend it for their March number, and, if worth having at all, should probably appear quickly; but I own to a general constitutional aversion to such hurry. An offer that might be made useful for the Navy I could not well decline.

[P.S.]   I saw Roosevelt today, and understand he has finished his notice.[3] I was glad to know he thought the 2d book equal to the former.

To William T. Sampson[1]

Naval War College, February 13, 1893 [NA]

My dear Sampson: I enclose herewith a list of some pamphlets and also of some drawings which our torpedo man, Chambers, has submitted to me by my directions. Blue Prints of the plans, if such exist would doubtless answer our purpose, which is to prepare large scale drawings for the lecture room.

By the scheme adopted there will be presented *1* a general outline history

---

1. "Admiral the Earl of St. Vincent (Jervis)," *Atlantic Monthly* (March 1893).
2. "Hawaii and Our Future Sea Power," *The Forum* (March 1893).
3. Theodore Roosevelt reviewed *The Influence of Sea Power upon History* in *Atlantic Monthly* (October 1890), pp. 563–567; and *The Influence of Sea Power upon the French Revolution and Empire, ibid.* (April 1893), pp. 556–559.

1. Sampson had succeeded W. M. Folger as Chief of the Bureau of Ordnance.

of Torpedo Warfare *2* a sufficient description of the principal submarine weapons, now in good standing, to enable the hearers to follow intelligently the plans for their use under the heads of "tactics" and "strategy"—each of which have been organized under a somewhat elaborate outline.

Of course whatever injunctions of secrecy you impose will be carefully observed.

I want also to ask if you will not give a general Bureau order to supply the College with the technical information coming to the Bureau, in all cases where the Bureau gives it any circulation. For instance, I obtained once from Folger the elements of the trajectories of some of the new guns—and a table of penetrations of the same. All such data are useful to us.

What will be the best way of attaining this end you will know—possibly to couple the College with the Intelligence Office. You will readily see that we not only may not have such data, but in some cases may even not know it exists. If you can fix a *routine* by which they will always reach us you will much help us.

To William T. Sampson

Draft   N.P., N.D. Probably, Newport, Rhode Island, circa
February 15, 1893 [NA]

Pamphlets prepared or issued from Torpedo Station
Lecture on drifting and movable torpedoes   Lt. F. M. Barber
    ″   ″ Whitehead Torp.   ″ ″ ″   ″
Notes on Torpedo Fuzes   Lieut. G. A. Converse
Lecture on Submarine Boats   Lieut. Barber
Notes on Movable Torpedoes   ″   ″
Issued
History of Torpedo Warfare—Lt. Comdr. Bradford
Notes on Spar. Torpedo   ″   ″   ″
Notes on Towing Torpedo   ″   ″   ″
Lecture Notes on torpedoes etc   Newell

Specifications & plans of Service Whitehead Torp. & Disch'g Apparatus
    ″   ″   ″   ″   ″ Howell   ″   ″   ″   ″
    ″   ″   ″   ″ Pneumatic Gun & Projectiles
    ″   ″   ″   ″ Submarine Gun & Projectiles ("Detachable Ram")
    ″   ″   ″   ″ Proposed Ram for above (Mentioned in Folger's Report)

Any official or authentic information concerning trials, performances or trajectories of above torpedoes.

The above are much needed at War College

To Theodore Roosevelt[1]

Washington, D.C., March 1, 1893 [LC]

My Dear Sir: I present to you herewith the written statement of my wishes, and the arguments pro and con, which you asked me to make.

I have for the past seven years been engaged in the study of matters connected with the Conduct of Naval Warfare, a question entirely distinct from that of the development of Naval Material. Upon the latter, it is safe to say, professional attention has been exclusively concentrated; very few, save myself scarcely any, have attempted the systematic investigation of Naval Warfare and Naval Policy.

You are acquainted with some of the results of my work. I have now in contemplation, 1. For the Naval War College, a Systematic Treatise on Naval Strategy, formulating its theories and illustrating its practice, by the historical examples collected in my previous studies. 2. An historical study of the War of 1812, upon the same general lines as my other historical works. I have on my table a request from a leading publishing firm of New York to write a Naval History of the Civil War.

The continuance of my work depends upon my not going to sea. The absorbing administrative work of a modern large ship of war would impose an interruption, which, at my age—53—and for two years, would probably prove final. I propose, therefore, to retire, as allowed by law, after forty years service, in 1896; if, in view of that intention, I am not meanwhile ordered on sea duty.

The argument *in favor* of this indulgence to me rests upon the character of the work I propose to do, for which that already done by me must be the guarantee. Interrupted now, it is probably interrupted finally; nor, as far as I know, is there any one else likely to take it up.

The argument *against* thus excusing me will probably be that every man must take his turn, that I throw upon others sea service which I should do, and which is essential to my own professional education. The reply is that I will get out of the way as soon as the law allows; and that the experience is not necessary to me, if, as I engage, I retire from active service.

---

1. At this time, member of U.S. Civil Service Commission.

The main argument, however, must be the utility of the work, past and future; the fact of my fitness for it; and the improbability of any one else undertaking it. In support of this I forward to you letters and criticisms, both American and English, which will adequately show the estimation in which the work is held abroad and at home.

In view of these indorsements (all of them unsought) it might also, I think, be safely urged that editors of leading magazines are now seeking from me articles on questions of naval policy, and civil societies asking me to address them on kindred subjects. It is therefore not improbable, seeing the favorable opinion held of me, that I shall by these means be able to contribute to the intelligent comprehension of naval necessities by the country at large.

The question then is: May I not, for the reasons given, be even more useful to the navy by the proposed course than by commanding a ship? And should the simple, and perfectly just, tradition, that each man must go to sea when his turn comes, prevail to prevent me from what is practically a change of profession, probably beneficial to the navy, but which my means will not permit me at my age to risk, except in the way indicated.

It will be important to note that my term of forty years expires in 1896, that is, within the term of the coming administration, upon whose decision my plea rests.

To Horace E. Scudder

Naval War College, March 15, 1893 [HUL]

My dear Mr. Scudder: The proof of "Saumarez" goes to you by this mail,[1] and it was my intention to accompany it with an explanation of the cause of delay, although I had not realized that it would cause inconvenience. The morning after I saw you I received a telegram that my mother had died suddenly during the night compelling my immediate departure for her home in Elizabeth, N.J. I only returned here Monday afternoon, and I desired to read Saumarez twice before returning it to you. Ordinarily I make other avocations give way to proof reading, so that the proofs may go back at once.

I have received both Admiral Ammen's letter and also the pamphlets, which I will look into carefully.

1. *See* Mahan to Scudder, January 25, 1893.

To Francis M. Ramsay

Naval War College, March 17, 1893 [LC]

Sir: I wish to make the following request to the Navy Department. For seven years I have been engaged in a close study of Naval History and Naval Warfare. Of the results of this study much has not been published; but the greater part has been and is now before the Department and the Navy. It is my desire to devote myself henceforward to the development of the same line of thought; and in that view it is my purpose to retire in 1896, after forty years of service, as now allowed by law.

Meanwhile I become liable to sea service for a period of at least two years. I apprehend that at my age—53—such a diversion is not merely a loss of two years of fruitful effort, invaluable at any age and especially in the later prime of life, but that also the consequent entire interruption of my line of thought may prove to be final. The complicated administration of a large modern ship of war is a task too absorbing to admit of sustained mental effort in another direction.

As far as I know, there is no other officer who proposes to do that which I here propose. I therefore ask that, upon the understanding that I will retire as above, within the term of the present administration, the Department will rule that the contribution I may be expected to make to professional thought, by such studies as the above, outweighs the advantage that can result from the experience of two years of command, when these so shortly precede my final retirement from active service; and that the Department will for these reasons excuse me from such sea service.

To Theodore Roosevelt

Naval War College, March 18, 1893 [LC]

My dear Mr. Roosevelt: I have delayed until to day making my application, on account of Mr. Herbert's[1] absence; and would have waited still longer, until I knew he was back, but that to day I have heard "on good authority," that there was thought of ordering me to temporary command of the *Baltimore*, whose captain, I believe, is ill.[2] Independently of the fact that temporary orders have a tendency to become permanent, the applica-

---

1. Hilary A. Herbert had succeeded Tracy as Secretary of the Navy on March 7, 1893.
2. A 335-foot, protected cruiser of 4,600 tons mounting four 8-inch, eighteen 6-inch, and six 3-inch guns. Launched in 1888, her twin screws drove her at 20 knots. In March 1893 she was on the Asiatic Station commanded by Captain William R. Bridgeman, class of 1861 (ex-1863).

tion would come with less grace when under orders. I accordingly sent it by the last mail—three hours ago—and I enclose you a copy, as finally mailed.

I also enclose a clipping from the well known service paper, *Broad Arrow*,[3] chiefly because of the last sentence. Concerning our rise in naval power, Mr. Herbert, I fancy, inclines to think "quorum pars magna fui"; and the connection may touch his convictions. I will ask you to return it to me carefully, as it is one of several sent me by the London publishers with a request to return.

I have thought of only one possible thing to add. It may be objected that other captains might have to go to sea a second time, if I dont. To this I believe an adequate reply can be made that, owing to the retirements of this year, and especially of 1894, there will be a sufficient supply of captains who have never been to sea as such.

I thank you most sincerely for the kind interest you have taken in this matter. It is to me vital—the question, probably, of a career made or a career lost, and I trust that any proper appeal to Mr. Herbert's mind may be made. Other you would certainly not make, and I, I trust, would not ask.

Frederick Singer[1]

Naval War College, March 24, 1893 [NA]

Sir: It is respectfully requested that the matter bearing upon the following subjects be furnished temporarily for the use of the Naval War College.

(a) The instructions or requirements issued to the Board upon merchant vessels as to the qualities necessary to make merchant vessels fit for transport duty.

(b) All available matter concerning the mobilization and maneuvers of the English fleet during the summer of 1892.

To Horace E. Scudder

Newport, Rhode Island, March 24, 1893 [HUL]

My dear Sir: Will the enclosed be acceptable to the *Atlantic*?[1] It is of course very slight, and I may well mistake the interest I feel in these specula-

---

3. *The Broad Arrow; the Naval and Military Gazette*, published in London from 1868 until 1917, when it merged with the *Army and Navy Gazette*.

1. Lieutenant Singer, class of 1868, was Chief Intelligence Officer.

1. The enclosure cannot be identified. Each issue of the *Atlantic* had a section called "The Contributors Club," which contained anonymous short pieces. There is nothing at this period which seems to have been written by Mahan.

tive questions as indicating an interest on the part of others which does not exist. The incident occurred substantially as I say—though the conversation has been considerably elaborated. Fiction founded on fact. The committing it to writing and sending it to you is due to a sudden impulse when thinking the subject over during a morning walk. You will know whether it is worth anything.

The sketch of Exmouth is well forward,[2] but if there is any urgency please notify me. Not more than a day's work remains barring polishing and some clean copying from a very rough draft.

I thank you most cordially for your words of sympathy upon my recent loss.[3] Such expressions are very grateful to the sufferers, and I have appreciated yours extremely.

To Francis M. Ramsay

Naval War College, March 25, 1893 [NA]

Sir: Articles of value and importance to the College appear occasionally in the different English, French and American quarterlies and magazines, but not of sufficient frequency to justify an annual subscription to these periodicals.

I therefore respectfully request authority to purchase for the College the occasional numbers that are needed through some reputable dealer, the whole to be covered by open purchase requisitions every June 1st. and Dec. 1st., and the amount to be expended not to exceed an average of $10.00 a month.

To Theodore Roosevelt

Naval War College, March 26, 1893 [LC]

My Dear Mr. Roosevelt: I thank you most gratefully for your letter and for the effort you have made on my behalf. I understand exactly the state of the case, as it now stands i.e. no promise on the Secretary's part, but apparently a disposition to take a view favorable to my wishes. I consider it a particular piece of good fortune to have had my case advocated by you, prohibited as you are by your reputation from seeking to further it on any other ground than the merits of the case, as you see it. It gives you a unique weight when you see reason for speaking.

2. *See* Mahan to Scudder, January 25, 1893.
3. *See* Mahan to Scudder, March 15, 1893.

I shall wait the issue quietly, though not without grave concern; but sure that in you I have all the support that I ought to desire, and a really interested friend.

I sent you a letter from Laughton, addressed *1215* Nineteenth St. for which I depended upon my memory. I mention it only because you have not. Don't trouble to acknowledge, for unless I hear to the contrary I shall be sure you received it.

To Horace E. Scudder

Naval War College, March 27, 1893 [HUL]

My dear Mr. Scudder: I have the sketch of Lord Exmouth finished, but would be glad to know how long I may postpone sending it in, as the fair copying it is a mechanical process I find rather a relief, if not too much hurried.

My object in writing, however, is to know *when* you want the Nicaragua article.[1] Though not wholly novel to me the subject is large. I daresay I could rush off an article similar to that I sent the *Forum* on Hawaii—but I doubt if either you or I would be satisfied with such hasty treatment.

Personally, I should prefer to let the subject mature in my mind—I am a slow thinker—and to go into print in the early fall, so that if I had anything worth saying it might come before the country fairly, but not too long, before the meeting of Congress.

According to the general plan you had in mind when I saw you, Saumarez appearing in the May number, Exmouth would come in July. Nicaragua and Howe could then follow in the fall.

I am extremely occupied now with my College lectures; but at the same time I am writing fairly easily and rapidly. Nevertheless, I feel that Nicaragua is a subject on which I ought not to feel myself under too much pressure, for discomposure is not conducive to good thinking.

Will you let me know, at your convenience your views in this matter. I go to New York Thursday—but will be back again on Monday—April 3d.

To Endicott Peabody

Naval War College, April 14, 1893 [HUL]

Dear Sir: I write to ask of you when an opening will occur for my son, Lyle Evans Mahan, to enter at Groton; and if you can tell me the probable

---

1. Published as "The Isthmus and Sea Power," *Atlantic Monthly* (October 1893).

number of years he will need to stay, before being fitted to enter College. Without having a fixed plan so far ahead, I incline at present to send him to Columbia.

I know there must be great difficulty in foreseeing the probable stay of a boy, of whose capacity you know nothing; so I must say my reason for asking is, to make arrangements beforehand for covering his expenses throughout his stay. An opportunity for so doing offers at this moment, and I therefore ask you to give me such approximation as you can.

He was twelve years old on Feb. 12 last. I can doubtless obtain for you fairly precise information of his present acquirements from his teacher.

To Horace E. Scudder

Naval War College, April 18, 1893 [HUL]

My dear Mr. Scudder: I forward you today, by express prepaid, the manuscript of Exmouth.

I fear you may think me an alarmist, as I have once before warned you, but Roosevelt writes me that the new Secretary[1] seems decidedly inclined to force me to sea, despite all arguments so far adduced to the contrary—even though I assure my retiring, as the law gives me the right, after three years more. It will therefore perhaps be as well to hurry the article with proofs— no vessel, however, is likely to leave the United States till after the Review.[2]

If the affair take a more favorable turn I will let you know at once— as well as of anything else of consequence to my work for you. The case seems to me so clear that I still hope; but it is useless to ignore the fact that I have to do with men to the last degree routinier.

To Francis M. Ramsay

Naval War College, April 18, 1893 [NA]

The Bureau is informed that I have this day received the Department's order of April 17, 1893, to hold myself in readiness for sea service.

---

1. Hilary A. Herbert.
2. The International Naval Review in New York in April 1893 commemorated the four-hundredth anniversary of the discovery of America by Columbus.

To Endicott Peabody

Newport, Rhode Island, April 20, 1893 [HUL]

My dear Sir: I shall be extremely glad to have Lyle put down for 1894. I have not your letters of the past here, but my impression was that that was his year. In the fall of 1894 he will be thirteen and a half; the following autumn still under fifteen. Nevertheless, I should greatly prefer his beginning in 1894; as I imagine you also would.

If you will kindly let me know that I may count upon this as a probable arrangement, I will look upon the matter as settled.

To Francis M. Ramsay

USS *Chicago*, New York, May 11, 1893 [NA]

The Bureau is informed that in obedience to the Department's order of May 3, 1893, I have this day reported to Commander-in-Chief, and Commander 2nd Squadron, Naval Review Fleet, for duty as Commanding Officer of the *Chicago*.[1]

To Hilary A. Herbert

USS *Chicago*, New York, May 11, 1893 [LC]

Sir:

1. I have the honor of informing you that in obedience to the order of the Bureau of Navigation, dated May 3, 1893, I have this day assumed command of the U.S.S. *Chicago*, relieving Lieutenant Commander C. S. Sperry,[1] temporarily in command.

2. In compliance with Article 362, *Naval Regulations*, I have made a

---

1. A 4,500-ton steel protected cruiser commissioned in 1889. She was the largest and generally regarded as the most handsome of the ABC cruisers. Her load waterline was 325 feet, extreme beam 48 feet 2 inches, mean draft 19 feet, and her twin screws drove her at 15.33 knots. She had a well-proportioned, three-masted bark rig, high sides, and a bowsprit. Her main armament consisted of four 8-inch, eight 6-inch, and two 5-inch breech-loading rifles. At this time, the *Chicago* was the second largest ship in the U.S. Navy, surpassed only by the *Baltimore* at 4,600 tons.

1. Charles Stillman Sperry, class of 1866.

thorough inspection of this vessel, in company with Lieutenant Commander C. S. Sperry.

3. The crew were exercised in my presence, and the exercise and inspection were in every way satisfactory to me.[2]

[Enclosure]

Received from Lieutenant Commander C. S. Sperry, U.S. Navy, upon assuming command of the U.S.S. *Chicago*, the following publications:—

2. Notes on the English Navy, Register No. 48,

Notes on the French, Italian, German, Russian, Navies, Register No. 48,

Notes on the Navies of the Lesser European, and South and Central American States, Register No. 48,

Corrections and Additions to notes on the English Navy, Register No. 48,

Instructions and Questions, Register No. 48,

Letter forwarding "Instructions and Questions,"

Report on Comparative Merits of Coal,

Notes and Diagrams of Naval and Coast Defense Guns of the Principal Foreign Powers, Register No. 48,

Corrections and Additions to Notes on the Foreign Navies, Register No. 48,

Notes on Torpedo Boats of all Nations, Register No. 48,

One (1) file case,

One (1) press copy book.

[Enclosure]

Received from Lieutenant Commander C. S. Sperry, U.S. Navy, upon assuming command of the U.S.S. *Chicago*, the following signal books:—

Two (2) copies of "General Signal Books of the U.S. Navy,"

One (1) copy of "Introduction to Revised Signal Code,"

One (1) copy of "International Code of Signals,"

Ten (10) copies of "Fleet Drill Book."

To Horace E. Scudder

New York, May 13, 1893 [HUL]

My dear Mr. Scudder: I do not know whether you follow naval orders sufficiently to have seen mine to the *Chicago*—on board which I now am. I have delayed communicating with you in hopes I might learn something

---

2. When John McGlensey, commanding officer of the *Chicago*, became ill, Walker allowed Sperry to keep the ship for the Naval Review at New York.

definite about our movements, but as yet I have not. I *think* I shall be able to complete for you the Nicaragua article.[1] That is, I shall continue reading & studying, & I imagine shall probably in the end rush off the paper at white heat, which is contrary to my usual custom; but ship life is unfavorable to my usually methodical habit of writing. If you attach so much importance to the subject as to wish to feel surer, I beg you will feel at liberty to assign the subject elsewhere, especially if you have a writer in view—otherwise you have, say, 75 chances out of 100 that I can do the work. If anything decisively adverse occurs I will inform you at once. My address for the present 75 East 54th St. N.Y.

To Stephen B. Luce

USS *Chicago*, New York, May 22, 1893 [LC]

My dear Admiral: Your letter enclosing Col. Snowden's[1] to yourself was received yesterday. The flattering opinions expressed by Mr. Gladstone and Mr. Balfour are among the most gratifying I have had—coming as they do from men so conspicuous not only in political standing but as men of intellectual force.

The lack of recognition in our own country—either official or journalistic—has been painful; not to my vanity for that has been more than filled by the superabundant tribute from all quarters in England, but as showing the indifference to service matters among our people.

I am not very sanguine about my possible resumption of work. I propose it indeed—but the failure of momentum, the fading of prestige in this age of rapidly changing impressions are all against it. Our own navy—by its representatives, Herbert and Ramsay—has rejected both me and my work, for I cannot but think that an adequate professional opinion would have changed the issue.

I thank you most sincerely for your thought in sending Mr. Snowden's letter which I here return.

[P.S.]   The *U.S. Magazine* for May has a very appreciative notice of the last book by Col. Maurice[2] the author of "War" in *Ency. Brit.*

---

1. *See* Mahan to Scudder, March 27, 1893.

1. Archibald Loudon Snowden, Lieutenant Colonel in the Pennsylvania Volunteers; minister to Spain, 1891–1893.
2. Sir John Frederick Maurice, an instructor at the Royal Military Academy, Sandhurst, England, and author of *Military History of the Campaign of 1882 in Egypt* (1888).

To Hilary A. Herbert

USS *Chicago*, New York, May 29, 1893 [NA]

Sir:

1. I have the honor of informing you that the following vacancies exist in the complement of this ship for the week ending May 27th, 1893:—

2. Seamen   12
   Ord. Seamen   3
   Landsmen   2
   Plumber & Fitter   1
   Coal Passers   7. TOTAL 25.

To Hilary A. Herbert

USS *Chicago*, New York, May 30, 1893 [NA]

My dear Mr. Herbert: An impression prevails that the War College building may be transferred for the purposes of the Training Station, and I have reason to believe that an effort to that effect will be made. While sure that you will not make so serious a change without the careful consideration natural to you, I wish to contest before you the argument based upon the comparative emptiness of the building, for which neither the officers of the institution, nor the nature of the case, is responsible; and to ask your attention to at least two other considerations, which to my mind are of much consequence.

In my original apprehension, the college needed an adequate staff of instructors—four in number; space for instruction, provided by lecture rooms; and finally a corps of resident students, probably six to eight—selected from the annual classes, for a longer and more profound study of the Art of Naval War. For this purpose, the extra rooms of the building would serve as studies.

In pursuit of this end, I had with much trouble collected the instructors, men of excellent capacity, who are not as copiously housed as at Annapolis, and they are now usefully at work. My own detachment leaves a vacancy.

That a class is not forthcoming is not the fault of the College. In this connection I beg to advance my two arguments, against the alleged inutility of a work which has not been given a chance to prove its usefulness:

1. Have laid before you a list of the line officers of the navy on shore duty or unemployed, with their respective occupations, and inquire whether

the latter are of such comparative importance that it is impossible to cull from among them an annual class of fifteen to twenty. Two years ago there were 250 so situated, *below the rank of commander.*

2. Do the College the favor to consider the proposed programme of instruction, copies of which are in the hands of Commodore Ramsay and of the Assistant Secretary[1]—transferred from Mr. Soley—and ask yourself whether the service can afford to dispense with the only means provided for compelling such instruction.

For be assured, Sir, that you will have to bring your horses to the water. Once there, they, or a large part of them, will drink. I have plenty of testimony from the usually silent opinion of the navy to the value of my own work at the College. But for the College that work would never have been produced; and without the College, or its equivalent, you will get nothing on these subjects. To speak coarsely—all important though they are, the pursuit of them "dont pay." They receive no recognition. Though [a] great part of my association with the College it has been a foot ball for sneer and prejudice. The question before you is whether its aims, as indicated in its programme, deserve such treatment, and whether you will constitute yourself the champion of its objects. Unless you do, they fail—they will "not pay."

To John M. Brown

USS *Chicago*, New York, May 31, 1893 [LC]

My dear Sir: I thank you very much for sending me the enclosed,[1] and for your effort on my behalf. Whether I can do *anything* on the cruise remains to be seen; at best I am very very seriously handicapped. A naval officer has no grievance in being ordered to sea—but that is not the question. The question is whether the navy will receive more benefit by my continuing my work, which no one else is prepared to carry on, than by my doing duty for which a score of men are equally fit.

I thank you very much for the copy of the circular and trust that the sale of the books may be satisfactory.

The enclosed correspondence will be regarded as Confidential according to your wish.

---

1. William G. McAdoo replaced Soley as Assistant Secretary of the Navy in 1893.

1. Enclosure not found.

To Washington I. Chambers

USS *Chicago*, New York, June 1, 1893 [LC]

My dear Mr. Chambers: I was pleased to receive your letter, although I am so harassed by the various ship's calls as to be hardly in case to extend help or useful advice. What you say about the Training Station is very true & I was sorely tempted yesterday to write an article for a newspaper showing up the absurdity of Bunce's grievance about quarters when he refuses to occupy those provided for him on board, is supplied with others on shore, and gets sea pay &c. Upon the whole, however, while this *might* be wise, (I dont say it wouldn't), I don't like to embark in attacking a fellow officer, even though he is giving so bad a precedent—for the *Times* account is evidently supplied by him.[1] I prefer to enlarge upon the positive merits of the College, and I yesterday mailed a letter (unofficial) to Herbert, contesting the argument against the usefulness of the College founded upon the fact that Ramsay has steadily refused to utilize it. I called his attention to the immense number of line officers unemployed or on shore duty—then to our programme in Ramsay's and McAdoo's hands and asked whether it was really impossible to spare men for the course. I also explained that the resident instructors were less amply housed than at Annapolis & that the extra rooms in the College proper were for those whom I expected to cull out of the annual classes for a more advanced and profound study of our subjects.

Now I am far from saying that an attack upon the Training System methods would not be advisable; but if made I would make it direct to the Secy, in the nature of a reply to the *Times* article—which is evidently inspired—and not in a counter press article. The latter only injures the navy, and dirties one's own hands. It would be perfectly proper, and in accordance with precedent, for Stockton to take that for his text, calling for a personal explanation & ventilate the whole matter. You too could help him. I cannot, partly because I am now much preoccupied, partly because one of your strongest arguments is that the College has produced, directly, one of the first, if not the first, authority on naval warfare in English, if not in any language. *I* cannot say this, but plenty have said it of me. Unfortunately, my work is made to appear as chiefly of literary excellence, when really its military value is its chief title to reputation. I enclose a circular just sent out from the publisher and if more quotations are wanted they can be found. The work is now being translated into French. It is not pleasant to be egotistic but in fact the programme & my books are the chief Cards

---

1. *The New York Times* article referred to is a long letter titled "Uncle Sam's Naval Schools" and signed "E.G.D.," published on May 29 (p. 9). The author attacked the War College on a variety of grounds and suggested that the postgraduate education of naval officers be conducted at the Naval Academy.

of the College—the rest is both argument and assertion which may be contested—the others cannot. A copy of the programme is in the letter book.

I mentioned your idea to Walker, but like all men he is not willing to enter a doubtful struggle. Above all things keep your tempers and if defeated go down with your colors flying. I can conceive no more miserable feeling than that you have deserted, through discouragement, a cause in which you believe. It would be to me a regret through life. But if, after every proper effort, you are beaten by the folly and indifference of second-rate superiors you have no more cause for mortification and shame than a man who is cut down at his post because the rest have run away from his support. Herbert is a cautious, slow man; and if a strong representation is made him the College will probably last over till its present great enemy has lost his Bureau, & a friend taken his place. All delay makes for the defence—and Robley Evans is thought to have best chance for the Bureau of Navn. He is a friend.

To John M. Brown

USS *Chicago*, New York, June 1, 1893 [LC]

Dear Sir: In dispatching my letter yesterday, amid much confusion, my dominant idea was to return at once the letters you were good enough to send on; and I consequently forgot to say what I would like you to know, (uninteresting as personal explanations are), that my retention at my particular work, by Mr. Tracy, was not, as Mr. Herbert seems to think, the result of either political or social influence. I neither exerted nor possessed the one or the other. Mr. Tracy retained me simply because he believed in my special qualifications for special work. I never entered his house, except on a New Years; we had no close mutual friends, and I knew him only at the Department. He valued me also as an adviser under some circumstances. I would be glad if, at any fitting time, you would convey this truth to Mr. Fairchild.[1]

The fact is Mr. Tracy was a man of ability, used to affairs on a large scale, which Mr. Herbert is not. The latter, with the officer who has the reputation of being his chief adviser,[2] belongs to the class of men who take narrowness for principle and rigidity for firmness. Such are incapable of exceptional action.

I should be glad to have your opinion, based upon the comparative demands for my works in the U.S. and in Great Britain, as to whether the

1. Charles Stebbins Fairchild, New York State Attorney General under Governor Tilden; U.S. Secretary of the Treasury under Cleveland, 1887–1889.
2. Rear Admiral Francis M. Ramsay.

projected work on 1812 or a Life of Nelson would be the more profitable undertaking. There is no good life of the great admiral.

I should also like to ask whether the semi-annual settlement—in July next—could be made by cheque to Mrs. Mahan, I leaving with her a signed blank receipt to be filled up. The *Chicago* is ordered to get away hence, for Europe, on the 15th inst.—and I see no reason why she should not do so.

You will be interested to know that I have it through our Minister at Madrid,[3] from the wife of the U.S. Secy of Legation in London, that both Gladstone & Balfour had spoken in the Secy's house in the highest terms of the second book.[4] The first called it one of "the books of the age." *

* He said "the book of the age" probably a polite exaggeration, if not a misunderstanding.

To John M. Brown

USS *Chicago*, New York, June 9, 1893 [LC]

Dear Sir: Your letter of the 2d was duly received. My own inclination is to take up the Life of Nelson, and I think I shall do so; but while my present preparation is on one side good—i.e. as regards his military character and exploits—I feel a deficiency in appreciation of his personal traits, and in that fund of anecdotes which is so large a factor in a biography. I mention this chiefly to disabuse you of any impression that I am ready at once to write. When we get to England I shall probably provide myself with a copy of his Dispatches &c, and principal lives, and soak in them before putting pen to paper.

I am also obtaining a few volumes of American State Papers the perusal of which is essential to the War of 1812.

I cannot yet judge of the probable size of the Life, but I should say about 400 pages of a volume like Sea Power—perhaps 150,000 words more or less. For illustrations, those in my last work would answer for the battle plans—beyond that I cannot yet say. My aim will be to make the work thoroughly *interesting*.

There is no authority for any statement that I contemplate the War of the Rebellion. I had spoken of it as a thing I might possibly attempt—but my disposition, never very strong thereto, was pretty much quenched by the decision to send me to sea. It will, in my judgment, involve work much in excess of remuneration, and with two years wiped out of my life my present intention is to close my book-making with 1812 and turn my at-

3. *See* Mahan to Luce, May 22, 1893, and Footnote 1 thereto.
4. *The Influence of Sea Power Upon the French Revolution and Empire.*

tention in future to the magazines. But there is no wisdom in formal purposes that can not have effect inside of four years.

I am very much indebted to you for your readiness to accept my suggestion about payments to Mrs. Mahan, and will ask her to notify you betimes of her exact address at Quogue, L.I. where she will spend the summer.

I wish also to repeat my sense of obligation for the action of yourself and Mr. Fairchild in the matter of my orders.

[P.S.] The ship sails on the 15th inst—and our address will be: "Care of B. F. Stevens, 4 Trafalgar Square, London."

To Horace E. Scudder

USS *Chicago*, New York, June 9, 1893 [HUL]

My dear Mr. Scudder: Amid unusual difficulties I have completed my article on the Isthmian Canal, which I have treated mainly from the politico-historical point of view; so much so that I think a title such as "Our Policy at the Isthmus of Panama" or "Political Aspects of the Central American Isthmus" would express the drift—but that is a question you will settle.[1]

We sail hence on the 15th for Europe, probably England. Mrs. Mahan will therefore take the paper with her to her summer destination—Quogue, Long Island—typewrite and send it, so that you will be pretty sure to have it by June 25. If it is set up speedily and forwarded to me (Care B. F. Stevens, 4 Trafalgar Square, London) I will proof-read and return at once, so that the corrected proofs may perfectly be in your hands by July 20. My wife's careful type-writing etc., will minimize printers errors.

I wanted to ask, as I shall not be here when Exmouth[2] comes out, if you could either send me cheque now, or make it out to Mrs. Mahan's order, (Ellen L. Mahan), I leaving with her a blank receipt to send you upon receiving it.

Now for the future—I believe you will be willing to take an article on Howe, if up to standard. Would you be willing also to take two more on British admirals?

I had an idea to submit to Houghton, Mifflin & Co. viz: that these half dozen articles might be made into a book under the title of Six British Admirals and with portraits and possibly a few battle illustrations make a good

1. *See* Mahan to Scudder, March 27, 1893, Footnote 1.
2. *See* Mahan to Scudder, January 25, 1893, Footnote 2.

Xmas book for 1894.[3] If necessary, they could be expanded so as to reach 90 to 100,000 words. I had in truth to compress a good deal & omit somewhat of interest.

We start with the impression that our absence will not exceed a year—but though seemingly well founded, these things are not dependable. Our address will always be to B. F. Stevens.

I am preparing to exert myself in the literary way; but what I can accomplish under these difficulties remains to be seen.

To Hilary A. Herbert

USS *Chicago*, New York, June 9, 1893 [NA]

Sir: I have the honor to request permission to leave an allotment of Three hundred dollars ($300.) per month.

To Augustus T. Gillender

New York, June 13, 1893 [HUL]

Dear Mr. Gillender: Mrs. Mahan, having forgotten about Quogue house fire insurance, wishes me to remind you, in case of time being up.

Also to say: that we are about to put, this week, an addition to the rear extension of 12ft. x 22, the full breadth of the extension, and full height; the lower story to be a laundry, upper additional rooms.

In this addition there will be a laundry stove, connecting with the existing chimney, which was put at the end of the extension, as it now stands, to admit of this addition, if desirable.

The addition will cost us $465.

In great haste, train being late. We return to Quogue, Thursday.

To Augustus T. Gillender

New York, June 14, 1893 [HUL]

My dear Mr. Gillender: I received your letter with enclosures this morning. Am I mistaken in thinking that the policy to which the enclosed is

---

3. The book was eventually published in 1901 by Little, Brown under the title *Types of Naval Officers Drawn from the History of the British Navy*. It contains the sketches of Hawke, Rodney, Howe, Saumarez, and Pellew.

to be attached is in your hands? If you have it—will you see it attached. If not, send it here to me; for we do not sail till Saturday and anything coming Friday will reach me.

I am glad you caught your train, for I feared it was a close thing. I am very much obliged to you for the power of attorney which I will give to Mrs. Mahan today. She leaves town tomorrow and her address will be Quogue, L.I.

[P.S.] We sail Saturday, at 10 A.M. so will get nothing that day.

To Ellen Evans Mahan

USS *Chicago*, At sea, June 28, 1893 [LC]

Dearest Deldie: We are now about 500 miles from Cape Clear, whence sixty more to Queenstown. It is therefore a toss up whether we get in on Friday. I hope we may, because that will give us Saturday to clear up and get to rights—not to speak of the fact that I always prefer port to sea. We have had upon the whole a very unpleasant passage, a good deal of rough weather and threatening with low barometer. Little rain, however, and above all almost no fog, that greatest of trials to seamen. I have been very well and for me unusually free from anxiety or nervousness, but then a big ship gives much less cause for uneasiness. Nevertheless we have taken a good deal of water on board, have been pretty well salted up, and shaken up too. I was talking to the admiral[1] in the door of his cabin when his desk pitched away and caught my leg between it and the door frame. Both the knee joint and the leg underneath were a good deal bruised, and the latter still has and for some time will have a broad belt of black and blue. Of course I have had to be up a good deal at nights, but I have slept well in the day time. The servants are satisfactory as far as my own simple needs go, how they will answer for any entertaining I dont know. Carl laid in fresh grub which lasted over a week, so I might have saved much of my sea stores. However, they are always there, and being American products will probably be as cheap as those to be had abroad. I must not forget to tell you that the old maids positively refused to accept the three dollars I sent by Carl. I have tried to do some reading since we left and really have accomplished something; but the interruptions are numerous. We left the navy yard as you know on Saturday but you may not know that we waited over night at Sandy Hook for the gale then blowing to subside. Leaving

1. Henry Erben, class of 1855, Commander, European Station.

after it, and in June, we rather ex[pected] good weather across, but we reckoned without our boat, for I have rarely seen more slop though often more wind.

Thursday [June 29]

We have been doing very well (for us) the past 24 hours are now within 300 miles of the port and so with a very fair prospect of arriving before dark tomorrow—for it is daylight up to 9:30 P.M. Before I forget—your allotment $300 is made payable in N.Y., first payment end of July. Address Navy Pay Office, Stewart Building. Your address I gave as Quogue. The Admiral told me today that he intended to remain in Queenstown until about July 10—then to Southampton till August 10—then south by way of Lisbon etc to the Medn [Mediterranean]. L'homme propose. I think I shall upon arrival get to work upon Lord Howe for the *Atlantic*.[2] You can scarcely find this a very satisfactory letter, but there is really so little going on, unless I chronicle the petty mishaps of sea going, there is nothing to say. You would not thank me for saying I had forgotten what a beastly thing a ship is, and what a fool a man is who frequents one. I have not actually minded a great deal either the disagreement or the separation, but as Nelson remarked in one of his letters I read two days ago, he got along without his intended very well for a few days—not so well afterwards. Nelson, however, never really cared for his wife after the first few years & fell a victim to Lady H. chiefly because heartempty. I hope to mail this in Queenstown Saturday, which should reach you July 9.

Queenstown July 1

We anchored here about 8 P.M. yesterday, sweetest Del, and may congratulate ourselves upon a fairly good passage. Although rough we had neither fog nor rain—and met no accident. We are of course much concerned over the loss of the *Victoria*.[3] Adml. Tryon was the one of whom a Br officer said he slept with my books. Nellie's letter was handed me upon my arrival and Helen's of the 21st came this morning. The *Eturnia* which left N.Y. the 24th stopped off the harbor today and I hope to get one from your dear self by 6 P.M. today—which will give me time to reply to anything needing reply. I am perfectly well but just now very drowsy—having been up almost all Thursday night and on my feet [the] great part of yesterday. I have written Aunt O.[4] by this mail, addressing 111 Bway. *9 P.M.* I have been disappointed of your letter, dearest, & find it hard to

---

2. "Admiral Earl Howe," *Atlantic Monthly* (January 1894).
3. By collision with HMS *Camperdown* off Tripoli on June 22, 1893, during Royal Navy maneuvers. Admiral Sir George Tryon went down with his ship.
4. Mrs. Cadwalader E. Ogden. Ogden, called "Caddie," was the son of Gouverneur Morris Ogden, called "Gouv," and Harriet Verena Evans Ogden. The last was a sister of Manlius Glendower Evans, Mrs. A. T. Mahan's father.

[114]

understand the delay of the P.O. here; for no mail came and we are told there will be one tomorrow at 9—but I will not risk this not going by tomorrow's steamer. So, good bye. Much love for the children and for yourself.

To Helen Evans Mahan

USS *Chicago*, Queenstown, Ireland, July 3, 1893 [NWC]

My darling Helen: I was greatly pleased to get your letter and Nellie's a day or two after our arrival here—to know that you are all well and with a fair prospect of comfort for the summer. I myself can have but little news for you having as yet not left the ship. This has been partly because of a great disinclination thereto, but still more particularly because of some trouble with my leg which was bruised on the passage over. I paid no attention to it and supposed it was all right; but for some days it has been hurting me and I find that one or more of the glands underneath—that is, back of the knee are swollen. This is always tedious and may materially prevent my enjoyment of Ireland. My intention is, if well enough, to start for the Lakes of Killarney on Thursday to be absent until Saturday night. I think I can make the trip without bringing much strain on the knee. Tell mamma there is nothing ailing the knee cap. Tell her also to let me know as soon as she learns from Little & Brown how the book[1] has done this year. I see that the London agents are still advertising, which I think a good sign. I feel so poor both for you and myself that I hope something helpful may turn up—I cannot but regret if I have to lose my last chance of seeing something of Europe.

During the passage over I read very diligently at the *Sonnets of the Century*[2] & want to caution you against what I think a very common fault in readers of poetry, viz: to read for melody and sweetness, without the mental effort necessary to realize the meaning. Such a method, robbing poetry of its intellect, soon ends in dullness. Try you and do differently. Take the very first sonnet, and bring before your imagination the two women, the garden, the rock hewn tomb. See them as in a picture. See

1. *The Influence of Sea Power upon the French Revolution and Empire.*
2. William Sharp, *Sonnets of This Century*. London: W. Scott Ltd., 1886–1887; New York: T. Whittaker, 1887. The first sonnet is Dean Alford's "Easter Eve." Of the four Mahan condemns for their hedonism, two are by Wilfred Blunt; the contrasted groups are by Matthew Arnold, Hartley Coleridge, de Vere, and Hamilton. The "lofty" one is Louisa S. Bevington, "Love's Depth," the sinful love is Herbert E. Clarke's "Assignation," and the sweetest is Meredith's "Lucifer in Starlight." His other selections include Keats, Rosetti, Wordsworth, and Symonds, among many of lesser poetic stature but impeccable sentiment.

also, what you have often seen, the faint dying light of the day—the full moon shining in the sky—the distant hum of a great city which you have often heard—then the coming up of the band of armed men to watch over the sepulchre—the passing of the word—the slow departure of the women. I myself seemed thus, by the aid of the musical language, to realize that scene as I never had before.

I think too I may safely say to you—Contrast the hopelessness of unbelief, the "Eat and Drink for tomorrow we die" of sonnets like 18 and 19, of 92 and 95, emphasized by their very beauty, with the victorious strain "Oh pain where is thy victory?" of 5 (which try to realize like 1) of 46, 58, 96, of 135. Contrast too the hopelessness of a sinful love, in that otherwise exquisite sonnet 41, with the loftiness of 13, the purity & loveliness of 57, of 137 (the latter one of the very sweetest in the book to my mind) of 152, of 190. Among those that struck me also as most sweet or strong are 8, 15, 56 (requires much thought), 59, 70, 76, 84, 97, 117, 130, 136, 247, 248, 261. But indeed, my dear child, each that appeals grows stronger & sweeter as read & reread. The old wine is better, as our Lord said; and I think the educational influence upon not only your mind but your character of frequent reading of these sonnets would be great and good.

Wednesday. July 5

I shall close now, dearest Henny, so as to be sure to catching tomorrow's steamer—to-days from Liverpool. I was much disappointed not to get a letter from mamma by the White Star steamer which passed here yesterday, having left N.Y. on the 27th. You see by the enclosed slip that I am spoken of as an Irish American captain. Also, tell mamma, I have had a letter from my friend O'Connor Morris,[3] who has read my *Farragut* with "the greatest admiration and wishes I would write a proper biography of Nelson." *Farragut* he will review for the Academy. I will send mamma soon a review in the *Guardian* which I think was done by Major Clarke,[4] & also the second part of Col. Maurice's article.[5] Tonight a party of us are to dine with an Irish (or English) regiment about three miles from Cork by water, and tomorrow the admiral & myself are to take dinner with the Lord Lieutenant,[6] whose yacht is lying in the harbor, on the occasion of the marriage of the Duke of York. You know I am not very fond of this sort of thing—but it is considered de rigueur not to refuse the invite of so high a functionary; both occasions will also possess a certain interest of novelty for me. I am forced

---

3. William O'Connor Morris, Irish historian whose articles and reviews appeared in the *Edinburgh Review* and the *Times*. Mahan was almost certainly in correspondence with him, but his papers have not been found.
4. A most flattering review of *French Revolution and Empire* in the (London) *Guardian* (June 7, 1893).
5. Probably his article "Army and Civil War," *Blackwoods* (May 1893).
6. Robert Offley Ashburton Crewe Milnes, 2nd Baron Houghton, Viceroy of Ireland.

thus to postpone till Friday my start for Killarney but upon that I mean to put my foot down, if my knee, which is much better, will permit. The Admiral now expects to get away on Wednesday the 11th. Nous verrons. With dearest love for you all.

To Henry White[1]

USS *Chicago*, Queenstown, July 6, 1893 [LC]

My dear Sir: I am sorry that I cannot very well accept your kind invitation for the 18th inst; but our movements are somewhat too uncertain. The admiral intends to go hence to Dublin on the 14th afterwards to Southampton—and if at sea, I could not fill my engagement.

We shall probably have to be in Southampton for three or four weeks.

To Ellen Evans Mahan

Queenstown, July 7, 1893 [LC]

Dearest Deldie: I write this line to leave here for Sunday's mail having the intention of starting for Killarny today for a three days absence. I feel some doubt as to the wisdom of spending the money, but I shall never again have the chance. Please let me know as soon as you hear from Little Brown as to this halfyear's sale. We dined last night on board the Admiral's yacht *Enchantress* as guests of the Lord Lieutenant—fourteen at table—mostly military & naval men and his personal staff. He is a very good looking sweet-faced young fellow of about 35, I take him—tall and slender but not slab-sided. Reminds me more of Bertie Harvey than any one I now recall but with more presence, dignity & height. His name is Lord Houghton. He and Col. Jekyll of his staff both complimented me very much on the books—which they had read—as did also Adml. St. John[1] who is Comd. in Chief in Ireland with head quarters here. The latter spoke to me of Frank Blake, who was a close friend of Admiral Mayne[2] lately dead, two of whose daughters are now staying with St. John. I received the enclosed telegram last night. I at first wrote an acceptance; but afterwards reflecting on the expense of the journey back & forth from Dublin, hotel bills etc I declined

---

1. Secretary to the U.S. Legation in London.
1. Rear Admiral Henry Craven St. John, in command at Queenstown.
2. Rear Admiral Richard Charles Mayne, who died in March, 1892.

by telegraph. From Southampton I could go. The Adml. now intends to leave here for Kingstown (Dublin) on the 14th. The Lord Lieutenant has promised him a good time there. For my part I little enjoy these dinners. They are well enough at the time, but are either dull if I take nothing, talking to absolute strangers, or disorder my digestion. If I could travel, get away from the ship, without the incessant thought of money, I should prefer that. However, shortness of cash seems our trouble always. My leg is decidedly better, but troublesome from the eruption produced by the strong counter-irritants used. I am well barring the heaviness consequent upon the compelled loss of my usual exercise. I shall stop here. Yours of the 25th was received just after I closed my letter to Hennie.[3] I wrote yesterday three pages of Howe.[4] We have no news. I may have something to tell you when I return, though descriptions of scenery are tedious. On Tuesday we go to Cork guests of the Corporation and will be driven to Blarney Castle. Thursday the Queenstown people take a sail up some river. Wednesday we have an entertainment on board. Sounds like "a good time" commonly so called. Goodbye dearest love to the children.

To Ellen Kuhn Mahan

Lakes of Killarney, Ireland, July 9, 1893 [LC]

My darling Miss Nellikin: I have just time to start you a letter from the Lakes of Killarney on this day before your birthday, which I may perhaps finish on the day itself. Tell dear mamma that having had the forethought to order my letters sent here, I was so happy as to receive hers of June 30, written on Mr. Scudder's sheet, upon my arrival yesterday from my circumvendibus. I had not been out of the ship since our arrival a week before, except to call upon the Consul, when I came ashore on Friday at 11, and went up to Cork. There I secured my tickets, and then passed two hours in a jaunting car which is a vehicle peculiar to Ireland. The drivers seat, single, is in the middle; behind him there are two seats, back to back, running lengthwise. Each one holds two persons who sit facing outward, with their backs to those on the other seat. In case of need there is room for a fifth who sits with his back to the driver. So you see it is all very compact and convenient, only in a jolt or turning a corner you feel as though you might be thrown out on your nose. I found Cork a bright cheerful town, but nothing about which I need talk to you. At 3 in the afternoon the train started for Bantry. It had begun to rain two hours before, the

3. Mahan's nickname for his daughter Helen.
4. "Admiral Earl Howe," *Atlantic Monthly* (January 1894).

first rain I had seen since leaving N.Y., and I thought I was in for bad luck; but it cleared by 5.30 when we reached Bantry, which is on the sea shore at the head of Bantry Bay, a name mamma has type-written pretty often. Here we took a car, as they call, which is exactly like a five seated buckboard, only higher. The people sit in exactly the same way. We had fourteen passengers and four fine horses, with which we drove two hours, circling round the head of Bantry Bay till we reached Glengariff on the other side, where we were to sleep. The scenery reminded me of Soames's Sound, only on a longer and grander scale—a long narrow Bay between lofty hills on either side—and in fact the general impression was much that of the ruggeder part of Mt Desert. At 9.30 next morning we started again, in a like conveyance, with the same number of passengers, for a drive of nearly eight hours to this place. The road was most excellent, firm and smooth, and winds up and down, over and through mountains, giving many beautiful views; but the hills and the valleys present a constant succession of magnificent Green Mountains, the same blending of scanty verdure with brown, base rock; an occasional lake, or distant glimpse of the sea relieved the prospect. It would have been a most delightful and instructive drive but for the threatening weather, which from time to time came down in showers. There was no cover to the car, so we had to up umbrellas, despite which my trousers were soon wetted, but I managed to keep my feet dry and having my overcoat was protected in the upper part of my body. The road lay through the Counties Cork and Kerry. You may fancy what it would be for people to make a living out of Green Mountain, so the shanties were few, far between, and wretched. The West of Ireland is one of the poorest parts of the world, at least where people are at all civilized.

July 10

Here I had to stop yesterday dear child; and this early morning I have but five minutes to remember your birthday. You have been a [sic] such a dear good child to us that it is always a pleasant anniversary for us to meet. Remind mamma, if she can, to give you the *Life of Mary Washington*[1] by I think Marion Harland for your baptismal day. I had a memorandum of it—price $1.00—and a Boston firm; I think Houghton Mifflin & Co. I am leaving in an hour for Cork & the ship—and there goes the breakfast bell.

9 P.M.

Here I am back to the ship, and I am going to complete my story, because my time is so occupied I dont know when I can get another minute. The road was beset with beggars, mostly children from 8 to 12, both girls and boys. They had a curious way of waiting till the car drove by and

---

1. Mary Virginia (Hawes) Terhune, *The Story of Mary Washington*. Boston: Houghton, Mifflin & Co., 1892.

then running after it. The cry was "PennioverpleaseSir" said very much [like] Jimmie Brown's "morenmillion" which was repeated incessantly. They would keep for a couple of miles and then give over, others almost at once taking their place. One could scarcely blame them, everything looked so poor. The walls of the houses are of stone of which there is plenty; they are thatched with straw, and look wretched. It is said that the poultry and pigs run in and out all over the floor, and that in many the fire just burns on the open floor, and finds a way for the smoke as best can by a hole in the roof. About 3.30 we came in sight of the famous Lakes of Killarney looking down upon them from 1200 feet. The road ran for some time in plain view and then plunged into the forest through which we rode till we reached the town. About four it began to rain hard, and soon after to *pour*. To make things worse passengers began to get off for hotels, ours being the last— and in every case there was a great Irish to do about the luggage which seemed always to be at the bottom; so the whole pile had to be taken down and then lashed on again. The passengers' temper became bad, but I am proud to say Papa was unmoved, although when we arrived my overcoat was wet through from the waist down—also most of my trousers and my drawers. I was *sitting* wet great part of the way. At the hotel they have a drying room which speaks volumes for the climate—in fact the people dont mind rain. As I came down in the train today I saw a child not over five standing in the rain beside its mother as she weeded the potato patch. However, the day after arrival was glorious—clear blue sky with great white clouds and a brisk west wind. I went to church in the forenoon and in the afternoon spent three full hours on the lake, being pulled round in every direction. It is a lovely sheet of water, surrounded by grand hills, and full of islands.[2] On one of them, called Innisfallen, are the ruins of a monastery said to have been built fourteen hundred years ago—which is very probable. For Ireland once was a great seat of piety and learning, called the Island of the Saints.

And now dear child I must stop. I shall try to add a few lines on the 12th saying how I am. You will all be interested in the telegram[3] which came Saturday but was only seen by me on my return. I have replied that we will be in Southampton by the 28th.

I want however to caution you very particularly about the surfbathing at Quogue. The L. I. beach I understand is much less safe than Newport. Do not go out far, and try to learn from the men in charge what the conditions of safety are—each day what you can do safely.

---

2. From here on, this letter is written on verso of a telegram from Henry White relaying to Mahan a dinner invitation from the First Lord of the Admiralty, Earl Spencer, when the *Chicago* reached Southampton.
3. White's telegram referred to above.

July 12. 1 P.M.

I shall close here. Tell mamma that we go to Kingstown day after tomorrow and to address to Stevens hereafter. B. F. Stevens 4 Trafalgar Square London. The doctor says I must go on the sick list for a fortnight and keep my leg perfectly quiet, so if the *Chicago* does anything amiss in that time I shall not be the culprit. Good bye. Dearest love to all.

To Ellen Evans Mahan

Queenstown, July 13, 1893 [LC]

Dearest Deldie: I dont think you treat me very well in the matter of letters. Today I got a scrap from Nellie, evidently written perfectly perfunctorily, without a bit of news, on Sunday as the day when nothing else can be done, and nothing later although the steamer did not sail till Wednesday. I dont think that is the way to treat people who are away or to expect much from them in return, either in words or in spirits. I shall have to leave this here tomorrow, unless the weather promises remarkably fine, so as to assure our reaching Kingstown on Saturday. The distance is small, but fog if it occur may delay us. If we arrive on Saturday, our letters would catch the Sunday steamer from here. The Killarney trip seemed to give my leg a set back; it is now bound up pretty tight, painted with iodine, and I am on the list. I have not left the ship since my return—nor the cabin for 48 hours—and this time so far as depends on me I propose making a sure thing of it. I have today a letter from Mr. White of the Embassy with an invitation from Earl Spencer, the First Lord of the Admy, for Erben & myself to dine with him on the 31st. White says he purposes (he thinks) to have some distinguished people to meet us, & that he has telegraphed to Erben. The latter came in to see me today but made no mention of the fact.

The misfortune about my leg has entirely deprived me of seeing anything, or bearing any part in what is going on. The doctor desires me to take perfect rest as far as possible, and I cannot walk with facility even if I wished; so of course I can give you no news. The entertainment given by the officers yesterday in return for civilities shown them, I am told went off very well—although there was a lack of men for the many women that came. Although not fond of such games I was sorry not to be able to get around and see the people. I surrendered the body of the cabin, retreating to my room. The weather was fine and has been since. I have been working Howe[1] but with only very moderate progress, and indeed with my usually

1. *See* Mahan to Ellen Evans Mahan, July 7, 1893, Footnote 4.

active habits this entire quiet inevitably disorders both my digestion & my head. It is I believe quite settled that we leave tomorrow afternoon. Carl seems to be succeeding pretty well in keeping the bills down as they have been not over $1.50 per diem, and he considers this expensive above the average. I have today recd. through Mr. White the invitation . . . [sentence struck through].

Friday, June 14.

The weather is overcast, and while we may have no delay, I think best to leave this here. We are going about two. A telegram from Mr. White just recd. asks me to keep two or three days after Aug 1 disengaged as he wants to ask some interesting people to meet me, but not sure when those in Parliament can come. I have a slight feeling of absurdity in being thus lionized even in so small a way, although of course recognition is pleasant particularly after the almost entire absence of it at home. Except Roosevelt, I dont think my work gained me an entrée into a single American social circle. I fear that there may be unavoidable expense incurred, but I think it worth while for if reputation is *any* good it is when rammed home by a certain amount of attention from people in position. Dearest love for the children and your darling self.

[P.S.]   Let me know as soon as you hear from Little & Brown.

To Ellen Evans Mahan

Kingstown, Ireland, July 15, 1893 [LC]

Dearest Deldie: I can write you but a line to say we got here this morning after a perfectly quiet and uneventful run. I enclose you the First Lord's letter to Mr. White & you can amuse yourself deciphering the postscript. I doubt if I shall get ashore here; the doctor dont think my leg will be *perfectly* well under a week and I shall run no more risk of a set back. It is not only the local trouble but my general health suffers from the want of exercise. Caution Nellikin not to use "most" for "almost"—as "most always" or "most all the girls." In conversation it is bad enough but particularly so in letters.

I dont know when this will get out. The steamer leaves Liverpool today and Queenstown tomorrow—and there is nothing to say but that I am well, barring the one trouble & that I love and miss you.

[P.S.]   Scudder has never sent me a copy of the July *Atlantic* with Xmouth.

To Ellen Evans Mahan

Kingstown, July 21, 1893 [LC]

Darling Deldie: I have just had a visit from His Honor Judge O'Connor Morris, who is by no means the formal person we would have expected from that very curiously formal note that came last winter. Did I tell you that upon reaching Queenstown I recd. a letter from him sent back from home, speaking about *Farragut* & saying that he himself was desirous of writing a life of some great Commander for the series?[1] I replied, and he wrote at once to ask me to visit him at Tullamore. I was then going to Killarney, and could not—but upon our arrival here he again asked me. In my enforced quietude I was obliged to decline, but said I would be very glad if he would visit me here which he has just done. From things he said he must be well on in the sixties, but he dont look it and he is a gentleman. It is a great disappointment to me that I cannot avail myself of this probably my sole visit to Ireland—and with such favorable conditions, for much hospitality has been extended. However—I seem to be getting decidedly better, only a thing of that sort is very slow. Now, I never know just what I have said before to you or to others, so that if I repeat you must forgive me. Your letter of the 7th did not reach me till the 19th. It got to Queenstown on the 15th so the delay is unaccountable and inexcusable. However now I have it, it is all right. Tomorrow I hope for one of the 10th or 11th from some one of the family. Pray disabuse yourself at once that letters all about yourselves are uninteresting. What interest have I at all comparable to you all, and especially to yourself? I am glad to know that Dr. Dix[2] thought well of Exmouth—for he is a judge of style. I have not seen it in print—why I cant imagine; for Scudder knows my address and it is just as cheap to send it here as to N.Y. I fancy it may be one of those which Stockton says he sent to 54th St. If you have it, please send it me, for I want to speak to the English publishers here about publishing in book form as "Six English Admirals." I have had a letter from Stockton & from Jane—the latter as Mrs. Aldens. Nothing particular in either. I replied to both at once. The College prospects seem gloomy, but I have washed my hands of it and of the Navy, and my only concern is on account of those whom I induced to go there. I must have told you in my last of my invites from Earl Spencer and Mr. White, & of my having to recall my acceptance on account of the uncertainty of my leg. The former has renewed the invitation for Aug. 9 and I have accepted again—the other has not and I dont wonder. He was evidently exciting himself to collect a company—and al-

---

1. *Great Commanders Series*, edited by James G. Wilson for D. Appleton and Co.
2. Morgan Dix, Episcopal clergyman and author.

[123]

though I really was not to blame it looked so. Besides the London season is now over. Cowles[3] said: "Pardon my insistence but you really owe it to yourself to leave Dublin & come here if you possibly can." We start on Sunday (23d) for Cherbourg—thence to Southampton where we will be by Aug. 1. The yacht races take place the following week and there will be a great crowd. The Queen I believe is at the I. of Wight, and the Emperor of Germany is to be there though officially incog. So far I have stood out of everything. The proof of the Isthmus paper reached me today. I have Lord Howe more than half finished, but it progresses slowly perhaps because the subject is not perfectly congenial. I must by all means finish it ere I am off the list, for it is evident I shall have very little time after reaching Southampton and getting well. My plan is to go to London about Aug 7 and stay a week—& with that to conclude my spree except what may turn up at Southampton. If I had been in England in July—from all indications I would have had a rattling time, for there seems no question that the books have taken wonderfully. Have you heard from Little & Brown? I trust I shall hear that Helen went to Madeleine Lewis, for, though I want her to enjoy herself her own way, I think that the habit of being with others, and the fact of being known to and liked by others, are considerable elements in the interest and enjoyment of life. She is one who is likely to be more valued and more interesting as she is better known.

July 22.

I am completely broken up today by the failure to hear from you—the last letter being July 7 and there being dates on board since yesterday of the 14. If you wrote again to Queenstown the fault may be there, for your last did not reach me till three days after it must have got to Q. town whether the fault of the Consul or of the local mail I dont know. Yours of the 7th however gave me to hope that you would thenceforth address Stevens. Let me remind you that the time of mails leaving N.Y. is daily advertised in the *Times* and I should think that a letter mailed the afternoon before at Quogue in time for the afternoon mail to N.Y. would certainly come by the next day's steamer. Even if you missed last Saturday's steamer, however, there should have been a letter somewhere in the middle of the week but nothing has come. There is another caution—always repeat in two successive letters anything of importance. I am most particularly anxious at this time to know what the returns from Little & Brown may have been. There is no news since yesterday as how should there be confined as I am to the cabin. The galleys of the Isthmus which have come postmarked Boston July 10—by Stevens. I send them back by this mail. Love to the children.

---

3. Lieutenant Commander William S. Cowles, class of 1867, U.S. Naval Attaché at London.

To Helen Evans Mahan

Cherbourg, France, July 25, 1893 [NWC]

My dearest Helen: I have to begin my letters with excuses for no news, for in the way of personal experience I have nothing to record beyond confinement to the cabin & a sorrowful failure to get any letters from home. My last date is still the 7th, others have them of the 14th and I am at a loss to account for it. It will be two weeks tomorrow that I have not been out of the cabin—but the doctors think I have really progressed very far, and today for the first my leg is not in splint. I myself recognize a very decided improvement and hope to be around pretty freely in a week. We left Kingstown Sunday morning early, and arrived here at 11 p.m. last night, having had a very pleasant passage with a minimum of fog, the great drawback to the English Channel. It is thirty years this summer since I was last here, in the old sailing ship *Macedonian*, of which Adm. Luce was then Captain; and it is a quaint feeling to see still the same old mole with its fortifications which will doubtless be here thirty years hence when I shall likely have gone the way of all mankind. I have little association with the place although I was also here in 1858. I only landed in /63 to go to Paris and thence by land to Cadiz. The country side as I see it from the ports is lovely. "The pleasant land of France"—never were truer words written. We will remain till Saturday or Monday and then to Southampton. From the latter place the Adml. tells me he means to cross to Havre, remain there till about Sept 1—then to Lisbon—Gibraltar the end of September, and Nice in October. There he will tie up for the winter.

I am greatly interested in your poetry—for I cannot but think that an *intelligent* reading of it will tend to develop you all round.[1] I would like you for instance to compare the following sonnets 9, 18, 217 which have all the same motive, and are in my judgment pitched upon a false key, because a half truth—the impermanence of the deepest love between man and woman. Study them, so as fully to apprehend their meaning, and then contrast them with three others, 57, 190, 247 whose theme is fidelity and constancy. See which rings truest to your truest self. Compare with these again the *Golden Treasury*, 194; and again the words on the enclosed slip,[2] written

---

1. *See* Mahan to Helen Evans Mahan, July 3, 1893.
2. The slip read:
   Mr. Seladine comes in with your letter, whom I am engaged to entertain a little; besides it is supper time, or else I should bestow one side of this paper in making love to you! and since I may with modesty express it, I will say that if it be love to think of you sleeping and waking, to discourse of nothing with pleasure but what concerns you, to wish myself every hour with you, and to pray for you with as much devotion as for my own soul—then certainly it may be said that I am in love; and this is all that you shall at this time have from your

   D. Leycester

   Kiss my boy Algernon for me, who sent me a very prettie French letter.
   Mahan may have been reading Frances Moore, *The Leycesters*.

[125]

by an English lady over two hundred years ago to her husband, a woman who was mother to the most charming woman of her generation and who had been twenty years married when she wrote. To my mind, despite the 20 years of married life it is the sweetest love letter I ever read. Where does truth lie with the first three—exquisite as they are—or with the sentiment that inspired the other. I have been very much struck with the way *study* upon this volume of Sonnets repays—for in truth it is not the *new* things that feed the soul, but those which often reading has made familiar friends.

Tell mamma that I have read and dispatched the proofs of the article for the *Atlantic* and I find that between you you have avoided any mistakes. I had to make more than my usual corrections, due I think to the disturbance amid which I wrote. Howe is well forward. I hope I may finish this week before coming off the list or reaching the distractions of race week at Cowes. With dearest love for our sweet mamma and very much for yourself and Nell and Lyle.

To Horace E. Scudder

USS *Chicago*, Cherbourg, July 25, 1893 [HUL]

Dear Mr. Scudder: I write to say that the galleys of "The Isthmus and Sea Power" were received by me at Kingstown (Dublin) on the 21st, read and remailed on the 22d.; so I expect that they took the steamer from Queenstown on the 23d.

It has occurred to me that two articles—not exactly a sequence, but in close connection—are needed to complete the treatment, viz.: one on the general drift of the negotiations and contention, that went on subsequent to the Clayton-Bulwer treaty. Mr. Blaine developed the idea, which I think would find echo with many Americans, that the treaty had become unequal in its bearing upon us, because our strength (potential) was land, Great Britain's (actual) maritime. Hence, he argued virtually, as she controlled the water, and we, as well as she, were forbidden to occupy the land by armed force, the game was left in her hands. To this the reply, from my point of view is twofold. 1 Had we a million men in arms, we could not maintain an occupation of a tropical dependency against maritime force preponderant in the surrounding waters no more than Napoleon's legions could cross Dover straits; and 2, that nothing prevents our building a navy of any power we wish. As a purely diplomatic question this is of course out of my line, though not impossible; as a mixed question of diplomacy and arms I think I could handle it.

The second article would be a discussion of the geographical features of the Caribbean Sea and Gulf of Mexico with reference to their military and naval significance; or in other words the Strategic features of that region.[1] On this I have lectured at the College.

If you think well of these propositions, it would be desirable to send me at once a proof of the "Isthmus and Sea Power" so that without expressing connection I may avoid iteration & preserve some continuity of thought. "Howe" is well on toward completion.

[P.S.] I never got a copy of Exmouth—was any sent me?

To Ellen Evans Mahan

Cherbourg, July 28, 1893 [LC]

My own dearest: I am inexpressibly vexed and a good deal worried at getting no letter. Dates of the 15th were recd a week ago—and today a Washn. offl. envelope postmarked 17th—yet the latest I have from you is the 7th. Your last said you would address to Stevens—but I took the precaution of a special letter to Queenstown to insure forwarding from there. Today surely at latest would have brought that, but it has not and I am now forced to think that in ten days July 7–17, in which at least two letters should have started, either some did, or were wrong-addressed or understamped. I beg you to be most careful on these points, for I trust you may not have to know either the anxiety or bitterness I have undergone. If it were a case of one letter, a thousand mischances might arise, but the failure of two cannot be explained by any assumption except neglect to write or carelessness in sending.

My leg is now really much better and the doctors think me out of the woods. I go on deck a little, and will probably come off the list when we get to Southampton. We shall leave here Sunday 30th. Howe is about finished but has run longer than I wish—11,000 words. I am trying to cut down but see little place.

In view of this trouble about letters, remember my caution always to repeat essential themes. Except understamping I cannot imagine accident—remember that foreign postage a single letter is only ½ oz. I am driven to

---

1. "Strategic Features of the Caribbean Sea and the Gulf of Mexico" was published by *Harper's Monthly* in October, 1897.

think that for some reason you have not written, and imagine illness and that you consider suspense better than knowledge.

I have no heart to write more.

[P.S.] We get a mail package daily from Stevens, and there are steamers from N.Y. at least four days every week.

To Ellen Kuhn Mahan

Cowes, Isle of Wight, August 1, 1893 [LC]

My darling Miss Nellikin: It seems to me that your turn for a letter comes just when I have most to say—last time from Killarney and today just after I have been to dine with the Queen, like the pussy cat that went to London. As there were 54 people at the table the compliment to me personally cannot be considered very exclusive. You see we only arrived at this anchorage on Sunday, and yesterday I received the biggest invitation envelope that *I* ever had. I looked at it very carefully, lest it might contain dynamite and on the seal I observed "Board of Green Cloth." That sounded very royal and upon opening I found myself informed that "The Lord Steward had received her Majesty's Commands to invite Captain Mahan to dinner at Osborne on Monday, the 31st July at 8.45 o'clock." That was the same evening, and as the Admiral was also invited we of course went together. You must understand that when people dine with Majesties they have to wear all their clothes special full dress, epaulettes &c &c, including swords—so I ate dinner with my sword on for the first time in my life. After we arrived—having driven about twenty minutes from the landing—we were led through long passages to the reception room, I suppose it would be called, where we all gradually assembled. We two were almost the first arrivals. The foreign officers are more covered with lace than we are, and besides that they wear orders, generally crosses, on their breasts, all which makes them very magnificent. At last a side door opened, and an old lady—the queen—made her appearance. She simply bowed to the company and then took the arm of her grandson the Emperor of Germany, and led the way to the dining room. There were not enough ladies to go round, so we superfluous men, admirals of the fleet, generals captains &c followed "promiscadres." The dining room was grand all in white, carved I presume, though I could not tell—and one long table. The queen was seated in the middle, on her right the Emperor, on her left another grandson the Duke of York who was married last month. The other men with ladies had their places assigned them, but we seated ourselves as we pleased at the two ends. I found myself between an Austrian admiral and a German captain both of whom spoke English very well. Second on my left was an old Admiral of the Fleet whom I recognized as Sir Henry Keppel, who commanded in China when I was there in 1868. I presented myself to him, and then to our admiral who sat next him on the other side. The dinner was like other dinners—neither more nor less. The champagne was too sweet for my taste so I drank little of it. The most interesting feature was the waiters. The English were mostly dressed in scarlet swallow tailed coats with double rows of brass buttons, buttoned up, and gold epaulets. There were some more elegant looking in black evening dress. Then there were some in Highland dress, and some Hindoos or Mussulmans in their Indian costumes and turbans. In the midst of the dinner two pipers in full Highland costume came in, and marched twice round the table, playing their bagpipes—then out of the door. When dinner was over the queen arose and of course all others, we all turned toward and bowed as she went out, according to our capacity for bowing. Some ladies curtsied very low. We all returned to the drawing room, and stood round chatting until the queen rose to retire. I forgot to say that before dinner was over two healths were drunk all standing viz: the Queen & the Empress. In the drawing room, she sat; all others (I think) standing; and one and another were taken up and presented to her—papa among them. She was kind enough to say she had heard of my books (I think that Royal people are always coached for such occasions). It was very easy to stand inclined very low, for had I not she could not have heard me, nor I her. I suppose the conversation lasted five minutes she then bowed her head, and I backed out as naturally and I daresay as ungracefully as if I had been doing it for years. When she rose to go the Emperor again gave her his arm, as she went out of the door she turned toward him—he bowed very low and kissed her hand. This was the end. We were taken into a room and there signed our names and rank, with the date of the dinner and place, in a birthday book, each man on the day on which he was born. Besides the queen, there spoke to me very flatteringly about my books, Prince George of Wales (the Duke of York), Adml. Commerell,[1] General Ponsonby,[2] Lord Roberts.[3] The latter is considered to be one of the two best, some say the best general in the British army. He told me some one had sent him the first book, but he himself had bought the second, and after some flattering words I said, Yes, my Lord, but it is better to have done something as you did in Afghanistan than only to have written something. The Ger-

---

1. Sir John Edmund Commerell, commander-in-chief of the North American Station, 1882–1885, Admiral of the Fleet, 1892.
2. General Sir William Francis Ponsonby.
3. Frederick Sleigh ("Bobs") Roberts, 1st Earl Roberts of Kandahar, Pretoria, and Waterford.

man Count von Arnim, who commands the Emperor's yacht, also spoke to me of the book. I was presented to the Prince of Wales, who talked very pleasantly for some time, but did not allude to that interesting subject.

The bad side to all this is that I am kept jumping so I have no time. I write now in utmost haste to save this mail. Yesterday we fired 105 guns—and at the end of the day when I was tired and lying down I was jumped out to meet His Royal Highness the Duke of Connaught,[4] who came on board without a moments warning. There was something funny about it, but I have not time to tell. To morrow I go to London to dine at Mr. White's, our Secy of Legation, returning next day.

Give my love to all. Tell mamma I at last got her Southampton letters and please never again address to a point without my knowing it. I am delighted with the news about the books and will tell her what I think in my next.

To Ellen Evans Mahan

Southampton, England, August 4, 1893 [LC]

Dearest Deldie: The ship came to Southampton, where she now is, yesterday from Cowes. I had at the latter place recd. a letter from Mr. Henry White, our Secretary of Legation, asking me again to dine with him on the 2d. This was the day he had first fixed and I accepted, and afterwards I had to cancel the engagement because of the uncertainty about my leg. I now accepted again and went up on Wednesday, taking a train that would bring me in not much ahead of time. I arrived in London about 6, went to Cowles's apartment, and got round to White's sharp on time—not ahead —to find no one yet arrived. His wife and himself were however on hand. She is a tall, slight, quite pretty woman not looking over thirty, tho she may have been set off by the light. The company duly arrived. I passed a very pleasant evening though the pleasure was less than the interest. I was very glad indeed to have an opportunity of seeing a number of people belonging to the London monde, and I believe Mr. White *did* as he said invite them mainly with a view to meeting me. The Whites I fancy are the kind of people who are both fond of entertaining and kindly. I enclose a list which he gave me next day of those present. I took down Lady Gwendolen Cecil, an ideally pretty name to my fancy. She is not pretty but is both intelligent and agreeable, and besides her father, the Marquis of Salisbury,[1] is one of

---

4. Arthur William, third son of Queen Victoria.

1. Robert Arthur Talbot Gascoyne, Lord Cecil, 3rd Marquis of Salisbury, became foreign secretary in 1878, and was prime minister on several occasions.

the most prominent men in England at the present time. I saw of course more of her and of Mrs. White who was on the other side of me than of anyone else but I exchanged a few minutes talk with most of the ladies. Only one, except Lady Gwendolen, whom I decidedly liked was to me particularly attractive, and that was Lady Elcho,[2] a married woman. The others as I saw them were just the average, but those two and Mrs. White ranked well up among agreeable women. Mr. Balfour,[3] the leader of the Opposition in the House of Commons was one of the party, and also Mr. Asquith[4] who is a member of the present cabinet though a very young man. White told me that these two were very desirous to meet me; & also Mr. John Morley,[5] after Gladstone[6] the leading man in the present government. In fact I can scarcely believe all that White says about my reputation here although I can on the other hand give no reason for my hesitancy. Morley was to have been at the dinner, but was detained in Ireland. I dont think we got to table before 8:45, and I did not get away till after twelve. White told me to remain to the last, but I went five minutes after the last woman. The next day I called on Mr. Bayard[7] our ambassador, and that was all I did, leaving London at 3 and reaching the ship at 6. On Monday I am going again to town and purpose remaining through the week—but it is possible that my expected enjoyment will fall through—every one having left town. I fear this is not a very pleasant letter, not nearly as interesting as it should have been, but I am put about and my day upset by again failing to get my letters, although dates a week later than your last (July 18) are on board. I most confidently expected to hear today and the disappointment threw me off so that I have not been able to regain my equanimity, and a concurrence of unpleasant circumstances on board has not helped me. I hope you have not again undertaken some new address, as you did to Southampton. My knee I think is really decidedly better—though once in a while I get a little discouraged about it. It has been a bad set back. I was very well when I reached Queenstown & feeling full of vigor while with it I have lost my grip and feel no energy nor interest. The sea trip singularly enough seemed to stir me up but all that has been lost and the simple detestation of the navy remains. One of our officers met Gouv. Ogden ashore yesterday—just arrived in the *Paris*. He told him that I was in London, which was true, but apparently he did not know that I was so soon to return. Love to the chicks—pretty big chicks now. I intend writing to Helen on her birthday.

---

2. The wife of Francis Wemyss Charteris Douglas, Earl of Wemyss, British politician.
3. Arthur James Balfour.
4. Herbert Henry Asquith, 1st Earl of Oxford and Asquith.
5. John, Viscount Morley of Blackburn, British statesman and man of letters; editor of the *Fortnightly Review* and biographer of Cobden, Gladstone, and others.
6. William Ewart Gladstone was Prime Minister at this time.
7. Thomas Francis Bayard.

[P.S.] I never told you about the money & can scarcely do so now without missing the mail. Fortunately there is no immediate hurry. I purpose however to pay my clothes bill from it—for I shall be too skimped without. In the long run I think I can come out all right on my share, but I want to spare myself the additional wear & tear to my most distasteful situation of perpetual worry about money. Then I want you to have about $400 at the beginning of a month in the Bank. The rest could go to Savings Bank only hesitate to put all in one bank. Will try to put a slip in Helen's letter. The money should be tithed for church.

To Ellen Evans Mahan

Southampton, August 5, 1893 [LC]

Dearest Deldie: I felt yesterday that my letter was a failure and I was very sorry for it. I can only say that I get very galled and distracted by the various calls upon me. I have found out where the missing letters almost certainly are—at Cowes. Either by mismanagement or misunderstanding they were sent there by Stevens on Wednesday—the 2d—arriving after the ship left on Thursday, and the portmaster apparently has not cared to forward them. I wrote him last night again & he has been telegraphed this morning, so I hope but do not at all expect we may receive them this evening. Now about the money. It appears to me, first, that we should give a tenth—$87—to the church, and it appears to me the pew rent, certainly for a half year might come out of it. Then I want my clothes bill paid from it. To do this I purpose sending the bill, when rendered, to you, and you can arrange through Hart to get a bill of exchange for the amount—sending him your cheque on the Chemical. I find it absolutely necessary to get a new blouse and cap—the old not only are shabby but cannot possibly last the year. Lastly, I think that to leave in the Chemical enough to make your balance at the beginning of a month $400 would be worth your while. I do not think you will be led to extravagance, and you will gain, in feeling easy about paying bills, more than the petty annual interest. When you go to town I would fix this so that, say Oct. 1, you would have $400. The remainder I would put in savings bank, only it might be well to take some other than the Greenwich, so as not to have all the eggs in one basket. You might ask Mr. S. [Scudder] to recommend one in Boston, desposit there and gradually raise it to an equality with the N.Y. Bank. You will have the cheque—scarcely less than 100—for the article already gone to the *Atlantic*, and Howe is now finished all but revision—I hope to mail it you for type writing by Aug 15. How small the little amounts are and yet how

[132]

happy they make us. I felt as if I wanted to tell every one the good news, for at most I hoped for $500. Last night I recd. Helen's of July 25—no. 14—Nellie's and presumably one of yours, 12 & 13, are still missing. I shall write to the dear child tomorrow, her birthday—the same mail will also take this. On Monday I go to London about 3 P.M. wishing next day to try on my new clothes, so that I may as soon as possible have the use of them. On Wednesday we dine with the First Lord—whether other attentions await us remains to be seen. It may possibly be difficult for me to write you to any extent while absent. A letter from Stevens, about the mail, tells me that Gouv left a card for me and that they are at Long's Hotel. I shall hunt them up of course. My intention is to return on Saturday or Monday but I shall be guided by circumstances. Capt. Clark[1]—a Pacific acquaintance—has asked me to pay them a visit at Plymouth, and Major Clarke's wife—he being in Malta—has asked me there to lunch—in Winchester, about 20 miles hence. He has become Sir George Clarke since I last wrote him.

6 P.M.

I have just finished revising Howe. The delay has been partly due to my carelessly destroying some of the rough copy. With my usual caution, I dont want to risk $125 worth of brain work, without a duplicate; and you also after sending your type written copy to Scudder had better keep the original until the article is published. The slight inconvenience of shoving it into a corner is nothing to the great one of losing the whole. I also will keep mine, which is complete but exceedingly rough—and far away from Boston. Goodbye my dearest.

9 P.M.

[P.S.]   The letters from Cowes have come, and I have Nellie's—No. 13 but not No. 12. I am very glad to get hers which was a very nice letter indeed, but I do so miss yours and it seems so long since I last heard from you yourself.

To Helen Evans Mahan

Southampton, August 6, 1893 [NWC]

My darling Child: Today is your birthday and you are out of your teens. It seems hard to realize, by simply thinking of the intervening time, that twenty years have passed since I heard your first feeble wails; but when I compare myself as I am with what I then was, the dints of twenty years on my physical powers are perceptible enough. Well, you have been to us a great happiness and very little trouble. You have been spared serious

---

1. Bouverie F. Clark.

illness, mercifully both to yourself and us and you have given me no anxiety, all which we gratefully and lovingly remember.

Tell Lyle that though it is his regular turn, he must be content for a while to stand out of his letter. I wrote to mamma yesterday so have very little news. I greatly miss mamma's advice in the various matters to which I have to attend; I have got so in the habit of depending upon her that I seem lost by myself—though I daresay I shall do fairly well. My clothes have been measured for, and are to be tried on upon Tuesday. I shall be rather shabby for my London visit for I fear they will not be ready for use then. I have written this morning to Aunt Ogden and told her that I should be sure to look them up when I got to town. In Southampton I have not been ashore, except when I went to the train on Wednesday, because we lie so very far off and our boats are so poor and few. I greatly regret it for I am sure I suffer for want of proper exercise on shore—perhaps when I come back I may make up my mind to try it, but I look longingly to the day when I shall be able to get to the beach in five minutes. We are like to be here till Sept 3d, when we are to go to Havre. Goodbye my dear child—enjoy your summer and dont *over* work yourself.

To Ellen Evans Mahan

London, England, August 11, 1893 [LC]

Sweetest Deldie: I always feel like a thief when using the stationery of a club to which I do not belong; but all the same I shall steal a little from the United Service, which has made me an honorary member for three months, in order to write to my darling. I came to town Monday the 7th with the Admiral. That evening we dined at the Club with Cowles, but the next day Mr. White asked us to dine with him at the Marlborough Club. When we left his office and came out on the pavement, Erben said "Well I suppose it is go just as we are" his just as we are being a blue serge coat and waistcoat, brown trousers with a very perceptible large check in them, and brown pot hat. Not much, I replied, I shall dress—whereupon he began to stamp and to snort, to blow and to rage with many expletives I must leave you to imagine. He wouldnt, he wouldnt, he wouldnt. Soon Cowles came out and the same question was propounded to him. Of course he should wear evening dress. Renewed objurgation, in the midst of which I left them to go to their lunch, while I went to Long's Hotel to find Aunt Ogden. Of course Erben dressed, and we had an excellent dinner. I purposely went at Aunt O's usual lunch hour, found her in, and went to lunch with her and Miss Ogden. She asked me to come again next day. She was looking very well and in good spirits. Gouv. came round to my lodging later in the afternoon. Next day—Wednesday—I lunched with them again and after lunch said good bye, for they were leaving next day for the lakes; but Gouv drove down to the city where I left a card upon Frank Blake, who was out of town—tried to see Marston of Sampson Low, who was also away. (Here, before I forget let me tell you that I left Howe with Carl to send by mail on Monday last) I parted with Gouv about 5 and went home to lie down. This was our day to dine with the First Lord, and White came for us at 8:15. I believe the Admiral had no scruple about dressing for this. Mr. White came for us at 8:15—the drive being only five minutes. The company was nearly all assembled. Now White says that the dinner was entirely in my honor, but Erben tells me that it was due to the fact that we were so civil to the Lord Lieutenant, who wrote over for them to do something for us. You may select your own version, but do not spread this, for *such* variance as to who shall be greater is nothing but ignominious. The First Lord, Earl Spencer, is grandson or grandnephew of the Earl Spencer concerning whom I wrote so much. Besides him, there were three ex-first-Lords, the Marquis of Ripon,[1] Earl Northbrook,[2] and Lord George Hamilton.[3] Erben was placed on Earl Spencer's right, and I on his left so the dinner was evidently for the two of us—waiters (if so common a name can be applied to such gorgeous mortals) in powdered hair and short clothes attending on the table. There were about 24 guests, admirals etc etc; among them Colomb, and Dennis' China friend Richards.[4] During the evening after dinner, and during a reception that followed I received a great many kind speeches about the books, which I wish I could adequately repeat for your pleasure. It was a man's dinner; but empty as London is very many ladies were there in the evening. Among them was Miss Russell that was, I dont know if you recall her, of Boston—now Lady Playfair[5] who was also complimentary. I was presented to Mrs. Gladstone, who looks like a crazy woman. She was kind enough to forget the fact in five minutes, and to my great amusement I was trotted up to her *at her request* a second time. As her memory seemed so bad, the old conversation answered again. While talking with a Lady Hayter,[6] she asked me out to spend next Sunday, which I accepted somewhat to my present regret. I go tomorrow afternoon. Last night I dined by appointment with Prof. Laughton who has given me some points about

---

1. George Frederick Samuel Robinson, Marquis of Ripon, who was First Lord of the Admiralty in 1886. At this time, he was Colonial Secretary.
2. Thomas George Baring, 2nd Baron Northbrook, who was First Lord of the Admiralty from 1880 to 1885.
3. Lord George Francis Hamilton, who was First Lord of the Admiralty from 1885 to 1886 and from 1886 to 1892.
4. Possibly Rear Admiral G. E. Richards, RN, who had been employed for many years on the Surveying Service.
5. Edith Russell, wife of Lyon, 1st Baron Playfair of St. Andrews.
6. Widow of Sir George Hayter, portrait and historical painter.

Nelson. Tonight I am to dine with Sir Francis Jeune[7] (pronounced June) I have not seen him, but he called and the invitation came en règle from him. This will probably finish me up, and I shall return to the ship on Monday or Tuesday next. I see by the Paris Ed *N.Y. Herald* that the College and Training Station are amalgamated. If so you had better write to Bunce about your furniture.[8] I will drop him a line too—I presume you will send for it Oct 1. Have you ever had any account from your carriage and harness sale by Lawton. And now dearest I am very tired and hot and must stop. Love to children.

[P.S.]   Have written to Bunce.

To Ellen Evans Mahan

London, August 12, 1893 [LC]

I mailed you an envelope this morning, dearest, containing two letters I thought would interest you. Had I waited, I might have acknowledged the receipt of yours of the 4th which I found at Stevens—only 8 days old— probably the quickest I shall get for a very long while. Among the guests at Lady Jeune's last evg. was Lord Chas Beresford—Fighting Charley—none other in the mention of whom you would find interest. I am tiring a little of the racket—a quiet hour over a book suits me much better and I had rather see your dear faces around me than hear any more compliments. The retiring and reserved side of my character undoubtedly predominates, and I see no use in forcing my inclinations.

I return to the ship Monday or Tuesday at the latest—barring the unforeseen. No further news. With dearest love—always devotedly, yours and the children's.

To Ellen Evans Mahan

Southampton, August 17, 1893 [LC]

Dearest Miss Deldie: I must begin today or I will not have a letter for tomorrow. Now business first. The combined bills of Stovel and Starkey

---

7. Francis Henry Jeune, Baron St. Helier, judge, President of the Probate Division.
8. The northeast quarters of the building were given to the Training Station in 1893, but not until December; and the orders of consolidation were issued on March 14, 1894. At the date of this letter, Captain Francis M. Bunce was commandant of the training ship *Richmond* and the U. S. Naval Training Station, Newport; Stockton was still president of the War College, and Commander George A. Converse was commanding officer of the Torpedo Station.

amount to £27. 2s. 6d. In this total are included a new blouse, a low cut uniform waistcoat, a new cap and a sword knot, all which were imperative upon me. Of civilians I have an evening suit, a morning suit with spare pair of trousers, and an Angola suit with do. I can pay this myself, but it will leave me very short indeed, and I find so much harassment of other kinds that I do not think best to undergo it. You have owing to you the pay from the "Isthmus & Sea Power," and probably from Howe which has gone forward—the two probably aggregating at least $200. So I want you through Hartman to get a bill (or draft) of exchange upon London for the above amount to *your own order*. They will give you it in duplicate—called first and second of Exchange. Endorse upon the back of the first—as upon an ordinary cheque—"pay to the order of Stovel and Co.," and send it to their address—23 Conduit St, Bond St London—with a line saying it is in payment of my bill to them and to Starkey, and requesting them to send receipted bills to me Care of B. F. Stevens, 4 Trafalgar Square. The second of exchange send by following mail to *me* endorsed to pay *to my order*. In case the first miscarries I will then have the second at hand. The amount of American money required to pay for the draft will be at the rate of $5 about, per pound; so, if you send Hart your cheque for $135, the difference one way or the other can readily wait till you meet. I on this side will instruct Stovel and Starkey to this same effect, of which I have already told them. Having read this over it seems so clear that I will say no more.

I hardly know what I have, and what not told you or Lyle already. In my account of my stay at South Hill Park[1] to him I did not speak of a few things which are more likely to interest you. Among the six or seven guests there was a Mrs. Adair,[2] an American, formerly Miss Wadsworth—who is sister to the beautiful Mrs. Post. The latter is now Mrs. Smith Barry, her husband a rich Irish landholder. Mrs. Adair, I understand is widow to a second husband, and has an estate in Ireland as well [as] England. She also is handsome, though not to my style, and was decidedly the most companionable, woman of the world, one of the lot. The others and the men were mutual acquaintances—as was she with them—but she alone seemed practically to realize how very much "out of it" was a person situated like myself, and bore me in that way on her mind. The hostess also was reasonably attentive—but without great resource. It was not a strong party—consequently—socially; their talk running mainly to society matters and others of mutual experience. Another of the party was one of Helen's sonneteers—Mr. Wilfrid Blunt—a decidedly odd fish as poets I presume have a right to be. The two other men were in Govt. service, and very pleasant in their own way; but I was quite taken with our host, who probably will not set the

1. Home of Lady Hayter.
2. Cornelia Adair, daughter of General Wadsworth of New York.

world afire, but such a cheery healthy rosy wholesome little English gentleman as it did one's heart good to see. I walked home with him from church on Sunday and was delighted with him. On my return here I found a stack of letters, one your long lost No. 12, containing the Artillery Institute notice of my books—also a singularly pleasant letter from Aunty[3] to whom I hope to write by this mail. I must tell you that in London I exchanged visits with Mr. Loudoun Snowden, late our minister to Madrid, now on his way home. He told me that what had *decided* my being sent abroad was my Hawaii article in the *Forum*[4]—that it had *slipped* out from Mr. Josiah Quincy, who is Cleveland's factotum in the State Dept. I am rather loath to believe this, for if meant as punishment it would fail of its object, if I only knew the reasons alleged in Herbert's letters; yet, if not true, how could such a rumor start. Snowden said "dont give me away," so you are not at liberty to repeat this. On the other hand, if they want to stop my further writing—the step has failed, for Isthmus & Sea Power[5] is in type. Keep your ears open & say nothing. Out here they scout at Cleveland as a civil service man, and Mr. Quincy was the other day characterized to me as the most dangerous of party men, whose reputation for being a "gentleman" emboldens him rather than restrains. I have declined to write for the Artillery Institute on the plea of over-work; and I have from the British *U.S. Magazine* a request to contribute the leading article for their Oct. number,[6] for which they pay. I replied that I had no time to undertake new work, but that if among my manuscript of unpublished lectures I found anything I could easily work up I would send it. I have an idea but dont know how it will pan out. Since my return I have been most disagreeably busy and the weather is hot enough—almost—for N.Y.—and muggy. Yet I peg away at Nelson and I find people are already interested. The [London] *Chronicle* wants to interview me on the subject. What about the carriage you left with Lawton with the single and double harness?

Friday

I shall start this by this evening's mail so as to be sure of taking tomorrow's steamer. I am simply deviled to death with papers & such; and as for the unfortunate executive officer[7] he is almost a fixture to his desk. I really pity him. Last night I was rejoiced to receive Nos. 19 & 20, from Helen Aug 6 and yourself Aug. 8, very good time indeed. Since you are so comfortable at Quogue will you not take refusal for next year. It is a great gain to have

---

3. Probably Jane Leigh Okill Swift.
4. "Hawaii and Our Future Sea Power."
5. Published in *Atlantic Monthly* (October 1893).
6. Mahan's "Two Marine Expeditions" was published in *United Service Magazine* (October 1893). The expeditions involved were the Athenian attack on Syracuse and Napoleon's expedition to Egypt in 1798.
7. Lieutenant Commander William W. Gillpatrick, class of 1866.

so little travel to pay if you are equally comfortable. It is certainly excellent for Helen & Miss Nell will come along in time. I have nothing new since yesterday. The days seem to alternate one fairly easy another the devil to pay. I have written to Aunty by this mail & I hope that among the three of you you will keep up some touch of Elizabeth [N.J.]—or rather of the people there. Tell Helen I think her closing words 'I am so glad you are my father' a very pretty compliment & wish that I could turn as neat a one, though I know she was not aiming to do so. And now goodbye. If I have forgot anything it must keep till next time. Always fondly thine.

To Ellen Evans Mahan

Southampton, August 18, 1893 [LC]

Dearest D.: I have been struck by a bilious fear lest I may have misstated the exact amount to be sent to Stovel, in my letter mailed this forenoon. It is Twenty-seven pounds two shillings and sixpence (£27.2s.6d) or about $135.

I have a letter today from Scudder, an envelope rather, wh. enclosed a letter to another person, who doubtless has recd. mine. I was sorry for I wanted to see what his proposals, or views about my other articles might be. If however the other man is in America, he has doubtless sent my letter back ere now and I will have it soon.

[P.S.] Remember to tell me in two or three letters what you have done about the draft.

To Ellen Kuhn Mahan

Southampton, August 21, 1893 [LC]

Darling Miss Nellikin: I was greatly pleased last night to receive your letter of the 10th. It had reached London that morning and was brought down by one of Mr. Stevens' employees so that I received it at 9 P.M. I have not this time very much to tell you for I have not left the ship since my return from town on Monday last. I find myself very much occupied with all the petty details of the ship, for she is both bigger and of a very different kind to any with which I have been heretofore associated. I begin at times to despair of ever again accomplishing any literary work—now because I am so busy and afterwards because I shall have lost the run of it. It seems hard at times to have to do what you do not do well, and to be prevented from that which you do well. I am surprised you should all think so much of my dining with the Queen, when I was only one of fifty odd who did the same. It was certainly very interesting to me. As for the Duke of Connaught I forget what I wrote you—but what happened was this. It was my first day on duty after my leg got nearly well, and so many visitors &c had been on board that by 5.30 I was very tired, and having the dinner at 9 before me I lay down, and took off my shoes. I had scarcely done so when it was reported to me that a German Captain was coming on board, so I sent up word to excuse me because I was undressed. Immediately after came the Duke of Connaught, and the same message was given him—or rather they said the admiral was dressing & I also—upon which he naturally remarked that it was a long time beforehand, and said perhaps the admiral would see the Duke of C. That of course stirred everyone and Mr. Nazro[1] came flying down to me with the news, and of course I would have felt bound to get up even had I not wished to see our unceremonious visitor. Two ladies of the royal family[2] had come on board in the same sans façon manner in the morning. I had been expecting to get down to see my friend Capt Clark of the English Navy, on Thursday of this week to stay with him over Sunday while we coal—but the admiral told me he wants to go to London and wishes me to remain during his absence—so you see. As regards what I said to the Queen, as far as I remember it was merely something complimentary to the British Navy. I am delighted that you are all so enjoying yourselves at Quogue—it seems as if it might after all become the place I have long wished, not too far from N.Y. and to which we could go every summer.

Tuesday, Aug. 22

It is time now to bring this to a close, I have very little to say more. Last evening the Yacht *Enchantress*, the one on board which we dined in Queenstown with the Lord Lieutenant, came in having Earl Spencer on board—the First Lord of the Admiralty—I was only too anxious to call, as a kind of acknowledgment of our dinner at his house in London, and he asked me to dine again—so I did, one might almost say "en famille" there being only Lady Spencer, his secretaries, and two officers of the *Enchantress*. He told me that his colleague, that is, in the British cabinet, Mr.

---

1. Lt. Arthur Phillips Nazro, class of 1869.
2. Mahan's guests of July 31 at Cowes included Rear Admiral Fullerton, commanding officer of the Royal Yacht *Osborne*, Prince Henry and Princess Beatrice of Battenberg, and Princess Victoria of Schleswig-Holstein.

John Morley, one of the foremost literary men in England had wished to come in at the reception on the 9th to see me, but had not felt well enough. Mr. White had also told me Mr. Morley wished to meet me, but I find it always hard to believe. Mr. White also sent me yesterday an invitation from Baron Ferdinand de Rothschild, one of the great bankers to spend a couple of nights at his splendid place at Aylesbury, but I could not get away. I must [save] a line for mamma duplicating some instructions I sent her by last steamer. I believe I told her that there came for me a letter from Mr. Scudder but he had put the wrong letter in the envelope. And now goodbye dear child.

Aug 22.

For Mamma

Dearest Deldie: According to habit I send you duplicate instructions about Stovel's bill. With Starkeys it amounts to Twenty-seven pounds, two shillings and sixpence (£27.2.6). Send Hartman[1] a cheque for $135 dollars, and ask him to get you a bill of exchange upon London. They give these usually in duplicate. *Send the "First of Exchange" to Stovel. Have them made payable to your order*, and endorse on the back "Pay to Stovel & Co." as in endorsing a cheque. Send this to Stovel with a line saying it is in payment of my bill to him and Starkey, and ask him to send receipted bills to me "Care of B. F. Stevens, 4 Trafalgar Square." The second of exchange endorse payable to *my* order and send it to me by the *following* mail, so that in case of accident to the first the second will be secured. $135 may be a little more or a little less than needed, but nothing to matter till you two meet. If Hart is away for long I daresay Gillender would do it for you.

I believe I have given Nellie pretty much all my news. I have a letter from Lady Hayter, an answer to my bread & butter letter, which seems a superfluous piece of civility—but as it is pleasantly and prettily worded I will send it to you next letter. It would overweight this.

To Ellen Evans Mahan

Southampton, August 24, 1893 [LC]

Dearest Deldie: I must start a letter to you today, for I am so harassed with pretty administration & other cares that if I do not I may fail to get

---

1. Hartman Kuhn Evans, brother of Mrs. Mahan.

anything done. Yours of the 14th came today—No. 22. First, I feel you are perfectly right about Lyle, and especially he must not be allowed to take the bit between his teeth. He must obey implicitly up to the time he goes to boarding school, & so turned over. After that we may possibly gradually relax our control, but I hope that his good sense will then lead him not to distress us. But, however we may refrain from commanding, when we do command we must be obeyed in our home. You are perfectly right about the bathing rules. Of course I am delighted with Hennie's growing favor. The child is so self distrustful that it is hard to conceive of her ever being puffed up—still human nature is weak in that way—and while encouraging her diffidence to more self confidence I would not tell her too many flattering things. I had a letter from Chadwick today in which he says: "I have one piece of good news for the end of my letter—the College is safe. The Secy read your last book (on Sea Power) and that convinced him. He told me some time since he was opposed to it. He now tells me that *he has informed Ramsay* that he has changed his mind." I scarcely knew till I got this how keenly I had felt the report of the College abolition—the tears came to my eyes of mingled relief and exultation. Like an ass I have allowed myself to be persuaded against my will to go ashore to visit this aftn., and stay for dinner and the night—at Lord Radstock's—an Irish peer. When invitations come by letter one can wiggle out, but by word of mouth one is tied up. However my resolution is now taken. I accept no more day invitations, nor will I again land on this beastly beach here, which has no landing. Hereafter my reply shall be my time does not permit—my whole day is wrecked by the sense of hurry. I have undertaken to write an article for the *U.S. Magazine*,[1] and, although I shall crib it almost entire out of my old lectures on Strategy, even the licking into shape requires time. I have not left the ship since my return from London & I get no good from a few hours absence. I simply lose time & hate to return to her. A few days or a week gives some respite though largely countervailed by the arrears of work. As regards Captains dining with the Queen there were half a dozen besides myself—the invitation was in no sense special to me, and the rest of the dinner was probably arranged before we were known to be coming. There is no discount, however, on the compliments from many people. That from Mr. John Morley for instance has great value—from Sir Geo. Trevelyan & Mr. James Bryce[2] also—they are all eminent men—as for naval and military men there is but one voice, and had we arrived here a month sooner I should have been quite a second class lion, I believe. The story of the theft is indeed very sorrowful—I trust people have been

1. *See* Mahan to Ellen Evans Mahan, August 17, 1893, Footnote 6.
2. Sir George Otto Trevelyan, historian, biographer, and statesman; and James Bryce, historian, diplomat, and jurist.

sympathizingly kind to the father, & mother if there be one. I can scarcely conceive Lyle's erring that way, though I fully endorse your teaching of self distrust—but on the side of truthfulness or purity he may find the battle harder, and temptation more insidious, than he at all imagines. May God protect him then.

Aug 25

Lucky I wrote so much yesterday. I went ashore at 4:30, stayed the night and as their breakfast was not till 9:15 I did not get back to the ship until 10:45. The visit was uneventful and uninteresting except they showed me half a dozen letters from Nelson to the grandfather of the present lord. They are all printed in the Dispatches but it was interesting to see sheets over which the hero's hand had actually passed and after 90 years they are in wonderful preservation. Mainly I think because not folded. One of the ladies staying there was a Mrs. Elliott who is a daughter of the Mrs. Wheeler who used to appear at St John's in Newport, & whose sister married Count Poppenac. The face struck me as familiar, though she has hazel eyes & darker hair, but I did not learn who she was until walking down to the boat with the elder son, Mr. Waldegrave, who told me. I mentioned to him Chart's[3] dinner. Returning on board I find yours of the 15th very delightful to have. I shall write Lyle (in turn) on Sunday, but I dont want to lecture the lad in my few letters—a scolding is but an incident in an entire day, but a letter once in three weeks should not have much preachment. I must leave that to you in my absence. Today I am going ashore to make some necessary purchases, hoping that tomorrow I may manage a nearly clear forenoon for my *U.S.* article. And now dearest I will say good bye. The letter after all is not so short. One from Stockton today dated 14th confirms what I hear from Chadwick but naturally (both from his disposition & from the facts) remarks nothing is certain while Ramsay is in Bureau. He has asked Taylor[4] (Harry) if he wont get the presidency, and Taylor is willing provided he can have virtual independence. He is a good man, will be a captain next year, and [is] Bob Evans'[5] brother in law. Many kisses for all.

---

3. Possibly, Edwin Chart, Resident Architect for Hampton Court and District.
4. Henry Clay Taylor, class of 1863, who was President of the War College from November 1893 until December 1896.
5. Robley Dunglison ("Fighting Bob") Evans, class of 1863, who married Charlotte, the sister of H. C. Taylor. He commanded the *Yorktown* during the Chilean trouble, 1891–1892, the *New York* in 1895, and the *Iowa* in 1898. In 1902 he commanded the Asiatic Fleet, and in 1907 the Great White Fleet, until he fell ill and was relieved by C. S. Sperry. His two autobiographies are *A Sailor's Log* (1901) and *An Admiral's Log* (1910).

To Stephen B. Luce

USS *Chicago*, Southampton, August 24, 1893 [LC]

My dear Admiral: Your interest in the College entitles you to hear as soon as may be that a letter from Chadwick, received to day but written Aug. 10 ends thus: "The War College is safe. The Secy read your last book (on Sea Power) and that convinced him. He told me some time since he was opposed to it. He now tells me he has informed Ramsay that he has changed his mind." "In quietness and in confidence shall be your strength."

I have received many very flattering expressions here. Earl Spencer & Mr. Henry White both told me that Mr. John Morley was very desirous to meet me. He would have attended the reception of the First Lord so the latter told me, had he been strong enough. Mr. Bryce (the *Am. Commonwealth*) and Sir Geo. Trevelyan—both distinguished authors and members of the govt. spoke very flatteringly. At Osborne, Erben & myself were invited to one of the Queen's dinners—54 guests, mainly naval & military, so nothing peculiar to us—but I was presented to her Majesty afterwards and she said she had heard of my books, and the Duke of York the *nouveau marié* apparently made a special point of complimenting me on them. There is I believe no discount upon their success but the best of all will be if the College really triumphs over its difficulties.

With kind remembrance to the ladies [etc.].

August 26

I see in the Paris *Herald* of the 25th that Taylor will be ordered as president. This agrees with a letter recd. yesterday from Stockton, who said he had proposed it to Taylor & the latter would accept, if left independent. But I think that Hilary A. Herbert should be the Saviour of the College, against Ramsay, Bunce and its other enemies.

To Gouverneur Morris Ogden

Southampton, August 31, 1893 [LC]

My dear Gouv: Your letter was received this morning, and I am delighted to know that your trip was so successful. I fear, however, that we shall not meet again on this side, as the Adml. has fixed Tuesday for going to Havre. Therefore, unless the cholera, which is in Nantes, turn up, I fear we shall be off. Independently of liking to see you all again I am sorry to leave—chiefly perhaps from native inertia.

I have the best accounts from Quogue in every way—but just now I am a little anxious to hear how this terrific hurricane has treated them.

Since I saw you we have *certain* news that Herbert, so long the enemy of the College, has turned completely round, and utterly routed the rest of the hostile camp at the moment they thought victory secured. He was converted by the books, which he read on board the *Dolphin* during his cruise. He has said that when I return I must take it up again, but that he intends me to see the cruise out. McCalla[1] writes that he said the books repaid all the money hitherto expended on the College. I am hoping that Harry Taylor may take the presidency.

Give much love to Aunt Ogden and remember me kindly to Miss Ogden. I hope you will have a good passage, which is not unlikely when the present cyclones are blown out.

To Stephen B. Luce

Southampton, September 1, 1893 [LC]

My dear Admiral: Yours of August 24 was duly received. I got my clerk to draw up a table of the nationalities of the seamen class on board. The result is that of a total of 178, 88 are returned as Americans. Of the total, 17 are ex-apprentices, of them 12 Americans; and we have besides 45 apprentices still carried as such, 27 Americans.

Since my letter of last week I have heard from McCalla and Stockton, both confirming the news of Herbert's determination to maintain the College. The former says that Herbert said my books justified all the money heretofore expended. I dont know how far this is mere rumor—but Stockton's is clear, his information coming from Harry Taylor, who with Sampson had an interview with the Secy, in which the latter stated his purpose positively.

Stockton says he thinks Bunce disposed to leave, a disposition that this conclusion will likely hasten. His argument which has, I believe, produced most impression upon officials, is the difficulty of controlling sodomy among apprentices on board ship; and the need of greater supervision.

The saving of the College is the chief thing and that seems now assured. The rest we can await—but when people fancy that I can pursue my studies on board ship they deceive themselves.

Kind remembrances to the ladies.

---

1. B. H. McCalla.

To Ellen Evans Mahan

Southampton, September 1, 1893 [LC]

My own dearest Deldie: Now that I have settled on board after London dissipation there really is little in my life to record. The good people about here are very hospitable and pleasant to meet, but I dodge all I can, except dinners, for I really have not time with the ship waiting to be put to rights. I dont mean that she is in bad order, but on certain points I have my own ideas the realizing of which means constant attention. I must devote myself also to economizing, for the month has been expensive. Upon the whole Carl does fairly well, not quite as successful as an economist as I could wish, but I can do—yet I feel the wish to entertain more liberally and with less pinch than I do. Day before yesterday I went to Winchester to call upon Lady Clarke, the wife of my correspondent who till lately was Major Clarke. I had not been in the old town since I was here in the *Worcester* before we were married & I remembered very little about it except the Cathedral. They are very interesting these quaint ancient English cities. The Clarkes have one daughter of fifteen a good looking girl. He is in Malta, but they are afraid to take the child there, because the island is not healthy—malaria and bad water. Goodrich spent two days with him last month. On Tuesday I was rather roped in for a party on board—informal—among them the Darwins[1] whom I had met at the Elliotts last Saturday, & who brought with them—of all people—Mr. & Mrs. Godkin.[2] Her I had not seen since we dined at the Jack Millers. He told me he had been surprised to find how generally Englishmen, even though not directly interested in naval matters had read my books. They have been staying at some country houses lately, where "every one" had read them. Last night I went to a dance at Col. Crichton's the present owner of Netley Castle. You may imagine how I enjoyed it—all strangers to me but they have been so kind. I was partially repaid by the sight of a typically handsome English young woman—superb complexion, coloring and development; rather too massive for so young a person, promising bulk for the future, but a superb creature as she stood. Tonight I dine at Capt. Yorke's,[3] and that I fancy finishes me, as we go to Havre on Tuesday—weather etc permitting. I had an extremely nice letter from Helen on Wednesday, enclosing also one from Lyle, which I was also very glad to get—with his war-cries. I am immensely pleased to know you are having such a good time at Quogue and hope you will take the refusal of the cottage, unless you think you can do better. The sur-

---

1. This could have been either Sir Francis Darwin, botanist, or Sir George Howard Darwin, astronomer and oceanographer. Both were sons of Charles R. Darwin.
2. Edwin Lawrence Godkin was editor of the *New York Evening Post* and *The Nation*.
3. John Manners Yorke, a retired Royal Navy officer.

roundings seem to realize for you, socially, what I have so much wished; pleasant friends, living simply and enjoying simply—sociality—not "society." A letter from Stockton, recd. at the same time, quotes this from Taylor who had an interview, together with Sampson, with the Secy: The latter "announced to us positively that he had definitely decided to retain the War College as an institution—that Mahan's book had caused this—that Mahan must go there as soon as he came back from sea, and much more that indicated to me qualities of perception and appreciation which are most rare in the politician class etc. He said he meant Mahan to make his full cruise etc." If the latter sentence be carried into effect I shall not be home next summer, and you may as well at least get a refusal at Quogue, for I dont think you will be called to Newport. I have been looking over your more recent letters but find nothing for reply, except to repeat my opinion that it would be a pity for Lyle to miss any school. We who have a life of work before us should not crave over 3½ months holiday which he will have had. I quite agree with you that if the servants cant use the elevator you had better take the 3d floor. I am glad to know Howe reached you. The *Atlantic* with the Nicaragua article has not yet come to me. I did not know it was out & Scudder's blunder in using the wrong envelope leaves me ignorant whether he wants the continuations. I have made little progress with Nelson, being so occupied; but I have twisted some of my old lectures into one for the *U.S. Magazine* here[4]—the proceeds of which I shall keep for self—turning over to you the American articles. I had yesterday a letter from Gouv, saying they had returned to London, after a very pleasant trip in the North, and would sail on the 16th. I greatly envied them this. He hoped we might meet again on this side but this is plainly impossible. And now good bye dearest one. My letters seem to me disconnected and uninteresting; but I am very busy with uninteresting matters & seem to myself to live pen in hand. With love to the children, always most fondly.

To Helen Evans Mahan

Southampton, September 3, 1893 [NWC]

My dearest Helen: Mamma tells me you find that I do not take sufficient notice of the contents of your letters—I suppose because from the time that must elapse between their writing and my reply, it seems as if the occur-

---

4. *See* Mahan to Ellen Evans Mahan, August 17, 1893, Footnote 6.

rences would have passed from your mind. I have heard of Jomini's[1] fracas on the beach and loss of his collar from mamma; also of Uncle Fred's[2] letter telling his interview with Chadwick about the College. This as you now know I have learned from several independent sources. From you I hear of your various friends and goings on but as it seems to me nothing very particular. We ourselves have been rather uneventful—although I have felt compelled to relax my sticking to the ship under the pressure of the persistent hospitality of the countryside around Southampton. I think I told mamma of my going to the Crichtons to a dance Thursday. I did not care for it, in fact found it stupid. The next evening I dined at Captain Yorke's a retired officer of the Royal Navy—where I had a very good time being myself in a happy vein and we had a good deal of fun at our end of the table. Yesterday I stayed on board and this afternoon went to call at Lord Radstock's—where I had dined ten days ago—finding no one at home but his daughter, Miss Waldegrave. From there I walked round with one of our officers to Captn. Yorke's where I found them just finishing five o'clock tea under the trees. The walk being two miles and dusty, the tea was very welcome. I bade all these goodbye, for we sail on Tuesday morning for Havre. The consul writes from there that they are ready to make a great fuss over us—but I don't think it will be as bad as in England. *I* want quiet. The Admiral says that after a week in Havre we will go to Lisbon—stay there a fortnight—thence to Tangier for two days—then Gibraltar and afterwards along the Mediterranean coast of Spain. Tomorrow I go to a tennis party at the Crichtons, but only for half an hour to pay a call and say goodbye. They have been most exceedingly civil to us all. I am waiting curiously your letters to know whether you have suffered great inconvenience from the storms of which we hear such dreadful accounts. The weather here has for the most part been very good, I hope it may last us so to Lisbon. Tell Mamma I send the enclosed so that if she has any church money to spare she may, if she likes, send something. Ever since Nellie was so benefited by moving from Annapolis to Bar Harbor it has been my purpose to help this charity, but first want of money and since then forgetfulness have too often prevented. Tell her also that I see no reason why she should not pay her pew rent out of her ch. money. I find myself unable to do much writing but have written an outline beginning for the Life of Nelson. A letter from Scudder says the Canal article[3] will be out in the Oct. No. And now goodbye my dear child—with love for all [etc.].

[P.S.] Sept. 4: 1 P.M. Well—just closing my mail.

---

1. The family dog.
2. Frederick A. Mahan.
3. "The Isthmus and Sea Power."

To Ellen Evans Mahan

My dearest wife: I have found by sad experience that unless I begin betimes to build up my weekly letter, it is sometimes hard to get up, so I begin today, to mail the 8th. We left Southampton yesterday morning at 5 and entered the docks here about the same hour p.m., having had a very pleasant run, neither sea nor fog. I saved myself carefully during the day from the time the Southampton pilot left us, till we took the Havre one, but the process of getting to a place in the dock was much complicated and I became excessively tired—more so than I remember being in a long time, both mentally & physically, slept badly and am a bit of a wreck today. I managed however to get up and call on our Consul; and tomorrow hope to be all right for I am then to make half a dozen official calls along with the admiral.[1] It is tiresome, and sometimes, although I know the strain is less here, I long for the obscurity and let alonedness of the South American ports. I have had no letter since Helen's of Aug. 23, nor indeed is one due before tomorrow or next day, but I anxiously want to know how the storms treated you. No trace of them reached the other side where the weather was persistently fine, with rare breaks, throughout our stay in England. We will remain here just a week from today, when the admiral now proposes to sail direct for Lisbon. Friday Sept. 8. Lest I forget, and if it be not already too late, in taking your apartment consider how the fire question is affected by the elevator, whether there is a free access to a stairway—and how far the fire escapes might aid. I have always relied mainly on the roof escape, as you know; but from the third story I suppose the fire escapes might answer. In any event, if we have the fifth floor, it would be well to ask Cruikshank to give orders that the access to the roof be kept accessible & not blocked in any way. When on the floor we can do it ourselves. My friend O'Connor Morris in his last letter to me asked that I would read his Life of Napoleon[2] and give him my candid opinion about it—a rather delicate request. However I bought the book—a dollar—and have nearly finished it, and happily can write a complimentary opinion. In the closing paragraph of the preface he gives me a send off which I copy for your benefit. "After these sheets had been corrected for the press, I have had an opportunity of reading the second part of Capt. Mahan's admirable

---

1. On the 6th and 7th, Mahan, Erben, and the latter's flag lieutenant, William P. Potter, class of 1869, called on the Prefect, the Mayor, the Customs Officer, the Commanding Officer of the Port, and the Senior Naval Officer.
2. William O'Connor Morris, *Napoleon and Revolutionary France*. New York: Putnam, 1893. The Library of Congress lists it as *Napoleon, Warrior and Ruler, and the Military Supremacy of Revolutionary France*.

work on Sea Power. I have made no changes in my text; but it is gratifying to me to find that my views as regards Napoleon's projects of a descent on England, and the operations that ended at Trafalgar, & as regards the Continental System, coincides with those of a writer, who is not only the first living authority on naval warfare but also possesses remarkable political insight." Your letters of the 28th and 29th came yesterday—the latter only nine days old. I was relieved to find that the storms which have evidently been tremendous had done you no more harm. You mention having written Hart for the draft. Dear little Miss Nell I am dumbfounded to find that *she* should be backward in making friends. I will write to her about it. "Ce n'est que le premier pas qui conte." Let her go to the Club a week and you will find she will make chums. Next year, if she dont do better, I will have to ask that she postpone inviting her other friends until she has become so familiar with the Club that she can take them there to have a good time. It has been the greatest error of my life to shun people, but then I am also more self sufficing than most; and at best it is a loss. By the way, speaking of friends, when you next write Mrs. Powel,[3] be sure to send my love to her and Sam and tell her how much I came to enjoy my evenings with them. Your letters mention also sending Howe to Scudder and what you got from Lawton for the carriage. I *think* there was single harness—but if I were you I would write at once to Stockton. I cannot remember whether the harness ever went to the barn, but Flanders will probably know. I had thought that Lawton took everything. You are quite right about Helen's charges—I cannot have the child racing herself to make money at her age and under present conditions. She has not yet full maturity and will not for three years; till then let her husband her strength by quiet development, avoiding hurry and needless worry, which always accompany doing too much. Her first duty now is to let nature perfect her—she can do that while working steadily, but not when working under pressure. It is worry, not work, that kills. I dont wonder she finds very young men flat, though very young girls dont usually find it out. Yesterday I went with the Adml. to pay visits on a number of French officials, and in the afternoon they returned our calls. It was a dreary business, not without its humors. The Consul knows little or no French—his son however being educated in France went along to interpret. Being only 17 he was shy, and the flag lieutenant, Potter, who fancies he speaks French, cut him out. Potter's accent I think is worse than mine. The Secretary is very fluent, but as Frenchy as a Frenchman much to the Admiral's disgust. So far I think the European Squadron wears less than the others. The everlasting visiting is a nuisance & a distraction but I fancy helps matters by breaking the monot-

---

3. Mary Edith Powel, wife of Samuel Powel, Jr., was a naval collector and historian who lived in Newport. She was greatly respected by the officers associated with the College.

ony. We having a flag ship, however, is an uncompensated bore. Erben is as little trouble as possible, I suppose; but as adml. there is practically nothing to do, except visiting, on this ridiculous station; so he is a kind of supernumerary captain, to fret himself about trifles and talk shop. I find it almost impossible to accomplish my writing—and see little prospect of betterment in that subject. Good bye sweetest—love for the children.

To Ellen Kuhn Mahan[1]

Havre, September 11, 1893 [LC]

...these things before I needed only a moment to renew my acquaintance. In Rouen Joan of Arc was burned and I went to the spot. A statue of her stands there now, while in the Cathedral is the tomb of Richard Coeur de Lion, who loved the Normans much more than he did the English. I was almost perished on the boat, though I had my overcoat. A very keen East wind was blowing hard, and there is nowhere to go except outside, no shelter. My hat had to be held almost all the first two hours—the breakfast at eleven was dear and *very* bad. They call the boat Bateau-Omnibus, and it looks for all the world like one of our summer street cars without a covering—catch me in another unless I am *sure* of a clear and a warm day. In reaching places they have no landings—a boat comes off from shore with passengers and takes away others. They manage it very cleverly and it is amusing to see them go and come. One old man with a tall soft white hat, a gaunt face and long white beard looking like the Wandering Jew; an old woman with spectacles and four or five bundles who has a great to do getting on board—then a mother with three girls of 8 to 12, all dressed in red plaids, with grey worsted hoods and balls over their heads. Another party comes with a little pug dog, who looks very puzzled and seems to feel as you do at the Club. You never saw so many ugly women as there are in this country—Havre is dreadful for them—not plain but downright ugly. Havre itself is a squalid unpleasant seaport town, and it was a great relief to me to get to Rouen, where, besides the ancient houses, there are broad, bright streets with handsome shops. I am glad we are not to stay here long, being [scheduled] to leave on Thursday 14th for Lisbon, weather permitting, and when you get this I hope we shall be at the other port i.e. Lisbon.

Sept 12.

Tell mamma I have just written Mr. Scudder, asking him to send her the cheque for the Nicaragua article. It will be due about Sept. 25. I have told him that her address would be Quogue until Sept. 28—so if there be

---

1. First part of letter not found.

any change she must notify him. I gave him her name, Ellen L. I went this afternoon to call upon Lady Beauchamp. She is an old Englishwoman, over 65 I should say, sister to Lord Radstock whom I met in Southampton. Though well off she has settled herself in Havre in the sailors quarter of the town, and devotes herself to doing good among them, has started a coffee house and reading room, where she attends personally during the forenoon, and lives above in the third story. She has had nine children, but they are now all settled in life, the last daughter lately married, and so for years back she has given herself to this work. It really raises one's ideas of mankind to see people so full of charity, as thus to separate themselves from all the world has to give. I did not find her an interesting woman, and she has, I think, fads about drinking wine &c; but as I told Lyle, John Baptist came neither eating bread nor drinking wine. People in those days said he had a devil. Now men are so wise they don't believe in devils, and they say such people are so odd. We need not adopt her fads, but we cannot but admire her self sacrifice, unless we are very queer Christians indeed.

After this letter reaches home I suppose a week at the very least will pass before another comes—probably ten days. We will be about five days getting to Lisbon and from there three to five days to catch a steamer in England or France.

Tomorrow a lot of us are to breakfast at 12.15 with the mayor of Havre, and in the evening to attend a reception at the sous préfet's. Perhaps I may be able to give you an account of these affairs before closing. I myself gave a lunch to our Consul and his family on Saturday, which is the third little entertainment—two dinners in Southampton—by me. When I took a seat in the public gardens the other day I had to pay one cent for my chair for which I recd. the enclosed card.

Wednesday Evg. Sep. 13

Everything in this world seems to end in a hurry, whether it be a family going to the country or a ship going to sea—so I have now little time to do more than say I breakfasted at the mayors with a large company this noon, only getting away at 3—then he with some of the company visited the ship, and at 5 I started for a brisk walk to get rid of the possible effects of the big meal. Now, 8 p.m. I am getting ready for a reception at the sous préfet's. Tell mamma I have recd. Stovel's and Starkey's receipts to day—Also I mail you a photo of the *Chicago* taken as she was drawing up to the mole at Havre—I happened to see it in a window and it struck me as so good that I bought it. Good bye dear child.

[P.S.] Whole heaps of love to dearest mamma, Helen, and Lyle, all by name.

Thursday, Sept. 14. 8 a.m.

Just a line to say that I am well and the weather seems fair so I suppose we will be off at about 11.

[152]

To Horace E. Scudder

Dear Mr. Scudder: I write to ask if, when payment for the Nicaragua article comes due, you could send cheque to Mrs. Mahan drawn to her order. Her name is Ellen L. Mahan. She has a power of attorney to receive money due me, if any such formality is needed in a case of this sort. Her address up to Sept. 28 will be Quogue, Long Island, N.Y.

Your letter of August 9 was at last duly received. I am still tempted to try the two articles,[1] if I do anything at all; but in truth I am so hampered by my work of petty administration that I have little power to do intellectual work. It is not merely want of time, though there is that to some extent; but what I most feel is the mental weariness caused by sustained, yet disconnected, occupations. These occupy the forenoon, always my working period, and in the afternoon my brain refuses to construct. For these reasons I have abandoned, for the cruise, my Six Admirals idea. I still cling to the hope of producing the articles mentioned, and of at the least assimilating Nelson's life, which shall be my next large endeavor.

To Henry Erben

USS *Chicago*, Havre, September 14, 1893 [NYHS]

Sir: In obedience to your order I have to submit the following:
The flag of the Commander-in-Chief was hoisted on June 1, 1893. From that date until June 17, the ship remained at the New York Navy Yard making preparations for a foreign cruise. On June 18, the ship left the lower New York harbor and arrived at Queenstown, Ireland, June 30—distance steamed 2907 knots,—average speed 10 knots.

1015

Amount of coal consumed 584 2240 tons, cost $1624.80. As regards general condition and efficiency, the hull of the *Chicago* is in serviceable condition as are also her engines. The boilers are in very indifferent state. In view of the fact that five-twelfths of the boiler power of the ship is now not in fit condition for service, I should be inclined to look upon the state of the boilers as critical, but the Chief Engineer tells me he does not so regard them. They will require great care in use and probably frequent repair; the Chief Engineer estimating their endurance at not over four or five months of actual steaming with certainty, though they may last

---

1. *See* Mahan to Scudder, July 25, 1893.

longer. The general condition and causes thereof are understood at the Navy Department.[1]

The ship having been only one month under your flag—a month spent either at the Navy Yard or in making a rough passage, no target nor torpedo practice has been held, nor have there been any tactical maneuvers. The drills have been ordinary routine for instruction.

The discipline of the ship has been very good. Summary of enlistments, courtsmartial, petty punishments etc. from June 1, until June 30;—

Courtsmartial: Under influence of liquor, 4.

Leaving ship without permission, 5.

Enlistments, 21. Discharges, 14.

Petty punishments 63. Desertions 6.

The sanitary condition of the ship has been good.

Percentage of sick 1 1/60. Number of Deaths 0.

Number invalided home 0.   ″   sent to hospitals 3.

To Ellen Evans Mahan

Havre, September 15, 1893 [LC]

My own dearest and sweetest Miss Deldie: I closed my letter to Nellie yesterday morning fully expecting that by noon we would be out of the port; but this morning French papers announced the outbreak of cholera in Lisbon 30 cases and 10 deaths in four days, so the admiral decided to hold on and telegraph to our consul there. We are still awaiting a reply. There is always some doubt as to the first diagnosis but the sudden appearance of so many cases and the percentage of mortality looks Asiatic. We will

---

1. On March 22, Rear Admiral J. G. Walker, commanding the Second Squadron of the Naval Review Fleet from the *Chicago*, wrote to Rear Admiral Bancroft Gherardi, Commander, Naval Review Fleet:

I have to acknowledge the receipt of your letter of the 20th instant, asking to be informed at what time, after the 1st of May, the *Chicago* will be ready to make a foreign cruise. In reply I have to say that it will, probably, require one year to fit the *Chicago* for an extended tour of foreign service. Both boilers and engines would require such extensive repairs that it would, probably, be found more judicious to replace them with new. Two of the six boilers are now considered unsafe for general service; the others have been repaired for a short term of service, and are fairly efficient.

I consider the *Chicago* in fairly good condition for eight months' duty on the North Atlantic Station. It is possible she may go for a somewhat longer period, but in her present condition she should not be sent to a distant station.

On May 5 Walker further stated that the *Chicago's* bottom had had one coat of paint in February, which had been knocked off during her anchorage of February 22, by swinging with the tide across shad-poles; and that she should be docked and properly attended to.

doubtless exercise the utmost prudence, for the admiral keeps his eye steadily upon the matter. I dont think he will either go, or remain in an infected port, and as autumn is already here I trust the disease will soon disappear. In case it appear in N.Y. after your return, please avoid all raw food that has not passed under fire. It is not that such (salads fruit & the like are in themselves dangerous) but their moist condition facilitates the adhesion of the germs. Water distributes them, & however pure otherwise should always under such conditions be boiled. All food should be thoroughly cooked.

There is no further news. I have not left the ship in 24 hours. I have tried to write upon Nelson, but make practically no progress. My forenoon work leaves me tired out mentally, and I fear all constructive work is at an end for the cruise—mais nous verrons. Goodbye dearest.

11 A.M.

[P.S.]   Well it is decided that we go. The newspaper report cannot be traced & we get nothing from our consul in Lisbon. We shall leave in about an hour. Before I forget let me repeat that I have received Stovel's and Starkey's receipts. I shall not get your letters till we reach Lisbon. Ever thine, my own love.

To Ellen Evans Mahan

Lisbon, Portugal, September 22, 1893 [LC]

Dearest Deldie: When I closed my letter to Lyle, I believe I had not received your letter of the 7th—nor his of the 3d. It is hardly conceivable, but the Vice-Consul who was in charge of the office allowed us to remain 48 hours at the quarantine ground, and although a party offered to bring the letters to us never sent them. You have indeed very little news, but I am glad to know that you continue to enjoy yourselves at Quogue. You do not say, but I hope Nellie has made out to throw off her shyness and make some friends. By the same mail came a letter from the editor of the *Forum*[1] hoping I might have something suited for the pages of their magazine—also one from the English *United Service* acknowledging receipt of proofs. I had also one from Luce, rejoicing over the College and saying they might be in Nice this winter, in which case we may meet them. The Second Exchange came all right, but as I have Stovel's receipts I destroyed it as useless. I was much gratified and a little relieved to find Scudder liked Howe so much. I myself thought it very heavy, perhaps because it caused

1. Walter Hines Page, editor of the *Forum* (1890–1895) and of the *Atlantic Monthly* (1896–1899).

me so much labor. Hard writing may have made easy reading. If that be so, my few pages on Nelson ought to be lighter than puff paste, they have been wrung out of the sweat of my brow. It is very provoking about the apartment—I wonder if it will not suggest itself to you to move into your mothers for Oct. Everyone would be pleased, I fancy and Hart not least so. I am averse to our getting in the way of looking upon the summer vacation as elastic—principally of course on account of Lyle, but as we all expect to be workers, irregularity is for all to be deprecated. I think it a very good thing for us to feel that Oct 1 should always see us back in town ready for work. As for news I at present am singularly without any. I told Lyle what little there was to tell about the trip from Havre. We had beautiful weather, not only quiet but very clear; and here also it is very pleasant, warm but dry, and cool enough at night for a blanket. There are excursions to be made from here but I question much their paying me for the money I must spend. The city itself, and surroundings, with the exquisite air & sky and sunshine, as seen from the ship promise enjoyment enough for our short stay. We are to remain until Oct. 1, and then go to Gibraltar. I have already written you, but repeat, that I have asked Scudder to send you the money for the Nicaragua article when due. I believe I have recd. all the newspaper clippings you have sent me together with the *Times* account of the *Atlanta* business.[2] It seems pretty bad. Some allowance should be made, but will not, for the unguardedness of men who were dealing with ships of which they had no experience. It is not exactly a valid excuse, but still people do blunder over new things. I am really at present very well. The making and work of the passage round seem to have produced no effect, unless some rather increased irritability, for which, however, I have much provocation.

Saturday Sep. 23

I am rather at sea as to when my letters will take steamer, but as there is a fast train this p.m. for England, I hope this may catch Tuesday's or Wednesday's steamer. I have really nothing more in the way of news. You will be amused that a Clipping Bureau has actually tried to get me in by sending a lot of extracts like the enclosed. We seem likely to leave here Oct 2 for Gibraltar, where we are to meet the *Bennington*[3] & the *Monongahela* the latter of which will transfer to us some boys. A few ideas about Nelson have been striking in lately and I begin to hope I may conceive a correct and harmonious portrait of him—but it is very slow work. I get so tired that my brain is little use. Farewell, my dearest—always most fondly thine & the childrens.

---

2. On September 7, 1893, *The New York Times* published the Board of Survey report concerning a fire aboard the cruiser *Atlanta*.
3. A 230-foot, 1,700-ton, twin-screw steel gunboat commissioned in 1891 and mounting six 6-inch guns.

To Helen Evans Mahan

Lisbon, September 28, 1893 [NWC]

Dearest Henny: I received three days ago your letter of the 10th and that of dear mamma's of the 11th with the enclosures of deed etc. I have not attempted to send this back because of the uncertainty as to when you will be in N.Y. I dont know how even to address this letter—as mamma doubts whether she will be in 54th St. I cannot but hope it may be found practicable for you to hang out in grannie's apartment[1] for a while, so that, if needs must, mamma can seek a new home unhurried. We have been here now a week out of quarantine & I find the place grows on me very much. I was rather sniffy in a letter I wrote Aunt Jenny[2] two days ago, but my repeated wanderings increase my liking for it. I am sorry that we must go away—probably on Monday Oct. 2. for Gibraltar. The climate is simply exquisite, clear, bright, sunny; warm but not too warm, and exhilarating. I have met nothing like it since Coquimbo—and then Coquimbo itself was a hole. The city is built on a succession of hills, along the river side about four hundred feet high, the houses rising one above the other, mostly white but many of them also blue, red, yellow or pink with mixture of other colors— a great deal of green hillside and the most delicious light blue sky and white clouds. It is really a dream—like what we hear of Italy. Ashore the place has no particular beauty, although there [are] a few—very few—handsome shops—and some fine residence streets of the Spanish and Portuguese type; but what is perfectly delightful is the older parts—the streets about twelve feet wide, wandering round up hill and downhill, round corners and up lanes, just as if they had started out for a walk and had no particular reason to go one way rather than another. The houses in those parts are pretty high, and the windows all have verandas of different bright colors—usually green and the picturesque effect is immensely increased by an artless way they have of hanging their wash on poles stuck out of the front windows— mingled with trousers, chemises, children's petticoats, etc. The windows not thus occupied are largely filled with the heads of women, peering out to see what is going on. On Sunday I found my way to a garden to which mamma and I were driven when we stopped here on our way home from South America with your useless little self on the front seat, and I think I can maintain without exaggeration that you often stayed on it as much as two seconds at a time. As I came down from the Jardim da Estrella, as it is called, I passed a scene which recalled your babyhood in Montevideo, when you went out every morning in your nurse's arms, cup in hand, to get your milk

---

1. Mrs. Manlius Glendower Evans maintained an apartment at 120 East 34th Street.
2. Jane Leigh Mahan.

[157]

fresh from the cow—at what is there called a Tambo. I saw a nicely tiled stable with ten cows, all beautifully groomed, feeding from a semi-circular manger, all their heads together in the center, and tails out. As there was plenty of hay for all, all seemed happy, and I suppose the milk is sold on the premises. It was called Vaccaria Normanda. The language here is quite a study for me. I dont know it but its changes from the Spanish are of a pretty regular kind so I can spell my way through pretty well. It rejoices in vowels, discarding consonants e.g. union—uniao; concepcion, conceiçao; but could mamma tell what means "Irmaos" from her knowledge of Spanish —"hermanos." It is quite funny to contrast with French thus: without, sans (Fr), sin (Sp), sem (Port). The gardens are a very charming feature of this attractive town—many plants that could not live with us growing freely and large out of doors—chiefly great palms of different kinds, in addition to which they have many of our own plants. These public gardens are scattered all over, and from many you get beautiful views. As for me, I simply gander all over the place, starting for some point and getting there but hardly knowing how. I miss seeing any pretty faces on the streets, possibly there may be some somewhere but they dont show up. Tell mamma I will send the deed back as soon as I know *where* to send it, but as Dodie[3] is also to sign I suppose there is no great hurry.

September 30

I have kept my letter open until now thinking I might hear from mamma again, and her letter of the 14th was recd. today. It calls for no notice, however, and I can only hope she may have thought of taking you to 34th St for October, which might solve many difficulties. I have nothing more to say but that I am well. Give my love to dearest mamma and to the rest.

To Ellen Evans Mahan

Lisbon, October 1, 1893 [LC]

Sweetest Deldie: Your letter of the 14th received yesterday gave me less unmixed pleasure than yours generally do, for it was evident you were harassed by the uncertainty about your quarters for the winter. I am very sorry I am not with you, for just to be able to talk over matters is a great help; but anxiety is our portion here, if it dont come one way it does another, nor can any one entirely relieve another. You are so capable that I have perhaps relied overmuch upon the fact—yet I cannot but hope still that what occurred so quickly to me will have ere this suggested itself to you, viz:

---

3. Rosalie Evans.

If 54th St is impossible, go to 34th, if only with Lyle, sending the girls to Elizabeth. I have already mentioned this, so it seems at this late day a waste to dwell further upon it in a letter which you can scarcely get much before a fortnight, when your plans will probably be fixed. I doubt not that this will add another to the experiences, from which we all learn so slowly, that we are provided for and that things do come right somehow. I think I myself am really somewhat better than I was, and I attribute it wholly to the fact that I no longer strive to be composed, but merely ask to be made so and then turn my mind away as much as possible. We are leaving here early tomorrow, and if the weather hold as good as it now promises we should be in Gibraltar by Tuesday night. Never in my life do I remember such perfect climate as this during our stay—neither Coquimbo, Bar Harbor, nor Montevideo at its best equal it, it is not merely that the weather has been magnificent but the tone of the air unrivaled, and I say this not of a past enjoyment, but of the present, which so commonly seems inferior to the past. There is very little news—the place is quiet enough, and I have said all I need about it in my letter to Helen, mailed yesterday. This I shall hold till we get to Gibraltar. Last night we dined at the American minister's— a Mr. Carruth from Arkansas. He tells me, by the way, that the correct pronunciation is Árkansaw—accent on the first syllable; that that is the true Indian pronunciation, and that the State Legislature has so ruled. They are great church people—he was delegate to the last General Convention, and sat right behind the New York crowd—Pierpont Morgan, Cutting etc. Dead opposed to divorce—which is refreshing in a Western man. On my birthday I gave a dinner to the Admiral, inviting five other officers. I did not say it was my birthday, as that seemed to me very stupid to do. Carl manages my little affairs very well—not quite as low bills as I want, but only exceeds by about five dollars a month, so I think I can keep quite within limits, allowing myself a little latitude for sight seeing. Here I have gone only as far as Cintra a mountain resort about 17 miles distant. It is surmounted by an old Moorish castle about six hundred feet above it, over a precipitous cliff; from the parapets you can see the plain country "Vega" stretching in all directions, and realize Irving's descriptions in the *Conquest of Granada* how the good knight Don So and So[1] looked from his castle on the height, and saw in the distance such or such a party of enemies upon whom he descended. This trip cost me inside of $3.00 and with my run to Rouen from Havre composed all my sight seeing—and in fact all my expenses, except board washing & sundries. I work away at my life of Nelson, but the interruptions are so numerous, and the mind so preoccupied that progress not only is slow, but I feel the want of that inspiration without

---

1. The "good Count de Tendilla, who was in truth a mirror of knightly virtue." Washington Irving, *The Conquest of Granada*. New York: George P. Putnam, 1850, pp. 465–466.

which I doubt of success. The mind does not have time to become enkindled, and I fear I am commonplace. The length of our stay in Gibraltar is doubtful, but Erben intends it to be short, and as he wishes to go to Malaga and be in Port Mahon by the 15th, it can scarcely be long. He purposes Barcelona also, but I dont know whether before or after Mahon. I enclose you two faire-parts of death and gratitude—it may amuse you to notice that they are stuck indiscriminately among other advertisements.

Oct. 3 [At sea]

I snatch a moment, dearest, from the random of pettifoggery in which my days are spent[2] to finish this so that I may mail upon reaching Gibraltar—about six hours hence. We are now just off Cape Trafalgar, with Cadiz in the distance, and I have swept with my glass the field of the great battle, which naturally looks much like any other bit of sea. We have had a very favorable run down, leaving Lisbon at 6 A.M. yesterday fine weather, no fog—but we meet a great many steamers which keeps me on the drive for I have no idea of another collision & I off deck to undergo again the worry of last cruise. I have no more to say to you, except that I hope you are not worrying about money—we have every reason to hope that enough will be forthcoming—the return petty as it is from mother's bequest will go far to meet the difference in rent and you have my two *Atlantic* articles also on which to count with certainty.[3] I am very hopeless of accomplishing any further literary work until the cruise is over, but will not finally give up until we get to Nice. If I then find I can get no more chance than I do here I will have to give up—it is useless. The folly of the Dept. is incredible—but I believe it is more that pedant Ramsay than the Secy. Goodbye dearest one. Love to the chicks.

To Ellen Evans Mahan

Gibraltar, October 3, 1893 [LC]

I write just a line, dearest, to tell you that in my uncertainty as to your movements I sent a letter today addressed to your mother's care, 120 E. 34th St., thinking that Hartman would certainly know where you are—and I shall continue so to address till I know your whereabouts. Nothing new, I am pretty tired tonight—and very sleepy—must go to bed early. With dearest love to you all [etc.].

---

2. The *Chicago* displayed unexpected eccentricities. For example, on September 27 holes were found in the bulkhead of her forward hold. The bulkheading, which had been cut too short, was pieced with plugs, and the plugs had fallen out.
3. "Admiral Earl Howe" and "The Isthmus and Sea Power."

[P.S.] Just think what historical scenes I have been viewing—Lisbon, St. Vincent, Trafalgar & Gibraltar—and right opposite is Ape's Hill on which one of Jervis fleet was wrecked drowning 600 men.

To Ellen Kuhn Mahan

Gibraltar, October 6, 1893 [LC]

Dearest Miss Nellikin: I was so glad to hear by dear mamma's letter of Sept 21, which I received yesterday that you have begun to go to the Club, for I am sure that it is only breaking the ice that is needed to make you find friends and intimates. As you will probably know before getting this, we reached here on the 3d. We had very fine weather from Lisbon, and it has lasted us so far—we have indeed been most fortunate and I cannot feel too thankful to be spared bad weather. This, as you know, is an English fortress —a huge rock that rises abruptly a thousand feet out of the sea, & is joined to Spain by low neck of sand only half a mile wide. Across this ruck there is a broad belt which is called the Neutral Ground, bordered on one side by Spanish and on the other by British territory. The Rock of Gibraltar, as it is commonly called, once belonged to Spain, but the English captured it 190 years ago and have held it ever since. It has indeed had a wonderful history, for not only did the Romans and Carthaginians hold it in ancient times, but afterwards the Moors for seven hundred years, and it was from a Moorish general it took the name it now bears, Gib-al-Tarik, Tarik's Mountain. There is a Moorish castle still remaining. As in all English ports people have been very hospitable. Our Consul asked us to dinner the night after our arrival. He is an old gentleman of seventy, very nice, who was born here and has lived here all his life. His father was an American who came here in 1801, and the two have been Consuls in succession for at least sixty years. This one was last in the U.S. in 1849, and I suppose never expects to go again. The next day we lunched with the senior naval officer, Captain Lake,[1] who spoke very nicely to papa about his book, and after lunch showed me a copy, which had been given him by Admiral Tryon who was drowned in the *Victoria*. Two or three other officers— army and navy have also asked about the books—whether they "had the honor" of speaking to Capt Mahan who wrote them. Gibraltar, as you may know was one of the places about which I had to write a great deal and I have had much interest, consequently, in seeing it. Capt Lake lives now at the place where my historical friend, Earl St. Vincent, once lived—though it has doubtless been greatly changed and beautified since then. Just now

---

1. Atwell Peregrine Macleod Lake, RN.

the place is very much burned up by drought, but we have delicious grapes that come over from Spain, and which I wish you little beggars could have. You would enjoy them so much and not have to think as I do whether the sweet will give me gout in my toes. They are only three or four cents a pound. To day I lunched together with the Admiral, at the Artillery Mess and then with three of the officers went round the galleries, which have been tunneled through the rock on the side toward Spain. From these long tunnels at intervals holes are cut in which guns can be mounted. It is a very fine protection, but I own it did not impress me as the best kind of fortification. These galleries were begun a hundred years ago.

I hope I shall soon hear something definite about mamma's plans for the winter, for now I dont know where you all may be nor how to address my letters.

Sunday Oct 8.

I shall close my letter here, Nellikin dear, as we are to sail tomorrow for Tangier. My letters will probably come quite irregularly now for some time, perhaps until we are settled at Nice, which I hope will be by Nov. 15. Not only do I have to catch my opportunity when I can, but I fancy the Spanish post-offices are not very dependable. I am the more sorry because of the uncertainty about where mamma is to be this winter about which I wish to hear. Goodbye, dear child—love to brother and sister and sweet mamma.

To Ellen Evans Mahan

Gibraltar, October 11, 1893 [LC]

Dearest Deldie: I must seize a moment for writing you a line, for we start tonight for Malaga, about sixty miles off, I shall be up most of the night and so rather fagged to write tomorrow. The following day I shall try to get away for Granada, on forty eight hours leave. Day before yesterday we ran over to Tangier, about thirty miles hence, on the Morocco side of the Straits, and were to have left there this evening for Malaga direct— but this morning the doctor reported to me that one of the naval cadets had broken out with measles, so we ran on here to put him in the English hospital. It is our second case—the first appearing in Lisbon in one of the ensigns whom we left there twelve days ago.[1] He took it from the Con-

---

1. Charles Searns Macklin, class of 1892, was sent to the hospital in Gibraltar, and the ship was placed in quarantine. Charles Butler McVay, Jr., class of 1890, had been sent to the hospital in Lisbon with measles on September 28, and all his effects destroyed.

sul's son in Havre upon whom it appeared the day before we left. The two are messmates, but we are informed all the other steerage officers have had the disease. I did not get ashore in Tangier which I little regretted—in fact I had intended not to go. It was arranged, however, that I should accompany the admiral in his official visit to the head Moor of the place yesterday; but it came on to blow very fresh from the Ed [Eastward], what they call here a Levanter, making a rough sea, so the visit was deferred. From Malaga we are to go to Port Mahon, and will probably remain there until it seems certain that we are free from measles—say a fortnight. I have received your letters of the 17th and 21st Sept. I can of course have no objection to your settling yourself where you are most comfortable—our means permit little picking & choosing—but I shall be sorry if you have to go east of Park Ave. I still hope that you may be able to go to 54th St again. A corner is a matter of such advantage—that it makes up for much. However all will probably be settled before you get this. It is one of the misfortunes of our separation that we can neither advise nor support one another. So much for the Navy—hang it. I have had another pessimistic letter from Stockton, elicited by one from Ramsay to Taylor in which he speaks most disparagingly—and most ignorantly—of the College and its work. I reply and cheer up as much as I can; but I am not, and *will* not, be fretted. I did what I could while there, I do what I may here and the result must be as God wills. In fact, I dont find myself caring how it turns out— and I try to have the same spirit about the future of the cruise.

I cannot say I am displeased that you miss me—but I hope it may not cause you much distress. Ramsey will do me all the harm he can—not of conscious malice but because he looks upon me as one to be disciplined. I represent a movement with which he has no sympathy. Consequently, I dont dare to look upon [the] cruise as ending even with the *Chicago's* return—if he is then in power. He would be quite capable of transferring me to another ship. I only mention this lest any sudden disappointment should befall you— I do not *anticipate* this but simply regard it as a possibility.

With love for the children, dearest, I am always your fond husband [etc.].

[P.S.]   I have forgotten to say—you should inquire whether Lyle follows the prayers I gave him after his confirmation. Find from him what they are and what he does.

To Ellen Evans Mahan

Málaga, Spain, October 12, 1893 [LC]

I have no time to write at length, dearest one, but send the enclosed without delay. I left a letter for you yesterday at Gibraltar. We reached here at 4 P.M. after a six hours run & will remain a week. I am off tomorrow for Granada on a three days leave. Your letters of Sep. 24 & 28 were recd here also one each from the two girls. Yours enclosed Lyle's. I am most sorry for your trouble about the apartment, but we know these things always do come out right. My only wonder is that you did not go at once to your mother's. Love to all.

To Ellen Evans Mahan

Málaga, October 17, 1893 [LC]

Dearest Deldie: The witnesses to my signature seem to me to have signed in an unfit place but I suppose it will not affect validity. I send herewith just a line, to say I am well, intending to write Lyle the letter due him in course. I returned yesterday from Granada, delighted with the Alhambra, indeed, but with the climate simply enchanted. I will not call it divine, for that seems almost profane, but I will say that on this earthly sphere imagination can scarcely get nearer the ideal of heaven. No wonder the Moors wept when they looked their last on such a vale of delights. Ever fondly thine [etc.].

To Henry Erben

USS *Chicago*, Málaga, October 19, 1893 [NYHS]

Admiral:
1. I have to make the following report:—
2. Yesterday Chaplain F. F. Sherman reported to me that in the course of a discussion at the mess table that day, P. A. Surgeon E. R. Stitt made to him the remark, "If the men of the ship respected me as little as they do you, I would resign d——d quick."
3. I have this morning investigated the matter, hearing Dr. Stitt's side, and then receiving in his presence and that of the Chaplain the statements of Passed Assistant Engineer Eldridge and Lieutenant Rodgers,[1] who were present when the alleged words were used.
4. It appears from these two gentlemen that in the course of a discussion, which originated with the Chaplain, the latter said that he would probably resign at the end of the cruise for certain reasons; whereupon Dr. Stitt said:

---

1. Frank Harold Eldridge, class of 1875, and Thomas Slidell Rodgers, class of 1880.

"If the men of the ship held me in the contempt they do you, I would resign too."

5. It appears that Dr. Stitt afterwards went to the Chaplain's room, and said: "Mr. Rodgers tells me that I should apologize to you for the language used at the mess table, and I apologize for it."

6. As a personal reparation this apology lacks the elements of being made as publicly as the affront was offered. There remains also the offence against discipline. The limited range of punishment allowed to a captain of a ship is not adequate to check offences of this sort, where the will to refrain from them is otherwise wanting. I therefore refer the case to you—remarking, however, that Dr. Stitt appeared to me to regret sincerely the error he had committed.

To Ellen Evans Mahan

Málaga, October 22, 1893 [LC]

Dearest Deldie: We leave here tomorrow for Barcelona, a two days run; and it had been my intention not to write you till on the way mailing from there, but as the admiral is sending a mail ashore in the morning I will drop you just a line to tell you how much I love and want you—leaving the rest for the passage up. The mails from this south of Spain are reputed irregular and it may be this will reach you no sooner than the one I hope to send from Barcelona. All our mails are at the latter place, the adml ordered them there, and then not sending for them when he decided to stay longer— so that last I have from you is Sept 28 received on our arrival here. Thomas[1] of the *Bennington* telegraphed for his & received some two days ago, but a captain of a flag ship is a nullity. Unluckily the adml's wife is in Europe, and home mails less valuable to him. I am going to write about your Quogue scheme, which seems to me to have much to recommend it, especially as pleasant places are getting more and more hard to find; but there are other considerations that I would want you to weigh. My experience this cruise prompts me more and more to retire—so long as God wills to keep me and I have no escape my course is laid out, but I do not think I should be justified in taking charge of a ship or ships when able to retire—not to speak of the fact of spending my years doing what I do indifferently when I might be doing something else well.

There is I believe nothing new of interest—in fact nothing new at all. I can probably run together a letter of what I have seen or noted in Granada

---

1. Commander Charles M. Thomas, class of 1865, Commanding Officer of the gunboat *Bennington.*

and Malaga besides what I wrote to Lyle, but of my personal concerns there is really no news, which they say is usually good news.

Farewell my own dearest and with love to the children I am always your devoted husband [etc.].

[P.S.] The enclosed[2] was given me by one of the young officers. It is from a Pittsburgh local paper. I suppose people *will* have it that the Queen made a special guest of me; but dont you fall into the folly of endorsing the story.

To Horace E. Scudder

Málaga, October 23, 1893 [HUL]

My dear Mr. Scudder: I sent you four or five days ago from here the corrected proof of Howe, which I trust you will duly receive, despite the alleged irregularity of Spanish mails.

I want to mention that the stamps on the envelope, which was sealed and therefore letter postage, were only for six cents, when this should have been twenty cents. The misfortune is that under the circumstances the letter comes to me as entirely unpaid, so your stamps are lost, and I also have to pay double postage upon delivery. I know of course that the mistake was made at the Riverside Press, but it might be well to caution them.

[P.S.] I found I had omitted to mention Howe's death, so I inserted paragraph, substance of which (except last sentence) is on enclosed slip.[1] The last sentence of the enclosed would, *I* think, improve the paragraph; if you think likewise, will you have it inserted?

In case of the corrected proof miscarrying, I think the original, with insertion, will do well enough, though I reconstructed two or three sentences.

To Ellen Evans Mahan

At sea, October 23, 1893 [LC]

My dearest Deldie: I left a letter for you in Malaga whence we departed today, and I shall keep this open after our arrival in Barcelona to see

---

2. A short account of Mahan's enthusiastic reception in England and the "unanimous" British praise of his sea power books.

1. Enclosure not found.

if your letters there recd. need an immediate reply. It has been particularly vexatious to miss my mail just now as you are left hung up (for me) homeless and apartmentless. At the same with yours of the 27 and 28, I received an envelope containing one from each of the girls written on my birthday. I was much pleased at the remembrance and also at the marked improvement in composition as well as in handwriting which they both show. Lyle's of the 24th was also very well worded for a boy of his age. Now as to Quogue, I think very well of the idea—only you must do a little calculation. There are not only taxes but insurance and repairs—still I should think that if you could rent for $500, in case of non-occupancy, that $200 would pay all annual expenses and leave $300 income which is 5 per cent on $6,000—as much as you are likely to average. On the other hand, if you occupy, you lose that $300; which is however scarcely more than you must ordinarily pay for summer lodging. Upon the whole, then, I must favor your plan—there is always an element of doubt; but if you will say your prayers and be thoughtful in what you do, we may hope for the best. It is to me a matter much to be desired that the children should meet habitually the same nice people summer by summer, so as really to know and be known by them. Your Dr. Carr appears very suddenly on the scene. I hear nothing of him till he suddenly turns up giving you heaps of advice. Who is he? I daresay all he says is true enough, but do be careful with the colchicum. As for the photo of the ship entering Havre, it was taken unknown to us, and thought I doubtless was on the forward bridge, I did not recognize myself. The taker did not bring it to our notice and I happened to see it quite accidentally while walking round the town. The second I sent you was taken at anchor in Lisbon—it is rare indeed to find a ship photo caught on the fly as the Havre one was. We have so far had most ideal weather in the Mdn.— too good to last, one fears. A little fog for some days in Malaga. Today we are coasting at a distance of three or four miles—with a brilliant sea and sky and smooth water. The high brown rugged coast is very effective in its contrast with the blue above and below—and the occasional green patches and white towns are also picturesque; but upon the whole I am disillusioned with Spain. I have scarcely seen a pretty woman—the streets are very narrow and smelly—Granada and Malaga alike unsavory.

Tuesday, Oct. 24

Another brilliant day, Dearest Miss D., rather more cloud, but the big soft white kind that drift lazily along—bright sun, cool air, blue sky and bluer water—lots of fishing boats with their quaint three cornered Mediterranean sail—about five miles off shore between Alicante and Valencia. A little north of the latter place is Murviedro, in attacking which my old school-friend Hannibal started the second Punic War. Spain is lovely to see under these conditions, but somewhat open, at near sight, to Mark Twain's reproach against the Queen of Sheba. I shall not write much for I am dreadfully drowsy. I dont go to bed these short runs. The coasts swarm with steamers & I am constantly called on deck by lights. I get a good many naps, but still sleeping in a chair, however easy, with frequent interruptions is not refreshing; and the worst of it is the day is as broken as the night. There are fewer sail, since we got away from the funnel leading to the Straits of Gibraltar.

Oct 25

I close in an immense hurry simply saying I am well and have your No 40. Arrived here, Barcelona at 9 this morning and can just catch mail for London etc. I want you to know I shall approve your Quogue plan, you using your judgment.

To Helen Evans Mahan

Barcelona, Spain, October 28, 1893 [NWC]

Dearest Hennie: Having been nearly a fortnight without letters when we arrived here day before yesterday, I then received quite an accumulation —four from mamma, one from you and Nellie from Elizabeth (one each) and one from Lyle. I also had one from Mr. Herbert speaking of my books in the highest terms, most flattering—and one from Little & Brown asking when Nelson would be ready, that they were having many inquiries both from home and from England. I shall not be able to give them a satisfactory reply—which is not my fault. They add "We are glad to report a good demand for the Sea Power both at home and abroad"; this I presume refers to the period since their last formal return of sales. The Paris (N.Y.) *Herald* on Friday last, the 20th, published a letter from its correspondent in Malta, giving an interview he had had with Adml Tryon just before he sailed in the *Victoria* and was drowned. The Adml. himself made first mention of the books saying "they were the best things ever written etc etc. We Englishmen are grateful to him; we owe him a large debt." As he was considered the first officer in the British Navy, this is a very satisfactory compliment. I wrote to mamma on the passage here, telling her I very much approved of her plan for building at Quogue. I mention it again in case the letter miscarry. In planning the house it would be well I think to have it so constructed as to admit of an addition, as something we would, or might, wish some day to build. I was a little startled to hear of your reading a novel of Zola's. I believed he has accidentally written one or two things that are fit for decent people to read, & I suppose your friend knew what she was giving you—but for the most part he writes, I am told, the very vilest matter rendered none the better by his great power. I once tried to read a novel of his, but found it impossible from utter loathing—a moral feeling resembling physical nausea. He is a beast. Tell mamma that I shall send her a cheque for $15, probably by my next letter. That I want her to have a nice dinner on her birthday and a bottle of good champagne. If she should want to invite the 34th St. people[1] she would want two bottles. Besides this I want her to get herself a present. I intend to have a little dinner party on that day—probably of the people who know her, Nazro, Dewey, and Rodgers.[2] Also, I want her to send me the October *Atlantic*. I had hoped Houghton and Mifflin would have sent it to me. The price for the article was more than I had hoped—as Exmouth was less. Now I think I have attended to business first—next pleasure so far as letter writing can be so considered. I did not say anything about Malaga, I believe; Granada is so much more interesting, and I saw Malaga only by tramping around it. It has very little of interest. The cathedral is reputed a fine building, I believe, and it was certainly impressive from some points of view. It is, I believe, in what is known by architects as the Renaissance style—that is, the style which came in between 1450 and 1550. At that time the capture of Constantinople by the Turks sent a great many Greek scholars into Western Europe, and this concurring with Luther's Reformation, caused a great intellectual movement which is spoken of as the Renaissance. The architecture of that day has round instead of pointed arches, and is distinguished by profuse and rather exaggerated ornamentation. Malaga was taken by the Christians only in the end of the fifteenth century, so its cathedral was built under Renaissance influence. Though to my mind less distinctively reverent and Christian than Gothic architecture, still the massive pillars and their great height produced a solemn effect. The same reasons caused the Granada Cathedral also to be of Renaissance style; but there the fluted pillars were of whiter marble increasing much the impression of vastness. Besides this, in the crypt under the building there were the tombs of Ferdinand & Isabella—the Catholic Kings as good Spaniards still call them—with their effigies in pure white marble evidently very good likenesses, for they closely resemble portraits I had elsewhere seen. Granada moreover was one of the spots consecrated by my early dreams—a place full of poetic association, which was not wholly disappointed. I am, it is true, quite désillusionné about Spain. Granada, Malaga, and Barcelona are all dirty, smelly, and rather insignificant in general appearance—always excepting special features like the Alhambra etc. Then I had always a great idea of the beauty of the Spanish women, but I have seen scarcely any. The prettiest, and she had a charming face, was a

1. Mrs. Manlius Glendower Evans, Rosalie Evans, and Hartman Kuhn Evans.
2. Lieutenant (j.g.) Theodore Gibbs Dewey, class of 1880, and Thomas S. Rodgers.

young peasant woman at the station in Granada, when I came away. You perhaps know that the Spaniards have on hand a little war with Morocco, and are sending troops over. A number of soldiers were in the third class carriage of our train and the women folk had come to see them off. The poor souls were doing as most women do everywhere. Here some were crying unrestrainedly—there two old women, probably mothers, were standing quietly, wiping their eyes from time to time. The pretty one, with a sweet pure creamy complexion & dark eyes, good features—really very attractive, seemed grave but cheerful. There was no apparent excitement in her manner, but I noticed her put her arms from behind around the neck of an older woman, who doubtless had a son in the car, in a caressing way. Whether he was her brother or her lover I of course dont know. She held out bravely, however till the train moved off, and then I saw her face all of a sudden begin to work and the tears ran down. There was then an old gipsy woman who must have had some [one] belonging in the train. At the moment of departure, she lifted up her voice and howled—stretched her arms out after the train and then flung herself full length upon her face; but I regret to say my sympathies were wholly given to the pretty-faced woman. Tell mamma that I entirely approve of her putting money in the savings bank, but entirely disapprove of her cutting her bank account down so as to feel skimped. The worry will be poorly repaid by any interest, & I dont believe she will spend more lavishly because her balance is good, she is not that kind. I confess I am very glad to hear you are going back to 54th Street. I know where you are and how you are, and I never believed you could much better yourselves. Mamma must keep her eye on the exit by the roof and appeal to the authorities, if it be not secured.

Oct. 28

I am about to mail this. Mamma tells me that you feel somewhat overwhelmed with undertaking a pupil independent of Mrs. Morgan. It is a distressing feeling, which you inherit from me, but that self distrust though a weakness, is not altogether a bad thing—particularly if it leads you to throw yourself back upon God, to ask His assistance and to look for success only to His constant help. Speaking humanly, and thinking of yourself "soberly, as you ought to think" you have an adequate knowledge of music, and probably a faculty for teaching—all which is in your favor. I have no further news—am well. Love to all.[3]

---

3. Enclosed in this letter was an unsigned review of Mahan's *Farragut* from the London *Guardian* of September 20, 1893. The reviewer was surprised that Mahan compared Farragut with Nelson, but otherwise liked the book.

To Nathan Appleton

USS *Chicago*, Barcelona, October 29, 1893[1]

Dear Sir: I have received your letter of Oct 12, and thank you both for your kind mention of my article, and also for your own enclosed,[2] which I have read with much interest.

It is unnecessary to say that I feel the urgency of maintaining our own priority of interest in everything touching the Isthmus. I think, however, this will readily be conceded by Great Britain, when she sees that we are prepared to make our position good—1. by putting in our money, 2. by supporting a navy adequate to back our assertions and insure the peace in those regions. I deeply deplore any alienation between the two Anglo-Saxon states, whose interests I think largely mutual; and regret that lack of time prevented my adding a paragraph to that effect. I have, however, said the same in more than one published article.

Hilary A. Herbert

USS *Chicago*, Barcelona, October 31, 1893 [NA]

Sir: I have to report that on entering Malaga harbor a pilot was employed for the *Chicago*, the Commanding Officer considering it necessary to do so.

To Ellen Evans Mahan

Barcelona, November 1, 1893 [LC]

My own dearest: I shall send you but a short letter this time, chiefly because I have but little to say—partly because I hope to have more time at Marseille, and that a letter from there will not be much behind this, for we leave day after tomorrow for there and should arrive the 4th. Before I forget —you wanted me to bring some gloves. Please send me a separate mem.

---

1. This letter was made available to the editors through the courtesy of Professor Arthur M. Johnson of the University of Maine. Professor Johnson found it tucked in a second-hand book he bought in Boston.
2. Nathan Appleton, "Clayton-Bulwer Treaty and the Ship-Canal," *Harper's Weekly* (September 30, 1893).

of number sizes, color etc. It seems to me it would be well if you have any woman friend in Paris who could select and send them to me in Nice—or you might yourself write the particulars to the Paris firm, directing to send to me upon my writing to them. I feel as if I would rather not undertake to bring in for any one else, having still some scruples about the Customs, infamous though I consider it to be. Hurrah for Le Nain.[1] Athanasius[2] Contra Mundum. My uncle[3] used to say he would back Athanasius against a General Council; and though it sounds conceited, Le Nain's is the first *entirely* adverse criticism I have met. True, people are not apt to bring such to one's notice. I hope you will look to Lyle's *habits* of devotion in my absence—his preparation for communion etc. We may not expect deep vital piety in a lad of his years—it would be precocious and abnormal; but a reverent and dutiful observance of forms is an invaluable discipline and preservative. When the fire is well stacked, it is ready for the kindling when the flame falls from Heaven. I purposely & carefully appointed to him short prayers and forms. The enclosed cheque contains the $15 I wrote Helen of, for your birthday—i.e. to have a good dinner with champagne, and to buy something for yourself. The twenty more are tithes upon Exmouth and the next article in Atl. [*Atlantic*] Send to the Seamen,[4] unless you have already done so. There is a kind of fitness in their recg. from those maritime articles. By this mail I send a letter to Jenny—asking that the silver may be divided now that Dennis is home, and saying you can act for me. I added what you may differ from, but I cannot but feel to be right—that I would not take it away during Aunty's life.[5] To force, unnecessarily, upon one so aged, another change in familiar surroundings, seems to me cruel, emphasizing what she has lost. I also said, referring to a remark of Fred's that he would like to buy in the silver if he could, that I would be willing to meet such a plan by taking equivalent manufactured silver, as determined by a good silver firm. I am now trying to arrange my hours so as to be able to write more regularly upon Nelson, but it is very difficult. My mere correspondence involves so much writing that I come wearied to the task—but I shall make a fair trial. I dont wonder you are lonesome, particularly during this month without a house & I fear you may find Pomfret trying—though it is by this [time] over. You must indulge yourself with some theatre going, & when the house is started visit your friends frequently, seek reasonable

---

1. Le Nain de Tillemont, *The History of the Arians and of the Council of Nice*. Translated into English by T. Deacon. London, 1721. Or, perhaps, his *Ecclesiastical Memories of the First Six Centuries*. Translated by T. Deacon, 2 vols. London, 1733–1735.
2. Athanasius (286?–373), Greek Bishop of Alexandria, identified with the Christian theory of the Trinity, which was promulgated as dogma at the Council of Nicaea in 325.
3. Milo Mahan.
4. Seamen's Church Institute of New York.
5. Jane Leigh Okill Swift.

diversion. I hope that when settled the money losses will be less trying than the gain from the settled feeling and the interests about you.

Thursday Nov. 2.

I shall send this off now, even though there may be things I should have said. The more I think of your Quogue plan the more I like it. Even if it should prove a little more expensive the gain would be great in the intimacy year by year with the *same* pleasant people—but I think the chances decidedly are that it will pay. Proceed with reasonable care—be sure of your title, and of your house plans. In the latter, contemplate possible addition, both as to site where you put it and its own plan. Goodbye dearest. Love to all.

To Ellen Kuhn Mahan

At sea, November 4, 1893 [LC]

Dearest Miss Nellikin: I have, or seem likely to have an unusual holiday this morning. We left Barcelona yesterday—had target practice in the aftn. and as that dirties the ship very much this forenoon is being given to a general scrubbing in which I have no share. We are about forty miles from Marseille and going very slow so as not to reach there before one, giving time for the cleaning and for the men to get their dinner first. I wrote to mamma two days ago from Barcelona, and now I cannot certainly recall to which of you children I last sent a letter—but I think 'twas Helen and so write to you. I made a bit of a failure of Barcelona, having intended to make an excursion to a place called Montserrat, about three hours distant; but instead of going at once I postponed to a certain day, bad weather came and threw me all out. We have such extraordinary fine weather since we got to Ireland that we seem unable to realize any other, and a rainy day takes us unawares. The last letter I had from you was the one written in pencil— Oct 9. I am sorry—very sorry—for your disappointment about Chicago, but you may be sure that in accepting mamma's judgment as sweetly as you did you will be in all ways happier in the end. I am glad to think of you all as back in the old house, I dont think it easy to improve upon— despite all drawbacks. Plenty of light and air, and the fact that we have had good health for three years, are advantages to be very seriously considered when contemplating a change. I have been looking over all your letters and find nothing to which to reply. I may say however that I am pretty pleased to see your and Helen's handwriting coming out so nicely. I think that if you will be at the pains to take care of it for a few years you will both have very good hands—and, when once formed, they are not likely ever to be spoiled. Lyle's is still unformed, but when he takes time—is not hurried—

he expresses himself so well that I think he will have a very good style, and you all have greatly improved in the wording and matter of your letters. I sent mamma a cheque for $35 in my last letter—$20 of which is church money. I hope she has recd but I mention it. Just as we were leaving Barcelona poor Mr. Nazro, Uncle Dennis' friend, recd. a telegram of his wife's death. He had been prepared for bad news by one that came the day before saying that she was very low. She has been a great invalid for many years, frequently at the point of death, so that outsiders find it easy to say that it is far better so; but it must be very hard for him, away from home & to know he will never again see her in this world. He is a very fine fellow and for many years has borne this burden of a sick wife, with an expensive illness and narrow means. I wish he may find a turn in his luck, but to be a lieutenant in the Navy at 45 offers poor promise of betterment.

Monday, Nov 6

I must bring my letter now to a sudden close dear Miss Nell, to catch today's mail. We arrived here, Marseille, day before yesterday, and today are in all the hurry of visits. I found letters from mamma, Helen & you, and today I have recd. those from mamma & Helens of Oct 27. You are dear good children to keep me so well supplied and I much appreciate it. Mamma must try however to pick me up some gossipy news, now that she has her type writer again. I shall try to get away from here soon to visit Arles and Avignon two curious old cities within 75 miles of Marseille. Good bye—dear. Love to all.

To Ellen Evans Mahan

Marseille, France, November 10, 1893 [LC]

My own dearest Deldie: I must write you today as I may not be able tomorrow. I went off day before yesterday for a two days leave to visit Arles and Avignon. You will remember the stop we made at Nismes, in '75, with Rosie along. It and the two other places had long been objects of my intentions, but not until now have I succeeded. Granada, Arles, and Avignon, added to Carcassonne and Nismes are very comfortable achievements for me. The trains are slow and somewhat far between; & rather than wait till ten, I took an "omnibus" at 6:30 to catch which I rose at 4:30 leaving the ship an hour later, before daybreak. It was a raw cold day, threatening rain. By the time I reached Arles there was a strong mistral—north-east wind—blowing, cold and raw. They make a great fuss over them here, but this seemed to me little worse than one of our bleak days in late October.

Fortunately while it lasts rain dont come—but the inconvenience of managing the paper of a guide book, getting glasses on your nose—keeping your hat on your head and your umbrella under your arm are quite considerable. There is at Arles an amphitheatre much larger than that at Nismes, and also, a little distance from it very considerable remains of an old Roman theatre. Also an ancient church about 800 years old, built upon the spot where a church has been from the earliest times. Much more attractive than the church itself are the cloisters, an equilateral quadrangle surrounded by arcades, whose differing styles show the periods at which they were built from 1100–1400. What most interests me, however, there as in Lisbon and Barcelona, is to wander through the narrow streets noting here and there the houses whose exterior shows that they are centuries old, and often by their ornamentation betraying the family pride of the local provincial noblesse. One seems in that way to enter into the life-conditions of those days which we call the middle ages. This is much emphasized when, as at Avignon, the town is surrounded by the old walls and towers of five centuries ago. You see the contracted and insecure condition of life, and how the poor creatures were necessarily huddled together, losing great part of the advantage which the lovely nature of the country gives them. I was dreadfully sleepy and tired that night—but I got to a good hotel, had a good dinner, and a delightful bed. You know how cold French houses are apt to be on cold nights, especially if you are tired. Well my room felt cold as ice—but there was a duvet and the bed as warm as toast. I slept from 9:30 to 6:30 profoundly—had my café complet at 7:30 and at 8 was out. Walked all round the ramparts of Avignon which were built between 1300 and 1350—in very good condition & so far interesting, but not at all to be named alongside of Carcassonne. The great feature of Avignon is the palace of the Popes—for it was the seat of the papacy for about 100 years, beginning 1305—during great part of the century there being two rival popes. The palace is a huge, vast and most austere looking fortress. Whatever its luxury or ornament within, without it is sheer unadorned military grandeur—exceeding anything I have ever seen. The inside has undergone so many changes that it now looks—and is actually used for—a barracks, bare and rude. It stands on a great rock—to which the foundations are secured—the joining of the masonry and rock being often visible. From the summit of the rock, beyond the palace is a most extensive and beautiful view, but the day was too hazy for me to have the full advantage. I could only see the "pleasant land of France" extended for a great distance before me with all its beautiful cultivation. Toward night it came on to rain. My train left at 7:08 due in Marseille at 10:52; but at Tarascon there was a long delay and I finally learned that we must be passed by the Rapide from Paris. It being evident that we should be very very late, and my boat waiting in the rain,

I went to the Chef de Gare who was most polite authorized my changing into the Rapide ordinarily not allowed even to first class passengers, and my return ticket was second-class to Arles—thence first class. Second class fatigues me over much for long distances. The Rapide itself was late, but I slept most of the way—got to Marseille at 11:20, and was on board at 12:10. I had not been in my room fifteen minutes when it came on to rain hard, and has continued to do so till a short time ago (now 4 P.M.). The other train did not arrive until 12:30. Carl was at the station for me but missed me, and waited for the train. I enclose you a picture of the lady whom I went to Arles to see, but she had an engagement and did not appear. Your letter of the 26th came a few days ago—from Pomfret. I hope you will put together for due meditation, two sentences in it. 1. "the disagreeable, worrying fortnight I spent in N.Y." and 2. "everything seems to have happened to suit." In the end everything does seem so to happen, but we seem never to learn the lesson. I think, I am more patient than I used to be and less worrying—but I have about given up any expectation of making myself any better. I try now simply to keep on my guard and when temptation comes ask not for strength, but to be carried over it. I have lost all faith in the power of my will, and am only thankful that I can believe in His power. I think when you are settled in N.Y. you may add to the interest of your letters by giving me a little more of the more trivial details of your day—or news of you and your neighbors. When one is away trifles of this kind are very acceptable. Oh! one thing I want to urge on you—to take some pains to insure dryness and adequate warmth in your rooms; for I feel sure, having developed this gouty tendency, that while it is primarily constitutional and shows acidity, that it is much aggravated by cold and damp. Do look to this—saving on fuel will be poor economy if the cold checks the due action of your skin. I have thought somewhat of getting a duvet in France. Would you advise it? I realized in Avignon that the warmth of the bed was my principal restorative, while on board here the dampness tends to rheumatism.

Saturday, Nov. 11

Six months today since I joined this ship. I must close now hastily as we are to breakfast at the prefecture at 12:30, and unless I now mail this it will have to lie over until tomorrow. There is no further news. Do mind my injunctions to keep warm, for gouty people need to diminish as much as possible the work thrown on the inward organs. Nothing helps me like sufficient warmth to the skin—short however of perspiration. Good bye— Love to all the children.

To Francis M. Ramsay

USS *Chicago*, Marseille, November 11, 1893 [NA]

Sir: Referring to the target practice for the quarter ending December 31, 1893, which was held on November 3, 10 miles east of Barcelona, Spain, I enclose herewith the reports of the Division officers.

2. The firing of the Secondary Battery was too rapid for the observers (two in boats and two on board) so the officers of divisions were obliged to estimate the "Merit off Target."

3. The 6-pdr. ammunition referred to as having given trouble is among the lot that is reported to have been slightly damaged in time past by partial accidental flooding of the ammunition room. In the future this bad ammunition will be served out and used for target practice.

To Ellen Evans Mahan

Marseille, November 12, 1893 [LC]

Dearest Deldie: I received yours of Oct 30 yesterday. While you have to use your hand I must submit—but otherwise I must really protest against the exceedingly short commerce of news that you send me. Remember that I am entirely dependent upon letters for my knowledge of what goes on at home, and four pages of small note paper in a sprawling hand is not quite what one has a claim to know, when wholly separated from all for which he cares.

I mailed you a long letter yesterday. Love to all.

To Ellen Evans Mahan

Genoa, Italy, November 18, 1893 [LC]

Dearest Deldie: I received yesterday your letter written in Pomfret and mailed in N.Y. It is a satisfaction to think of you as being all together and in a place so familiar to me. Now that you have your typewriter again I hope you will give me all the news you can—you are too often very scrappy as if writing were an unmitigated bore. It did not occur to me till lately that you might possibly be alarmed by the news of the Barcelona theatre explosion. As it turns out we have had an escape, which is never the less real because so absolute. Others may think it far fetched, but you and I will gladly recognize the merciful providence of God, which has so far covered us. The occasion of the bomb throwing was an opening night at the principal theatre in Barcelona. We were to have had a box placed at our disposal, and probably many would have gone. I myself would likely have had to go, and, though usually caring little for plays when I cannot understand the language, would have been willing to do so on the chance of seeing the fashion and beauty of Barcelona, pretty sure to turn up on such an occasion. The consul writes me no fewer than 18 fragments of the shell drove through the box we were to have occupied. It is therefore most fortunate that the admiral had decided to sail. We arrived here Thursday morning, day before yesterday, after a rather unpleasant passage and the weather has been gloomy and raw ever since our arrival. We are rather spoiled by the almost unchanged good weather that has attended us, and are enervated by the delicious yet not excessive warmth of the Southern Mediterranean. I have only been once ashore but am delighted with what I saw. Marseille was so dirty and commonplace, the people so unrefined and "common" to use your word— there was nothing to attract. I saw only one decent looking woman during our stay, and scarce one that looked thoroughbred. Here the well dressed people look like ladies and gentlemen, & without asserting great good looks the women have pretty complexions, refined features, and the air of well bred people. It is like the transition from the Bowery to the Avenues in N.Y. Even the poorer working people have an air of self respect and dignity that the French have not—as a rule. They say that these northern Italians are very much superior to the Neapolitans & Sicilians. I had a letter from Mr. Marston of Sampson Low, yesterday, answering one or two questions mainly about the best paying size for the Life of Nelson. He says that the books continue to sell well—and proposed to me to undertake editing Campbell's *Naval History and Lives of the Admirals*[1] an old work you may remember to have seen in my hands. It is utterly impossible—but there is interest in seeing how literary work opens out before me. 1. Nelson. 2. War of 1812 etc. 3. War of the Rebellion. 4. This proposition. It gives me the feeling and hope that I shall be justified in retiring at the end of my forty years—even tho I do have to make this unlucky cruise; and that it will be better to do so than to waste more time waiting for promotion. God will teach us what to do when the time comes. Meantime, do my best, I advance but very slowly with Nelson—and my night work moreover seems uninspired—no flow of thought or words—ideas inarticulate and formless—and worked into such shape as they get by most arduous labor. By a curious coincidence I meet here, on his way to Nice with the appointment of Consul there, Hall,[2] No 1 of my class at the Naval Acady. He came on board yesterday to

---

1. John Campbell, *Naval History of Great Britain, including the History and Lives of the British Admirals* . . . London: J. Stockdale, 1813.
2. Wilburn B. Hall.

see me, but I was away, not knowing of his being here. This consul told me, and I called but he also was out. I have asked him to lunch for tomorrow, with his wife & family, if any be with him. I used to know her well, and I think before he did, for he was much of a book worm and went out little. She was a S.C. girl, daughter to Com. Ingraham[3] of the Navy, and pretty with the prettiness of youth and the soft attractiveness of southern women. The last time I saw her was immediately after my graduation, the evening before I left Annapolis, at a little party given by the Gills. What a change of the outward man, she certainly and I probably, will have to see. Of course they were rebs. I have just received an answer to my invite—they will come, one son with them. I forgot to say that Mr. Marston is negotiating a translation of *the* books into German. On your birthday I shall have Rodgers & Dewey to dinner & three others—as to whom I am hesitating—probably Jasper[4] whom I think you would prefer. Now I shall close this with dearest love to you and the dear children.

[P.S.] We have just had a visit from the commanding general and staff— such magnificence you never see; but the interesting feature is they are all like gentlemen. The aide-de-camp a picture, tall handsome, distinguished, but the mildest, most, deferential tone. You will think I have a craze on the Italians, but really the revulsion from France is too great. I trust the Italians will lick them well in the approaching war, but I fear they wont.

To Hilary A. Herbert

USS *Chicago*, Genoa, November 19, 1893 [NA]

Sir: I have to report that on entering and leaving Marseilles a pilot was employed for the *Chicago*, the Commanding Officer considering it necessary to do so.

To Ellen Evans Mahan

Genoa, November 21, 1893 [LC]

My own dearest Deldie: It is Helen's time for a letter but in honor of your birthday she must wait a spell. I wish you and myself many happy returns of this day, my dear; we have had much happiness & love in one

---

3. Duncan N. Ingraham. The daughter who married Hall was Harriot.
4. Robert T. Jasper, at this time Executive Officer in the *Bennington*.

another, and I trust it may long continue. I shall have a small dinner tonight —of whom you will know only Jasper, Rodgers and Dewey—two others, making in all six. There are others here who know you, but never on terms on [of] cordial intimacy—Kenny[1] though, I believe, is the only one. I should have asked Nazro, but his own wife having so recently died I did not feel it tactful to ask him to celebrate the birthday of my own. My friends Hall and his wife lunched on board on Sunday, as I wrote you I expected. Him I have seen in the meantime, she not. It is my first experience of meeting after so very long a time a person I had known well. Over thirty-four years. I remember it as though yesterday—the week after my graduation, the latter part of June, 1859, a little evening party at the Gills', whose house you may remember, though you never entered it, on Main St. in Annapolis, next the City Hotel, but on the side toward St. Anne's Church. She cannot be more than a year—or, at the very most, two years—younger than I—so to leave a person—particularly a pretty woman—at eighteen and next see her at over fifty is something of a sensation. She has worn well however—not of course that she looks young—not even particularly so for her years but she has not gone to pieces. Figure trim and graceful, complexion clear, plenty of hair—but gray. Being brunette, of course she has no color, and the skin is brown. However, you cant feel much interest in a person whose chief interest to me is that I knew her as a pretty girl, in the days when, like Narcissi, "N'est-elle pas fille?" was a sufficient reason for sentimental regard. He is much stouter, a little prone to monopolize conversation and particularly when you would prefer to talk to his wife. He wrote me a letter in reply to my own invite which I will send you some time. For me it would be rather gushing, but all people are not alike and I am always somewhat drawn to people who speak of our Lord, as he did, as Our Lord. I remember that my Sunday in the country in England, one of my fellow guests, who reminded me of Annie Ward somewhat, turned to me and drawing my attention to the East window said "that must be some of So and So's work—you notice the figure of Our Lord"—I felt my heart warm to her at once. I had to meet them Erben, Potter the flag lieut, and Thomas of the *Bennington*, so with their son—we were eight in all. They came to church and I think the breakfast was very successful. I just recd. a very nice note from Jasper asking me to make you the compliments of the season. But for your inveterate procrastination, making your entry into the world a day late, you would have had your birthday yesterday well celebrated, for we dressed ship and fired a salute for the birthday of the Queen of Italy. Please dont forget to send me the *Atlantic* with Isthmus and Sea Power—and Howe when that comes out.

---

1. Albert S. Kenny, who was serving in the *Chicago*.

Our little entertainment went off very neatly last evening dearest one. We drank your health, and I was happily thankful for the day that brought you into the world as well as for that which gave you to me. The admiral's wife and daughter arrived last night from Switzerland, a circumstance which will probably keep us here a few days yet. We have been having bad weather, but it has now cleared off and is beautiful—cool and clear. The place is surrounded with high hills which allow variety in walking and give fine views. The people also interest me much. Night before last I received a cheque for my article for the *United Service Magazine* £10. I had only expected £6—not that it was not worth more, but I always anticipate poverty in service periodicals. As it was, I had to wait so long that I began to think I was to be done out of it. It puts me on my feet very nicely—for I can just about manage, fulfilling the entertaining I can scarcely avoid. I live rather better than I care to—not in quantity but in quality, but I do not care to discourage Carl by making him cut down—the saving would be trivial and I should have to nag him.

10 P.M.

I failed to get this off by the mail by inattention, but will close for to-morrow. Every one seems coming to Genoa; whom do you think I met in the street today? Sarah Elizabeth. She and the Dr. have arrived to take the steamer of the 24th for home. I dont like the account she gives of him, although she seems untroubled. Symptoms seem to me something like your mother's. I have today two letters—one from a Mrs. Clymer and another from her daughter Mrs. Gurney—inviting me to visit them if we go to Spezia. They had heard from yr. uncle Charles.[2] There is no immediate likelihood of our going to S. Hence the intention is to go to Nice. Good bye my own darling. Much love to the children.

Nov. 23

Will close for mail.

To Samuel A. Ashe

USS *Chicago*, Genoa, November 24, 1893 [DUL]

My dear Ashe: I had the unexpected pleasure, I may say the very great surprise of seeing here Hall and his wife, on their way to Nice—and through him I heard of you and, as I was glad to understand, of your well-being and cheerfulness. I will not pretend to apologize for my long neglect in writing you. I have so much work to do with my pen, that my very hand-

2. Charles Kuhn, brother of Mrs. Manlius Glendower Evans.

writing shows the trace of it; and if our modern letters do not aim at being the epistolary models which those of last century present, they do demand some effort of mind, which I am often too jaded with other composition to give. Separated now from my family, but resolved to keep myself a living reality in their life, I have as much as I can do in maintaining my regular correspondence with wife and children. It is however a real satisfaction to hear of you, and I beg you to believe that my regard is not less if less often expressed.

Hall I had met fifteen years ago, but his wife I had not seen since we said goodbye during the week after my graduation in 1859. It is the longest period that has ever elapsed, for me, in renewing an acquaintance. Nor do I know of any now alive whom I have not seen since that time. To say she had changed but little would be absurd. Some may look thirty at fifty—but it is not given any to carry the color and expression of 18 to middle life. Otherwise I found her the same person I had known and so warmly liked. In a way he had changed more than she, for he has put on a good deal of flesh and that since I last saw him. We are likely to see a good deal of each other—off and on—during the winter for we expect to spend two months at Ville Franche, four miles from Nice and within his consular jurisdiction. We talked over old friends and I was surprised to find that he knew more than I did—even of those who had remained North.

It is now nearly six months since we left the United States, and despite the reputed charms of Europe I hopefully expect that we may return next summer. I have become exceedingly interested in professional literary work, and have now a fair promise of success in it. Last spring I asked the Dept. to excuse me from further sea service, on the ground that I could do work more useful for the Navy in the line I was then successfully following, and I undertook to retire, as the law allows, at the end of forty years service, in 1896. The last Secy would have granted the request, but Herbert did not see his way. The work therefore dropped and I am now amusing myself with a Life of Nelson, which the publishers think will be a pecuniary success backed by the reputation I have acquired in England. For it is a singular fact, due probably to the broader maritime interests of Great Britain, that I have achieved much greater standing there than at home—wherever I go I am complimented on my work by their people, while at home few know it.

For the rest while blessed in health and so far in spirits, and with all happiness in my home ties, I am forced daily to realize that I am growing old, and especially that all charm ship life ever had is utterly gone. I am enduring, not living; and have the painful consciousness that I am expending much labor in doing what I do but indifferently, while debarred from doing what I have shown particular capacity for. It is not a pleasant feeling—especially when accompanied with the knowledge that the headstrong folly of my youth started me in a profession, which, to say the least, was not the one for which I have the best endowments.

Hall could of course give me but few details beyond those broader outlines of your lot that I already know—except, perhaps that I was not aware you are the political power he tells me you have become. When you find time to drop me a line, tell me what you can—of your own self more particularly—for in that I have and shall, I am sure, always have a most affectionate interest. My address is Care of B.F. Stevens, 4 Trafalgar Square, London.

This station possesses the advantage of much to occupy the mind & to some extent prevent it from dwelling upon the temporary loss of all that makes the truest happiness of life; but still, the pleasant home letters continually remind me of the loss of days and experiences—a break in associations—which can not be replaced. You, my dear friend, have had to bear a yet heavier trial—but I am glad to know that in a numerous and satisfactory family you still have much of the best earth affords. I thank God I have never shared the folly of our days, which affects to see in anything else the happiness which family ties bestow.

To Helen Evans Mahan

Genoa, November 26, 1893 [NWC]

Dearest Hennie: It is a delicious rainy Sunday—not one of those disconcerting days which keep you in doubt as to its intentions, but an honest gentle downpour which puts my mind wholly at rest as to going ashore. I have latterly adopted a plan for my day's work to insure, if possible, doing some daily writing on Nelson. The time up to 2 p.m. I give to the ship's work of all kinds. At 2, about, I go ashore, walk etc until 4.30, and when I return I lie down giving orders not to be disturbed, before 6.30, my dinner hour. I try thus for sleep as well as rest so as to be fresh as may be for an evening's work, which I try to make from 8–11. It is by no means the equivalent for my morning hours at home. Do what I may, my mind is jaded, and I not only fall short in quantity but am tormented with doubts as to the quality of what I do. Words fail me, & the ability to find substitutes for those that dont just express the idea, & I have not that power of mustering my phrases which has before conduced much to my success.

I want to tell you, dear, that I am very much pleased with your letters. They are very full, chatty and interesting and bear their own witness to what mamma and Aunt Jenny have written me of your progress toward

[183]

maturity during the months since I came away. There is of course a slight element of sadness to think of the child being really grown up, and also that I should perforce be away during these changes, but I cannot really complain that you are growing up to your years and taking your place in the world. You may be sure that letters such as you send me will be welcome to any one and your handwriting also is taking on form and character. I was pleased to hear that it was decided you should take Rosamond Tuck, for it would extend your "connection" a little; but at the same time you must bear in mind that you are not yet at your full strength or with your full equipment for successful teaching. For some years to come, say three or four, it will be wiser for your future success to avoid wearisome work, hurry and drive—and also to devote more time to perfecting your music than to making money. I have wanted you never to acquire simply the habit of teaching. Three years hence, if mamma approves my purpose to retire, we may want to make a combined effort to increase the family re- sources—and I hope Lyle also will look to this by making sure of his fourth form, if diligent study will do it. With regard to the Quogue house tell mamma, if possible, to arrange that each of the family have his or her own room, unless it should seem a decided advantage that she and I be together, in which case let it be large enough—spare on the furniture at first rather than on the building. Of course you will want a spare room. As to my making any detailed suggestions, it would from this distance cause only confusion —and mamma has good judgment enough if only she will remember that skimping is out of place, when you cannot remedy any fault caused by it. I still continue to like this place very much although the weather is not pleasant for a ship. We have had several magnificent days but almost always more wind than I want. I still think well of the good looks of the women, and it is really a pleasure to be moving among those who look like ladies, even though you may not know them. There is lovely coloring among many of the younger ones. I am surprised however to find many cases of decided red hair—not carroty but distinctly reddish and sandy. The shops are very nice. It is the first place where I have been able to suit myself with neck ties— though even here they are not *just* what I wish. Being a silk country & having to pay only 75 cents for a nice one I thought best to indulge. I find Jaeger's here only four dollars a suit, so I think that also will pay me.

Tell Lyle I will not object to his having a rifle—but I will not permit his using it with ammunition until he or rather mamma has found some one—expert—who will teach him how to use it and especially how to carry it when moving about in the country so as to be secure from accidental explosions. I shall expect of him a promise that he will never point it at any one, *whether loaded or unloaded* & that he will try to carry it when moving, so that if it be discharged, it would go into the ground or far above people's heads. I think, as he is so soon going to school, when he cannot use it it will be a mistake to ask for it, and for any shooting he may do a shot gun would be far better. This is not a very interesting letter, but when I have been a week in a place there is little left to say. It is only by frequent change of scene, or by mingling with other people that the material for letters accumulates—and here, though content enough, I have neither resource. Good bye dear child—Love to mamma, Nellie and Lyle.

Nov. 28

[P.S.]   I forgot to mail this yesterday—I am always forgetting something but close it now. Tell mamma I recd. yesterday hers of the 14th—no further news.

To Ellen Evans Mahan

Genoa, November 30, 1893 [LC]

My dearest Deldie: I seem somehow to have got a little at odds with my time and sit down now to write to you feeling hurried and driven. First of all I must remind you that you have not sent me again the measurements, or rather the numbers of the gloves for you and the two girls—and in connection with that I suggested, if you had any friend in Paris who would choose & send them to me, it would in my judgment be better than trusting to any selection of mine. You must lose no time, whatever you do, for the admiral told me today that he wanted to leave Nice early in January, where for I dont know. I gather he has received some orders from the Dept. & he spoke of an "interesting" trip—in the interest whereof I take little stock, but it is all in the cruise which wears steadily away. We are keeping today as Thanksgiving and I suppose it really is so. I received yesterday your letter of the 17th in which you mention your interview with the architect. I think with Helen that you want a great deal, and with you, why not? You will get no less by being more modest. I wish you would ask Mr. or Mrs. [Henry] Saltonstall if they know anything of a Mr. Gardner F. Sanderson—his wife and two daughters are here, and I met them rather oddly. They have been abroad quite a while, but one daughter has just been home for six months, returning in the steamer which brought Hall. He gave them a card to me which was left when they visited the ship. Sorely against my will I felt I had to call; but I found the two daughters, whom I should take to be not less than 22 nor more than 28, bright conversable women—one rather pretty, the other not at all so. I spent a pleasant half hour which I rarely do in society—the worse luck; for it is unquestionable relief to have half an hour's bright conversation but I find it oh! so rarely that it really dont pay me to seek it. When it comes it is always unawares—the time before and the next time being as a rule dull as ditchwater. I had yesterday a letter from Mr. Marston saying he had arranged for a translation of the books into German, but there will be no money, unless perhaps they will give me a royalty after clearing expenses. We are to leave tomorrow for Nice, and must then lie by to repair one of our boilers—a five or six weeks job. I am somewhat sorry to leave here for I like the place very much, but there is so much blowing weather that it reconciles me somewhat. I will write soon to Little, Brown & Co. about sending you the money. I shall look with curiosity to know the amount, and also what success *Farragut* has had in his second year. I have bought four Jaeger undershirts for $8. They seem perfectly up to the standard, and I *think* that is much less than N. Y. prices. Possibly in London I might get them cheaper but then I may not get to London again—I am sure I hope not if it means longer from home. I have also bought a number of neckties this being a silk region, at an average price of 70 cents. The quality seems to me good, and if I could have found more to my taste I would have bought more—but there is a dearth of plain colors and the patterns dont often suit my eye. I distrust my taste. I have taken ties into an affection something like yours for cheap calicoes—rarely passing a window without looking over them. It is astonishing what a lot there are, I should think every Italian must wear three at a time. I was ashore this aftn. probably for the last time of my life in Genoa—although it is storming so this evening that we may not get away tomorrow. I shall be glad to find myself again in a place without stern lines, as we have to be in most Medn. harbors. I am perpetually uneasy lest ours should part as one did soon after our arrival. Most harbors here are artificial, protected by moles and therefore very contracted, so that ships have not room to swing but tie up at both ends. I enclose you the advertisment of the books, evidently intended to catch the Xmas market. You may know they are now having an excitement on the question of their naval supremacy in England, which may help us in our sales. Upon the whole I will make this a double letter, with its enclosures and as there is no more news I will tell you a funny incident. When the general from shore came to return Erben's visit, in great magnificence, there came along his aide-de-camp, a tall six footer whom Rose would call a beauty, splendid looking chap, in gorgeous uniform and a long cloak down to his heels. When they started to leave it had begun to rain hard, but the young man lingered to talk to me—no blame to him—while Erben was standing in the rain, anxious to get shelter. Well the aide stalked to the gangway, & instead of hurrying over, he stopped majestically in front of the admiral, drew himself up to his full height, carried his hand to his cap in military salute, and stood motionless I think while you could count ten; then he extended his neatly gloved hand, bowed profoundly and went over the side. It was too cute, and the rain coming down.

Goodbye dear love. Kisses for children.

To Hilary A. Herbert

Villefranche, France, December 3, 1893 [NA]

Sir: I have to report that on entering the harbor of Genoa, Italy, a pilot was employed for the *Chicago*, the Commanding Officer considering it necessary to do so.

To Ellen Evans Mahan

Villefranche, December 6, 1893 [LC]

Dearest Deldie: I have had no time to write since I came here, nor shall I today at least in time for the mail, even if later. Consequently instead of a letter to Nelly, whose turn it is, I just drop you this line to say that I am well and have recd. your letters up to Nov. 24. The last brings sizes of your gloves which I will this time try to keep. I see every reason to believe we will be in the English Channel again before going home and think therefore best to postpone buying for the present. Your Uncle Charles[1] came on board day before yesterday and I am to breakfast there today. Had I foreseen that the drive would still last I wd. have made it Thursday or Friday. He shows his age. I had not seen him since Pia's[2] funeral. Love to all.

[P.S.] We shall (must) be here till Jan. 10.

To Ellen Kuhn Mahan

Villefranche, December 7, 1893 [LC]

My dearest Miss Nellikin: I would be ashamed of myself for my failure to write if I had any just cause for feeling so; as it is I am only distressed that I have not been able to get the time to write to you, for I dont want people to forget me. Your letter of Nov. 20 reached me a few days ago. I am delighted to hear you three girls—if I may call mamma so—are to have such fine feathers for the street, and I hope someone will tell Miss Fanny Jones how much I appreciate her kindness to those I love. All these little matters about you all interest me very much and of course I am profoundly delighted at the prospect of our having a country home of our own. What

---

1. Charles Kuhn.
2. Probably, Charles Kuhn's wife or daughter.

perhaps pleases me most is that you will be meeting each summer much the same people, already known to you and liked—so that you may be to make among them permanent and intimate friends. Some say they like continually [to] meet new persons—to me nine out of ten so met are disappointing, and for that reason I prefer to meet the old and tried friends trusting we may find something new to talk about. Nothing like old friends, after all. I was amused at your interview with Aunt Lina.[1] She is a foolish woman, and I fear with a bad temper; but I was glad that you turned back rather than answered back. Even between equals answering back is a bad *habit*, though it may at times be necessary; but she is much older than you and your aunt—at least by marriage. We hope to remain here—about four miles from the great winter resort, Nice—until about January 10, as our boilers must be repaired. This is a beautiful anchorage—a round bay, about three quarters of mile in from the shore line, surrounded by lofty hills thick with olive trees. The town Villefranche is a funny little place, looking something like a small patch cut out of old Genoa or Barcelona, such as I have described them in my letters—tall houses, crammed close together, with narrow streets. On Monday I drove from here to Nice by the sea route, along with the admiral in full uniform, to call upon the officials in Nice. Twenty four years have passed since I last travelled that road, and despite the ridiculous frumpery in which we were dressed I much enjoyed it. The road rises high above the water and gives a beautiful view of Villefranche Bay and the ships; then at an altitude of four hundred feet it turns the point which separates us from the beach on which Nice stands. Nice has greatly changed and grown; but the mountains, the lovely sky—and the Mediterranean blue are still as of old. That afternoon after our return—your uncle (granduncle) Charles[2] came on board for a moment to see me. I had not seen him for eight years and found him a good deal changed—beard quite white—and it seemed to me manner a little more fussy and more talkative. Yesterday I breakfasted there at 12 o'clock—only himself and Dr. Huston Bache. At 2 I left the apartment and found time to walk around those parts of the city with which I had formerly been familiar. It was the same yet changed, and even improvement does not wholly commend itself to one who finds his associations marred. I passed by a little pastry shop where I used at times to eat some cakes and drink a glass of wine—in days when my toes knew not gout, it was the same old corner but the shop had grandi and the middle aged Italian woman who used to run the affair had disappeared. I myself did not feel up to the cakes, so there could be no illusions as to the years come and gone. This evening I am going—at 5—to the reception of the American clergyman, whose wife's day it is. He had called personally—so I must go—though I detest receptions. My mind is made up that I will decline all

---

1. Angelina Corse Evans, daughter-in-law to Manlius Glendower Evans.
2. Charles Kuhn.

invitations that come to me simply as Captn. of the *Chicago*. Personal invitations from people who know me, or about me, I shall act as the case demands & to purely official ceremonies and entertainments I must submit—but I will *not* be made a social martyr because I am victimized to be captain of a ship. Tell mamma I have to day received a letter from the Editor of the *Fortnightly Review*—London—asking me for an article. I fear I shall have to decline, for if I would write any article it had best be for our home magazines—but I will think over it two days. This month's *Fortnightly* has a review of my books.[3] I have just completed Nelson as far as the beginning of the French Revolution, and am thinking of sending to mamma to type write, after revising. It is but a small part of the whole, but the part with which I was least familiar. I am very doubtful of the quality. As to quantity no doubt remains I cannot accomplish one third what I do at home.

Goodbye dearest Miss Nell. Much love to mamma and the other children.

[P.S.]   I hope you have some church into which you can drop for your prayers before drawing hours.

To Ellen Evans Mahan

Villefranche, December 11, 1893 [LC]

My own dearest: I mailed today a letter to Stevens asking him to send three books, one to each of the children, which I hope may reach you about Christmas. I give you the names now, but you need not tell them—*Sacharissa*[1] for Helen, *Meh Lady*[2] for Nellikin, and *Heroes of the Goodwin Sands*[3] for Lyle. I dont know how they will turn but hope they may be interesting. For yourself I would be glad if you would buy some particular thing you want—for yourself or for your room to the amount of ten dollars and call it my present to you. The books, if they fail otherwise, will tell the children I thought of them from far away. I am glad to think of the relief to you by the extra servant and by the little extra cash. My father always

---

3. W. L. Clowes [pseud., "Nauticus"], "Sea Power, Its Past and Its Future," *Fortnightly Review* (December 1893). The author compares Mahan's histories favorably with Colomb's *Naval Warfare*, not for originality of thought, but for cogency and lucidity of expression.

1. Mrs. Julia Mary (Cartwright) Ady, *Sacharissa; Some Account of Dorothy Sidney, Countess of Sunderland, Her Family and Friends, 1617–1684.* London: Seeley and Company, Ltd., 1893.

2. Thomas Nelson Page, *Meh Lady.* New York: C. Scribner's Sons, n.d. When reprinted in 1901, the work was subtitled *A Story of the War.*

3. Thomas Stanley Treanor, *Heroes of the Goodwin Sands.* London: The Religious Tract Society, 1892. The book is about life-saving and shipwrecks.

told mother "Dont save on servants nor on the substantial part of your table—clothes, finery, and household adornment can wait." I trust therefore that in putting into Savings Bank you will not reduce your balance at the Chemical sufficient to keep you fretting. If you began each month with $450 including allotment, it is probable that you would be free from worry. I dont at all approve of your opening the children's letters in their absence. I want them to feel they are their very own from papa, and not merely a general way of communicating with the family. Of course they will share, but I want their own prior right of property fully recognized. As to neighbors, I dont mean the people in the same street, but those whom you meet from time to time, direct or indirectly—and particularly if I know them. Everything that recalls home and N.Y. is welcome at this distance. We seem likely to have here what is commonly called a good time—I trust it will not interfere with my health. I get my exercise most irregularly and find myself very much tied down. Yesterday—Sunday—I lunched at the Pollonnais[4] Villa on the east side of the bay—a lovely place. The old gentleman is said to be a Polish Jew—they are certainly Jews—but they have been tied with all our admirals from Leroy to this. I was principal guest and had to *lead* in the old lady—a clever woman I daresay, but very deaf. Luckily I had on my own right a quite pretty & bright English-woman—wife of an army officer—so I had some distraction. After lunch, towards 2 P.M. (you understand of course the lunch at 12 was déjeuner) a company began to assemble mainly English—but mixed—and I was pleas-antly surprised to find among them quite a lot of pretty girls. The first doing was a piece of music—comic I presume, certainly quite taking—in which almost all of these girls took part—four or five playing the violin, others other instruments—neither the name nor the description of which can I undertake to give. It seemed to me well done. Afterwards dancing—half a dozen or more of our junior officers came in and made themselves agreeable. I find American dancing has a good name here, largely due to our officers. Luckily I fell in with some people to whom I could talk—and much of my afternoon was passed jawing bad French to a Hungarian and an Italian lady—the former pretty, but neither in their première jeunesse. Wednesday I am to dine at the Schiffs[5] who have a villa at Eze some four miles east of this—opposite side from Nice—and to take ten of-ficers with me. Tom Rodgers will be here. I have not seen Mr. Kuhn[6] since Thursday when I was at the reception at the Am. clergyman's. Fri-day and Saturday I was ill—bilious. Today Mrs. McCrea, Phila.,[7] gives a

---

4. Pollonnais was Mayor of Villefranche.
5. Mr. and Mrs. George Schiff, an English couple who frequently entertained Mahan when he was in Villefranche.
6. Charles Kuhn.
7. Mrs. Charles McCrea.

small tea to Ad. and Mrs. Erben. I should have gone but for the weather—which is rainy. I am away behind in visits, & find that my resolve to accept no invitations except from friends is impossible. People catch you on the fly and then where are you? I received today from Mr. Marston a copy of the Dec. *Fortnightly*, which has a simply gushing article on my books by a Belgian naval expert, who under the nom de plume of Nauticus[8] has quite a European reputation. I am sorry to add that he cudgels Colomb—calling him verbose, obscure, and unreadable. Marston wishes me to write if I would like any part of the article used in the advertisements. The day of reckoning for me will come I fear when Nelson is published, if it ever is.

9 P.M.

I stopped here to go to a reception at Mrs. McCrea's given to Adm. & Mrs. Erben. It was raining hard and I at first intended not to go, but feeling the need of air & change I went. Absurdly enough, starting in a hurry I forgot to make sure of the address & when I got to Nice could only remember it was in your uncle's street—Boulevard Victor Hugo. I stopped at his apartment, but he was out & the man could tell me nothing—so I walked along, speering about, and seeing three cabs standing at one door, and a man coming out I asked if Mrs. McCrea lived there. It proved to be the place, and I went in. People were all very nice—I landed among Philadelphians and jawed away for ¾ hour. Your uncle was there and had been put out at my not coming as he wanted me to dine with him and some others on Thursday—afterwards to go to the reception of a Mme. Something—Russian —put a lot of letters together & choke over it is the way you speak Russian—So that is fixed for Thursday. If I can be sure some of our younger officers will go to the reception of the Am. clergyman, the same afternoon, I intend going there to make sure of their being started fair—in which case I am to send my evening dress to Mr. Kuhn's and dress there. Mr. Wurbs-Dundas[9] was there, asked me to go to the opera Tuesday or Thursday—but I declined both—I may drop in at his house at 5 P.M. Your uncle seems inclined to take hold of me—so I suppose I pass muster as reasonably presentable—and he is quite a feature in the place I understand. I think I shall ask him down to lunch and bring his own party—and fix his own day. Do you know—it seems quite absurd—I have really enjoyed the receptions which considering my aversion to them I think speaks well for the people I have met—but in truth they have been comparatively small, and in their foreign way I suppose there is a kind of camaraderie among the sets that form. I want to tell you an incident that struck me as very funny—I meant to tell it to Nelly but it slipped out of my head. While we were paying our official calls—one of the party, the Consul I think, said "Why is it that after passing a redhaired woman you

---

8. *See* Mahan to Ellen K. Mahan, December 7, 1893, Footnote 3.
9. Mrs. Wurbs-Dundas was a Philadelphia Lippincott whom Mrs. Mahan knew.

always meet a white horse?" The admiral said, "I dont know *why* it is, but its so, it has often been remarked and discussed in the papers." As a geographical fact I had never before known that a redhaired girl is bounded on one side by a white horse, so I smiled incredulously and held my peace. Half an hour afterwards we were returning to the ship, and I was sitting quietly, like the young waterman thinking of nothing at all, when my eye hit upon a redhaired woman looking in a shop window. Unconsciously I turned my head and on the other side came trotting along a white horse pulling a bob-tailed car. I assure you at this moment, a week after, my eyes are full of tears of laughter, as I think of that grotesque combination of the redhaired girl and the white horse thus ridiculously brought before me. I told the admiral about it when we got back to the ship and he became quite excited—swore it was always so. I haven't seen a redhaired woman since, so that my inquiry into this scientific fact has progressed no further. And now dearest I must wish you all a very merry Christmas. Where I shall be or how pass the day I don't know but you may be sure I shall think of you all lovingly. This little fling in Nice & elsewhere may be all very well, and I shall be hereafter glad of it when back by your side.

[P.S.]   Dec. 12—Closing for mail—Well.

To Hilary A. Herbert

USS *Chicago*, Villefranche, December 12, 1893 [NA]

Sir:

1. I have to acknowledge the receipt of the Department's letter of November 27, 1893, desiring an explanation of my discharging Max Hessel, Ordinary Seaman, without the approval of the Commander-in-Chief, required by Article 803 of the *U.S. Navy Regulations*.

2. In reply, I have to state that my action was taken purely in inadvertence—the paragraph in question having either escaped my attention or slipped my memory. I may add that the man's time of enlistment had expired and he had requested his discharge; and I have so generally before this cruise acted on my own responsibility in matters of this kind, being either alone or Senior officer present, that an act of this sort came naturally. As an excuse for ignorance, or infraction of regulations, this is doubtless invalid; but as an explanation it may help the Department to realize how I fell into my error.

3. I beg to express to the Department my regret for this unintentional infringing of its orders.

To Ellen Evans Mahan

Villefranche, December 18, 1893 [LC]

My dearest Deldie: Your two last letters have been delightful—long and full of details which may be trivial in themselves but are most interesting to me at this distance. First, to answer them, I am extremely sorry to hear about Rosie. I think you should consider whether you could take her place for a time this year as last. It is dreadful to think of her taking so much stimulant—dreadful I mean that at her age she should need it—and especially that she should *go* on the strength it gives. I have always understood that the effect of stimulus is to restore quickly, as rest alone does slowly; but that it should not be resorted to in order to protract effort. When possible, of course, it is better to let rest alone restore; but when stimulus is taken, it should, I think, always be succeeded by repose. As regards the Bunce affair at the College, I think Sears and Chambers erred by being too precipitate.[1] A full and careful representation should first have been made to the Secy of the engrossing character of their College. If he had then persisted it would have been in order, in fact obligatory, to say that it was not fair to the College to occupy its quarters without doing its work, and ask for detachment. They were right enough, except in allowing their act to have any appearance of haste, or of temper which Ramsay doubtless attributed to it. Both my nose & my eyes give me infinite annoyance. I console myself by believing that this running carries off some of the gouty humors. I have been puzzling myself to know how Helen made $14 per week, your last letter explains that Miss Fisher has a lesson everyday. You may be sure I intend to hold my peace tight about Mrs. C. I feel as if such a piece of news was like a bag of dynamite. You were very right to give Mary anvil cloth—I do believe in making people comfortable. Now I have answered most of your letter & hope you like the fun—I will proceed to my own news. A letter from Little & Brown is sure that the interest in Nelson [is] even greater than appears and hopes they may have the manuscript in early summer. If they will send me a few months composed of days thirty hours long, and insure me seven hours sleep & four hours of my old inspiration daily—it might be done. They say they will have a satisfactory remittance for Mrs. Mahan on account of the last six months' sale. Little do they know Mrs. M. I said, if they think her so easily satisfied in the matter of money— but I trust you will have the grace to seem so. I wonder what it will be— you will know very soon after getting this. You will be interested to know that I have gone to several receptions with a certain amount of enjoyment.

---

1. Lieutenant James H. Sears, class of 1876, was assigned to the War College from October 1892 to November 1893, and W. I. Chambers was so assigned from November 1892 to November 1893.

[193]

They have not been large & the people seem all to know one another and be at ease. I believe I told you I had met Mrs. Charles McCrea—she seems very well off and her girls are decidedly stylish & attractive—thoroughly ladylike, without any flippancy. There are also two Schiff girls here at Eze both pleasant. The elder laughs somewhat too much—but the younger is really charming—frank and unaffected without a shade of pertness or forwardness. She is one of the rare instances of a name fitting—being Rosie and her complexion even rosier than Nellikin's. I find both mammas also pleasant, though I fancy the elder ladies feel it taken out of them by the go. I am to dine at the Schiffs on Xmas. The other women I meet are all well enough—with exceptions of course. Among others, (did I already tell you) I met Miss Lee whom I used to know "before the war"—a daughter of the great Confed. general. She is staying here with a Mrs. Tom Willing, née Lee, a cousin of the General's—a woman now of ninety. Her husband was one of the Phila. family—died at the age of 37—so half a hundred years ago. Mrs. W. has lived abroad for fifty years, without going home but is still intensely American—living on her memories. I breakfasted there on Sunday—12:30—and afterwards walked with Miss Lee. I think I told Lyle what Tryon had said to her. She said also that the mother of a young officer in the Br. fleet had sent him a copy of the second book, which happened to reach the ship in advance of any other. He held it up in the wardroom, and—so this lady said—there was a general hurrah. You must remember this was told Miss Lee long before my coming here was thought of, or she expected ever to see me again. Yesterday I went to the Schiffs' day—my dinner call for last week, and there fell into conversation with a Mrs. Baird—English —who used to know "Marcy Breese," when she was Miss Curtin at St. Petersburg—was very desirous to hear something about her, and said—so I understood—that she had introduced her to Breese. So you see the world is small—to think of the Robiglios quietly living next door to your Uncle Charles. I cant remember what I say from letter to letter—but I dropped in there for afternoon tea on Thursday last, they came on board on Saturday & she left for you a photo of the three children of whom Robina alone is left to them. I have a general understanding that some day I am going to them for a "family dinner." Also, I have a like understanding with Nazro that some day I am going with him to breakfast with Pulitzer[2] of the *World*, who has a villa close by Villefranche Bay. I detest the *World*, but I like Nazro, and fancy also that it may possibly be useful to him, as he does newspaper work. Your uncle Charles had an accident on Sunday which might have been nasty. He was driving a pair of horses, one stumbled and fell, and he was pitched over the dash-board. Fortunately he fell on the horse which did not struggle very hard. His forehead was bruised, and the horse's hoof cut him underneath the chin through to the bone. The

2. Joseph Pulitzer, owner of the New York *Evening World*.

doctor came and sewed this up and wanted him to stay quiet—but he persisted in going to a reception to which he had undertaken to take me. I was willing enough to stay out—but not a bit of it. Next day he did withdraw from a dinner engagement. This morning I walked to Nice and stopped at his apartment about ten. He said he now was undergoing that battered and strained feeling which does not come always at first. He has really been extremely nice to me, I have not seen a sign of disagreeableness of temper—but of course I shall not let him see too much of me. We begin tomorrow with fortnightly receptions for which our probable stay will allow three. The adml. gave a small affair on Saturday, & I think the officers are sufficiently started to give a fair prospect of success. The *Bennington* arrived today which will increase our resources in young men. I have been so bilious—too much food and drink & no time for proper exercise—that I have taken again to early rising. I go ashore at seven thirty and walk to or from Nice—the other way by train. I shall vary this programme somewhat by going up the hills. This morning I walked *in* ordered a duvet—a meter and ⅓ square—about four feet, and a kilogramme & a half best feathers (dearest) total 55 francs about $10.50. "Ballon" they call it. Of course I haven't the faintest idea whether the bargain is good or bad. From the duvet I went to the dentists—and thence to your uncles. Huston Bache came in while I was there, but I have often seen him before. Your uncle would come down to the door and charged me to send love to you and your mother when I wrote—so there you have it.

Wednesday Dec. 20. 11 A.M.
No further news. I close this now for today's mail with assurances [the last two words are crossed through]. I must have been thinking of something else when I wrote those words. Dearest love to all and Happy New Year—may it see our meeting. Europe is all very well but there is nothing like home.

To Helen Evans Mahan

Villefranche, December 25, 1893 [NWC]

My darling Child: The sun has just set, so I am in one way a little late in wishing you and all a merry Christmas for this year. I trust it has been so to you, though you as well as I, if not so deeply as I, must have felt that the separation of a family greatly mars the expected pleasure. Last year I was in San Francisco; and uncertain as I knew the future to be, I assuredly did not anticipate that this would find me in Europe. I am to dine tonight with the Schiffs, as I perhaps have already said—certainly I have mentioned the family often enough. They seem as if they could not do too much for us, and, while I daresay that a dozen or so of reasonably pleasant & gentlemanly men are an addition socially there is a cordiality in their way that shows there is real kind-heartedness and good will behind it all. On Saturday I went to Nice to square up a lot of visits which I owed, & in returning I met at the station the two elder daughters[1]—who are at home—and the third, who had just come from school with papa for the holidays. Mr. Rodgers (T. S.) was also there, but he was looking for other friends and so did not travel in the train; consequently I went alone in the compartment with the three young women. I think you would have laughed—I nearly did aloud at the time—to hear them all chattering as hard as they could, half the time all at once, all different and yet all with that odd family resemblance, which strangers note so easily. It is odd to see how young girls go about by themselves here in Europe—so contrary to the impressions I had. This was 6.15 two hours after sundown—of course they would be met at the home station by a servant and their house is close by—but still we dont expect such freedom here. I was very tired that evening, and had already something like influenza—so yesterday, Sunday, I stayed in bed and took quinine. Today I am better, but very shaky. The running from eyes and nose on Saturday morning was excessive—showing either malaria or a touch of influenza, which is about. If the latter it was very slight. Your letter of the 10th came three days ago—but I am really puzzled how to answer your question about books. My knowledge on the subject is very slight. Have you tried to read any of the selections from Keats and Shelley in the *Golden Treasury*?[2] They are great poets certainly—but perhaps might not interest you. A book like Agnes Repplier's[3] might be suggestive to you—and I daresay that Imbert de St. Amand's[4] sketches of women would be useful in giving you ideas of that time—or those times. Well done memoirs give more life like ideas of periods than history usually does—for the greater motives of men, by which history is made, remain much the same from age to age, the superficial details alter and this memoirs give or may give. The book I have had sent you from London, *Sacharissa*, is in the line you speak of. Have you seen the *Love Letters of Dorothy Osborne*?[5] These two were good women of the olden time. I can only

---

1. Marie and Rose, daughters of Mr. and Mrs. G. Schiff.
2. Francis Turner Palgrave, *The Golden Treasury of the Best Songs and Lyric Poems in the English Language*. Cambridge, Mass.: Sever and Francis, 1863. During the 1880's, Macmillan, Lippincott, Crowell and Stokes brought out editions.
3. Agnes Repplier, *Essays in Miniature* (1892), *Essays in Idleness* (1893), *Points of View* (1891). Or perhaps, since Mahan was speaking of poetry, *A Book of Famous Verse* (1892).
4. Baron Arthur Léon Imbert de Saint-Amand, *Famous Women of the French Court*. New York: C. Scribner's Sons, 1892–1893. This was a series, translated by Elizabeth Martin, which included his works on the court of Louis XV, the Valois court, etc.
5. Dorothy Osborne Temple, *The Letters of Dorothy Osborne to Sir William Temple, 1652–54*. Edited by Edward Abbott Parry. New York: Dodd Mead & Co., 1888.

say that I will now try & keep my eyes open to note books for you, and would advise you not to be in too great a hurry. Buy to read—and as for Quogue be content for a time to have books on the table—dont aim at filling a case all at once. There is a book now in 54th St, *Memoirs of Madame d'Oberkirch*,[6] which with a lot of twaddle gives also much curious gossipy information of somewhat celebrated people—Marie Antoinette —Dorothea, the wife of the crazy Czar Paul, and mother of Alex. the ally of Napoleon, and incidentally of many celebrities, as well as of aristocratic provincial life before the Great Revolution. With regard to reading in French or English—the former is better, if you can read easily—but dear child where are you to get the time? You dont know enough French words to read without frequent recourse to the dictionary. I am deeply interested, and upon the whole pleased at your money-winning and pupils, but dont take any more now, and beware about getting yourself hurried. You have not yet reached the age when you can undergo drive without injury, and as no necessity exists it would be wicked to hurt yourself. Beware then of accumulating employments—you may find they leave you no time for quiet thought or prayer. It would be in every way bad for you, mentally and physically. Young organisms need spare time just for growing, which those who have attained maturity can dispense with. I do wish, too, that you would, as a kind of religious duty, save a tithe every month. Say $5 out of the $75—it is not so much the amount as the habit of laying by for the future, which all should attempt. I have failed herein—I wish you would do better. I am also much pleased to hear about your voice—it is a nice gift to possess—but dont waste time, or get hurried unless it really is fine enough to repay you. I went today to church in town, the first time I have been to a service in church since the Sunday I spent in the country in England. On the way I met Mr. Frank Ogden[7] and his wife—the latter I had never before seen. Another visit for me I suppose. On Thursday I am to dine at the Robiglios to meet Mr. Kuhn, and that evening a dancing party at the De Groots, where I suppose I shall have to show up. Tomorrow is their day, and as I have not yet been I must do that. Then Friday there is a Toy Symphony[8] at the Schiffs, and the following Tuesday I am to breakfast here nearby, and (if I survive) a dancing shindy at the Schiffs that evg. I count for nothing in the dancing, of course, but I rather like the meetings with the women. All are very cordial and the society is so small you feel quite at home. For the small numbers there is a remarkable proportion of pretty young women—which always is an attraction to me—

---

6. Baronne Henriette Louise d'Oberkirch, *Memoires of the Baroness d'Oberkirch, Countess de Montbrison*. Edited by her grandson, the Count de Montbrison. London: Colburn, 1852.
7. Brother of Mrs. Mahan's uncle-by-marriage, Gouverneur ("Gouv") Morris Ogden.
8. This entertainment form is attributed to Joseph Haydn who, in 1778, wrote a score for toy instruments and led his orchestra in its performance.

as it was to my father. It is frivolous kind of existence, but no harm for me coming incidentally for a little while. I recognize its charm with this delicious surrounding, but I should think it might easily pall and become flat. I have not envied the girls for your sake, being persuaded that occupation, good earnest work with an object and an interest, such as yours possesses, is a surer and more durable happiness than the plainest existence here. For while in itself inadequate, it leads to nothing. For one year or two years very well—but after them what? With regard to your occupations you must remember there is not only the drive, but that no one can do many things *well*; you must concentrate on one or two, and touch all others superficially only. I am so pleased to hear of Lyle's efforts about his French—it shows thought and determination with which he will do well; for he has plenty of brains and health, if he only uses them diligently. When thus away from home, and myself crippled for the work to which I am best fitted, my greatest happiness is in hearing of you all doing so nicely, and trying so hard.

Tell mamma that if she wishes to acknowledge the photo of Madame de Robiglio the address is Boulevard Victor Hugo, Number 11. She will remember that she is the Comtesse de R. I enclose a note from Mrs. Schiff actually written by the eldest daughter, who does her mother's writing. Is it not an extraordinary hand?—there certainly ought to be a patent taken out on the "M"—and the D and O are not without certain eccentricities of merit. In fact if you will not be content with merely making out what it is about, but will really study it out and note the formation of the letters it will repay you, & suggest ideas as to the Origin of the Alphabet.

And now, dear, this is a very long letter. Give my best love to your dear mother and the other children.

To Ellen Evans Mahan

Villefranche, January 1, 1894 [LC]

My own dearest Deldie: I must start my letter today, if I do no more, to wish you and all our dear ones the hopes of the new year, chief among them that its course may see us again united, and before our Buster[1] takes his departure for school. I am almost driven to death here now, and shall continue to be unless I put my foot down hard. I have for this week declined two invitations to dinner, and one for an evening party—but even so tomorrow I breakfast out and spend the evening—on Wednesday have

---

1. Family nickname for young Lyle Evans Mahan.

a party breakfast with me, then our own reception on board—evening dine out. Thursday, Friday, no, Friday I breakfast at the McCreas and today I have saved by refusing—but I have many visits to pay. Of course, if at leisure, this would be a small matter, but with ordinary ship duties, and Nelson to boot, you will realize I have no time left. Tell Lyle that I was very much interested and pleased by his account of his studies, and that I am equally though not so intelligently interested in what he says of his football etc—for I do not well understand these new games whose scientific character has come up since I used to play them as a boy. I hope he will always tell me of all these things, for I want him to have a hand in all in-nocent amusements—only I hope he will not make the mistake of some boys, and make them the chief instead of the secondary concern of his school. They wont help him much in life, whereas a trained mind will. Although a holiday, my forenoon has been spent in work. This afternoon I purpose paying some calls. I shall not go on for under my present drive I shall not write a pleasant letter.

8 P.M.

I dont remember whether I ever said to you that I went to the Wurbs-Dundas on their reception day, by invitation from him, whom I met at the tea given by the McCreas to the Adml. I did not at first remember but think I do now to have heard you say that she was a Miss Lippincott. She walked me over [a] great part of their house which seems very handsome, but she made such an impression upon me that as I came out, I laughed to myself and said "That's the last time I get in there," and so it shall be. My circle is now fairly well fixed and small, and I hope to keep my engagements well under, especially the evenings. Tomorrow I lunch at the Cutler's, English with a Hungarian wife, the latter rather pretty with attractive ways—no longer young. I must then stop in Nice at the reception of the DeGroots, Americans, who gave a dance last week—two quite pretty daughters. In the evening a dance at the Schiffs my going to which will depend on two or three considerations. Wednesday the Schiff girls—three—and their papa lunch with me. Mrs. S. has heart trouble & as much as possible shuns mount-ing ships' sides. That evening I dine with them, to meet a Major French of the Br. Army, whom I already know, but who wishes to see me more intimately—a great admirer of my books, who told me they swear by them at the Staff College. Thursday the Frank [Uphens] had asked me to dine but I de-clined. Friday lunch at the McCreas—breakfast rather—and for Friday evening have declined a dancing party near here. I see I repeat myself—so much for letters written in scraps. Last Thursday I dined at the Robiglios, your uncle Charles being of the party which numbered five besides the R's. It was rather heavy I thought—he has little to say and she though talk-ative enough and excellent is not brilliant. The rest were strangers to you—from there I went to the DeGroot's dance and next afternoon to the Toy Symphony at the Schiffs. The latter as you see figure for most, and they are rattling girls, without giving one the least impression of fastness or anything unbecoming—simply boiling over with exuberant health & spirits. I met Hall[2] and his wife on the street this afternoon and was surprised to see how much older she looked than I at first thought. I believe it is now fixed that we go from here to Naples toward the end of this month & later to Malta to be docked—but I would not mention it. My one desire being to get home I care but little for the intermediate steps— my chief wish being to be where I can get ashore easily for a two hours walk in the afternon, have to see but few people and work in the evening. I cannot get on here with social calls, ships duties, letters home twice a week etc. Like yourself I prefer to see your hand to the type-writer—but besides hurting you it has the disadvantage that your letters are much shorter that way—which disappoints me. I think this place is getting played out and yet I hate to leave for unknown diggings. Your calendar for me came, but in bad shape. The boy however has patched it up and I think it will do; and now dearest I will close because somehow, the spirit of writing does not move freely. I fear I am a little worried about Nelson going on so slowly. Dearest love to all. I add a few lines for Hennie.

Dearest Hennie: In thinking about your books it occurred to me that one of the most interesting memoirs ever penned is Boswell's *Life of Johnson*. It is a famous work, and still considered the best biography ever written. Presents a vivid picture of London literary and general society in the last century. A new edition is lately out. It is however an expensive as well as long book, and it might be well for you to borrow a volume from some one to see if you can like it.

I see also advertised *The Letters of Sir Walter Scott*,[3] and *The Letters of James Russell Lowell*[4]—both very highly spoken of. Of the two the latter would be better for you. They are very recent publications.

I would advise, however, your making a list and getting only one at a time. I will probably have more suggest[ions] when I next write to you. One of Robt Louis Stevenson's novels might be a good thing to have on hand, to read at anytime when you are kept at home or in bed. He is an admirable writer.

The three books above are only suggestions to add to your own list.

---

2. W. B. Hall.
3. Sir Walter Scott, *Familiar Letters of Sir Walter Scott*. Edited by David Douglas. Boston: Houghton, Mifflin & Co., 1894.
4. *Letters of James Russell Lowell*, edited by Charles Eliot Norton. New York: Harper, 1894.

Miss Pardoe's *Court of Louis XIV*,[5] and some other such by her were once well thought of—but I suppose are now a little out of date. The memoirs of Madame de Remusat[6] give an inside picture of Napoleon the Great's Court.

To Ellen Evans Mahan

Villefranche, January 5, 1894 [LC]

My dearest Deldie: I enclose a letter I have written to Herbert, after many doubts and misgivings. I will ask you to typewrite it, including my signature, and forward to him, addressing envelope to "Hon. H. A. Herbert, Secretary of the Navy, Washington, D.C." and writing on the upper edge *Personal* broadly underlined.

If after reading it you should think there is in it any failure of respect or deference, I authorize you to withhold it. I have had it under consideration for a fortnight, have written & rewritten. I should not of course have meddled at all had I not been asked. Stockton wrote me & said Taylor thought I might help. I have by no means taken the line suggested by S., and do not intend that any one, save yourself, shall know what I have said. My own impression is that S. may a little have lost his head, not to be wondered at under circumstances of such irritation—and as you know I have long said I recognized Nelie's[1] petulant turn in her father. Of course I dont know the circumstances—but it seems to me Sears & Chambers might have been induced to wait until every argument had been exhausted with the Secy. Had he then persisted, an application for detachment was perfectly correct.[2]

I have nothing much to say about myself—except that on the one hand I am very tired out with ganging—notwithstanding I have regretted on many invites; yet on the other I shall be sorry to leave here. Such are our inconsistencies. Shall write Nellikin in a day or two.

[P.S.]   The short note to H. to accompany the type-written letter.

---

5. Julia Pardoe, *Louis XIV and the Court of France in the 17th Century*. New York: Harper & Bros., 1855.
6. Claire Elisabeth Jeanne Gravier de Vergennes, comtesse de Rémusat, *Memoirs of Madame de Rémusat*. With a Preface and Notes by her Grandson, Paul de Rémusat, Senator. Translated from the French by Mrs. Cashel Hoey, and John Lillie. New York: D. Appleton, 1880 and 1888.
1. C. H. Stockton's daughter by his first wife, Cornelia Carter. Born in 1876, she was between the Mahan girls in age.
2. *See* Mahan to Ellen Evans Mahan, December 18, 1893.

To Ellen Kuhn Mahan

My darling Miss Nellikin: Your poor papa has rarely if ever in his life had as much to distract him, certainly in the social line. Just think of my having an invitation to dinner for every day this week, except Saturday. I have dodged them all but one—some because I really had another engagement evening—others because I did not want to go. Major Wurbs-Dundas asked me for last night "to meet Lady Anglesey[1] and niece," but I didn't fancy the entourage at his fine house & gladly availed myself of an excuse. I consider that to dine out two days hand running is ruinous to me, and when such occurs have no hesitation in alleging the previous engagement. Besides these dinners I had some ladies and officers to lunch with me Wednesday—and I myself am breakfasting out yesterday—today—and tomorrow. I am enclosing two notes[2] from the Monsieur and Madame, to whom I go tomorrow after church. They are French Jews, but most amiable, kindly people—dont look much like Jews. My "aimable réponse" was that I would go. You see my hosts are on terms with Lord and Lady Salisbury, who come here with the avowed purpose of avoiding social engagements and resting. I am so busy and often so tired that my home letters have to be worked in at such times as I can which does not improve them.

9 P.M.

I had to stop here and dress, and went to Nice, where I took breakfast with a Mr. John P. King, cousin of Mrs. Stockton,[3] and his mother at the Grand Hotel, where I lived during my visit to Nice in 1869–70. Afterwards I took the train back to Villefranche and from the station walked up to Lord Salisbury's villa. It is called La Bastide, which if it means, as I believe, a kind of fortified place against intruders is by no means amiss. It is not visible from here, and not knowing where it was I had sent my steward, two days ago, to find out. By his directions I followed a steep stony path, till I reached a small chapel, to one side of which a footpath led to a gate, where La Bastide was written. The gate was locked and no one in sight, but I could see the house. I therefore went back and continued along down hill, until on the other side I came to another gate, quite a distance below the house, which proved to be unlocked. I then toiled up a zig-zag ascent, passing a middle-aged gentleman, who bowed to me, but who I knew was not Lord S., having seen the latter's portrait very often.

1. Third wife of the 4th Marquess Anglesey, née Minnie King Wodehouse.
2. Enclosures not found.
3. After the death of Cornelia Carter in 1876, Stockton married Pauline Lentilhon King.

A little way ahead I saw a stout, red faced elderly woman, whom I could not think Lady S., but one can never tell from external appearances; so as she went back towards the house I walked very slowly to let her escape if she wished to—and she did, went elsewhere in the grounds. After some perplexity as to which was front of the house, I found it and rang. Of course the family were all out—so I left three cards—and knowing that they were closed to visitors generally I thought I would take a chance, and said to the servant that I had called because Lord S. had said he would be pleased to see me (see note). The servant said they had gone to the consecration of a new English church just opened at Beaulieu—the next station to Villefranche. I then asked the shortest way to Beaulieu preferring to go back that way to the very rough road that I had come, and in descending, not very far from the house, I met Lord Salisbury coming up. I knew him by his portrait and therefore stopped and introduced myself. He was very polite, and for an Englishman, who had doubtless looked upon me at first as one of his persecutors (beasts the Ogdens used to call them), reasonably cordial. Said he had read my books and was glad to know me—also that he regretted not having been able to come to our dance on Wednesday. He did not ask me to go back, which I thought he might have done in civility; and I daresay he would, had he known that I would decline (as I should). I did not hold it against him, however, for it was so like my own self—besides the old gentleman, he is 63, was pretty well blown, for it is no fool of a hill. I thereupon said I was very sorry he could not be with us, asked him to present my compliments to Lady Gwendolen,[4] whom I had had the pleasure of meeting, and wished him good afternoon. The whole expedition from the time I left Villefranche station till I got back to the ship took me only an hour and a quarter. There is no carriage road to La Bastide—with the express object, I understand, of keeping visitors away—all must climb the hill on foot. I have done the civil thing, having been doubly invited, by themselves through the Pollonnais and by Lady Gwendolen in London, so now, as the lawyers say, the "onus" is with them. I have taken a great fancy to a young girl here—a year younger than Helen—one of the Schiffs the family that have shown us all, and me in particular, more attention than any other persons. I have dined there three times, and find them all nice, father mother and three daughters. The youngest is still at school and about your age, but my favorite is Miss Rosie—number two. She is extremely pretty the only one of them that is, but what I like about them all is an extreme frankness and ease of manner which never reaches familiarity, and a go and vitality which seems as if it might at a moment get to romping, but does not. They are just as cordial to middle aged fellows, like myself, as they are to younger men, and seem as pleased to talk to them, but of course I dont give them credit for such superhuman virtues. Miss Rosie

4. Daughter of Lord Salisbury.

did by me a thing which seems so characteristic of the whole lot of them—and so nice—that I must tell it you. She had been playing on the violin to her sister's accompaniment on the piano, and when some one else went to play, she sat down on a sofa. The seat by her being vacant, and the younger men talking elsewhere, I sat down by her and told her—what was true—that her playing had given me much pleasure; for whether it were the instrument or her skill there was something extremely sweet in the effect. "Oh" she said "I should be so glad to play for you at any time—what kind of music do you prefer?" Not much you may say; but still, when you consider that there were at least three very presentable young fellows in the room, and that the merest commonplace acknowledgement was all that most would have made, there was something in it and the cordial sincerity with which it was said that was very pleasing to an older person, who are not bad judges of the young. It is amusing, almost touching, to one who like myself has little real faith in the interest of persons in strangers—and takes little stock in professions—to see so much apparent cordiality and pleasure in meeting others. God forbid I should doubt its sincerity—but I cannot believe in its reality. One of them asked me about the future movements of the ship. I replied that I knew little, but believed the admiral intended to be in England in May. "Oh," two of them exclaimed, "then you will be sure to come and see us in London, and we'll have such a good time,"—as though I could possibly add an iota to the existence of girls in the swim of London society. Yet I am quite confident that at the moment they fully meant it. It is only fair to say nothing could be more real in act than their kindnesses to us here—and the mother, though naturally more subdued than those vivacious girls, is equally cordial.

Monday Jan 8.

I think my dear Miss Nell, I had better close today. I was out much of yesterday and there are some things I could say more—but I had better close for the mail and leave for another letter. I enclose a slip for mamma whose letter written Xmas I have recd. Love to mother and sister.

[Enclosure]
Dearest Deldie: Your Christmas letter was recd. I entirely approve all you have done about the house. As regards money, you will not I hope forget to tithe the receipts from books and articles at Jan. 1.—and I think whatever comes from *Farragut* after being tithed should go on your Chemical account. I think I shall be able to get through without asking any more from home; or if necessity arise I may be able to work off a magazine article. I have after some deliberation decided to confine my literary work to Nelson, thinking that probably in the end I shall make more. But I get on slowly, and it may happen that I shall find it utterly impossible to get it out this year, I have in fact very little hope of it—under any circumstances

—although I blame myself a little for the social distractions which I can scarcely avoid. I think there were other things I wanted to say but cannot now remember—Always lovingly [etc.].

To Hilary A. Herbert

USS *Chicago*, Villefranche, January 6, 1894 [NA]

Sir: I have to report that a pilot was employed for the *Chicago* in entering Villefranche harbor, the Commanding Officer deeming it necessary to do so.

To Ellen Evans Mahan

Villefranche, January 11, 1894 [LC]

Dearest Deldie: I dont know how far you are inclined to allow Nelson, with its prospective thousands (of dollars) to interfere with my writing to you. It is now near ten p.m., and I have just put him aside after a period of unusually easy writing. I have now something over 160 of my usual manuscript pages done, but it is very slow work. I am of course immensely interested in Helen's progress, but do be careful that she dont overdo. She is not yet fully matured, nor will be for four years yet, and an unbroken nervous system & bodily strength is full as important as acquisition, and far more important than any haste in advance. Now we can support her, she can measure her work; but the day may come when all of us, who can, must do some share to the common support. I greatly fear the action of the Democrats in the House, and despite the enormities of the Republicans I believe now, and I believe finally, that the latter represent the progressive party of the nation. The Democrats still have both feet in the tomb of Jefferson. I should not be surprised to see any attack made upon us, pay, numbers or retired list. We need not fear—God will provide, but let us economize our strength now, that we may keep it for the day of need. I believe, but I forget almost every thing, that I wrote you to keep *Farragut* proceeds on your bank book. I think we should tithe all these little extra incomes, if only because we must recognize how we are cared for. I begin this year putting aside 1/20 of my ship income for church. In reading of all your presents and pretty surroundings, a feeling of sadness crept over me to think of our happiness amid so many who suffer and want—especially in these times. It seems almost unfeeling not to bear something too—but

[205]

at all events let us remember the poor—practically. Today Lord Salisbury came on board and luckily I was here and the admiral away. Lady Gwendolin Cecil (my dinner companion in London) his daughter, came along, with two of her brothers. I had a chance to see her face thus by daylight, and found her better looking than I had thought; not pretty but a sweet face, and looking like a lady—for which as the Irishman said, "Devil thank her and why shouldn't she?" with three centuries or more of good blood behind her—only, as we know, that rule dont always work. I took them all over the ship—catching hold, en route, of Nazro, Rodgers, and Dewey, our three most presentable men. Then they sat for fifteen minutes in my cabin, talking—Rodgers with the lady—trust him! I with Lord S. and the others promiscuous. We went on deck just as the colors came down & the admiral then came on board. I had already a boat manned, as they had expressed their purpose of leaving, and after a few moments talk between the Ad. & Lord S. they departed, Rodgers *volunteering* to steer the boat ashore. Lady G. was in deep mourning, and as she shook hands for good bye she said that her mother had wished her to say she regretted not having been able to come on board, having just lost a sister. You may suppose that such a message rather overwhelmed me coming from a lady, who is not generally supposed to have any explanations to make—but it certainly was a civility pleasant to receive, the more so as she is reputed rather exclusive. One thing with all my faults she can count upon I am not likely to *intrude*. I was not prepared to find her father so big a man. He is taller than I, and very much bigger, brown, large features, though not prominent, heavy iron gray beard. Looks his age in figure (63) but not in face. She is slight not over medium size, colorless, grayish brown eyes, features not noteworthy, but perfectly refined, and as I said, sweet. Nazro talks of going there tomorrow, with Rodgers & perhaps Dewey to ask them to our negro minstrel show. They are said not to want callers, but we have the advantage of committing them to nothing—we come, go, and return no more; and also have less desire to hang round a Lord than the native Englishman of the snobbish type. 10:15—I must stop now and go to bed, or I shant sleep well. I go tomorrow to Mentone for lunch, or bkft. I think people must like me here. The Schiffs have had me *four* times to dinner, & a couple living on the point near by have asked me a second time to Bkft. Mrs. Schiff had a very bad attack—heart—last Sunday night, & you will be pleased to know that when I heard of it, I sent Carl with my card to ask for her. Today came yours of Jan. 1. and Nellie's of Jan. 2. I am so pleased that Howe brought so much. It will help you out of your scrape in sending so much to Mr. S.[1] I have received a letter from Taylor, that the College is in a bad way the Com. having decided to refuse an appr. There is still room for hope, and I thought if you could see Dr. Derby, & stir up Hart and

---

1. Possibly the contractor who was working on the Quogue house.

Gouv it might be well. The fight must be first upon the the merits of the College, of what it has effected against bitter opposition; & then there must not be too much thin-skinnedness in asking people to back us simply as a matter of friendship. *What is wanted is direct political influence* brought upon the members of the Naval Committee in the House of Representatives. The justification for asking this must be the value of the College, in support of which I advance my reputation which is now world wide in naval circles. I write today to Roosevelt, Brown (of Little, Brown) and Fred.[2] Shall write to Cummings[3] of the Naval Committee. To Roosevelt[4] I enclose a letter to Cleveland if he sees proper to deliver it. If Derby, Gouv or Hart, knows any person by or through whom a strong word to Cleveland might be got—get them to use it—making a *personal* request based upon my assurance of the merits of the College.

I close in an immense hurry & very tired for writing always wearies me. Keep the College on your mind, & do what you can for it for absent *me*. Love to children.

To John M. Brown

USS *Chicago*, January 13, 1894 [LC]

Dear Sir: I learn from home that the Naval Committee of the House of Representatives proposes to strike out the appropriation for the Naval War College, asked by Mr. Herbert, the Secy of the Navy.

If you feel at liberty to do so, I would esteem it a great favor to have you ask Mr. Fairchild if he will write to any member of the House Committee, but above all to Mr. Cummings, the chairman, who I believe is from New York. The occasion justifies such action, for that the College contains the promise of the utmost benefit to the Country, as involved in its naval interest, I stake all my reputation as an author and expert upon naval history and naval warfare; and I gather, from sources I cannot mention, that the attack upon it by enemies has been both secret and indirect. You are able to bear unbiased evidence to the esteem in which its work is held abroad; for it cannot be too often repeated that but for the War College I would never have put pen to paper.

If with any other man in political life, especially of the dominant party, you have any influence, I shall esteem it the highest personal favor if you will ask him at once to stir in this matter. Did you know the narrow

---

2. Mahan's brother.
3. Amos J. Cummings, Democratic congressman from New York and Chairman of the House Naval Committee.
4. No Mahan letter of this date was found in the Roosevelt Collection.

and almost malignant opposition which the College encounters, from prejudiced men of a somewhat antiquated type, I am sure you would be disposed to do all you can.

[P.S.] Mr. Fairchild might like to feel sure that Herbert favors the College. Of that I can give *full* assurance. The arch enemy is said to be one of his chief understrappers.[1]

To Grover Cleveland

USS *Chicago*, Villefranche, January 13, 1894 [LC]

Sir: For venturing to address you at all, my reputation for knowledge of the matter I deal with is my sole justification. To that reputation my friend, Mr. Theodore Roosevelt, can sufficiently speak.

Upon that ground I venture to assure you, from my intimate knowledge of my subject, that the maintenance of the Naval War College at Newport is of the first importance to the proper development of the United States Navy; and as there seems a disposition on the part of the House Naval Committee to refuse the small annual appropriation, I ask your powerful personal support.

I know that Mr. Herbert, the Secretary of the Navy, favors the College. The opposition comes from elsewhere.

To the Department of the Navy

USS *Chicago*, Villefranche, January 13, 1894[1] [LC]

1. I ask the attention of the Department to the records of the Summary Courts Martial held on board this ship on the 6th and 8th of January, 1894, in the cases of Patrick Boyle, J.A.G. Simpson, and John Laffan: with particular reference to the offenses charged, the sentences passed, the action of myself as the officer ordering the courts, and to the final action of the Commander-in-Chief.

2. Believing the latter to be such as must result in injury to the dis-

---

1. Henry Cabot Lodge wrote in a letter to Luce of January 22, 1894, "There is a movement headed by Commodore Ramsay and Captain Bunce to endeavor to break down the War College. . . . The Secretary, although not hostile, is very lukewarm."

1. This letter was enclosed in Mahan to Herbert, January 25, 1894.

cipline of the ship, I ask the Department to consider that two men, Boyle and Simpson, who had taken upon themselves to be absent from the ship without permission for periods exceeding six and seven days respectively, escape with a punishment scarcely more than the Captain himself is authorized to inflict. The reward of the deserving is diminished greatly, if the undeserving can thus seize for themselves so long an indulgence.

3. Upon first arriving on the station several cases of gross overstaying of leave occurred. After due deliberation, warning was given that any one overstaying over forty-eight hours would be tried by Summary Court— a rule which has since been followed. Under it several cases have been tried, and sentences of loss of pay have received the Department's approval. Between July 7 and September 5, when the first trial was held, there were fifty cases of overstaying for over 48 hours. From September to the present writing over four months, there have been 11.

4. I am perfectly aware that the approval of the Commander-in-Chief is required by statute, in all summary courts held in his presence; but his action in discharging this function is subject to comment by the Navy Department, and I think the matter one of sufficient consequence to the discipline of the ship, to ask the Department to consider it—the more so as the Commander-in-Chief has informed me he will not approve sentences of loss of pay, although such are authorized by law.

5. As regards the case of John Laffan, steerage steward, found smuggling liquor,—there have lately been several cases of drunkeness on board, an offence from which the ship had been exceptionally free. The steward of an officer's mess should be particularly trustworthy. Whether the sentence is exactly the best that could be assigned, may or may not be so; but I respectfully submit that it is in accordance with law and was practicable, and that, being so, the decision of the Commander-in-Chief, by which so grave an offense, the parent of so many other offenses, escapes punishment, is a serious injury to the discipline of the ship and to the position of her captain.

6. I would like also the Department's consideration that Summary Courts are evidently intended to reinforce the power of the captain, while submitting it to the check of a board of officers, who may be supposed not to lend themselves to injustice or hasty action on his part. The approval, directed by law, by a superior, perhaps a chance "senior officer present," really weakens the original purpose of the statute. But as I am not here seeking a change of law, I would respectfully submit to the Department that by approval was never meant that the senior entirely agrees with the court, or with the officer ordering it. Captains, being primarily responsible for the discipline of their ship, should, I submit, be allowed to seek it according to their own ways and personal views within the limits of the law—

for the reason that every man acts more efficiently upon his own lines than upon another's, even though the latter's may be in themselves better. The simple opinion of the Commander-in-Chief that a punishment—though legal—is "not suitable," should not, I submit to the Department, be held to justify him in summarily setting aside the decision of the Captain, in a matter affecting the discipline for which the latter is immediately responsible.[2]

To Ellen Evans Mahan

Nice, France, January 14, 1894 [LC]

Dearest Deldie: In thinking over what I wrote you yesterday—do not understand that I want you to become a political woman for the College. I thought you might speak to Derby, Gouv, and Hart, saying that the great point is to bring to bear on Cummings (Amos J.) Chairman of House Nav. Committee & upon Cleveland, any proper influence which would induce them to listen to the College plea, and to rest that very largely upon my own now established reputation and my *positive opinion* that no one thing is so essential to the proper advance of the Navy as the maintenance of the College. I dont want you a wire puller—but you might perhaps see Gillender also, & Dave.[1]

Jany. *Atlantic* just recd. Is little Sedgwick[2] still at St. Georges?

[P.S.]   Drop a line to Harry Taylor saying I have written Herbert.

To Ellen Evans Mahan

Nice, January 22, 1894 [LC]

For Yourself Only

Dearest Deldie: I hate to give you trouble, but as you may hear any way—it is best to hear from me. Erben has reported to the Department that my professional ability is "Tolerable"; and "Attention to Duty" the same—and has added a long statement as to my lack of attention to certain

2. On January 8, Erben had also mitigated a sentence passed on an apprentice seaman, J. J. Kelly.

1. David B. Ogden, son of Gouverneur Morris Ogden.

2. Possibly, William Parker Sedgwick, Jr., class of 1903.

things.[1] You know me too well to believe there has been any willful neglect & if there has been any due to natural incapacities, we can well believe God will bear me clear—for I have kept my work before Him. I could not of course trust my own judgment alone, so I have put before Nazro and Tom Rodgers both Erben's report and my own proposed reply. So far they are not able to see any ground for it (Erben's statement)—by tomorrow, when I shall see them again, they will be able to tell me if I am anywhere weak. You recognize of course that the word of a senior has great weight, but I think I can make the Department see the absurdity and injustice of letting stand—alone—the accusation of one man only six years my senior & of no *particular* reputation when the means of investigation are at hand.

Now, dearest, please dont worry. It is one of the rubs of life, to be taken as they come. Erben is a man who is rash in his statements, and I think has gone beyond the beyonds—and my two advisers seem to consider his statements substantially unfounded. The Chief Engineer told me the other day no captain had taken as much interest in the engines—& I have been in the habit of going round more than Erben at all knows. At the same time, one cannot ignore the seriousness & disagreeableness of such a charge from a senior. Back me with your prayers & dont worry. Of course, if you want comfort talk to any direct adviser—Gouv, Dave, Hart or Rose.

Jan. 23

I have returned from the ship (I am staying with your uncle Charles) and Nazro tells me that he and Rodgers, after carefully talking & thinking the matter over are of the opinion that there is no ground for Erben's statement, and that my rejoinder is admirable and dignified. This may, I think, entitle us to the courage of a good cause. I enclose my rejoinder, with Erben's statement, and advise your taking them to Dave by an evening

---

1. On December 31, 1893, Erben had submitted the following fitness report on Mahan:

Professional ability	Tolerable
Attention to duty	Tolerable
General conduct	Excellent
Sobriety	Excellent
Health	Good

Efficiency of men under his control. Tolerable, except in the matter of divisional exercises where her condition is good.

Regarding my answer "Tolerable" to question No. 1—I state herewith that Capt. Mahan always appears to advantage to the service in all that does not appertain to ship life or matters, but in this particular he is lacking in interest, as he has frankly admitted to me. His interests are entirely outside the service, for which, I am satisfied, he cares but little, and is therefore not a good naval officer. He is not at all observant regarding officers tending to the ship's general welfare or appearance, nor does he inspire or suggest anything in this connection. In fact, the first few weeks of the cruise she was positively discreditable. In fact, Capt. Mahan's interests lie wholly in the direction of literary work, and in no other way connected with the service.

[211]

appointment. I have sent them to Theodore Roosevelt asking him to consult Sampson & Evans, and that I would tell you to communicate with him if you thought advisable. His address: Civil Service Commission, Washington D.C.

Erben's animus in this is not easy to make out. He *may* be honest, he may deceive himself. He is petulant, unreasonable and impulsive—thinks one thing one day and another the next. This, however, is immaterial. What I want is investigation at once, while the matter is fresh. If Ramsay defeats this, I want to be kept in command of the *Chicago* until she goes home this summer, so that the Board of Inspection there may pass upon her condition under my command. She can stand it, I am sure. Ramsay is quite capable of detaching me, and as an injury to my reputation will injure the College he will do anything he can for that.

God bless you my dear love. I am sorry you should have this to bear; but with a reasonable certainty that I am right you will take courage & God will help you.

Of course you may tell the children if you think best. They need not blush for me. Give them my love. When I have done all this requires, I hope to write a decent letter to you.

What Dave can do is to give advice & possibly rouse some influence if there be hesitation to investigate.

3 P.M. Jan 24

I shall send this today, dearest, and tomorrow the papers. It may probably be that the latter will need to be copied by type-writer—and one sent to Roosevelt by you—so stand by. Meanwhile, if this comes before the papers, drop him a line to say that I should object to either Bunce or Ramsay being on a board to investigate me. I closed a letter to him today—but in truth I am here so interrupted that I forget things I mean to say. Tomorrow I shall try to get everything perfectly correct, and after mailing dismiss the worry from my mind.

Yours of Jan. 12 came today. Is it possible there is so much time between my letters? It seems to me I do nothing but write to some one.

To Hilary A. Herbert

USS *Chicago*, Villefranche, January 25, 1894 [LC]

Sir:

1. With reference to the statement made by Rear Admiral Erben,[1] under the head of "Remarks" in his report upon my professional ability and attention to duty, I submit the following statement;

---

1. *See* Mahan to Ellen Evans Mahan, January 22, 1894, Footnote 1.

2. The part that most painfully impresses me is the allegation of lack of interest. I think it hardly fair to press a casual remark whose precise words I can not now recall, to the implication that I take no interest in my duties. A man may say, as I have, that details of administration, which make up so much of a Captain's duty, are to him uninteresting; it by no means follows that he does not interest himself in the proper discharge of them when a Captain. There are few men, I presume, whose daily work does not bring much that is uninteresting or distasteful, but which they yet do faithfully and well. The question is not what I feel, but what I do; and the test of what I do is the results obtained. That is the question of the present condition and efficiency of the ship.

3. For the first few weeks Admiral Erben states that she was positively discreditable. I joined the ship May 11, 1893, he on June 1. Up to the 15th she was at the Navy Yard; she went to sea on the 17th, reaching Queenstown June 30. During the whole of July I was incapacitated, more or less, by an injury received to my knee on the passage across, but which I did not give in to until in harbor. I was under treatment throughout the month and actually on the list from July 12 to August 1. How much farther the indefinite period, "first few weeks," extends, I do not know.

4. The ship was inspected by Admiral Erben in Barcelona at the end of October. If any serious failure occurred in her various drills, or in other respects, I was not informed of it. It is to be supposed that within the three months, August–October, she made some progress to efficiency.

5. As regards her present condition and my own reputation I submit to the Department that as I am entirely responsible for failures, so I am entitled to full credit for success. The question is not as to the methods I have used —if lawful but to the result I have reached.

6. This, under head 6,—"Condition and efficiency of Command"—, Admiral Erben states is "tolerable," except in the matter of divisional exercises, where her condition is "good." This concedes the most important part of a fighting ship's efficiency, her divisional exercises. As regards the indefinite residuum of cleanliness, order, discipline of crew and officers, I offer the following remarks.

7. Admiral Erben and myself are men not greatly apart in either age or rank. He has been in the Navy eight years longer than I, and from that has three years more sea service. He left his last ship in June, 1884; I mine in September, 1885. I was given to understand by the inspecting officers of the latter, the U.S.S. *Wachusett*, at Mare Island, about September 1, 1885, that her efficiency was found exceptionally high and that the report was very complimentary. This report should be on file at the Department; if not the three inspecting officers, Captains McNair and Kempff, and Commander Glass,[2] are within easy reach of the Department. I refer also

2. F. V. McNair, commandant of the Mare Island Navy Yard in 1885; Louis Kempff,

to the replies of Rear Admiral Upshur, the Commander-in-Chief of the Pacific Station, to which the *Wachusett* was attached, given to the Examining Board when I was examined for promotion to Captain, in October, 1885.

8. Appealing to this past record, I submit to the Department that it will not be fair to me to allow the opinion, however officially expressed, of one but little my senior, to go on record now, without a mature endorsement on its face of the opinion of the Department. The condition of the *Chicago* on January 1, 1894 is open to investigation. I am aware of the inconvenience of such a course, and do not formally press it; but I do ask it. The testimony is here—will the Department refuse to receive it? And I add, with a certain proud humility, that my reputation is now so identified with that of the United States Navy, not as a mere literary man, but as one whose military opinions are quoted with respect throughout the world, that an undeserved stigma upon me will more or less hurt the service too.

9. Admiral Erben's remarks upon my literary tendencies involve—intentionally or otherwise—an implication I must meet, viz, that my ship duties are affected by my literary work. On this point I beg to say that I have kept clearly before my mind the possible danger of falling into such a snare, and that I have not only conscientiously, but systematically, provided against it. My rule has been not to touch my literary work until the ship's work for the day was over; and the practical result has been that there have not been a dozen days since Admiral Erben joined the ship, in which I have put pen to paper before the evening meal—except when I was confined by the before-mentioned injury. The consequence has been that the work actually achieved is very little.

10. Satisfied myself that the ship in cleanliness, order, and discipline, is in very good condition, I feel compelled to submit to the Department further the enclosed letter, marked "A," affecting the question of discipline, as viewed by Admiral Erben and myself.[3] This letter was drawn up prior to my receiving the report on "Fitness." I had decided not to send it; for I recognized that, whatever the opinion of the Department, it could scarcely fail to sustain the senior. I submit it now, not to challenge an expression from the Department, but to enable it to form its own opinion as to the comparative disciplinary tendencies of Admiral Erben and myself.

11. This report on my "Fitness" came to me with all the shock of a surprise. In common with other Captains, I have found the office work of ships much more confining than formerly; but after all allowance for that, I feel that the quiet, steady doing of each day's work has brought the *Chicago*, on December 31, 1893, to a condition of efficiency in all the chief

---

class of 1862, Ordnance Officer at Mare Island in 1885; and Henry Glass, class of 1864, also on duty at Mare Island in 1885.

3. *See* Mahan to Department of the Navy, January 13, 1894.

essentials of a ship of war. Her hull and material generally are clean, well cared for and in all respects as good as can be expected after near five years in commission. Her crew are well-ordered, healthy, and well drilled. With the exception of the time I was laid up—from Queenstown to Southampton—I have always been in charge of her when at sea or underway. She has met with no accident, and I believe has been handled with reasonable discretion.

12. If this is substantially the case, the Department will, I am sure, feel that the statement that I am not a good naval officer can not be allowed to stand upon the say-so of any one man, merely because his rank is senior to my own. It must be substantiated from other sources. At the time when distinguished officers of other navies are saying that my treatment of naval warfare is better than anything ever yet done, to have said that I am not a good naval officer gives an odd impression. Granting even, which I do not expect, that investigation should show me to be an indifferent administrator, I should only share a defect that has been common to some very distinguished seamen.

13. I earnestly hope that the Department will see its way to ascertaining, through the evidence of those on board, what the condition of this ship actually is—or was on January 1. The immense injury a senior may do a junior by what he considers an honest expression of opinion is incalculable; and I do not believe I err in asking the Department that if the opinion, however honest, is not accurate—not supported by the facts—the paper itself may bear the Department's stamp to that effect.

14. It is unfortunate for the eliciting of the whole truth, that three watch and division officers of the *Chicago*—Lieutenants Cresap, Rodgers, and Dewey—should at this moment be detached. Personally, however, I should be satisfied if the Department will send them the "Remarks" of Admiral Erben with my own rejoinder, and ask their opinion, upon honor, as to my efficiency and attention as Captain of the *Chicago* and generally as a naval officer.

15. I respectfully ask the Department to order a general inquiry into the condition and efficiency of the *Chicago,* and my conduct and action as her captain.

To Ellen Evans Mahan

Villefranche, January 25, 1894 [LC]

My own dearest Deldie: Enclosed are the documents. A copy goes to Roosevelt by the same mail.

[215]

Do you avoid partisanship or excitement, which will be best done by observing the law of Christian charity. God will defend the right.

I have been staying with your uncle Charles—having had a light attack of influenza, which left me pulled down. Your uncle has been kindness itself. I cannot thank him too much.

I shall not affect to write more. I am much better in health & quiet in spirits. How a thing like this teaches one to know God and the power of the Holy Spirit. It is worth all the trouble.

To Ellen Evans Mahan

Villefranche, January 26, 1894 [LC]

My own dearest Deldie: I feel almost as if I owed you an apology for having given you nothing but my troubles in my last letter or two—for when one is so far away from home & those at home would like pleasant news it seems too bad to send nothing but such disagreeables. However, you may content yourself with knowing that I had sedulously for months kept before me, and acted upon, the idea that at all reasonable costs I should avoid any difficulty. This having been really forced upon me, wholly unawares, I feel that the quarrel is none of my beginning and that I may have good hope that it is sent from above, and that I will be seen through it as shall be best for us. With that reflection good bye to it for the present. I believe I told you I had had an attack of influenza which prevails here, almost every one suffering from it, but in no way of a severe type provided any care is taken. I was very well indeed on the 9th of January—Tuesday— when I was invited to dine with Mrs. Willing and Miss Lee. I accepted with great reluctance, being already engaged for Wednesday & having made a rule I would not dine out two days handrunning; but I did not see any way to refuse and so went. Mrs. W. is the old fashioned kind, not happy if you dont eat, and I exposed myself I suppose to the night air. At all events, on Wednesday night, as I came back in the train, I found my throat scrapy. I kept along till Monday when I had an engagement with the dentist, but that night I went to bed and stayed three days, including in them our last reception on Wednesday the 17th.[1] Your uncle came to the last and came in to see me, and asked me to come up and spend some days with him—and so I went on Sunday—the adml. giving me leave in very grudging manner & exacting that I should come to the ship every alternate day. Your uncle was, as I said, most kind; and although the re-

---

1. For the British consul.

striction prevented my getting the utmost benefit I did derive much and am now so far restored as to be practically well. I returned to the ship for good this morning, Friday—shall probably dine with your uncle tomorrow and at the Schiffs Sunday. Unluckily the weather has been very bad, & that, combined with the necessity to come to the ship, prevented my working off all my scores of visits as I had expected to do. I met some of your uncle's French friends, one of whom told me that he seemed as pleased as a boy to have me—though I could not but wonder in that case that he had not had me up before. However, nothing could be nicer than he has been to me. This evening I have been dining on board the French flagship *Formidable*, and talking French throughout.[2] Tiresome, you know, though I think my facility has much increased—but after all à quoi bon?

Saturday Jan. 27.

I have just (4 P.M.) returned from a round of visits to all the French ships in harbor—about ten, talking French all the time—so my French certainly becomes more glib. Before I forget I want to say that if anything occurs to you or Dave, I dont think it should be done except through Roosevelt. If the latter will undertake the cause, he ought not to find people striking in independently. As time runs on, I begin to feel as though it was perhaps a tempest in a teapot. Nevertheless, it wont do to let such an expression stand, even if by such a man. I have had to pay 60 francs more to the dentist or about $15 altogether while in Nice. Today I was happily surprised by receiving your letters & Helen's of the 15th & 16th. The returns from Little & Brown are satisfactory—although my covetousness was wanting more. If you have the data I would like to know how many of No 1. have been actually sold. I had also a very nice letter from Jane. As I remain so long in one place the news gets less & then being confined so long to my cabin etc made things worse—but in truth I now see few [people]. We expect to be ready for sea a week from today & Erben is in a hurry to get off. He has not been well and is never satisfied—has no resources. We will go to Naples & Malta—perhaps toward Constantinople. I had a letter ready for mailing to Herbert, suggesting the waste of keeping me here—but when Erben's accusation came, I had to withdraw it. I could not retreat before such a charge, until met.

Tell Helen that the author of *Sacharissa* has published the memoirs of Henrietta—duchess of Orleans—daughter of Charles I of England—a woman who had a varied & romantic career chiefly at the French Court.[3]

Goodbye my darling—always most fondly thine.

Love to the children.

---

2. The French fleet had arrived in port on January 19. The *Formidable* was the flagship of Vice Admiral Boissondy.
3. Mrs. Julia Mary (Cartright) Ady, *Madame, a Life of Henrietta, Daughter of Charles I and the Duchess of Orleans.* London: Seeley and Company, n.d.

To Ellen Evans Mahan

Villefranche, January 28, 1894 [LC]

Dearest Deldie: I enclose the first letter from Capt. Borokenhagen of the German Navy. The preposterous attempt to make my reputation to be that of a merely "literary" man may have to be met—and you might put yourself in communication with Roosevelt, who could easily in Washn. ascertain the reputation of Boisse[1] & Borokenhagen in their own navies. The latter is apparently in charge, or second, at their Naval School which speaks for the estimation in which he is held by the most military of nations. It is desolating to be attacked for such twopenny grounds as Erben alleges to me for his opinions; but a great comfort to know that God rules all. Believe me dear I do not worry—in fact the power to worry seems departed from me—I am not indifferent, set on vindication, as I should be, but not depressed or unhappy. That source of anxiety can be spared you. And in the opinion of Rodgers & Nazro you may depend with much certainty. I shall write again in two or three days.

[P.S.] I asked a French Captain about Boisse. He has a first-rate repute.

January 28

In the present vexatious time I thought the enclosed might doubly please you. I heard from Dr. Diesbach last night, and he has half finished Sea Power No 2. Not improbably his and Boisse's translations may appear about the same time. I am quite well. Diesbach wanted Boisse's address which I sent him. With dearest love always fondly.

[P.S.] Preserve enclosed carefully—they may become useful.[2]

[Memorandum]

USS *Chicago*, Villefranche, January 30, 1894 [LC]

At 7.30 Admiral sent me word that the battalion was to land at 9 a.m. but not to use the steam whaleboat. I went on deck a few minutes before 8 (was on deck when colors hoisted) and found that the order about the steam whaleboat was countermanded through the Ex Offr. (who informed me) no message to that effect having been sent to me.

I note this not for the sake of raising points, but to show how the admiral jumps in independently.

---

1. Mahan's translator for *Revue Maritime*.
2. Enclosures not found.

To Helen Evans Mahan

Villefranche, January 30, 1894 [NWC]

Dearest Helen: I told mamma that the same woman who wrote *Sacharissa* has also written the memoirs of Henrietta, Duchess of Orleans and daughter to Charles I, and so a contemporary of Sacharissa's. I have also noted *Old Court Life in France*, and *Old Court Life in Spain* both by Frances Minto Elliott, which sound as though they might be interesting.[1] A Mr. King a first cousin of Mrs. Stockton told me today that he had read and liked the former. I am now paying my good bye visits, for we are nearly ready to depart and will sail probably Monday the 5th. Our plans have been upset by the injuries to the *Normannia*.[2] She sailed with stores to meet us in Naples about Feb. 10; after getting there we were to go to Malta. Now the stores will not reach Naples before Feb. 21, and the admiral thinks that will be too late to go to Malta afterwards. Consequently, his decision is to go to Genoa from here, put the ship in dock there to have her bottom painted and thence to Naples, giving Malta the go by until we return from the Levant. I trouble myself but little about it, although I regret going again to Genoa. I liked the place very much, but the weather was detestable; and it is rather sad leaving a place with so many friends to go back to an old resort. An entirely new place would present some distraction. My friend Mrs. Schiff has given me a group portrait of her three daughters and also at my special request a single one of each of the two eldest—so I want mamma to order from the man in Newport who took me when last at the War College one of those he then took, and to send it to me—as I promised I would give one. You have seen of course how many of our officers are being taken away and sent to the *Bennington*. We get very good men in their place,[3] but I feel much annoyed by the change. I was used to and valued those I had & I dont like having to break in with new ones. Tomorrow I am giving a breakfast to the four departing ones, having asked to meet them the four young ladies of whom we have seen most, the two Schiffs and the two McCreas. Mr. Schiff and myself will make ten. I suppose they will leave the ship the following day and the *Bennington* probably sail from here by the end of the week. On Thursday, the 1st I am to breakfast at the Prefecture—a naval affair, I understand, officers of the French fleet etc. This will bring us pretty near the end of our festivities here, though I am to dine one of my last days at the Schiffs—again! I in-

---

1. Frances Minto Elliot, *Old Court Life in France*. New York: G. P. Putnam's Sons, 1893; and *Old Court Life in Spain*. London: Chapman and Hall, 1893.
2. Pride of the Hamburg-America Line, the *Normannia* sailed from New York on the 18th, and was struck by a tidal wave on the 21st, when 760 miles at sea.
3. Lieutenants Chauncey Thomas, class of 1871, John Bernadou, class of 1880, John Ellicott, class of 1883, and Sumner E. Kittelle, class of 1889.

tend to sleep at your uncle Kuhns on Thursday after the breakfast, and hope that day to wind up all, or nearly all my obligations. Your last letter complained of the interval between mine, but I think you found that it was due to irregularity in the mails & not to my fault, though I have found Nice to swallow up more of my time by visits and give less news to write than when I have been moving about. I wish you would ask Marraine[4] if little Mr. Sedgwick is still at St. Georges, and tell Mamma to send me 100 more cards to Stevens—unless she hears on good authority that we are going home.

Wednesday, 31st 10 P.M.

My breakfast went off nicely—the Schiffs arriving from one direction at 12.05, the McCreas from the other at 12.12. I was at the station and brought them all off in the gig. All are bright talkable girls. Having had the Schiffs before, I put Miss McCrea on my right, Mr. S. on my left and scattered the others along. Mr. Rodgers, Dewey, Cresap & McVay were the officers who are leaving for the *Bennington*. In the midst of the breakfast Mr. Raymond Rodgers[5] came in & drank a glass of wine with us. The guests left the ship about 3 and I went ashore with them. I am to send now three of my photos—one for mamma and the others to each of the two young ladies—rather absurd for an elderly gentleman with no hair to speak of; but as I was asked & promised nothing is left but to fulfill. You have very tolerable reason to be jealous of Rosie Schiff—if Lyle were the right age I should like him to go in for her, and would be very willing to have her for a daughter. As it is, she will pass beyond the limit of my future. There is one thing, however, that I would fear for; and that is the pervading religious feeling without which no human character is on the road to perfection. I fear they have it not. This reminds me of your friends the Holts—I did not know you had any relations with them. I have heard that they were unbelievers. Now I have no wish to control your choice of friends, nor to limit your range of thought—but do be careful not to allow that miserable doubting feeling, based upon no reasonable convictions to find its way to your mind. Remember that I, certainly a man of brains, find the truths of Christianity satisfying to my intellect & my only firm support in doubt & trouble. Beware, therefore of the nerveless doubt of our age. If such come to you, pray and study, God will not leave you in the dark—but if you have not time to study, shut out doubt & refuse to listen to those who suggest. Remember that I, as my experience of life, tell you that the truth of the Gospel is my firm conviction. God is, and is the Rewarder of them who diligently seek Him.

---

4. Rosalie Evans, Mrs. Mahan's sister, who was godmother to Helen Evans Mahan.
5. At this time, Naval Attaché at Paris and St. Petersburg.

To Ellen Evans Mahan

My dearest Miss Deldie: Like yourselves I find myself with little to say. Events are scarcely numerous enough to fill two letters a week. It seems pretty well decided now that we will get away on the 6th Tuesday, and just now the admiral seems disposed to resume his plan of going to Naples and thence to the Levant, postponing our visit to Malta to his return or about the first week in April. We will see. The *Bennington* left here for Genoa day before yesterday. We have from her a very nice set of fellows but none whom you knew. Raymond Rodgers has been on board two or three times this week looking well & quite thrilled the McCreas when he came to the breakfast table in grande tenue the day they breakfasted here with the Schiffs & the departers. On Thursday I breakfasted at the Prefecture—fifty two men and one woman—reversing Father Maturin's[1] proportion of the sexes. The lady was the Prefect's wife. I was seated between the Maire of Villefranche, M. Pollonnais, and the captain of the French flag ship, both of whom I already knew. My French is getting much more glib. I asked the captain of the *Neptune*, their newest vessel, to let me visit her & he replied by inviting me to breakfast next day—where I accordingly went and then walked all over the ship, in and out, including a visit to the tops on the masts out of which peep the little guns. Later in the day I went to town and dined with your uncle, sleeping at the house. He was going to a costume dance at Mrs. Bishop's, the object of the costumes being to be somewhat incongruous; so he went as Abraham with a white turban and long white beard, wearing also a short [illegible] cloak of blue velvet trimmed with broad gold lace braid. I was to have returned to see him, but I went to the McCreas where the two girls made themselves so pleasant that I lingered till too late. It seems they have a falling out with Mrs. Bishop & so were not invited. I could scarcely believe my ears, when I heard they would receive me. I returned to the ship at 10 this morning. Tomorrow I take my farewell dinner with the Schiffs, and on Monday, if nothing prevents, will dine for the last time with your uncle. You must get your mother to say to him how much I have appreciated his kindness during my stay. He has seemed in good spirits—excellent—but I find the impression prevails that he is aging much. He certainly is *very much* older looking and acting than when I last saw him, just after Pia's death. I called also upon Madame Robiglio, but found her out—and Miss Lee who, with Mrs. Willing was at home—the Consul's too, but he was out and she in. I have

---

1. Basil William Maturin, British clergyman and preacher, known as "Father Maturin." From 1876 until 1888, he was rector of St. Clements in Philadelphia, where Mahan may have known him.

lost my interest in them. I should imagine from the earnestness of Lyle's exhortations to cultivate the Schiffs that there has been a divergence of opinion upon that subject between his sisters and him. I dont know why—but there has been creeping over me a conviction that I shall not get to London again; no reason only a feeling. I hardly see how the girls can be called homely. The eldest is certainly not at all pretty—perhaps even plain. Rosie I consider very pretty and quite charming, while the school girl is a dear little thing, with honest brown eyes that quite win your heart. The two youngest look alike a great deal of color, eyes & hair both dark brown. I see that *Blackwood* for February has an article on Sea Power—which generally means me—so I have sent for a copy.[2] Both Taylor and Stockton seem much impressed by Ramsay's hostility to me—appear to think he has affected the Secretary; while Walker[3] wrote to Raymond Rodgers that he heard R[Ramsay] and Bunce were almost insane in their vexation over my reception and reputation abroad. I do not affect [to] undervalue the importance of this, especially in view of Erben's action, but somehow I cant worry, and without defiance feel quite sure of protection. Let us shut our eyes and say our prayers. Stockton seems in fine fighting humor, and upon the whole I feel as if the atmosphere of strife were becoming quite natural. I hope I may be kept in the same constant frame—neither defiant nor cast-down. Deliverance, not victory, is my prayer. But oh! darling, I do feel as if a few minutes with you would be a great help.

Monday Feb. 5

I shall close this now, dearest one, and let it take the mail. We sail tomorrow afternoon for Genoa then to go into dock & from Genoa will go to Naples—thence probably to Smyrna & it may be to Constantinople. I dined last night at the Schiffs and said good bye—also in the afternoon paid some other calls. Tonight to your uncles and am to see Adml. Luce at 5:30 by appointment. He says he has something to talk to me about.[4] Good bye— dearest love to all the children and yourself.

To Ellen Evans Mahan

USS *Chicago*, At sea, February 9, 1894 [LC]

Dearest Deldie: The Secretary, to my surprise, answered the letter you type wrote for me.[1] He announced his continued interest in the College,

---

2. A. Alison, "Armed Europe: Sea Power." *Blackwood's Edinburgh Magazine* (February 1894). There is no mention of Mahan in this article.
3. Rear Admiral J. G. Walker, at this time a member of the Board of Inspection and Survey.
4. Luce was in Europe as head of the American exhibit at the Columbus Exposition in Madrid.
1. *See* Mahan to Ellen Evans Mahan, January 5, 1894.

[222]

criticised severely the actions of Sears & Chambers, whom he will not rein-
state, and said he intended to put me again at the head of the College upon
the conclusion of this tour of sea duty. It is not worth while for me to
make up my mind now, but I rather think he is reckoning without his host
if he expects me to go there again under Ramsay as Chief of Bureau, or
under circumstances at all similar to those I have heretofore experienced.
True, we are so much at the Secy's mercy that I may acquiesce in bad lest
worse befall me, but at present one thought and purpose dominates my
mind viz: to retire the instant the law allows me. Even before Erben's
action I felt the impossibility of bearing the double strain of ship and
writing—since then, even the ship, under the conditions, seems to overtax
my attention. I am unfortunate in my executive. He is a good seaman &
a hard conscientious worker; but he has not the faculty of running a ship's
company. With the malevolent aspect of the admiral and the difficulty of a
junior maintaining his cause against a senior, this inadequacy makes my
position very trying. Happily, all is in God's hands; and, if I am not always
as trustful as I should be, this thought greatly helps me. I sent a letter off
to Nelly this morning before leaving Genoa—not much in it. I did not go
ashore at all while there, feeling it necessary now not only that things
should go well, but that I must get appearances on my side. Funnily
enough, since the row, the admiral, who had told me he would approve
no more sentences of loss of pay, has approved *three*. Can one understand
such vacillation? How put your foot down, if not decided upon what was
right? I was very sorry to leave Villefranche, but think likely the change
may benefit me. The faithful Schiffs came down to see us off—father,
mother, & girls—she remaining in the boat as the doctor forbids her going up
stairs. I believe they are as much favorites with the others as with me. I
had no time to write her from Genoa but shall certainly do so from Naples,
if not on the way down to acknowledge our indebtedness for their most
cordial hospitality. I shall at the same time write your uncle Charles, who
seemed really pleased to do what he did for me. He seems to like his life,
but to me it has a most lonesome and forlorn outlook. If he outlive his health,
what will become of him. He several times said, how much it would add
to his happiness had he nephews or nieces near him.

Feb. 10

We are at sea still—but should arrive tomorrow forenoon. As for your intentions of taking me to teas, receptions etc—you must remember that not
only am I here entirely alone, except chance conversations with an officer
here & there, so that even I feel lonely, but also that the society in Nice was
very small (that which I frequented) knowing each other well, & in intimacy
somewhat like a large family. As you yourself said the sans gêne disappears at
once when at home. Here we are on equal terms, quite irresponsible & nothing to do but amuse one another. I see no reason to hope from my ex-

perience here that I will find N.Y. & Washn. receptions less dreary than of old. Another thing I have never seen young girls so cordially welcome elderly men as here, the McCreas and Schiffs notably. It was not merely politeness of manner, but an apparent readiness and pleasure in talking to you. I shall stop here—intending to mail this letter in Naples tomorrow & write to Laddie on his birthday.

For yourself only

About your England project—so many things you suggest turn out well that I cannot wholly reject the idea, and I should dearly love, if only a glimpse, to break the absence. But I am convinced the captain of a big ship in commission can scarcely have his family in the same port. If you came, I would ask one or two weeks leave, & leave the ship wholly for that time—but as to going every evening, I had to stop the Ex offr. who undertook to do so, & am satisfied he would have done better had his wife not been here. I have said openly that the captain of a ship should not have his wife in the port; & besides I have not an Ex. who can take my burden off my hands. He is not bright nor quick. You can have no idea, I had none, of the enormous increase in a captain's labors—sometimes I fear breaking down under the uncongenial load, & indeed but for the support God gives me I believe I should go to pieces. It is to me a "vale of misery," and my one hope is that I shall so pass through it as to "go from strength to strength"—that & that only.

Feb. 11

Arrived Naples. Well. I should add I think the chances are against our returning to England.

To Ellen Evans Mahan

Cablegram   USS *Chicago*, Naples, Italy, February 12, 1894 [LC]

Reply Dave wish such investigation as Department chooses. Consult Roosevelt.[1]

---

1. David B. Ogden had telegraphed Mahan from New York, February 11, 1894: "Do you wish court of inquiry letter not so understood." Library of Congress.

To Ellen Evans Mahan

Naples, February 14, 1894 [LC]

Dearest Deldie: I mailed you on our arrival here a letter written mainly on the way from Genoa, and on the 12th I wrote Lyle for his birthday. I have sent you also notices of *Farragut* from the *Academy* & *Spectator*[1]— possibly Farragut[2] might like to see them. Day before yesterday I had a telegram signed Ogden—I presume from Dave—asking if I "wanted a Court of Inquiry, for my letter was not so understood." Not being quite sure of his address I replied to you that I wished "investigation such as Department chooses. Consult Roosevelt." My idea was, if the latter would act, to let him *control* action, others contributing such assistance as they might—but *through* him. I had experienced so much trouble from the erratic, ill-concerted, movements of others about the College that I wanted to secure a head, and Roosevelt on the spot would be in touch with the best advice, Sampson & others. My own idea was not to worry the Dept. if it was for any reason very averse, while yet to insist firmly that I must not be pilloried on the ipse dixit of a man of Erben's calibre. I therefore suggested to R. that if the Secy. did not wish to order an investigation (as to the form of which I was not particular) that I should be kept in command of the *Chicago* if she went home—so that an unbiased board might pronounce there on her condition etc. All I believe I made clear—so farewell for a while to this unpleasant subject. I only trust you are not worrying, and will not even if the thing gets in the papers. If it does, unpleasant things are bound to be said. The natural envy of men will prompt many to make reflections upon me from the very fact of my reputation—to do what they can to drag me down. But we have the assurance that all things work together for good. Where I come short—and who never fails?—we will bear the reproach; when I have done well, it will in due time be clear as the light. Only dont worry, remembering that I do not.

I dont care very much for this place. The weather, it is true, has been against us—dull, misty and heavy until today which has cleared. The natural features are less grand than I expected, except Vesuvius, which is larger & finer than my anticipation, and the endless cloud of smoke or steam rolling from its summit is impressive. The city is dirty—very—and in all respects less attractive to me than Genoa—few pretty women, too. There is a remarkable museum, which I have not yet seen, and an aquarium, which I visited today. I cared for it less than some I have seen, but the cuttle fish

---

1. *Academy*, XLIV, p. 287, and *Spectator*, LXXI, p. 522. The *Academy* review was by W. O'C. Morris.
2. Loyall Farragut, USMA class of 1868, who retired from the Army after three years' service. His biography of his father, *The Life of David Glasgow Farragut*, had been published in 1879.

[225]

were extraordinary and hideous. The eight long tentacles two to three feet long, extending from the small gelatinous body—the horrible bag which contains the digestive apparatus—the writhing and twisting of the tentacles, perfectly lithe and looking like so many snakes, were monstrous. People liable to delirium tremens would do well to keep clear of the sight. I dont expect anything in a social way here, but have already half a dozen cards which I must return. A most singular meeting with Capt. Henderson R.N. We had tried to meet in England, unsuccessfully, but he came in here the very day we arrived, en route to Egypt, where he is to take command of a ship, the *Edgar*. He left the same afternoon by steamer for Alexandria but got on board to see me. Was it not odd? really quite a coincidence. Today I had a visit from a crazy man, a monomaniac. He sat down and after first asking me if nobody could hear, told me in the first place a story I am unwilling to put to paper—most extraordinary yet not unprecedented— and in that quiet, plausible, selfpossessed way that is characteristic of perfect sanity & of delusion alike. Though incredulous from the first, it was not till he began to tell of how he was followed, and persecuted, and the way in which everywhere the persecution showed itself that I recognized (though not an expert) the signs of an unbalanced mind. His idea was that we might take him to America & so he might elude his pursuers. Poor beggar, it was too evident they are in his own brain. I explained to him that the ship was not now returning to America, and that even if it were our orders would not permit us to take him. On this point and all others he was reasonable, but asked of me a promise that I would not tell his story— which he probably is driven to confide to some one whenever the fit comes on.

Feb. 15. 9 P.M.

This afternoon I received Helen's of Feb. 2d, and as it seems mine have been coming at long intervals I will close this and dispatch it tomorrow. I cannot remember now about my writing, but although I felt pressed for time, I was sure I had sent my letters with fair regularity. Now of course my social calls will be pretty diminished, and if nothing else occurs to preoccupy me I shall have more time. Three hours this afternoon, however, were spent in returning calls, and to my disgust I found two more cards upon my return. I have however only one invitation to dinner, for Monday next, at a Mrs. Vickers, whom with her husband I met at Lord Radstock's at Southampton last August. Under the conditions, and with the change in our officers, I feel necessary to tie myself much more closely to the ship and its duties. You will have seen that Clover is ordered here as Executive. If he prove a man of greater go than Gillpatrick he may make things easier for me—but he has always struck me as one of the heavy kind. For myself I get very tired, but still, as far as I can see my health and nerves bear the strain very well—for it is a strain, work uncongenial, petty details always distasteful to me, and my liked work stopped. Of course it is a grind, but so far I bear it better than I could have hoped. The bay and surroundings here showed up very well today—brilliant sky and air like crystal, blue water bold rugged shore teeming with houses, snow capped mountains in the back ground and Vesuvius smoking in the front—very fine. If only Nelson would drop in for a moment with Lady H. Good bye— dearest love to the children all. You must settle the enclosed. Fondly A.

Friday morning Feb. 16

Well—Goodbye again.

[*Memorandum*]

USS Chicago, Naples, February 15, 1894 [LC]

On Feb. 14 Mr. Montgomery[1] came to me for permission to be absent from quarters on the 15. As that was general quarters day I declined.

The next morning Mr. Kittelle came with same request. I held in abeyance until doctor expressed opinion on the case of the patient DeVeaux. When he recommended no quarters (on account of noise) I decided to have boat drill, and upon consultation with Ex. Offr. said Kittelle or Montgomery might go—settle between themselves. Kittelle went.

Mr. Montgomery came to me & asked permission to see admiral and tell him he was unable to join his (admiral's) party. I allowed him. The next thing I knew Montgomery was on deck in plain clothes going with admiral—no word of any kind having reached me.

To Henry Erben

USS Chicago, Naples, February 17, 1894 [LC]

Sir: My verbal interview with you yesterday having given rise to an incident extremely unpleasant to me, I beg leave respectfully to submit in writing the following résumé of what occurred.

1. I expressed my dissatisfaction with the excusing of Mr. Montgomery from the morning exercises of the day before, contrary to my own decision in the matter.

2. I asked that, when you should wish officers excused from any duty, I should be clearly notified as early as possible, in order to avoid misunderstanding such as had occurred in the case of Mr. Kittelle and Mr. Montgomery.

---

1. Naval Cadet William S. Montgomery, class of 1892.

3. I have to regret that my allusion to your report on my "Fitness" seemed to you out of place; but I must disclaim having had any wish to re-open that subject. I spoke of it as fact which necessarily increased my exactingness with the officers of the ship, and entitled me, in my own opinion, to be rather supported than overruled in such a case as that of Mr. Montgomery.

4. The above, I believe, covers all the points raised by me. At the end of our interview, which lasted at the outside ten minutes, you said to me, "If you are dissatisfied, you have only to apply, and I will send you home by the next steamer." I submit to you, Sir, that as I had not even hinted at any wish to leave the ship, as nothing in my requests called for such words, their address by the senior to the junior, and the obvious implication contained in them, make them distinctly provoking. I beg to recall them to your memory, as well as the tone and manner in which they were uttered.

To the Department of the Navy

Draft   USS *Chicago*, Naples, February 17, 1894 [LC]

I beg to make the following statement to the Department.

I yesterday morning sought an interview with Admiral Erben, on the subject of a permission given by him to a naval cadet to be absent from quarters and exercise the previous day, when I had refused such permission.

It may be well to say that I fully understand, and admit, the right of the Commander-in-Chief to permit the absence of any officer he chooses; but, independent of a certain grave impropriety in the part of the young gentleman himself—immaterial to the present subject—I remarked that the report the Commander-in-Chief had made as to my fitness to command rendered my position as captain somewhat delicate, and therefore entitled to the greater consideration in the exercise of my office.

The commander-in-chief replied that he considered that incident (the report) as absolutely closed. I said, (in effect) it could hardly be so, while his statement was on file and I captain of this ship; not that I wish to discuss it with him, or have done so since sending in my rejoinder, but it inevitably makes me feel the necessity of being more exacting with the officers than has been my wont. After a short conversation, in which I affirm no disrespectful expression crossed my lips nor disrespectful action marked my bearing, the commander-in-chief said that if I was dissatisfied I had only to apply, and he would send me home by the next steamer.

I had used no expression of dissatisfaction except with his action in the case of the naval cadet; as to which I presented the remonstrance I am entitled to make. The Department will realize that it would be folly for me to desire detachment, with the stigma of his report against me unremoved.

Upon due consideration, the expression used by the commander-in-chief appears to me so grave an insult, official and personal, that I am compelled to refer it to the Department; and to remark that those who know him personally can realize what extreme provocation his manner can give—and did give—to such words.

The Department will remember my rank and position, that I am fifty three years old, and as far as I know (except in the opinion of Admiral Erben) an officer of good standing in the service.

I respectfully submit to the Department that the use of such an expression shows an absolute unfitness to exercise the authority of commander-in-chief, for there was for it no adequate provocation, merely the uncontrolled temper and tongue of the person using it.

But if the Department is not prepared to take so extreme a view I respectfully ask that, if my request for an investigation be granted, the investigation may be made to include the bearing and action of the C-in-C towards me and on board the *Chicago*.

To Helen Evans Mahan

Naples, February 18, 1894 [NWC]

My darling Daughter: I will begin by saying—tell mamma I am sending my precious manuscript of *Nelson* by the hands of Lieut. Thomas,[1] late of the *Bennington*, who leaves us on the 21st en route to N.Y. I have asked him simply to give it to some good express, charges *not* prepaid by him. I own to a pang of fear as I think of the dangers of the sea etc—but there is no reason I should keep it longer here. After type-writing, please keep the original in some separate place—as 34th St—I can do little here, and have done little; but I intend to make the life of Nelson the *great* work of my own life—if given by God the time and opportunity. It is a very great subject, and very hard it is for me to bear the enforced abstinence from working steadily at it. But that, too, is as God wills—so we will not complain. Our weather continues dull, & quite cold. The mountain tops of the Apennines in the distance are covered with snow and two days ago even Vesuvius was heavily dusted with it. In clear weather, the steam rising from the summit is very impressive; but when overcast, as now, it looks just like any other vapor, and when not attentively regarded might be taken for a series of clouds. Your letter of the 2d is the last I have from home, but very possibly we may have a mail this afternoon. I am glad to hear of your going to the theatre, but still more of the number of visitors you are having

---

1. Chauncey Thomas, who had been assigned to the Hydrographic Office.

on your afternoons. That and the little society about Quogue are a source of real pleasure to me, as I have felt our want of social surroundings—not so much for myself as for you children. For myself, however, I realize now that, though a dreadful consumer of time, the gadding of Nice kept my mind diverted. At home I dont miss it. My darling Miss Rosie (Schiff) is disappearing into the dim distance—in truth however I saw but little of her, fond as I was of her. The youngsters naturally monopolized her, and I talked to mamma. Two days ago a letter reached me, forwarded from Ville-franche, from a very old friend—Mrs. Harry Blake,[2] Kitty Blake as she signs herself, because her name is Sarah—whom mamma will remember. I dont recall meeting her since Nellie was born and very sorry I was to miss this chance. She wrote from Cannes—near Nice—and expected to be in the latter shortly. We left just too soon. She asked about mamma, whether she was in Europe or not. Her husband was a cousin of Mr. Frank Blake who you may recall was at Newport when we were in the Hall cottage & again in the new College building. I am so delighted to see that the College appropriation will probably pass—more, I fear, for love of victory than any other reason. I am prone now to feel that a navy which has at its disposal the kind of work I have done so well, and can find no better use for me than commanding the *Chicago*, dont deserve much interest at my hands. I have also had a letter from Mr. Laughton,[3] who tells me he has accepted an invitation to write a short life of Nelson for the series "English Men of Action." He says he hesitated as he "did not want to come in contrast with me"; which was a prettily turned compliment. I am immensely interested in Nelson, and the way I have taken of developing the subject seems to me the right one; at any rate it grows upon me and I think the portrait, as I give it, will grow upon the reader. I have seen the review of a book on music[4] which I think I will order for your birthday—but send early in the summer so that you can read it at Quogue if you like it. I imagine it to be a treatment of the historical development of music. At any rate the author, Doctor Parry ranks among the first musicians of England. I fear the look out now is that the *Chicago* will not go home till toward fall—and also that Com. Ramsay is to remain Chief of the Bureau of Navn. The latter will be a misfortune for me & still more so for the navy.

Feb. 19

This mornings mail brought me a letter from Lyle of the 4th to which mamma added a few words on the 5th. That makes 14 days getting here which is longer than I have yet had. When we leave here for Smyrna

---

2. Widow of Henry Jones Blake, class of 1863, who had resigned in 1866 and died in Paris in 1880.
3. John K. Laughton.
4. Sir Charles Hubert Hastings Parry, *Art of Music*. New York: Appleton, 1893.

(or thereabouts) probably on the 24th I shall have a long wait & you too. Tell Lyle that I think the only thing the matter with his handwriting is haste. The letter recd. today is perfectly legible, and very fairly written. The only thing is that with writing, as with other matters, one must first learn to do well, slowly, afterward you can become rapid. I am very pleased to know that he is doing so well in all his lessons. Mr. Thomas, who takes my manuscript, will probably leave here on the 21st, day after tomorrow, by the *Wieland*, a freight steamer which however takes some passengers & which is expected to arrive in N.Y. about March 4 or 5. He said he would, if possible, take the package up & see mamma. I told him she was likely to be at home about 1 P.M.; & she would I presume want to ask him to stop [to] lunch. His wife may be in N.Y., and if he calls, it would be nice if mamma went to see her. I have no further news. It is bitterly cold today for this part of the world—down to 37. I have looked over your letter but do not find in it anything particularly requiring an answer—but do not think I am not interested in hearing of all your visits and your visitors, as well as theatres. Dont forget to let me know if Mr. Sedgwick is still at St. Georges, for I keep sending him the *Guardian*. And now goodbye dear Child. Much love to mamma & the other children.

To Ellen Evans Mahan

Naples, February 19, 1894 [LC]

My dearest Deldie: Your two letters of Feb 6, acknowledging my budget and detailing your interview with Dave reached me this afternoon late—and as I was going out to dinner I had no time to answer them. Mine to Helen had been closed in the forenoon. You were quite right in advising against Soley—and also against Gherardi. If any admiral would help me it would be Walker but even touching him I warned Roosevelt that admirals would naturally side against an appeal against one of their number, even though the natural right of the accused was clear as we think mine to be. In truth, Erben's great error was in incorporating such vague remarks in a paper which, to use the legal phrase, should be privileged. There was no call to do it—and if he wanted to make such a statement he should have done it in a formal charge, or set of charges, specifying facts, as to which an investigation would follow as a matter of course. As regards his motives, they matter little. He protests, somewhat too much, that he has no personal feeling. My own belief is that he has gradually imbibed an extreme dislike to me, because I am very different from himself, and I cannot but think he feels the contempt with which I regard his ebullitions of temper. He is petulant, uncontrolled, boorish when annoyed, stamps and swears. I look on with a silent disapproval which I fancy he feels. As the eldest Schiff girl said one day, when he was making a particular ass of himself, he acts like a baby of two years. With this dislike he has fastened upon certain occurrences, mostly trivial, in which there has been neglect, either mine or another's, and has gradually persuaded himself that they show inefficiency—judged mainly by the standards of the old fashioned ways. Then he hates Walker, & looks upon the *Chicago* as an evidence of Walker's misrule. Upon this state of feeling supervened a bad attack of influenza, in which, either from lack of good sense or from economy, he persisted in remaining on board ship and out of bed. He was perfectly unbearable, blustering, rude, irritable to the verge of insult, sometimes crossing the line. This, I think, finished the matter and he committed himself to the paper in question. He was rather startled at my reply, I think; and I am enormously mistaken if he does not realize the error he made in those Court Martials. I should not have referred them to the Department, except to aid in justifying myself; but his action had kept me awake nights wondering how I could maintain discipline. However, he has plucked up heart, being I believe convinced that the array of lapses—almost all trivial—can substantiate his charge. On the other hand, I believe him unaware of the positive proofs of efficiency and interest that I can bring forward. It is impossible to diagnose the Dept's action. An investigation will be troublesome. If I were Secy, I should write to him that such vague allegations had no place in such a paper: that if there were adequate foundation he should prefer charges: that it was evident from his action in the C.M.s that he had interfered injudiciously with the discipline of the ship, and that it was impossible for the Department to allow such a paper to go on file against an officer of my previous reputation, unless supported by specific facts which must be proved.

A most gratifying evidence of the discipline of the ship's company was given when in dry dock in Genoa. Such occasions, as men have to leave the ship freely, day & night, to use W.C.'s on shore, often—generally—give rise to straggling and drunkenness. In 48 hours but two men of our whole ship's company are known to have left, and we had not one man drunk. I was so pleased that I seized the occasion—telling them that such a record was not only a credit to each man but to the character of the ship as well—to put all on the first class conduct list, for leave etc. Here in Naples their conduct has been excellent also. Of course we shall have more trouble—but still, after all allowances & drawbacks, the showing is good, nor can I be denied some credit for it.

I cannot tell you, dearest, what a pleasure and source of strength to me are your confidence and sympathy. Of course I knew you would stand by me, but one, especially when so much alone, craves the assurance of others confidence & trust. Both Nazro and Rodgers feel strongly with me, Thomas also though he said little, expressed utter surprise when I showed him the charges.

I will repeat to you that the manuscript of *Nelson* goes home by the hands of Lieut. Chauncey Thomas, who sails hence on the *Wieland*, on the 21st expecting to reach N.Y. about March 4. He said he would if time allowed call upon you and I named one p.m. so look out for her in the papers & for him. I cant do much more with *Nelson*, this cruise. Under the circumstances, I must be doubly watchful over my ship duties. You need not therefore hurry the type-writing.

Love to all the dear children.

To Ellen Evans Mahan

Naples, February 22, 1894 [LC]

This being a holiday, dearest Deldie, I sit down to write a few lines, though I scarce know what there is to say. Day before yesterday I went out to Pompeii, more from the feeling that I would be very wrong not to go than from any strong interest. In fact my interest in sightseeing under these conditions is almost nil. Black care sits behind the horseman, and if I am not accompanied by that drive, I find at least that there is no sense of enjoyment in gadding from the ship for a few hours. Give me a few days and I found at Granada and Avignon that I could still find pleasure in novel scenes. I am, however, glad I went to see the ancient city, the sight of which, ten years ago, would have seemed to me an irresistible temptation. I came away with a realization of what its streets, & their aspect, were that I could in no other way have gained—I saw its surroundings and the kind of deposit with which it was covered. Prominent among the feelings with which I came away was that it must have been a very dull place to live in. For the most part no windows on the street, & the style of house in general, though not in detail, such as we are accustomed to in Spanish towns —patios, etc. Streets very narrow and blank walls to gaze on. The most of its art treasures & relics of all kinds are now in the Museum at Naples. Our life here is astonishingly monotonous after Nice—not that I regret the change, unless it affect my spirits as so far it has not. I dined out on Monday, a gentleman & wife whom I met at Lord Radstock's in Southampton—an extraordinarily dull affair & poor dinner. Tonight I am to dine, semi-officially,—by which I mean as Capt. of the *C.*—somewhere with some one, to meet our minister to Italy.[1] My going ashore is for the most confined to

---

1. William Potter.

[233]

two hours walk in the afternoon, which I dont in the least enjoy as I did Genoa. This place is not to compare—very dirty and smelly.

Feb. 23 8 A.M.

I had to stop here for some twopenny detail, and afterwards the minister and a party of five others came on board, remaining two hours. Among them was Dr. Nevin[2] whom you will remember. Much changed, being now quite bald and grown full beard which is iron gray. There came also a Mr. Chas. H. Marshall, whom I did not at first recognize, nor he me; but we were classmates at Columbia 1854–56. I then left and he graduated in 1858. By the way I forgot to say that among the dinner company on Monday was Frank Macauley—bigger & heavier than ever. I understood he lives now in Florence. The dinner last night was fairly enjoyable, given by the two consuls, Naples & Castellammare, to Washington's birthday, the minister, and the admiral. The minister is a very gentlemanly man named Potter from Phila.—said to be indebted to Wanamaker for his place. His remplaceur will be here within a fortnight. Yours of the 9th came yesterday—also one from Roosevelt. Of course neither he nor you could have any news as yet—but he said Lodge would go to see the Secretary at once. They—R.[Roosevelt] L.[Lodge] and Davis look upon the matter as a kind of conspiracy. I confess I dont—possibly because I find it hard to believe in such things—partly because there is a rude kind of good humour about Erben, which, though perfectly compatible with malice, does not seem so. At any rate, whatever others may think, it does not become us, the injured parties, to impute motives. The attack is venomous and dangerous, because there are few men whose derelictions cannot be made to appear great, if you look upon them only and not upon the career as a whole. This is especially true in a charge by a senior against a junior in a military service—so we must not minimize the danger. In asking an investigation I have done all I can, and what I ought. Whether they give it or not is not my concern. If the thing becomes known, the service will divide into two camps—according as they like or hate the College—and the affair will be a ten days talk. Such at least is my reasoning. Tell Gouv when you see him that I am obliged for the slip from the *Evening Post*, (about Draper etc),[3] but that to enter upon such discussion when two weeks must elapse between each rejoinder is impossible. I promise myself, if I can ever get rid of my naval shackles, to take up that line of life—advocating one true policy by article writing. Meantime a year of this administration has convinced me, I think finally, that the future is with the Republican party. Jimmy Van Allen's nomination was a small incident—but the outward necessary aspirations of

---

2. Robert Jenkins Nevin, rector of St. Paul's American Church, Rome, from 1869.
3. Possibly, William Franklin Draper, Republican representative from Massachusetts.

the U.S. will only be fulfilled by the Republicans. With rare exceptions the Democrats know nothing of Sea Power—neither by knowledge nor by instinct. I am greatly distressed about Fred[4]—there is politics in it doubtless, which is rough on so ardent a Cleveland man, and probably due to Ludlow[5] influence & the discontent of the Engineer Corps with Fred's friendly attitude toward the Navy in the Board. Thank Hart for his note to you. And now dearest goodbye. I will try to send another line before we sail—for Smyrna—on the 25th or 26th. Love to the children.

To Ellen Evans Mahan

Naples, February 24, 1894 [LC]

Dearest Deldie: I hope our darling Miss Nell will forgive me the delay in writing her in her just turn. I will write on our way to Smyrna, if the weather is good; if not upon our arrival there. This is simply because it will take us four days steaming away from you to get there, and then four days more for the letter to retrace its way—so that a week will elapse between the receipt of this and of my next. I want therefore to give you the last before sailing. I am quite well, but with scarce any news. Yesterday, Mr. and Mrs. Henry Russell (Hope Ives) of Providence came on board—an utter surprise. I dined with them & some friends of theirs last evening, and today they came again and went over the ship. Twenty four years since we met; the May before I met you at Sharon we crossed in the *Russia*, your aunt Grace[1] being on board. I feel a little sad at the idea of going a thousand miles further from you all and from my letters—but try to console myself with the reflection that the admiral intends to be in Malta about April 5— so that then, not so far off, we will be on our westward way. Ten months by official count I have now been on this cruise. I will leave here a little space to close tomorrow morning.

Love to all my darling children.

[P.S.]   I am so sleepy (9:30 P.M.) I can scarcely hold my eyes open.

Sunday—Feb. 25 8 A.M.

Our mail goes ashore early, so I will close with renewed assurances of my fondest and tenderest love for all.

---

4. Mahan's brother, an Army captain, who wrote a paper on lighthouses which was praised in *The New York Times*.

5. Nicoll Ludlow had had two tours of duty with the Light House Board.

1. Grace Evans, sister of Manlius Glendower Evans.

USS *Chicago*, Naples, February 1894 [LC]

In case of investigation I ask the adml. for qualities of good naval officer.

To Henry Cabot Lodge

Naples, February 25, 1894 [MHS]

Your very kind letter has this moment reached me, as we are in the very act of getting under way for Smyrna. I have therefore no time for more than to express my warmest gratitude to you and to Roosevelt for your kindly interest and action, and to express my entire satisfaction with all that you have done, or may do, in my case. Even on the spot, a man is not the best judge of what should be done in his own quarrel—at a distance of four thousand miles he is only too fortunate in having two such discreet and yet sincere friends, as yourself and him, to act for him.

In reply to a telegram, received here on the 12th, to know if I wished a court of Inquiry, I replied: "I wish investigation *such as Dept. wishes. Consult Roosevelt.*" My purpose was to enforce my demand for some kind of investigation—and as I had already indicated to R. that I would be satisfied if the *Chicago* went home under my command for inspection, I felt that left him full freedom of action.

Would you kindly show this to Roosevelt. I feel most deeply grateful both to him and to you for your support.

[P.S.] It is perhaps unnecessary to warn you that Ramsay has innings with the Secy. of which none are witness; and I think sometimes of Bishop & Mrs. Proudie in *Barchester Towers.*[1] The Commodore has great influence.

[Memorandum]

USS *Chicago*, At sea, February 25, 1894 [LC]

On Sunday Feb. 25, leaving Naples, the Adml. was on deck without a cravat at all—and blouse one button (the 2d) only, buttoned.

I make this note, not to attack him, but to defend myself if attacked, as, e.g. he has criticized much smaller matters of men's uniforms.

This is not the first time.

---

1. In Anthony Trollope's novel *Barchester Towers*, the Proudies are politicians and social tyrants in their small ecclesiastical world.

To Ellen Kuhn Mahan

USS *Chicago*, At sea, February 26, 1894 [LC]

Dearest Miss Nellikin: To make hay while the sun shines is a good proverb, and although at sea we have not much more hay than I have hair on my head, it is advisable to use good and sunny weather for your letters, for one can never be sure how long it will last—especially in the Mediterranean. This has the reputation of being a very changeable, treacherous sea. Being, as you know, narrow with a burning desert on the south and snowy mountains on the north the movements of the air currents are violent and give little warning. However, we will have no rights to abuse the weather, if it continues to treat us as well as it has so far done. We left Naples yesterday at 2 P.M. running down during the night to the Straits of Messina. On the way we had the chance of seeing the ancient volcano Stromboli that has been blazing and throwing up lava ever since history began. I did not see it when near, but when over fifty miles away I two or three times saw the dull crimson glow, twice as big as a full moon flare up on the horizon. Those who later saw it nearer say that at those times it seemed just like a pot that boiled over, the lava not being so much ejected as slopping over. At a little before 8 this morning we passed through the straits where were the Scylla and Charybdis of the ancients. They were doubtless dangerous to the old clumsy sailing ships, but of not much consequence to a powerful steamer. After passing Messina the clouds that had hung over Sicily lifted and let us have a fine view of Aetna—a superb mountain ten thousand feet high, and now covered with snow so deep that scarcely a dark patch can be seen as low down as two thousand above the sea. This was very fine. For the next twenty four hours we shall be out of sight of land, crossing from Cape Spartivento, & then we hope to see the southern capes of Greece—Gallo and Matapan. Just before sailing we very unexpectedly had a mail from the U.S. by which came mamma's letter telling of Cousin Dave seeing Mr. Tracy, &c; also one from Mr. Lodge and one from Mr. Roosevelt. I was very glad to have had these before leaving, for though I worry astonishingly little for me I find my letters from home very much more grateful than even they formerly were.

March 1

It was just as well, my dear Miss Nell, and a good deal better, that I made hay when I did, for we have had anything but haying weather since then. Tuesday was fair with a fresh fair wind, but toward nightfall, just as we were rounding Cape Matapan, the wind suddenly changed, and as we came to Malea cape it freshened from right ahead and blew so hard all night as to reduce the speed of the ship from 10½ knots to a little over 5. It was the most disagreeable and exhausting night that I have passed on board, the spray flying over the bridge like a hurricane—for the wind was blowing fully 25 miles an hour to which the ships speed added 5 making thirty miles, or the speed of most railway trains, with which the showers of spray struck our faces. I could with great difficulty pull myself against it. I dont think I slept an hour all night, though I was much in the cabin, and both Mr. Nazro & myself were very tired next day. We anchored, as the gale still continued, in a small bay not far from Athens, just west of Cape Colonna, of which the ancient name was Sunium. This is one of the localities in Greece that is quite famous, from an ancient temple of Minerva which stands upon it about 300 feet above the sea. I remember to have seen an engraving of it at some time. Near here also occurred, about the year 1750, the shipwreck of a small merchant vessel which has become very celebrated, because one of the few survivors, named Falconer, made it the subject of a poem, The Shipwreck, considered the finest purely maritime poem in our language.[1] He, poor fellow, was unlucky; for less than twenty years later he was again wrecked in a ship which has never since been heard from.[2] The land about was part of the world famous Attica, renowned evidently on account of its people rather than itself, for it is rugged and rocky, thinly clad with vegetation, few trees & seemingly unproductive. Picturesque it certainly is, wild mountains, many of them heavily capped with snow and deep gullies. It was an odd contrast as we lay at anchor yesterday—the beautiful ruined marble temple of Minerva, with many of its white pillars still standing on the promontory on our right, while immediately in front was a nearly finished, but still unpainted modern frame house, of the strictly cubical and unadorned style of architecture, with the regulation three windows on each story, with a door in the middle on the ground floor. We left there at 5 this morning & have since been passing among the islands of the Archipelago on our way to Smyrna. The islands closely resemble what I have said of Attica—rugged and abrupt— the sea apparently breaking right against the cliffs, with here and there huge snow capped mountains. We expect to get into Smyrna sometime during the night. Fortunately the wind, though still fresh, is no longer violent.

Friday March 2. 9 A.M.

We got in last night, or this morning, at 3. I am desperately tired not having got to bed till 4, and send this by first chance.
Goodbye my darling child. Love to all.

---

1. Passages from William Falconer's "Shipwreck" are included in the *Oxford Book of Eighteenth Century Verse.*
2. Falconer was lost in the *Aurora,* when she went down between the Cape and India.

To Hilary A. Herbert

USS *Chicago*, Smyrna, Turkey, March 2, 1894 [NA]

Sir: I have to report the death on board this ship, while at sea, of Jackson
S. De Veaux, Mess Attendant. The deceased died from the effects of
pyaemia, on the 26th day of February, and was buried at sea the following
day. His effects have been sold and his accounts closed and forwarded to
the Fourth Auditor of the Treasury.

To Ellen Evans Mahan

Smyrna, March 4, 1894 [LC]

I was most delightfully surprised, my dearest Deldie, to receive upon
our arrival here your letter (no date) apparently of the 12th or 13th
February. As we are here nearly at the end of creation, as far as the station
goes, and had a mail the morning we left Naples, just a week ago today, I
had no hope of anything till at least three or four days after we got in. This
was only a day later than the Naples mail, but when away from home a
letter is always a letter. This was the one written on the blank pages of
Dave's note—mentioning his interview with Tracy. There seems to have
arisen in all minds a feeling that jealousy, conscious or unconscious,
prompted Erben's action. It is a matter of small moment, unless to put me
on my guard. The man is impulsive, entirely uncontrolled, very tolerably
satisfied with himself; those who know him better say he is very warm
hearted. I am satisfied he is full of prejudices, and quick to form them on
very slight grounds, and to this attribute an action in my case that strongly
reminds me of what he has said or done in others. But the subject is hateful
—let us have done with it. The same mail at Naples, arriving only two hours
before we sailed, brought very satisfactory letters from Roosevelt and
Lodge. The latter has always struck me as one of the chilly-tempered New
Englanders—and I was the more impressed by his letter of 8 pages, detailing his interview with the Secy, at part of which Ramsay was present.
The general result you know. He writes besides: "The Secy requested
me to say, what he could not say in an official letter, that he had nothing
but the kindest feelings towards you, that there was no reason for you
to make yourself uneasy, & that when the ship went out of Commission
she would be rigidly inspected by a first class Board, & that you would then
have an opportunity, if you desired, to meet all the criticism of Erben, &
to receive vindication in the report of the inspectors. He also told me that
he had carefully read your books during the past summer and greatly ad-

mired them." "Before Ramsay left the room I said that I thought [the last word is crossed through] regarded this slur upon you as not only unworthy, but a great misfortune, for as an American I took great pride in your work and thought it an honor to the American Navy. The Secy said, very warmly for him, 'So do I, and that is the reason I do not want to give publicity and set controversy going upon so slight a matter.'"

I consider this settlement satisfactory, for the present at least; though something will depend upon the actual endorsement made by the Dept. People dont always fulfill what they have said in the first warmth. Still I indicated to Roosevelt my willingness to accept the test of the Inspection Board, as an adequate investigation, and trust the matter will have so eventuated. In fact, a Court of Inquiry is almost blocked by the detachment of Dewey, Cresap,[1] and Rodgers. The Ex. Off. also leaves in a fortnight, so four most important witnesses would be unavailable. I consider also that while a man owes it to himself to protect his good name—professional or other—there is such a thing as being morbidly sensitive upon expressions of opinion. For the most part Erben's charge is vague. There is but one clear allegation viz: "that for the first few weeks the ship was positively discreditable"—and this I believe could be absolutely disproved. My request for investigation was unmistakable in letter and spirit. No one can say— while that is on file—that I shirked inquiry. My telegram was equally clear —I asked investigation, careless as to the method. The Dept. has chosen one way indicated by me, and I see no reason why I should insist on anything further. Personally I think no vindication could be more conclusive than a satisfactory inspection; and with regard to the interests of the Service I believe the Secy is right, for these public scandals (they inevitably become such) do harm to it.

I sent Lodge a letter of thanks at once. We were so near getting underway that I had to send Carl in a shore boat to mail it. To Roosevelt and Dave I shall write from here—I hope by the mail which takes this; but do you see Dave and tell him how deeply I appreciate his kindness throughout. You will see the propriety of not letting Lodge's letter transpire—but there is no reason that Dave should not hear everything. Replying to your own letter—the account of sales January—1893—could scarcely have been sent me in Newport as I spent all that month in N.Y. I think there were about 250 of No 1, for that month and 160 of No 2. Adding the 500 copies for which I get nothing brings the sale of each close to—if not up to—2000. My attention was drawn to my own teeth by the cutting of the silk, and a few pieces of amalgram fell out. My bill ran up to over $15. I am delighted at the turn the College affairs have taken. Despite all my past experiences I can even now scarce refrain from hallooing as though it was out

---

1. Lieutenant James C. Cresap, class of 1871, was ordnance officer in the *Chicago*.

of woods. What Taylor proposes to Adm. Weaver[2] is not only eminently sensible and useful—it is also well calculated to attract popular approval, for which I showed, perhaps, too little aptitude. Thank Mr. Saltonstall for his interest in the matter. Your answer to Dennis about the silver is perfectly in accordance with my views. I think the question of ownership should be at once settled & if Gillender will raise the matter it would be better. I dont quite like Dennis's tone, but then Jane also may have seemed—not unnaturally—loath to part with such long standing associations. Not having been ashore, I have little to add to my letter to Nellie. Never in my life—at sea or elsewhere—have I passed such a night as last Tuesday, nor been more exhausted. There was not much sea, the waters too narrow—but the spray flew pitilessly, drenching those on the bridge from head to foot and almost blinding us. Had it been in a frequented channel there would, I think, have been great danger—but we met nothing. I did not get a half hours sleep. I have seen much worse weather—but never in a ship that could steam in the teeth of the wind as we were doing. In the cabin there was scarcely a sign of motion—so little the sea—the sheer force of the wind reduced us from 10 knots to 5. The Archipelago is disappointing—though the combination of land and water may be fine in warmer weather. It is bleak, rugged and almost treeless, as are the historic shores of Greece itself, so far as we saw them. Striking—but neither grand nor attractive—would about express my opinion. The beastly northeast wind is the worst of all. We are in full view of the Tomb of St. Polycarp, the good bishop of Smyrna, mentioned in the 2d chapter of the Book of Revelations. He was burned here and buried near by. Good bye my dearest. Always fondly thine. Love to the children.

March 5 9 A.M.

Going to mail. Am well. Goodbye again.

To Henry Erben

USS *Chicago*, Smyrna, March 8, 1894 [NYHS]

Sir:

1. Replying to your letter 5A of March 6, 1894, relative to the breaking away of the 3d Cutter from the booms on the morning of March 3d: I have to report that I was awaked about 3.15 a.m. by the orderly with the report from the officer of the deck, Lt. Hodges,[1] that the 3d Cutter had broken a-

---

2. Aaron Ward Weaver, class of 1854, had retired in September 1893.
1. Harry M. Hodges, class of 1875.

drift, and that he was manning a boat to send after her. I began dressing, and in a minute more the orderly reported that the officer of the deck thought that it would be hazardous to send the boat under the conditions of the weather. I replied "Then don't send her"—as I would soon be on deck myself.

2. When I got on deck I found the anchor watch clearing away the 4th Cutter, and the quartermaster at the same moment reported that he had lost sight of the missing boat. I directed the 4th Cutter sent away after her, which was effected with some delay—sending with her a crew for the missing boat, and putting Naval Cadet Clark[2] in charge.

3. The 4th Cutter returned unsuccessful: and as daylight was not far off, and the boat could not, with the wind prevailing, be lost, I ordered the then officer of the deck, Ens. Norton,[3] to put all glasses in the ship at work as soon as light made, and to send the two whale boats, with an officer and extra crews in each, in search of the missing boat as soon as things became visible.

4. Towards daylight Ens. Norton reported to me that he had of his own motion sent the 4th Cutter with the Chief Boatswains Mate in search, having arranged signals by which the direction of the boat could be controlled from the ship, in case of the glasses picking up the missing boat.

5. The boat was brought back to the ship at 8 a.m. by a boat belonging to the Turkish man-of-war lying within the mole, at the point farthest from this ship—a distance of one mile. Being within the mole, (where we could not have expected her to drift) prevented our seeing her whereabouts.

6. As to the result of the investigation, I found that the boat had been secured with a bow and stern line—that the boom pennant parted at the thimble and the stern fast also gave way under the sudden strain brought upon it.

7. Naval Cadet Clark returned to the ship without, in my opinion, having pushed his search as far as he should have done. For this I reprimanded him privately.

8. To Ens. Norton I said that as I was up and about—though not on deck—he ought to have reported to me before sending the 4th Cutter as he did—there being then no necessity for hasty action.

9. I sent for Lt. Hodges twenty-four hours later and told him, that while admitting the propriety of his not lowering the boat, when in his judgment risky, I thought she should have been ready for lowering when I got on deck, which I might be expected to do rapidly after being called. He replied that the boat was being cleared away by the anchor watch, which was on deck and awake at the moment the accident happened—that at the same

2. Frank H. Clark, class of 1893.
3. Albert L. Norton, class of 1888.

time he sent below to rouse out the boat's crew, and that the delay occurred there, through the difficulty in rousing men in the middle of the night, not expecting a call. He added that he thought he had done all he could, but that, in the light of what had occurred, he should on another like occasion turn up all hands, as the surest means of rousing the force needed.

To Ellen Evans Mahan

Smyrna, March 10, 1894 [LC]

Dearest Deldie: We had to wait long for our last mail, but en revanche it came doubly full. The latest was your type written of Feb. 19—also there was one from Helen, to which you added & that from Nellie, describing the plans. The latter were received safely, and I shall send them back by this mail. Of course I was greatly interested, and sorry when I came to the end. I think you have done very well, very well indeed and I have no alterations to suggest, even were any permissible. I hope we shall be permitted many happy summers in the first home that in any human sense can be called our own. As regards the desk, the one I now write at is 4f. 2in. x 2f. 4 in. I do not find it large enough, and should think that from 5 to 6 feet long and 3½ to 4 wide would be better. The question of expense must be considered—barring that, the larger the better. You know my fancy for bright colors, therefore a brightish wood, oak or ash, would best please me, and I incline to think a dark cloth covering, of color not to show ink spots easily would be best. Above all no ingenious subdivisions. A few substantial roomy drawers suit my habits best. This desk is cut up into a number of trivial spaces, no one of which is good for anything. Of course the particulars of the desk must be subordinated to the general impression of the room. I shall not attempt to buy for the house, partly because I cant trust my judgment of materials, partly because I am too short of money. Villefranche entertaining, my dearest, and dentist's bill cut in pretty heavily. I also bought some wine for I find myself generally better in health and spirits for the use of a light white wine. As you must have noticed I do not feel the depression this cruise that I did last—owing partly, I trust, to spiritual growth but also doubtless to better physical condition. You must not let yourself exaggerate the annoyances of my position, nor Erben's actions. Affairs are bad enough, but he is not willfully disagreeable, nor do I think consciously malicious. Substantially, his action was malicious, uncalled for, and his statements in my belief false; it does not follow that he is a liar. He is a man naturally impatient and self satisfied, who has never controlled himself—consequently, in old age, he has no self control whatever. When pleased, or his sympathies aroused, he is genial and impresses people as kindly; when annoyed by the merest trifle, he is intolerable, and the cause of his annoyance is often not only trivial but unreasonable. He is loud mouthed, blustering & profane. You may imagine my mental attitude to a man of that sort—for the uncontrolled person is simply a big baby. They say his wife never attempts to withstand him, but simply allows his fits of sulks and bluster to blow over. What Madame de Robiglio refers to I dont know. Whether he talked against me, or whether she refers to difficulies with Nice people, I cannot say. You need not make a martyr of me, though I am most grateful for your confidence & sympathy. Wives sometimes are more unjust to those who injure their husbands than who hurt themselves. A little à Kempis might aid you, as it has me. Much he writes is to my mind overstrained, but you can scarcely read ten pages without finding words that go straight to the root of feelings that nature arouses under provocation such as we are receiving. And I am thankful in reviewing my feelings and conduct to recognize that I have, not so much controlled myself as been lifted up and controlled to show a degree of patience and calmness I should not have expected. This experience has been well worth the trial—le jeu a bien valu la chandelle. In thinking over the present distress I have recalled my feelings in the winter of 1888-9, when the College seemed hopelessly gone—yet see the result, the big building on Coaster's, and life, albeit struggling still, despite all Ramsay's and Bunce's machinations. By the way, what an odd perversion of facts to attribute that $100,000 to him. Whitney got it, as *we* all know, for Goodrich, with the evident purpose of clenching the nails in my Collegiate tomb. Really, men will say anything. I am sorry Stockton should be so bitter, but you must remember he has been in a state of contention, which he could not avoid, for three years, & with men more powerful than he and of very nasty dispositions. Bitterness comes easily so, but if a Christian man, as he is, will read a little à Kempis he will find much help. There is of course plenty in the Bible, but when you are weak the dilution that comes through a fellow sinner seems to suit even better. I am distressed about Fred. Poor fellow; now is the time wife & children come in—and one says heartily—it is indeed not good for man to be alone. I fear too that Fred, without meaning it, has by his mistaken abstention from church etc lost touch with God, who stands by one so marvellously under such trials as the present. "His (not our) faithfulness & truth shall be my shield and buckler." I shall write him again. I greatly question the Secy's seeing anything except through Ramsay's spectacles, and so far as man goes have few expectations. Put not your trust in princes, but I rejoice with trembling to find how my mind

[244]

keeps going beyond and behind them all to One whom I can trust. I say again, though bitter, the experience is worth all, and more than all it costs. I sent off yesterday a letter of congratulation & welcome to Bishop Hall, and mentioned your address to him, in case he should get to N.Y. Of course he is not likely to have time to call. I hope *Nelson* is by this in your hands —I wonder how you will like it. It is the driest period of his life and career, but my manner of treatment can be realized from it. I think somewhat of offering Mr. Brown to see it, & express an opinion on its general plan. I have just glanced over your letter written on Helen's unused pages. I cant imagine anything so base as conspiracy such as the others fancy—I may be too guileless but I cannot believe it. Nor did I realize that I put on any airs of superior knowledge—so perhaps both surmises may be true. Tell Matthews that we also know enough to come in when it rains, and also, and better, to stay out when it rains if any useful end is to be served. As regards the Cottage name I am at a loss, but I do not like One Acre—dont be in a hurry, better wait nameless for a while than hastily equipped with a bad name. I want to caution you about underpaying your letters—I have to pay *double* what you fail to put on, so last week I had tenpence English to pay. I find Smyrna uninteresting, the only thing I really find amusing are the long strings of camels filling up the narrow streets, walking with that long gandering strut in single file each attached to his leader, and No 1. to a little donkey not much bigger than my thumb. We have however had lovely weather for a few days past—real spring sunshine. I found at the Club a series of articles on the dissatisfaction of daughters with the narrowness of their life and interests, & as I read I could not but feel how providentially we have been guided, for the desires of the girls seem to be summed up in the wish to be somebody, having some interest and doing some work, with an individuality of their own not merely merged in the family. I cannot but think our girls must feel that that is what we have been trying to do for them. 8 P.M. We leave here tomorrow, 1 P.M. for a place on the south coast of Asia Minor, thence to Alexandretta & Beirut to be in Alexandria about the 21st. I shall close here for tonight adding a few words tomorrow. I enclose an absurdly Frenchy letter from our hostess at Villefranche Mme. Pollonnais. She gave me a book by herself[1] and I felt I could do no less than send her a *Farragut*.

March 11, 8 A.M.

Ten months on board today. We leave about 1 P.M. bound down the Syrian coast (but I see I have said this). Now put away any bitterness in your heart, dont trouble about the motives of others, and indeed since

---

1. Amélie Pollonnais, *A travers les mansardes et les écoles*. Illustré par Menta. Paris, 1886.

nothing now is to be *done*,[2] as far as possible dismiss the matter from your mind. If I have the right, my vindication will come in time. Goodbye again. Love to the dear children.

[P.S.] I wish you would send Taylor your copy of my rejoinder to Erben's report, asking him to send it to you again.

To Ellen Evans Mahan

Mersin, Turkey, March 14, 1894 [LC]

Dearest Deldie: Helen will excuse this taking the place of a letter to her which I have not had time to write, and I hear a mail goes from this little place today. I shall say nothing except that I am well and very tired. This is the seaport of Tarsus, St. Paul's city, you will find it in the northeast corner of the Levant, but on the south shore of Turkey in Asia—not far from Alexandretta. That is, you will find it, if it be on the map, which I doubt. Good bye. I will write to Henny at length, when I can—but I am up so much as never to be better than half awake. Love to all.

To Helen Evans Mahan

Alexandretta, Syria, March 16, 1894 [NWC]

My darling Henny: I sent mamma two lines from our last port, which may or may not reach her before this does you. My last long letter, to her, was from Smyrna, which we left on Sunday last, the 11th, at about 2 P.M. We passed through, or by, many places and names familiar enough to all of us who have read much of ancient history, however cursorily— Chios and Samos and Rhodes the coasts of Asia Minor etc. The most interesting to me, both in itself and from the attending conditions, was the island of Patmos, in which St. John was a prisoner when he saw the vision in the Revelations. I was called just before daybreak by the officer of the deck, to say that there was a steamer's white light, very bright, nearly ahead. As I have to go on deck when steamers are met, and my clothes were on, I got up almost immediately, and then I saw a light, hanging apparently, a very little above the horizon, as brilliant and big in appearance as a large

---

2. In the background, things were still being done. On this date, John M. Brown wrote to Charles S. Fairchild that he had no influence with Congressman Cummings, but would try to exert some with other members of the House Naval Committee.

electric street light. The officer said, "I am sorry I woke you, Captain, but it came in sight so suddenly, I could not do otherwise—it is the morning star." The words flashed at once in my mind—almost the last in the Bible—our Lord's—"I am the Root and the Offspring of David, and the bright and Morning Star." It was thus rising—if not immediately over Patmos, as I think it was—over one of the same group lying within a mile or two. The lustre and apparent size, and the suddenness of the rising, all due to the extraordinary lucidity of the air, conveyed to my mind, as never before, what the force of the image must have been to St. John, who must often have seen exactly what I was then gazing on. Our course from Smyrna led us continually among the isles of the Grecian Archipelago, until Monday afternoon about four, when we passed the north end of Rhodes, and soon after struck the South Coast of Asia Minor, where are the ancient Lycia and Cilicia—St. Paul's native land. The islands are not beautiful except with a certain severe and abrupt beauty—rising sheer and craggy straight from the blue water, scarce an offlying rock breaking the immense depth of the latter. We were wholly within the Turkish line, and misgovernment keeps the whole region poor, while centuries of mismanagement leave the people with little hope, or even desire, for better things. The slopes being great, I suppose there is little soil—here and there we saw places of more gradual decline, and even approaching plain country. These were often well cultivated and more beautiful—as man's hand generally, not always, makes Nature. There remains always, however, the incomparable clarity of the air and the brilliant blue of the Medn. sea and sky, which would enrich any landscape; and we were favored with perfect conditions from Smyrna to Mersin. The latter place, though said to have 6000 inhabitants is a mere strip of buildings, some two streets deep, lying along an open bay about eighty miles west of this Alexandretta. In itself, its chief interest is as the sea port now, and probably in olden times, of Tarsus, St. Paul's city. We were there two days, from Wednesday morning to Thursday (last) night, and I did not go ashore until yesterday afternoon, when several of us accepted the offer of the railroad manager, and took a special train to Tarsus. The latter is now merely a dirty, tumble down, Turkish city, under which lie the remains of the streets and buildings in which the childhood and youth of St. Paul were passed. Of those nothing is to be seen, except possibly one Roman archway, still standing, though a wreck in appearance. The new town is, however, built largely of stones quarried from the old ruins, and therefore much of its materials is probably contemporary with the Apostle. But when you lift your eyes from the ground, you see in all directions the striking features of the landscape amid which he grew up—the broad Cilician plain—fertile then as now—the steep and lofty hills of the first range from the coast (Anti-Taurus) and beyond them rising far higher the Taurus mountains, rising I suppose to 8,000 feet

[247]

and now deep clad in snow for 3000 from the top. These Turkish towns have not in themselves a redeeming feature, dirty, tumble-down, uncared for, but the people and animals amuse me. We are all familiar with engravings of Mussulmans—the turbans, flowing robes etc etc. but we do not realize the bright yet tawdry colors, the general shabbiness, raggedness & dirt. As far as I can see, those who keep themselves in good condition wear European garments, except the usual fez, and possibly the shoes. A string of camels too is an invariable delight, their long awkward stride, the gandering motion of the head and neck, as they crane their face and nose from side to side, & above all the almost infinitesimal donkey who usually heads & sometimes also closes the procession, of ten or a dozen of the slow-moving, awkward brutes. Each is attached to his predecessor by a chain & No 1 is fast to the jackass. But when all is said, one soon wearies—for the novelty quickly passes, while the dirt remains. This is the most out of the way part of the station—we shall get no mail till we reach Alexandria probably a week hence. How long we will be there remains to see, but we hope to turn westward thence, and the Admiral expects to be in Malta about April 10. I have little or no personal news, and shall get out your letters now to see if they need answer. By the way, how does your singing come on? I have looked over your last letter & find nothing that wants reply. I have answered about the house at Quogue etc. I am doing nothing and see no hope of doing anything literary. I dont suppose the Secy wished to paralyze my activity, but he has done so effectively; as for Ramsay, his right hand man, I have little doubt that he considers that result positively a happy one. And now good bye. I shall send this ashore to take its chance & probably not write again until Alexandria, for I dont think anything would be thereby gained. Love to mamma & the two rapscallions.[1]

To Ellen Evans Mahan

Beirut, Syria, March 18, 1894 [LC]

Dearest Deldie: I wrote you a line from Mersin, and Helen quite a long letter from Alexandretta—both which, I shrewdly suspect, are on board a French steamer which has followed us down, and arrived here shortly after us this P.M. The present writing, I understand will catch a mail leaving here tomorrow for Alexandria, direct, and so may outstrip the

1. Mahan enclosed a picture of Tarsus, on the back of which he wrote: "The view of the town is worthless. Throw out the minars [minarets], all but one or two, and add indefinite dirt and squalor, it may give a remote idea—but the landscape—especially the foreground range of hills & the snow covered background conveys a very good general idea."

others. I know not, like the old woman in the train, I ask questions and
dont understand the replies. We left Alexandretta yesterday & had rather
a rough night down. As usual I was up all night—though only occasionally
out of the cabin. I hope our dear laddie will not be such a fool to take up
this absurd profession. Of course I am very sleepy after the experience. It
is a wonder to me I bear it so well. I am cross and irritable next day and
somewhat nervous; but I usually get a good sleep and then am all right. At
Smyrna, unluckily, my long night was broken by an accident occurring
& from this I did not regain my composure for days.[1] It is a profession, now,
of wretched frivolities and banalities such as I should most deeply regret
any intelligent boy, whom I cared for, taking up. I am hungry for letters—
none for a week and will get none till next Friday—Good Friday—if we then
are happily in Alexandria.

Goodbye dearest, Always lovingly. Love for the children.

                                                        March 19, 8 A.M.
Closing for the mail. Well.

To Ellen Evans Mahan

                        USS *Chicago*, At sea, March 23, 1894 [LC]

Dearest Deldie: Our Levant trip leaves me literally at sea as regards my
letters. I have sent off three since leaving Smyrna, two short ones to you
and one to Helen. Where they went and how they have fared I know
not. Tomorrow we expect to be in Alexandria, where a fortnight's mail
should await us. Clover also is believed to be expecting us there. I shall be
glad of the change, though the results may disappoint me; but as I had no
hand in seeking it, I am hopeful. The present incumbent is a good seaman,
very diligent and hardworking—but very dull—forty in a class of nearly
70—slow, and forgetful at times, and a rough somewhat resentful manner
of speech when I interfere. Between him and the admiral (who perhaps
looks on me as I do the other) my position is unusually unpleasant, for I
have been used to efficient executives & smooth relations with every one.
Well, both will change in six months, for the admiral retires about Sept.
5. I have no news for you. None of the Levantine ports possessed interest
for me—the look the smell, the dirt is more than an equal drawback against
the novelty that soon passes. I am almost glad that I have not seen Jerusalem.

> We have a vision of our own.
> Ah! why should we undo it?
>   (Wordsworth)

---

1. *See* Mahan to Erben, March 8, 1894.

Today is lovely—real old *Potosi* weather. Do you remember how that ran, day after day, in the trade winds? This is the very ditto. Blue sky, blue sea, jolly breeze—not too much although the cabin is rising and falling uncomfortably for a sickly stomach. I want by the way that you should write to Comd. C. M. Thomas U.S.S. *Bennington*, Mare Island and enclose him 70 cents in two cent stamps. In sending me 100 francs he sent a cheque for $20, which is 70 cents too much.

Alexandria Easter Day.

We arrived here yesterday forenoon, darling, and my heart was rejoiced, not only by a large mail of arrears but also to know that you were all well. The dates were up to March 5, your last. I deplore this frequent outbreak of gout, first wrist, then foot—should you not get advice? or might it not be well to take a month of baths at Richfield—say in that month of broken time, June. What you have so far is not bad but it may need attention & you cannot well be more prudent in your eating than you now are. I am glad you refrained your lips from speaking Erben's war record to Ireland.[1] I have the feeling that God's protection on which alone we rely may be withdrawn if we revenge ourselves. Do not, however, put too much faith in what the Secy says, or will do. It is always hard for a junior to be righted against a senior. As yet he has not acted, to my knowledge, and Ramsay will very likely undo Lodge's work. It is not very material. I promptly asked full investigation to which some reply must be made. If not investigated, the result will depend upon professional opinion, which will divide into two camps, according to its prejudices or sympathies, and the final outcome will probably not be far from the truth. Meanwhile let this, and our suffering at separation convince us more and more of the advisability of retiring as soon as may be. I feel at times unhappy at this loss of time, and I have felt very much the monotony and lack of interest since we left Naples. I scarcely realized how much the Schiffs and my other acquaintances did for me in Villefranche. I shall take up going ashore again for my walk, and I hope that the new executive, Clover, may prove one who will enable me to feel that I can leave things greatly in his hands. This Gillpatrick could not do. He is a good seaman, very diligent and hardworking—faithful—but very dull and slow. Much was neglected, and officers of *all* services agree that the captain cannot bring his ship up to the mark with an ineffective executive. The faults Erben found were mainly of a character that Gillpatrick should have corrected. They were often trivial, they did not affect the actual efficiency of the ship, and to say she was discreditable was a gross exaggeration. It was, moreover, most unfair, and jaundiced, to look wholly upon unimportant lapses, and overlook, will-

---

1. This may have been a bit of private scandal. Erben's Civil War record in L. R. Hamersly, *The Records of Living Officers of the United States Navy and Marine Corps* (1898) indicates honorable service. Ireland was Lyle's tutor.

fully or otherwise, the positive good work done. But Gillpatrick did not pervade the organization of the ship, as he should; & the trouble was not in his industry, but in his capacity. He is a dull, heavy man — voilà tout. Erben said to me frequently "G. does not help you, as he ought"; but I thought he appreciated, to use Goodrich's phrase, that the captain may do his best, "the executive officer sets the pace." I am sorry for G., but for myself perhaps Clover will put me at some sort of leisure. As it is I am on the strain continually, to provide against oversights the Ex. should save me. Of course you will not say this, for it is G.'s misfortune not his fault. Poor Lyle! I remember my earache of 8 years ago & sympathize with him, but happily it is over now. Tell him he is an absurd brat with his cards. I was very pleased to get his letter and much appreciated the compliment Mr. Dodworth paid by selecting him to learn the new dance. It shows at this early age that he has perseverance, which in his case has overcome great natural awkwardness— and I trust this will encourage him to equal diligence in more important matters. I was amused at Bunce's going back on my books—though it is really no laughing matter to see prejudice carried so far. I can hardly yet admit to myself that I have enemies, personal or official, so set to do me harm. 8 P.M. I have hastily decided, dearest, to go to Cairo tomorrow, and as I have had two bad nights I am going to bed now. I feel great need of a change, and intend to be away three days. Love to all.

To Ellen Kuhn Mahan

Alexandria, Egypt, March 29, 1894 [LC]

My darling Miss Nellikin: I mailed a letter to mamma very soon after our arrival here, on the 24th, but for the life of me I cannot remember what I said in it. I either am, or seem to be, so hurried & preoccupied in these present days that almost everything slips out of my mind and I can now only pray continually that God may soon relieve me from cares and duties which I discharge with so much labor and trouble. On Sunday I decided very hastily to go next day to Cairo, partly because I thought a party was going with whom I could enjoy myself, and partly because I felt the immediate need of change. So I started the next morning by the 9 A.M. train, the members of the party upon whom I most counted having meantime changed their minds. The ride is about three hours and a half, but our engine broke down about five miles from Cairo, and we did not arrive there till 1.30. The country is as flat as one's hand, and flatter—much like New Jersey on the old road, only not nearly so heavily wooded. It is in fact the Delta of the Nile, which begins I believe about Cairo. The land, which is now being ploughed looks very rich & heavy—but the huts and hamlets in which the peasantry live are almost all merely mud walls and covered with corn-stalks and straw. It does not rain often or much, nor is it ever very cold, so that they do not need the protection from weather essential to our people. They are mostly of a dark chocolate color, not shiny black like our negroes nor with flat noses nor woolly hair—and the Eastern style of dress the flowing robes and turbans, the colors of which are often garish give life and animation to the scene. I puzzled sometime to tell the difference in dress between men and women, and finally concluded that, besides the head gear, it consisted mainly in the fact that the women wore trousers and the men went bare-legged. Then the women wear a cloth or shawl like a hood instead of the turban. We were very unfortunate in our weather, as we have been in port since leaving Naples. On Monday it blew very hard in the afternoon raising clouds of dust, and we found very little to interest in the places we were then taken to see. The most amusing incident was that we passed a little donkey foal, about as big as Jomini, except his head and ears which were huge, and the little beggar, losing sight of his mother, trotted after us hard as his tiny legs would suffer him. It caused a good deal of fun and we had at last to stop the carriage to enable the farmer to overtake him. The country is so dusty that a high wind envelops it in a cloud like a light fog through which it is impossible to see far. Happily the following morning, Tuesday, the wind had fallen, and with it the dust, so we had one fine day for the drive to the Pyramids and the Sphinx, about nine miles from the city, and the great wonder of those parts. We started about nine in the morning and were away until nearly sundown, lunching at a hotel, quite modern at the foot of the monuments. I could not but smile as I remembered how Napoleon said to his army "Soldiers from the summit of yonder pyramids forty centuries behold your actions." Now their forty centuries look down equally unmoved on British and American tourists with their bottled beers, brandy and soda, puggarees like towels tied around their hats and other outlandish costumes—pretty girls, sour old maids, grizzled bachelors & fin de siècle young men & women, all assembled to astound the 40 Centuries, which to do them justice show no particular amazement. On the way out we stopped at the Museum, an immense building, filled with the innumerable finds that have been made by excavation in all parts. Of course I cannot begin to indicate to you the smallest part of the whole, & can only say that what most fascinated me was what bore a clear impression of the human living being of those far away days. There was one mummy of a woman who had been dead near three thousand years—but who had not been "laid out" before embalming—the process evidently having been applied to the body just as it lay upon the breath departing. The limbs lay loosely, not extended and the head, instead of being with face turned up, lay upon the side, the mouth slightly open. One seemed to be present at the death scene; and, ghastly as mummies usually are, the human interest of the whole with me outweighed the repulsion. Then in one large domed room there were arranged, lying in the original coffins, the mummies of some fifteen or twenty ancient Pharaohs, all which with many lesser persons were found eight or ten years ago piled in a sequestered cave near the upper Nile, where they had lain concealed for centuries. Among these is the coffin & mummy of Rameses II, the Pharaoh of "the Oppression" as he is supposed to be, the one from whom Moses fled into the land of Midian. You may suppose I was much interested in this person, who was a mighty man in his day, celebrated among the Greeks as Sesostris—a great conqueror; and I was amazed to find that the face that was alive some 1500 years B.C., was so preserved that its features could be distinctly realized. The cartilage of the nose even was quite perfect, and we could see that he had had a high Roman nose very marked and thin, that the whole face was clear and severe in outline, the frame tall slight and gaunt, and the neck extraordinarily long. The whole appearance of the man was that commonly associated with an intellectual, despotic, ascetic—like, we may suppose, Cardinal Richelieu. I was also interested to see on some mummy cases, much later, only two thousand years old, during the Greek ascendancy, the portraits of the dead, one of whom a woman of 35 was quite handsome. This, and another of a girl of 16, were quite life like and artistic—others were very wooden.

March 30

I must now draw my letter to a close, my darling child. I am so harrassed [*sic*] and driven in these days that I find time with difficulty and my trouble is increased now by the very bad weather which detains me on board ship. Except Sunday we have not had a decent day for boating. I must go on to say that I was not much impressed with the Great Pyramid. It is doubtless a huge, grand mass of stone but I did not care for it. An English officer, however, suggested that it grows upon one, which may perhaps be so. There is a passage about four feet high which leads first down and then up to a chamber left in the interior. Three of our officers entered and they describe the air within as astonishingly hot & oppressive. One of them went in alone with the guide, and when in the chamber which is, I believe only fifteen or twenty feet square, the candle went out. He had to sit still in the dark till the guide got another candle, probably for ten minutes—for, though a smoker he had with him no matches. He says he never knew what darkness was before, hundreds of feet of masonry on all sides between him and the light. He held his white straw hat close to his face but could not see it. I must tell you that I have received here the photos of the family and Jomini, as well of the streets & apartment. The latter I find good, and it was a great pleasure to look again upon even the shadow of home—but I did not think those of the persons good. To begin with, why should you all hold your heads *down*. Jommy is tolerable, but not quite like him. Those of myself also came. I think they are horrors, but that may be only wounded vanity. I had a letter a few days ago from Rosie Schiff—much to my surprise. I have not yet answered—nor do I see when I am to find time unless at sea. I am sorry for you all having to part with dear mamma, but I suppose by this time she will be back with you all again.

Love to all [etc.].

To Hilary A. Herbert

USS *Chicago*, Alexandria, March 30, 1894 [NA]

Sir:

1. Replying to the Department's (Office of the Assistant Secretary) letter of March 7, 1894, (no number), relative to the painting of the bottom of the *Chicago*, and the endorsement of the Bureau of Construction and Repair, stating as its opinion that International anti-corrosive and anti-fouling paint should not have been put on over McInnes, I have to state that this was done by order of the Commander-in-Chief.

To Ellen Evans Mahan

Alexandria, March 31, 1894 [LC]

Dearest Deldie: I sent off quite a long letter to Nellie yesterday, but as we are to start tomorrow for Malta, according to a very bad habit into which the admiral is falling of sailing on Sunday, I will drop you just a line of my latest news and of my loving thought of you and all. I am much moved by this last sorrow that has befallen poor Rosie, and send the enclosed rather as a token of my sympathy and affection than for any help it is likely to be to her. If your mother continues to feel as she does it might be unpleasant to write direct, besides I have no time for a letter. There is nothing new. I am sorry to have made so short a stay here, but glad to be again travelling westward. We shall be pretty steadily on the go, as the admiral wishes to be in Gibraltar by the 13th of April—a distance of 2000 miles—besides two or three days at Malta. I detest this hurry; besides in these short stays so much time is occupied in official visiting that little is left for any enjoyment. It is too bad to send to the Mediterranean a man absolutely without sympathy or interest in the objects which make that sea worth visiting, and utterly selfish as regards the wishes or likes of others—but I am not a fair judge for him & have no right to judge him at all. The wardroom has been giving a dinner to the captn. & offrs. of the British ship *Edgar*, my friend Captn. Henderson, and I have just stolen away to write these lines. I dined with him last night, and after dinner to my utter astonishment he proposed my health in a most flattering speech speaking of my books and my distinguished reputation. He told me that the revival of interest in their navy and its fostering and right direction was mainly due to the books which had come out just in the nick of time—in fact, he said, "We owe to them the £3,000,000 just voted for for the increase of the navy." All the guests present were English, except Potter, our flag lieutenant. The British Consul-General & Adm. Blomfield,[1] who holds some position ashore, both spoke of them—the latter made a special call upon me & invited me to lunch tomorrow—which of course I cant accept. Sunday Morning 8 A.M. I shall close now although we do not sail till 1 P.M. as the day will be full. It is trying thus to lose the one day of rest. Pray for me, dear, that if God will this seagoing may soon cease for me. Love to the children.

To Ellen Evans Mahan

Malta, April 5, 1894 [LC]

My dearest Deldie: I should be writing this time to the dear laddie, but there is going to be here so much hurry that I shall not, probably, be able to do more than scratch a few lines to you, and try to get a little more time to write him as nice a letter as he deserves, for his to me have latterly been very nice and much improved in handwriting. I should probably have begun a letter to him on our way from Alexandria, but we had very disagreeable weather—not positively bad but rainy and uneasy. We arrived last night about 10 p.m., when I found waiting for me yours of March 16—and this morning Lyle's of March 18. The admiral has announced his intention to sail tomorrow evening—whether he will do so or not remains to be seen, but in any event you can imagine there is no room for either rest or interest in this rushing headlong into port and then headlong out—dirty from head to foot when you arrive, barely time to clean up to get dirty again, & paying official visits instead of seeing the sights, for which no adequate time is afforded. However, I have settled in my mind that the present is for us a time of tribulation—sifting—for that is the meaning of the word; and I shall endeavor so to pass through it as not to miss the spiritual profit. Sometimes, certainly, I feel depressed, but not for long. A letter from Stockton telling me of the order of consolidation. I shall give no notice,

---

1. Sir Richard Massie Blomfield was Deputy Controller General of Egyptian Ports and Lighthouses from 1887, and later Controller General.

[255]

but in their place I should, after a decent interval of compliance with the new orders, ask for detachment. Personally, while I cannot but regret the defeat of my policy, I feel some relief that my obligations to the College are now ended. It is, however, clearly my duty not in any way to influence the decision of Taylor or Stockton either directly or indirectly. Do you therefore hold your peace. The admiral has just told me that he wishes to get to the English Channel—or to Antwerp—I cant quite make out which —towards May 1. A little early for comfort. I have had a note from Sir George Clarke, & am to dine with him at 7:30 P.M. today—at his mess, for his family is in England.

April 6

I think I had better close and send this today. Last evening upon re-turning from my walk with Clarke I found yours of Good Friday and Helen's of the Tuesday before both which mentioned the sad news of Dr. Parker's death.[1] His has been a noble life. I shall of course write to her, but being ignorant of her address shall have to send it under cover to you. You mention in one of your letters what Thomas said about Erben's in-terference. You may be sure I have no intention of making any row. I know too well the impossibility of a junior making head against a senior to de-liberately choose that line of action. I assure [you] I fully share your de-sire for the end of this separation. Since we went to the Levant some of the old *Wachusett* weariness has visited me. I trust it may not get the upper hand —for I am afraid that there is even a chance of our remaining out next winter—a contingency for which I was till lately wholly unprepared. Let us not, however, borrow trouble over it. We will be separated just as long as God wills and no longer, and today's burden should not be increased by speculations about tomorrow's. Goodbye dearest. Love to all.

[P.S.]   We dont sail till Sunday, the 8th.

To Ellen Evans Mahan

Malta, April 8, 1894 [LC]

We are to sail today, my own beloved, maintaining our bad and wholly unnecessary habit of Sunday work. I mailed you a letter day before yester-day, and so shall only drop a line to say I am well, and enclosing one for poor

---

1. Stevens Parker, rector of St. John's Episcopal Church in Wilmington, Delaware. He was the husband of Mary (Maime) Lewis Parker, Milo Mahan's step-daughter.

Mrs. Parker. I think I have material enough for one fairly interesting letter for the laddie, which I shall try to write on our way to Algiers; but in truth it seems to me I become more and more busy (with trivialities) each succeeding month. Time is harder and harder to find. It is partly due to a kind of harassed feeling, which coexists with a general cheerfulness of feeling. There is no news, beyond the accounts of Malta which I reserve for my next, to Lyle. People have been very nice to us, and complimentary to me. Goodbye dearest; love to all the dear children.

To Ellen Evans Mahan

Algiers, Algeria, April 13, 1894 [LC]

My darling Wife: I received Hart's telegram conveying your mother's death last night, about ten. I had fallen asleep in my chair, according to a bad habit I permit myself now and was awakened by the orderly entering. I own that with all the surmises that ran through my head & caused my hands to shake, she, the most fragile in health of all was the last name to occur to me. I wish with all my heart that I were with you at this time, for although you have in the children much to comfort you, and they are of an age to do so, still the severance of a life long tie is always keenly felt, and one would fain have around all those that are still left. The admiral made a miscalculation about sending our mail here, so I will have no letter before Gibraltar—say next Wednesday—and my last from you is dated Good Friday, three weeks ago today. You were then in 34th St., and had before mentioned your mother's confusion of speech, but there was in it nothing unprecedented & I had taken no alarm. I shall write to dear Rosie today. She will I suppose feel more keenly than almost any one else, and particularly from the strange aversion your mother had latterly taken to her; but time is merciful and there can be little doubt that the alternate relief will be great, for the strain had gone beyond her strength. For yourself I cannot have much to say. Now she is gone you will happily remember more vividly the times before illness had made her less reasonable—time softens all outlines and all severities. You have not, I think anything with which to reproach yourself towards her, & she was always the fond, if peremptory, mother toward you. I had just finished a letter to Lyle, but knowing his fondness for his grannie I closed it without allusion to her death. It went by this morning's mail. This will take tomorrow's, and I will try to leave here a few lines on Sunday. We sail for Gibraltar on Monday, the 16th. I am extremely pressed and I think overworked, but trust that ere long God will lighten the load. For your mother I cannot but think it is better so, her life might at any moment now have become a burden to herself as well as others. Love to the children—especially the laddie who will perhaps most miss the one that is gone. With fondest love, I am always, my dearest one, Your attached husband.

To Ellen Evans Mahan

Algiers, April 14, 1894 [LC]

I wrote yesterday to you, my darling Wife, and also to poor dear Rosie; but as you are much in my mind just now I write another line to leave here tomorrow—the more so as I imagine Algiers may be in closer communication than Gibraltar where we expect to arrive on Wednesday. Today I imagine you all to have been to Philadelphia, though I cannot recall the name of the cemetery where your father & Caddie were laid—perhaps at this moment about 4 P.M. you may just be returning thence. I have no news whatever to give you of myself nor of the ship—I have simply cancelled the one or two invitations that I had accepted in the port, as well as one I had given, neither act involving any great sacrifice. I wish ever so much I could be with you, for though I do not apprehend undue or morbid grief on your part, I know that the presence of those upon whom you can depend is very welcome at a moment which, when every deduction is made, cannot but be one of great sorrow. The oversight by which our mails were not ordered here leaves me, as I told you with no news later than March 23, so the message by the telegram found me quite unprepared. We have no clue as to our future, whether we shall go home in the summer, or the fall, or remain over the winter. I cannot but hope the latter, for I feel, as one of the girls said, it would be better to see you all again, even if I soon left again to finish the routine two years. You must turn over in your mind whether we can manage to allow me to take six months or a year's leave of absence, after the sea service is over. The pay is only 2800 per an, but I estimate that by undivided attention to *Nelson* I could complete it in little over six months and that it would sell 2000 copies at (probably) 75 cents a copy to us. This of course is not certain, but there would be the further advantage that it would renew my ties to literature, and be in the direct line of the future I propose to myself. Furthermore, I despair of ever doing any good work unless fully at leisure to allow my mind to steep in the subject. I cannot take it up and lay it down; and it was the recognition of this fact—that either *Nelson* would crowd the ship out of my head, or the ship *Nelson*, or else, most likely of all, that both would alike suffer—which determined me to drop the book, though bitterly against my will. I think probably I shall have to ask you to send me $100 by the time we get to England. I am struggling ahead again, but I want to be able to take a fortnight's leave in London, for I need rest. The burden of entertaining is unavoidable. And now goodbye again darling. Love to the children.

Sunday, April 15

Well.

To Helen Evans Mahan

Gibraltar, April 19, 1894 [NWC]

My darling Helen: We received two or more mails upon our arrival here yesterday—never having been sent to Algiers. Along with two or more from mamma I have yours of Easter Day & April 1—but where are Miss Nell's? Lyle also has sent me two, for which I thank him very much, as I do you. You seem to have been having a famous succession of sprees— it does me good to hear of them—and I am glad to know that this little burst of innocent & healthful dissipation was enjoyed before poor Grannie's death came to put a temporary stop to your gaieties—not that I believe that these incidental bereavements should be allowed long to cloud the lives of survivors, but there is a certain element of decent observance which un- derlay the exaggerated mournings of our ancestors. I should be sorry to see you going to large entertainments or marked gaieties during the short remainder of the spring. It gives me also much satisfaction that you can see the humor of things. Your description of our dear McCarty Little was ex- cellent & brought him right before me—you caught the characteristic traits very well, and 'hit off' to perfection. A person without a good sense of humor is not half developed, and is sure to be deficient in sympathy [with] the most Christlike of all the natural traits of mankind—not to speak of the absurdities into which one is often betrayed by the want of humor. You are quite right in saying that most people are more or less funny if one only has an eye to the fact. I have very little news for you—in fact I may say none at all. Nothing has happened nor seems likely to happen. We are to leave here tomorrow night for Lisbon, where we are likely to remain a fortnight & I hope even three weeks; for these modern ships, with their coal and their many requirements need an occasional long rest, and we have been on the steady go ever since we left Naples. From Lisbon it is intended that we go to England—to a place called Gravesend, on the Thames, about 35 minutes by rail from London. It is my intention then to ask for two weeks leave—for so only do I see my way to any rest. If I go away for the better part of a day, I dont get the ship off my mind, and simply find arrears of work on my return—whereas when I am away for a spell my daily work is done by others. A disgusting rumor has reached us that the ship is to be sent to Rio Janeiro and thence to the U.S. to be home in June. The latter of course would delight me—but I have no mind to the Southern trip. I scarcely expect it to happen, but it is a case of who knows. It certainly would be most improper, for the engines are in no state for so long a trip.[1] If this does not come off, and we go to England, we will after a stay there of probably not less than a month, go to Antwerp where there is an exposition this year. I dont care much for the latter, but I should much like to visit the Low Countries, where I have never been. The drawback is that, although I have read Motley's[2] famous works, I have no associations with the region & little sympathy with the Dutch character. I cannot as yet help you to a name for the Quogue cottage—and can only suggest not to be in too great a hurry. Like some infants it might have a temporary nom de guerre pending the final settlement. A delay is far better than fastening upon it some appellation we should afterwards regret. I wish, my dear Child, you could just conceive the hurry and drive I am always in here, and particularly since leaving Nice. It has been ever so much harder for me to write letters, not only on account of want of time, but from sheer distraction of spirit. When I have anything to say—business—I can sit down & write it, but for an ordinary chit-chat letter the difficulty grows from day to day. I long eagerly for my release from one of the most disagreeable and arduous duties that I have ever known, but I shall have to possess my soul in patience for some time still. A letter from dear mamma has come since I began this. It is dated April 6, and mentions Grannie's increasing weakness, but without immediate apprehension. I trust Rosie got home before her death. As I said —no news. I had a very nice letter from Dr. Woolverton[3] by the mail. I enclose one I recd. here from Genl. Nicholson[4] of the British army, in Malta. I sat by him one night at dinner there & liked him very much. He is probably three or four years older than I. He had then, though I knew it not, recd. a telegram of his daughter's dangerous illness. She died two days later, having a little baby—she herself not yet nineteen. I sent him a short note of condolence, which drew out the enclosed. And now goodbye, dear Child. Love to all from your hurried and driven but always loving father.

[P.S.] April 20. Well.

---

1. The *Chicago*'s boilers had last been repaired by yard workers at Villefranche on January 17.
2. John Lothrop Motley.
3. Theron Woolverton had retired in 1891.
4. Stuart James Nicholson, commander of the Royal Artillery Brigade, Malta.

To Ellen Kuhn Mahan

My darling Miss Nellikin: What has become of you this very long time in which you have written me no letter. I dont know just how long it is but it must be several weeks. I have just received here the letters about Grannie's death and Cousin Emily's.[1] For the former I had been prepared by the telegram received in Algiers, nor would I have been greatly surprised had no such warning reached me, but the other almost stunned me, as indeed it must have all others, for there seems not to have been the faintest premonition. It is the most sudden death that has ever come within my experience. Aunt Lil's[2] of course was sudden, but then we had long known that it might happen—that her heart was weak. I see very little to soften the blow to Mr. Livingston—but the one child and she it is scarcely possible can begin to fill the place left by one so exceptionally bright and alive as Cousin Emily. I enclose a note for Mr. Livingston which I hope mamma will forward to him. Thank Lyle for his letter telling me of Grannie's death. I have since had one from mamma, written the previous day; and though I hope, I scarcely expect to hear again for two or three days more—till after the funeral. As this is our second visit to Lisbon I have not much to tell you about it now. They say we always arrive at a bad time, when the summer season is over, or the winter—never when either is at its height. It matters little to me, I haven't money enough to go in for everything, and so I prefer to save up for places where I may know people. I am glad to believe that we may now be in London during "the season," though whether I shall really enjoy it remains to be seen. I dont want to leave here until about May 10—but I fear we shall get away sooner. At Gravesend we shall have to be a month or more. We cannot even start across the Atlantic without certain repairs that will take that long—and we are by no means certain that we are to go home this summer, much to my disappointment. Nothing is fixed—but I hear Com. Ramsay wants to keep the *Chicago* here till next spring. It will be a great blow to me—but how happy we are to know that all these things are ordered for the best by One who knows far better than we. What would we otherwise do?

April 27

The weather here even is very cold—under 60 in the cabin—yet warm in the sun. It is to this condition of the climate I think is owing the sickness

---

1. Emily Evans Livingston, daughter of Mrs. A. T. Mahan's paternal uncle, William E. Evans; second wife of John H. Livingston and step-mother to his daughter, Katherine Livingston.
2. Lillian Evans, a younger sister of Mrs. A. T. Mahan.

ashore, which the doctors have announced is an epidemic of cholera mor-
bus—though our doctor says he never heard of that disease being epidemic.
It will decide our leaving here as soon as we can—probably on Wednesday
next, May 2. We are wholly without news. I go ashore for a walk, about 3
in the afternoon, returning about 6, and already feel the benefit of it, for
the place amuses me. In the East—Smyrna & Beirut, and in Alexandria even
I found little amusing, and could walk little. Algiers the weather was bad.
Lisbon has a further advantage in my eyes—it is all up and down hill—no
flat walking is equal to that.

2 P.M.

I am now going to close for the mail having really nothing more to say.
We have newspapers to April 14 but no letter for me. I am not however
surprised or disappointed—knowing how busy and painfully preoccupied
you must all have been in the days following Grannie's death. Give my
love to all and write soon to your loving father.

To Ellen Evans Mahan

Lisbon, April 29, 1894 [LC]

Dearest Deldie: I was rejoiced today to see again your handwriting
though but the scrap appended to Nellie's letter of the 16th. We have
had our letters rather irregularly here this time. You have been passing
through a very trying season, and I cannot but rejoice that it is now
over; for the prolongation of your mother's life under the conditions, in
which there seems to have been no possibility of change, could have been
only misery for her and exhaustion for all around. For Rosie the relief,
though she may not so regard it yet, must have been even more necessary
than for you. The case had become like that of my mother's last year, when
those who loved her best could scarcely desire her continuance here. You
will believe that I was struck aghast and dumb by the shocking news concerning Emily. There *is* a tragedy, without relief from the merely human
point of view. When his first wife died he was so young and his child, a baby
—at their present age there can be no prospect of any one filling Emily's
place so completely and satisfactorily as she did that of her predecessor.
Their life is broken up. I am sorry to hear that the Colgates are renting
their house in Quogue and Nellie thinks none of your pleasant friends of
last year will be down there. I suppose, however, there is good reason to

hope that the place has a future and that nice people will generally be found there—but I could wish a little more permanence, for I greatly desire our children to contract durable friendships. Is Mrs. Colgate's health the cause? Nell must remember her foolishness of last year and determine to go in for the society she finds around her. The week here has been singularly uneventful, except the scare about Cholerine. Yesterday our doctor satisfied himself, on grounds not to me convincing, that the epidemic is a mild form of true Cholera. This rests almost wholly upon the opinion of a Spanish physician, sent by his government, that the bacillus, which is admitted to exist, is the same as that of Cholera, but in an attenuated form. The Lisbon doctors say no—that it possesses distinct characteristics—but they admit the disease is abnormal and as yet give it no decisive name. The fact remains that there are scarcely any deaths, that the attacks are soon over & leave no bad results—all which the Spaniard attributes to the "attenuation," or debility, of the bacillus. However, our doctor recommends that we dont go ashore, except on duty, and excludes all uncooked food, which I feel chiefly in the deprivation of fresh butter. We cant get away until Thursday, on account of repairs to engines. We have a report, which you may have seen, in N.Y. *Herald*, that the *Chicago* will remain here till spring, without an admiral after Erben goes. Of course I dont relish this, but things turn out so different from what I expect that I dare not feel discontent, if it prove true. The thought occurred to me—"Possibly the Secy. may mean thus to evidence confidence in me, despite Erben's report," for it would certainly bear that construction. You may possibly not be surprised to learn that he never wrote that letter he said he would. It is a serious step thus directly to disavow a superior—and this other action would reach the end of justifying me without overt snub of Erben. I cannot believe that the latter's reputation as an officer is good. Certainly I do not consider him an officer, and the favorable impression made upon outsiders by his blustering manner is a singular evidence of the shallowness of men's judgments.

April 30

The Adm. has decided to remain till Friday the 4th and as I shall write again for that I will close here for the mail. I really have no news, and the sooner I get my love to you the better. For the present farewell. Love to children. Fondly.

[P.S.] The enclosed seems worth preserving—from N.Y. *Sun* of Jan. 1.[1]

---

1. Nothing in that issue of *The Sun* seems worth preserving. Its contents included: "Property Rights in Seals," "Kaiser Wilhelm's Policy," "Hopeless of Promotion—Gray-Bearded Lieutenants in the U.S. Artillery Service," and a lengthy political editorial on the coming year.

To Ellen Evans Mahan

USS *Chicago*, At sea, May 6, 1894 [LC]

Half-way across the Bay of Biscay, two days out from Lisbon, and hoping to be at Gravesend on Wednesday morning—such, most dearest Miss D., is about the size of things with us at this present writing. We have not had very pleasant weather, having a decided tendency to haze and fog much of the time, but in the English Channel and its neighborhood all are beggars for good weather and cannot be choosers. Up to an hour ago today has been mizzling and drizzling—pretty thick withal—recalling my favorite story from Marryat which you may perhaps remember, of the old British seaman entering the Channel from four years in the West Indies. As the fog shut down and the rain descended, he said, "Now this I call something like—none of your d-d blue skies." While thus disagreeably damp, we have to console ourselves with thinking that there is no high wind, and with the barometer steady near 30, a good chance of escaping the proverbial seas of the Bay. My last letter from you—any of you—is yours of April 20, which reached me at Lisbon on the 2d. twelve days. I can imagine how unutterably dreary and lonesome to poor Rose must be the hours spent now in the deserted apartment. I do not know for how long it was taken but suppose its lease expires on May 1. Perhaps she may then get off somewhere. Her going to Quogue suggested itself to me at once, but at this distance I thought best to make no suggestions to you. As you say, things shape themselves; we are often rather compelled to accept the solution which alone is practicable than the one we would ourselves choose. I should think the noise of the trains, to one in Rosie's condition would in May be too trying; but when the windows are closed I should doubt their annoying her.

Gravesend, May 9

We arrived today, darling, in fact got into the Thames last night, but the tide did not allow us to come up until this morning. I have received your letter and Helen's of the 24th and Lyle's of the 22d. H. mentions that you had two from me, but you only say that you had a "scrap" enclosing one for Maime Parker—the scrap seems to have made more impression than the two. You do not tell me how Lyle's drill turned out, which is really too bad, unless, as I hope, you are leaving for him the pleasure of chronicling a success. I was greatly pleased by his expression that he did not expect the prize of the best driller, but that he meant to try. If he sticks to that principle, he will do well and go far. Nelly must combat her tendencies to discouragement, and I am quite sure she will. Let her go in for friends at Quogue this summer—it will be a good discipline. The cards from Tiffany came all right —but were somewhat delayed by being addressed Mrs. Mahan. Stevens got an idea you were coming out. I am sorry you all judge Rosie Schiff so hardly —but whatever she be, sweet or sour, you may be very sure there are no attractions this side the water to keep me a moment longer than the Dept compel me to stay. To do Miss Rosie justice, while she is extremely civil and attentive to me, she has no unnatural preferences for elderly gentlemen and enjoys her flirtations with the young men to the full—nor are there any absurdities going on. I own I think the taste for Schley somewhat indiscriminating, but I believe women generally do like him, and he really is amusing. We have dropped, as always in England, into a crowd of kindly attentions. How far they will go remains to be seen—I fancy in my own case the bloom is off the lily, but if relegated to obscurity there will be compensations in more freedom of movement. Home and congenial work are the things I ever sigh for, and am more than ever convinced give all the happiness this earth has to bestow. I hope Taylor cherishes no hope of my going back to the College. It is not best for us to proclaim my intentions, but my purpose is fully formed not to accept the presidency under the present conditions. I dont *want* it under the best of terms, have had more than enough of it—but to be an immediate subordinate to Bunce & work under Ramsay's wet blankets and procrastination is certainly a choice to which nothing but dire necessity will reconcile me. I wrote to Taylor, in reply to his request, that I would deliver my old lectures on Strategy this year, if the *Chicago* went out of commission in time—but as for any other work I could not undertake it. My wish is to get a year's leave and at once take up my literary career on my return—but I shall make no such decision until you and I have taken sweet counsel together. I dont wonder the Torpedo people were disgusted—the thing is all wrong and will be worse under Bunce than under most people. My own relations with Bunce were always good, and they were, as you know particularly nice and very hospitable to me; but he is of the aggravating kind. Besides which I feel as if my reputation now forbade my accepting such subordination in my own line. If this seem to you overstrained, say so. I am glad to know, how glad you may imagine, that you are feeling strong again after your exhausting month. I know that my return would be a help, and did I not so earnestly long for it for my own sake, I should be eager that the ship might return this summer. We do not know how it will be. Do you think you do well to write with your hand to me? I fear for it, and I sometimes think I am cut short of news by it. Dont worry about *Nelson*. I have no hope of writing any more on it until I leave the *Chicago*. Good bye. Love to the children—also to Rose and Hart.

To Ellen Evans Mahan

Gravesend, England, May 11, 1894 [LC]

Dearest Deldie: The enclosed appeared in the London *Times* of this morning.[1] It has struck me that—in view of Erben's action and the enmity of others—it might be a good thing to get published. The banquet in our honor is fixed, I believe for the 24th. This will reach you therefore in time to get inserted in the same N.Y. daily that has the telegraphic report of the affair & the combination might possibly be good. I hate such self-pushing & nothing but the desirability of showing the strength of my value, as a military thinker, in the face of Erben's report would lead me to do it. In short it is defence not glory I aim at. Dave, Gouv, or Suydam[2] might help you—but use your judgment and dont excite yrself and dont insert if thought unwise.

[P.S.] The *Evg* [*Evening*] *Post* would be the best probably—but beggars cant choose.

To Helen Evans Mahan

Gravesend, May 11, 1894 [NWC]

My dearest Helen: It is a year today since I joined the *Chicago*, an ill-omened anniversary in some ways, and what manner of letter I can write you, my dear daughter amid the present drive, I can hardly see. My mail, twice a day, is something portentous, but you need not imagine that they are all invitations. One thing, however, is gratifying. Almost every one of many who have written and asked me to come to them is among those I have known—or rather, have known me—before; friends, old or new, but still friends who know what they are to expect in me. It is more gratifying to be wanted *again*, than merely wanted once. But before going on, dear child, I want to thank you as well as your sister & brother, for the faithful and affectionate persistence with which you have kept up your letters to me. All children do not do so. You cannot yet fully realize how

---

1. *The Times*, p. 9, has an article on the arrival of the *Chicago*, and the projected banquet and reception. It praises Mahan for expounding the "principles of what may be called the philosophy of naval history . . . ," calling his sea-power books a major event of that time, and pointing out that within five years they had had a potent influence on British foreign and naval policy.

2. Possibly, John Howard Suydam, minister of the Reformed Church in New York, New Jersey, and Pennsylvania; under the pseudonym "Knickerbocker, Jr.," author of *The Wreckmaster, Cruel Jim*, and other books.

much it is to me, but I trust your own children will some day repay it to you, if you have the misfortune to be separated from them. I may say the same, too, to Lyle, with reference to Mr. Ireland's report of him. I can wish him no better than that he may some day be as proud and happy over his boy, as I at this moment am of him. Now for my news. I sent off my letter to mamma upon arrival, so you know of that. By the first or second mail, I recd. an invitation from Lady Jeune, where I dined last year, to spend Sunday with them in the country, also from the Schiffs to dine Sunday. I accepted the former, a decision which I hope will meet with all your high approvals, and then pled previous engagement on the latter. Today I have a note from Mrs. S. asking me to fix my own day next week and shall name Friday. I had also a letter from my old friend Mrs. Harry Blake asking me to lunch when I could, so I have fixed Wednesday for that. I haven't seen her for, I suppose, fifteen years, but I am very fond of her. Sir Geo Clarke wrote to welcome me & come to dinner, which I have set for Wednesday—you know who he is, where I met him etc. On Thursday the 17th I dine with Mr. & Mrs. Poultney Bigelow[1] (brother-in-law I think to Charlie Tracy) to meet Mark Twain. That is all, so far, for next week. It carries me as you see to Saturday, which I have left open on the chance of being asked to the country for that day. Five clubs have sent me entrances, among them the Athenaeum, an exceedingly high-tone literary club, which only opens its doors, by the letter accompanying, to a "strictly limited number of distinguished visitors" and therefore wanted to know whether or not I could use the privilege. Although a little inclined to poke fun at such very select respectability—the compliment of being invited to the Athenaeum is I believe unimpeachable and I was most glad to accept. We were boarded, within three hours of arrival by Mr. David Clowes, the avant courier of a negotiation to settle upon a banquet to be given to Adm. Erben & the officers of the *Chicago*—to arrange time etc. The meeting of the projectors was held that aftn. Wednesday, committee formed, and May 24 is fixed. Clowes came into my cabin after being with the admiral, and said to me, "This really is to welcome you more than anything else but we put it on the general ground." So Erben is happy in believing it is simply (solely) a return for the Naval Review hospitalities of last year, just as in August he assured me Lord Spencer's dinner was merely a return for civilities shown by us to the Viceroy in Ireland—said civilities consisting only in firing the salutes de rigueur on such an occasion & eating two of the Viceroy's dinners. "You're not in it," he assured me, a speech which has caused me many a sly snigger since. This morning the *Times* has a swinging article —Editorial—in which it begins by saying that "the arrival of the *Chicago* bearing the flag of Rear Adml. Erben .. affords a fitting opportunity of

---

1. Poultney Bigelow, correspondent for the *New York Herald*, who had just published his third book, *The Borderland of Czar and Kaiser*.

[267]

paying a friendly compliment to the United States Navy, and doing honour to the greatest living writer on naval history. This may be regarded in some measure as a return for the cordial hospitality (in N.Y.) but more particularly it is designed as a special compliment to the great writer" etc. for a full column. I fancy Clowes is in that too. Well, flattery is pleasant, particularly when no discord is heard, but let us keep it to ourselves and engage in no unseemly contention, or desire, to engross attention. The *Pall Mall Gazette* interviewed me [the] first day, and gives a column of interview, beginning: "American ships come & go, and people take little account of their movements. It would have been the same with the *Chicago, although she is the flagship of the European squadron.* But her captain etc."[2] I had also a visit from Mr. John Mahoney, who represented so he told me the Irish of East London and came to welcome the American ship on account of the sympathy of America with Ireland. I told Mr. Mahoney, who I gathered was in the tailoring line, that I was very glad to see him personally, but was not just now doing any political sympathy. He thanked me & left me his photo, as grand something or other, with a scarf. You see my friends are mixed. Capt. Yorke of the Navy also wrote asking me to stay with them after his return to town next week, an offer I value chiefly because given, as I said, after knowing me. And now, what will interest mamma, I have had a letter from Mrs. Hoskins asking me to come & see them. I own after all these years & amid my many other calls, I would have preferred to escape this extra duty, but of course I shall, and indeed must, go. My plan is after returning to the ship on Monday to go to London for a week on Tuesday—15th. I wanted a fortnight for I need the rest—recreation; but the adml. is curiously unwilling to have me away. But that he, at least, retires in Sept. my position would indeed be nearly unbearable. He is—but I will not say my opinion of him. The educational value, spiritually, of being under the dominion of such a man, is very great, and I must not lose it by unbridling my tongue. I have taken lodgings for a fortnight, and after the week shall go and come according to circumstances. I wholly lose, however, the benefit of relaxation—for a week will barely suffice to meet my duty calls—and as to getting benefit from running to the ship for work & rushing to town for dinners or what not—it is out of the question. The Chief Engr.[3] says he does not think it will be possible to keep the ship out beyond August, and in fact she will need some fairly extensive repairs to cross the ocean. I have just glanced over your letters. Tell mamma I entirely approve of all she has done & is doing & that Nelson was born 1758. I am glad to hear such favorable opinions of the Quogue mansion. Nellie I hope will be better long ere this; and I want to tell her & you, dear, that mamma & I have

2. Quotation not exact. "Our Naval Supremacy: Captain Mahan's Opinion," *Pall Mall Gazette*, May 10, 1894. Scrapbook at Naval War College.
3. Henry W. Fitch.

planned to provide for you by giving you good health & the means of gaining a living & have spent for those objects rather than save. Now you owe it to us, & to yourselves, not to undo, by overwork, the foundation of health. You must husband your strength till you are 25, at least, & while you still have my income to fall back on. So doing you will be strong when the time for labor comes.

[P.S.]   Tell mamma to send me the $100, if she has not already done so, and the number of your gloves, if [sic] I have mislaid them.

To Ellen Evans Mahan

Gravesend, May 14, 1894 [LC]

My dearest Deldie: Your letter of the 4th reached me today. I recd. it at Stevens' office where I stopped on my way back from the country where I spent Sunday at Lady (or Sir Francis) Jeune's. She seems to me rather more of a figure than he, although he is an extremely intelligent man, who has reached his judgeship comparatively early and stands very high in general estimation. She is a Scotchwoman, a little short of fifty, I fancy, small of stature, but of indefatigable energy, & quite a figure in London society. You may remember I dined there last August. She wrote me immediately upon our arrival asking me to dine with them in town on the 23d, and come out for Sunday if I could. I was very glad to accept both, for she is a woman who cultivates all the distinguished in intellect etc. The weather which had been bad for some days cleared very nicely for the Sunday, a most beautiful day, like our own country Mays, but much cooler. The company was pleasant—much more so than those I met at the Hayters, where the conversation depended wholly upon current society topics in which I naturally was out of it. Lady Jeune pressed me to stay over today which is a bank holiday, awful for traveling, and when they were to make an excursion to some naturally old English house, fifteen miles distant. Had I been captain only of the ship I would have stayed, but being responsible to a not very friendly admiral I felt I could not. I had a couple of notes from Mrs. Harry Blake who now lives in London, and as I passed through on Saturday, I went to see her, to get straightened out on some invitations she had sent me. She was much the same, though looking badly for a cold, but manner much the same. I think, however, I recognized the inevitable deterioration of a person who lives only for the world, with no necessary occupation, nor specially elevated aims. It has been a hard life. Harry was only 37 when he died, and she lost her daughter at 17. Both of them are now invested with a halo of imaginary excellence. The boy still lives—is about 27. He married an Australian girl,

[269]

and is now in Australia—so that she, poor woman, is all alone. The young man is delicate also. With all this & no strong religious feeling—life seems to me to become so aimless. Its best interests gone, and the holiest vanished. Tomorrow I go to town for a week. Well my dear, the bloom is *not* off the lily, as I expected it would be. People vie with one another in compliments—and while of course it is a very small fraction of London society that cares about me at all, and it is all ephemeral, it still gives me a feeling of a dream. A young fellow of 22 or 3, sitting by me at table, said his tutor at Oxford (or Cambridge) mentioning a very well known name advised him to read the book as being the best he had read ever. The *Saturday Review* gave me a column headed "Capt Mahan" saying that while all desired to show friendly feeling to the U.S. that it was the presence of Capt. M. which would attract the interest of many who would wish simply "to do direct honor to one of the officers who will be present. They will see the chief interest of the occasion in the presence of Capt. Mahan."[1] However I will send you the article and forbear the stupidity of writing my own eulogisms. On Wednesday I dine at Sir Geo. Clarke's—on Thursday at Mr. Bigelows—Friday the Schiffs—Saturday go to Lord Chas. Beresford's for Sunday. Monday I have suggested to Mr. Marston in reply to a letter from him to dine with him—not yet settled. Tuesday I return to the ship. Wednesday dinner at the Jeune's—Thursday the "banquet"—Saturday dine at Mrs. Blake's. There I stop—unless the 30th for which I have an invitation to dine at Mr. Shaw Lefevre's[2]—but I am not sure whether I can go—whether the ship will be here. Sounds very gay doesn't it? But oh my darling I get very tired. I feel such a drive, I long just to be quiet to put my feet up and be free from care, and above all to be back with you. This jumping from place to place, and above all this disquiet of the mind is to me infinitely wearing, and while adulation is certainly pleasant to weak human nature, it dont for a moment compare to the delight of doing congenial work. Do you remember my quotation from Lowell:

'Tis not the grapes of Canaan that repay
But the high faith that failed not by the way.

The high faith I fear was not there—can you ever forget my own distrust of success?—but the honest work was and no delight can equal it for en-

---

1. *Saturday Review* (May 12, 1894), p. 492. This article further states: "In his hands naval history ceased to be a mere series of picturesque but disconnected facts, and became the exposition of a great force working by law, in a universally intelligible manner, to definite ends." The same issue, p. 485, comments: "The U.S. man-of-war "Chicago," commanded by Captain Mahan, the most distinguished, perhaps, of living naval historians and critics, having arrived in the Thames, a movement has been started to entertain Captain Mahan, with his Admiral, of course, and his officers."

2. George John Shaw-Lefevre, Baron Eversley, Liberal politician.

durance. Praise however prized is cloying contrasted with the process of production, of the free movement of the intellect. I wonder for whom were you looking for apartments on 52d St and Broadway—Rosie or for all hands. I had a letter from her by the same mail & am glad to see that mine to her had the effect I designed of giving her the assurance that she had to grieve only for her mother's loss, and not in any way to reproach herself for any failure of duty. I trust that Quogue may have some congenial people— with change of scene & air and surrounded by quiet social people she will, unless her strength collapses, obtain a relief that will be greater than she has known for years. I trust you may not have been ill-advised in leaving it [your mother's estate] to me unconditionally. I hope I may be trusted but greatly question if any one should be. However, I am not so young or attractive as to induce any woman to marry me for so little money as I can in any way control. By the way, among others, I have a note from Lord Tennyson, the son of the poet: "My Father would have welcomed you. Your naval histories are era-making books"; and then says that if I would like to visit either of their houses "to propose myself," which I suppose means to fix my day for a visit.

May 15

I shall dispatch this by this mail, my dearest one. I hope the £20 will be along soon, for though I expect to keep within my balance, I have had the misfortune to break one of [my] teeth, & I have also my overcoat to pay for. Mention again the size of your gloves. Goodbye my darling. Mr. Marston wants to see me about my books—present & future. I trust July's returns will at least more than cover the £20, and that I shall then be on my way to you all.

To James R. Thursfield[1]

United Service Club, London, May 17, 1894 [RL]

My dear Sir: I write to say that it will give me great pleasure to lunch with you at the Athenaeum on Tuesday next, as by your kind invitation— at 1 I think you said.

---

1. A naval historian and journalist who, from 1881 on, was the leading editorial writer for *The Times* and in charge of the "Books of the Week" section. He popularized the works of Mahan.

To James R. Thursfield

Dear Mr. Thursfield: I regretted extremely having to break my engagement to lunch with you on Tuesday next. My doing so was due simply to a letter recd. from the Admiral that he wanted me to be on board Tuesday forenoon to consult about something. Great believer as I am in concentration of force, I am disposed to question the advisability of concentrating an admiral's command into a single ship, which is the condition of the U.S. European Squadron. My chief regret, however, is the loss of this opportunity of meeting you, yourself, whose friendship I should have been so glad to cultivate.

To Ellen Kuhn Mahan

London, May 19, 1894 [LC]

My darling Nellikin: Your turn has come for a letter, and sorry I am that the conditions are so unfavorable for my writing you one as good as you deserve. I am simply harassed and driven to death, and the case is made much worse by the fact that I am sleeping really dreadfully. Never was there a week in my life that has had more distinction and less solid enjoyment than the present, & my own constant thought and hope and prayer is to get back to my quiet home and my beloved work. Twice a day I get a mail of a half dozen to a dozen letters, most of them to little or no purpose, but all requiring answers and I cannot at any moment look forward to two or three hours quietly and enjoyably my own. I dont think I should mind so much, my dear child, if I could only hold my weary eyes open and if my dulled brain were capable of giving you a clear and bright report of my daily doings. There is not much to them it is true—racing from one end of this huge town to the other in pursuit of calls or to lunch or dinner, mainly of course to people whom you do not know & often perhaps have never heard. I might perhaps enjoy it for a little while, but it seems to me nothing could possibly be more unsatisfactory for a continuance. Before I forget, let me say that I have received both first and second of the drafts mailed to me by mamma, for which I am very much obliged to her. To day—two hours hence—I am to lunch again at Mrs. Harry Blake's who intends I believe to have some people to meet me. I had understood I was to go out this evening to Lord Charles Beresford's but from a note I got this morning I gather I am not expected till tomorrow. If I go, I shall sleep Sunday night there. On Monday I am to dine with Mr. Marston, whose house publishes my books on this side of the water. I believe he wants to talk business about the books present and to come. I am to call that evening—or aftn.—by appointment on a Lady Stanley of Alderley, at 5. (no short name you see) an old lady of 85, who it seems wanted to see Capt. Mahan before she died. She is the mother-in-law of Lady Jeune, whose first husband was a Stanley, and from the accounts is by no means nearer death than is compatible with being very much alive now. Tuesday I have to go back to the ship—but I am to dine in town on Wednesday, Thursday & Friday—the first at Lady Jeune's the last at Mrs Harry Blakes. Thursday is the banquet at which to my dismay I am expected to make a speech. I have had two or three other invitations which looked speechy but I declined them on sight. By mail this morning I received a letter from Mrs. Tyndall, whose husband[1] was quite celebrated as a scientific man and died but a few months since, saying that he would so have welcomed me & had been so stirred by my books. All this seems to me utterly incredible, but of course it is true. I dont seem to know myself at all, nor do I feel much elated. The thing begins to pall now, and I would far rather be working again than recg this praise—nothing like good and honest work for happiness. I cant say that the work of answering letters is happy—especially as I toil in vain; no sooner is one batch off my hands than another replaces it. "What it is to be so sought after" said Sam Weller to his father. "I dont take no pride in it, Sammy," said Mr. Weller senior. Last night I dined at the Schiffs, whom I then saw for the first time in London, and on Thursday met Mark Twain at Mr. Bigelow's. Mr. Clemens (Twain) is a most remarkable looking personage, in no prepossessing sense of the words. An immense head of long floppy hair, quite gray, which stands out in admired disorder from all parts of his head—rather insignificant otherwise both in feature and figure. _I_ never admired his books as you perhaps know. Yesterday I went to Greenwich, where the Royal Naval College is, with three other of our officers. We were very kindly received & shown all over. There was not much to interest you—but there were many portraits of persons in whom I was much interested, and some relics of Nelson, among others the coat he wore when killed &c. Near by there is a great school for the children of seamen who have died in the Navy, and we were taken over to see them do their exercises. They are drawn up—five or six hundred in long rows, about four feet apart and perform various motions with dumb bells and sticks. These are painted red and yellow each alternate boy having the same color. It makes a very curious and rather pretty effect to see these contrasted colors waved about in the air as each boy does the same movement. Afterwards we saw them at the mess, of which the most interesting feature was the saying grace.

---

1. John Tyndall, famous for his work on the nature of glacier motion, radiant heat, electrical phenomena, and the various forms of water. His wife was Louisa, oldest daughter of Lord Claud Hamilton.

[273]

When all was ready, there was one bugle call—Silence—and when all was quiet a second call, when every one uncovered, and the boys clasped their hands and chanted, or monotoned, a grace the words of which I could not catch—but it was very pretty and effective—above all when one remembered they were orphans. Adml. Luce & his family sail to day for home. They should arrive about with this letter. And now goodbye my darling daughter. My letter began gloomily, but writing has roused me a bit. I am to take a strong dose of bromide to night & shall probably feel all right tomorrow. Love to mamma, Henny & Lyle.

To Ellen Evans Mahan

Gravesend, May 22, 1894 [LC]

My dearest Deldie: I fear you will get but a scrap of a letter this time. Never in my life have I been so driven; luckily it is but for a short time. I am so sorry I cannot write fully, because it would interest you so much. Let us see what I have done. I mailed my last, to Nelly, on Saturday. By Lord Chas. Beresford's invitation I was to have gone that aftn. to his place near Richmond Park, but in the morning a letter from Lady Charles, *assuming* that I was coming Sunday morning. As I preferred to go to church I waited till aftn. reaching there about 5. It was a little annoying upsetting some of my plans. You will I hope be pleased to hear that I declined dinner invitations from two countesses in twenty four hours, and that I have today, an invitation from the Marchioness of Salisbury to stay from Friday till Monday at Hatfield House—one of the famous houses of England. This I should promptly have accepted but by the baddest of luck comes an invitation to be present at the state dinner, cabinet I believe, on the Queen's birthday—the 26. We are in doubt whether we *must* accept this. It will be an awful nuisance for I shall never again have the chance that this offers & I could tear all my hair out (no *great* sacrifice) with vexation. I am engaged to dine with the Schiffs on the Sunday, but wrote to Mrs. S. with the freedom of friendship to excuse me. Meanwhile I wait the result. Last night I dined with Mr. Marston, a dinner given me by the house very good indeed. He spoke to me about the advisability of getting out a cheaper edition of the two books, which he thought would have a very large sale. Meanwhile, the time he said was hardly ripe for this, as the extant editions are still selling very well—so I hope you may get some money in July. I returned to the ship this morning and shall sleep here tonight. Tomorrow I dine at the Jeunes and I believe shall there meet Mr. Balfour. On the 24th comes the "banquet" to Adml and officers of the *Chicago*. There is little doubt this was started about me, the originator told me so. I dread it horribly for I must reply to a toast— & I cant think what to say. Friday I lunch with Mr. Bryce, a member of the cabinet—afterwards shall call upon Mrs. Hoskin, unless Clarke makes an arrangement for me to call upon Lady Carnavon[1] who it appears wishes to meet me. I called there Sat—Friday, but she was out and at once sent me an invite to dinner for the 24th wh. I had to decline and wrote C. [Clarke] that if he could arrange for the visit on 25th I would go. She was one of the aforesaid countesses—the other being Lady Shrewsbury whom I met at Beresfords. The latter is a grandmother, though young looking for it, and the other must be middle aged. Yesterday I called by appointment on Lady Stanley of Alderley—a very vigorous old lady of 87. She had invited a number of people to drop in all of whom [were] most complimentary. One lady must tell me what Sir G. Tryon had said but I cannot now recall it. Marston made a few remarks after the dinner & therein quoted or rather read a letter from Stanley the African Explorer "What a pity—the one man I should like to see. I join in all that the *Times* says." I believe I mentioned that Mrs. Tyndall had written. In truth dearest I am gagged with flattery—it seems puerile almost for me to repeat it even to you. Well Friday night I dine at Mrs. Harry Blakes who has assembled a company to meet me. Saturday to Monday will be Hatfield unless I am miserably disappointed. Monday I shall have a few friends to lunch, and shall sleep aboard—one of the friends I believe to be the author of the *Times* article. Tuesday (today week) I dine at Frank Blakes and spend the night go to the dentist next day—and, probably—shall drive with Mrs. Harry [Blake] to leave my cards. That night I dine at the Shaw Lefevres (Wednesday) a member of the cabinet. I have before me an invitation from another of the Treasury lords to dine in the House of Commons, wh I am advised to accept. I can name for it either the Thursday 31, or Friday June 1. So you see dearest the time is *very* full. One thing I *do* desire above all and that is to go home. I am weary and frightened lest by chance this headlong whirl of excitement and movement should carry me off my feet and in any way become necessary to me. Now at least my chief longing is for home and my work. On this point I fear we must reconcile ourselves to see our hopes dispersed. It was inexpressibly bitter to me, but I fear the statement in the A & N *Register* last recd. here is too explicit for doubt that the Secy has decided to keep us out another year. Another blow has fallen in the opinion of the Ambassador that we *must* accept the cabinet dinner. Hang the cabinet! I say—moreover I sympathize with Salisbury's politics and must dine with his opponents for none of whom do I care—indeed quite the reverse

---

1. The wife of George Edward Stanhope Molyneux Herbert, 5th Earl of Carnavon.

towards most—and I have lost my dinner with the Schiffs—so it is a mess all round as some of my other affairs are. I have an invite to write a paper for the Royal U.S. Institute £30—and am inclined to do it.[2] Oh my dear sweet wife what is all else to seeing your face & the childers. God send me soon home to you, but I can never forget the great kindness of these Englishers.

[P.S.]   The draft for £20 is recd.

To Ellen Evans Mahan

London, May 25, 1894 [LC]

My darling Miss Deldie: It is of no use my pretending to write a decent letter under my conditions at present. I may save the mail tomorrow with one for Lyle, whose turn it now is, and for whom I reserve the descriptions of last night's banquet etc, together with such other events as may [occur]. Tomorrow the Queen's birthday is kept in London. There will be at 10 the trooping of the colors to which several of us are asked, after which I must go to the ship and at night I have the official dinner at the Prime Minister's—Lord Rosebery's "Levee Dress" so will be very swell. Lady Salisbury kindly wrote me to come visit anyway on Sunday, so I shall take the 9 A.M. train which will bring me in time for Church. Now my own dearest dont think I have you less in my mind for all my frivolity—my own desire is to be back with you all again & at my work. I am concerned to hear Nell is droopy. Is she discouraged? I wish I could talk to her a little. Tell the dear child not to doubt for one moment that there is a place in life for her and that by God's help we shall find it—to keep up her heart & be patient to wait and to watch. We shall pull through. Think how long it was before I was guided to the work which is now so overwhelmingly praised. Think of Lord Roberts one of the two first British Generals saying in his speech last night that he wished I could be induced to do for the army what I had for the navy. My darling it is all for you all—I wish father & mother could have heard it—but let Nell take courage that is the lesson; Papa thinks she is good for a good deal.

---

2. "Blockade in Relation to Naval Strategy," Royal United Service Institution *Journal* (November 1895). Also published in the U. S. Naval Institute *Proceedings* (December 1895).

To Ellen Evans Mahan

Gravesend, June 1, 1894 [LC]

Again, my own dearest Deldie, my letter has rather to be in the form of an excuse for a hurry & a drive that I cannot avoid nor control. I had purposed to sleep on board last night so as to put in a long night's rest—but upon coming down in the morning I found a note from Lord Rosebery, the prime minister, asking me to dine very quietly with him either that night or the next. The opportunity of a dinner nearly tête à tête with one of the most prominent men in England, and at present the head of the govt, was too tempting to be resisted so I surrendered my intended rest. The dinner was at the usual hour, and then sat down only Lord Rosebery, Mr. John Morley one of the foremost literary men in England—and a member of the govt— and myself. Mr. Lecky[1] the celebrated historian had been asked as fourth, but could not come. Morley went off to the house of Commons at 10, and after that we two sat and talked till 12, when I took my leave but Lord R. walked round with me to my lodgings, and took me by the way into one of the most famous of the last century clubs. He told me upon my first arrival that no literary work in his time had caused such enthusiasm as *Sea Power*—to which Mr. Morley assented. Tonight I dine at our ambassador's, Mr. Bayard—tomorrow at one of the old naval clubs, & Saturday at a Mrs. Beaumont's which concludes the racket. On Monday I hope to return to the ship for good—but there is some talk of our being presented at the levee to be held on that day. I have an offer to write two magazine articles, each of which will pay be $150. I shall make the attempt so as to recover, if possible, more than the expense of my stay here. Today I received yours enclosing Nellie's from Newport—also a very nice one from Helen & from Lyle. Mr. Marston came on board yesterday with all his family staying two hours. I returned with him in the train to London. He says that the reception here has reacted very favorably on the sales, although the latter had been steadily satisfactory before—so I trust your cheque from Little and Brown may relieve some of your anxieties. On Wednesday I dined at Mr. Shaw Lefevre's, but I think in the company there were none with whom I had any previous association that would be interesting to you. The Marquis of Ripon an elderly gentleman whom I met at the First Lord's last year came up & spoke to me—told me he had never understood *how* England had crushed Napoleon till my books made it clear. But my dear I am getting tired of singing my own song even at second hand. God keep me in vivid recollection of my own nothingness. I was more than pleased that my letters to Maime Parker & Rosie had seemed

---

1. William Edward Hartpole Lecky.

to be to them such comfort—after all I am some use in the world so far. It was one of the signs foretold of our Lord, you remember—"The Spirit of the Lord is upon me, that I should know how to speak a word in season to him that is weary." It is better than writing successful books. And dearest, let us keep our eyes open to the uncertainties. After all, storm does succeed sunshine—be not high minded, but fear. Lord R. made a curious remark last night. "I like the way your admiral bears himself," he said, "for the position is difficult—for after all he is much in that of chaperon to a débutante." Some admirable photos of me have been taken—free of expense & I am to have some copies. If you like them, I may get more. Each of the Schiffs selected alone, as best, that which I prefer. And now dearest with heaps of love for all [etc.].

To Helen Evans Mahan

Gravesend, June 5, 1894 [NWC]

My dearest Helen: If you at home only knew how much writing I have to do, I think you would forgive me if I cut you shorter than I do. Ten letters did I mail today—mostly short it is true and then the evening mail brings six more. But a truce to complaining—only you must not be surprised at any traces of hurry. I think my last to mamma was on Friday the 1st and that in it I gave an account of my dining with Lord Rosebery, and that I happened to have the evening vacant because I had reserved it for a day of rest. The temptation of dining almost tête à tête with the Prime Minister, a man who being little over 45 now should be prominent for many years to come was too much for my weak powers of resistance. Next evening we dined with our ambassador, Mr. Bayard, who, as you may have seen, and at least will see when I have time to send the papers, spoke very handsomely of me at the "Banquet."[1] Adml. Erben was taken suddenly with a severe congestion of the throat—commonly called cold, but I believe stomach —which prevented him from speaking, so that when I stopped for him in the carriage he commissioned me to make his excuses. There were I suppose twenty four guests, English and Americans—among them being Mr. Whitney formerly Secretary of the Navy. I sat on Mr. Bayard's left and next to Lord George Hamilton, who was first lord of the Admiralty under the last administration, Lord Salisbury's. He was very complimentary, as they all are—in fact he had written me a note some days before complimenting me incidentally on my speech, the which I own surprised me. The

1. Of May 24, 1894.

trouble is that so many things pass I cant remember all from day to day. Mr. Whitney also made some complimentary remark to which I replied, as far as I recollect, that the work was pretty much all done for the War College. He has aged, more than the intervening time, since I saw him last. That night after dinner were perfected the arrangements for our presentation at the levee the following Monday—a presentation which I understand followed upon the express invitation of the Prince of Wales. The following night, Saturday, I dined with the Royal Navy Club, an organization which has existed since 1765, though never with a club house. They simply dine together several times a year, usually upon the anniversaries of naval victories. We had been asked—Erben and I—for the Queen's birthday, by a special exception to their rule, which allows only one guest at each dinner. They then already had one, and were anxious to take us two in. We were however already engaged then and so they asked us again for Lord Howe's anniversary,[2] this year his centenary, whereof mamma by typewriting knows somewhat. The admiral remaining indisposed again excused himself, so I was the sole guest and as such was seated on the right of the president, Adml. Sir Vesey Hamilton while on my other side was Sir Houston Stewart also an admiral. I remember well the latter's father, who was commander-in-chief at Plymouth when I was there in 1863—a man who had been ship-mates with Marryat, the celebrated novelist, in 1806, under the command of Cochrane one of the most dashing captains of that day.[3] I mentioned the fact to Sir Houston, who is a ruddy robust man of 68 to 70, of medium height and sturdy frame, aquiline nose and iron gray hair. He assured me his father would have welcomed me most heartily, and went on to tell me he had never thoroughly understood the [battle of the] first of June, 1794, till I had explained it. He added that my last chapter was wonderful—or magnificent—I forget the exact word, but it was a large adjective. Meantime the president told me I should have to answer to the toast of the guest—which took me unawares, but I am getting hardened and dont care much. So when the time came for "The Guest" to be toasted Sir Houston got up and made a speech that was really quite eloquent, about England and America and poor papa's writings—concluding with a call for three cheers for me and again another. It was really quite overwhelming to see this sturdy quiet old gentleman so enthusiastic. The attendance was large about 100 admirals and captains—nearly double the usual they told me—and cheered very heartily, while I stood bowing and rather abashed by my reception. I had found something to say in the fact that almost all the famous old naval worthies of whom I had written so much had been members of the club, and while I cannot flatter myself that what I said was brilliant, it was said steadily and without embarrassment, and was well received. This

2. Of the Battle of the Glorious First of June, in 1794.
3. Thomas Cochrane, 10th Earl of Dundonald.

closed the evening's proceedings, but a great many both then and before dinner, came up to be introduced to me. I came home that night to the ship, but by bad luck got into the slower of the two trains that leave nearly at the same time. I slept most of the way down but still was late in bed. The next day I had promised to lunch with Mrs. Harry Blake, which I did, greatly grieved that the trains ran so as to deprive me of church. Indeed, I fear church is being put sadly in the background of English society of the upper class, & I myself am ill at ease over the occasional neglects into which I have been betrayed. I do not think, however, I would willingly or willfully omit church and into this I was unwittingly led by circumstances not necessary or interesting to relate. There was nothing specially interesting in the lunch—unless the fact that we had to wait a half hour, as commonly happens at all London meals. I passed the afternoon at a musical reception, which emphasized to me the unfortunate drift of London society. I am no sabbatarian—yet I could not but think that people who labor at society the six days might spare the 7th for better use. From there I went to the Schiffs for a cup of tea, sat with them for an hour much like 34th St.,[4] then home to dress for the dinner which was to conclude my London spree, at a Mrs. Beaumont's whom I met at Nice last winter. The company was middle aged which always vexes me, who am prone to forget I am the same and would prefer to take down some pretty young woman. However the one assigned to me, though grey even to whiteness, had a delicate refined face, once pretty, and was bright. Though I did not take our hostess down I sat on her right. She said to me during dinner what struck me as odd— I wonder will it you? She said "I was particularly interested in your works for a special reason. Did you ever hear of Sir George Colley?"[5] I replied— "Do you mean the one who was killed in South Africa?" "Yes," she said "he was my husband, and he was Chief of our Staff College and had a turn of mind I thought much like yours etc." I thought her eyes moistened a little, and wondered how number two at the other end of the table—a rather odd sort of man—would appreciate the situation. However, everything cannot be romance, and Englishwomen are quite right in not suppressing allusion to their first husbands—when they have had such. It saves blunders. Nothing very remarkable happened at this dinner—the same cordiality I receive everywhere. I think now my dear I will stop. I enclose Lord Rosebery's note, which must be carefully kept. As our friend Brown used to say, in his mysterious way—"It is autograph" and may some day be most interesting. I will only mention that I have mamma's telling of her visit to the house and satisfaction with it. Our present arrangement is a re-

---

4. The home of Mrs. Manlius Glendower Evans.
5. Sir George Pomeroy Colley, governor of Natal, killed in battle against the Boers at Majuba.

ception on board on the 11th—our wedding day—and sail on the 13th. Nous verrons. Love to all.

June 6

Closing for the mail. Take a good rest at Quogue dear child, and now that you are losing your old pupils be careful not to take too many new ones. Overwork is much to be deprecated before the physique is thoroughly matured—do you guard against it.

To Theodore Roosevelt

USS *Chicago*, June 6, 1894 [LC]

My dear Mr. Roosevelt: By some unknown detention your letter of March 27 only reached me within the week. I hasten to assure you that I did not take in the least amiss what you said to me about extreme care. I fully recognized both the spirit and wisdom of your advice and have directed myself assiduously to carrying on duty thoroughly.

By this same mail I write to Mr. Lodge a letter he may probably show you. Being still in ignorance of the terms of Erben's indorsement, I can make no comment on it; but if it be as the press say, he has, so to say, introduced new matter in the cross-examination without allowing me the opportunity to rebut—which is contrary alike to justice and to reputations.

You will have seen how heartily we have been received over here. It has been a great pleasure, but has also involved a good deal of a burden. Nevertheless, I confess to have derived great satisfaction from the lavish expressions of appreciation given to me personally—that is, to my work. To have an ex-first lord say he never had understood *how* they downed Napoleon, and a veteran admiral that he had never before comprehended the first of June [battle], gave me ground to hope that I might yet be of some use to a navy, despite adverse reports. Still a clear writer may not be a first rate officer.

Rest assured I shall do my best to deserve the confidence you have so graciously expressed—and I believe I may truthfully say the *Chicago* is—and has always been—a well looked-after ship.

To James R. Thursfield

United Service Club, London, June 6, 1894 [RL]

Dear Mr. Thursfield: If you could on Monday take the train leaving Charing Cross about 11 (11:07 I think) you would arrive about 12 and

[281]

be on board about 12:30. I write simply because I have asked Clarke and Clowes to come also with their wives. Pardon me that I do not know if you are married—but if you are and Mrs. Thursfield would like to visit the ship I would be most happy.

To Henry Cabot Lodge

USS *Chicago*, Gravesend, June 6, 1894 [MHS]

Dear Mr. Lodge: You will not perhaps be surprised to learn that Mr. Herbert never wrote the letter he said he would address to me. I was not surprised, nor should I have made of it an occasion to disturb you again, with complaints—especially as no investigation is now practicable before the *Chicago* returns.

An incident, however, has occurred which raises the question whether I may not finally be forced again to ask, insistingly, for investigation. The enclosed slip appeared in the *Army and Navy Register* of April 21,[1] and has been given to me by a friend. In the passage marked by me with red ink occur three allegations, two specific, the third vague. If they are the mere newspaper gabble collected in lobbies by reporters, I take no heed of them; but if they were actually made by Adml. Erben, I now learn them for the first time. They do not occur in his original report on my "Fitness," and must therefore be in the endorsement *which was never shown to me.*

That I failed to go on deck when my presence was required may be (certainly suggests) a most damaging charge. That I failed to investigate complaints of enlisted men is less so, but is only less serious. Before moving in this thing, I wrote to the Executive Officer who belonged to the ship during the time covered by the report, who assures me unqualifiedly that he knows of no foundation for either statement. The Navigator (next in rank) says the same. In my belief both statements are untrue—yet they are specific, while the report on Fitness, which alone I saw, was vague and had to be met by a general denial and demand for an enquiry.

Assuming that the statements were made, I would draw your attention to two points. *First*, both natural justice and Naval Regulation (*U.S.N. Regulations*, 1893, p. 222, par 1035) require that I should at once have been notified of these specific charges, which but for newspaper gossip would now be on file unknown to me. *Second*, there has been a grave and gross

---

1. Citing the *New York Tribune* throughout as its source, the *Army and Navy Register* under the heading "Erben and Capt. Mahan" (p. 261) stated that Erben reported that Mahan failed to be on deck on occasions when his presence was required; that he frequently omitted going to the mast to investigate the complaints of enlisted men; and that he failed in most instances to show the zeal and interest about the routine duties of the vessel required of a commanding officer.

indiscretion somewhere in the Department that such charges should become the property of the Press, while the person accused is ignorant of their existence. To the best of my recollection Erben did not allege them to *me* in the least. If there is no foul play in the matter, it looks badly like it.

My present idea, subject to such friendly advice as you may give me, is to learn through you, if possible, whether such statements were made, if so, to represent to the Department that every consideration of justice demands that I should have—and from the first should have had—a copy. I fear that they are charges which no inspection can remove and that investigation must be asked and accorded. Nor can they be sheltered under a report of "fitness." This is an expression of opinion only, upon which Adml. Erben has seen fit to seize as an occasion to make charges, partly vague, partly specific, but which have no claim to that privilege which might be asserted for a routine report which he is required to make, as expressing his opinion.

I trust you may be able to tell me that no such statements were made. I have no desire to stir up a fuss, or petulantly insist on vindications—but there are things men cannot with propriety allow to stand against them. I think you cannot but recognize that a vague accusation of neglecting duty is very different from a specific charge of failing to go on deck—possibly in serious conditions of emergency. As the account of my own rejoinder is not very correct, I hope I shall find Erben equally misrepresented.

I shall be very glad of any suggestions you may do me the honor to offer. Will you return the slip in time? [2]

[P.S.]   My address is always B. F. Stevens, 4 Trafalgar Square, London.

To James R. Thursfield

Gravesend, June 7, 1894 [RL]

Dear Mr. Thursfield: The bound volume of the *N. American* came all right. Please excuse my delay in acknowledging. I do have so much distracting writing to do. I am ever so much obliged for your kindness and will try to master Mr. Carnegie's positions before leaving England. They strike me as rather vaporous. In any event I will be careful to return the book to you.

I have found Sir George Clarke's which are bound.[1]

With kind remembrances to Mrs. Thursfield.

---

2. Lodge wrote on the letter: "Make a memo for me to see Sec. of Navy."

1. George Sydenham Clarke, "A Naval Union with Great Britain," *North American Review* (March 1894), answered Andrew Carnegie, "A Look Ahead" *ibid.* (June 1893). Clarke agreed with Carnegie's aims, but found his historical reason faulty, and his suggestions for Anglo-American political union impractical.

To Ellen Evans Mahan

My dearest Wife: There seems nothing for it but to write to you to-night, although but two days since I wrote Helen. Tomorrow night I must go to the State Ball, the Queen having "commanded the Lord Chamberlain to invite me." I dine at the Schiffs and sleep there, go to the ball about eleven and shall get away I presume about two. I had hoped then to return to the ship in the forenoon but the admiral told me he thought I ought to go to the Royal Military Tournament to which we have been invited—which is between 2 and 6 pm. I dont care to return to the ship for that small time so asked permission to remain away till Sunday evening. I dont know just how I shall manage all, having given up my room in town. My dear, my head is a maze, I am so tired at times, and now, that I can scarcely think. I returned to the ship Monday after the levee and have remained ever since & am pleased to note that there is still power of recuperation—but the deluge of letters with the ship business permits me no rest, and my sleep though better is not yet good. I told Helen about my Sunday dinner at the Beaumonts. Monday I broke up from my lodgings which I had kept along for three weeks—sending my special full dress to Mr. Bayard's where I had been invited to dress for the levee and to lunch. The latter finished we drove at once (I lunched in full tog) to Erben's lodgings, picked him up thence to the Palace—passed through rows of red coated officials & the "beef-eaters" of the Tower, clad in the dress of Henry VII's time, to an ante room where the diplomatic corps were assembling with those who, like the adm & myself had the privilege of the diplomatic circle. The other officers of the ship mustered somewhere else—where I know not. Presently we saw great state coaches arrive, coachman & two footmen in three cornered hats and scarlet and gold liveries—coaches also I believe scarlet, not sure. In these came the members of the Royal Family the Prince of Wales being [there] to receive. I must tell you our invitations came by express direction of the Prince—or rather I should say our presentation was asked of the Court upon his intimation—though whether Erben is his pet or I, I dont know—most likely the former who had really seen something of him while I have not. When the time came we marched in, the successive ambassadors in order of local rank with their presentees. We were told to unglove our right hands as the Prince would shake hands with us. The Prince and others stood along the far end of an oblong room, the prince on the right, next him the Duke of Connaught, then two foreign royal princes, then the Duke of York then the Duke of Cambridge—cousin to the Queen and a man of 70—then one or two others. The Prince, Connaught and York each shook hands with us, and remembered having met us before. The first was dressed in scarlet soldier rig, the second in dark green—Rifles I think, the third as a naval captain—all covered with orders. After filing by, having the privilege of the circle, we fell in a crowd between the door by which we entered and a corresponding one on the opposite side of the room and thence for two hours watched a continuous procession enter by the door we did, file by the princes and out at the other door—soldiers in all the uniforms man ever dreamed of, generals, admirals, captains, civilians in court dress, clergy, Hindoos & other Asiatics—all sorts & kinds from the Empire on which the sun never sets. I got dreadfully tired—though I found several to talk to —mostly aides de camp; among others Captain Noel who you may remember wrote me a nice letter about book 1. I was very glad when it was over— it was too monotonous to sustain interest. Yours of the 28th and postal of 29th reached me this evening. McAdoo's remarks were funny, but after all who is hurt.[1] "What hast thou that thou hast not received? Now, if thou have *received* it, why glory as if thou hadst not received it?" I try to keep in mind that the gift and the call to write both came from outside—let who will, then, claim the glory. I am glad you are pleased with the house—may we see in it many happy days! I am still more pleased to know that little Nell is feeling better. I am feeling unusually sanguine for me about the sales this six months—perhaps because I feel poor as do you. The trip back to Cambridge [word crossed through] Oxford will cost me $25 or 30—but I thought the honor worth it.[2] I stay with the Schiffs in London, and with the President of Trinity College in Oxford. My purpose is to arrive there P.M. 19th and leave A.M. 21st, stay over 22d in London, and have then 23d for Antwerp again—but nous verrons. I really think Mrs. Schiff likes me better than does any member of the family, though I think all like me—she asked me to stay and is always most kind. Being 50, you need not be alarmed—and I fear she is a very ill woman liable to be carried off at any moment. I have sent you by this mail, a *Graphic*,[3] a *Times* with full reports of the speeches—mine excellently reported—also containing an editorial, and a number of clippings. And now, dear, I must close & go to bed. I am really tired. I shall close in the morning for I shall have no further chance for this mail. On Sunday I dine at the Club with Bouverie Clark, my old

---

1. Mahan probably referred to McAdoo's press statement published in *The New York Times*, May 26, 1894, p. 1, on the London banquet of May 24, in which he praised Mahan's work, and continued: "The department has the right to participate in the triumph of Capt. Mahan. In the production of his great work every possible facility was extended to him. He had at his command one of the finest and most complete libraries on naval and professional subjects that could be found anywhere, and he was given by his connection with the War College ample time and every opportunity for the closest, most exacting, and analytical study of the great subject upon which he has thrown so much light. . . ."
2. Mahan received honorary degrees at both Oxford and Cambridge in June 1894.
3. *The Graphic* (June 2, 1894) carried a cover picture and a description of "The Banquet to the American Naval Officers at St. James's Hall." On June 9, it ran a brief article on "Our American Visitors" with portraits of Erben and Mahan.

chum in the Pacific. He comes for the ball where I shall perhaps see him—but the crush I fear will be greater. That is rot about what Erben said, tact etc—but I must say he shows no bad feeling whatever and he told me that he had meant to say something but Bayard took the wind out of his sails. There never was the slightest indication of anything like bad feeling anywhere that evg.

Friday Morning

I must close now. To think of my not writing you about the Hoskins but that will keep a little. I most heartily echo your wish for my return. It has been the most fatiguing month of my life—and for enjoyment not to be weighed against a day with you all. Goodbye. Love to the children.

[P.S.] If Little and Brown run over 500 I may ask for some more. Will do my best. Shirts going.

To Ellen Evans Mahan

Gravesend, June 11, 1894 [LC]

Our wedding day, my darling, to which you have not yet waked up, but to send you a line on this likely busy day I must seize the flying moment. May God always bless the day which gave you to me, and make our happiness in each other in the future all that it has been in the past. I dined last night in London at the Club with my old Pacific friend, Bouverie Clark, who had come to London for the State Ball, and returns today to his station at Davenport. This is dear little Nell's turn for a letter—but the present will bridge the interval that may most probably elapse before I can build one up for her. I have left London for good, except the passing through en route to and from Oxford next week. Well darling it has been quite an ovation etc etc—but it is over now and I can assure you being lionized in this way is not the real substantial enjoyment that the quiet doing the work was. It is like a diet of sugarplums contrasted with our simple table. My one longing now is for rest—to get way to some quiet place, where you all are, and to do nothing for a week or two, then to resume the old even tenor of my way. May God so will it soon—till He does may I have patience & acquiescence. Goodbye. Ever fondly thine with love to the children.

To William T. Sampson

USS *Chicago*, Gravesend, June 11, 1894 [NA]

My dear Sampson: A requisition went forward last week, which, but for a misunderstanding in the Admiral's Office, should have gone three or four weeks ago, for a quantity of Rapid Fire Ammunition. I have ascertained from the Hotchkiss Company, in Paris, that it can furnish all but the 1 Pdr., either in Antwerp or an English port; needing, however, to have the initial velocity stated in the order. My present purpose in writing is to suggest, as so much time has been lost, that you might cable the Admiral authority to purchase the 6 Pdr. and 37 mill. ammunition, and initial velocity required. The 1 Pdr. would be a comparatively small bulk, that could be brought in any vessel ordered to this station.

We expect to leave here on the twelfth, Wednesday next, and will be in Antwerp a month, needing imperative and extensive repairs to boilers; and in any event could stop to receive at some channel port before going south.

If the ship is to return very shortly, the matter is immaterial—although we are very short of 1 Pdr. R.F., owing to several boxes so marked proving to be for the old light gun, and so unavailable for the heavy gun which was substituted for it at some period prior to my coming on board. But, if the ship is to remain out over winter, with all the contingencies involved, her rooms should be filled, as she carries none too great an allowance at best.

Had the requisition gone forward when first sent in, my idea was that you could decide whether to send by a vessel coming from home, or order us to purchase by letter; as it is, if the latter, we should know speedily.

In case we are to remain out and no vessel is coming here, the cartridge cases for 1 Pdr., I gather from the Company's letter, might be sent them and the requisition in that manner completed by them. We have probably three months in this neighborhood before us.

To James R. Thursfield

Gravesend, June 11, 1894 [RL]

Dear Mr. Thursfield: I am sending back, through the Post Office, the volume of the *N.A. Review*, so kindly sent by you.[1] The article was the one I wanted & I have had it copied. I am immensely hurried and must close with brief but hearty remembrances to yourself and Mrs. Thursfield.

[P.S.] I hope we may be seeing you on board this P.M.[2]

---

1. *See* Mahan to Thursfield, June 7, 1894.
2. Erben was to give a reception.

[287]

To Ellen Evans Mahan

Antwerp, Belgium, June 15, 1894 [LC]

My dearest Deldie: We arrived here this forenoon after a very quiet passage, having left Gravesend at 5 P.M. yesterday. As I left a letter for Nellie there, my chief reason for writing so soon to you is about the plaint the child herself makes about her depression etc. I cannot of course judge certainly at this distance, but I am inclined to think the trouble is less in herself than in her surroundings. The two other children are more self sufficing, and have less need of change etc. The difficulty is how to evoke a remedy with our small means. There may possibly be physical conditions, but I doubt that. I have always thought Nellie, despite her pepperiness, to be essentially meek, lowly minded and self distrustful. She has shown a lack of spirit in confronting the rubs of life which is very different from what I had expected to see in her—she seemed as a child so bright, cheerful and comparatively enterprising. But the home has for her great sameness, & while she is too lowlyminded to lay the blame there, (not that there *is* blame, but it is the probable cause of trouble), she feels it without knowing what ails her. My absence doubtless tells, for women somehow all feel the support of a man in the house. Now, what to do, I cannot tell. I shall of course write to the child soon. The fact that she felt so much better at Newport is significant—change of air may do much, but change of scene is alone immediate [tonic] as in her case. I here get so harassed and tired that to leave the ship seems to me an impossible effort—yet no sooner am I away and in the train than all my clouds vanish. It is then, in my opinion, the conditions of the house which unconsciously weigh upon Nellie—and as of her love for all there is no doubt, the secret must lie in her manner of life. Too monotonous, I fear, too little interest, too little variety of companionship. Perhaps we have made a mistake in her drawing, and this I think had better be ascertained by direct question to her teacher "Is it worthwhile to go on?" I was struck by Jennie's remark on her drawing; and writing so well. Yet I know not. Who could have dreamed Nellie would not make friends?—there again Jane used to say "Nellie is sure to make her way," and our fears were for Helen. What then to do? In the first place, surely to pray that God will send her friends and teach both her and us how to order her life. Then you must watch, not taking for granted too easily that physical trouble, malaria, accounts for all. If we can learn what kind of life and occupation best suits her, where her interest lies, provide occupation congenial, and pleasant social relations, we may solve the problem. Helen's advice and help too must be sought, and she must learn to recognize that Nellie's difficulty in gaining friends proceeds from natural peculiarities, which may not be harshly judged, as though they were not the very greatest obstacles to success. I may be making a mountain out of a mole hill, but if Nell at all correctly depicts her feelings, there can be no question our duty is to watch carefully and diligently—not anxiously—for the cause and the remedy. I am persuaded the cause is external to her—not in herself—she needs change in her mode of life.

I never told you of my visit to the Hoskins. I found them living in one of those monotonous rows of houses in the far west of London of course in a very plain way. Mrs. H's elder sister, 77, lives with them. I saw, besides Mrs. H., Ada, Bertha, and Clara. Mrs. H who will be 70 her next birthday is more unchanged than any, after her Clara looks more like herself. Ada has become very like her father, quite the old maid with that peculiarity of drawing the upper lip till the gums show well that he had. I am so annoyed to find that I have either mislaid or destroyed Mrs. H's letters; for while continued correspondence is impossible, it would have been kind and graceful for you to have written & sent, say, your and the children's photos. There was not much to tell, Florence and Lily are in S.A., the latter having married a widower with eight children. They showed me Reggy's photo, a young man with a moustache, face not very distinguishable; also one of Mr. H. in his later years with a full gray beard, very much better looking than in the former flesh. I stayed about an hour. The address is—"Finsboro Road Kensington W." but I cant recall the number. Mrs. H. seemed somewhat tearful which was not unnatural for the sight of me recalled past days and circumstances wholly changed.

Dont allow Nellikin to charge herself with vague sinfulness or wrong doings. If there be anything specifically on her conscience, hear it patiently and lovingly; but tell her that vague feeling of wrong doing, without specific wrong act, is but a snare of the devil. Her trouble may be physical, or may be due to lack of correspondence between her natural bent and her actual work. In any case the remedy is patience, prayer and watchfulness whereby the cause of trouble will be found—for they who seek find. But in neither case is her suffering to be considered her fault. God in His own time will reward faithfulness.

To Hilary A. Herbert

USS *Chicago*, Antwerp, June 16, 1894 [NA]

Sir:

1. I have to inform the Department that, on the 13th instant, the body of William Davis, enlisted as a Coal Passer on board the *Chicago*, at Gravesend, England, May 15, 1894, was found in the River Thames, at Cliff-at-Hoo, County of Kent, England, supposed to have been drowned in attempting to desert. After being certainly identified by a member of this

crew, the deceased was buried at Cliff the day after his body was found. He left the ship without permission ten days previous to the finding of his body.

2. According to information derived from members of the crew, Davis was once an Apprentice, known as W. H. Davis, and an Ordinary Seaman on the U.S.R.S. *Vermont* in 1893 as—Lambert; served on board the U.S.R.S. *Minnesota* and on board the U.S.T.S. *Portsmouth*.

3. A letter has been written to Mr. Thomas Davis, Elizabethport, N. J., his nearest relative, as given by him when enlisted, informing him of the facts in the case.

To Ellen Evans Mahan

Trinity College, Oxford, June 20, 1894 [LC]

Dearest: I am going to write you only a line to say that I am here & well. I left Antwerp Sunday morning, reached the Schiffs that aftn. about 5, on Monday went to Cambridge for the day, recd my degree and passing a few hours very pleasantly and yesterday came down here where I am to receive my degree today at noon. I go in uniform, full dress (without epaulettes because they might tear my gown) gold lace trousers, cocked hat and *red* gown—the latter being of scarlet cloth with silk sleeves & trimmings, the combination of which with the military paraphernalia strikes me as excessively odd. I lunch today at All Souls College, and dine at Christ Church. I have no news to give you—I am trying to be as quiet as may be, but the Schiffs are having three rather large dinners whereat I am to meet, or have met, one or two celebrities—and on Friday, surely against the grain, I am to lunch with Baron de Rothschild,[1] where Levi P. Morton will also be. And now good bye beloved. I trust you are all *settled* at Quogue & resting. It is Lyle's turn for a letter but he may have to wait till I return to Antwerp.

To Ellen Evans Mahan

London, June 23, 1894 [LC]

My dearest Deldie: I have decided to leave my writing in full about this week's doing to my arrival at the ship again, when I hope to send a

---

1. Sir Nathan Meyer, 1st Baron Rothschild, banker and philanthropist.

long letter to Lyle whose turn it now is. It will be sufficient to say now that I have passed a very flattering pleasant week at Cambridge, Oxford, and here in town, where I am indulging in two days of doing absolutely nothing—loafing—a pleasure, or rather relaxation I greatly need. Tomorrow I return to Antwerp and again begin the grind, whose end God knoweth. I trust you need not fear to find me changed. I am indeed aware of a kind of restlessness which defies quiet, and which to a certain extent craves the "adulation" which I at the same time despise; but I do not think that the disturbance is other than superficial, or that I have really had my head turned, or lost my relish for the simple home life and steady work which I have long loved. Certainly there would not be an instant's hesitation as to what I would choose, instanter, were the choice mine to make. How, if long continued, my character might be changed, I dont know; but in my fear and dread of such a change, which I should think debasing I dont believe God will let me be overcome. The thing must now soon come to an end, & I trust Mr. Herbert may see the propriety of soon calling us home. Good bye dearest—be sure that, if I could, the next steamer would be taking me home. Love to the children.

[P.S.] I hope our book returns may be good. If they run over $500, I shall ask you for the surplus, up to $100—more, I dont think I shall need. It has not been current expenses chiefly—but overcoat shirts & other permanent acquisitions which have drained me—but I could have fetched all right but for the Oxford & Cambridge trips—yet I thought I *ought* to take the degrees. Lord Rosebery said I had beaten the record.

To Hilary A. Herbert

USS *Chicago*, Antwerp, June 26, 1894 [NA]

Sir:

1. I transmit herewith the first sheet of Enlistment Record and Shipping Articles for Charles William Smith, with the signature added as directed in the letter of the Bureau of Navigation No. 30900A of June 7, 1894.

2. Replying further to the same letter, Par. 2, in regard to Timothy O'Riley, Boilermaker; Timothy O'Riley states that the original spelling of his name was O'Reilly and that an l was dropped out and that it is now properly O'Reily. He was shipped in 1888, when his name was signed by a Writer as O'Riley, his finger being too much injured to allow him to sign for himself. As his name has been carried as O'Riley for six years a new Enlistment record has been made out the first sheet of which is herewith transmitted with the name spelled O'Reily. He has also changed the spelling of his name on the last duplicate shipping articles to agree therewith.

To Ellen Evans Mahan

Antwerp, June 27, 1894 [LC]

Dearest Deldie: I have just heard that a long letter I mailed to Lyle this morning, not being marked via London will not go by the shortest route. I have no time for more now than just to say it has gone and that I am well, but awfully tired. Goodbye dearest. When will this long cruise come to an end?

To Ellen Evans Mahan

Antwerp, June 29, 1894 [LC]

My dearest Deldie: Yours of the 18th and Lyle's of about the same date reached me yesterday. I do not wonder that you find the occupying of the new cottage expensive. I have always heard that nothing outruns calculations more. It is, I suppose, partly due to a lack of facing the music when making our calculations. We unconsciously look at as favorable a state of things as we can. However, having done your best, as I am sure you did, it is needless and useless to worry. I must hope that either the books bring in well, or that I go home soon and get a chance to work. I have now propositions for magazine articles which would bring me in $500 but I cant write a line—and my expenses mount malgré moi. It is an expensive station, but then one is kept too busy to brood which is a help. I find this place rather—indeed, very—uninteresting; but if I can only avoid being entertained and having to entertain in turn, I shall not mind. You have probably seen a rumor that Erben is to be succeeded in command of the station by Ramsay. How very distasteful to me this would be you can imagine, but there seems some foundation for it. It would be out of the frying pan into the fire—with the compensation only that Ramsay is a gentleman, though a very trying one. The other is scarcely so. It has become very hot all of a sudden, not our N.Y. heat, nor unendurable, but very distinctly hot. The paymaster's clerk tells me my allotment is made out for *three* years. I have twice asked him. If any doubt remain in your mind, inquire of the Navy Pay Office in N.Y. With regard to the photos I sent you, I had myself decided the fuller length to be the best, before consulting the Schiffs, each of whom independently selected the same. In returning to the photographer I marked them in order of my preference A.B.C. so that C, which you prefer, stood last with me; so opinions differ. I think C at once the most severe and most intellectual of all, for in it I had not tried to look pleasant.

You did not mention Rosie & Elsie[1] being with you—so I suppose Hart's illness stopped that. A letter from Nell came today. I hope she will find friends at Quogue—surprising she has so little enterprise in that way. Tell Lyle that while I had hoped he would reach the fourth form, I am not disposed to grumble at any time, provided I can feel that he is not careless, but conscientiously trying his best. What I most fear is that the start he has may make the third form year too easy & so encourage idleness. He removes now from us, may he try to feel that he is always with God. How people who do not believe in God find any adequate motive for doing right I cannot understand—I should be helpless. Good bye dearest. I have no news for you. Not only have principalities, potentates and Universities left me—but everything else. Love to all [etc.].

[P.S.]   I wrote you that if the books brought in over $500, I would want the balance *up to* $100. That is, you would have 500 in any event, and also any excess over $600.

To Helen Evans Mahan

Antwerp, July 3, 1894 [NWC]

My darling Helen: I begin a letter to you with very little material with which to fill it. It is a pretty sudden, though not wholly unwelcome, comedown from the rush and gaiety of London to find ourselves in this quiet place, lying a mile and a half from the city in a river which looks for all the world like Passaic Bay which we pass on the way to Elizabeth by the N.J.C.[1] And yet there is this difference, that here there is not even the semblance of a hill, such for instance as is to be found at Aunt Jennie's in Elizabeth or over on Staten Is. The Scheldt runs very swiftly between low meadows, protected by the famous dykes of the low countries—and the moment I looked at them I said "malaria probably, mosquitoes certainly." The latter we have had, though not nearly so badly as I feared, the former not. I find Antwerp quite uninteresting, which is due largely to the fact that I have lost interest in places, and in sight seeing for the most part. There is a fine Zoological garden upon the track of which Mr. Livingston[2] put me, and I find a weird interest in watching lions and tigers crunching bones—then there are many fine pictures which I have not yet seen. You may perhaps have heard already from Katharine Livingston of my meeting with them. It was rather a curious combination of incidents. I had gone to the

1. Elsie Smith, a friend of the Mahan family.
1. New Jersey Central Railroad.
2. John H. Livingston.

postoffice to buy some stamps which I rarely do—but finding a long queue waiting I soon got tired and started to come away and at the swinging doors I met Mr. Livingston just about to enter. He recognized me, whereas I failed to know him. It is four years since we met and he is looking gaunt and rather wan, which is not wonderful after the terrible affliction and strain he has undergone. He had also the advantage over me of knowing that I was here, while his appearance was totally unexpected to me. At his proposal I went to the hotel, a few steps away, where we talked for half an hour, then went again to the P.O. where I bought my stamps. As we entered I met our Consul just coming out, who gave me a late Paris *N.Y. Herald.* I dont know what curious feeling prompted me not to mail one of my letters in which I had asked Mr. Herbert to detach me in case Adml. Ramsey was coming to the *Chicago;* but I did withhold it, and on coming out and opening the paper I found that the command of the station was said to be offered to Adml. Kirkland.[3] Had I not first met Livingston and then the Consul the letter would probably have been sent. Of course you will not speak of this letter. The next day—Sunday—Mr. Livingston came on board with Katharine, Mrs. Gore, the latter's daughter, and a lady whose name I forgot. I took them over the ship and they remained about an hour. Katharine was looking very well and pretty, but I was distressed to see signs of discoloration running along her upper teeth, which are already a disfigurement and look ominous for the future. Mrs. Gore I had never known but slighty. My pretty English friend Rosie Schiff has also very delicate looking teeth—a great pity for she has a most attractive smile. Mamma's letter of June 22 reached me a few moments ago. I dont myself quite know the difference between L.L.D. and D.C.L. The former is commonly had Dr. of Laws, the latter Dr. of *Civil* Law, i.e. *Roman* Law. In both cases as applied to most recipients it is of course a purely honorary appellation. You have a house full sure enough, but I am glad of it. I thing it good for you all and would wish that Miss Elsie, or some other, were going to stay. You seem to make your way very well, but dear little Nell, from whom we never expected such a trouble, seems to have a diffidence towards strangers, which having them in the house wd. tend to dispel. The mixing easily with strangers is sometimes a natural gift, but where it is otherwise custom soon rubs off natural shyness. There are few men naturally more retiring than myself, yet this cruise has resulted in making me perfectly at ease in all companies and all places, except when making a speech, and even that was getting easier. I am going very shortly to order for you Parry's *Art of Music* which you must regard as a birthday gift. If I only knew of something for Nelly I would send it her also. I think I will anyhow and if "Ships that pass in the Night"[4] is not too expensive I

---

3. William A. Kirkland.
4. Beatrice Harraden, *Ships that Pass in the Night.* New York: G. P. Putnam's Sons, 1894.

will send it to her for her birthday. We are greatly fearing—at least I am—that the *Chicago* will have to stay out over the winter. I trust it may not be so. Tell mamma that was all nonsense in the *Times* about our repairs.[5] The truth is the boilers were known to be in bad condition when we left home, but it was thought they might last a year and then home. When we got here they were found to be in such bad shape that they could no longer be tinkered and it has been necessary to spend $15,000 which renews them so much that they can run on until she goes home for new boilers, engines and decks. It is a dreadful disappointment for me. Tell mamma to bear up for she seems to feel it more than last time I was away. Tell her also to remind Will Harison that *Harpers*, on declining my first book, wrote that their professional reader, while speaking well of it, advised against publication. He evidently was not the accomplished littérateur of whom the *World* has a story that he at once recommended it. Who he was I dont know—Soley alone can claim that. Love to mamma & tell her that if it is any comfort to know I am as anxious to get home as she is to have me, she can have it. I have secured another copy of that London *Times* [editorial] she gave the *Evg. Post*.[6] Love to the children.

To Ellen Evans Mahan

Antwerp, July 6, 1894 [LC]

Dearest Deldie: If life could be a burden to me with all my family blessings it would be now—such an interminable round of the pettiest yet most exasperating calls, which fill up all my time & tax my brain as much as the most important matters. Scarce 5 minutes ever elapse without some running into the cabin—between 8:30 and 3:30. At the latter hour I take flight ashore in order to get some rest. I am trying to wring out of my exhausted brain the *North Amn.* article[1] for I greatly need the promised $150. If by the time this reaches you, nothing definite transpires about our prospects I must ask you to order 100 more cards from Tiffany. A letter from Marston today tells me they have not been able to get copies of the books from Little & Brown, who write they have sold more within six weeks than in the previous six months (in America) and that Sampson Low's orders for 500 of the 1st and 250 of the second could not be executed till they had reprinted. All which I fear shows that Little & Brown are not quite enterpris-

---

5. "Chicago: Antwerp visited; Boilers will be repaired; salute acknowledged," *The New York Times*, June 24, 1894, p. 5.
6. Probably the editorial of May 11, 1894 which the *N.Y. Evening Post* republished.

1. "Possibilities of an Anglo-American Reunion," *North American Review* (November 1894).

ing enough to capture a boom. However, Marston adds he has notice that supplies are now (July 4) coming forward. I had today a very nice letter of congratulation from Kennedy,[2] who says inter alia that "the class is very enthusiastic." On the night of the 3d our minister in Brussels gave an entertainment, including a skirt dance by Loie Fuller, to which we were obliged to go.[3] Almost every one present was a stranger to me. Mrs. Adam, wife of one of the British Secretaries of Legation, I had known thirty years ago as a little girl of seven, Juliet Palmer, daughter of Dr. Palmer of the Navy and sister of Aulick.[4] When presented to her I said "I am one of those dreadful people who remember you as a little girl" but she seemed rather pleased and repeated it to several. I rather stuck to her through the evening, for though not pretty nor particularly bright she is entirely the *quiet* lady, and one never knows what one may drop on in these mixed assemblies abroad. We have been having very hot weather the past week, almost as bad as N.Y., but it is less excessive now. I have been a little upset by it—but nothing to mind were it not for the dreadful grind that every day brings. I am quite sure that I have something else to say but it cant be of much importance. I would be glad if you would send for Nell's baptismal day for a copy of Kate Douglas Wiggins' "A Cathedral Courtship." You can get it probably from any bookseller at not more than 75 cents—but I think Houghton & Mifflin are the Am. publishers. There are two dear little stories, but of course if Nell wants something different, give it her. I am so glad you find the cottage satisfactory and that you asked Elsie Smith. At present— alas! almost everything points to our remaining out till spring, but a letter from the Bu. Stm. Eng. (private) says fall—& our chf. engr. says the builders of the new engines will need to take measurements from the ship herself. Nous verrons. Always, my dearest, your fond husband and the children's loving father.

To Jane Leigh Mahan

Antwerp, July 8, 1894 [NWC]

My dear Jennie: It is very nice to hear such pleasant accounts as you give of the girls, and very tantalizing not to be able to see them for myself. However!

---

2. Lieutenant Duncan Kennedy, class of 1868, who was assigned to the Torpedo Station, 1893–1895.
3. Mahan's obligation led to a very pleasant exchange with the young American dancer. *See* J. M. Ellicott, "With Erben and Mahan on the *Chicago*," U.S. Naval Institute *Proceedings* (September 1941), p. 1238.
4. Juliet, daughter of Surgeon-General James C. Palmer, USN, had married Charles Fox Frederick Adam.

I did intend to try to write you some account of the doings in England—but to tell the truth I shrink from the labour, in view of the bulk of writing and think[ing] I daily have to do. I seem intellectually spent with each day's work. The University honors were doubtless the extreme of those formally bestowed upon me; yet I have myself been inclined to place two others, less formal, at the head. First, there was the dinner at the Navy Club, an organization dating to 1763, to which Nelson and all the naval swells have belonged. It has no house, but meets some half dozen times a year, generally on anniversaries of naval victories, for dinner. One guest only is invited—considered to be that of the President for the evg. On the Queen's birthday a guest had already been asked, but they broke their rule (conservative Englishmen!) and asked Erben and me. Both were engaged and could not come. On June 1, Lord Howe's Victory in 1794, they asked us two. Both accepted, but Erben was ill so I was the sole guest, and, I understood the first foreigner ever entertained by the Club. *Strictly for home consumption*, I believe they wanted me chiefly—in fact at the banquet May 24, one admiral said to me "Of course you understand your admiral being here prevents our giving you the prominence we wish," but be very careful not to say this. Well—to return to the Club—after dinner the last toast but one is "the Guest," and I was told I was expected to speak in reply. A veteran admiral, Sir Houston Stewart, whose father was a midshipman with Marryat under Cochrane in 1806, proposed the toast; preceding it with really a quite eloquent speech about the U.S. ending with me and my works. As I rose to reply, he proposed three cheers with really astonishing warmth and animation, leading himself, and closing the three with another —"tiger" as we say in America. If not modest, I am at least bashful, so you may imagine I was somewhat overwhelmed at being thus greeted by a hundred British admirals & captains. I think it was perhaps the most spontaneous and affecting testimonial I received while in England.

More quiet, but to my mind an equal distinction, coming from a single person, was my invitation to a tête-à-tête dinner—nearly—with the prime minister, Lord Rosebery. The admiral & myself dined at a state dinner he gave May 26, the official celebration of the Queen's birthday. On that day all the Cabinet gave dinners. First Lord to naval men, Foreign Affairs to diplomatic body, etc; but the Prime Minister to a select miscellaneous party —Prince of Wales, Archbishop of Canterbury, Head Master of Eton, Dean of Christ Church (Rosebery's College) Oxford, Lord Lieut. of Ireland, Huxley[1] and Lord Kelvin[2] great scientists etc etc. Erben and myself included—20 to 24. Not being very ranky, I was on the opposite side of the

---

1. Thomas Henry Huxley, English biologist.
2. William Thomson, President of the Royal Society. He had been electrical engineer for the Atlantic, West Indian, and Brazilian submarine cables, and invented the navigational sounding machine that bears his name.

table from the Minister, and did not fall in with him till just before leaving. After a few words, as we were moving off, he said "Well Captain Mahan when can we renew this conversation?" I, looking upon it as a polite façon de parler, said "Perhaps we may meet again this evg," at the Foreign Office reception to which most were going—and thought no more of it. The next Thursday, May 31, I had reserved for a rest, but in my mail came a letter from him saying he was sure it was nearly hopeless, but could I dine with him that day or Friday en petite comité. Of course to see closely so distinguished a man with a probable future, (he is only 45), I pitched the rest overboard, and, being engaged for Friday, telegraphed I could come that night. Was it not lucky I had it? He asked to meet me Mr. Lecky the historian, & Mr. John Morley, his colleague in the Cabinet, whose name you probably know. Lecky could not come, but I think to be asked to meet those three, and considering Rosebery's position, was one of the most distinguished compliments paid me. Morley had to go off about ten to the House, and I sat till nearly 12, the conversation between R. and myself continuing animated till then. When I left he walked round with me to my lodgings and on the way took me into one of the last century clubs, showing me a table at which Charles James Fox[3] used to play, the circumference of which was hollowed out to allow his fat paunch room. I met Lord Rosebery again at Oxford, at dinner at Christ Church on June 20—he being a D.C.L. of the University. When I spoke to him, he answered your question of himself, saying: "Well, I think you have broken the record, in taking a degree from each University the same week (or year)." I fell in with him again later in the evg., not being by him at dinner, and after some conversation he again asked me to dinner for the next night, but I was engaged. On the 22d I lunched with one of the Rothschilds, half a dozen only and very simple. One guest came late, Sir Francis Knollys, and as he took his seat he said to me "I have just come from Lord Rosebery who asked me to remember him to you" so I suppose he really took a fancy to me. I hope that Elly, Lyle etc will have kept my letters, which will certainly interest you. You know perhaps that I was invited to Hatfield House, Lord Salisbury's, the late Prime Minister, from Friday till Monday, a customary period in England. Rosebery's state dinner being official & royal, on Saturday, clashed with this—so I only got there on Sunday. The other Prime Minister still living, Gladstone, took no notice of me. Some say that not his eyes only, but his unwillingness to increased naval expenditure caused his retirement, when he found his colleagues obstinately set upon it. If so, I had a hand in his resignation, for all agree in telling me that the increased vote for the navy was due to the books. Many naval officers said this, and Rothschild said "You are responsible for our increased taxation this year," in part of course. The Hatfield invitation was simply one of dozens they are con-

3. English Liberal statesman, rival of Pitt.

stantly giving, but it was pleasant to see a family, that has so much, so simple. The Marquis [of Salisbury] himself has less social facility than Rosebery, more English diffidence of manner, and a huge man. They have a private chapel, Holy Communion at 9:30 AM Sundays, Evensong about 4 or 5. I arrived too late for the former—went to the parish church, about a stone's throw from the house in the forenoon, but to chapel in the afternoon. The family & servants all there, I suppose 40 souls—choral service—men all on one side, women on the other, & very little less than filling the chapel. In front the Marquis, now sixty-odd, a son in law with two lads of six or so— half a dozen younger men butlers valets etc behind. On the opposite side Lady Salisbury, daughters & daughters in law, maids & maidservants of all degrees in their caps etc. Singular lack of beauty in the family; the only pretty woman, & she quite attractive in looks and manner, was the eldest son's daughter—the future Marchioness. It is a house where Mary of Scots was confined; and the oak still lives, though sadly declined, under which the Princess Elizabeth was sitting when she saw riding furiously towards her a man whom she supposed came to summon her to the tower, but on the contrary announced her sister's death.

Well, how do I feel about it all. Of course I have been immensely gratified and pleased. It is but human, and I cannot think wrong so to feel; but elated, I think not. It is constantly ringing in my ears "What hast thou that thou has not received?" So feeling, withal, there has been an absence of self-consciousness or embarrassment that has fairly surprised me. Smalley[4] did me there no more than justice—I have really not felt any conceit, for the simple reason that my knowledge of the success of my work is wholly external. I know it as a fact—but I dont realize it, nor, somehow, identify it with myself. Again, as regards embarrassment, I have never seemed to *realize*, even with the Queen, that I was speaking to other than a lady who was entitled to certain forms of respect. All that kind of self-possession seems so unnatural to *me* that I dont understand it; for I think you know I inherit father's disposition to withdraw into the background—and indeed I do so. I think the British flunky comes much nearer overwhelming me than the biggest lord in the puddle. The look of calm surprise that can evolve from their faces, e.g. if you take a wrong direction, is extraordinary, & particularly as they effect it without moving a muscle or winking an eyelash. I own I think them the most formidable members of British society.

Of this place I shall say nothing and for the rest of my news I must refer you to the letters I trust are in Quogue if you care to read them. Except fatigue, there was scarcely a drawback to the English stay. The weather

---

4. George Washington Smalley, who was in charge of the *Tribune*'s European correspondence from 1867 to 1895, when he returned to America to act as American correspondent of the London *Times*, 1895–1905. He was a proponent of strong Anglo-American friendship.

was vile—but there was no contretemps. We stayed long enough but had not I think outstayed our welcome. In fact we were given to understand it was the Prince of Wales' special request we (Erben & I) should attend the Trinity House dinner—the night before we sailed—when half a dozen members of the royal family were present—and I had refused several dinners of three & four weeks' notice, because of our going. The books are booming. The Eng. publisher writes me he had an order in Boston for 500 of the first and 250 of the second, which Little & Brown could not fill till new copies were printed. They had sold in six weeks more than in six months previous. This did England for us.

Give my best love to Aunty.

To Ellen Evans Mahan

Antwerp, July 12, 1894 [LC]

Dearest Deldie: Your letter of the 3d was recd. this morning. I shall be glad when you have your type-writer again, for I am very hard worked, worried and dispirited, and it is disheartening to get such short letters with no news beyond the barest announcement of how you all are. However I myself can do little more than write a line or two—there is nothing occurring of personal interest, and I am more and more harassed every succeeding day with the most insignificant details yet all requiring diligent attention. I dont know why or how things seem to go so much harder than they did— but they certainly do. Undoubtedly I recognize that all work—being appointed by God—is equally honorable and good; but the wear and tear at present is very great. I live in the midst of repugnant surroundings—all which tells. Yet I am well—quite well; and come up again the moment the strain is off. But my mind sets firmer and firmer to retire and on no account—if I can help myself—to do any work for a service that can do no better for me than waste these two years of my life. You are very right to have the children's friends there and I hope that the cheque from Little and Brown will relieve your anxieties in part. Dont send me the $100 unless you see your way clear —which I should think would be the case if the cheque exceeds 500. I have nearly completed an article for the *North American Review* for which they promise $150. I should never have attempted it but for the need of money. I am sorry to learn that an exaggerated account of our collision day before yesterday was in the home papers, and may have caused you anxiety.[1] It

---

1. Excerpt from the *Chicago's* log for July 11, 1894: "At 7:30 A.M., the English S.S. *Azov*, Liverpool, coming from Batum, Russia, Capt. Richard Jones, struck the ship

might have been serious but was not—about $5000 damages but no danger. The fault in no way ours. I wrote Nellie three days ago and this must go this evg if it is to catch the English mail. Good bye dearest.

To J. B. Sterling[1]

USS *Chicago*, Antwerp, July 18, 1894 [LC]

Dear Colonel Sterling: I have not forgotten my promise to undertake the paper for the United Service Institute.[2] On the contrary, it has been much on my mind, as I have gradually realized how large and intricate were the conditions with which I had to grapple; but I find it ncessary to write to you that you will have to allow me a great deal of time—quite indefinite, in fact. All the best part of my days is taken up with the ship routine, which I find exhausts my brain force to a very crippling extent. I can only find opportunity to work at night—which I *never* do when ashore. This all means not merely less work, but,—a far more serious matter,—work of inferior quality, if too doggedly persisted in. Such an article as you have asked should be the best I can do, and I cannot hasten it. In fact, while I will not say I have no ideas on the matter, they are unformulated; and I must run through the actual experiences of the naval manoeuvres of some years back, or else I may assume conditions contrary to hard facts.

If master of my time, I would give myself up to the subject, and my three or four morning hours would, I dare hope, fetch me on with reasonable speed; but that is just what I cannot do. It would be somewhat different, too, if I had all my ideas fixed and had only to shape them, but actually I have just run off a short article—5,000 words—involving ideas I have long held, and yet found much difficulty, under my conditions, in linking them together.[3]

---

on the starboard bow at the forward sponson for the 6″ gun, cutting through the sponson." A Board of Investigation convened by Admiral Erben to report upon "all the attendant circumstances connected with the collision" met on July 14, and rendered the opinion that the *Azov* was "wholly responsible for the collision." The time for repair was estimated at twenty days. When the accident occurred, the *Chicago* already had fifty workmen from ashore repairing her machinery and boilers.

1. A colonel in the Coldstream Guards, editor of the Royal United Service Institution *Journal*.
2. "Blockade in Relation to Naval Strategy," Royal United Service Institution *Journal* (November 1895).
3. "Possibilities of an Anglo-American Reunion," *North American Review* (November (1894).

To Ellen Evans Mahan

Dearest Deldie: I received yesterday yours of the 11th enclosing Rep. Hale's and Mrs. Powel's, and I write now—though I mailed a letter Friday— to beg that you will accept her invitation and go to her for the better part of a week at least. Home is very sweet—but home is also your place of business with its frequent little worries and I think it would do you good to get away. Helen could run the house and Rose being there would help her in case of any real emergency. For the same reason I could wish you would go to Rebecca's[1] in the fall, after Lyle is off to school; & it is an argument the more for carrying out the plan I suggested about Europe—should it be otherwise feasible.

Please also dont read or trouble about any publications concerning my affair with Erben—dont hunt them up. The public will have little interest in the matter unless indiscreet friends of mine warm it up. I hope Luce wont be a firebrand—I suspect him of being "Retired List."[2]

I enclose you Higginson's[3] letter. It will have the value of showing you that professional opinion cannot be biassed by the ex parte statements of a man like Erben. If I am able to conduct myself throughout like a gentleman and a Christian all will doubtless go well in the end.

The disappointment about going home is inexpressible, and not less so that I believe the decision, or rather the influence that has urged the Secy. to his decision—to be malicious. But none of that is our affair. We have a bit of tribulation and sorrow to pass through, in doing which we must keep up our hearts. You seem less cheerful than your wont, and I think change will do you good.

I will say no more now, lest I trench on Helen's letter.

[P.S.] Yours of the 13th saying the $100 had been sent just came. The same mail brought the enclosed from Meade[4] which I am sure will please you—particularly taken in conjunction with H's. While both peculiar men —no one will deny them the character of good officers in the sense in which Erben tried to condemn me. I did not know you would want so much money but my great desire that your mind should be easy is attained. I shall try to help myself out with magazine writing.

There is no reason that Jennie or Eloise Derby should keep you from Newport, under the circs.

1. Rebecca Lewis Evans, of Philadelphia, wife of Allen Evans who was the son of Mrs. Mahan's uncle Edmund C. Evans.
2. Luce retired in 1889. Mahan feared that Luce, being free of possible retribution, would espouse his cause too vigorously.
3. Captain Francis J. Higginson, class of 1862, stationed at the Navy Yard, Mare Island.
4. Richard W. Meade, who was preparing to assume command of the North Atlantic Station.

To Little, Brown and Company

USS *Chicago*, Antwerp, July 24, 1894 [LC]

Gentlemen: I beg to acknowledge with thanks your letter of the 10th inst, and to congratulate you as well as myself on the very favorable returns of sales during the past six months.

I grieve to say that I can give you no satisfactory reply in the matter of the *Life of Nelson*. I have for some time been wholly unable to do any serious head work—my brain seeming to get over-tired during the fore part of the day, and not answering my calls upon it in the evening. All my previous work—*Sea Power* &c—has always been composed before 1 PM, and that is precisely the time which I now have to give to the infinitesimal details of the ship. Were it only a question of working harder, I might undertake it; it is the discouraging conviction that the work would fall below what I have heretofore done that deters me. I have recently attempted a magazine article,[1] simply because I wanted the money—the experience has been painful and instructive.

It is my purpose when I leave this ship to ask for a year's leave of absence and devote myself wholly to *Nelson*. If granted and, as now seems probable, the ship does not return till next May—a year will bring me close to my period of retirement in Sept. 1896.

All this postpones my undertaking very indefinitely—but while disappointing to you, I can assure you it is in every point of view a far greater trial to myself. I am, however, quite helpless. I can neither quit the ship nor do good work on board.

To Hilary A. Herbert

USS *Chicago*, Antwerp, July 26, 1894 [NA]

Sir:

1. I have to acknowledge the receipt of the Department's letter dated July 9, 1894, in regard to the failure to fire the 5″ B.L.R. guns of this ship at the Great Gun Practice held during the last two quarters.

2. Target practice was not held with the above mentioned guns by the order of the Commander-in-Chief.[1]

---

1. *See* Mahan to Ellen Evans Mahan, July 6, 1894.

1. The inquiry concerning the failure to fire the 5-inch BLRs actually came from Ramsay. Erben also answered it, stating that for ordinary target practice he did not deem it advisable to go to the expense of tearing down bulkheads and moving the heavy furniture.

To Helen Evans Mahan

My darling Helen: It was my intention to write you last night & mail the letter this morning; but the mosquitoes were so bad as to make impossible to do so. It was slap-slap, all the time, I could read with the book on my knee, but could not spare the use of my hands to hold the paper and pen. I have protected my sleeping room with bar door and window, but the main cabin is open to their invasion. We are lying in quite a narrow river surrounded on all sides by flat plains—the general characteristic of the Netherlands, both Belgium and Holland—the surface of plains being little above, if it be not actually below that of the river. They are protected by the dykes of which you hear so much in Dutch history, or will hear if you ever read Motley. I am heartily tired of Antwerp which does not possess interest for over a week, and our surroundings are not pleasant. The weather has been exceedingly bad, raining every day, which is bad enough ashore but very much worse on board ship—and besides renders drills & neatness almost unattainable. Then, too, the cause of our detention—the repairs—keeps us topsy-turvy; we are in a din and disorder comparable to a navy yard without the satisfaction of being at or near home. It has also been hot much of the time, but not enough to mind, and sufficiently cool at night for sleep. I am remarkably well, despite everything—not very alert or strong but that I attribute mainly to the soft damp climate which makes the Dutch and Belgians the slow phlegmatic people which they are. Your letter of the 15th inclosing one from Lyle, has just come. Though very interesting in the account of yourselves there is nothing that seems to call for reply. I want you to urge mamma to go to Mrs. Powel's; while Rosie is in the house there will be always a person of sufficient experience to act in case anything unusual arise during a short absence. Mamma may be never so happy at home & yet be better for the entire change and release for four or five days from the "trivial round." I *particularly* wish her to go—and preferably before you go to Bar Harbor. Tell Nellie that I think I have track of a "solid book" for her—but not before fall. I dont want too much solidity in summer. I dont find anything to do here, and dont feel at liberty—either from duty or from economy—to go away. In fact I dont want to go away—have not the slightest desire or interest to do so. I have to go ashore most afternoons for the same reason that I want mamma to go—to get rid of the trivial round. I go generally to the picture gallery where there are several hundred pictures—many of them masterpieces of the Dutch & Flemish school, notably of Rubens who was born here. I cant appreciate them but I moon away my time in a half interested way. Other times I stroll round the streets or sit gaping in the park thinking of nothing at all. There is a fine Zoological Garden to which I have been twice. Tell mamma that I have received the draft from C & [illegible] Randolph for £20.8s. I must close now, for I have to read and dispatch an article for the *North American Review*,[1] which I have held on to till the last moment. Good bye dear child. Ever so much love to mamma, brother, sister and Dodie.[2]

[P.S.]   The enclosed may interest though you know the facts.[3]

To George Sydenham Clarke

USS *Chicago*, Antwerp, July 29, 1894 [LC]

My dear Clarke: I only saw today, and then by accident, your orders to Woolwich. How far they are otherwise agreeable to you I cannot know, but they will at least have the advantage of bringing you back to England, and from that point of view I beg to congratulate most heartily both yourself and Lady Clarke. You are ahead of me in escaping from your trouble, for I grieve to say the *Chicago*'s return is postponed for another year, and by so much, I fear, retarded my resumption of the work with which my future seems most hopefully identified. Happily, the past is secure, unless wrecked by my own mistakes in the future; only myself can deprive me of the recognition which your country men have obtained for me from my own, who were at last waked up by the reception you gave me. This the sales showed, being more than double the most prosperous previous halfyear; and the English publishers had to wait for their orders owing to the American demand.

As I mentioned in my last I have dispatched, after many hesitations, the article Bryce[1] asked of me. You will find points in which I differ from you; nor could I accentuate our points of agreement as I could have wished (they are much more fundamental than the differences) owing to the way our government looks on the expression of political opinions, however general, by officers—particularly if diametrically opposed to the traditions of the party in office. I am quite one with you about the necessity of broadening our sphere, but it would be imprudent to say so too explicitly. Besides, it might antagonize our people who must be warily converted. But what I started to say in this paragraph was that I had of course to read your paper several times—and each time I did so with increasing admiration for the matter itself and for its presentment.[2] Carnegie is nowhere—and vaporous.

---

1. "Possibilities of an Anglo-American Reunion."
2. Rosalie Evans.
3. Enclosure not found.

1. Lloyd Stephens Bryce, owner and editor of the *North American Review*.
2. George Sydenham Clarke, "Naval Union with Great Britain: Reply to Mr. Andrew Carnegie," *North American Review* (March 1894).

[305]

To Ellen Evans Mahan

Antwerp, July 29, 1894 [LC]

My dearest Deldie: Very little news have I for you, my darling; and Sunday though it be my time has been all broken up from the quiet hour I had hoped to give you. The mosquitoes make it quite impossible to write at night. They are very stupid, as compared with the Jersey species; I think I kill 20 or 30 every evening; but they keep the hands too busy and annoy too much for me to be able to write. Delay succeeds delay & it now seems probable that we may not leave here before the 12th or even the 15th of August—for a telegram has been received that a number of officers and men are to arrive on the 11th to relieve those of ours whose times are out. Our great misfortune, speaking humanly, has been that our boilers would not hold out—bad—for a few months longer. Then we might have got home. Now, having had to spend £3,000 on them, the Govt. must justify the expenditure by getting service out of them. We are a little exercised with the fear that the troubles which exist all over the world may call us some-where—notably just now Corea is on our mind. Well—as you said about your worry over the finances—it is astonishing how hard we find it to trust God. The large sales of the last six months were certainly due—and due only—to the furor over me in England. My exile here led to that, and it is quite certain the returns would not otherwise have exceeded those of January —$500 or so. Yet I find myself harassed and agitated about the future. I think, however, with both you and me it is infirmity and not willfulness. We try to trust, though we succeed ill. We shall miss the Cowes Regatta, almost certainly, through having to wait here for the above steamer. The admiral will telegraph for a change, but I question his getting it. Our friends, the Schiffs, were quite counting on this ship being there, and till today I ex-pected it; now they must go lamenting. Antwerp is certainly for me a used up place. I go ashore every afternoon for three hours—just to walk and lounge—no amusement but the change seems a relief from the dead monotony of the ship. I strongly suspect that hostility to me has much to do with our movements from the Dept. Herbert has written me very pleasantly, as you know, but Ramsay handles him. Fortunately the Clovers and Ramsays are great friends, and as Mrs. C. has come to Europe, Clover would be worse hit than I at any change. He is a good and capable officer, but deadly slow. A letter from my French translator of Book One, M. Boisse, tells me he hears it said that the *Revue Maritime* has not in a long time published so interesting an article (as the Introductory Chapt.) [1]

---

1. Alfred T. Mahan, "Influence de la puissance maritime sur l'histoire," *Revue Maritime et Coloniale*, CXXI, p. 339–375; CXXII, p. 344–373, etc. The translation ran from February, 1894, with the preface by Boisse, until December, and concluded

I shall close my letter & mail this p.m. dearest, for there is no use in keeping it. News there can be none. I have ordered myself two dozen shirts at 10 francs each—rather less than 2 dollars. I fear I may be deceived on quality, but they seem to me to look well enough, and so I thought best to secure them. Linen goods are cheap here and the fit is good. If I dared trust my judgment of material I daresay I might buy to advantage, but I cannot. Dear me! What an element of happiness is in congenial work—which here is wholly wanting to me—that and being with you and the children seem to me the chief ingredients. With such good general health as I fortunately now enjoy and our other mild prosperity there seems as if little else could be asked. Well I have been on board nearly 15 months out of the 24—let us hope the remaining nine will pass quickly and happily. Goodbye dearest. Always fondly thine own.

To Ellen Kuhn Mahan

Antwerp, August 3, 1894 [LC]

My darling Nellikin: Your letter of the 22d. July reached me yesterday. It is not often that letters come to me just à propos for answering. Usually I have a hunt for the last from the one to whom I am about to write, but this came just as your turn did. The mail leaves here tomorrow though I fear the steamer is a slow one. I also had a delightfully long letter from mamma and very glad I am to see the type-writer once more, that I may not have to put up with such shreds of letter as latterly. Tell mamma I believe every one who builds a house has the same experience as she of the costs running up. I was sorry, though not surprised, to hear it. I am feeling very poor tonight myself. I had with great difficulty written an article for the *North American Review* which I sent by mail a week ago. In considering it since I became forced to the opinion that its publication would probably hurt both me and the Navy; so to day I cabled not to publish it, and instead of being $150 to the good, I am out of pocket four dollars. But my mind would not rest, and the more I prayed for guidance the more uneasy I became; so I think I must have done right. I have not, in truth, the time to write well; and when handling a delicate subject which this was, one needs to have all one's faculties in good order. Now as regards your drawing or taking up something else I am, I confess, somewhat perplexed. I think, perhaps, it might be better to get some one's opinion—your teacher's best—

with the section "Conditions mises à la paix par l'Angleterre." No more appeared, in spite of the "à suivre."

as to whether there is any promise of your doing better, or rather of your really doing well. However that may be, I cannot look upon the time spent as lost. You will derive some benefit from it, undoubtedly. Yet, if your teacher says that you can never attain excellence, it would be a waste of time to continue. I think I would like to get his opinion, if possible. For writing I look forward with distrust, although I myself have been fairly successful. Excellence therein depends—as in art—upon two principal things; the originality which has something to say, and the power of expression, form, what they call technique in music & painting, by which you are able to say clearly, perfectly, and elegantly what you have to say. Both are natural gifts—but the latter can be cultivated to a high degree, whereas no amount of cultivation will ever give originality of idea, if the gift be not born in you. To acquire the gift of expression, or to improve your own gift of that sort, you need training, the use of models—that is, the reading of authors with good styles, and not others—and also someone to point out to you what is good and what defective in your models. Now I dont know how to set about getting you that training—nor do I know enough to lay out a course of reading. If I were home, I could make inquiries. Mamma, however, might speak to Dr. Dix, and ask if he could recommend any person who could either give you instruction, or recommend some one to do so. It would undoubtedly be very safe for you to read, even unsystematically, some authors celebrated for their style, some really great poets. For example, Macauley's Essays which Dodie has, and Milton and Shakespeare. If you really like any of these they may, in style, make a great impression upon you. A most important thing will be to acquire the power of reading steadily. This must be done gradually—read with strenuous attention, not wandering, as long as you can without tiring; but when really tired, stop. You will thus soon learn about how long you can read at one spell *at first*. Take that as your measure, and give that much time every day, *no matter whether you feel like it that day or not*. Bind your attention to it for so long, and no longer. After some time you will be able to do more, but I should suppose that two hours at a stretch would be the most you could do, even after a year or two—at first perhaps not over ¾ hour. This amount of reading, solitary, should I think be your aim—two hours a day whether in one, two, or three sittings. Classes for literature are sometimes formed & are doubtless good—but nothing can take the place of one's own individual, solitary, struggle. Being still only seventeen, you have before you three or four years in which to acquire the mastery of expression—that is of writing perfectly clearly, simply, and correctly—thus learning to use an instrument without which no thoughts, however admirable, can be properly set forth. This clear, precise, accurate writing of good English is a very different thing from style. Good English and its rules are the same for every one— style is characteristic of the individual and is different for each one. In fact the attempt to imitate, consciously, another person's style will only ruin your own and not give you his. A Frenchman once said, truly, "Style is the man himself." The writing of good English consists indeed rather in the avoidance of faults, and is a matter of rule. It is most important to acquire this so thoroughly that you dont have to think about it—just as you dont think of your feet when you dance—and it can be acquired very much as the steps of dancing, by attention and pains. When you have gained that—and three years is none too long—your style can work unconsciously, and you can get out successfully whatever is in you. I think myself it is quite probable you have something in you; what I cant tell, and you are too young to show; but bear in mind that the conditions of all success are patient drudgery in mastering the rudiments, and even genius can never fully express itself unless it has learned the technique of its art, be it painting, or music, or writing.

Now this is a pretty long preachment and resolves itself to this: you should have a guide, teacher, and then you must read under his or her guidance (preferably a man) and also write. By writing your faults will appear and can be gradually corrected.

I have really no news to give you. We hope to leave here on Monday for Cowes, so as to see something of the regatta, and then the admiral talks of going to St. Malo on the French coast, returning later to Southampton when he will haul down his flag, thank goodness, on Sept. 6, and get out. The next one may be worse, but it will be a relief to get rid of this one. I see no prospect of any further enjoyment in Europe—but so long as I have to be on board ship it is better than other stations. But my greatest need now is rest and work. Rest from the hideous trivialities of my present daily life, and work of a character to occupy my mind healthfully.

Give my dearest love to mamma & the children.

To Helen Evans Mahan

Antwerp, August 5, 1894 [NWC]

My darling Helen: Despite the mosquitoes, I must write you tonight a line for your birthday tomorrow; for we are to leave here in the afternoon and I fear the morning will be too occupied otherwise. I am most heartily glad to get away. We have now been here over seven weeks, weeks of disorder and discomfort without a single relieving feature except the general good health with which God has blessed us. We go to Cowes & hope to reach there late Tuesday afternoon. So you are twenty one. Twenty one years since that squawking little brat was cared for by Mrs. Oliver, Carolina,

Pepa et alia. Well, as I am by way of being complimentary tonight, I will say you might have been worse! I had this morning Nelly's letter of the 27th July, and one from mamma of the same date. Neither gave much news but then I know there is not much going. We also have very little. I hope that in Antwerp we have touched bottom for dullness, and, what I much more care for, that I have turned the corner of my long absence. It is an inexpressible regret to me to be away so much, and also to have such a break in my writing. I had a letter from Mr. Scudder today, hoping I had not forgotten the papers I was to write for the *Atlantic*;[1] but in truth I am so much discouraged over my slip up for the *North American*[2] that I have little hope of accomplishing anything. It is impossible to effect anything amid such interruptions and mental fatigue. Goodbye dear child; many happy returns! but remember that to have them in happiness you must not *over*work while you are young. Dearest love to mamma, Nellie & Lyle.

To Ellen Evans Mahan

Cowes, England, August 8, 1894 [LC]

My dearest Deldie: I had very nearly forgotten that my letter for you was overdue—having sent one to Helen for her birthday instead, three days ago. But in truth I have been in no state for writing nor am yet. We left Antwerp day before yesterday, about 4 p.m., and were so fortunate as to have very pleasant weather coming between two gales of wind, the latter of which began to pipe when we were about twenty miles from here, and has been making itself disagreeable ever since. The sun is now breaking through the clouds but the wind is high and boating rough, which is bad for me, as I am to dine again at Osborne this evening at the ultra fashionable, but I suppose wholly palatial hour of 8:45. As I said to Clover if the invite were to Captain Mahan I might appreciate the compliment, but to the Captain of the *Chicago* accompanying the Admiral Commanding a squadron of our ships, there is an impersonality in the matter not at all flattering. On Friday I am to dine (the admiral also) on board the Royal Yacht—where we will meet the Emperor of Germany. Tomorrow night, if not officially called off, I dine with the Schiffs who have come down for the races. This morning Mr. Geo. Gould[1] pulled alongside with two ladies who had become frightened & wetted trying to get to the *Vigilant*. I was just seeing

1. "Admiral Earl Howe," *Atlantic Monthly* (January 1894), was the last article Mahan wrote for that publication.
2. *See* Mahan to Ellen Kuhn Mahan, August 3, 1894.

1. George J. Gould, American railroad entrepreneur.

the admiral to the gangway, and seeing Gould backed out for I confess the name is distasteful to me—so it fell to Nazro to take them to Erben's cabin, where they were to wait till a boat could be given them to go to the yacht. Nazro thought one of them was Mrs. Gould—though oldish looking for him and so addressed her, but she said "I am not Mrs. Gould, I am the Duchess of Manchester." I did not see her and only mention the incident inasmuch as I believe you knew Constance Iznaga. Your long letter of July 21 was a great satisfaction to me, though I wish I could hope never again to have a letter from you. I quite sympathize with your feelings about having people in the house, as you know people bother me also, but I did not know you felt the same; it is not amiable but very natural. Your experience with the house is that of every one who builds, so at least I understand. The only thing that troubles me is that you have had to trench upon the money given for Lyle's schooling. It was for that object only, and the sole reply we can make is that a mortgage can at any time be put on the house, if necessary. No—you must not grumble about the appetites from fresh air—they are too good a token. It is delightful to hear what you tell about Lyle's perseverance. Under God's continued blessing it will be the assurance of success to him, for I am sure he has ability. About Jomini, I must leave the decision to you about his remaining at Quogue—only dont engage it for the following winter, or give him up. I cannot willingly contemplate ever having to treat another dog as we did poor Major. My heart is very tender and doubly so when thus away from all for whom I care. Think what a disappointment to me having to cable not to publish my article —150 dollars given & all that grinding labor—but I think now that the very grind showed that I was not fit to work. God knows His own way—but it seems hard at times to be thus fettered. I had a letter from Scudder last mail, urging the two articles that I once said I would write for him. I shall have to reply, as I did to Little & Brown about *Nelson*, that it is hopeless. My whole nervous system is in a state of exasperation hard to control at times. Before closing today, I want to say how pleased I am at your asking people like Esther and Emma,[2] who can make you no return.

Friday Aug. 10

Yours of the 30th with Helen's and Lyle's came yesterday. It dont seem to require an answer. I quite agree that it would be desirable for Rosie to be in the same building with you, and devoted as Elsie and she may be, she needs more than one person's company. I dined at Osborne as I wrote above. The proceeding differed from last year's in very little. There were fewer ladies than before—I sat between Sir Edmund Commerell, one of their most distinguished admirals, a Victoria Cross man and very agreeable, and a

---

2. Possibly, Emma Totteral Evans, second wife of Mrs. Mahan's uncle William Elbert Evans.

Colonel Philips of the Royal Marines—also very pleasant. The occasion was somewhat more pleasant to me than last year because I knew many more people, and so had some one to talk to all the time. I also fell in, rather than was presented to, the Emperor of Germany. As I told you last year, after dinner we gathered in a long drawing room, the Queen (who appeared to me much aged in the twelvemonth) seated in the middle, the company divided at either end. I was talking to some one when an aide de camp came to me and said several of us were to be formed and pass before the Queen, and to follow him. So I passed on the opposite side from her making a half reverence as I passed, to join the group of presentees, and as I reached the other side the Emperor spoke to me. I cannot now recall either how he came to speak, whether I was presented, or what he said. My mind being wholly bent on following my first orders I was taken unawares, and we had not exchanged two sentences when the aide said "I beg your Majesty's pardon, but the line is being formed to pass before the Queen & Capt. Mahan is wanted." So I was whisked round and followed in the queue. When I stopped and bowed before her, she simply said that she remembered having seen me last year—to which I replied that I had then had the honor to be presented & passed on—but to the other side from the Emperor. His aide, a rear admiral, had spoken to me before dinner and said the E. was much interested in my books, and the Captain of his yacht told me next day that the Emperor had wanted to have some conversation with me, but that I was carried off. Now that I am back in England the compliments begin again, though of course less formal and more incidental. I went today to return my visit to the Captain of the Prince of Wales's yacht,[3] and while I was talking with him in walked Sir Henry Keppel,[4] a retired admiral of 86, who said he had seen my name on the Prince's book, (each visitor to the yacht puts his name on it) and had come in to see *me*. I said to him that he was looking very well, (which he is for 86) and he replied that reading the books would do anyone good! I could only say laughingly that I did not know I had appeared in the medical line, but I was very glad the result was such in his case. As I wrote my name in the book, I added U.S. Navy only and said to the captain "Is it necessary to add the ship's name?" "Well, not in *your* case, I should say," he answered—which was not badly turned. It seems puerile to repeat such things, but I know they interest you, and you will see they dont get into indiscreet hands. Imagine a man like Commerell saying to me "I wish you would study up the question of Gibraltar, for your opinion would have great weight over here." I had a curious interview in the grounds of the Club House. A youngish man—35 or so—came up & spoke to me having

---

3. Rear Admiral Fullerton.
4. Sir Henry, admiral of the fleet and first and principal naval aide de camp to the Queen, was not retired. By special dispensation, his name was retained on the active list until his death in 1904.

the tact to add—"I think we met at Hatfield." I then caught on to his being one who had acted as a private secretary to Lord Salisbury. He said a little later "From your name you must be of Irish blood." "Yes," I replied "my father was Irish." "Are you any relation to Parnell?"[5] "Not that I know of" I answered. He then said "You are so much like him—less in coloring than in feature—as to suggest the idea of relationship. After you left Lord Salisbury said to me—'What a remarkable looking man Captain Mahan is' (have not the Irish the knack of blarney) and I then mentioned the resemblance which he also recognized." Last evening I dined with the Schiffs at their hotel— Erben & his wife also there—after which the party returned to the ship to see the illumination & fireworks had in the Regatta. They were very pretty but nothing extraordinary. Yours of the 31st has just come in. I dont know much about prices in Nice, and would upon the whole rather prefer Beaulieu as being nearer Villefranche, but I own I rather shrink from the extra expense, seeing the uncertainty of our movements. There is always the possibility of missing me. It is extraordinary that Ramsay should be jealous of me—but I think I am more likely to be feted out here than at home. My sole desire is to be quietly with you all. I care for no fetes. Meantime I will try and learn about prices etc etc—& when you go to N.Y. you can find what the return ticket to Genoa will be. How long are Lyle's Xmas holidays? I am rather averse to any cheap camping out project also—but I dont know how I shall bear the additional separation. My own opinion is that Ramsay will try to keep the ship out just so long as he can keep me—but I will have a try at Herbert to bring me home when two years are up. As to promotion it is wholly secondary in my view to getting at my writing again.

Love to the children.

[P.S.]   Keep enclosed.[6]

To Horace E. Scudder

USS *Chicago*, Cowes, August 12, 1894 [HUL]

My dear Mr. Scudder: Yours of July 26 has been received and I thank you very sincerely for your congratulations upon my reception in England. That the entertaining process did absorb some of my attention is certainly true, but the diversion did not extend over five weeks. My failure to accomplish any work is due not to that, but to the absorption of my time by the petty details of ship economy, having only an overfatigued brain for mental effort, with results disastrous to the quality of the work turned out.

---

5. Charles Stewart Parnell, Irish political leader.
6. Enclosure not found.

Since I sent you *Howe*, I have made an attempt to get on with the *Life of Nelson*; but was forced to abandon it with the conviction that it was too far below my best to justify continuance. A month ago I accepted an offer from Bryce to write a short article for the *North American*, tempted by what seemed high pay for the amount turned out; but the result was that after mailing I became so dissatisfied with the work that I cabled not to publish—a back out that never happened to me before.

It is pain and grief to me, but I fear I am condemned to silence as long as our sapient department rulers keep me here. Do you know I have on the best authority, that the naval officer who keeps me here, and has most influence with the Secy., had never (at least up to three months ago) read my works which have set all the professional men in Europe thinking and talking.

[P.S.]   I must not forget to thank you for my election to the Histl. Society.[1]

To Hilary A. Herbert

USS *Chicago*, Southampton, August 15, 1894 [NA]

Sir: I have to report that on Saturday the eleventh instant while manning yards in honor of the Prince of Wales, who was visiting this ship, First Class Apprentice C. F. Hill in jumping from the rim of the fighting top of the foremast to the topmast rigging lost his hold and fell to the deck, receiving injuries from which he died eight hours later.

To Ellen Evans Mahan

Southampton, August 17, 1894 [LC]

My own dearest Deldie: I have but little time to write you, for I am starting tomorrow early for the country, and must start this before I go. I have little news, which is of small consequence—what I chiefly lament is that I [am] able so little to help you by talking about your own problems. As regards Pomfret I think very well of your going there, provided you

---

1. New York Historical Society.

have the money and you think the children need it. I hope that you will soon receive some income from your mother's estate, for it is evident that I can earn nothing by my pen during this cruise yet I cannot live within the allowance I have made myself. The absolute necessity of relief for me from the wear of the ship must be borne in mind, for upon me depends for some time the best prospect of income for the family. Relief I can only get from the distraction of outside society, & if I accept that I must make some return; and this I cannot do on my monthly allowance alone. This contingency must be kept in mind in your expenses—I am sorry to say it, but the alternative of a breakdown would be worse. I feel deeply for you in parting with our darling laddie,[1] and the more so because my tired and harassed brain does not enable me to write you and him as at happier moments I might do. He is a dear good boy, and I am very grateful for his frequent letters to me. I have received the cards from Tiffany—not much too soon, for I was down to my last dozen. We are quite without news. The last two days have been full of exasperating work and worry—the details of which, however, would not interest you. I believe I wrote Lyle that I am going to stay over Sunday with Mr. Henry White who used to be our Secretary of Legation. Two days is not enough for much benefit—yet the change is something. We have been alarmed over suggestions that the *Chicago* might be sent to China. The idea, judged by all *rational* considerations, is absurd; but then that is really no ground for foretelling the Dept's action. Nothing could be more absurd than keeping the ship in Europe, except indeed the first sending her here. God send me soon home, for I am very tired. Good bye, my dearest child, love to all the chicks.

To Ellen Evans Mahan

Southampton, August 20, 1894 [LC]

My dearest Deldie: I am just back from the Henry Whites, where I spent Sunday, and as I thought you might like to hear something of your ancient friend Minnie Hartpence,[1] (if that be the spelling), as well as to get an extra letter, I will write you a line before my impressions wear off— for upon the whole I was much pleased with her. I of course did not know whom I was likely to see, nor did the Whites have any clue to my possibly

1. Young Lyle had gone to Bar Harbor, Maine, on vacation, prior to entering Groton School in September.
1. Mrs. Mahlon Sands, a schoolmate of Mrs. A. T. Mahan.

knowing anything of her—so that we met as absolute strangers to each other's antecedents when I arrived on Saturday at 5 p.m. There was nothing about her to draw my attention, but something suggested (probably the chance mention that she was an American) that it might be your quondam friend. White and I went out to stroll before dinner and I then asked if it was Mrs. Mahlon. As you know, I had never seen her. At first I intended to say nothing of your acquaintance, but as we talked she seemed to me not at all the simply worldly airy woman we had heard she was become—so after dinner I sat down by her on a sofa while the others engaged in a round game of letters, and after a little talk I said to her that I thought she knew my wife. She looked naturally a little puzzled, but on my mentioning your name I assure you she awoke to very cordial interest, and was very animated in her recollections of you.

She must have been a very pretty woman. She has now lost in the main the pallor I have heard you mention, and is become fat (in moderation) fair and forty. While without color her complexion is not pale, and her features are still delicate and refined. Her expression, however, is very sad, at times particularly so—not the look of a person who *has gone* through much, but of one who is perpetually conscious of sorrow and disappointment the lines deepening from time to time, as if she were brooding. Mrs. White spoke to me afterwards about her—said she had been very much misjudged. That she had been overpersuaded into marrying a man much older than herself, when she cared for another, had been brought to London where she had attracted more admiration than any other woman in Mrs. White's long acquaintance, and that she *had* thrown herself into it in reaction from her disappointment. Sands was all that was kind, but of totally different character & never understood her; but that she herself, some two years before his death, had withdrawn gradually from the swim, deepening her home life, and the husband & wife were drawing closer when his terrible death came. Mrs. W. said she thought her life was a constant sighing over what might have been.

It is always pleasant to think better of those you have once liked, and I think you may feel sure that Mrs. White, who is bright and clever judges her more fairly than the common rumor that reached us. I saw a good deal of her for a short time, and while I did not like everything, I do not believe that she is unusually worldly, and I do think she is unhappy—the latter perhaps more than she ought to indulge. She is certainly pleasing to men & I think would be to women who were congenial.

Goodbye dearest. What a funny world it is for meeting people. Dr. Nevin was also there as a Sunday guest. Love to all.

To Hilary A. Herbert

USS *Chicago*, Southampton, August 21, 1894 [NA]

Sir:

1. I have to acknowledge the receipt of the Department's letters, Nos. 33179 and 33180, of the 7th inst., concerning the enlistment of William Thomas Ryan and Charles G. Anderson, alleged deserters.

2. The above named men have been questioned and examined, and their identity as the two deserters mentioned in the Department's communications is fully established.

3. I would respectfully represent to the Department that these men are yet in debt to the government upon this enlistment, and also that, if discharged as they now are, they will be landed penniless on the shore of a foreign country. They themselves have of course no claim to consideration; but as the time of the ship's remaining in this port will admit of the delay without injury to the service, I have decided before carrying out the order to ask whether the Department is willing as a matter of international comity that we should bring men from Antwerp to England and land them there without money, especially as there is said to be considerable distress from lack of work ashore.

To Helen Evans Mahan

Southampton, August 26, 1894 [NWC]

My dearest Helen: Although I have written two letters home last week, they have both I believe been on special subjects rather than connected with my own little daily doings. I begin today therefore with the short trip I took from Saturday to Monday, 18–20. I had an invitation from an Englishman to visit him because he had seen I was purposing a Life of Nelson & his father had served on board the *Victory*, Nelson's flag ship at Trafalgar, and while I was intending this visit I had a letter from Mr. Henry White to pass the usual Saturday to Monday with them—so I determined to combine the two. Leaving here at 10 on Saturday, an hour brought me to Fareham where I was met at the station by my correspondent, Mr. Edgar Goble, a man of from 55 to 60. I had only three hours, and he had arranged to do more than I had expected; for he drove at once not to his own house but to that of Sir Wm. Parker,[1] the son of an admiral of the same name, who

---

1. Sir William later sent Mahan a portrait for his *Nelson*.

himself was the last to survive of the English captains, who actually served as such under Nelson. The present Sir Wm. is a man a little older than I and he has some very interesting relics etc., which he showed me. Chief among them was a portrait of Nelson of which I had never before heard, taken in Sept. 1805, when he returned to England after an absence of over two years, remaining only three weeks, and then leaving it for the last time— for he was killed Oct. 21. The artist presented it to Parker in 1838, with a note which is pasted now on the back giving the particulars. There were other interesting things, but nothing I can stop to mention. This portrait of the great admiral shows a worn sad expression which I have not noticed in others. We then drove to Mr. Goble's. His father was clerk to the captain of the *Victory*—Hardy[2]—and in that capacity was near Nelson throughout the day—heard the talk about the famous signal "England expects every man to do his duty," and being near the admiral when shot was one of the group that stood round him as he lay on deck before bring carried below to die. Owing to this he was called upon to aid Mr. Benjamin West—an artist of American birth but long resident in London—to group his picture of the Death of Nelson, where Goble's own face appears. He has handed down a singular story. The day before the battle, while they were trying to close with the enemy's fleet, he dined at Nelson's table, and the admiral then said, "Tomorrow I shall do that which will give you young gentlemen something to think about and talk about for the rest of your lives, but I shall not live to talk of it myself." This confirms the remark he also made next morning to a captain who took leave of him to go back to his own ship —"Goodbye, Blackwood,[3] I shall never see you again"—and shows that he had a real presentiment. Mr. Goble had asked to meet me at lunch Admiral the Hon. Maurice Horatio Nelson, the brother of the present Earl Nelson,[4] who descends not from the great Nelson but from one of his sisters, but the patent which permitted the peerage to descend in the female line provided also that its holders should take the family name Nelson. The present admiral is a quiet commonplace man enough, who has long since retired from active service—but to my meeting him I owe an invitation from Earl Nelson to visit him at his seat, appropriately called Trafalgar, which I shall of course try to do. From Fareham I took the train to Portsmouth whence I had to take a fresh start for Guildford, the station of the Whites. I met in the train a young English army officer whom I had known in Nice last winter, and had with him a short talk—then got forty winks of sleep, which greatly refreshed me, and from the station a drive of half an hour brought

---

2. Sir Thomas M. Hardy.
3. Sir Henry Blackwood, who, in the *Euryalis*, commanded the in-shore squadron at Trafalgar, and was given command over the frigates by the wounded Nelson.
4. Horatio, 3rd Earl Nelson.

me to the house now occupied by my friends, a charming old English country seat, built between three and four hundred years [ago] & having still traces of the moat which was needed in those peaceful times. It has a great hall two stories high, full of portraits each of which has its history, several of English sovereigns who have from time to time been guests there. Mr. White told me that he had been telegraphing to all sorts of celebrities to meet me—chiefly statesman—but all were engaged. I was not particularly sorry to have a quiet time, without any mental strain, and the very small company gathered were easy and pleasant. One, as you already know, was an old admirer of mamma's, a Mrs. Sands. I think she was genuinely pleased to hear of mamma again, though I fancy she is pretty well settled to be English the rest of her days. Mrs. White told me that she had had a succès fou when she first came out in London, but it is easy to see she is not happy. Mamma will be interested and grieved to hear that her husband, who was an utter unbeliever, completely destroyed his wife's faith, so that she is like so many other poor creatures that now grope wistfully through life. As the prophet Isaiah has it: "We grope for the wall like the blind, and we grope as if we had no eyes: we stumble *at noonday* as in the night." I had a good deal of talk with her first and last—she goes in for psychological research & all that, but she shows the evident trace of association with clever people. I doubt her being clever herself. She seems to have seen a great deal of Gladstone & to be really attached to him; and she told me that his chief interest in life was in religion—so that, though now off duty forever in this life, he has the solid founda[tion] of peace and happiness before him. Quite a contrast to Mrs. Sands was Dr. Nevin, the American clergyman who has been in Rome for near thirty years. Smug, smiling, quite self-satisfied, though not unpleasantly so, an interesting talker, yet always about his own doings—a man who has been successful, moderately important and likes to feel so—in all respects a singular foil to the sensitive rather brooding and evidently uncontented face of Mrs. Sands. Besides these there were two or three young American men of means—one of whom asked me to come and stay with him at a place he has taken near Cambridge. Mrs. White spoke again of the number of distinguished men who had been carried away by their admiration of my books—mentioning names; and Mrs. Sands said she had sent to her library for it and received the reply that there were a hundred copies *out* and none *in*; but it seems to me there must be some mistake here. A letter from Mr. Marston yesterday says they are still selling well, and he enclosed me a circular he is sending out to all schools, calling attention to their suitableness for prizes. On Sunday afternoon the Duke of Connaught rode over with one of his staff to 5 o'clock tea. We were *not* invited to dine with the German Emperor—although he gave a large dinner on his yacht—and I am inclined to fear that we omitted some mark of attention. Possibly, it was in a failure to write our names in his book; but however it lies of course dont mention my surmise outside. After all, there was no reason why we should be asked.

Tuesday Aug. 28

I will close now dear child—simply saying I am well. Much love to mamma & the others.

To Hilary A. Herbert

USS *Chicago*, Southampton, England, August 28, 1894 [NA]

Sir:

1. Referring to the detachment of Carpenter Chas. H. Bogan, I wish to say, that the ship loses a most efficient officer, whose services have been indispensable; and in view of the constant repairs that are occurring on board, and of the length of time the *Chicago* is likely to remain abroad, I consider it very desirable to have another Carpenter in his place.

To Ellen Evans Mahan

Southampton, August 29, 1894 [LC]

Dearest Deldie: Your letter of the 20th came today, a rather longer interval than usual having elapsed since the last. I dont suppose this will get off before Saturday, but I must write now for I can only get quiet time in the evening, and tomorrow I have the Yorkes and Clovers to dinner, while on Friday I expect to go for 24 hours to Earl Nelson's. I have, however, little or no news, nor prospect of any beyond what I sent in Hennie's letter of yesterday or day before. First I will reply to some of your questions. I should think well enough of Nellie's joining a literature class, because association with others helps one forward and *may* lead to friendships mutually helpful; but it seems to me that as Nelly is to take up literature as a profession—at least on trial—that she must also, and principally, study and read by herself, *under good guidance*. I feel very powerless to help in this matter, never having myself had systematic training. This is a serious defect. My success has been due to natural clear headedness, which has translated itself into style—to a habit of omnivorous though desultory reading, which has given me a large and pretty precise vocabulary—and finally, to the happy seizure of an idea to all intents original and unworked. But I should doubtless work to better advantage—more easily, rapidly and correctly—had I been trained. As I explained to Nelly, training gives the mastery of the tools, without which the cleverest man cant get out all that is in him. Now your surest way is to consult Dr. Dix, and probably through him the professor at Columbia College who represents literature, saying plainly what is wanted viz: a competent guide, who would carry Nelly through a course of reading, and of study of the construction of English sentences, which would at once develop her mind and give her the mastery of what I may call the *mechanical* part of good writing—faultless grammar, correct placing of words, the avoidance of the errors of construction, so frequently found, which are not bad grammar in the ordinary sense but bad syntax. I am persuaded this sort of thing can be acquired by any painstaking person of good capacity. In itself it is not much towards success, if the student have no individuality, no originality of thought, or fancy, or perception; but if such qualities exist the mechanical training is a sine quâ non to their utilization. If you feel any difficulty in *saying* all this, why not type-write it, and go to Dr. Dix, either in Quogue or in N.Y., and then to such persons as he may recommend. A person fit to undertake the work will more than understand my idea. He will know, as I dont, how to carry it out and to impart to it much of which I have but a glimmer. You might say that, Nellie being now 17, we counted upon giving her at least three years, of 8 months each, till she is 20. I should by no means expect her to do nothing but work. Three hours—perhaps two the first year—would be enough daily. She would give other time to reading the best novels, for style or fancy, essays like Macaulay's etc—& reserve enough for exercise and entertainment other than mental.

So much for Nell. Now as regards Helen, I beg she may not undertake too many pupils. At twenty-one girls are still too young for prolonged strain of teaching. Time is not gained, but lost by disregarding the demand of nature not to be overtaxed while maturing. Twenty-one will be injured by work which twenty-five can undertake with impunity. I should say that two hours a day teaching should be enough—considering that for the present practising also must go. Adopt some *rule* which will enable you (and her) to resist the temptation of a few more weekly dollars. Besides, it dont altogether hurt one not to be had too easily.

I felt some self reproach about your sending me the $100—but if I dont spend it it will be on hand here as well as there &, as I wrote Helen, Mr. Marston says the books continue to sell well. I am not without hopes that the excess of No 1 over No 2 for the *last* six months, prophesies a considerable sale of No 2 during the *current* six months. You would not be able to stay at Villefranche because there is no hotel—that I know of; but at Beaulieu, about five minutes away by train, on the opposite side from Nice, there are hotels. I should myself prefer to have you there to Nice, for we could be more alone, & if you dont stay *with* your uncle, independence will be best. We must not, however, set our hearts too much on your coming. It is impossible to foresee what Kirkland will do, but there seems reason to fear that he will avoid any place where there is social racket—which is the particular characteristic of Villefranche. I confess I look forward to his coming with apprehension. He is irascible, profane and gouty—a warm heart, but that is of little account when the temper is violent & uncontrolled. However we must hope for the best. I will keep you informed of prospects, and upon going to N.Y. you must arrange at the Cable office a cable address—a single word—which will embrace your name and residence. Very likely Mahan, being unusual, may be unappropriated. If so, being registered at the office, Mahan, New York, would be all, and I will arrange a code sufficient for this one purpose—to notifing you when and where to go. The steamers on the slip you sent are the ones—and the trip is interesting. We expect Kirkland about the 8th on which day also Erben sails for U.S. I hope they will not meet, for, though I dont think they love one another, I would prefer the present man should not poison the new one against me. However unjust, it would be very bad for me to have another report against me. If Ramsay sticks to his two year rule, my time will be up next May, and I must do my best to soften the heart of the new Adml.

Friday Aug. 31.

I must close here dearest, as I am going away this aftn. until tomorrow evening and shall have no time to write. My fondest love for you and all.

To Hilary A. Herbert

USS *Chicago*, Southampton, August 30, 1894 [LC]

Sir:

1. I received three days ago the Report on Fitness made in my case by Rear Admiral Erben and dated July 1st, 1894. I should leave it unanswered but for the fear that—notwithstanding my full reply and request for investigation made in January last—my silence might be interpreted as implying my acquiescence whatever in its terms.

2. As an expression of Admiral Erben's opinion, I have no occasion for remark. His opinion is his opinion, and the Department demands it. But I beg to be clearly understood as claiming that, as an estimate of my professional character, it is substantially erroneous, taking into account, as I think,

only what seems amiss to the person criticizing, while either blind to or ignorant of the work actually done, and the results actually achieved.

3. Into these results I in January requested the Department to inquire at once. So many important witnesses have since then departed that the necessary investigation could now scarcely be held on board; and as, by Admiral Erben's admission, the present condition of the ship is good, enquiry into that present condition is not needed. I must, however, protest against the implication, that credit therefore is not due me, by the wholly unnecessary intrusion of Lieutenant-Commander Clover's name into a paper dealing with my efficiency. I am far from wishing to ignore the merits of that officer and the valuable assistance he continually gives me, nor yet the diligent work of his predecessor, Mr. Gillpatrick, who was loaded down with such a heavy burden of arrears.[1] It is conceded in all navies that the Captain cannot attain the best results if the Executive Officer is deficient in ability or zeal, so much so that in France and England the Commander is allowed a voice in the selection of his chief assistant. Neither do I affect to feel independent of the willing support I have received from my other subordinates in general. I heartily acknowledge all that they have done; but I assert that the efficiency, cleanliness and discipline of the ship have been good and progressively better, and that, as I am responsible for bad results, I cannot be denied credit for good, merely because an officer, slightly senior to myself in rank and age, does not approve my way of reaching results.

4. It is repulsive to me to be forced thus to assert in words my own competency; but, while lamenting the necessity, I am obliged to say that I have not only nominally but actually commanded this ship—that, while I have purposely tried to let each officer manage his own business, indicating the points which I deemed most important, I have known what was being done, and have used such means as seemed to me best adapted to insure advance without persistent interference, which I believe tends to defeat its own object—and that the result has been, and is, a ship clean, well disciplined, and perfectly fit for her work, so far as is consistent with the inevitable deterioration that follows over five years of steady commission.

5. I feel that the perspicacity of the Department scarcely needs to be informed that the test of my work is the result, and not my liking for the work.[2]

---

1. A reference to the condition in which Sperry transferred the *Chicago* to Mahan.
2. On September 1, Erban wrote the Department objecting to Mahan's rejoinder to his fitness report, especially the section on Erben's small advantage of age and rank. He stated that he would welcome an investigation so that he could explain his charges more fully.

To Hilary A. Herbert

USS *Chicago*, Southampton, September 6, 1894 [NA]

Sir:

1. I have to inform the Bureau that I have to-day forwarded to the Bureau of Supplies and Accounts a requisition for 8-inch and 6-inch charges and shells to replace those used in target practice during past twelve months. Unless they can be obtained, it will be necessary to curtail the practice this next year, and not to expend any more 6-inch ammunition at all.

To Ellen Evans Mahan

Southampton, September 6, 1894 [LC]

Dearest Deldie: I write only a line to explain that I can do no more, and to apologize to darling Nellikin for failing to give her due letter. I am too driven this week, and am tomorrow cut short by going on a visit to Lady Jeune's who has again invited me most pressingly. I am to stay from Friday to Monday & I assure you I need the change badly; not because of my general health, but from the drive, worry, and at the same time the wearing monotony. Like yourself, I feel if we could only be together all would be so much easier. I am sorry that I seemed to you worried about money. I am scarcely that, and I am sorry you dont go to Pomfret for I believe the change to dry air would be good for you all.

Erben hauled down his flag today and went ashore. He was slopping over, a thing which always rasps me, particularly when it follows a jollification & champagne, which they had in the wardroom—very nice & kindly of them all right but one hates to see tears after wine. I was not invited, which showed Nazro's good sense. I would not have cared to refuse —yet would have had to do so for I will do nothing that can be twisted into an acceptance of what Erben did by me.

I had a letter from Gouv, saying that they would be in Ryde, near here, next week & would sail on the 15th; so when you get this they will be on the briny. I shall make a point of seeing them. We expect Kirkland next Monday & then our plans may develop.

Friday Morning Sept 7.
I must mail this now my own dearest. There is no other news. I trust you will agree with me in my determination to retire, quand même, at 40 years. I am worse than wasted here. If my brains survive the sooner I get them to work the better—nay indispensable.

To Ellen Kuhn Mahan

Southampton, September 10, 1894 [LC]

My darling Miss Nell: Things pressed on me too much last week to allow time for a long letter—the departure of the admiral coinciding with some other business too important to be postponed. I was kept on the anxious bench as to whether the new admiral would arrive so as to prevent my accepting Lady Jeune's invitation from Friday to Monday. The first report was that he would arrive on Saturday, but by writing to the steamer office in London I found that she would not reach Plymouth until Monday, about 4 am, and that he could scarcely get here before that afternoon. So I decided to go. My state of mind is that of detesting to go away—but when gone I soon hate the thought of coming back to the ship even worse than I did the leaving her. I took the train from here at 4.50 pm Friday, due at Newbury at 6.30. I knew that I was to meet His Royal Highness the Duke of Cambridge, the Commander in Chief of the British Army, and to my surprise he got on the same train—I think at Winchester, but of course he had a reserved carriage & I saw nothing of him at the time but his cocked hat &c, with a bevy of following aides. I drove humbly behind them in a hack—fly they call them—and reached the house a little after 7. They always in England have a cup of tea awaiting you, so I got that, talked with Mrs. Harris who is wife to the Editor of the *Fortnightly Review*[1] and whom I already knew—also to Sir Redvers Buller[2] who is in the Duke's suite & and was presented besides to General Sir Baker Russell[3]—a cavalry general—who was present because the Duke was going to inspect some brigades of cavalry near by. Having thus got a start at knowing some of the people of the party, I went up stairs to dress for dinner. I had so little rank that I passed by the large comfortable room I occupied on my previous visit to Arlington & found myself in one not very much larger than my own in 54th St—but you know I am not exigent on such things. After the comfortable English style I found my clothes all laid out—everything unpacked & ready, hot water &c. The company I must say was exceedingly pleasant the women all good looking with perhaps one or two exceptions, the men fine manly and fairly handsome specimens of the race—mostly I fancy men of some rank. The Duke's aides were Lord Downe[4] a very good looking fellow and Col. FitzGeorge his (Duke's) son. The Duke of Cambridge married, religiously, a lady not of royal blood, and the marriage though perfectly regular in every other way, is not officially recognized. She was

---

1. Frank Harris.
2. General Sir Redvers Henry Buller.
3. Sir Baker Creed Russell, at this time Commander of the Cavalry Brigade at Aldershot.
4. Major General Hugh Richard Dawnay, 8th Viscount Downe.

not a Duchess but simply Mrs. FitzGeorge, and the children bear that name. Besides those I have already named, there was staying at the house Lord and Lady Arthur Butler[5]—the latter an American woman from Cleveland—about 30—decidedly pretty and ladylike, good to talk to, bright, good sense and right feeling. She is somehow mixed up with the Philadelphia Sturgises—Maisie &c but I did not get that straightened out. She was one of the kind you can talk to with pleasure on matters of more interest. Then there was a Miss Norton—English—quite handsome but not so light in hand conversationally. Besides these Lady Jeune's daughters by her first husband, two Stanley girls of 16 and 18, who really were first-rate to talk to, quite astonishing for their age. Not that they were particularly brilliant—though the younger is quite original in her way of thinking—but so much at their ease, so thoroughly companionable it was delightful to be with them. The elder is very pretty and I distinctly fell in love with her. Her name is Madeleine, her sister's Dorothy. Then there is a Jeune boy—a half brother. These were the permanents; but besides them there were other guests every day at dinner, so we sat down 20 to 24. I was pretty well placed every day. The first day Lady Jeune placed me on her left—the duke being always on her right. I saw she was very nervous, which was odd in a woman so accustomed to the world; but next day I learned that the duke, who is 76, has a way of going to sleep, and not infrequently subsides on the shoulder of the lady next him. This dont matter, but these naps interfere with his night sleep, so hostesses have to try and keep him amused and awake. The second night I was at the young folks table, between Col. FitzGeorge and a Sir Charles Fraser, an outsider. The former was very agreeable—the latter heavy. Your father, my dear, you would hardly recognize. I am persuaded that my sphere in life is to have plenty of money and to talk. I own, however, I have met some people to whom I cant talk. Last night I was between Lord Downe and I forget whom. The former is charming to look at, handsome most refined and a charming smile. It took him nearly 48 hours fairly to thaw to me, but after that he was lovely—but he is no great shakes for talk. I was a little disposed to be sulky at having no ladies to talk to, but things brightened up. There were on no occasion enough ladies to go round —but I got even after dinner. Well on Saturday there was a great drilling of cavalry to which we all went out—a beautiful sight and luckily a fine day; very wintry but pretty clear and no rain. The Duke was dissatisfied with some of the troops & Sir B. Russell said the grass for fifty feet round was scorched with his profanity—but I didn't hear it & fancy he is not so black as painted. He seems a jolly old gentleman, but of course it is ruinous always to have your own way—at times he is very noisy but he's distinctly

5. Arthur J. Wellington Foley Butler, heir of the 3rd Marquess of Ormonde, and his wife Ellen, daughter of General Anson Stager, U.S. Army.

likeable. He complimented me on my work, and one of the Cavalry Colonels told me it was the best book he ever read—that he would like to make every one read it.

Tuesday night, 11th Sept.

You can see that I was getting tired and sleepy last night—I have very much writing to do and some of it troublesome. I have now been on board sixteen months this day. Shall I finish my Arlington experience? On Sunday we all went to church in Newbury and put on tall hats because the Duke did. The church is quite old—after service the duke was shown over it by a local antiquary who told him that this was the first time a royal duke had been in the church since Prince Rupert nearly 250 years ago. There was great fighting in this neighborhood during that Civil War, when Charles I held his court at Oxford, of which the spires can be seen from Arlington in clear weather. There were indeed two Battles of Newbury, and in the afternoon we were taken to see an ancient house in the country where is still to be seen the mark of a bullet fired at the King while he sat in a window, while not far away are the ruined walls of a castle which held for the King to the last where also the marks of the cannon balls are clearly visible. Sunday was a beautiful day and the weather is still fine although at this moment the fog has shut in. I was very sorry to ... [remainder of letter lost].

To Jane Leigh Okill Swift

Southampton, September 13, 1894 [LC]

Dear Aunty: The past two or three months have seemed like a season of great quiet after our London "season." It is just three months today since we closed that by the Trinity House dinner—at which were present almost all the grown up males of the Royal Family—the Prince of Wales and his eldest son, the Duke of York, the two next kings of England—the Duke of Edinburgh, the Duke of Cambridge besides other lesser royalties—and a host of dignitaries, cabinet ministers past, present and to come, besides generals and admirals and judges by the barrel. After that crowning performance we blew out our social candle, & went quietly to Antwerp, where in seven weeks I only once, that I can recall, dined out. Of course when we came back to England—to Cowes and Southampton—the thing began again. We dined with the Queen at Osborne, and with the Prince of Wales on board his yacht. The Emperor of Germany also gave a grand dinner, to which we were not asked. I have besides dined at several private houses, and indeed people seem as if they could not be too kind and hospitable. We have now been back over five weeks, of which the four last at our present anchorage. I have thrice been away on the pleasant English invite "from Friday—or Saturday—to Monday." The first time, now nearly four weeks ago was to the house temporarily occupied by Mr. Henry White, our Secretary of Legation in London for eight years, but recently displaced by Mr. Cleveland. He told me he had been telegraphing in every direction to get some celebrities to meet me but in vain. Parliament was on the verge of adjourning, and every body was flying to their country homes. Being a man of large means and having his official position and an attractive wife—besides being himself good looking and hearty—he has a very large acquaintance in the best English society. Despite all these advantages he failed of his guests and curiously enough we were a purely American party. Mrs. White was a N.Y. Rutherford—he being a Baltimorean. Besides themselves there was a Mrs. Mahlon Sands, whose husband was very tragically killed in London some years ago. She is a Philadelphian & as I happened to know an old school fellow of Ellie's. The other guests were Dr. Nevin the Am. chaplain in Rome and two youngish men of means. On the Sunday afternoon the Duke of Connaught rode over from Aldershot, their military camp where he commands, for afternoon tea. Like all the royal family he is an agreeable man, unaffected and with much savoir faire, qualities that stand royalty in good stead in these days. I should not forget to tell you that en route to the Whites I stopped by invitation to see a gentleman whose father was on board Nelson's flagship at Trafalgar, and was one of the group that surrounded the great admiral when he fell and before he was taken below. He had some interesting relics to show me, but besides he had invited to [meet] me a present Admiral Maurice Nelson, great nephew to *the* admiral and brother of the present Earl. This meeting, and the knowledge that I contemplated a life of Nelson, brought me an invitation to visit Trafalgar, the Earl's country seat, which I of course accepted, though I could only go for 24 hours. The place has no direct association with the hero but is beautiful and in a beautiful position—wonderful old trees. England is really a most beautiful country. There were here many most interesting relics— principally likenesses and a bust, but other things as well. Lord Nelson gave me an autograph letter of the admiral and also a copy of one to Lady Hamilton, which is of distinct value to me & has never been published. The family is not interesting, rather shy and stiff—except the Earl himself who talks along easily. It is woeful to think how much of what I hear I lose, and that while in the midst of interest, much of which might repay research, I am so tied to the ship that I can do nothing. Last Saturday and Sunday I again spent in the country at Sir Francis Jeune's. You may perhaps have seen occasional magazine articles by her. She is a clever woman, Scotch, not yet quite fifty, much given to society and particularly found of collecting celebrities about her. She has been very kind to me & this was in fact my second visit to Arlington, their country seat. She had written once or twice for me to come, & finally fixed these days as the Duke of Cambridge was to stay with them while inspecting a brigade of cavalry then encamped about six miles from the house. As he came with his retinue of aides etc the house was very full and as neighboring gentry and officers from the camp were daily invited we sat down twenty or more to table. The ladies were much in the minority & as I had little rank I didn't get a lady to take in any time, but I revenged myself after dinner. The first evening I sat on Lady Jeune's left— the duke being always on her right. I noticed she was strangely nervous for an old society hand, and I found out afterwards that the duke, who is 76, has a habit of going to sleep, when his head drops on his neighbor's shoulder, and the two ladies who flank him have it on their minds to amuse & keep him awake. The little accident dont matter, as his infirmity is understood; but if he sleeps so, he injures his night's sleep. The house party was very nice. One or two distinguished—all men of position & party, intelligent, agreeable, and of good presence. The interest never flagged, it was "go" throughout. There are two daughters—by her former husband Colonel Stanley—very talking girls quite the reverse of what we commonly, and I believe on the whole justly, fancy English girls of 16 and 18, to be. I suppose the number of bright people constantly coming and going brings them forward. They were quite able to give and take the light badinage of society, without a trace of forwardness on the one side or of gaucherie on the other. They quite won my heart. There was also there a young American woman, of 30 I suppose, married to a lord but quite evidently the reverse of what we commonly fancy the fate of such marriages; evidently devoted to each other and leading a fairly quiet life with their four children. She belonged to Cleveland, Ohio, so of course our acquaintances scarcely touched. They were Lord and Lady Arthur Butler, and either he or his boy will be Marquis of Ormonde as the elder brother has no sons. I fear you may think I deal heavily in lords etc; but in truth I think a little quiet fun might be poked at our English friends on the score of the frequency of titles—like our militia colonels. Plain misters seem almost a minority—but while all lords are not so, those whom I have met have been quiet, unpretentious dignified gentlemen, their rank serving only to give external assurance of their social standing.

Friday Sept. 14

I wrote last night dear Aunty, till my hand and head were both tired, and today I must close for the mail, for I have no time to write by day, and tonight I am dining with Mrs. Ogden, Ellie's aunt who sails for home in tomorrow's steamer. It makes me feel very envious for I find such glory and excitement as I have had here a very poor substitute for home affection and my preferred work. With much love to Jane.[1]

[P.S.]   We go from here to Havre in about ten days and thence south towards the Mediterranean.

To Ellen Evans Mahan

Southampton, September 13, 1894 [LC]

My own dearest Deldie: There is no absurdity in writing two letters as close together as yours of the 3d and 4th, the former of which reached me this morning and the other tonight. I am amused at your wishing me to take care of you, as if you had not been taking care of me all our married life. However, so long as each feels that the other is necessary, our married life is not a failure. This evening's mail also brought me the cheque for $100. I *feel* mean in taking it, yet my reason tells me that upon the whole it is not unfair—the chief advantage I derive from it is the power to accept, without feeling too great onesided obligation, the kindnesses shown me here. The society of these English folk is for the most part very pleasant to me. Although I should find it hard to define, I fancy there must be a slight difference from our own folk which gives a zest to my intercourse with them. I have rarely enjoyed two days more than those spent at the Jeunes on Saturday & Sunday last; but Lady Jeune is great in getting cleverish people about her. Being herself clever this society reacts favorably upon herself, while her two daughters show distinctly the advantage to young people of seeing so much of intelligent elders as they do at their country home. In town I suppose they have been less to the fore. They are quite unlike our idea of English girls—entirely free from stiffness, gaucherie, or mauvaise honte, and equally so from forwardness. It is entertaining as well as pleasing to see two children of 18 and 16 give and take as they do—reminding me of Stockton's impressions of our own babies when left on his hands at dinner that time. He never forgot it. I devoted myself so to the elder the last night I was there, that I extorted an amused nod and laugh from Lady Arthur Butler, an American and herself quite a pretty woman, when she caught my eye. She said nothing but was plainly entertained—but I thought that with the disadvantage of 36 years seniority and a wife and children at home that I was very safe. I hope you wont construe that sentence grammatically, as it makes the wife and children a disadvantage, which I assure

---

1. Mahan's sister, who lived with her aunt in Elizabeth, New Jersey.

you my darling is far indeed from my very lightest thought. How gladly would I give up all the scanty pleasures of this racing life to be once more quietly with you, with my children, and with my natural work now wholly stopped. Sir Francis Jeune himself is a man of very considerable distinction—the chief judge of a very important court and promoted to that position, I believe, at a comparatively early age. I take him to be about my age but I should say older looking, though he has more hair, (not much). One of the girls said their mother was 49. She looks older, also; but she is doing too much. A heavy social racket and at the same time doing much charitable work and writing for magazines etc. She is a small woman, slender, dark eyes, hair now grey and approaching white, ruddy complexion but she looks fagged at times. She is Scotch by birth, a Mackenzie. Jeune is her second husband, and the two daughters are Stanleys. I wrote much of this to Lyle last night, in a letter I timed to reach him as near as might be immediately upon his arrival at Groton. Tomorrow night I am to dine with Aunt Ogden in Southampton and as they sail next day I hope you may meet them in N.Y. and so get late news of me. The doctors all say I am looking better than this time last year, but I feel the strain very much. Happily sixteen months are passed and I trust the goodness of God may carry me unharmed through the next eight. That will fulfill the two years and if Kirkland reports well of me I can then ask for detachment. He came on board yesterday looking much the same; but has shaved his cheeks leaving only moustache and a pointed chin beard which become him better. He seems in excellent health which I hope may continue, to our comfort as well as his. He appears disposed to leave much more in my hands than did Erben—but on the other hand he is a much more masculine and decided man than the other, and may be worse if I make mistakes. You have no idea how hard it is to keep these ships straight, and how hard for me to be as hard as I ought to be. I fear trouble indeed I do, and am constantly repeating "in all our troubles to put our whole trust and confidence in Thy mercy." I still receive compliments about my books from time to time, but naturally not so many as I did. Kirkland gave me an outline of what he proposed to do. Havre, Lisbon, Cadiz, Madeira then the Spanish coast, Naples, Palermo, Messina and ending up at Nice. No Levant—but I fear he may be ordered to go there. And now dearest I will stop, having already written more than I expected to do. As I dine out tomorrow, I cant carry this to the last date—but en revanche I hope you will see the Ogdens in N.Y. Good bye—love to the girls. I shall have now to write Lyle independently, which increases my already heavy burden of correspondence—but I must not let him feel dropped.

To Cyprian A. G. Bridge[1]

USS *Chicago*, Southampton, September 18, 1894 [NMM]

Dear Admiral Bridge: Your letter was duly received, and ought, of course, to have been sooner answered, but in truth I have so much other writing to do that my correspondence suffers. It is needless to say that I entirely agree with your view—perhaps even go too far to my own extreme of exalting the Art of War, in its various branches, over the absorbing attention to matériel on the part of naval officers of the executive branch. But while this is true, it is also unfortunately true that I am perforce so immersed in the petty duties of administration that I can command no power of concentration to produce such a paper as you suggest. I am a slow, meditative kind of writer, perfectly incapable of dashing off my ideas on such a subject, or even of saying with precision just what my ideas are. While my mind is reasonably active and fruitful, it deliberately refuses to be "bossed"; and when tired out with the details of ship economy it strikes work and can be neither persuaded nor bullied into action.

At the present moment I feel as if from word to word I would have to lay down my pen from sheer mental lethargy. I have abandoned all forms of literary production, save one unlucky paper which I cannot lick into shape for the reasons I give. Nothing I fear can be expected of me until this cruise is over.

I trust that the station assigned to you[2] by rumor is in all ways satisfactory, though I fear your departure for it may prevent our again meeting in the near future. With best wishes for your success and happiness in it, and with my compliments to Mrs. Bridge—believe me [etc.].

To Helen Evans Mahan

Southampton, September 18, 1894 [NWC]

My darling Helen: I hope I may be able to send you a decent letter, but somehow everything seems to become to me harder and harder as the cruise goes on. I feel very tired & have so many letters to write of all kinds that I seem to do that and everything else mechanically. I have just returned from a short trip about twenty miles from here to see a gentleman from whom I hoped to get some information about Lady Nelson, the wife of the great admiral, but he was unable to give me anything of any particular

1. Admiral Sir Cyprian Bridge, RN.
2. Bridge had been assigned as Commander-in-Chief of the Australia Station.

value. He had been trustee for her three granddaughters & had known their mother, who was daughter in law to Lady Nelson but never seems to have received any particular information about the latter. You know that she & her husband were separated, owing to his infatuation about another woman —one Lady Hamilton. About the latter everything is known but poor Lady Nelson seems to have sunk into utter obscurity, and I cannot even begin to find out what sort of woman she was, except that her life was blameless. My host lives in the New Forest, which has been the "New" forest ever since William the Conqueror turned it into waste land for the sake of the deer which he was so fond of hunting; and I think that showing the neighborhood to me was more attractive to my entertainer than imparting his scanty knowledge. It is a wild, sparsely settled woodland, interspersed with many open spaces, over which long gallops after the chase could have been had. On Friday last I met Aunt Ogden and Cousin Gouv, dining with them at a hotel in town, and the next day I saw them again on board the steamer. I think she looks older—Gouv had not been well. Edith when she first came into the room I thought looked pretty, but the impression disappeared after a little while. The weather has been good since they sailed and I hope has been so for them, but I felt very homesick when the steamer was leaving the harbor. You will now soon be going back to town, and I hope, my dear child, that you will not overtax yourself with teaching or other work. I wish this, of course, primarily on your account, but I also look to the future of us all. There is no necessity for laborious work now laid upon you, but I have fears lest in a not very remote future the pay of retired officers will be reduced. It will in that case be necessary for us all to work and possibly pretty hard—but by then you will have your full strength if you do not impair it now. Of course, if you marry, you will transfer both your work and your support elsewhere—but we have at present to contemplate the other contingency. The same distrust of the future of the retired list, with other reasons also, compels me to retire as soon as I can, in order that I may more surely fit myself for gaining a support independent of the navy. I tell you this simply that you may feel that the gaining a few dollars more just now is not to be weighed against husbanding your health against the day of need. I would not indeed have you idle, only measure your work and aim at regularity of effort; above all avoiding the fatal habit of doing things by fits and starts. A person who regularly and steadily employs four or five hours a day can without great difficulty increase to eight or ten; but one who does not work systematically can rarely acquire that valuable quality in later life. I hope both you and Nellie will try to write regularly to Lyle—say once a fortnight, and without expecting a reply always. It is most important that a boy should feel all in his home near to him continually; yet he cannot write so many letters in reply. I myself have felt the pressure greatly during this cruise in which I have so much else to do—& now I must try to write

[333]

to him also without neglecting you all. It seems easy, perhaps, but it is really at times very hard work. We expect to leave here within a week for Havre to go into dock, and then we will work gradually, but I trust also rapidly towards the Mediterranean. Since we must remain out I wish we were at least as far as Lisbon now. I have no news, and am so preoccupied with the increasing worry of the ship that I feel as if I never should. Goodbye dear child. With dearest love to mamma and Nellie.

Wednesday morning

Am closing for the mail. Well.

To Ellen Evans Mahan

Southampton, September 20, 1894 [LC]

My own dearest Deldie: I am so tired, not so much mentally or physically, but morally, that were I not so well I dont know how I could bear it. The wonder grows on me continually that with all the effort I keep things as well, or rather that they are kept as well for me, as they are. Kirkland has now been with us a week & nothing could be more cordial and liberal than his action towards me;[1] but I am too old to trust to first appearances & knowing him to be gouty I look out for squalls. One thing however seems certain that there is no bias against me. How odd it is of you never to have alluded to my meeting with Mrs. Sands. I wonder did you get the letter. I asked the Jeunes to visit the ship and bring with them the Butlers—Lord & Lady Arthur—whom I had met [at] their house. They appointed to come Wednesday and I invited some officers to meet them, going myself to the train, but only Sir Francis & the boy with Miss Stanley appeared. Lady Jeune & Miss Dorothy not able—the Butlers had never promised. I was sorry—but the officers did nobly and we had quite a jolly lunch and then showed them everything. The girl who came—Madeleine—is my special favorite in fact has displaced all previous fancies except yourself for the time being—until the next one comes along. I am writing tonight because tomorrow I must go to London to have a tooth fixed which is crumbling under me. Have I not had luck this time? The *North American* printed my article in proof and returned to me, with the hope that I could permit it to go with some toning down and as I want the money I shall try to do it. There is very little news. We are now in the midst of a dense fog & in fact England is getting very disagreeable. We start on Sunday evg, if the

---

1. A few days later, Kirkland performed a vital service for Mahan. He telegraphed the Department that the Captain's mess attendant, Emmanuel Frendo, had syphilis and was unfit for present duties.

weather is good, for Havre where between docking and other diversions we shall remain for ten days or so. Then we must return either here or to Plymouth to coal and to receive a visit from our minister—ambassador I should rather say. I am awfully sorry to come here again—but why cry? Today our dear Buster begins his school—bless his heart he will have a few days homesickness I fear. I shall try to write him every ten days or so busy though I am. I will endeavor to deserve his love whether I keep it or not. Good bye dearest with love to the two girls and looking wistfully to the time when I shall come back to you.

To Ellen Evans Mahan

Southampton, September 23, 1894 [LC]

Dearest Deldie: I have no time to write but thought the enclosed might interest you. We are off for Havre this afternoon. Dearest & fondest love to all. Lady Jeune's hand will puzzle you.

[P.S.]   Having a little more time than I thought I add that I went to London Friday had my tooth fixed, spent that evening & night at the Schiffs' and left next morning. Dentist said tooth would soon have ached but being taken in time cost only one guinea for repairs, to which however must be added the cost of the trip seven or eight dollars. No news since I last wrote. A curious thing—a press reporter found me out at the Schiffs at 8 P.M. and wanted my opinion on the Korean war.[1] Schiffs all very cordial & nice. Recd. yours of Sept 11 in London. Will answer queries some other time.

To Ellen Evans Mahan

Havre, France, September 27, 1894 [LC]

My own dear Deldie: Again I have no time for more than a line to you and an apology to Nellie, to whom a letter is due—while I am bitterly grieved at losing the opportunity of writing to our dear boy—to whom it is my purpose to write as often and as amusingly as I can. I am dead with sleep and so tired I can hardly see—harassed & driven almost to death with

---

1. *The Times* of London published an interview with Mahan on the war on September 25, probably the one he gave at the Schiffs' on September 21. *See* Mahan to Clarke, September 30, 1894.

the conflicting duties of my position. You must indeed forgive me, dearest one, and believe that the burden seems to increase daily and I never know what it is to have a mind unpreoccupied. I assure you I dont enjoy it. I got today—my birth-day—your letter announcing Aunty's death.[1] I have written to Jenny. It surprises me to see how much I feel it—my eyes quite filled with tears especially when I thought of her freed from the burden of those sorrowful illusions which made the misery of her life & of so many others. And withal there is a sense of loneliness in that all the elders whom I knew intimately as a child have passed away and that I now stand in the front rank of the unending procession, which also is moving on to the inevitable common end. Well dearest I am so sleepy I can scarcely form my letters and though only 9 P.M. I am going to bed. We are going back to Southampton on Saturday and a week later will, I hope start for the south. Goodbye my own dearest. Love to the girls and to our dear lad.

To George Sydenham Clarke

Southampton, England, September 30, 1894 [LC]

My dear Clarke: I received your letter three days ago at Havre where we spent most of the past week, returning here yesterday preparatory to our departure for the South shortly.

I have not seen the report of my interview—which you will believe I did not seek—but suppose it is substantially correct, as I made the man read over what he had written.[1] I fancy the divergence between you and me is less great than may seem—but I certainly have thought for some time that there was a something taking about the phrase "a fleet in being," which was leading English naval thinkers to press the significance beyond its due value. I have myself in more than one writing both published and unpublished, laid great stress upon the strategic bearing and importance of a body of ships not hopelessly inferior, properly massed and stationed with reference to the theater of war. Such a factor in the situation is most imposing and imperatively forbids the scattering of the enemy's forces, which are thereby prevented doing much harm by the mere fact of being kept together. E. G., I have instanced the effect that would have been produced on our blockade of the South by such a fleet in being, and again I have developed the idea

---

1. Jane Leigh Okill Swift, Mahan's aunt. Her death left Mahan's sister, Jane Leigh Mahan, alone in the house in Elizabeth.

1. *See* Mahan to Ellen Evans Mahan, September 22, 1894, Footnote 1.

in an article in the *U. S. Magazine* for October 1893.[2] Per contra, the case of Torrington, who gave the phrase birth, would exemplify my later contention.[3] I was imperfectly familiar with Torrington's action when I published my first book. I thought him guilty of carelessness as to lookout and culpable exposure of his fleet in an advanced position without lookouts. I criticized also his tactics at Beachy Head. Further information modified my views as to this conduct. I think upon the whole he managed well, and certainly was perfectly right in not risking a battle which could have availed only to destroy his force. So far, good. But I have never subscribed to his plea, nor those of his partisans, in thinking that his fleet in being *should* have prevented the descent of the French. It may have done so, but ought not. Were they ready, Tourville had only to spread, within mutual support, his superior fleet to form a curtain behind which the operation could have gone on. Without risk? Surely not. But do you purpose to make war without running risks? Was not Napoleon quite right in his sarcasm "my admirals have learned, I know not where, that war can be made without running risks." He didn't of course mean risk of having men killed but risk of disaster. What effect the landing of 30,000 men in England in 1690 would have had I don't know—but, was that effect great, Tourville (in the French) was certainly censurable for not attempting it, despite the fleet in being, and the risk of disaster.

So at the Yalu. The Japanese fleet in being did not deter the Chinese, who nearly made a success of it. Whether it was worth while to land the men is another question. If it was, a fleet superior, though not greatly, to the "fleet in being" attempted an operation in its despite and so nearly succeeded as to justify the risk. War can't be made without them.

And was it not so in 1796. The British channel fleet was surely very much in being then; yet Hoche not only attempted but, so far as the fleet in being went, actually succeeded in an enterprise that would have shaken the British dominion in Ireland to center had not the weather interfered.

I think that in the "fleet is being" you fellows have got hold of a perfectly sound general idea, but by overlooking the necessary qualification they are erecting it into a dogma—a fetish—which involves the danger of becoming "doctrinaire." Now of all dangerous conditions a military doctrinaire is in one of the worst. He is a quick match and gunpowder. It is however only against the unqualified reliance upon the fleet in being that I object. My natural tendency is rather to magnify my profession, and I readily admit that a gigantic operation like an invasion of Great Britain would require much more caution than a sudden raid. In short my position

---

2. "Two Maritime Expeditions," *United Service Magazine.*
3. In 1690 Arthur Herbert, Earl of Torrington, was ordered to engage the French fleet off Beachy Head. He was court-martialed for holding back, but was acquitted.

is that while the principle is sound, much depends upon the application. It is not a panacea.

The history of my article is this.[4] After writing and mailing it, I repented of some expressions and cabled not to publish, at the same time writing the editor. He printed it in galleys and returned to me, with the hope that I would tone down and allow publication, this I think I shall do. I expect you will go gunning for me when it appears, but by that time I shall be in Gibraltar and will take refuge under the guns of the fortress, if our friend Lake[5] will permit. Seriously, the article as a whole is indifferent. Many of the ideas I think suggestive but I am dissatisfied with their concatenation—a sufficiently long word; but believe it can't do harm and may do good, I shall let it go. I am too horribly driven for any decent work. Yours in the U.S.[6] I shall look up.

Kind remembrances to Lady Clarke and believe me [etc.].

To Hilary A. Herbert

USS *Chicago*, Southampton, September 30, 1894 [NA]

Sir:

1. I have to submit the following report upon the instruction and exercise in signalling for the quarter ending today:-

2. The five special signal boys have been instructed and exercised weekly in the Meyer Code, the Ardois Night Signals, and in handling and working the Search Lights, and less frequently in the flag General and International Signals. No instruction has been give in the new Introduction to the General Signal Book, there being no new set of flags yet furnished the *Chicago*.

3. The Quartermasters have been instructed in the Meyer Code, in the use of the Search Lights, and have also been exercised in the General and International Flag Signals, and are proficient.

4. The Coxswains have been instructed in the Meyer Code and in the use of the Search Lights, but in some cases it has been found impossible for them to learn the Meyer Code owing to their limited knowledge of English, or entire inability to read or write.

5. The apprentices, exclusive of the Signal Boys, are divided into two sections in charge of the Naval Cadets, and during the quarter have been instructed weekly (average).

---

4. "Possibilities of an Anglo-American Reunion."
5. Captain A. P. M. Lake, RN.
6. "A Plea for a Policy," *United States Magazine* (September 1894), p. 455.

To Hilary A. Herbert

USS *Chicago*, Southampton, October 2, 1894 [NA]

Sir:

1. I have to inform the Bureau of Ordnance that out of sixty (60) 6 Pdr. Hotchkiss caps furnished by the company in Paris, five (5) exploded in priming the cartridges for saluting charges, and in backing out twenty-nine (29), eight (8) more exploded.

2. Under the same circumstances no explosions occurred with those brought out from the United States.

3. I therefore deem it expedient to send the accompanying requisition, trusting to catching one of our vessels coming this way to bring them out, or else that they may be sent otherwise.

To Ellen Kuhn Mahan

Southampton, October 2, 1894 [LC]

My darling Nellie: I really had no time to write you last week and so just sent a scrap to mamma. We started for Havre on Sunday week—Sept 23—arrived there next morning, and went into dry dock the following afternoon. It is called a *dry* dock because, after the ship has entered it and been placed, all the water is pumped out and then they are able to clean and paint the bottom which in steel ships like the *Chicago* become covered with grass and small shells. This roughness of the bottom causes the ship to go much slower than she ordinarily would. I wrote you all about Havre last year. It is primarily and above all dingy—I know no other word that so aptly characterizes the impression made by it upon me. I had what I felt to be rather bad luck there. The French Minister of Marine, who is a Havrais, was then stopping in town with his family. He asked us to dinner, which was dullish, though all of them speak English fairly well—but unluckily the admiral, forgetting the disarray of a ship in dock asked them to visit her, which they did on Friday bringing some twenty or thirty people with them. We had to haul out of the dry dock, the men got their dinner late and everything was much as it should not be, which I regretted. We also took breakfast at our Consuls—which I did not find much more interesting. The first intention had been to sail from Havre to Plymouth—there take in coal—and thence to Lisbon, but the admiral, when last in London, contracted some sort of engagement with the Am. Ambassador & wants to salute him when he sails for N.Y. next Saturday. There we are taking in stores, and are having a boat built to replace one of ours which is worn out. All this will detain us till at least the 15th of this month, much to my regret. Places become to me not only wearisome but depressing when, as is here the case the people whom I know have mostly gone and the animation of summer is succeeded by the winter's monotony. Admiral Kirkland impresses me favorably—he seems kind hearted and considerate. As far as I see now there is no indication of the sour surliness which characterized Erben—but he has hardly been here long enough yet to judge. I have had mailed to you Overman's *History of Europe 1598–1715*[1] as the serious book you are to attempt to read and which Marraine was to give you. I have not myself read it, but it is well spoken of & the period one of which you should know something. I am going to look up a map and have it sent you. Marraine may pay mama $1.25 and call it square. If any one would give you a subscription to the Mercantile Library[2] which has a branch on 5th Ave near 38th St, you might try reading with it Miss Pardoe's *Court of Louis XIV* &c. But I say this with uncertainty, because you cannot attempt to read too much. The great thing is to acquire the *power* to read— that is to maintain your attention well fixed for a certain length of time. Like all other powers it is partly natural, but also can be acquired. I think you ought to have better guidance than my own, especially when I am so far away and with my mind so painfully occupied with distasteful details. Under any conditions it is perfectly impossible for me to give you the attention & help you need in these matters. I might recommend you Macaulay's Essays or History[3]—because they are very interesting and the style is so good; but then he is very prejudiced—and even though I tell you not to believe half he says you would not know what half you could believe. It is a pity, too, for they are admirably written & interesting, and it would do you no harm sometime to borrow a volume from Marraine and read one when you want just a short piece. For it is true of reading, as of everything else, that you need variety—not always the same thing. What is objectionable, especially for a beginner is dawdling over books, dipping here and there; later in life a practised skimmer like myself can sometimes make even dawdling pay, but it is dangerous for the young. Try to attain the power of fixing your attention for one hour and then gradually for two. I dont think many can go beyond this at a sitting, but you like others must get your own experience. But my dear child I really dont want to be reading you a lecture and must stop. All I can say is that I have scarcely any news, so you have lost nothing. Tell mamma I think it very strange she has never even mentioned my letter about Minnie Hartpence. Good bye

---

1. Citation not found.
2. The Mercantile Library Association furnished good reading for young business employees at low rates.
3. Thomas Babington Macaulay, *The History of England from the Accession of James II*. Various editions, from 1849 on, in the U. S. and in England.

darling. This is a poor letter—but one cant make bricks without straw. Love to mamma & Helen.

[P.S.]   Ask mamma to send me 1 doz tooth silk by post addressed U.S. Consul Gibraltar & marked "keep till arrival of *Chicago*."

To Ellen Evans Mahan

Southampton, October 5, 1894 [LC]

Dearest Deldie: I received last night your letters of the 24 and 25 September, telling of your journey to and from Groton and leaving there our dear laddie. I gather from what you say that he had not up to the time you left received the letter I wrote with the view of getting to him just after you left. I am glad to know the country is beautiful as well as healthy. The latter I expected, and for the former I know that, though rugged and not very fertile, New England is often fair to look on. I do not trouble much about him—it will be strange indeed if he fail of happiness among so many well regulated boys. It is we who suffer and will suffer most in the departure of the child to return a child no more. Kirkland has now been on board more than three weeks and has been very nice to me—although I see indications of an impatient temper which may become uncomfortable. All who have experience of him, however, agree that he is really warm-hearted, and he seems disposed to make a companion of me rather than of his staff[1]—asks me to walk with him etc. Of course, for one of my reserved and solitary temper, this has its inconvenient side, the more so as he walks slowly whereas I go fast. He is besides extremely profane, to a degree distasteful to me; but I am determined, as far as in me lies, to avoid any occasion of coldness or dislike. I feel as if I were a bootlick but I believe it is really right to repress that offishness which is so obstinate in me, and which perhaps had something to do with Erben's dislike of me. Kirkland messes wholly by himself—his staff in the wardroom—and seems independent of society for amusing himself. He tells me that Dr. Laurie is dead, and that Mrs. Laurie is living somewhere in the country—in the Argentine I think—upon property bought by her father which has appreciated greatly in value. We have been startled, and I myself amused, by a rumor in today's Paris *Herald*, which you have probably seen, that I was talked of for the Naval Academy but that Mr. Herbert was averse to the change. The last is probably true enough, but what even started the rumor passes my understanding.

---

1. Admiral Kirkland had reported on board with his personal staff, Lieutenants J. A. Nickels, class of 1869, and York Noel, class of 1874. Noel was Kirkland's son-in-law and his secretary. His wife was Florence Kirkland.

I will of course send my photo to Mr. Saltonstall with a letter, and my autographs for your friends. I am glad to say that—quite contrary to our expectations—Kirkland seems socially inclined, talks of two months at Nice etc. All absence from you is against the grain, but if it must be so where better than Villefranche. I think I can stand it better than last year, for I am really getting casehardened to dining, and have now some acquaintances & even friends—though upon reflection they seem rather summed up in the Schiffs. I will miss the McCreas, if they are not coming back. We are now waiting for the completion of a boat to replace one of ours that has been condemned. It will not be ready in time to permit us to sail before the 20th, which I regret not wishing so late a crossing of the Bay of Biscay. The weather too is gloomy now, and the days grow short apace although for two weeks the sea must have been smooth—very little wind and what there is from the N.E. fair for crossing the Bay. There is no news. The London *Times* has been calling me Copernicus again. Shall I sue for libel? I find what their meaning is—Copernicus taught that the sun was the centre of the system—not the earth as was believed before his time, and I have been the first to show that sea power is the centre around which other events move, not it around them. "In the philosophy of the subject," says my unknown friend, "we must all sit at the feet of the eminent writer—the one man who has taught us that sea power is the central factor of our national polity—*That has been done once for all.*" My dear, do you know that is your husband they are talking of? Even my speech at the banquet was quoted against a man the other day. I have a letter from the Editor of the *Contemporary* asking for an article on the Eastern War. That makes the *Contemporary, Fortnightly, North American, Forum, Century*,[2] and *Atlantic* and I think the *Nineteenth Century* (verbal) but am not sure. I have no news—everything here is dead quiet our friends all gone. The Ed. of the *N. American* sent me back galley proofs of my article[3] expressing the hope I could tone it down and allow its publication. I have so done, sent it back, and purpose to allow it come out. It dont touch naval matters & both Clover & Nazro advise its publication. I find myself so unexpectedly saying things that attract favorable comment that I shall try & hope for the best. Goodbye. Love to the girls, and to Buster when you write.

Oct 6—8 A.M.

The mail closes shortly. Pray for me, dearest that my strength do not fail during the remaining time. I feel sometimes almost done out—mentally & morally, not physically.

---

2. "Lessons from the Yalu Fight," *Century Magazine* (August 1895).
3. "Possibilities of an Anglo-American Reunion."

To Ellen Evans Mahan

For yourself only

Dearest Deldie: I have only time for a line to say that I hope you will be careful about yourself and the girls in going about after dusk, if the present lawlessness in N.Y. continues.[1] I trust Helen will not be frightened—and at the same time I think it well not to be imprudent till the police gets its grip on again. I wrote Buster last night and will to Helen in a day or two.

To Helen Evans Mahan

Southampton, October 9, 1894 [NWC]

My dearest Helen: I must leave behind me tonight a letter for you, as I go tomorrow to Devonport, near Plymouth, to spend a few days with an English naval officer[1] who was in the Pacific with me ten years ago. He had more than once asked me and last year I had "named the day"; but Erben went to London and with his curious wrongheadedness in such matters objected to my being away while he was. However, all seems for the best, for I am nearly tired to death now yet wd. have nowhere to go but for this. London in the foggy season now upon us, in bachelors quarters and without friends wd. be very different place from May last, in the height of the fashion, and with all the halo of distinction with which I was then greeted. The Schiffs are breaking up for the winter—going back to the Riviera— and not even a club is now open to me. But moreover I want to see my old friend, and his wife whom I have never met. I doubt it will be for the last time for I scarcely think I shall ever again see England after this leaving. Devonport is near Plymouth & the admiral who there commands was also in the Pacific[2] at that time. We were to have gone there before leaving the Channel, but have been so long delayed that we shall not be able. I purpose staying till Monday morning next. I received letters from mamma & from you last night for my birthday. I wish you did meet some of my friends but you are mistaken in thinking of the men as young. Those of whom I spoke as being at Lady Jeune's were mostly well on in the

---

1. Senator Clarence Lexow's committee was investigating New York City departments, especially the police. According to one comment, the police were reluctant to perform their duties for fear of reprisals from criminal elements.
1. Bouverie Clark.
2. Sir Algernon Lyons.

forties—one or two approaching at least my own age. The two Stanley girls—Lady Jeune's daughters—are sweet; not insipidly so, but very attractive. The elder, my favorite, quite disputes the ground with Rosie Schiff. In truth my reason and better judgment is all in her favor, but Rosie certainly has that rare gift called charm. We are all getting bored to death with Southampton. We have been here two months with the exception of the short trip to Havre, and we have exhausted it long since. All our friends also are gone away. I go ashore at 3, walk till 5.30, and then back on board— see no one and hear nothing except what is in the papers. You see we waited till Sept 6 for Erben, and afterwards had to dock, paint etc.; but withal we might by this have been away but for the necessity of having a new boat built here. We shall I hope start by the 20th, and I am happy to know that the admiral intends to spend two months in Nice. I have been trying lately to get abreast of my correspondence but it is a hard thing to do—so many letters turn up continually. I am sorry your children seem so unable to come to you but anything is better than that you should be run too hard at your present age, and if others dont turn up, as I dare say they will, why, you will have more time for practice. Tell mamma I sent my photo to Mr. Saltonstall and at the same time wrote him one of my best notes. I addressed Lynnfield Mass, which I hope will reach him. How absurd it seems that Lyle had no paper! Had he no tongue to ask for any, or no money with which to buy? It seems so inconsequent—so like me & so unlike mamma, if she was responsible for it. I prefer that he shd. write to her oftener than to me. It is more natural & mothers should be first, but at the same [time] fathers often make a mistake in leaving such matters wholly to the mother. And now dear child I think I am at the end, not of my budget, for such it is not, but of such rambling ideas as I can conjure out of my wasted head. I hope I shall some day be able again to do better. Goodbye. Love to Mamma and Nellie.

To William H. Henderson

Devonport, October 11, 1894 [NMM]

My dear Henderson: Your letter reached me two days ago, anticipating the fulfillment of a purpose I have been nursing three months to write to you. Thank you very much for your congratulations upon my reception in England. I assure you it was very deeply felt by myself, & will, I am persuaded, remain by far the most distinguished period of my life.

I am paying a two or three days visit to Bouverie Clark, an old chum of mine in the Pacific ten years ago. I find also stopping with them a Kings Ballard, brother to one of your young officers who invalided home. I gather that he is doing well and tomorrow goes to London.

We should by this have been back in the Medn., but have been delayed by various circumstances. I fancy we shall get away by the end of next week. I must tell you that I was unable to deliver any of the letters you kindly gave me, except the one to Thursfield—my time was so occupied, I could not fit them in. Thursfield I met by quite a lucky chance my first evening in London. I had gone to the Athenaeum to find him and while waiting there was introduced to Col. Stirling[1] who, without knowing my quest, asked me to dine with him at the U. S.[2] to meet Thursfield. We had a very pleasant partie carré, Sir Geo. Clarke being the fourth. Clarke and Thursfield afterwards lunched with me.

Please make allowances for my writing. Clark's pens seem all to be quills, to which I am unused. Hoping we may meet again this winter believe me [etc.].

To Ellen Evans Mahan

Royal Naval Barracks, Devonport, October 12, 1894 [LC]

My dearest Deldie: Here I am on a visit to my friend Clark, as I think I mentioned in my letter to Nellie—that is—said I was coming. I left a letter for her, (or was it for Helen?) before quitting Southampton on Wednesday. That *my* memory should be at fault on a point of that sort may serve to convince you of the mental fatigue and distraction which seems to increase upon me as the cruise goes on. It is at present I think largely due to the immense monotony of lying so long in Southampton Water, coming as that did immediately on top of our no less tedious stay in Antwerp. Variety is the spice of all life—but nowhere is it more essential than to ship life the burden of which I feel continually more and more. I wrote to Stevens to send my mail here & so was rewarded yesterday by recg yours of the 1 & 2. Of course you miss Buster and the case is the worse in that I am away—a house full of one sex only is in a bad way. Fortunately I have now 17 months complete and we may fairly hope this is our last year of separation. Please dont call home the horrid little flat—it is not so to me. I hope we may see our way, however to taking one with more room sometime. As regards your coming out—if Kirkland sticks to his present idea, Jan 10 more or

---

1. J. B. Sterling.
2. United Service Club.

less will do very well. My idea is to cable you if necessary, as follows: "Mahan New York Genoa Jan.—." The full meaning being "take the steamer *due in Genoa* Jany—." You should arrange with the Company that "Mahan" would indicate your full address. The name is rather unusual except among the very poor and is probably unappropriated—but if taken you might substitute "Deldie." The reigning idea is to be in Nice for Carnival, which would involve our being not far off at Jan. 20–30 in which you would probably be due. I think to ask a fortnight's leave and to take rooms at Beaulieu about two miles from Villefranche—a pretty situation where we could be much to ourselves. Your uncle of course would want to see something of you—but there are frequent trains—and I am sure the Schiffs will also want to see you. I think you will like them—especially Rosie & Marie—but I trust they will not have round a friend of theirs in whose looks etc they take great stock. I believe she is all right and certainly most amiable—but to me she looks like one of the demi-monde. Queer I cant recall her name, (Mrs. Bingham) knowing her so well. Tom Rodgers and I used to exchange wondering surmises about her. She is immense, nearly six feet—well proportioned—blonde & hair that looks champagned far past her première jeunesse—altogether not at all the sort of person I would care to walk with in the avenue. Yet when you talk with her she is so kindly—perfectly quiet and never a word in the least risqué—that I suppose she is simply one of the phenomena of English life. I have no news for you dear. You wont care to hear how lovely the country is, soft and mild as our April. The Clarks had a dinner last night and tonight I dine with the admiral, who is the same that commanded in the Pacific when I was there. I am still a bit of lion you see. I stay over Sunday, returning to the ship Monday. I am glad you did not scold Hennie about the house bills. I dont think likely she can improve on you, for she probably inherits my dislike for bargaining but the money is not ill lost in rest to you and experience to her. The rest, change and pleasure of new scenes weigh with me in asking you to come out, as well as my desire to see you. But we must not be too sure for anything may happen to interrupt our plans. A letter from the Bureau of Const. to Kirkland spoke of the movements of the ship as uncertain. The same has been said for months past and I dont [know] what to make of it. It is inconceivable folly to think of sending her to China —for, though her boilers would stand it, I doubt if the Engines would the 25,000 miles steaming entailed by the mere going & coming. And now dearest—good bye. Love to all. I shall write often to Buster—but have bid him write you in preference to me—to me only occasionally.

To Edward C. Mann

USS *Chicago*, Southampton, October 16, 1894 [NDL]

My dear Sir: Your letter was recd. by me only three days ago, and the above heading will sufficiently explain the delay in replying & the impossibility of my attending the opening exercises of your proposed Post Graduate School of political science. There is no likelihood of my returning to the United States before next spring and I should prefer therefore to defer any positive promise to undertake the lectureship you suggest. I can do no work here. I can only say now that your proposition falls in with ideas I have long held, as to the desirability of putting before the public the relations of the Navy to general policy of the country, which I have thought of attempting by a series of magazine articles. May I add that the general tenor of your Post Graduate course has my heartiest sympathy.

[P.S.]   My foreign address is c/o B.F. Stevens, 4 Trafalgar Square, London.

To Ellen Kuhn Mahan

Southampton, October 18, 1894 [LC]

Dearest Nellikin: I am ashamed to have to write you such a short and hurried letter as I must to day—but I am driven almost beside myself by the accumulation of work and petty annoyances attending it. My six days leave was grand but it is followed by such arrears I could almost regret it. My postponing writing you is also partly due to an opportunity of looking over a number of letters of 1804 and 1805 relating to Lord Nelson which must be done now or perhaps never—loaned me by the Radstock family here. I must tell you that I found your last letter, recd. yesterday evening a great improvement—written more deliberately, and therefore much better as to handwriting, and very well expressed indeed. I trust this may lead you to more care, or perhaps I should say to less haste; allowing yourself more time. Not even in letter writing should a young person who hopes to write well, write in a slovenly or hurried manner. Of news I have very little or none, and indeed my mind has to receive so many passing impressions and I am so hurried that even things that might possibly interest you pass away from it. I have great difficulty at times in recalling the simplest things. All this is excessively trying to a man of my temperament, and who would fain keep in touch of his family by a minute record of daily doings; not to speak of the debt I owe you all for your constant loving thought of me. It is discouraging to find that work seems rather to increase than diminish as the time goes by; but it is partly due I think to my anxiety on account of my reputation, to insure accuracy and perfectness as far as may be throughout all things. This anxiety is of course incurred by previous circumstances of which you know something. Of course, under these circumstances, the end of the cruise seems to me [to] offer inexpressible relief; but God knows what is best and I think I can see that amid many shortcomings the trial does tend to correct certain faults of my character. I shall close this now (8.30 a.m.) in hopes it may somehow catch an earlier mail than the one I intend to send by the *City of Paris* from here on Saturday. Give my dearest love to mamma & Helen, and say to the former that I know no depth of folly or wrong into which I might not fall, but that if I should fail to be content with the fifth flat with you all, it would be the saddest misfortune that could happen to me. Certainly I long for it now, though I would be glad if it were bigger, so only that it is *home*.

To Ellen Evans Mahan

Southampton, October 19, 1894 [LC]

My own dearest Deldie: Here I am again pen in hand but what shall I find to say? Your last really made me sad when you spoke of the looks of your bank book and your loss of Lyle. Bear up yet a little longer, the time cannot, probably, be very far off when we shall all be together again—and our expenses, if not actually lessened, will be easier to bear together. True the lad must go away again, but if you will consent to my retirement I hope we shall not again be severed till that day when death do us part—only, we will hope even then, for a little while. Nellie's last letter was extremely nice, much better than mine to her. And to think of the underrunning fear that I shall not be satisfied with the fifth flat when I come back. Dear child, what I shall in the future become I know not—nor do I deny that much in the conditions of those with whom I have been thrown here seems to me to be pleasant and desirable—but I have always felt the same: that the inability to mix freely with society on account of our means not being sufficient has been the chief manque in our life—depriving it of a certain variety which is very much to be wished. But at the same time I fully recognize that, like everything else, this is consciously enjoyable only while the novelty lasts—and indeed, while I do enjoy the animation of a crowded room or dinner my chiefest pleasure has been—a queer confession for a graybeard—has been in watching and talking with pretty young girls principally Rose Schiff and Madeleine Stanley. Like my father I love young things from young girls to puppies & kittens. Now as regards the question of money & your coming here—if it will involve you in any anxiety you shall not come & I shall leave it to you to decide—feeling only that—while I greatly desire it for my own account I still most especially desire that you should have the holiday, the change, and the strength that women & men get from such a meeting as ours would be. We are leaving here tomorrow—at least I hope so, for it is getting cold damp and horribly dull and depressing. We go to Lisbon. I dread the passage—the probable fog and very possible bad weather but I shall be glad to get to a milder climate. I am astonishingly well. While at Clark's in Plymouth I was able to see myself in a bright light and a long glass, and I was surprised to see how clear rosy and unblemished my skin was—not a roughness on it the very picture of health and as fair as a man of thirty five. *I quite admired myself.* With reference to money you must remember that Mr. Marston wrote that the books continue to sell well, and although we must not expect the returns of July, I still hope to see the sales of No 2 approach those of No 1 behind which they now are by about 900. You may be interested to know that after much hunting I have a chance of getting a likeness of Lord Nelson's wife—unluckily only in old age—but perhaps I may yet find one younger. Also, I have found at Lord Radstock's some interesting letters which passed between his father and grandfather the latter an admiral in 1802 the former a young officer who served on board Nelson's flagship. I have got some interesting things from them & hope more may turn up for they say they have a great many letters. I am glad to know about Auntie's will though it seems strange you should have forgotten to tell me before—also about Tom Ogden's[1] death though I knew him very slightly and just recall the old people so long ago. I suppose you have seen the talk about my being ordered as Supt. of the Academy. Whether there is anything under it or not, I dont know. Certainly I have not moved a hand in the matter. I incline to think that Mr. Herbert means to move the College to Annapolis and thinks it would work well to put me over both. I make no assertions, but, while I might *now* consent to take the Academy alone in order to get back to you all, if they leave me to finish my cruise away from you I have no intention voluntarily to assume any such nigger work as the Academy. A year's leave & then retire that is my present aim; and I hope that with Auntie's and your mother's leavings and my hoped for earnings that we may get on. One of our new officers who has been with Ramsay, says Goodrich[2] will not be ordered home until the superintendency is filled. He wants it & they fear his importunity. McNair[3] also wants it & evidently they dont want to

---

1. Brother of Gouverneur Morris (Gouv) Ogden.
2. C. F. Goodrich remained in command of the *Concord* until 1895. He was never Superintendent of the Naval Academy, but became President of the Naval War College in 1897.
3. F. V. McNair was made a member of the Naval Examining and Retirement Board on November 21, 1894. He finally became Superintendent in 1898, and held the position until his death in 1900.

give it to any of the applicants—hence I am trotted out as a "dark horse."[4] I have ordered Stevens to send Nellie two atlases and two maps to accompany her reading of the book. Dear I fear my letters are less interesting than they were and incoherent. I am always in a hurry and always pressed. I dont know what it is to feel at ease. To tell my vexations and cares would only worry you and weary me. The only thing is I keep very well and recognize that as a matter of spiritual discipline it is doing me good. And now, my own darling, my dearly loved and sadly missed wife, I will close again, leaving space only for a last line tomorrow. God bless and keep you always, and grant us, if He will many days together, happy as the past, and to share together His rest in the better days to come. Love to the girls.

Saturday 20. 8:30 A.M.

All well—good bye again my darling.

You will realize, with regard to the Academy, that I should for many reasons be unwilling to take the girls there—would go there alone. I cannot deliberately close Helen's teaching career nor postpone the plans we have made for the future, if God leaves any choice in my hands. There are many other reasons pro and con, of which I would like to talk with you, but can scarcely write clearly. I rather hope no choice will have to be made.

To Horace E. Scudder

USS *Chicago*, Southampton, October 20, 1894 [HUL]

My dear Mr. Scudder: I have lost, I know not how, unless by injudicious lending, the *Atlantic* of January 1894, containing Howe. Will it be too much to ask you to send me a copy care of Stevens 4 Trafalgar Square London. As you know, it is with a view to ultimate publication that I want them. I have the rest safe enough. We leave here today for Lisbon & the Medn. and glad I am to get south, though the Medn. is not quite a bed of roses at this time. I rather expect an article by me will be in this *North American*.[1] It is far from being up to the mark, and if you knew how I had to labor as it was, you would appreciate the impossibility of my pledging myself to work now. I think it has some good and suggestive ideas—it is the coordination of them I find fault with, but could not better. I dont think they will please the spirit of this age.

---

4. Captain Philip H. Cooper was the real "dark horse," being appointed Superintendent on November 15, 1894.

1. "Possibilities of an Anglo-American Reunion."

To Ellen Evans Mahan

Lisbon, Portugal, October 27, 1894 [LC]

My dearest Deldie: It is Helen's turn for a letter, but yours of the 12th requires an immediate answer so I will send it at once. You are substantially right as to what I told you about my grandmother's will. My recollection is quite distinct that my mother told me that Auntie's share was, by her mother's will, to go to us children—but I am not sure as to the *equal shares*. As all wills are, I believe, filed or recorded, the facts can be ascertained. Auntie was always so righteous in all her ways of thought that it seems to me improbable that she would ever have thought of willing otherwise than within her clear right. I fancy Jane's estimate of *our* portion included the Tenafly property. Concerning this I mean to write to Gillender and ask his opinion whether it would not be well to have it divided now, by mutual consent of us three joint owners. I thoroughly dislike joint ownership, especially between relatives, as likely to lead to differences & quarrels. As things stand, I suppose no one of us can do anything—sell, let, etc without the others; and either wrongheadedness or mistakes might stand in the way of a wise action.

We got in here yesterday afternoon, after five very disagreeable days. We left England with threatening weather which came on that night, and we had strong head winds, amounting at times almost to a gale, with frequent rains, all the way down. Night before last we anchored fifty miles north of here, not having time to reach here before dark. Next day we came down against almost a gale, with thick weather. With great difficulty we got a pilot and ran in. During the night it blew and rained furiously, and I was so thankful to be inside, for I was awfully tired. Today I have felt even more tired than yesterday—although Clover says he wonders how I stand it as well as I do. But at 54 it does come hard. The *Chicago* behaves admirably—but so many wakeful nights and constant wetting of salt and fresh water do tell. Unluckily it is still raining here—detestable weather, soft, muggy and enervating.

The mention of Aunt Margaret's[1] death was also in one letter today recd. This is a merciful release all round, for from the accounts she has been as good as dead these months past. The generation before us is fast passing away.

Kirkland dont intend to get to Nice before January 15, which will suit us very well, if you decide to come. I shall try and find out my chances, for if I am to return in May the expense may be unadvisable; but I rather hold to your coming—not only because I so want to see you, but because I think it will be good for you as well as me. You must bring a dress to

---

1. Margaret Evans, sister of Manlius G. Evans.

dine in for you can hardly refuse to dine with the Schiffs, after their kindness to me, and they will be sure to ask you. I dont know of any one else likely to trouble you, or to prevent our being much by ourselves. Mrs Sands (Hartpence) begged me to let her know if you came—as she expects to be somewhere in the Riviera, but I see no necessity for doing so, unless you desire it. I suppose your uncle[2] may make some fuss over you, but I trust he wont want to drive you, for I dont think he is any longer safe to drive. I had, and may still have, many acquaintances in Nice, but none sufficiently familiar to be likely to bother us with attentions. And now good bye dearest. Dont trouble about my affections. My one desire is to get home to you and the children, and to my work. I trust God will soon release me from this chastisement—this dead grind. Love to the children.

Saturday morning—Oct. 28.

All well, and a bright day which I hope may last.

To Helen Evans Mahan

Lisbon, October 28, 1894 [NWC]

My dearest Helen: I wrote to mamma two days ago instead of to you, because there was a question she wanted answered. I did not say much of our passage south, reserving that for my more regular letter—not indeed that there was much to say. For nearly ten days before we started the weather had been exceptionally fine, with an unusually high barometer —indeed the previous month had been very quiet despite the very heavy storms you had in the U.S. During my visit to Plymouth it was beautiful. Three or four days before our sailing, however, the barometer began to fall getting as low as 29.50 and when we left on the 20th the sky was threatening, and the pilot said we were sure to have very bad weather. The wind was then east, but by nine at night it had got round to South West and freshened very considerably. The admiral thought of going into Plymouth, but I didn't want to, so we kept on, and on Sunday evening rounded Ushant Id. with a more moderate sea, and stood across the bay of Biscay for Cape Finisterre. The weather behaved very curiously, now clearing up and again clouding over and blowing hard, always from SouthWest. When it did clear it was wonderful to see the extraordinary lucidity of the atmosphere. It seemed to be of infinite depth yet perfectly transparent, and the stars seemed to swim in it, while the great white clouds sweeping by intensified the effect by the contrast. I remember while sitting on a chest and looking at the sky I recalled some lines of Byron's, which made me

---

2. Charles Kuhn.

[352]

think again of what I once said to you: that we are too apt to rest in the mere melody or sweetness of poetry, without making the mental effort to appreciate its intellectual quality. The deep dark sky and the placid stars shining, not so much brilliantly as intensely, for they did not twinkle in the least, showed me how carefully Byron had worked out his words from what his eyes had seen of dark & bright

> She walks in beauty, *like* the *night*
> Of cloudless climes and starry skies;
> And all that's best of dark and bright
> Meet in her aspect and her eyes;
> Thus mellowed to that tender light
> Which Heaven to gaudy day denies.

You will find the rest in his Hebrew Melodies if you care to follow the verses, *Golden Treasury* p. 206, and trace the same idea worked in and running through the whole. Well, in three or four hours that brilliant sky misted over, a rainbow came round the moon and the next day was blowing and mizzling, the barometer dancing a jig—up & down. At night I was very tired and the weather so thick you couldn't see more than half a mile so I wrote orders to the officer of the deck that he must look out—I could not get up in time if wanted—and I lay down to sleep. At quarter before twelve I was waked with a message that it was blowing a gale, raining very hard and impossible to see any distance. So I got up put on some clothes, and when I got on deck there was the same old blue sky and white clouds— everything had cleared off and the same lustrous calm eyes looking down from heaven. Notwithstanding, the next day was also unpleasant raining and drizzling, and the night after we passed Finisterre we stood along, scarce able to see anything at times—only knowing that steamers would pass, and they did pass, very close to us. It was an anxious time and I kept saying to myself "Oh thou of little faith, wherefore dost thou doubt?" but it was hard to prevent the feeling of uneasiness. I got Mr. Clover to take four hours of that night for me—but two of them I could not sleep owing to the jarring of the ship as she plunged into the head seas. The next day it moderated and cleared—Wednesday—& we ran in for the coast which we made and skirted, but could not get to Lisbon before night; so we anchored about fifty miles north under a cape with good promise for next day, which however proved delusive. At 7 in the morning it was blowing harder than at any time during the voyage, and looking very nasty. I would have preferred to stay where we were but the admiral wished to go on, and so we started. When we got off Lisbon bar it was very thick and foggy and no pilots out, but we fortunately exchanged signals with a shore station which said a pilot could be sent us. So we closed in and got him, and he took us through rather a narrow and not very deep passage but we got in all right and here we are. The night of our arrival it blew harder than ever and misty. I just hugged

[353]

myself to be at anchor inside, and able to sleep quietly. Yesterday and today have been clear and pleasant. I am glad and much obliged to you girls for persuading mamma to stay a bit with Aunt Bartie. She ought to have a change from time to time if just to get wholly away from household cares. The monotonous strain of these tells heavily, and of course will be worse than usual this winter with Lyle and me away making the house so much more small and quiet. I had today hers of the 14th saying she was going to Aunt Margaret's funeral, and also Nellie's saying that she should keep on drawing a bit longer. I quite approve of perseverance, but think it might be well to ask Mr. Beckwith if her not getting on as fast as he thinks she might is for want of aptitude. I was sorry to hear of Jomini's fight—I trust he will not lose his peaceable temper.

Monday Oct. 29

All well. Goodbye dear child with love for all.

To Ellen Evans Mahan

Lisbon, November 1, 1894 [LC]

My dearest Deldie: I am afraid that in this paper, which I bought in Havre, I have made a slip-up similar to that which you made on your last type writing. However, we will hope that our foreign correspondence will not have to endure much longer. I suppose you will have seen the report which made its appearance in last Sunday's Paris *Herald*, that this ship was to be relieved on Nov. 15 by the *San Francisco*[1] and to join the North Atlantic Squadron. Of course this raised quite an excitement on board, for it was and is in entire contradiction to all previous indications—but, as the latter are by letter and this by telegram, it is quite possible that circumstances may have arisen causing a change. For myself I remember that the West Indies and Central America are in the N.A. Squadron quite as well as N.Y., and so feel no immoderate joy at the prospect. In fact, were it the admiral's purpose to spend the winter in the Western Medn. I should prefer that to the W.I., but as he intends going to the Levant in mid-winter I would far rather choose the islands. The really determining feature for me is that if we get back to the N.A. I am almost assured of my detachment in May, whereas out here they may—Ramsay surely will—keep me along from month to month on the plea that the ship is so soon to return. Taking all in all I trust the report may prove substantially correct. We are now having most beautiful weather—the Indian summer of the

---

1. A twin-screw armored cruiser, 324 feet in length, displacing 4,088 tons. Commissioned in 1890, she was rated at 19.5 knots. She mounted twelve 6-inch guns and carried four 18-inch deck torpedo tubes.

country, which is called here—and also to some extent in England—St. Martin's summer. Tell Helen, in reply to her question about the Schiffs going to the country, that their house at Eze is quite by itself, so near the sea that a child could throw a stone at it from a window. There is scarcely even a hamlet near them & they are about two miles from the nearest place Beaulieu. The villa is very unpretentious, though seemingly roomy. It reminds me somewhat of the Weed and Minot cottages at Bar Harbour, but is quite closed in with pines. You have stunned me with your idea of buying a house in N.Y. I have never dreamed such a thing could come within our means, nor do I now see how. I can only say take your time about it. The advantages are obvious enough, but the step is one hard to retrace when once taken unless great care and foresight is exercised in the choice of locality. I wholly fail to see where the ready money is to come from, upon even the most liberal estimates of what you may receive from your Aunt's estate. I received yesterday a cheque for £30+ from the *North American* for the article. I have now so many requests for articles it is tantalizing to be unable to comply—but I seem smitten with lethargy or paralysis after my morning's work. I cant think it is either indolence or fancy—in view of the steadiness of my brain work under better conditions. In looking over your last letter but one, I notice that I did not set you right as to us boys having ever been asked to consent to Jenny having an additional amount left her by Aunty. No such request was ever made but I am perfectly clear that mother told me Aunty could not will away from us—& almost equally clear that she told me Aunty wished to made a distinction in Jenny's favor of $5,000. I do not object in the particular case to the provision made for Jenny. It is not more than adequate to her support & that of the house; and girls—or women—are not yet ready to support themselves—besides she was the one on whom the burden of the two old people mainly—almost wholly—fell. You will remember that the suggestion came from me, though through you, that Rose should be specially provided for in your mother's will.

Friday—Nov. 2

I notice what you say my own darling about loving your own house but there are few of us I fancy that do not feel the same as we grow older, but I am persuaded that to yield too much to the feeling tends to age one, and to impair the health. Not only change of air but change of conditions from time to time is beneficial—just as change of position relieves fatigue. I most regretted your not going to the Powels on that account, and on that account I cling to your making the run out here this winter if pecuniarily feasible. You enjoy the sea, you could not but enjoy the beauty of the Riviera—combined mountain and sea—you would have meeting me to look forward to, and upon leaving would know you were returning to the children & that but little of my cruise was left. If the adml. sticks to his plan of spending Feb. in Nice, you will have time to receive the returns from Little & Brown—see Lyle back to school & yet come out betimes. But above all you would have *entire* change of scene and ideas. I am persuaded that what has made this cruise so much easier to me has been simply change of association with different persons. It has been in many ways enormously unpleasant—much more so than the *Wachusett*—but the wear & tear on me has been vastly less. You have had less sherry and bitters. You must take the girls into your confidence now, but enjoin secrecy. They deserve all our confidence. I notice, or think I notice, a slight depression of spirits very unusual to you, and the girls seem to feel that you are not as well and bright as usual. You must come if you can. Two of my girls—Rosie Schiff for one will be near Nice. Number 3 is—what do you think? A Portuguese Jewess- I believe I mentioned her sitting by me at dinner here last May; then sweet sixteen—now, perhaps, sweet 17. Her social position I suppose only ordinaire but she is really very pretty. I dined with them last night, and she was at the other end of the table so that I several times saw her profile in repose— thoroughly Jewish yet refined, and exactly like the general effect of the faces sculptured at Nineveh—the Assyrian—a Semite race kindred to the Jews. They are going to Monte Carlo for much of the winter so you may see her perhaps.

Saturday, Nov. 3

The mail goes out tonight, beloved, and I do not seem to have more to say. Nellie asked whether the history[2] I sent her was to be considered a gift from Marraine. I understood at the time that Marraine would wait for it to be sent—but there is no reason whatever that it should be considered any of her affair, particularly as she gave the child a birthday present. I shouldn't say a word to Rose about it. We are to leave here on Monday for Tangiers and thence go to Gibraltar. Neither are pleasant places to be at this season and at Gibraltar we are bedevilled with mess-dinners, things which I detest. And now good bye my own darling. Keep your heart. Ere this reaches you I will have been 18 months on board. Barring something most unlikely I must get home next summer. Try and reconcile yourself to coming here for a fortnight. Love to the two girls. Always most fondly [etc.].

[P.S.] Send me word if Lyle, or either of the girls, still care for Crake's[3] books. I cut a list of them from the *Guardian* on purpose.

---

2. Overman, *History of Europe, 1598–1715.*
3. Dinah Maria Craik, novelist.

To Ellen Evans Mahan

My own darling: I wrote at length Saturday, and now drop only a line to say that we are to sail by noon. We were pretty disappointed not to get our mail yesterday, but are expecting it by 10, and the adml. intends to delay so as to send up his on shore—so I will keep this open in case any immediate reply is needed to what I may hear from you. We are in a state of suppressed excitement over the rumors of the ship being relieved by the *San Francisco*, but as you are likely to know more by the time this reaches you than we can surmise now I will not enlarge upon the chances. God send I see you soon somewhere, somehow; but I cannot clearly discern what is best for us, as distinguished from what I would like. Happily, He knows.

10:30 A.M.

Well your letter giving account of Aunt M's will etc has come but as there is nothing to which I can reply in a hurry I will close now. Ever my dearest your loving husband.

Love to the girls.

To Ellen Kuhn Mahan

Tangiers, Spanish Morocco, November 8, 1894 [LC]

My darling Nellikin: I started to write to Helen today but I believe it is really your turn. I surely ought soon to be on my way home for I have so little now to say in my letters and am so easily upset, as I am feeling today. We left Lisbon on Monday, & reached here night before last—Tuesday. It is the ship's second visit but I did not go ashore last time the weather being bad and our stay short. Yesterday I went with the admiral to call upon the U.S. Consul[1] and the Moroccan Minister of Foreign Affairs who here represents the Sultan—the latter living at Fez two hundred miles inland. The minister is very old—it is said 85—but very well preserved; rather a handsome man of middle height full slightly aquiline features, a fair ruddy complexion in excellent condition, white hair and beard. His expression very amiable and benevolent. As he spoke no English and we no Arabic, our conversation naturally was disjointed and lacked vivacity, but was eminently complimentary. He has a Spanish name Torres, and is said to be a descendant of the old Spanish Moors who were forced to retire from Granada to Africa 400 years ago. He wore of course the turban and loose white robes of a Mussulman & looked as if he had just stepped out of the *Arabian Nights*. In the afternoon I went to call upon

1. John Judson Barclay.

[357]

the governor of Tangiers, a man of 40, splendidly handsome, rich dark complexion, black curling hair and beard & very strong firm features. He was very animated & courteous in his bearing, but seemed to know little or nothing of what was going on in the world outside Morocco—some idea there was a war somewhere—China & Japan—but plainly neither knowing nor caring who the Chinese & Japanese are. We were served cups of mint tea very sweet indeed, in after dinner coffee cups, and surprise was expressed that we only took one. Then we were showed the room reserved for the Sultan to sleep when he comes to Tangiers—in the Alhambra style but a poor come down to one who has seen the Alhambra or the Alcazar palace in Seville. In going to these places we naturally passed through many of the streets of Tangiers, narrow and dirty, paved with irregular cobblestones that must have been agony to the admiral's gouty feet. I felt them most uncomfortable in all but my thickest shoes. Someone said Tangiers is just like a picture from the Bible, with its quaint Oriental dresses—its camels—its dark cavernous booths of shops &c; but I say to me it simply reveals, as did Granada and Smyrna and the poor old parts of Lisbon, the back ground of misery and squalor against which stand out the picturesque occasional features like the Alhambra, the tournament, the castle, the cathedral &c. The U.S. Consul is quite an oddity and a bore. He is about sixty, has lived much in the East, and is, unluckily for those who meet him, the possessor of a desk 214 years old, on which over a hundred years ago Geo Washington signed his father's commission as Consul to Morocco. He is so elated with this that in every conversation he manages to drag it in. I first met him in Genoa a year ago & he told it me in five minutes, told me again yesterday & in fact it & some ancient papers he has are like King Charles's head in Mr. Dick's memorial[2]—they will get in despite all. I dont find the place interesting and intend not to go ashore again, unless absolutely unable to avoid it—but the climate has certainly been beautiful these days. Unfortunately, it is quite an open bay and we are liable at any moment to weather which makes landing impracticable and the bay barely safe; and as winter is now drawing on the chances are doubly against us. I was interested in hearing what Mr. Beckwith had advised about your drawing. I think it wise to undergo another test before finally abandoning so many years' work; but should the decision then be against you we must not despond but turn diligently to whatever seems next best. I hope we shall leave here tomorrow. If we do we go to Malaga, because we have to meet the *Machias*,[3] which brings us stores, at Gibraltar. That is a disagreeable place to be, and so the admiral wants not to get there until the other ship does.

---

2. In Dickens's *David Copperfield*, Chapter XIV: "As I looked along the lines [of Mr. Dick's Memorial] I thought I saw some allusion to King Charles the First's head again in one or two places."

3. A 212-foot torpedo gunboat displacing 1,177 tons, commissioned in 1893. She mounted eight 4-inch guns and was driven by twin screws at 15.5 knots.

Besides, just now the British Channel fleet is there, and that would mean lots of official visiting, two or three dinners &c. There is also a great deal of formal ceremonial connected with the late Czar.[4] I dont understand the details of it but it is evidently complicated. At Malaga we shall probably find a sheltered anchorage—no visiting and though the place itself is dull enough we can get on pleasantly.

Friday, Nov. 9.

I shall close my letter now, dear little girl, and send it off to take its chance of reaching you. How long mails take I dont know. We are only thirty miles from Gibraltar & not much more from Cadiz—yet we do not yet know the result of the elections at home on Tuesday last. So you see we are rather far from the madding crowd. Dearest love to mamma and Helen.

To Cyprian A.G. Bridge

USS Chicago, Málaga, Spain, November 13, 1894 [NMM]

My dear Admiral: I see by the papers that you are to sail on the 22d. to take up your command in Australia, so I write a line to wish you a pleasant term of service and a good voyage out.

We have received information, wholly unofficial but apparently quite authentic, that another vessel already in commission will sail from home sometime this month to relieve us, and that we will then return at once. This is such a sudden reversal of the policy regarding this ship, and so opposed to the known wishes of a principal official,[1] that it may yet be reversed. Personally—in addition to the usual wish to see one's family, I shall rejoice if able to resume the work I have had in hand & to give it further development.

I will make to you the same request that I have addressed to some others. If you know of any family where there are likely to be letters *about* Nelson, from associates of his official or private, will you put me in communication with such. I am convinced that any unpublished letters of his own will add very little to the means of estimating afforded by those already published. It is in the casual mention of those living with him—friends, relatives or subordinates that fresh material must be sought.

For the present my *Life* of him is at a standstill. I hope to make it my best, and am unwilling to utilize for it the fag ends of time the ship allows.

Again wishing you bon voyage and all prosperity, and with remembrances to Mrs. Bridge I am [etc.].

---

4. Alexander III, who had died on November 1, 1894.
1. Secretary Hilary A. Herbert.

To Ellen Evans Mahan

Málaga, November 13, 1894 [LC]

My beloved Deldie: We are in tribulation about our mail which is much belated owing to various causes. In the first place there was exceeding bad weather at sea, which brought them late to London; then the traject to Gibraltar is long any way; finally the admiral while in Tangier was very uncertain as to his plans. We left there Sunday, having first sent a telegram to Gib to send the mail to Malaga, and we confidently expected it would arrive last night by the only mail, but it did not. In consequence, at present my latest from you, Oct. 23, is now three weeks old. As so often happens the obscurity occurs just when interest and curiosity are most awake. There is the question of the elections, but even more of our own movements. I believe I have before alluded to the report of the *S.F.* [*San Francisco*] relieving us. This came first by telegram to Clover from his wife in Paris, where she had seen it in the Paris *Herald*. Thereafter followed a telegram from Mrs. Noel, (Kirkland's daughter), saying that our marine officer's[1] wife would not come with her, as intended. Then we saw the revocation of Dorn's[2] orders, who was booked for this ship. All this seemed to point the same way but Mrs. Clover's telegram was Oct. 28, and consequently was, and still is, later than any public or private news from the U.S. by letter. Mrs. Noel however, reached Gib on Saturday last, & her husband, who had gone to meet her, telegraphed the admiral that the *San Francisco* was to sail about Nov. 17, and the *Chicago* to return immediately. En attendant, all the adm. knew officially was that he must meet in Gibraltar the *Machias*, which is—or was—to bring stores for us. He did not want to go there till there was a certainty of her coming, partly because the anchorage is unpleasant, partly because the British fleet is there involving dinners, which he dreads for his gout and also a participation in the very excessive mourning for the Czar which they are carrying on. He therefore decided to come here—only sixty miles from Gib—and await developments. After so much disappointment one begins to feel as if letters would never again come, but I suppose reliable news can scarcely be long delayed. If the rumor prove true, I think things will turn out about this way. The *S.F.* can scarcely sail before the 20th and will be a fortnight to Gibraltar. Meanwhile, before starting for a mid winter approach to our coast—the *Chicago* will need three or four weeks careful overhauling of machinery. This can best be done at Marseille —and I think likely that, after calling at Gibraltar—the admiral will go there, via Barcelona, lay us up for repairs, and order the *S.F.* to the same place. There he will shift his flag, leave us and continue his cruise in the other

---

1. William F. Spicer.
2. Lieutenant Edward J. Dorn, class of 1874, was assigned to Ordnance Instruction, Washington Navy Yard, on November 3, 1894.

ship. We might thus start for home early in January. Of course all this is mere conjectural calculation on my part—but I dont think it far out, if the good news prove true. Of course I would much rather have come home in summer; and I a little regret your not having the projected trip. I believe it would have done you good—much good. However I will try to flatter myself, by believing my coming will be almost as good. It is not sure that the ship will go out of commission—but if kept along I am pretty sure to be relieved in May when my two years are up, while I could not be sure out here. *Do not mention my calculations*, for if they knew of the delay they might keep us out. Oh my darling I am so tired of it all. Kirkland is very nice to me—a singular man, very; but manly and masculine which the other was not. I said little of Tangier, but I am going to recommend you to read "The Exiles" in *Harper* for May 1894[3]—a story of Tangier, admirably told and most interesting. I saw one of the characters there. Now about the purchase of a house. I had no idea you could get together so much money, and I quite approve of the idea. Even if I did not feel so, I have much opinion of your good sense which is of course fortified in this instance by Gillender's experience. I also entirely coincide with you as to the importance of locality; indeed you may remember I never smiled on the idea of going east of the bridges. The great defect in our family life has been the want of external social relations. In ourselves we have been most happy always; but association with others, whether they come to us or we to them, is a needful addition. Not only does it afford the necessary change of routine, but from it the family brings back more substance on which to maintain its own life. I believe I have attended to all in your letters. The floss silk came in the mail to Tangier. If we dont come home I think your proposal of the *Kaiser Wilhelm*, Jany 19, very good, but there will be more than enough time to discuss it, if the present news prove deceptive. We are—I am—astounded over the elections. I myself became a Republican, I think finally, after Cleveland's action about Hawaii. I became convinced that the Democrats are buried in the grave of Thos. Jefferson beyond all resurrection, and that, with all their faults, the future of the country rests with the Republicans. I had however no conception that so vast a number had, for whatever reason changed their camp.

6 P.M.

The mail came two hours ago & as it goes out in a half hour I think better to close saying only that a letter has come from the Dept. saying the *S.F.* would be out in about two months (from Oct 29) and that the C. would then go home to go out of commission. Thank God! May we remember Him in this prosperity as in the past adversity, and with our new money remember also the Giver. As regards the position of the house I dont think I can add much to what I have said above. I would rather pay $5,000 more

---

3. Richard Harding Davis, "The Exiles," *Harper's Magazine* (May 1894).

and be suited in position for the reasons I give—I would even take a smaller at the bigger price for the sake of promoting social relations. Of the particular neighborhood I know little.

Good bye my darling. Love to the girls.

[P.S.]   Remember how long after my orders to go home the *Wachusett* was kept out.

To Hilary A. Herbert

USS *Chicago*, Málaga, November 17, 1894 [NA]

Sir:

1. Replying to letter number 36406 of the Bureau of Navigation, I have to say that the petty officers therein referred to, and mentioned by name, are all able to speak English quite well enough for the necessary duties of the ranks they fill, though in some cases they cannot read or write it, in others very little, and their vocabulary is limited.

2. They were selected for the positions they hold, because considered to be the men best fitted for the rating at the time given. The original acting appointment was not in all cases given by me; when by me continued, it was so because the man was so far satisfactory.

3. I do not find in the present regulations any one requiring the ability to read and write before rating. If it be in the Department's thought to impose that additional requirement, I would respectfully suggest that, judging from the experience of this ship, the time is hardly yet ripe for that step. It is certainly well that Coxswains should be able to read and write, and to make signals; but it is as yet far easier to find in a ship's company persons possessed of these capacities, than men fitted to manage a boat and control its crew under all circumstances.

To Helen Evans Mahan

Málaga, November 17, 1894 [NWC]

My darling Helen: I hope I am not wronging Nellie in writing today to you instead of her. My life is now become so monotonous in its daily repetition of the same routine, and the absence of all novelty that I seem quite unable to remember to whom I wrote last but one. In that way I still remember whether or no it is mamma's turn—the last I can recall but not farther—I shall have now to keep a memorandum. I yesterday received mamma's of Nov. 2 telling me that Lyle was put into the Fourth form. I see the drawbacks but upon the whole I am better satisfied to have it so. I deeply regret that I am not at home to keep nearer track of the boy's progress, but doubtless it is better so. I closed my last letter to mamma by telling her that the official word had come that we were to go home when the *San Francisco* comes. I am delighted from every point of view—both to see you all again and also because I sorely need rest. I am so tired of the daily small annoyances of our life. I have little or no expectation of getting back before February and probably I cannot get clear of the ship before March. This will so nearly close up my two years that even Ramsay will scarcely think necessary to send me again to sea. I remember, however, that in the *Wachusett* we received the orders to go home in March, but were afterwards so delayed that we did not get there until September; so I am not unduly elated, and keep myself calm. We were here a year ago as you may remember so that Malaga presents no novelty—I notice more than I did before that the Cathedral so dominates the city that the latter seems only an appendage. The weather, although upon the whole fine, is not nearly so much so as last fall. We shall leave here on Monday, 19th for Gibraltar, to take in coal. This will use up great part of next week, and I suppose we shall get away about the 24th for Barcelona, reaching there, if the weather be not bad, about the 27th. Thence we shall probably have to go to Marseille, but what beyond the admiral intends I dont know. He had plans before the *San Francisco* was ordered, but whether he has changed them or not is as yet unknown.

Sunday, Nov. 18

I dined ashore last night at the house of a Mr. Bevans the only American merchant here. His wife a woman somewhat older than mamma, is a Virginian from the parts where the Brodies now live and used to know Aunt Jeanette.[1] There were ten at table, two Spanish girls who spoke English perfectly, and one of whom, rather pretty, looked not at all Spanish. The mother of the other was an East Indian. On Friday the admiral invited a few people to come & dance. The few somehow increased to nearly a hundred. I was glad of the chance to see so many Spanish women together, and surprised to find so few pretty and so little different from other Europeans. There are two sisters, no longer very young, who went with us on a little drive on Thursday and also were on board Friday, who have really beautiful *red* hair. I never saw red hair before that I admired. One of them was generally pretty as seen through her veil; how she would have stood the unkind revelations of a garish sun I cant say. Funnily enough, there followed close behind our wagon for quite a way a white horse waggling a country cart. As she spoke no English, we felt safe in quoting the

---

1. Jeanette Katharine Murat Mahan, wife of Dennis Hart Mahan, Jr.

proverb.[2] Though there are plenty of carts and drays about Malaga a very large part of the carriage about the country is on donkey back, with big panniers as in the days of Don Quixote & Sancho Panza; a fact which speaks for the badness of the roads. It is not so very long since brigandage was rife, as commonly happens in a mountainous country and bad roads; but now they have a large army of country police—Guardia Civil—some 30,000 in all Spain, who have tremendous power. You see them every where in plain dark uniforms, wearing three cornered cocked hats laced with silver—a stalwart, dignified and often handsome set of men. I am told that the assurance of one of them that it was necessary—Era preciso—is accepted as justification for shooting an offender. I never saw a set of men who averaged better in looks. I am sorry to hear from mamma that you are uneasy under Dr. Warren's administrations. I do not find fault with you for it, and think I can understand it, but as I am coming home soon I hope you will try and put up with your grievance until my return, and at any rate talk about it as little as possible. If very badly tried you might go often to Trinity[3] with Aunt Ogden who I am sure would be glad to have you. But dont talk, if you can help it, it adds fuel to every flame. Besides, talk of that sort is often wearing to others who are not feeling at the moment just as you are, and I want you to think of sparing mamma as much as possible while I am away. I should think the magnificent project of buying a house would be a much more agreeable subject of conversation. And now dear child good bye. Pray for me that I may be able to bear up during what we may now hope will be the short remnant of this cruise. Love to mamma & Nellie.

To Ellen Evans Mahan

Gibraltar, November 21, 1894 [LC]

My dearest Deldie: I have little time to write more than a few lines upon your birthday, to show I have not forgotten it and how thankful I am for the day which made possible that you should be given to me. My time has been a good deal frittered away today, owing partly to my own fault, partly to engagements I could not avoid. It had been my intention to give a little dinner today in honor of the event, but we were to coal ship, so I last night invited our Consul and daughters also Captain Lake senior British naval officer and his wife and Mr. & Mrs. Noel (Florence Kirkland). All the last named declined, only the Consul's family coming—so our party consisted of these and three of our officers. We drank your health. Today

---

2. See Mahan to Ellen Evans Mahan, December 11, 1893.
3. Holy Trinity Episcopal Church, E. Walpole Warren, rector.

I lunched at the Consuls, and tonight am dining with the Governor, greatly to my regret as it is blustering and stormy with bad boating. Our coaling is greatly interfered with much to my disappointment. Kirkland declined the Governor's invitation. He suffers much from gout and has so drenched his stomach with purgatives that it is in very bad condition. He is continually upset, and is somewhat worried especially for fear least anything should hinder his promotion which is due in a few months. He is however very cheerful and plucky, and altogether so far very acceptable, though I should prefer to be quite by myself, no flag on board. I have recd. Helen's letter in which is inclosed Mr. Ireland's about Lyle. I confess it was a new idea to me that Lyle had a rugged aggressive independence. My fear was that he was too timid and retiring, and shrank from intercourse with others because of the attendant collisions. That certainly is my own trouble, and sorely harassed am I here by some of my surroundings. The station is beginning to weigh upon me as did the Pacific, and earnestly do I solicit your prayers that I may be upheld through the remnant of the cruise. At times I feel as if I must break down ere long. I shall not enter into nor enlarge upon my annoyances, for that would be tedious but I assure you they are real and incessant, and to survive them I need every help of grace that I can obtain. In vain, almost, do I repeat to myself the words of encouragement, the constant pelting of vexations drowns my voice—nor do I see any hopeful issue. My letters remain unanswered, my thoughts beyond my control, I live as in a dream and an evil dream at that.

Nov. 23

I am feeling somewhat better today having had a profound night's sleep. This letter will I believe go by the *Furst Bismarck*, one of the line by which you now will *not* come out, and which sails for N.Y. on Sunday. This has given me more time without delaying your letter. We—or rather Clover—today had a telegram from Hanford[1] who is assistant to the Commdr at the N.Y. Yard, that the *San Fr.* would sail about Dec. 20. This would bring her to Gibraltar about Jan. 3d, or to Algiers the 5th, if as Kirkland now inclines the ships meet there. We shall need several weeks—three or four—for repairs; but then these may be begun before the other ship arrives. The adml. is mainly dominated by the desire to reach a climate where his gout will give him less trouble, & now fancies Algiers. I have little choice outside of Villefranche. It has its drawbacks, but is a quiet harbor, good for the men in many ways, and offers some society the one thing that alleviates the monotony of our life. I had a letter from Mrs. Schiff the other day from Eze, where they have now been nearly a month. She said the McCreas were there in Nice on their way to Rome, where they will spend the winter. So they have not gone home—what a hopeless, aimless wandering life; but they

---

1. Franklin Hanford, class of 1866.

were nice girls. I wish I were sure of again seeing your uncle & the Schiffs. My last night at Malaga I dined with the American dentist and was placed by a very striking looking Englishwoman—a Mrs. Lockhart who spends the winters in Malaga; her husband[2] being a confirmed invalid. He is a cousin of the Lockhart who was Sir Walter Scott's son in law. She said he had so regretted not being able to come that night, as he was so much interested in the navy and my books. She herself had read them. I said I would have been glad to call had I known sooner, and it was arranged that I should next afternoon at tea if we did not sail; but we did. She had Nazro on the other side, and I am bound to say we are both pretty good company when we try. She said in leaving that it was her first experience with Americans, evidently meaning it for a compliment. So you see, my dear, we stumble along. I have a note from Sally Smith—I imagine not *your* Sally asking me to go for tea tomorrow. She is American from Newport I believe. The Masons were here last year.

Saturday, Nov. 24

I forgot to say that in talking with Mrs. Lockhart, I said what a miserable blunder a man's going into the navy was, and she replied "You surely are not one to say so." I suppose that is the way most people look at it, yet I increasingly feel what a shocking mistake I made; and in all my difficulties, when I might otherwise feel a fuller reliance upon being supported, I have to remember that my early perverseness was the cause of all, and I can never feel sure that I am walking in the way God would have me even now. So far our children have been very dutiful, and I trust therefore no such lasting sting may be in store for them. I dined last night with Captain Lake, the Senior Naval officer, who seems to have a liking for me, as do most of them. The truth is, as far as I know myself, that while delighted at the success of my books, I am not really elated or stuck up about them. What makes my weakness in other ways—my retiring disposition and shrinking from criticising or opposing others—helps me here. Lake's wife is a quiet, ladylike rather pretty woman—not exciting to talk to, but from what I see of her would I think grow upon you with increasing acquaintance. I said nothing about my dinner at the Governor's but in truth there was little to tell. The admiral not going I was the guest of honor, sitting between the Governor and his daughter-in-law, a colorless young lady. His wife is rather an invalid and shows up but rarely. The Governor is a full general in the army, a hale and attractive man of about sixty. I talked to him most of the time. As everywhere and with every one English I found the books to the fore, and it is really curious to see how in even such an out of the way place as Malaga I should stumble upon people who had actually read them. But, dearest, how the eagerness for home grows, now that the prospect of seeing

---

2. Graeme Alexander Sinclair Lockhart.

you all again is given. All here seems to recede like a troubled dream, and the things & even the people to which I looked for such compensation as might be afforded become forgotten. I abhor my conditions and long to be back in the old quiet life.

Saturday 3 P.M.

The mail has just come with your letter of the 9th, only a scrap but I know news is scant. Would God I were back with you, but we must temper our souls to patience for none can tell what delays He may ordain. I see no chance of our arriving before the middle of February. Goodbye my own darling wife always your devoted husband. Love to the girls.

To Ellen Kuhn Mahan

Gibraltar, November 27, 1894 [LC]

My darling Nellikin: Again I am in some doubt as to whether my letter is due to you or to Helen. However, I have now made a memorandum that this goes to you, so I will know next time. It dont greatly matter for I have so little to say. We have now been here a week, have finished coaling and are ready to proceed; but we are waiting for the *Detroit*,[1] expected tomorrow, in order to hold two court-martials, after which, I suppose, we shall proceed to Barcelona. I find little to amuse me, and I am suffering in common with many others from the relaxing climate. With them it takes the form of remittent fever of a mild type and easily controlled. So far I have only had general misery without any fever and am only good for nothing. The doctor's medicine also is pulling me together. Helen's letter of the 11th recd. yesterday, complains of not hearing from me. It is too bad, for I write regularly, and often when much pressed for time and I cannot understand how it has happened. Of course, after leaving Southampton, as it took five days to reach Lisbon, and at best three for our letters thence to get to England, there would be a break of a week; but we were in Lisbon on the 25th Oct., and you should have had letters on Nov 8. Since I have been here I have dined with the Governor, with Captn. Lake the Senior British Naval Officer, and with Mr. Williams one of the civil officials but nowhere have I met any of those particularly agreeable men or women— the latter especially—who make what amends is possible to one absent from

---

1. A protected cruiser of 269 feet, displacing 2,072 tons. Commissioned in 1893, she mounted nine 5-inch guns and three 18-inch deck torpedo tubes. Her twin screws drove her at 18.5 knots.

home. I have been thinking about Xmas presents for you girls and have decided that mamma be asked to get for *you* "The Burial of the Guns &c" by Thomas Nelson Page[2] and for Helen a volume of Richard Harding Davis's short stories.[3] I dont know the title of any of them but they are all good I think. At the same time if there be anything else you two prefer you may have it instead—only I am giving you things of small value simply as tokens. For Lyle I think to order a book from Stevens; but I have been so much taken with some of Davis's and Page's stories that I felt sure you would like them too. I have recd. a mysterious packet, addressed to me "from G. M. Philips" Westchester Pa and inside a copy of my *Life of Farragut*, bearing on the title page the name Geo. Morris Philips. No letter or message of any kind. Can mamma help me to understand it? At first I thought it must be a mistake, but the outside is perfectly clear addressed to me and "From G. M. Philips." I have today had a very nice letter from Mrs. Schiff expressing their regret at not seeing me again, if it be so, and inviting me to stay with them if I can get leave from Marseille which is only about six hours from Nice: I shall try to do so, for I am really fond of them and they have been most kind to me. Gibraltar is disagreeable at this time of the year—frequent blows which the Rock so far from keeping off seems to send down always in redoubled strength; but in truth Mediterranean winter cruising is disagreeable like all other winter weather. It is inconceivable to me that with half a dozen pleasant ports to choose from the admiral should persist in going to the Levant where the weather is almost always bad and no interesting port except Alexandria which is not to compare to others. At Cairo one might enjoy oneself, if there long enough to know people, but Alexandria is merely a commercial port. Fortunately, if the *S.F.* leaves on Dec. 20 the Eastern cruise will fall to her not to us—but if the fitting of the *Columbia*[4] for flag ship, for this station, now reported in the *Herald*, have any foundation she may not get here for months. I dont intend to believe any such bad luck, however. I shall have, dear child, to stop here, for really after cudgelling what poor brains are left me I cannot find another item of news. It is most painful to be thus unable to send anything that can be of interest except of my own condition, but I really dont think it my own fault. Good bye darling. Love to Mamma and Helen.

---

2. Thomas Nelson Page, *The Burial of the Guns*. New York: C. Scribner's Sons, 1894.
3. Richard Harding Davis, *Exiles and Other Stories*. New York: Harper & Bros., 1894; or his *Gallagher and Other Stories*, New York: C. Scribner's Sons, 1891.
4. A 431-foot cruiser displacing 7,350 tons. Commissioned in 1894, designed for commerce-raiding, her triple screws drove her at 23 knots. Heavily armored and armed, she mounted one 8-inch, two 6-inch, eight 4-inch guns; and four 18-inch deck torpedo tubes.

To Ellen Evans Mahan

Gibraltar, December 2, 1894 [LC]

My own darling: I sent off a letter to Nellie four days ago, which I then confidently hoped would be my last from this place, but the cruise is ending (I hope ending) in a series of annoyances & vexations. We are lying here under the Rock during a spell of violent easterly weather accompanied by rain, the most disagreeable and trying I ever remember at anchor since the blockade in the days of the war. It is a very curious experience unlike anything I ever knew. Outside and above the wind is strong from east, and also over the sand neck which connects the Rock to the mainland. Under the lee of that are anchored some thirty or forty vessels, mostly coal hulks— all which ride to the east. Round our end or the other of the Rock the wind eddies, so that we have it from North, South and West but very rarely from east. Such a heavy sea is running in the straits & probably throughout all the southern Mediterranean that it seems inexpedient to go out into it for we should burn much coal and probably make very little progress— not to speak of the discomfort. The squalls are something tremendous at times, all blowing from west for us—the water is driven as white spray in every direction and miniature cyclones of spray are to be seen mostly outside of where we lie. There is no sea, the Rock breaks that—but there have been torrents of rain. I have not been ashore since I mailed Nellie's letter. We are looking for the *Detroit* which we were expecting to meet here, but she has delayed at Cadiz and the admiral has decided not to await her. The gale alone detains us. To complete our contretemps the mail was diverted to Barcelona a week ago, so that one or two must now be there which might be here. I have just looked over your last which is very short but I quite sympathize with the impossibility of filling letters when no news is at hand. I myself have nothing. As to our starting as soon as the *San Francisco* arrives that depends upon the admiral—not on me. We must spend three or four weeks in repairs to make the engines fit for a winter passage, and the same time must be employed in preparing the ship for inspection. If Kirkland puts us where this can be done before the *S.F.* gets out, then we can start, if not we must wait. You must console yourself with the knowledge that all delays help fill out my two years, the pound of flesh Ramsay demands. We can scarcely get out of commission before March 1, and indeed I count upon the end of the month, which would give me the two years less one month. Of course I expect to be home a month sooner, perhaps Feb. 15. But dear, let us not forget the experience, nor suffer anything but dire necessity to change our resolution that I retire at 40 years. What God may dispose I know not, but I think we would be foolish & even wrong of our own volition to rescind this purpose. I am very distressed about Mr. Saltonstall—when he is called away a very noble life will have ended. I had from him a very pleasant &

cheerful letter, written I suppose by Miss W.'s hand. How many have passed away since I left. Dear how I long for you all. A year ago today we reached Villefranche. I wish we were there now, but I think the admiral has no intention of going. I miss society dreadfully. I know how much it did for me, but scarcely realized till I fell out of it. I trust God will strengthen me to bear the short remnant, & will make it short indeed; at times I feel as if my strength might fail. However I am not often thus, the deprival of my daily work has upset me, and there is something depressing to every one in a levanter at Gibraltar. Goodbye darling. Be sure I love you and long for home. Love to the girls.

To Ellen Evans Mahan

Barcelona, Spain, December 9, 1894 [LC]

My dearest Wife: I dont know whether my last letter was addressed to yourself or to one of the girls, nor can I remember whether it was sent from Gibraltar or from here. Can you conceive my head in such a state? I did indeed make a memorandum of my last two letters—but that I have lost. At times I worry over a confusion so alien to me, but I believe it mainly the fruit of a growing preoccupation, to the straining of the mind to forget nor overlook any of the ship duties, and I trust that when the release comes, I hope speedily, and one or two great objects take the place of the myriad petty ones which now distract me, that I shall regain the quietness and self possession that I had. I am older, true, and shall never again be quite what I was, but perhaps some faint simulacrum may survive the weary waste of the two years past. It is, however, fitting rather that I should now write you, for in the first place your letters recd. here seem to imply that you are waiting to hear further from me before going further about getting a house. If so, pray dismiss all hesitancy. Your reasons for the change are perfectly good, and if, as Gillender says, now is the time I would lose none. Only be not precipitate—choose leisurely and as wisely as you can. You already have my views, which are substantially your own. Secondly, I want you to be deciding as to whether I shall ask for leave of absence for one year. You know the leave pay is only $2800. My mind is fully fixed, D.V. [Deo volente], to retiring when I can, a year from September next. It appears to me best to devote a year to the pursuits to which I intend to give my life. It will be a year saved, and should the inexpediency of retiring be proved, that would be a gain. I can scarcely imagine anything but absolute necessity inducing me to pass again through the misery of this cruise, or to accept the ridiculous situation of admiral of one of our escuadrillas such as this—One ship!! Not to speak of the absence from those who alone make my life worth having. On all this I want you to meditate while I am en traversée. As time passes our probable movements become somewhat clearer. Assuming that the *San Francisco* sails Dec. 15., Kirkland says he will send orders to Gibraltar for her to meet us at Algiers. We go from this to Marseille, probably about the 20th, a week there, 27th, two days to Algiers, say reach there about the Jour de l'An. *San Francisco* about the same. We must have three or four weeks to repair which means, approximately, leave Algiers about January 25, reach N.Y. about Feb. 14. All this is subject to many doubts, not to speak of the possible changes due to naval vicissitudes. I shall believe I am going home when I see the U.S. coast—not before. Upon my arrival here I recd. all your letters to Nov. 23d and last night Helen's of the 25th. This recalls to me that I commented on Mr. Saltonstall's state, which again proves that I wrote to *you* and from *here*. The girls must forgive me. Dont let there be in our minds any rivalry with Goodrich. What he is, he is; poco importa what any other is. I am distressed about our dear Rose, I had not realized it was so bad with her, and then even Elsie gone. It is sad too for you to have no other house to which you are always welcome. I shall be curious to hear about Hart's going to Europe. I was much upset to know that he was out of a business I had come to look on as quite secure. It is my purpose to write your uncle Charles today or tomorrow, proposing to spend a couple of days with him, if the adml. permits me to run off to Eze for a week from Marseille. Probably his reply will mention if Hart be coming. I shant mention it. You are quite right in judging Madeline [Madeleine] Stanley the best of the three. My own opinion is the same, but when Rosie Schiff lays herself out, or perhaps I should better say is in the humour she has the most natural charm. As for the little Jewess she is very nice—only when she grows old! but that I shant see. That Ramsay had not read my books I had from Chadwick half a year ago. Dont let yourself be prejudiced against Bunce. They were invariably nice to me, personally, throughout my stay, nor do I believe the row would have come to a crisis, had I remained. Talking of your uncle Charles, nothing could have been nicer than he was while I was there, but then I was little in the house, and in no way tied to him. I am besides in no way of the obtrusive kind. Neither is Hart, but day in, day out, is a very different experience from that I had. Of course I have nothing on which to hazard any advice. Now, as regards your baby Grand, I said nothing because I know nothing. I am pleased, and grateful to the giver, and glad of Helen's pleasure whereas Minnie Hartpence was one who once loved you, whom you had known as a girl, & not even seen for years. To me the past with its memories always appeals, and I should have hailed such personal tidings of any long lost sight of friend as I gave you. I believe this about exhausts my news & my comments on your letters, so I may as well mail it. I shall make a mem. of its going which I hope I may not also lose. Good bye—my own darling. Pray God to hold me up through the closing days of this tribulation and bring us together for many happy days on earth, if He so will. Dearest love to the girls. I wrote to Lyle two days ago.

To Hilary A. Herbert

USS *Chicago*, Marseille, France, December 15, 1894 [NA]

Sir:

1. Charles O. Ryan, Seaman, of this ship has been found by a General Court Martial to be guilty of desertion from the Marine Corps, in which he was enlisted as a Private under the name of Charles Ryan.

2. Orders have been given the paymaster of the *Chicago* to close the accounts of Charles O. Ryan, Seaman, and to take up the accounts on the Marine Roll of Charles Ryan, Private, U.S.M.C.

3. The Commanding Officer asks if any further action is necessary in effecting the transfer of the said Ryan to the Marine Corps. He is now confined as a prisoner on board this ship awaiting transportation to the United States.

To Ellen Kuhn Mahan

Marseille, December 15, 1894 [LC]

My darling Miss Nellikin: I hope that this is your turn, but as I explained to mamma I cannot any longer remember to whom I wrote last, and I lost my memorandum. I only know that I wrote to her nearly a week ago & that it is a shame I have not written sooner; but my dear child I am so driven and worn that I can scarcely endure. My health fortunately continues seemingly very good, but the strain on my brain and nerves is so great to try and keep up with all the requirements of my position that I can bearly [*sic*] manage. You must all pray for me that I may not break down. The coming of the *San Francisco* is not merely a promise of the great happiness of seeing you all again, it is the prospect of relief from a burden fast becoming insupportable. Well, here we are again in shabby, sordid, common old Marseille—the commonest, cheapest great city I ever beheld. And we are here, apparently just in the nick of time, for there is the promise of a heavy north west gale, and the northwesters of the Gulf of Lyons are celebrated all over the world for their fierceness. We got into Barcelona just before one gale, having left Gibraltar just after another, & while in

Barcelona we had beautiful weather. We left there yesterday at 3 in the afternoon with all the promise of a superb night, which lasted up to midnight—the sea like a mill pond. I then sat down in my chair and fell asleep, but in an hour was wakened by a little quick rolling motion that had set in. I went on deck and found already quite a great N.W. breeze and rising sea. As these gales are apt to come on rapidly I ordered some precautions which we had been induced to omit by the deceitful sky. The wind increased during the night, but very slowly, the sea also getting; nothing very bad however, and at 11 A.M. we were safe in Marseille. To night a port officer has been off to inform us we must expect a very heavy mistral as they call the Norwesters. They blow hard with a clear sky. I have had a great disappointment. I had expected to go to Nice, tomorrow, for a week to spend part with Mr. Kuhn and part with the Schiffs; but this morning I received orders putting me on a court martial on Monday. As the admiral knew I particularly wanted to go it was not very nicely done by me; but, as he knew, I shall say nothing. He is generally nice to me, and I think is kindhearted, but from his conversation I judge him to be a person who likes at times to be crooked and disappoint others. I may be able to run down for two days. There was not the least necessity, in *my* judgment, for the orders, nor do I think I ought to have been on the Court, quite independent of my other wishes. I have had letters from both Mrs. Schiff and Mr. Kuhn saying they would be glad to have me, and indeed I need the rest and diversion it would have been to me. We are absolutely without any news of our own. Our stay at Barcelona was wholly uneventful, I merely went ashore two hours a day for a walk and for the rest toiled at my daily task. This place offers nothing better, nor indeed as good being in every way less interesting. I am very glad to hear that your criticisms are so much better & trust that they may indicate that your genius has at length burst its shell. Where is Dorothea all this time? I am delighted to see that the morbid feelings you seemed to have last year have disappeared and that the interest in life natural to your years has returned. Most people at times suffer from such moods, but they are painful both to [themselves] and to those about them. Well, as there is really no news, I may as well close. I still think that the ship will start for home about the end of January, but we will know more about things after her arrival in New York. Goodbye dear child. Love to mamma and Helen, as well as to Buster who will be with you before this comes.

To Ellen Evans Mahan

9 Boulevard Victor Hugo, Nice, December 19, 1894 [LC]

Dearest Deldie: I wrote to Nellie on Sunday, telling her my disappointment about getting away on that day. Our Court Martial was finished on

Monday night, I trust to the admiral's satisfaction, or I may be recalled, and I left yesterday at 10:30 reaching here at 3. I remain till tomorrow Thursday when I go to the Schiffs, where I will remain until Sunday morning. I then return to Nice, breakfast with your uncle at 12 and take the 1:40 train for Marseille. We are to leave there for Algiers the next day. Such is the programme, and I trust by the time we are a week in Algiers, we may receive such news concerning the *San Francisco*, as will obviate our leaving that port except for home. I seem suddenly to have lost all force to bear up against the recurrent annoyances of my position, and am incapable except of looking forward to deliverance. Of course I do my work but it wears me out. Your uncle seems very well and tells me he expects Hart about Jan. 15. He intends for him the room I am occupying—where I can assure the bed is very comfortable—and also will fit him a little drawing, or sitting, room. I dont see why the arrangement should not turn out well, *if* Hart can manage to assure *himself* interests, social preferably. Your uncle's time is full of engagements, & in many of them I fancy all he will ask will be to gang his own gait. If Hart has his preoccupations outside, as he has, their association will be only at the table and a little in the house. So far from wanting a companion Mr. Kuhn seems to me rather to wish some one in the house, & to be otherwise unfettered in his movements. But what is to become of Rosie in all this? I have no news except that the instant relief from the ship gives me hope that when she is for me wholly a thing of the past my mind will regain its tone. I have at times fancied I should never again be my old self. Good bye, ever dearest. Love to the children.

To Ellen Evans Mahan

Nice, December 19, 1894 [LC]

I mailed you a letter today already and I suppose these two cards[1] may need more notice. They were addressed to Mr. & Mrs. Yours of Nov. 27th just recd. (before leaving for Groton). I am glad you are moving about the house. As for Lyle's one lateness, I am both pleased by the punctuality he has achieved & by the spirit in which he seems to have taken what was a natural & severe disappointment. That is even better than success, particularly as the fault was scarcely his. Of course, the authorities could not properly accept his excuse.

---

1. This note was written on an invitation from Mr. and Mrs. Robert Lenox Belknap and their daughter to an "At Home" in New York on December 13. The second card referred to has not been found. Belknap was manager of the American Bible Society, trustee of Princeton Theological Seminary, and trustee and President of the Board of the Presbyterian Church on University Place, New York.

To Ellen Evans Mahan

Marseille, December 22, 1894 [LC]

My dearest Deldie: I have neither time nor opportunity to write a nice letter to one of the girls, whose turn it is, so I shall just dash off a hasty line to you. My holiday project for Nice came to a disastrous end, for besides the loss of the two first days by the Court Martial, of which you know, I have had to surrender the last two to the admiral's hurry to get away. I reached Eze at 12:30 Thursday and at 4:30 had a telegram that the ship was to be under sailing orders 4 P.M. Saturday—today. So instead of coming back by day train on Sunday, I was forced to take last night's train reaching here this morning. I am sorry for I wanted the change. Your uncle was very nice to me, as were the Schiffs, as usual, but I amuse myself rather better at the latter place. Of course your uncle is getting old and prosy—in those respects he has aged since last year though physically he seems as well as ever. The Schiffs on the contrary, gabble away about everything in the world, and as they are all really fond of me, I think, I listen or join in just as I like, which rests me. We sail tonight about 8 for Algiers. If we have good weather we ought to reach there Monday towards midday. There is little or no news & indeed my only purpose in writing now is to insure you a letter. I will try and write a longer one soon. I am so intensely eager for the arrival of the *San Francisco* to release me from my thralldom to this ship that I feel as if I cannot but be disappointed. I received by the way your letter, and what Mrs. McLean said, on Thursday just before going to Eze. Mr. Saltonstall's death was a loss to the world everywhere. I am so glad you went to the funeral though of course you could not do less. I hunger for a letter from you and ought to have had one today, but they rather mess the mails now & I fancy this has gone on to Algiers. I felt a little depression in bidding farewell, probably for ever, to the familiar and beautiful Riviera, to Mr. Kuhn and the Schiffs. Him I shall scarcely see again—them not probably. It is chiefly the question of affection but the sadness that attends all finalities, the end of the year or what not—a feeling to which I am very susceptible. I hardly think however that I shall bewail the last of the *Chicago* any more than I did that of the *Wachusett*. Goodbye, dearest, always with fondest affection for you and the children.

To Helen Evans Mahan

Algiers, French Morocco, Christmas, December 25, 1894 [NWC]

My darling Helen: I shall wish you all a merry Christmas and hope that you are having one, although I see from mamma's letter that you all also, though with one another and in the dear home, are having your tribulation & vexation—most natural—in feeling forced to go to Elizabeth. The only thing I can say is that poor Aunt Jennie could with difficulty have come to you, there being no room in the flat. Next year I hope we shall be better fixed, and I am sure that for her an entire change of scene on that day would be better than to pass it in the old surroundings where the human element has passed away forever. I wish she might see her way to give up the house, but the problem is one on which another cannot very wisely proffer advice. Have you remembered, my darling, that this is the third successive Xmas I have passed away from home? I had myself forgotten it. Of them all it has been the least merry—in fact, not only absolutely devoid of merriment, but crowded with vexation & disappointment. Two years ago at San Francisco it was dull enough, but then I was soon to return home and was at least unharassed.[1] Last year I really spent a very jolly evening with the Schiffs—and in the day there was the ever lovely Riviera. Today we could not have even a communion service in the cabin, because the ship was entering the port, and the whole forenoon was taken up with securing her, receiving official visits, and all the other flummery of entering port. To add to my désagréments the news is that the *San Francisco* is not to sail before the first. Accustomed as I am to the exasperating delays of the navy, I scarcely know now what to expect. To crown all, the admiral has asked me to dinner in that unexpected fashion which found me without an excuse ready. I had rather be kicked, yet as I feel it particularly important to keep on pleasant terms with him, I could not refuse without a thoroughly plausible reason. So I am stuck. He is not congenial to me—in fact, I fear I am not fitted to run in this double harness. He is a kind-hearted, well meaning man, meddles very little with the ship beyond his own comforts, and seems upon the whole satisfied with me; but he is essentially coarse, and seems at times to derive real pleasure from the feeling that he contraries another. However, let this go. Except I take to people I am unquestionably one who cannot bear the yoke of fellowship, a trait which makes me unpopular with the many, but I believe very cordially regarded by the few whom I too like. I wrote mamma a line on the 22d from Marseille, after my return from Nice. I cant recall just what I said, for I was greatly hurried, so I may repeat myself. I went down on Tuesday the 18th, to your great uncle Charles Kuhn's, and stayed with him that day and Wednesday. On Thursday I left him with the understanding that I would breakfast with him at 12 on Sunday, on my way back to the ship. I went to the Schiffs, arriving at 12.30. That afternoon Mrs. Schiff took me to call upon people in the neighborhood of Eze and Villefranche, who had been kind to me last year. At 4 we reached their villa again and half an hour later came a telegram for me that I must

---

1. Mahan had been sent to San Francisco on court-martial duty.

be back to the ship at 4 Saturday. It was a complete surprise as well as a great disappointment. After looking at the time table, I decided to take a night train which, leaving at 1 A.M. Saturday would bring me to Marseille about 8. I thus spent Friday with the family and Mrs. Schiff took me that day [on] a long drive along the Riviera, and up the mountains to a hotel where the rest of the family joined us by rail and we had lunch. It was one of those wonderful days the Riviera can produce, brilliant sunshine, cloudless sky, warm yet bracing atmosphere, with the gorgeous mountain scenery and bright blue sea combining in a beauty that only land and water united can bestow. I left the Schiffs at 9.30 took the train to Nice, where I went again to Mr. Kuhn's, saw him for a half hour and then again to the station, where I took the train for Marseille. It was a very cold night and I sat up through the whole. The train arrived on time, and at 8 P.M. that night we sailed. The promise of the weather was then fair, but the reports seemed to indicate storms at sea, so I had everything well secured. It was well I did for next morning we struck one of Nelson's north westers, which blew furiously all day Sunday. The adml. and I both agreed that only on two or three occasions had we ever seen it blow so hard. As it seemed likely the same gale prevailed at Algiers making it difficult to enter the port the Adml. ordered me to anchor under the lee of Minorca—to the south of it. It was nine in the evening when the anchor was let go, and I was so tired out, though the ship had done beautifully, that I was asleep before 10 and did not wake till 8 next morning. Even then I would gladly have stayed in bed some hours longer, and my feet felt like lead, but after breakfast I was all right and greatly refreshed. We started again yesterday at 1 and arrived here at 9 this morning, but the day has been one of toil, worry and vexation. Your letter of the 9th and mamma's of the 11th reached me here—neither contains much news requiring an answer. I am glad you are having so many musical sprees. I wish you could get an hour or two more pupils each week. Cannot Mrs. Morgan help you to any? We shall I suppose stay here a week, nor can I wholly abandon the hope that the *San Francisco* may yet relieve us here. I feel very much saying good bye to the Schiffs, all whom without exception have been most kind and seemed really to regret my going—but I have no wish to go back again to Villefranche now that the adieus are over. It is hard to think that I shall never again see that beautiful Riviera, for, as Shorthouse[2] truly says, things never again can be as they once were; but if I could only get back to you all, and to my natural occupation it would be all right. The dreadful monotony of uncongenial work is very wearing. And now, dear child, I will close and let this go to the mail. Love to mamma, Nellie, and Lyle who will still be with you.

---

2. Joseph Henry Shorthouse, novelist.

To Thomas A. Janvier

USS *Chicago*, Algiers, December 25, 1894 [HUL]

My dear Sir: Upon my return to the ship on Saturday from Nice, I found awaiting me your very interesting and acceptable present *In Old New York*.[1] It has given me what I have often wished, an account of the genesis & development of the City, in compact form, unencumbered with excursions into a thousand other matters by which histories of the City have heretofore so often been made impossible to the general reader. I have already dipped into it in my irregular fashion & found it full of interest.

As we sailed the same evening I could not amid the press of departure find time to acknowledge its receipt, but I beg to assure you that the favor is very heartily appreciated.

To Helen Evans Mahan

Algiers, December 26, 1894 [NWC]

My darling Helen: It occurred to me this morning in bed, that in writing you yesterday I had not remarked upon the impression of your doing too much, which I received from your letter; and here today mamma's letter, of Dec. 14, tells me that the doctor finds you run down from the effect of the winter's drive. Now, you are getting too old for me to insist upon what you should or should not do, but please consider that when I so strongly urged last year that you should not overwork with pupils, that I could not wish you to become overworked with music, visits etc which "worry you dreadfully trying to fit them in." I cannot prescribe what you had best do, and I know too well how occupations increase upon one; but I hold strongly that such pressure is not only bad for the body, but bad for the spirit, which is of greater consequence. It is hard for "God to be in all one's thoughts," when hurried from this occupation to that, as I know to my cost; but situated as I now am I trouble less about it, for my works are all against my liking. You are, however, considerably master of your own time and will have the backing of mamma & me. Excellent as music is for you, be moderate somewhat—and I think my old rule never to be out late on Saturday one worth your consideration, for how can you bring your mind and heart clear to early Communion, if you are up and excited, late the night before? Be moderate in all things is the Bible's own teaching; and be sure that the hurry we all are in in these days is essentially faithless. For your very progress in music, in friendship, and all innocent duties or

---

1. Thomas Allibone Janvier, *In Old New York*. New York: Harper & Bros., 1894.

pleasures, the promise is not to the careful and worried about many things, but—"They that *wait* upon the Lord shall *renew their strength.*" In writing these things I am not trying to give you rules, but subject for thought and, I hope, practice. Martha and Mary are two constant types, repeating themselves from age to age. Sitting at the Lord's feet, giving yourself time to hear what He has to say, is the path, not of holiness only, but of happiness and of true success. For what is any seeming success if there be not peace, and what peace is there—real peace—save in the knowledge of God, which cannot find its way amid the weed-growth of a driven life. My dear child think of these things, and trust Him to show you what to do.

To Ellen Evans Mahan

Algiers, December 30, 1894 [LC]

My own dearest Deldie: I should have written to you yesterday and purposed to do so but was unexpectedly called upon to go to a lunch up on the hill, which ran away with all my afternoon. The weather has been very unpleasant—rainy—almost ever since our arrival, and consequently I am very behind in my exercise; for though I dont greatly mind rain ashore it is very disagreeable going and coming and the streets of the town are disagreeably dirty. It took yesterday fifty minutes to drive from the landings to our entertainer's, and today I am going to lunch again even farther. Of course such distances are almost prohibitive of social relations, and nearly all the foreign society is on the hill, scattered in villas. Our stay is uncertain. The admiral thinks he may hear something by the mail today or tomorrow. I doubt it— but the Paris *Herald might* have news of the *S.F.* sailing. The Adml. talks now of Palermo and then Naples—he even once hinted at going to Villefranche to make the exchange there. I care not very much—try to be very philosophical in a Christian sense; in which I do not always succeed. This place has turned out much less well than I hoped. We have a poor berth—& the weather very bad. Naples would be better but then it is 700 miles away which between going and coming means 1500 more of steaming before our return. I wrote Henny a second letter about the drive she was in, for I own I felt deeply regretful that she should have lost her pupils without diminishing her hurry. Of course I dont find fault, for I know how occupations increase on one, but it is something strenuously to be guarded against, the nervous strain of constant ganging. And what more unprofitable than the hurry of formal visiting. Of course I intended to go and see Lyle, and am amused at the mathematical halving of the time. I fear it is very doubtful whether I can get away even at the date fixed by him. If we go to Naples we will not get home much, if any, before it, and at no time is a captain so wholly engaged as when going out of commission. I am glad to know that Rosie is improving & can quite understand the need of her going to a milder climate—for there is nothing like open air for the nerves, and open air in the North is only for the strong. But what is to become of her if Hart settles abroad? Sufficient unto the day I suppose is the evil thereof. I dont suppose Mr. Kuhn will last much longer, but may not Hart settle abroad? I feel quite convinced in my own mind that if we have our house next Xmas Jenny must come to us. Cheerfulness in the poor old house in Elizabeth is at that season almost impossible—besides the travel of a whole family is really a labor. In our house, consider seriously the question of warm baths. I feel myself much older in that respect and although I think when the worry of the ship is off I shall rejuvenate, I dont certainly know. A Russian ship just passes going out, and the band plays that noble national air—practically the same as "Rise crowned with light, imperial Salem!"[1]—I am always glad to have a Russian in harbor to hear it daily; but how ally two nations whose sentiment is voiced by such differing airs as the Marseillaise and the other. Raining again! what a detestable climate! but this is their worst season & after all one cant expect much in the way of weather in January & December—even in the Medn. As far as I can see Kirkland is doing his best to spoil his cruise by an obstinate disregard of all the conditions that make for pleasure. It is no use flying in the face of the weather & for a man to go to Jerusalem in January when he could do it in Easter tide is too absurd. That & a determination that the women (his daughter is here) shall see the squadron is not run for them seem to be his determining motives. Is it not funny? He is very nice to me however, and I fear that I am too prone to see folly in what I personally dont like. Nevertheless, what says the prophet, "Can two walk together, except they be agreed?" It riles me to see discomfort inflicted when comfort—comparative —could be had—which perhaps means only that I dont like other people's ways as well as my own. The calendar for 1895 arrived two days ago and in good condition. And now dearest I will close in order if possible to catch todays steamer. With dearest love to all—your devoted husband [etc.].

To Ellen Kuhn Mahan

Algiers, January 4, 1895 [LC]

My darling Miss Nell: I hope the sight of the enclosed may not too much excite the covetous expectations of the family before it is known

---

1. The national anthem of royalist Russia was "Bozhe Tsarya Khrani," by Alexis Lvov. The hymn mentioned by Mahan is a passage from Alexander Pope's "Messiah, a Sacred Eclogue in Imitation of Virgil's 'Pollio.' "

to be some church money which I have accumulated and am sending for mamma to apply as she may think best. Yesterday I received letters from mamma and from you, the former enclosing one from Mrs. Hare and one from Aunt Bartie. I must say that the Eleventh Street position seems to me very tempting from the nearness to the Hares. I feel very strongly the necessity of our having some established friends, or we really will be left quite alone. Now that the two grandmothers are dead and their homes broken up, there is scarce any one belonging to us any home to which we will not be strangers. And this will be still more the case if Dodie goes abroad with uncle,[1] for under all the conditions I feel pretty sure that, the Atlantic once crossed, they will not soon return. They would not find weather very much better here than on your side. Ever since we left Marseille it has been very bad, and in the ten days we are here there has been but one pleasant. All the others it has rained much and hard, with violent wind hail thunder and lightning. One morning in this supposed mild clime there lay two inches of hail on the ground and the mountains were covered. We have been twice struck by lightning, but being an iron ship and our conductors in good order, the current was dispersed without harm done. I am disgusted with the place, yet seeing the sea rolling outside & the tramp steamers trooping in for refuge I am prepared to choose staying here till the *San Francisco* comes rather than go farther and fare much worse. It seems now likely that we will remain here, and at once begin the overhauling of the engines necessary before going home. Besides, the Admiral's daughter, Mrs. Noel, who is here with her husband is quite seriously ill, and while the Adm. might not stay on her account, I fancy he is not sorry that needed repairs delay our departure. I am, you may suppose disgusted with the *San F*'s delays; for though I have had many pleasant moments there are no more here, and I am so tired of the ship, and I do long to be home. I am interested to hear of your bicycling & Helen's fencing. I dont see why women should not do both as well as ride horseback; yet I have an old fashioned dislike to both. What I chiefly wish, however, is that your lives may not become too driven, nor dissipated among too many pursuits. Some variety is needful, but too much ends in accomplishing nothing. So I am delighted that your dancing classes are so enjoyable, even while I trust that life may seem to you more meant for work than for amusement. But in truth one of my great desires has been that you should have associates, social surroundings, friends & intimates, and I dont see where you are to find them unless you two go where people gather. So it all comes back to the old cry *"Moderation* in all things"—"Use life as not abusing it" & pray God to teach you how to do these things—to "hear the voice behind you, saying, 'This is the Way, walk ye in it,' when ye turn to the right hand or when ye turn to the left."

---

1. Hartman Kuhn Evans.

My own doings possess nothing of interest. I am in a constant drive, but one that I hate and cannot avoid. The town of Algiers is most uninteresting to me, and in this wet weather the streets are a pool of mud. There is an English club a short hour's walk distant and well up on the hill. To walk there for exercise, read the papers and then back to the ship, such is my diversion. I have met a few people and lunched out twice but nothing and no one really interesting—no pretty young women who always while away my time—no Rosie Schiff nor Madeleine Stanley. The truth is utter monotony is wearing out my fibre; yet I look absurdly well—good color & all that and am putting on fat, not that I think that a good sign.

And now good bye darling child. Love to mamma & Helen.

[P.S.] I cant understand my letters failing to reach oftener, for I am sure I wrote oftener—busy though I am.

To Ellen Evans Mahan

Algiers, January 7, 1895 [LC]

Dearest Deldie: I am very sorry to hear that my letters reach you at such long intervals, for I know how eagerly I look for yours. Although I have not always kept a memorandum I have been under the impression that I wrote pretty regularly twice a week, although, going over the same ground again as last year I find little material for letters. But, still more, I am awfully tired and worried with desk work, and it may perhaps be that the aversion to the pen has caused me to procrastinate more than I realized. We are a long way off here, and the Medn. very boisterous so that letters take a fortnight to come. I have yours of Dec 21, but had hoped last night's steamer would have brought later. No more mail came, however; and no more will be till day after tomorrow. I have little doubt that Hartman will go out to Nice, for I think your uncle wanted it—and I think was right in aiming at a clear understanding of what was to be expected—but he may have put it less pleasantly than I understood. It seemed to me that his aim was that both he & Hart should be independent of each other's movements *outside* the house. I am sorry to think of Rose going for I shall miss her, but it is doubtless best. I suppose they will take the Genoa route. The weather reports say the Nice weather is very good. Here it has been something too terrible—like the rainy season in the tropics—tremendous downpours, accompanied with violent squalls, thunder, lightning, hail and snow—and now lasting for a fortnight without any serious interval of fine weather. I have never seen such uninterrupted continuance of bad. Everybody is discouraged, for bad as all this is on shore, it is twice as bad on ship board, and all I fancy are feeling how much better Nice would have been. I cannot feel quite certain why the adml. decided not to go to Nice—but it seems to me he did it out of sheer crookedness, because his daughter Mrs. Noel came out to join her husband, to show that the ship was not to be run for the convenience of the women. Well, Mrs. Noel is here, and ill with a low fever, and of course people will say that our remaining is on her account, though there are quite good enough reasons otherwise. For we are to remain here through this month, and have begun the overhauling of the engines and boilers which I told you must be done before our return. The admiral reasons that if we go to an Italian port we can only remain eight days, unless we beg the favor of an extension, and that the Dept. has said that the ship is to return as soon as the *S.F.* gets here. Where then do the repairs so well as here? This is most true—but it was true when we arrived, and we have lost two weeks. So of course, people will say Mrs. Noel's illness is the cause. Personally I am glad but most of the others regret. Certainly this place is uninviting and has no accessible points of interest. All the pleasant society live three quarters of an hour or more away—whereas in Naples we are near Rome etc and at Villefranche ten minutes railway takes us to charming society. So, with all the cards in his hands, the admiral flies into the face of the weather and all past experience and makes a dull winter where a pleasant one was in his grasp. We dined with the French admiral last evening—a mixed company of men and women. I took in decidedly the prettiest, indeed the only fairly pretty woman in the party, a married woman of two & thirty. She spoke only French, and although my French has lately gained in fluency, it tires my head to carry on long. Moreover the Gov. General was on her other side and he is a dignitary not to be neglected, so he got more than half her time, and I talked to a very amiable elderly Commissaire on my right. I could not but contrast my lot with the jolly Sunday dinner I should probably have had with the sans façon laughing Schiffs and the company they gather, had we been at Villefranche. I was always sure of three pleasant afternoons or evenings in the week at Nice, & what an inestimable boon is that in this monotony! I received your enclosure of letters from Rebecca and Mrs. Hare. I should be glad if the 11th St house suit you, being near the latter, for I feel how very important it now is for us to cultivate relations with others. You will have to open your economical soul for dinners etc; and I think I shall insist upon creating a dinner fund by two magazine articles per annum. The subject is really serious, for we are getting on and cant afford to lose time, but then we are all likable and if we give ourselves a chance, will, I think get on. Did I tell you I have received the new diary, which came in good condition? I shall miss Lady Anne Bingham's pretty mug.

I see by the morning paper that a mail goes at noon today and no other till Thursday, so I shall close this up now (Jan. 8./8 A.M.). As you see there is very little news. A telegram from Hanford yesterday says the *S.F.* probably sails this week. It makes little difference now as our repairs will take all this month, but they deserve to lose their European cruise for their sluggishness. Give my love to all the children—but Lyle will be off again—and *reflect seriously* upon the necessity of cultivating friends. I have this cruise experienced the immense relief that an aftn. or evening gives me. With dearest love. Fondly your own [etc.].

To Helen Evans Mahan

Algiers, January 9, 1895 [NWC]

My darling Helen: A very affectionate beginning to be followed by the truly touching news that the Isle of France is in the Indian Ocean—east of Madagascar, and is more commonly known as the Mauritius—the latter being its Dutch name. It is now an English possession. The same name Isle of France was before the French Revolution applied to a small district surrounding Paris, derived probably from the days when the power of the so-called Kings of France actually extended only over it—the remainder of their titular kingdom being really in the hands of nominal vassals. The name Mauritius—the Latin for Maurice—was given by the Dutch in honor of Prince Maurice of Orange, son of the great hero of Dutch Independence, William the Silent, and himself a very distinguished general about the year 1600. When the French got the island I dont know, you could find in the *Encyclopaedia Brit.* The English took it from them in 1810. I have this morning your letter and mamma's of Xmas. She mentions that Dodie was to sail Jan. 5, but does not say whether Hartman is also going. I suppose he is, but how strange not to say so. I hope she may have better weather in the Atlantic than the Medn. has given lately. It has been blowing a gale almost unintermittently since Christmas and Mr. Clover, who came in one of the same line last year, says the *Chicago* is more comfortable in a sea. Nice or the Riviera is of course her destination. Nice will pay best, but although less prosperous than formerly there is more going on than elsewhere, and of course her uncle counts for something. He will be very pleased to see her, and probably will often take her to drive, but the novelty will wear off, and he is not the man, nor of the age, to abandon his fixed habits to beguile the hours of an invalid. I hope Hart will be with her—the very knowledge of his being at hand will help. Then the climate, though unequal, is generally pleasant and often exquisite, especially after January. Here we have had it dreadful. This morning's paper says that more rain fell in the first week of January than the average for the whole month, as shown by records of fifty-four years. The last week of December was nearly as bad. The weather changed the day of our arrival. Till then people were wearing summer clothes.

Jan. 11

A mail goes tomorrow so I shall get this ready. I find upon enquiry that the *Normannia* will stop here on Monday or Tuesday next, so I shall hope to see Rosie then. Due Monday, they think she will not get here before the next day—arriving in the morning & leaving about 4 p.m. If I could have communicated with her at Gibraltar, I might have prepared her, but although only 48 hours apart, or less, there is no direct communication between the two places, and a letter takes near a week. Not knowing what she is well enough to do, I am at some loss what to undertake. After two days indifferent good the weather turned bad again last night, but it dont seem so bent on mischief as before and I hope we may near an end.

8 p.m.

I went ashore this afternoon and enquired at the office of Cook, whose tourists fill the *Normannia* what were the prospects of her stay. They say that if she arrives on time—Monday—it will be as above; but if behind, as they fear, then not more than three or four hours. In the latter case Rosie can scarcely land for a drive, as the fear of missing the steamer would scarcely allow pleasure to a nervous invalid. However, we shall see. We had a little dance this aftn. The admiral has a funny way of asking a few people in an off-hand fashion, and then wants the officers to stay on board and entertain them. Very young people perhaps are always ready for a dance, but men from 30 to fifty and over, as most of us are, dont care so much to have these things sprung upon them. I have not found here a single interesting woman, nor even one to me moderately attractive, and find continually cause to regret the strange decision of the admiral to avoid Nice where the American flag-ship has always heretofore wintered. There I could last year count upon two or three pleasant gatherings in a week, which powerfully lightened the monotony and brushed the cobwebs out of my brain—here nothing, dullness even duller. My only real pleasure is climbing the hill to the English club, reading the papers there, getting a cup of *four* o'clock tea and walking back. Not maddening, but refreshing and though under foot is bad, the air is fine and exhilarating. But even of this mild dissipation I am often deprived, by inevitable duty calls, or, as tonight, by some unexpected contretemps. What a pity that these next three or four weeks of inevitable delay, I cannot be where Marraine will be, and hear at leisure what she could tell me of you all.

I am eager to hear whether you approach any solution of the house question. I should be pleased if the 11th St one suit for it would be pleasant to be near people like the Hares. The family is good. The chief objection is

[385]

it is so near the Astor,[1] I should have no walk; but that could be overcome. Well, dear, I think I have now made as much brick without straw as I very well can so will say good night and good bye. Love to mamma & Nellie.

[P.S.] I had Lyle's report. While there is yet no reason to crow, I think there is evidence of diligence, and he had of course much to contend with. I shall write to him about it. I am pleased with him.

To Ellen Evans Mahan

Algiers, January 13, 1895 [LC]

My dearest Deldie: Although I sent a letter to Helen two days ago, as the *Furst Bismarck* is advertised to touch here tomorrow on her way to N.Y., I will take the chance and send this. I have just (6 P.M.) returned from my afternoon walk, and an inquiry at the Steamer office tells me that no telegram of the *Normannia* reaching Gibraltar has been received, so that she will not get here until Tuesday. Being thus behindhand she will hurry away after landing her passengers for this place, stopping probably for only two or three hours. This will give me the chance to see Rosie, but not to take her [for] a drive as I had hoped to do—perhaps not even to get her on board the *Chicago*. Yesterday we had a telegram from Stevens that the *S.F.* had sailed on the 10th, so that *seems* settled and by the time you get this she may be in Gibraltar. I look for her here the 27 or 28. The admiral intends to hurry off east with her, but *we* are not likely to start for home much before the middle of February. Until I have my orders I cannot reckon upon the probable time of our arrival, but I fancy March will have run its course before thus we are out of commission. If we run on over April 15, I get sea service for the month completing two years. I have had a letter from Taylor asking me to lecture at the College, and while willing to do it—because he deserves it at my hands—I am a little perplexed how to answer him. I want to devote all my energies to *Nelson*. If my time for retirement came sooner, I could see my way, but I am not sanguine that they will give me leave for over a year. I feel that to do a really fine piece of work I must give it all my energies—have no other occupation. It is very hard to make things fit.

I trust you are having some luck in your house hunting. While I would not have you hurry, remember you cannot hope to find ready-made perfection. If the locality is healthy and convenient, having regard to Helen's pupils and friends coming to us, much else may be borne with. It is evidently quite impossible to occupy the flat longer—indeed I have been thinking we

---

1. The Astor Library on Lafayette Place.

must go to Quogue as soon as Helen's pupils are over, simply because it cant hold us. I have, too, a feeling that I would like to start afresh with you all, under new surroundings, and with somewhat new intentions as to society, in a mild way. I feel that even you and I, but still more the girls, need now to establish not only the home though that first, but also other points of contact with our kind. I have felt the benefit of it so much during the cruise that I should be unwilling deliberately to put away all hope of such meeting with others; and although of course our home happiness is a very different thing from the desolate misery of ship life, yet a monotony too much unbroken is not good. What we can accomplish I know not, but our chief necessity is a house in a good position—that attained we may take our next steps. But at all events we must have some other place for next year. I realize of course that we cant go in for general society—but I hope we may make some way.

Dont fall into the mistake of stopping writing, until I tell you to. Any letters that come after we sail for home, Stevens will simply send back as directed to do.

With love to the girls always your devoted husband

Jan. 14. 9 A.M.
Have just received yours of Dec 31, with Helen's of the 30th. I am most distressed to hear of your sciatica. It is strange that Hart should not have heard from your uncle as I certainly understood the latter to say on the 19th (about) that he *had* written. However, we shall see.

To Ellen Evans Mahan

Algiers, January 15, 1895 [LC]

Dearest Deldie: The *Furst Bismarck* came in this morning & sails in an hour, but I find that the letter I mailed yesterday in the P.O. marked "per" her will not go. This will, upon delivery on board with two cents—so I hear. I try it, but have no time to say more than that I am well. The *Normannia* is due at 2 P.M. & I shall hope to see Rose then. Good bye. Love to all. There was not much in my "per *Furst*" letter but notice if you get it.

To Ellen Evans Mahan

Algiers, January 16, 1895 [LC]

Dearest Deldie: Rose passed through here yesterday, the steamer arriving at 2:30 & leaving at 7 P.M. I told her I would write you a line so that she need not feel hurried to do so upon her arrival at Nice. I found her look-ing thinner & paler than when I left home, but as I have not seen her at her downest I cant compare her with that. She says that her dyspepsia has been much better since the second day but that otherwise she does not notice much improvement, although they had a very good passage indeed up to two days before reaching Gibraltar. Owing to the delay in getting health probe given I did not really get on board until 3, and after the crowd had thinned a little we went ashore, and at 4 started for a drive of two hours, enough to give her some idea of the country about. As the hills rise some hundreds of feet she got several fine views & in fact saw as much, though less thoroughly, than I shall in my prolonged stay. It was a great pleasure to meet her, though the small bit of home trotted out, & at once withdrawn, does not leave me exhilarated. I realized too how much of a loss she will be to us, with our small social relations, for I doubt it will end in her & Hart remaining abroad. Life there is cheaper & easier in every way for foreigners of limited means—and once the nostalgia is over, I doubt their willingness again to take up the peine forte et dure of the American grind. I am glad to see that some bad weather promised for today has not come, so I hope she will reach Genoa with good conditions tomorrow—but one cannot reason from the south to the north of the Medn. You may fancy that her being in Nice & Hart makes me doubly regret Kirkland's cussedness in not going there. Good bye my own dearest. Love to the girls.

To Ellen Kuhn Mahan

Algiers, January 19, 1895 [LC]

My darling Nellikin: It is certainly well that I am soon to go home, for I never can find matter more to write home two letters a week. I had a little diversion in meeting Marraine on Tuesday last, though it was only three or four hours, not enough for us to get used to one another, much less to exchange any news—except that she told me how you were all look-ing. Of course having been in Morristown she had not been au courant of your daily lives. We here in Algiers have had quite good weather since she left—not only quiet as to wind but sunny and warm as our most spring like April days; but I see by the papers that it has been stormy in the northern Mediterranean. By this time, however, Marraine will be in Nice with her friends and, I suppose, Miss Elsie[1] will have joined her. The Algerians are of course telling us that what we now enjoy is the real winter climate of the place—each one for his own. Mr. Gladstone is expected to arrive tomor-

1. Miss Elsie Smith.

row, and I hear his two daughters are already here. We knew of his going to the Riviera, but I at least had no conception that he was coming here until I saw it announced this morning. The local papers are quite pluming themselves on the fact that this celebrity has had—as they believe—to fly from the south of France to their more favored shores. When the Empress of Austria, on the other hand, left here a week ago, three weeks before her appointed time, to go to Cap Martin near Nice, it was the result of the lies that were telegraphed about the better conditions of the Riviera—in all which, as you see, there is a great deal of human nature. Assuredly, nothing more fiendish in the way of weather was ever seen outside Russia, than that we had our first fortnight. I am engaged to dine on Tuesday at the Hotel St. George, where I hear Gladstone will stop, and as there is to be a hop there afterwards, I shall not unlikely see him. My hosts are a Mr. & Mrs. Ebbs, the mother of the latter a Mrs. Allderdice was last winter my pet aversion in Nice. I did not realize that I would meet her when I accepted. Of course she will fall to my share. Mrs. Ebbs herself is rather pretty and quite engaging—though ages younger than I am. I find no one here whom I like, which is a great misfortune and makes particularly trying my not getting to Nice. If there, not only have I friends, but Marraine would add much to my enjoyment and I too could help her. It is now reasonably sure we cannot leave here before February 10, and I should think we must get away before the 20th, barring accidents. I am delighted to hear that you and Helen are having so good a time this winter. Mamma seems rather out of it, but then she can always sleep, at least in the evenings. My last letter from her was January 4, but says nothing of the prospects of a house, a matter which exercises me much. I wonder whether she has yet received Little & Brown's account for last half year. I ordered a copy of the English edition for myself lately, and I find the second book marked Fourth Edition. Now if I knew how many in an Edition I might infer something. However, most people seem to know something of the "author." And now good bye dear child. Much love to mamma and Helen.

To Hilary A. Herbert

USS *Chicago*, Algiers, January 19, 1895 [NA]

Sir:

1. Replying to the Bureau's letter of November 21, 1894, (no number), concerning preparations made on board this ship in clearing ship for action, I have to report that the following dispositions are made:—

2. The topgallant yards are sent down and topgallant masts housed. The yards are secured up and down the lower masts.

3. The Surgeon's table and apparatus for care of the wounded are arranged in the fore hold, cot and whip rigged at hatch.

4. The ridge ropes and awning stanchions, if shipped, are unshipped and sent below to fore hold.

5. The binnacle for standard compass, with appurtenances, and that for the steering compass on the forward bridge, are unshipped. The former is stowed in the after hold, secured upright to a stanchion by the hatch. The latter with compasses stowed in Navigator's storeroom on after orlop. A boat compass is placed in the conning tower, as a rough, though very imperfect, guide, in case of smoke.

6. Endsails and awnings, if up, are sent down to the sail room.

7. Hatch railings (canopies) are unshipped and sent below; after canopy to Warrant Officer's Storeroom on orlop; forward ones to Yeoman's Storeroom.

8. The shot hole stoppers, with troughs, slings, tools, &c., are assembled under charge of the Carpenter abreast of the main mast on the spar deck.

9. The furniture in the gun room (5″ B.L.R. stern guns) is moved into the Admiral's and Captain's cabins, leaving a clear space for passing ammunition.

10. Furniture in the wardroom is moved aft clear of the Fixed Ammunition and Shell Room hatches.

11. Spare whips are provided for each ammunition hoist and placed on the berth deck handy.

12. Arm chests, Carpenter's chests, and various other chests about the decks, together with the mess tables and benches commonly stowed overhead on the gun deck, halliard racks and harness cask, ladders not needed in action, are stowed in the passage ways in compartments numbers 60, 61, and 63. The bulk of these are placed in the starboard passage way, and secured by close stowage. The water-tight doors of the starboard passage are closed in action; those on port side left open for ease of communication, men being stationed to close them if necessary.

13. At quarters at night the oil lights about the decks are lighted.

14. Pendant tackles, top burtons, and preventer braces are gotten up; lower and topsail braces toggled; lower and topsail yards and gaffs are slung; fore and main stays and topmast backstays are snaked down; top chests are securely lashed to the tops; rigging stoppers are gotten up; grapnels and whips are rigged from after boat davits to clear wreckage from screws; gratings are put on hatches; scuttle butt and division tubs are filled with fresh water; relieving tackles are hooked; steam steering gear thrown into action when steam is up; air ports are closed and screwed up, metal masks being kept ready for use; all water-tight doors are closed, except those through which ammunition passes, or those that are required to be opened for necessary communication through ship; davit boats are hung with extra

lashings; pumps are rigged and hose attached; extra lashings are put on the anchors; ammunition hoists are rigged and collision mats are gotten up; the collision gongs are tested; ammunition whips are rigged from the tops; and the electric circuit tested.

15. If at anchor a spring is gotten on the cable, the chain stoppered and gotten ready for slipping; boats lowered and dropped into the safest position.

16. With reference to the above programme, I must guard myself from being understood to say that all these things are always, or some even frequently done. The standard binnacle is never unshipped. I presume that no Captain of ordinary carefulness would in time of war be found cruising with awning stanchions up and ridge ropes up. The carrying of the mess tables and chests from the upper to the berth deck, must either be done with a deliberation greater than would be permitted by the rapid closing of two steam vessels, or else with a rush that would, if often repeated, hopelessly smash all the material involved. At night it would be almost impracticable.

17. With regard to the spring on the cable, it has been retained as possibly required by the Board of Inspection; but I am convinced from frequent experience, in the small Mediterranean ports, of manoeuvering this twin screw ship about an anchor, that a spring is not merely unnecessary but dangerous. Unless under very exceptional conditions I would not use it in action.

18. The question of the alcohol and turpentine chests upon the spar deck is one upon which I have formed no positive decision. Would it be possible to supply these inflammables in small packages that could be moved below? If not, it may be advisable to start the fluids overboard.

19. In conclusion, I would add that this ship carries a number of articles of furniture which would in action be not merely exposed to destruction, but would be sources of much danger. There are, for instance, no fewer than six desks in the Admiral's and Captain's cabins and offices. There are a number of chests on board which greatly add to convenience, but which could be dispensed with in case of absolute necessity. I see no reason for interfering now with this condition of things, which in no way affects the efficiency of the ship on peace service; but on the other hand I also see no reason for finding a place on board, in war, for that which would then be dangerous. A simple hinging-leaf writing table, easily moved, would then be a better substitute, the necessary papers being kept in boxes small enough to be readily portable.

20. The chairs are in excess of absolute requirement, and I should think unduly massive. There are on board a number of wicker chairs which after five years use are still serviceable. Their very lightness makes them more durable. The suggestion is inevitable that such might be fitter for war purposes.

21. These reflections may seem to be beside the question of clearing ship for action, but in truth the first thing to be considered is how to fit a ship so as to leave as little as possible for preparation, or as a source of possible danger, on the day of battle. This condemns the spar system of the ship, which, moreover, I am convinced impedes her way more with wind ahead than it assists her with even a gale astern.

To Ellen Evans Mahan

Algiers, January 25, 1895 [LC]

Dearest Deldie: Needless to say I am delighted at the news of the books' sales, which I looked anxiously for the last two mails, and the more so that my imagination never fancied they would reach the figures of last July. According to my rough running calculation the two *Sea Powers* have now brought in over $5000 of which, however, 3700 has been chiefly since my reception in England. I wrote to Nellie on the 19th and am ashamed to see by my notes that I have not written since. I can only say that I was perfectly sure not over four days had passed. This may account for some of my previous irregularity. I can only say that it has been entirely unconscious, due to changeless monotony with which day follows day; but I am glad it did not happen in London or Nice, for you then might attribute it to my Schiff friends. Agreeably to Mrs. Schiff's invitation I wrote to Hart a few days ago, that they would be glad to have him call. If he does, I hope he may like them, but I doubt, if he meets Mrs. Bingham, their great friend, whether he will go again. She is a most amiable woman and of a type I think English people generally think handsome, but I am sure Hart will be as startled as I was, when first we met. She is about six feet, built in proportion, though not exactly fat with hair of astonishing blondness, which dont look as if it grew there etc. She was a pet conundrum last year to the discreet Tom Rodgers, but I expect she's quite all right only not at all the type I admire. By the way did I ever tell you that Kitty McVickar has been left by her husband Lord Grantly. I believe you used to know her, so the fact may interest you. I had a letter from Marie Schiff yesterday. They have had the same dreadful weather that we had, and it with the consequent confinement has resulted in another severe heart attack for Mrs. Schiff. These are always dangerous, but she seems to have again pulled through this time. I dont wonder, darling, that your life seems monotonous, & that you are lonesome. I cant tell you how sorry on your account I have felt because of Hart and Rosie leaving. You may have seen little of them, but they were always among the possibilities of the day. Now you are almost without resources socially—nor do I yet see quite how they are to be supplied. I shall soon be home, God willing, and Quogue follows not far off—but we must seriously reflect what can be done next year. I am very, very sorry for Julia Tracy—failure must mean so much, so many daily rubs and worries. Dupont[1] I do not recall, except I think I met him once at Wilmington. Winterthur, if not their place, is probably an outlying village of Wilmington. I had heard of [illegible words] thing of a mystery of it I did not repeat. His French doctor, [illegible name], told me he judged from the symptoms, which to me sounded alarming, that the trouble was calculus. Are you wiser? But calculus or stone is not necessarily so fatal a trouble as Helen's information says. I hope it may be less serious than it seems, but your uncle was evidently alarmed for him. From the newspapers I fancy Rose has had only fair to middling weather in Nice— but it is sure to be better as spring draws on. This is much warmer & for a fortnight has really been beautiful in every way. You are quite right to suit yourself about the house. It is much the same case as marrying in haste etc. At the same time it is simply imperative that we find some place next winter. The flat is impossible any longer. I am rather glad Helen is fussy about you; and if she *is* overcareful you owe it to all of us to keep specially well—the more so as I am so near my return. If the Doctor is serious in saying 14 hours in bed he must see cause for so extreme a measure, for that would be, if you rose at 10 to go to bed at 8. Doctors are funny, and faddy—but I can scarcely fancy one advising so much rest for nerves. You must not stint yourself in money either. If I am so soon to be with you what will be the good to either of us to save a few dollars & find you ailing. I have no news. Our sailing will not I think depend upon the *S.F.*'s time. She is likely to arrive and depart again before we will be quite ready. My best expectation is to get away by Feb. 15. That would be three weeks from today. The weeks intervening between this and our meeting are not likely to be pleasant, but that will matter little when they are over & we together. Let us both do our best to insure that. Love to the girls.

[P.S.]   I have just had a visit from several gentlemen on board a yacht here, one of whom is Paul Stewart, son of your father's old friend, who told me of his mother's death, which I had not heard but suppose you know.

Saturday, Jan. 26. 8 A.M.

The mail leaves in an hour, and I have no more news, except that the *San Francisco* arrived yesterday at Gibraltar which you will know long ere this reaches you. It seems now to me another long step in our homeward journey, and I am, oh! so tired of the ship. Again dearest love to each and all.

---

1. Alexis duPont Parker, of Wilmington, son of Mary (Maime) Lewis Parker, who was Milo Mahan's step-daughter.

To George Sydenham Clarke

USS *Chicago*, Algiers, January 29, 1895 [LC]

My dear Clarke: I don't know whether you are by way of seeing the movements of our ships, as given in our service papers, and you may possibly not know that we have been ordered home. The first vague intimation reached us three months ago, soon after leaving England, and was confirmed a fortnight later; but our relief ship, the *San Francisco*, has but just joined us in this port. Owing to the general dilapidated state of our engines, etc., we are making a thorough overhaul with some repairs, prior to beginning a winter passage across the Atlantic. We shall not leave here before the 10th or 15th of next month, but I am beginning betimes to say good-bye by letter to my friends in England, whom I cannot again see in person before our return.

You will conceive that, besides the usual rejoicing over rejoining those who are dearest to one, I am heartily delighted at the prospect of once more resuming the work which is most congenial to me. The impatience and distaste for detail, which is at once my strong and my weak point, makes the duty of a modern captain especially onerous to me; and I have especially chafed at a multiplicity of requirements which I am fully persuaded tend to reduce the efficiency of modern ships, by preventing officers from concentrating their attention on the really important. Like almost all practical problems, I am convinced the efficiency of a ship depends not upon the number of things that are attended to more or less well, but upon the perfection with which a very few things of cardinal importance are executed. As in a position, there is a key to the situation, which if carried the remainder signifies little. Our friend Clowes credited me with the faculty of dwelling on all that is important and passing over all that is irrelevant. Whether I deserve such high praise may be questioned, but I admit great impatience of the irrelevant when I recognize it, and I think the insistence upon so many accomplishments, so many minutiae, in our service, not only shows an absence of all sense of proportion, but by dissipating the energies of commanding and other officers, is really inflicting vital injury. I told the Department the other day, in reply to a question looking to further infliction of needless work (needless in my judgment) that "faire peu pour faire bien" was the maxim of a first class authority—La Gravière.

However, they will not heed. Education—cramming—is in the air from elementary school to navies. The bell of the bell-wether jingles aloud and all the sheep are following. Here a little, there a little, the multitude of things to be done increases day by day—and the more of them they pile together, the nearer they think they approach perfection—wherein I think they are absolutely mistaken. For myself my mind is as bent as human purpose can be to get out of it all, when my time for retirement arrives, which will be in September, 1896. I hope that meantime they will let me take leave, in which case I hope to proceed with my life of Nelson, and having finished that, with the War of 1812. Each is a fairly long job of work. I hope to find myself sufficiently easy not to write for money chiefly; and if so I shall strive to bring my work to a level as high as the too kind criticism of your countrymen has given that of the past.

For, after all, it is to your countrymen that I owe the recognition of my own, and for this, as for the cordial and touching reception given in this past year, I must remain always grateful. I am glad now to recall that, approaching my task without serious bias, the more I read, not only in English but in French narratives, the more I learned to honor not only the virile qualities but the integrity and substantial justice which in its broad lines has marked the wonderful career of your country.

And now I will say good-bye—not very solemnly however, for the Atlantic after all is not very broad in these days. Please make my most cordial remembrances to Lady Clarke, and hoping soon to see you again, believe me [etc.].

To Helen Evans Mahan

Algiers, January 29, 1895 [NWC]

My darling Helen: I this morning received yours of the 13th, together with mamma's of the 14th; and indeed I had one of the biggest mails I have seen since the days in London when a dozen and a half was my daily allowance. First of all I want to thank you for making mamma send for a doctor as soon as she began to look run down. It dont do to trifle with weakness, especially so early in the winter; and of course mamma has a heavier load than usual this year, I being away, Lyle gone out of the house; and the family in 34th St. which was, after all, something that besides natural affection drew her out of herself, being entirely broken up, takes a great deal out of a life so quiet at best. It will, I hope, make a great difference when I get back, which I hope cannot be more than five or six weeks after you get this. I trust also that Uncle and Marraine[1] will again establish their home in the city. I had a letter from her this morning, replying to one I wrote after her departure. I fancy she is comfortably enough placed, but she describes herself as very homesick. Miss Elsie however had joined her and uncle was soon to arrive. Then as the lovely southern spring comes on and she gets used to her surroundings I think she will cheer up a great deal. I wrote also to uncle giving him Mrs. Schiff's invitation to call. I

1. Hartman and Rosalie Evans.

hope he will try it, but I never expect others to like those whom I do. Marraine does not find Nice as pretty as Algiers, in which I do not agree with her. I was greatly interested in your Boston experience. Speaking generally, I have always found the people of that city very pleasant and very much to my taste, and it seems your experience is the same. Although I had so many letters there was surprisingly little of interest in them. Little & Brown are concerned to get the manuscript of *Nelson* while the bloom is still on the reputation of the others. It would I suppose go off now like hot cakes—but I cannot do anything nor am I willing to hurry beyond the rate at which I can turn out my best work. Both the subject and my present reputation—not to speak of the buyers who have a right to expect my best —demand this of me. Mr. Thos. Gibson Bowles[2] takes me to task for some expressions in my article in the *North American*,[3] and another wants information about the role of frigates in battle. The U.S. Consul at Beirut hopes to see the *Chicago* again there this year and congratulates me on my reception in England, and the Army and Navy Club in Washington wants my annual subscription. I find little to do and less to interest in this place— yet if I had to stay out, I would be as content here as elsewhere except Nice; nowhere else would I have friends. As it is, our stopping here instead of at Nice has turned out for the best in all ways except one—that being that, if there, I could have seen and helped Rose and Hartman. They have had a very bad winter on the Riviera, Mrs. Schiff has been so ill that I could not have visited at the house, and here we have had, after the first two weeks, lovely weather with which we are rapidly getting the ship ready for inspection etc. I should have liked to see more of Marraine. Whom do you think I have asked to dinner on Wednesday? Take a long breath "His Serene Highness Prince Louis of Battenberg."[4] I got awfully badgered over it all, didn't know to address him etc. He is a captain in the British Navy and commands a ship now in port—a very quiet gentlemanly person of about forty. He has accepted. He paid me a very pretty compliment. I had met him once or twice in England, and one occasion was the dinner of the Royal Navy Club, at which I was the guest on June 2. "You know" he said "that no one not a British subject was ever before asked [to] be guest of the Club, (it is over a hundred years old) and I hope we shall hereafter stick to the rule so that you may remain the only one." I told him that in my letters home I had mentioned that as one of the two incidents which had been to me the most grateful compliments I had received—the other, which I did not name to him, being the Prime Minister's invitation to dine with him en petite comité. It is a great happiness to me, dear, to know that you

2. Bowles, whose *Maritime Warfare* had been published in 1878, was an authority on international and maritime law.
3. "Possibilities of an Anglo-American Reunion."
4. The flag lieutenant's call on HMS *Cambrian* of January 27 was returned by Prince Louis himself, a courtesy which likely led to Mahan's invitation.

[396]

all are all looking so eagerly for my return. I hope I may deserve all your loves, and that God may smooth all difficulties that lie yet before me on my homeward path. Good bye my darling. Love to mamma and Nellie, and tell the former I hope she will be very obedient to her elder daughter when she is taking such good care of her for me.

Jan. 29. 8 a.m.

The mail closes in an hour, & should leave for Marseille at noon, but as it is blowing very hard I have my doubts if the steamer makes her trip. It has turned very cold again & I feel for poor Rosie at Nice, where the thermometer ranges 15° lower than here. Still, they are sheltered from the Northerly winds. Good bye again. Pray for your father, dear child, during these coming anxious weeks, till I am quit of the ship.

I see I have not mentioned that the *San Francisco* came in on Sunday morning.

To Little, Brown and Company

USS *Chicago*, Algiers, January 31, 1895 [LC]

Gentlemen: Your letter of the 11th, inclosing statement of sales, was received a few days ago, and was, as you say most satisfactory—especially, to me, in the continued demand for the earlier one. I am rejoiced to know that your generous venture of 1890 has resulted favorably to you as to myself.

I agree with you that it would be well in future impressions to give me my degrees. I prefer to have the D.C.L. *prec*ede the L.L.D., because, although the latter was actually conferred two days earlier, the former had been offered and accepted some time before. Indeed I have reason to think it was the action of Oxford that suggested the idea to Cambridge. I value both equally, but the priority belongs to the D.C.L.

You cannot be more desirous to see the complete manuscript of *Nelson* than I am; but I positively cannot do efficient work on board. We are, however, to sail for home in a fortnight or so—and I hope to arrive in N.Y. by March 20. Some little time will be needed then to get my final release from the ship, after which it is my purpose to ask the Department for a years leave. There is ample precedent for giving it to me, but possibly I may ask you for help thereto. I have accumulated a few interesting data hitherto unpublished—but not the least of my tasks will be a somewhat extensive search by correspondence for matter.

I will mention here that I had some months ago a letter from the Century Co. asking if I had not something in hand that would answer for serial publication. I thought some rumor of *Nelson* might have reached them—as they alluded to Sloan's *Napoleon*,[1] now coming out—and spoke of the advantages the serial form had in way of pecuniary return &c. My prepossessiveness and reason are against it, believing as I do that if the work be first-rate its effect would be vastly weakened by coming out by jerks. At the same time, in its backward state, I did not care to decline; so I said I thought that there were portions of the work which would lend themselves well to such publication.[2] My impulse was to write you at once, but having reached this tentative conclusion it seemed hardly necessary. I now mention it, as a matter of the frankness due to our relations, and I think you will feel with me that the communication of the fact is a matter of confidence between us. The publication in that form of some of the picturesque battle scenes would probably benefit the book—but, unless harder pressed for money than I have any present reason to fear, I have no intention of weakening what I hope to make a powerful work by sending it out in installments. In all events I shall do nothing without consulting you.

To Ellen Evans Mahan

Algiers, February 1, 1895 [LC]

My dearest Deldie: Your letter of the 18th, just two weeks old today reached me last evening and was most welcome; but letters now seem almost to have lost their efficacy, for I have no sooner read one than I begin longing for the next. It is not so much that I look for news, but there is a faint suspicion of companionship in a letter, though it so ill replaces the bodily presence. I could not make any point in what you told me about Stoddard & his father, whose identity now escapes me. I had a very successful little dinner on Wednesday for His Serene Highness Prince Louis of Battenberg, Mr. and Mrs. Clover, Paymaster Kenny and Nazro—all, except Clover, people who talk well. He is dull, in some ways very dull. I was a little bothered how to seat the company—not knowing how social rank affected such matters, and wishing to do things as the Romans do in Rome. However, I remembered that Louis XIV always took off his hat to the women servants, and I gave the lady the pas. I asked the prince to take her in, & seated her on my right and him on my left. Nazro next him, Kenny next her, Clover opposite.

1. William Milligan Sloane, *The Life of Napoleon Bonaparte.* New York: Century Company, 1896.
2. *Century Magazine* published four articles excerpted from Mahan's *The Life of Nelson*, which Little, Brown and Company published in 1897. These appeared in the issues for February 1896, January 1897, February 1897, and March 1897.

[398]

Every one seemed to enjoy themselves and I was glad I had done it. I had worried over it somewhat & wished I had not asked him. My biggest worry was about the admiral. He has been very kind and nice to me—hospitable— and when I first invited the Prince I intended to dine him tête à tête not asking the admiral nor any one *because* the adml. is so dreadfully profane and at times coarse, I couldnt face the idea of his breaking out before this really very refined and sufficiently dignified gentleman. Then I felt tête à tête might be stupid, and thought I would ask Nazro—then I felt it never would do to ask any one else & not Kirkland. So I plucked up courage and asked him, intending, if he accepted to ask the Clovers, for I knew the presence of a lady would keep him in order. He declined, saying dinners upset him always, but I asked the Clovers anyhow and then the other two. I dont know if I was repaid for my worry, but just now my life is a constant worry, if not one thing then another. The approaching inspection is ever on my mind, and though I confess gratefully that I have so far been safely brought through every trouble I cannot get rid of the fear that some censure will fall on me. People talk to me as if my reputation was such as to make [me] invulnerable. I hope it may be so, but I certainly am not presuming on it. "What *you* say would carry such weight—you ought to write pointing out the absurdity of this or that" etc. The admiral's daughter, Mrs. Noel, who has been progressing nicely has had a bit of a relapse today—I hope it may prove only transient. It is very curious that with his violent dislike of ladies being on the station & his determination that the movements of the ship should not be affected by them that he is thus tied down. It is my own belief that his original decision not to visit Nice was due to sheer cussedness, because Noel was bringing his wife out, expecting that this ship would spend the usual period there. He got more set in this by the efforts of several of us to make him see the advantages of the place; but now, though I think he has very good reasons to give for detaining the *Chicago* here I am in my own mind persuaded that he is unconsciously swayed mainly by her illness, and the impossibility of Noel leaving her when the ship leaves. It is a very singular case of l'homme propose Dieu dispose. Last year we followed the regular routine, absolutely independent of the woman question. Erben did not half like his family being here, but I think they affected his movements very little. How sold I should have been upon getting you to Beaulieu! But then you might have stayed here. We have had some pretty sharp weather again—but it seems to have gone. I fear poor dear Rose is not finding Nice very genial—I have watched the reports & see that we range from 12 to 18 degrees warmer—and that our morning temperature is about the same as Nice noon. But it will soon be all right & if she can get rid of worry about money I think she cannot but love the climate. About our getting away I will tell you *entirely entre nous* that it will be about February 20, but dont give this out. We will do our best, but a rickety engine must be reckoned

[399]

with. I dont think that orders for us to go home have yet been received. I have no news for you dear and can only beg you to remember me more than ever in your prayers, for very very much depends upon the next few weeks. I greatly need support and help. The inspection is a terrible ordeal to me. You are, I hope, wholly reconciled to my intended retirement. And now good bye dearest. Much love to the girls.

Feb. 2d.

I see by the morning papers that snow is falling along all along the Riviera, thermometer at Nice 25°. Poor Rose, but it cant last long. No further news. Dont forget your prayers for me, I need them sorely, for if God dont help me, I dont know how I can manage all I have to do.

To Ellen Evans Mahan

Algiers, February 6, 1895 [LC]

Dearest Deldie: I last night received your letter telling of Lyle's German measles. Like you I feel there is no great cause for anxiety, but also like you I feel a certain anxiety from which I hope you by this time are free. It is Nellikin's turn for a letter, but I think it best to write you, chiefly to emphasize my feeling that the utmost care should be taken to prevent any injury to his hearing, but above all to his eyes. The temptation to read or study too soon becomes great for an active minded boy, impatient of enforced idleness, and masters & teachers have not the time to concern themselves about individuals who dont complain. You must write Lyle himself, cautioning him against any strain, & you may say to him & to Mr. Billings that deeply as I should regret his losing a year, I should esteem it as nothing alongside a continued weakness, which might last through life as the consequence of premature exertion now. A year now is a great loss, but permanently weak eyes are a drag for life. I have that confidence in Lyle that I am sure he will not willfully or willingly exaggerate any trouble his eyes may give—and let him feel sure I shall not grudge nor fret over the loss of a year to save them. Greek text is very trying to weak eyes.

I have nothing to say about myself. I am sending a cheque for $10 to the Army & Navy Club, Washington—my fifth annual payment—and have asked that the receipt be sent to 54th St.

With dearest love & hoping the house & home may be happily found [etc.].

To Ellen Kuhn Mahan

My darling Nellikin: I shall not I hope have many more letters to write home, for I have so little to say that it is really becoming quite a burden. We seem now to have a very good prospect of leaving here on or by the 20th. We shall stop at Gibraltar and fill up with coal, I think, but whether at any other place is doubtful. The orders will be to return to New York. I look forward with some dread to the voyage, as we can scarcely escape some bad weather and shall for the most part have head winds, and I am getting old for exposure. Besides the weather here, when good, as for the most it has been, is really delicious, so that I am not braced for our keen March winds. I find myself getting quite fond of this place, the scenery is so charming and the air so pure and clear; and had I such acquaintance and friends as last year in Nice, I believe I could even prefer it. It is not so, however; I have not found a single person, much less a family, that has really attracted me, nor has there been towards me the hospitable disposition that I met alike in Nice and in England. Of course I dont complain of this, nor wonder at it; neither do I care, as I would if I saw people I much fancied, but it makes just the difference between a dull and a good time. I had this evening a letter from Marraine, written two days ago. As I do not know whether you hear from her—she says she thinks she is better, and sees uncle daily. He arrived on Friday, the first, and is going with a great rush into society, but she dont think he enjoys it very much. Her letter was very short and she said she was not strong enough to write much. I wrote a reply to her by this mail. We gave a reception, with dancing, this afternoon, to pay off our social scores, and as the weather was fine we had a great many come, about 175. I talked to a great many people, and at the end of three hours, when they went away I was very tired of standing and shouting so as to be heard above the band. We have been very much shocked at the suicide of a French Colonel, whom I had met and of whom some of our officers had seen a great deal. He was at the French admiral's dinner a month ago, and it was his wife whom I took in, and whom, you may remember I found so pretty for a French woman and so attractive. One thing that struck me was that the French papers, "at the request of the family" gave no details, and did not even give the name. Just imagine how the N.Y. *Herald* or *World* would have had a half column of big head lines, with every harrowing detail, an attempted interview with every relative of the unhappy man, and probably a hideous caricature of a likeness. What makes this particularly dreadful is that although he can scarcely recover, or retain intelligence if he do, the poor man lingers on alive & his family are on the rack of suspense. He had fortune and everything to live for, wife and children, but as far as is known became unhinged through over sensitiveness to censure, which he had incurred through some negligence. I have just been on deck for an hour, walking with the admiral and looking at the city in the moonlight. I wish you could see it. It is built on a hill side, facing to the east, and the old Moorish quarter is composed almost wholly of white, square-built, eastern houses which look now as if built of pure white marble. Under them and to our side the French houses of a yellowish stone have a kind of dusky hue. There is something magical in the appearance, particularly in connection with the absolute quiet that reigns all around now—at half past ten. I have not any news to give you. People are still very complimentary, and it almost seems as if everyone *had* read the books. Well good bye dear child. I am so pleased to think of you as being so happy. Take good care of mamma and keep her quite well till I come back, for she has not even the little distractions that you have. Love to her and Helen.

Saturday morning Feb. 9

The mail goes ashore in a half-hour and leaves at noon for Marseille. Nothing further.

To Ellen Evans Mahan

Algiers, February 11, 1895 [LC]

My dearest Deldie: I sent a letter to Nellie by day before yesterday's mail, and this will leave, I hope, by tomorrow's, Lyle's birthday. Yours of the 28th, intended to come by *Fürst Bismarck*, came this morning, marked on outside "too late"; but its arrival was actually only twenty-four hours later than the *Bismarck* herself—indeed, I may say, it was not ten hours later, but being Sunday the mail was not delivered until this morning. I should gladly have heard something more definite as to Lyle's condition, not that I have any special fears, but I would be relieved to know that we were assured the care as to warmth of body, and care for hearing and eyesight which is apt to be lost sight of among so many boys. You will be prepared not to expect much in the way of news. The admiral hopes that both ships may leave here about the 20th or 21st—we for Gib, the *S.F.* for the eastward. You might, if you wish, arrange through Dennis or Chadwick to hear when the *Chicago* arrives or sails from Gibraltar; as we telegraph both events to the Navy Dept. You must not expect us to reach N.Y. in less than 20 days from Gib, for the wind is pretty sure to be against us all the way, and I must go slowly to economize coal. The distance is 3,600 miles, of which 3,000 to the point where we pass Bermuda. In case of coal

[402]

running short from bad weather I may have to put in there, but all this is contingency. I presume that upon arriving in N.Y. we shall anchor off Tompkinsville, Staten Island. If so I shall telegraph you thence, and tell you where to reply, and you will send me word how all are. You must not expect that I will come rushing up at once from the ship. However natural, I think there is something almost indecent in the way people seem to think no duty imposes any restraint upon getting home. We have our inspection to look forward to, and generally a certain sober propriety of conduct to observe. You will be sure that I will not delay an instant more than necessary in coming home. I have of course a special reason for caution in the fact of Erben's reports against me. You will be pleased to know that Kirkland today said to me that he intended when I left to write the Dept. to express his entire satisfaction with me, that he thought I paid the utmost attention to my duties etc. etc. and that he purposed more particularly to do so because of what he considered Erben's injustice in the matter. This was of course without any suggestion on my part; but with my usual caution I suggest your keeping the knowledge wholly to yourself; for, if known, malicious people might say he did it wholly out of opposition. I am glad to see by Shepard's[1] talk etc, that the confidence of the general service in me is apparently unshaken. Helen's letter of the 27th also came today, but nothing requiring an answer. Everybody seems much shook up about the measles, but it seems to me a case not for worry, but for care and nursing. If Lyle is told *how* to be careful, his inherited tendency to carefulness will probably keep him right. Well, for very dearth of news I must now say good bye, my own dearest. Love for the girls.

Tuesday. Feb. 12. 8 A.M.

The mail closes in an hour and I have no further news. Good bye again. Pray for me.

To Hilary A. Herbert

USS *Chicago*, Algiers, February 16, 1895 [NA]

Sir:

1. I have the honor to inform the Department that John James Ester-brook, Landsman, has been received on board this ship from the *San Francisco* without accounts or papers, for reasons stated in the letters of Com-

---

1. E. M. Shepard, commanding USS *San Francisco*.

mander E. S. Houston,[1] commanding U.S.S. *Machias*, of which copies are enclosed.[2]

2. With proper regard for his health and physical decency, I am compelled to order issues of clothing at once; and I respectfully request the Department to cause his accounts to be transferred by the Fourth Auditor to this ship to await her arrival at New York.

To Ellen Evans Mahan

Algiers, February 19, 1895 [LC]

Dearest Deldie: I cannot write very much to you today for I am so busy, my head gets so tired & there is really little or no news. I had a letter from Hart yesterday saying that Rosie seemed to improve, that he intended to call upon the Schiffs but had not yet had time and telling me he had recd. a telegram of Gouv's death. I had seen the latter the night before in the Paris N.Y. *Herald*, & was not wholly unprepared for it from Helen's letter mentioning her meeting with Aunt O. in the street. I wrote the latter immediately, a letter which will go by this mail, but no words can express the crushing character of such a calamity at her age, and in her condition. The indications now are that we shall sail for Gib tomorrow night or Thursday morning. We are now coaling and receiving water for the boilers. The admiral is still here on board the *San Francisco* & apparently wishes to see us off. I have little to add to what I have already said. I shall have a pretty large wash when we reach N.Y., too large for the home, you might arrange what to do about it. If we anchor off Tompkinsville I will telegraph you, and want a telegram sent to the address I will give, and you had better have a letter sent to the Navy Yard N.Y. on March 15. I am somewhat uneasy about you, knowing you had been run down, lest you should contract Lyle's measles and afterwards be exposed to the extreme cold you have experienced, particularly if caught en voyage. Then there follows Gouv's death which might involve your going out when you had better be in bed. I shall therefore have to endure a certain amount of anxiety during our passage. The length of the latter cannot be predicted, the weather at this time of year being so uncertain. I enclose two little quelque choses which may be interesting. News there is absolutely none and I shall not therefore weary myself multiplying words. Good bye my own dearest. The time is drawing short and I trust the same merciful care which has kept us so far will still keep us to a happy meeting. Love to the girls.

1. Edwin S. Houston, class of 1865.
2. The enclosures were two letters from E. S. Houston to W. A. Kirkland.

To Ellen Evans Mahan

Gibraltar, February 24, 1895 [LC]

My dearest Deldie: I shall write you but a very few lines more to assure you of my recollection and love than to communicate anything. The mail by the *Nedda* closes tomorrow, but sorry indeed should I be to think that you will not, long ere this reaches you, hear by telegram of our sailing from here for home. As I told you before I may stop at Madeira, or at Bermuda, or both—if I think more prudent on account of coal. The head winds and accounts of bad weather in the Atlantic make necessary to be forehanded in that most essential article. We left Algiers on Thursday the 21st at 2 p.m. and had a very pleasant uneventful run of two days, reaching here at 3 yesterday. One of our ever ailing boilers must be cleaned, and we have to take a hundred odd tons of coal, but I sincerely hope and expect to keep the time I have set for sailing—1 p.m. Wednesday. This is a wretched place to be this time of year, and the more so now that the English Channel fleet is here forcing us to take an incommodious berth. There is no news. Owing to the excessive rains, the railway communication in Spain is much disturbed. Letters take at least five days from England and even so there are now three mails overdue—hence my last is Nellie's of Feb. 3, three weeks old. This should be a warning to you not to miss writing me—as you might from Groton by the steamer of the 2d from N.Y. Dont lose your thought of others because the boy has measles. A letter from Hart told me he intended to call on the Schiffs, but had not yet found time. Pray for me dearest that I be supported during these few remaining weeks, and may close my sea service (I trust) without discredit. How I long for repose. The *Castine* is here, a forlorn looking little tub, but with a very good fellow for captain.[1] And now au revoir. Always with the utmost love and affection, my darling.

[P.S.]   Dearest love to the girls and to Lyle.

To Hilary A. Herbert

USS *Chicago*, Gibraltar, February 26, 1895 [NA]

Sir:

1. I have to inform the Department of the death of Nils Fredericksen, Gunner's Mate 3rd Class, which occurred on February 16, 1895, while

---

1. Sister ship of the USS *Machias*. *See* Mahan to Ellen Kuhn Mahan, November 8, 1894, Footnote 3. Attached to the South Atlantic Station, she had recently visited the east coast of Madagascar under the command of Commander Thomas Perry, class of 1865.

under treatment for dropsy at the Colonial Hospital, Gibraltar, where he had been left by the U.S.S. *Detroit.*

2. The funeral of the deceased, at the North Front Cemetery, Gibraltar, was attended by the United States Consul, Mr. H. J. Sprague, who had taken personal interest in Fredericksen's case at the request of the Commanding Officer of the *Detroit.*[1]

3. In accordance with the directions received from the Commander-in-Chief of the European Station, and in view of the fact that Fredericksen's accounts and papers had been transferred to the *Chicago,* I ordered Paymaster Kenny, of this ship, to discharge the bills and expenses incurred on account of the deceased, with the hospital authorities and others, which he has done and holds receipts for the disbursements.

4. There was small hope of recovery entertained from the day of Fredericksen's transfer to the hospital, where he was tapped on five different occasions; and although his life was prolonged for a while, he died on the date stated from general exhaustion.

To Hilary A. Herbert

Cablegram   USS *Chicago,* Gibraltar, February 26, 1895 [NA]

Revocation collision circular received.[1]

To Hilary A. Herbert

USS *Chicago,* Gibraltar, February 26, 1895 [NA]

Sir:

1. I have the honor to acknowledge the following telegram, received this date—

Mahan—Gibraltar.

Circular regarding new regulations for preventing collisions at sea revoked. Acknowledge.

H. A. Herbert.

---

1. J. S. Newell.

1. On July 6, 1894, Grover Cleveland, in accordance with the recommendations of the International Marine Conference of 1889, issued a Proclamation on Collisions at Sea, to take effect on March 1, 1895. The regulations met with so much protest in England, especially with regard to fog signals, that the Earl of Kimberley and Sir Julian Pauncefote, British ambassador to the United States, insisted on consulting Parliament, and desired the effective date to be extended until the following October. *Foreign Relations,* 1894, pp. 260–275.

2. I also confirm the following telegram sent this date in reply to the above—

Revocation collision circular received.

Mahan.

To Hilary A. Herbert

USS *Chicago*, Gibraltar, February 28, 1895 [NA]

Sir:

1. I have the honor to confirm the following telegram, sent this day, to the Navy Department—

Secnav—Washington.
New York
Mahan.

2. I beg to say, furthermore, that I shall sail at 1.00 P.M., to-day, for New York, and intend to take the southern route for west bound steamers as laid down in the Pilot Chart issued by the Hydrographic Office for the month of March, 1894.

3. Owing to the prevailing rough weather,—a strong south-westerly wind preventing coal lighters from coming alongside, and so made coaling ship impossible,—I was unable to leave this port on the afternoon of Wednesday, February 27th, as stated to be my intention, in letter No. 9, of the 24th instant, to the Department.

To Ellen Evans Mahan

Funchal, Madeira, March 4, 1895 [LC]

My dearest Deldie: I suppose this will get to you before we arrive in N.Y. as I am told the mail goes to England tonight. There is no news. We have had a very disagreeable, though not quite stormy, passage from Gibraltar & anchored here yesterday noon. Today we are coaling & I hope to get away some time before sundown. As we pass close to Bermuda, I may find cause to get in there, but my great longing now is to get the ship off my hands, or rather off my mind, so painfully do I feel the need of rest. I am too old—too old. Pray for me that my strength fail not. You dont know what a deprivation your failure to write has been to me under these conditions, nor can I account for it except by supposing you so preoccupied with Lyle, for I have too often charged you not to stop writing. Do beware of that so common fault with mothers of preferring their sons to all else. Despite my suffering at this time, it matters less for me than for the girls. It would be a dreadful thing for you if they should get such an idea in their heads, and especially if you were to lose me.

Despite my worry and weariness I am quite well except in my nerves & brain which are getting very overwrought. I carried away a touch of malaria from Algiers but the change of air & quinine with whiskey have nearly restored me. Although I keep on my clothes I am much less disturbed at night than in the Medn. etc, where we met so many vessels. But when every allowance is made I feel it imperatively necessary to retire as soon as I can, and on shore to avoid administrative duties as far as possible.

Have a letter waiting for me at the Navy Yard, N.Y., about the 20th, and you may as well, if you can, make some arrangements for my wash— as with Katie's aunt. I will telegraph you our arrival at Tompkinsville, Staten Is., where we will probably anchor, & shall expect a reply there. As I told you, I cannot set an example of rushing out of the ship before I know her future movements & inspection.

I was last here in 1863. What suggestion of changes to see certain familiar spots unchanged when so many persons have departed.

Dearest love to the girls and to Lyle when you write.

[P.S.]   Remember we shall have head winds, possibly very strong, and do not be worried if we dont arrive by the 25th.

To Ellen Evans Mahan

Bermuda, March 17, 1895 [LC]

My own dearest Deldie: I am not going to write you anything of a letter as I hope by today week we may be in N.Y. That of course depends upon the weather & other good fortune, but I trust it may not be much longer. I came in here to take a little more coal, & in entering an accident occurred to one of our engines, which will take a couple of days to repair, but I have every reason to hope I may get away Wednesday. The weather set in baddish on our arrival & so continues today which makes me hope it may be good for our passage. From Madeira on it was *very* good & I trust that the gracious Providence that has so far kept us will keep us to the end. The *Blake* (of the Naval Review) is here with Sir John Hopkins, also bound home like ourselves. I am to dine with the Adml Monday & the Captain of the dockyard on Tuesday. What a people they are for dinners! In Gib both the Commd. in Chief of the Channel Squadron[1] & the *second in command*

1. Admiral Alfred Taylor Dale, RN.

invited me, as did the *Governor* (informally). The second was the greater compliment—in fact the other invites were "to meet Capt. Mahan." Too bad I had to decline. The C. in C., however, greeted me by saying he was proud to meet me. So, dear, our good English friends were good to me to the end. Love to the girls & Lyle.

[P.S.] I am wondering whether we could get to the mountains anywhere, in May. I suppose you give up the apartment May 1. You need not be alarmed if we are later, as the ship is very slow now.

To Horace E. Scudder

75 East 54th Street, New York, N.D. Probably, March 25, 1895 [HUL]

Dear Mr. Scudder: Thank you very much for your kind letter of welcome received this morning. I hope now soon to get regularly to work again at the tasks which formerly gave me so much pleasure, but am still somewhat in the hands of the Department. I have been called to Washington by the Secretary whom I expect to see on Wednesday; and I hope the result of our interview will be to convince him that it will be best for this Navy as well as for myself to have me free to work on my own lines. Now that I have a little reputation, I find that the great trouble is to resist temptations to dissipation of energy.

To Hilary A. Herbert

USS *Chicago*, Navy Yard, New York, March 30, 1895 [NA]

Sir:

1. In view of the fact that the *Chicago*, under my command, will be put out of commission in the course of a few days, after the termination of the quarter ending March 31, 1895, I have the honor to request that all returns of the heads of departments of the ship may be omitted for the end of the present quarter, and be made up to and include the final date when the vessel is placed out of commission, thus saving the duplicating of returns when all departments will be more than usually busy.

To Robert U. Johnson[1]

75 East 54th Street, New York, April 1, 1895 [NYPL]

Dear Sir: A few days ago I recd. your note of the 26th ult, alluding to a former one of the 6th enclosing one from Miss Seawell.[2] The latter have not come to hand—why, I do not know. Are you sure it was mailed?

To Augustus Lowell[1]

USS *Chicago*, Navy Yard, New York, April 1, 1895 [HUL]

Sir: Your letter of the 25th ult. was duly received. I do not at present see any chance of my being able to accept your proposition of lecturing before the Lowell Institute[2] next winter. It is barely possible that the literary work in which I now hope to embark may suggest and promote the writing of such lectures, but it would not be right for me to leave you waiting a decision. I am just now too occupied with the details of putting the ship out of commission to allow me even to look about me—mentally—Would you like to name a time for a final reply?—or shall I now say "No," which is all I could now answer truly.

To Hilary A. Herbert

USS *Chicago*, Navy Yard, New York, April 4, 1895 [NA]

1. I have the honor to inclose herewith for the information and action of the Department a letter received by me through the mail.
[Enclosure]

New York, March 26th, 95

The Commander of the U.S.A. Cruiser *Chicago*

I have reason to know that one of your men deserted your ship while

---

1. Associate editor of *Century Magazine*, 1881–1909, and editor, 1909–1913. Johnson was coeditor with C. C. Buel of *Battles and Leaders of the Civil War*.
2. Molly Elliot Seawell, writer of novels and popular history dealing with naval subjects, whose "Paul Jones" was published in *Century Magazine* (March 1894).

1. Vice president of the American Academy of Arts and Sciences, and a trustee of the Lowell Institute.
2. The Lowell Lectures, endowed by John Lowell in 1836, were free to the public, and treated subjects in science, art, and literature.

visiting London some time ago, his name is Pease and is sheltered by his brother who is working for the Central R.R. of New Jersey as electrician and lives in Elizabeth Port.

I feel this my duty to state as a devoted Citizen.

To Robert U. Johnson

USS *Chicago*, Navy Yard, New York, April 4, 1895 [NYPL]

Dear Sir: I have found your letter enclosing that from Miss Seawell among a collection of other letters where it had accidentally been misplaced. Miss Seawell's idea strikes me very favorably, but in the confusion amid which I am now occupied, I find it impossible to take stock of what I can do in the immediate future. Probably not until the ship goes out of Commission (Ap. 15–20) can I tell what I can undertake to do.

[P.S.]   I may say that the battles of the Nile, Trafalgar & Copenhagen are bound to be written by me some time.[1]

Also I question the word "Decisive" & would support rather "Remarkable."

To Francis M. Ramsay

Navy Department, Washington, D.C., April 10, 1895 [NA]

The Bureau is informed that in obedience to the Department's order of April 3, 1895, I reported in person at the Navy Department on April 10, 1895, for special temporary duty.[1]

To Francis M. Ramsay

USS *Chicago*, Navy Yard, New York, April 12, 1895 [NA]

The Bureau is informed that I have this day completed the special temporary duty assigned to me by the Department's order of 3rd of April, 1895, and have resumed duties as Commanding Officer of the *Chicago*.

---

1. *See* Mahan to Little, Brown & Company, January 31, 1895, Footnote 2.

1. The duty may have had to do with a report on the condition of the *Chicago*. In his *Annual Report* of 1895, Herbert said that $300,000 was asked for refitting her with new boilers and engines.

To Hilary A. Herbert

USS *Chicago*, Navy Yard, New York, April 17, 1895 [NA]

Sir:

1. I desire to bring to the notice of the Department the case of James Whalen, Coal Passer, of this ship, who has been recommended by a Medical Board of Survey for transfer to the Naval Hospital, in a state verging on melancholia, superinduced by drink during his unauthorized absence from the ship.

2. Whalen joined the *Chicago* on June 1st, 1893, and almost from the beginning of his service his record is marked with serious offenses against discipline. He has overstayed his liberty 207, 50, 192, 34 and 53 hours, and on several occasions he has been drunk on duty. Twice he has been tried by summary courts-martial.

3. When Whalen is in a condition to leave the hospital, I recommend that he be discharged from the naval service, with an ordinary discharge, endorsed to the effect that he is an undesirable person for re-enlistment.

To Hilary A. Herbert

USS *Chicago*, Navy Yard, New York, April 17, 1895 [NA]

Sir:

1. Referring to the Department's letter of April 10, 1895, desiring an explanation of there being no target practice on board the *Chicago* after the second quarter of 1894, I have to say that during the third quarter the ship was in the English Channel, or immediate neighborhood, where the crowd of passing vessels renders target practice both difficult and dangerous. It was at first expected that the ship would go south before the expiration of the quarter, and would receive additional ammunition at Gibraltar, according to the Department's notification. She was, however, detained until the 20th of October. The passage to Lisbon was too boisterous to admit of target practice. At Lisbon information was received that the ship would return home shortly, to go out of commission, and that the ammunition would not be sent. These facts, with the difficulty of finding anchoring ground for the observing boats, outside the three miles limit, and the exceedingly boisterous weather of this winter in the western Mediterranean concurred to prevent target practice.

To Montgomery Sicard[1]

USS *Chicago*, Navy Yard, New York, April 22, 1895 [NA]

Sir: As it is generally understood that the present boilers of the *Chicago* will not remain in her, I would respectfully suggest that the Department be asked whether, in that case, it wishes that they be cleaned and scaled before going out of Commission, as the work of doing so would take two or three days and by so far delay her going out of Commission.

To Hilary A. Herbert

USS *Chicago*, Navy Yard, New York, April 24, 1895 [NA]

Sir:

1. Replying to the Department's endorsement of April 22, 1895, upon State Department's letter of April 19, enclosing communication from the Italian Embassy, relative to a one hundred dollar Confederate Bill said to have been passed in Alexandria by a person styling himself Lieutenant Engineer Rogers of the U.S.S. *Chicago*, it is probably unnecessary to say that no officer of that name has been attached to this ship while under my command.

2. As the *Chicago* left Alexandria March 31, 1894, and there have been many changes in the ship's company it will be difficult to ascertain the actual delinquent, even if the person who committed the misdemeanor was really one of our number, as he represented himself to be.

3. I will, according to the Department's instructions, obtain any information that may be practicable.

To Hilary A. Herbert

USS *Chicago*, Navy Yard, New York, April 25, 1895 [NA]

Sir:

1. In accordance with Bureau of Navigation's letter, W.A.M., of April 5th, 1895, I have to-day forwarded by express a box containing signal and other books as per enclosed list.[1]

2. One Fleet Drill Book of 1891, on hand January 1st, cannot be found.

---

1. At this time, Commandant of the New York Navy Yard.

1. The list consisting of 20 titles, arranged by year and by number of copies for a total of 97 volumes, may be found in Record Group 24, National Archives.

To Hilary A. Herbert

USS *Chicago*, Navy Yard, New York, April 26, 1895 [NA]

Sir:

1. Referring again to the Department's endorsement of April 22, 1895, upon State Department's letter of April 19, enclosing communication from the Italian Embassy, I have to say that the only case of a transaction, on the part of any member of this ship's company, resembling that reported in the letter of the Italian Ambassador, during my command of the *Chicago*, occurred in May, 1894, at Gravesend.

2. Joseph C. Pretti, Apprentice 2d Class, was accused of fraudulent attempt to pass a worthless bill upon a storekeeper, at Gravesend, at the time stated. He would have been tried by a General Court Martial, but it was found the parties ashore would not appear against him. The money, however, was refunded.

3. Whether Pretti had attemped the same trick, with better success, in Alexandria, I can obtain no information. There is no rumor to that effect on board.

4. He was sent home for discharge from this ship from Antwerp, on June 23, 1894.

5. The Department will remark that no description is given of the self-styled "Engineer-Lieutenant" Rogers, by which an identification could be made, and that it is perfectly possible that his connection with the *Chicago* was as fictitious as his name.

To Francis M. Ramsay

Navy Yard, New York, May 1, 1895 [NA]

The Bureau is informed that in obedience to the Department's order of March 29th, 1895 I was detached from the U.S.S. *Chicago* on May 1, 1895. My address is 75 East 54th St., New York.

To Francis M. Ramsay

75 East 54th Street, New York, May 7, 1895 [NA]

The Bureau is informed that I have this day received the Department's order of May 6, 1895, to special temporary duty in connection with the Naval War College and Torpedo School.[1]

---

1. This duty permitted Mahan to resume his research and writing.

To Augustus Lowell

75 East 54th Street, New York, May 9, 1895 [HUL]

Dear Sir: It is only for a week past that I have been fairly clear of my ship, and able to consider the amount of work, present and practically pledged, that lies before me in the immediate future. After so doing, I with great regret find myself compelled to decline your obliging offer, which I should otherwise gladly have accepted.[1] If in January or February next you should feel disposed to renew it for the following season, I may very possibly be able to give a different reply. I shall with that view keep the matter before me as regards subject, treatment & necessary time, as well for composition as for delivery. My safe address is always Navy Department Washington.

To Robert U. Johnson

Haverford, Pennsylvania, May 14, 1895 [NYPL]

Dear Sir: Your letter of the 9th was received by me here. As regards your proposition to contribute an article upon the bearings of the Yalu fight,[1] I have, most unfortunately for myself, been so much indisposed since the *Chicago* went out of commission,—May 1—that I have been unable to do any headwork, and I am unwilling to make an engagement which I may not be able to fulfill.

I expect to return to N.Y. Thursday, and will try to get in to see you on Friday. There is in my mind a hitch about the copyright of the Naval Battles,[2] about which, as well as about the time you want them, I should wish to see you.

To Hilary A. Herbert

75 East 54th Street, New York, May 31, 1895 [NA]

Sir: I respectfully request the Department's permission to change my residence to "Quogue (Long Island) New York."

---

1. *See* Mahan to Lowell, April 1, 1895.

1. Published as "Lessons from the Yalu Fight," *Century Magazine* (August 1895).
2. A series of four articles for *Century Magazine* that appeared February 1896 to March 1897 and treated Lord Nelson at the battles of Cape St. Vincent, the Nile, Copenhagen, and Trafalgar. *See* Mahan to Little, Brown and Company, January 31, 1895.

To Robert U. Johnson

New York, June 2, 1895 [NYPL]

Dear Mr. Johnson: It will give me great pleasure as well as interest to
see McGiffin's article,[1] and, if I can, to write some comments thereupon,
but I am much occupied this month & hesitate to make promises as yet. The
warm weather takes it out of me. We go this week to Quogue (Long Island)
N.Y., which you might note as my address.

I shall bear in mind the *Century*'s offer, but at present will only say that
I esteem it very highly in every point of view.

To Augustus T. Gillender

Elizabeth, New Jersey, June 4, 1895 [HUL]

Dear Mr. Gillender: Is there any hitch about the 86th St house? Mrs.
Mahan has been in New York for two or three days, but so far from well
that she has been unable to get to see you. The girls went to Quogue today
and we are to follow them on Thursday. The matter about the house
seemed so simple, and our suggestion for the terms of the contract having
met your approval, we have wondered if they raised any objection. We,
however, asked only what had been agreed between Mr. Platt and ourselves.

[P.S.] The said house to fulfill, in design and detail, the conditions of
the plans submitted by the builders, (or architects), and accompanying this
contract; and to correspond in all respects, as regards character of construction, (including plumbing), in quality of materials, and in finish, to
the dwelling house No 148 West 86th St, except in the particulars herein-
after specified; to wit:
Stationary basin in 4th story bath room
Fire place in 4th story front room
Have to be taken out
3rd story back room—
same 2nd story back room

---

1. Philo N. McGiffin, class of 1882, was Executive Officer of the 7,400-ton, armored,
German-built, Chinese battleship *Chen Yuen* at the Battle of the Yalu, September
17, 1894. His account of that engagement, which Mahan consulted, was published in *Century Magazine*, August 1895, under the title "The Battle of the Yalu."
Mahan's "Lessons from the Yalu Fight" was published in the same issue. McGiffin
lectured on this subject at the Naval War College during the 1895 session. He was
honorably discharged from the U.S. Navy, June 30, 1884.

To Augustus T. Gillender

New York, June 6, 1895 [HUL]

Dear Mr. Gillender: I enclose the contract which was received by us this morning and has been signed by Mrs. Mahan. Unfortunately her cheque book went away yesterday in our trunk to Quogue so she will have to wait till we get there this afternoon. We go down by the 3.20 train, but as there will be no mail up till tomorrow, I think likely the cheque will not reach you til Monday as you go out of town Saturday. It will be sent tomorrow.

We both thank you very much for your kindness, which we greatly appreciate.

To Robert U. Johnson

Slumberside, Quogue, Long Island, June 9, 1895 [NYPL]

Dear Mr. Johnson: Your note of the 3d, following me from place to place, was not recd. here till the afternoon of Friday, the 7th. I dashed at the business yesterday, though I detest a hurry, and was rather refreshed to deal with the old familiar subjects so long neglected. A telegram will warn you of the manuscript coming—I hope in time to go with McGiffin's.

My address for the summer is Quogue N.Y.

[P.S.]   I regret the number of words is near 4,000 exceeding that named in the telegram, but I had to make a guess in seizing the opportunity to telegraph from this rather out of the way place on Sunday.

To Robert U. Johnson

Slumberside, Quogue, Long Island, June 11, 1895 [1] [NYPL]

Dear Mr. Johnson: Your letter was received this morning, and I was very glad to know that the manuscript, having to make such a close connection, arrived in time.

---

1. From June 11, 1895 to January 22, 1896, Mahan kept a letter book. The editors have found 33 of the 321 items listed therein. Many of them were to H. C. Taylor and vanished with the War College correspondence and Taylor's personal papers. Some were to Kirkland, whose papers are reputed to be in Mexico City. Some were to publishers who have no archives. Since the letter book contains briefs, it is known that Mahan declined to write for the *Naval Annual*, to speak before the Military Historical Society of Massachusetts, and to review various books. It is also known that he was in Newport from September 10 to September 14.

As regards the payment, your proposition was for 2000 words, for which I think $100 fair payment. Had I intended to make it 4000, I would have asked for more, but my pen ran on beyond the limits suggested by you.[2]

May I suggest a modification in your title, which seems rather too comprehensive, viz: "*Some* Lessons *from* the Yalu fight." I dont think I quite exhausted the matter.

To Robert U. Johnson

Slumberside, Quogue, Long Island, June 14, 1895 [NYPL]

Dear Mr. Johnson: I enclose receipt for cheque for which many thanks. I am sorry that I made any mistake in counting the words which I made 3900, but owing to the tour your first letter made in search of me, from my abode, everything was done with such a rush that mistake was natural. I consider the amount paid entirely satisfactory.

As regards the title, I only meant to offer a suggestion in a matter which I consider the Editor's prerogative. The substitution of "from" for "of" conveys the qualification at which I aimed.

To Bouverie F. Clark

Slumberside, Quogue, Long Island, June 14, 1895 [LC]

My dear Clark: Your very kind Christmas letter and card reached me immediately upon our return to the U.S. and I thank you and Mrs. Clark most heartily for the remembrance. That is now over two months ago. I did not reply at once because I knew that my letter of goodbye from Algiers had crossed yours and must have been meantime received. The six weeks following our return were very full of occupation—due partly to my family being in New York, when we went out of commission, and yet more to the amount of clerical and other work involved in getting rid of a ship. I dont know how bad it may be in your service, but with us it has become very complicated & I have found by sad experience that to spare supervision during the process involves double trouble in subsequent official correspondence. "Why is this thus?" when the books and the people who can give replies have been scattered. We hauled down the pennant May 1; and by great bad luck I was taken ill four days before with what seemed a bad cold, but which I fancy now was at bottom due to the causes which lead to your Medn. fever, of which we had a good deal among our men last

---

2. Johnson penned on this letter, "Send $150. I will write."

winter. I was very well in Algiers till just before leaving when I was similarly indisposed and at Gib had to decline Adm. Dale's invitation to dinner. Fitzroy[1] was then laid up with gout, but he also asked me for a few days later. Unluckily, I had to go to sea before. I have been so fortunate as to find my family all well but during the passage across my son was lying at death's door for a fortnight or more—measles followed by pneumonia and threatened heart failure. He is only fourteen and over large for his age. Mercifully I knew nothing of it—my wife bravely keeping the burden to herself as I could avail nothing. He is now quite well again. We are here for the summer, owning a little cottage, about 200 yards from the sea in a country as flat as Holland and with nearly as many windmills—for pumping water. The wind practically never fails. Our address here is simply "Quogue, N.Y." In the city our home will be "160 West 86th St. N.Y." As far as one can lay out their future in this changeful life we expect to be here from June 1 to October 1, the rest of the year in New York. I intend to retire when my time for voluntary retirement comes. This summer I have to give a few lectures at our College in Newport, but I hope now within a month to begin serious and consecutive work on my *Life of Nelson*. During the cruise I got him down as far as the siege of Bastia in 1794 but there had to stop. I find the great want now is not Nelson's own letters—there are quite enough of them—but letters *from* persons serving with him, or associated with him in daily life, who may incidentally mention him. If Captain Hamond is still with you—I understand he is an East of England man—would you ask him if he knows of any descendants of Sir Edward Berry, who was flag captain at the Nile? Like Nelson he was a Norfolk man, and I am pretty sure married in the County. His home letters might have allusions, incidents of daily life etc which is the great desideratum now. I have received a few—but very few—new anecdotes of such character. If at any time you get track of any thing of the sort, or can suggest where I might turn up something, be sure and let me know. I want very much to write a *Life* that will be the standard, if I can. I trust Mrs. Clark and yourself are both well. I shall always remember the pleasant and refreshing days I spent with you and the renewal of my acquaintance with the delicious Devonshire scenery. Pray remember me very kindly to her and believe me my dear Clark [etc.].

To John M. Brown

Slumberside, Quogue, Long Island, June 20, 1895 [LC]

Dear Mr. Brown: I have before me your letter of March 26, in which you were so good as to offer to come to N.Y. and see me when I was set-

---

1. Robert O'Brien Fitzroy, RN.

tled. I never replied, partly because of our meeting at the De Florez's dinner, but yet more because from the time I had any leisure, through the severance of my tie to the ship, up to the day of my arrival here, I have been too much under the weather to be up to anything like business talk. The fortnight I have now been here has quite set me on my pins again.

I write now to say that I am to be present at the Commencement Exercises at Harvard, June 26 when it is proposed to confer a degree upon me, & that I shall probably reach Boston, from Newport, at 3.15 p.m. Tuesday. It is perhaps a little late in the afternoon, but I might then get round to see you if not too inconvenient. At the same time I have nothing very important to say, but in direct interview suggestions at times arise. As I shall be at the Alumni Dinner Wednesday, and must return to Newport by 7 p.m. train I should have no time on that day.

Quogue is rather out of the way—not far from N.Y. but poor communication. It would give us great pleasure to see you here at any time. How would you like to come for the Fourth of July staying over Sunday—we should be very glad to see you. The place is very quiet, but always cool and a good beach.

As I leave tomorrow will you kindly reply, concerning Tuesday, to 30 Kay St. Newport.

To Francis M. Ramsay

Slumberside, Quogue, Long Island, June 20, 1895 [NA]

The Bureau is informed that I have this day received the Department's order of June 19, 1895, to report to Commdr. Naval Station, Newport.

[Motto]

Slumberside, Quogue, Long Island, June 20, 1895 [NWC]

It is better to trust in the Lord than to put any confidence in man.

To Francis M. Ramsay

U.S. Naval Station, Newport, June 22, 1895 [NA]

The Bureau is informed that in obedience to the Department's order of June 19th, 1895, I reported to Commodore R.R. Wallace[1] on this date for duty in connection with lectures at War College.

---

1. Rush Richard Wallace, class of 1856, commander of the Naval Station, Newport.

To Francis M. Ramsay

Slumberside, Quogue, Long Island, June 29, 1895 [NA]

The Bureau is informed that I have this day completed the duty assigned me by the Department's order of June 19, 1895 to deliver lectures[1] at Naval War College and have assumed duties at Quogue N.Y.[2]

To John M. Brown

Slumberside, Quogue, Long Island, June 30, 1895 [LC]

My dear Mr. Brown: From the time you left me in Cambridge until my return here, yesterday, I was altogether too busy to find time to write and thank you for your kindness to me in Boston. The day at Harvard[1] your own experience will enable you to understand, while with me the lectures, to which I had to give myself in Newport, entailed an amount of illustrative preparation which occupied me wholly.

I passed at Harvard a most agreeable day, and was above all so specially pleased with the men that I met, that I have said to Mrs. Mahan if we were not already compromised to our house in New York I should want to settle in Boston at once. I have always had a hankering that way, but my lines seem cast in New York.

Will you be good enough to make my compliments to Mrs. Brown, and say to her what a pleasant remembrance of her hospitality I have carried away with me. I own, too, there is to me, in our country, something as refreshing as it is unusual to find a man living where his father did before him. I myself can never do so, but I envy the restful feeling I should think would accompany it.

I hope now to settle down to *Nelson*.

[P.S.]   I found my bag at Park Sq. without any trouble.

To Robert U. Johnson

Slumberside, Quogue, Long Island, July 9, 1895 [NYPL]

Dear Mr. Johnson: Your letter of Saturday was recd., but has unfortunately been mislaid. Answering from memory I can say it will give me

---

1. Mahan gave three talks on the Gulf and Caribbean and one on strategy.
2. These duties, research and writing, were performed in his own home.
1. The University gave Mahan an honorary L.L.D. on June 26.

much pleasure to look over the papers you mention, viz: the *Huascar* fight and other occurrences in the Chili-Peru War,[1] and Adml. Ito's[2] paper if he wrote one. As regards the *correctness* of my account—as of the *Huascar*, I have not the data to pronounce, though I might detect improbabilities.

As regards the papers on Naval Battles, I see no reason to doubt that I can in the course of /96 give you a treatment of the Nile, Copenhagen and Trafalgar—possibly also St. Vincent.[3] It would have to be understood that I do not impair my right to use the *text* in my *Life of Nelson*, of which they will form a part. The illustrations would of course be your concern— though I presume they would be almost entirely copies of existing originals which my publishers could also take as far as needed—by their own employees.

I am averse to binding myself too far beforehand, though I recognize that you are entitled to a certainty at a fixed time. Will you let me know, at your leisure, when you want a definite promise from me to supply the articles.

To J. Franklin Jameson[1]

Slumberside, Quogue, Long Island, July 11, 1895 [LC]

Dear Sir: I have received your letter of July 8. I have not happened to see any account of the projected *Historical Review* and should be glad if you would send me one if you have such in print. As regards the review of Froude's book[2]—I have no very special knowledge of the period in question, and cannot tell beforehand how far his treatment would lend itself to my comment, professional or otherwise. I would suggest, therefore,

---

1. C. H. Wetmore, "Famous Sea-fight; The Engagement in 1879 off the Bolivian Coast between Peruvian and Chilean Ironclads," *Century Magazine* (April 1898).
2. Sukenori Ito, commander-in-chief of the Japanese fleet during the Sino-Japanese War, 1894–1895.
3. *See* Mahan to Johnson, May 14, 1895, Footnote 2.

1. Professor of history at Brown University, 1888–1901; head of the Department of History at the University of Chicago, 1901–1905; director of the Department of Historical Research, Carnegie Institution, 1905–1928. He was managing editor of the *American Historical Review*, 1895–1901, 1905–1908; Chairman of the Historical Manuscripts Commission, 1895–1899, 1905–1908, and President of the American Historical Association, 1906–1907.
2. James Anthony Froude, *English Seamen in the Sixteenth Century. Lectures Delivered at Oxford, Easter Terms, 1893–1894.* New York: Charles Scribner's Sons, 1895.

that you should send me the book, with your proposed rates of payment. I will read it at once, and reply yes or no—returning the book, if the latter. My writing is a factor in my income, which I am not rich enough to disregard at a time that I am very occupied. Please address me Quogue, L.I.

To Robert U. Johnson

Slumberside, Quogue, Long Island, July 15, 1895 [NYPL]

CONFIDENTIAL

Dear Mr. Johnson: I return you the *Huascar* article, which I have read twice.

As a description of a naval battle for naval men, I should call it nearly valueless. As a picture of the scenes on board—an inside view, so to say—it may be accurate, and is certainly ghastly.

I have no authorities at hand to which to refer, and have had to depend wholly on my memory for such conjectural corrections as I have noted in the margin. I have seen all the iron-clads engaged—but over ten years ago— I think the writer has fallen into several errors. The Peruvian *Independencia* was not, I think, an iron clad, (p.3), but an old time wooden steam-frigate. I never saw her and may be mistaken.

The *Huascar* description tallies fairly well with my recollections of her, some time after the fight, when the Chilians had repaired her. The two Chilian iron-clads were not, according to my memory, "barbette" ships— i.e. the guns firing over the armored bulwark, or turret—but "casemate," the guns being in an enclosed armored space and firing through ports.

The term "rapid-fire" is inaccurately used. The rapid-fire gun of today scarcely existed then. Premising that naval terminology is at present in a fluctuating state, I understand a Rapid-fire gun to be one in which the powder and projectile form a single package, inserted one at a time by a single movement. They differ from the machine gun, in which a number of charges, in a receptacle or "magazine," are placed in connection with the gun chamber and fed into it *automatically*. Both classes of gun fire rapidly, but the machine gun as yet is very small. It is the increased weight, and consequent penetration, of the rapid fire gun, of very late years, that has given it its great significance in battle.

I am very doubtful of the writer's claim that the story of this battle is yet to be told. My impression is that it was told with great particularity in a publication by our Navy Department, which I read. We had then upon that coast a singularly capable admiral, with intelligent, active-minded, aides.

[423]

Lieut-Commander T. B. M. Mason,[1] and Lieut-Commander Duncan Kennedy were out there, and I am quite sure both visited the ships after the action, and furnished detailed descriptions of the results. Mason is now on the retired list, and I doubt if the article ought to be referred to him, but Kennedy is at the Torpedo Station, Newport, R.I. You might refer the article to him with my annotation, not giving my name. His knowledge being more first hand, his recollection is more likely to be exact, and besides he is younger.

I have of course not undertaken to correct the crudities of style, or of spelling. I should scarcely think the writer a naval man; also, if in Callao, as he says, (p. 2.), how could he see the *Huascar* after the fight, if she was towed to Valparaiso, as he also says, (p. 23.). Of course he may have seen her in Callao, after being repaired, as I myself did.

As regards my undertaking the naval battles, you shall have my definite reply in a fortnight from today. There is little doubt it will be yes.

To John M. Brown

Slumberside, Quogue, Long Island, July 18, 1895 [LC]

My dear Mr. Brown: I spoke or wrote to you some time ago, of my idea of publishing some parts of my *Life of Nelson* in a magazine. Since then I have recd. a proposition from the *Century* to contribute to it some articles on great naval battles. They have in contemplation a series of these in 1896. Before giving my final reply which I must do in ten days or so, I would be glad to hear from you any suggestions you would like to make to me. It is understood that I retain the right to use the text for the *Life*. I hope, though I am not sure, that I may have it ready for the market of Christmas/96, in which case the articles may help advertise it.

The *Century*'s letter says also "We should be glad to make favorable arrangements, as we usually do, with your book publishers to reproduce our illustrations by selling them plates of the cuts, if they so desire."

On the matter of illustrations my own feeling is rather averse to a copious use of them. I feel that, if the text be really first-rate, to break it up by a multitude of pictures is an injury to the work. I want, in short, the attention of my reader, which I dont think can be had under the magazine illustrated system now in vogue. The necessary maps and plans, and a few excellent full page illustrations from standard paintings, if such can be had—that is my idea. Of course there is a business side which you will understand better than I, & about which we will exchange views.

---

1. Theodorus Bailey Myer Mason, class of 1868, whose explicit accounts of the *Huascar* are in the National Archives, Record Group 74, along with those of C. R. P. Rodgers.

On second thoughts I inclose the page of the *Century*'s letter which refers to the conditions. They will want to advertise during the fall what they are to give during the year. Please return the letter.

To Henry C. Taylor

Slumberside, Quogue, Long Island, July 19, 1895 [NWC]

My dear Taylor: According to your request I have looked over the question of the comparative advantages of Eggemoggin Reach and Nantucket Sound, as the base of operations for the U.S. Fleet, under the conditions of the problem propounded this year by the College. I will consider the two places under the three heads, suggested by me in my lectures, into which the strategic advantages of a given point may be analyzed.

I. Position.

There are two possible *local* bases of operations, suggested by the problem for the enemy, viz: Provincetown and Casco Bay. The enemy's line of communication from Halifax, his *home* base, to either point, would pass near Cape Sable. Drawing lines from there to Casco Bay and Provincetown, respectively, it will be observed that not only is Eggemoggin Reach nearer than Nantucket Sound to the Cape, and to the line thence to Casco Bay throughout, but that also it is nearer to the line between Cape Sable and Provincetown during the greater part of its length. In the same way the Reach is nearer to all points of the British Canadian Possessions, upon which our fleet, if escaping to sea, might attempt operations. Confining my views to the scene indicated by the problem, I should say the Reach had the advantage of position.

II. Strength.

A. Defensive Strength. I should think that greater immunity from attack could safely be claimed for Eggemoggin Reach. The off-lying dangers in either case are considerable. Penobscot Bay is easier pilot ground, from its numerous landmarks; it has probably little change of conditions from year to year, and accurate surveys are in an enemy's hands; therefore, its natural defenses are less than those of Nantucket, with its shifting sands. But the narrowness of the entrance at either end permits an easy and efficient lookout against torpedo attacks and the soundings allow torpedo defenses against attack by heavy vessels, the lines for them being rather shorter than those which I apprehend would have to be laid down at Nantucket. It is, however, openness to attacks by torpedo vessels that constitutes the great defensive weakness of Nantucket Sound. This should be carefully looked into, because the numerous shoals on the chart impose upon the eye. One forgets that they can in moderate weather be traversed in many directions by torpedo craft, and that the fleet lying there would need elaborate preparations, and the utmost watchfulness, to avoid disaster—the more so as the offensive strength of the anchorage would cause great disquiet to the enemy. The latter if capable, will attack, and constantly. As Nelson said under like circumstances, in 1798 "I will fight them the moment I can reach their fleet, at anchor or under sail."

B. Offensive Strength. The menace to the enemy of a fleet stationed in Nantucket Sound may be stated thus. From the exit at Pollock Rip to that by Vineyard Sound, going round, is about 100 miles; roughly, the same as from Sandy Hook to Montauk, though rather less than that from the Hook to Plum Gut. But the offensive advantage of the Sound over New York lies in this: that between the extreme approaches there are several intermediate passages, and at such distances that it would be impossible, with the relative forces allowed, to guard all by detachments either large enough to fight our fleet, or in supporting distance of each other. E.G. From Pollock Rip to the exit by channel passing just East of Nantucket Id. is 44 miles; while from the latter to Vineyard Sound is 45 to 50 miles. Then there is the Muskegat Exit, 27 miles from Vineyard Sound, besides several to the eastward from Great Round Shoal Lt. (N.B. No U.S. Battle ship ought to draw over 24 feet). I think, by the way, we may assume that pilots for this ground would be better able to guide heavy draught ships than those of the Maine coast.

In short, our fleet, safe in Nantucket Sound, throws the enemy on the defensive for every exposed point he has—and they are many—and compels him to observe it with the largest force he can spare. To calculate this force—he must at the Eastern and Western entrances—that is, within controlling distance of them—station a division slightly superior to our force; and he must also provide a lookout, day and night, over our movements at all practicable exits. All these lookouts would be small detachments, more or less exposed, which it would be our business to cut off in detail, when possible, and at all times to keep as far out of range as possible.

I will not enter into the possibilities open to our fleet after it got out. From the coal mines of Nova Scotia to the West Indies, every unfortified place—and some fortified—would be open to attack; while our land forces presumably are finding full occupation in Canada for all the army the supposed enemy can raise.

Our fleet in Nantucket Sound would realize the effect of the position for the French fleet in Corfu, which I suggested in my lectures; and it may be interesting here to say that, since my return here, I find Nelson expressing his purpose to remain before whatever port they might enter, should they escape his pursuit. Our fleet in Nantucket *fixes* there hostile force more than double our own—leaving only the remainder of the whole available for their offensive operations.

Eggemoggin Reach has indeed several exits, but the extremes are distant from each other only 35 or 40 miles. I think two divisions, each, as before, slightly superior to our own, could be so stationed as to make escape, without a battle, almost impossible. One division I would place south of Vinal Haven Id., the other south of Long Id.; but even if the former be placed outside Matinicus R[ock] escape would for us be difficult. In case of a battle, even if the result were favorable to us, the other division would come upon us, crippled, before we could escape.

III. Resources.

In themselves, neither the Reach nor the Sound offers many resources; but the greater nearness of the Sound to the chief centres of the country give it evidently a great advantage. In order, however, to make these reasonably assured, our scheme of operations must contemplate extensive army support. Both Nantucket and Martha's Vineyard, probably also Monomoy, must be held in force against an enemy's landing, and possibly establishing great guns, very few of which would immensely slacken our grip. The rail-road and other communications with the Cape Cod shore of the Sound should be carefully studied, so as to decide to what points supplies can most easily and plentifully be brought, most safely stored, and most readily transferred to the ships and the two islands. The whole Sound should be regarded as a fortress, cut off from supplies by sea, and for those by land dependent upon a somewhat difficult and exposed route. Wharfage and lighterage on the Sound shores would have to be created. The question of the Elizabeth Islands might also have to be considered. Narrow and thrust out as they are, they cannot be held by troops, as the enemy's heavy ships would—unless they are heavily fortified, and supported by works on Martha's Vineyard shore—be able to range as far as Wood's Hole. Yet, in foggy weather, or in dark nights, a valuable occasional line of communication with Providence and New York might be maintained by the light draught steamers with which our coast abounds, handled by determined men of local experience. It would be simply running a blockade.

To sum up: As regards position, and having reference to the problem only, I think, upon the whole, Eggemoggin Reach has the advantage; but I do not think the difference great enough to be at all decisive of the question at issue.

As regards defensive strength the advantage is decidedly with Eggemoggin. For offensive strength it is still more decidedly with Nantucket, and as offensive is a weightier consideration than defensive, I should, on the score of strength, decisively give my vote for the Sound.

For Resources the advantage is with the Sound.

Striking a balance I believe the Sound to be distinctly the better; but, as I have said, to make it available, the entire ground bounded by the blue rectangle on the coast chart should be thoroughly studied. An enemy that has command of the water might much harass the railroads on Cape Cod by sudden dashes.

The great danger, however, the defensive weakness is from torpedo boat attack. All possible positions for our fleet, the defense thereof, and the lookout service, should be carefully studied. This, to my mind, is the crucial naval problem involved.

In conclusion I may add:

1. The possibilities opened by such an offensive position as Nantucket Sound, even to a force so inferior as that allotted to us—*taken in connection with our probable superiority on land*—affords a strategic study of the most interesting character.

2. As we can never in our generation expect to equal the great European navies, would not a good standard measure for our necessary force be the following: That it should be such that, occupying a position with two exits like New York, Nantucket Sound, or Eggemoggin Reach, the most powerful enemy could not spare a force large enough to keep before each exit a division larger than our fleet massed inside? In other words, our fleet should be more than half as strong as any force that could be sent against us. This strength to be independent of Coast Defense ships and vessels useful only for peace cruising.

3. While the position of Nantucket Sound, regarded only in comparison with Eggemoggin Reach, may be considered inferior—it is arguable that the combination of two positions like New York and Nantucket, possessing their other advantages and each having two exits far remote from one another by the exterior line, is extraordinary, if not unequalled. I know none such. A fleet retreating upon the line (New York or Nantucket) could with difficulty be headed off from both—at the least its chances would be exceptionally good. Perhaps this consideration which enters into both position and strength, would still here decide the issue in Nantucket's favor.

To J. Franklin Jameson

Slumberside, Quogue, Long Island, July 22, 1895 [LC]

My dear Sir: I return Froude's *Seamen* by this mail.[1] I have read the book attentively, and do not find that it is one I could very well review. The

---

1. *See* Mahan to Jameson, July 11, 1895.

treatment is not specially technical, and it seems rather a re-airing of Froude's special hobbies. I instinctively distrust his accuracy, yet have not the special knowledge of the subject that enables me to comment safely.

To J. Franklin Jameson

Slumberside, Quogue, Long Island, July 26, 1895 [LC]

My dear Sir: I today received your letter of the 24th and regret that it will not be in my power to undertake at present any such paper as you suggest. Independent of my regular duties, I have an unfulfilled promise to contribute a professional paper which can no longer be postponed. I can understand your dilemma, being unexpectedly left in the lurch by a contributor upon whom you depended, but though I am sorry I cannot help you.

To Robert U. Johnson

Slumberside, Quogue, Long Island, July 27, 1895 [NYPL]

Dear Mr. Johnson: I have heard from my publishers, and, as I expected, they have nothing to urge against my publishing the accounts of the naval battles.[1] Before absolutely concluding our agreement, however, I think it would be well to have an understanding as to the length of the articles, the room, that is, that you would be willing to allow for them, the time of appearance of the first, and the intervals at which the others should appear. With reference to the last, I may say that my expectation is to have the book[2] out in time for the Christmas season of 1896. I should like also to know somewhat definitely at what rate you would be prepared to pay me for them. I am well aware of the liberality of the *Century* but I think it is always better, when possible, to have agreements understood before hand.

I have mentioned the question of the illustrations to the publishers; and I think you will hear from them in due time. I shall have some suggestions to offer as to places, or rather persons, to whom you might with advantage apply in England, for portraits and other illustrative matter, if you care for such.

---

1. *See* Mahan to Johnson, May 14, 1895.
2. *Life of Nelson.*

[429]

To Robert U. Johnson

Dear Mr. Johnson: Your letter was received on Saturday evening last. I am satisfied with the terms of payment which you propose. In estimating the value of an article, I have of course to take into consideration the amount of labor which it causes me, and those which I am to write for the *Century* in this instance are not of the kind which give me the most trouble.

I am a little perplexed about the time at which you require the first copy, namely, October 1, for the January number. Familiar though the subjects for the most part are to me, there is a certain amount of anecdote and detail which I want to hunt up, and moreover I like to polish my articles as much as possible. Were I at present disengaged from other matters, I should of course have ample time; but it unfortunately so happens that I am involved in engagements that occupy my time quite fully up to the 20th of September. Can you not therefore, give a somewhat later date than October 1 for the copy? I do not say that I cannot get it in by October 1, but I am chary of making promises when I feel doubtful. At any rate, name the latest date you can for me.

I intend to begin with the battle of Cape St. Vincent, and upon the whole think it best to follow the chronological order—the Nile, Copenhagen, Trafalgar. Can you ascertain for me whether there is accessible in any of the New York libraries, Drinkwater's *Battle of Cape St. Vincent?* a contemporary account by an eye witness.[1] I don't think it is in the Astor. I wrote some days ago to England for a copy, but may slip up on it. As regards plans of the battles, my own opinion at present is that my own plans in my books are best suited to convey, to the unprofessional reader, the general idea which alone he can receive. To enter into too much detail merely produces confusion; but the essential underlying idea, or principle, upon which the battle was fought and decided is usually simple and can be grasped.

As regards the illustrations I have to suggest, I have not today time to particularize. Most of those to which I should refer are in England, and in the hands of parties whom, though I have met, I could not presume to send you to in my name. If, therefore, you think it would be an advantage to mention my name, (as in England it not improbably would, though it would not in this country) I should prefer to write a letter beforehand to them. My idea is, subject entirely to your own opinion, to present with each battle a portrait of Nelson as nearly as possible contemporary with it. There are other illustrations I will name.

---

1. John Drinkwater, afterwards Bethune, *A Narrative of the Battle of St. Vincent with Anecdotes of Nelson, Before and After the Battle.* 2d ed. London: 1840.

To Robert U. Johnson

Slumberside, Quogue, Long Island, August 8, 1895 [NYPL]

My dear Mr. Johnson: As your letter asking me if I could furnish the article on Trafalgar shortly to you, was crossed by mine of Tuesday, you will be prepared to learn that it would be quite impossible for me to do as you suggest. Even if I had all the material better in hand than I at this moment have, the press of immediate work would forbid it. I am very sorry, but it is quite impracticable.

To Hilary A. Herbert

Slumberside, Quogue, Long Island, August 10, 1895 [NA]

Sir: I forward to the Department today by registered mail one copy of the Fleet Drill Book, issue of 1891. This book could not be found at the time the *Chicago* went out of commission in May last. By the inquiries I made, I learned from Ensign R. L. Russell[1] that the book had been inadvertently taken by him to the *San Francisco*, when he left the *Chicago* for that ship. The book has been returned to me by Mr. Russell, through an officer of the *Columbia*; and I have now the honor to send it to the Department.

To Francis M. Ramsay

Slumberside, Quogue, Long Island, September 2, 1895 [NA]

The Bureau is informed that I have this day received the Department's order of August 31, 1895, to report at the Navy Yard N.Y. on Sept. 4th, as member of a General Court Martial.[1]

---

1. Robert Lee Russell, class of 1885.

1. Captain George W. Sumner, class of 1862, was accused of culpable inefficiency in performance of duty, hazarding a ship of the Navy, and neglect of duty, in failing to make proper preparation for dry-docking the *Columbia* at Southampton, England, where she was strained by improper placement of the keel blocks.

To Francis M. Ramsay

Navy Yard, New York, September 10, 1895 [NA]

The Bureau is informed that I have received this day the Department's order of September 7th, 1895, to proceed to Newport, R. I. and report to Commdr. Naval Station for lecturing at War College.[1]

To Robert U. Johnson

Slumberside, Quogue, Long Island, October 9, 1895 [NYPL]

Dear Sir: I enclose the manuscript of the Battle of Cape St. Vincent.[1] I have noted, in pencil, on margin, the approximate places where in my judgment certain illustrations would fit; but these marginal notes are merely *suggestions*, at *your* discretion. In the text I have entered, in ink, bracketed reference to Figures 1, 2, 3. These should stand, in the text, as essential.

I forwarded yesterday corrected proofs of Figs. 1, 2, 3, to Mr. W. L. Fraser[2]—and sent a letter concerning the illustrations for this article—also merely suggestions.

If possible, I would like an acknowledgment by postal—although I keep the rough draft as a duplicate till the article is in print.

To Robert U. Johnson

Slumberside, Quogue, Long Island, October 10, 1895 [NYPL]

Dear Mr. Johnson: In forward[ing] the manuscript of St. Vincent yesterday, I forgot to ask if a *duplicate* galley proof could be sent—one copy of which I could retain. It will be convenient to [have] in the preparation of the *Life of Nelson*, though the text in both must differ considerably. There will be more battle in one, and more Nelson in the other, but the study of the former will be most useful in the latter.

---

1. He remained in Newport until September 14. *See* Mahan to Johnson, June 11, 1895, Footnote 1.

1. "Nelson at Cape St. Vincent," *Century Magazine* (February 1896).
2. An employee in the art department of *Century Magazine*.

To J. Franklin Jameson

Slumberside, Quogue, Long Island, October 14, 1895 [LC]

Dear Sir: Your letter of the 11th has been received. The work on which I am now engaged, the *Life of Nelson*, being biographical in character, does not lend itself to such extracts as you wish, except the battles, which I have engaged to supply the *Century*. They are (two are) more "popular" than you wish. For the rest, I have met so many hindrances in the *Nelson*, owing to impendent promises, that I am unwilling to enter into any engagements until it is well forward. Thanking you for your favor I remain [etc.].

To G. W. Stadly & Co.

Slumberside, Quogue, Long Island, October 14, 1895 [UML]

Gentlemen: Your letter of the 12th is today recd. I have not answered the former, being unwilling to pledge myself to time, which I can ill spare, or to accuracy which in a naval battle is practically unattainable. The most that can be insured is a correct impression of the general, and decisive features; but, devoid of the natural, topographical, details that remain permanent, and can be described, on shore, the shifting scenes of a naval action leave no adequate trace of their passage. Neither my past nor my present purposes require me to follow the movements of the units of the fleet, & I have presented diagrams only, which convey indeed how the battle was won to an intelligent student, but no more.

If that will satisfy you, and your expected public, I will be willing to examine your plates when ready, and if it do not involve too much labor to determine their accuracy will consent to appear as an editor. Further than this I cannot now go—nor can the matter of two battles be of great importance to your prospectus.[1]

To Robert U. Johnson

Slumberside, Quogue, Long Island, October 23, 1895 [NYPL]

Dear Mr. Johnson: The first two diagrams of Battle of Cape St. Vincent being taken, with very slight change, from my book *Influence of Sea Power*

---

1. Stadly & Co., a Boston firm, noted on the letter, "Capt. A. T. Mahan—Napoleon Atlas." There is no evidence that Mahan subsequently served as an editor of the Stadly project.

upon the French Revolution and Empire, would it be possible to attribute them to it thus: (From Mahan's *Influence of Sea Power upon the French Revolution and Empire*). It would help the book.

I have completed the Battle of the Nile article[1]—which I understand you want in hand Dec. 1, for the March number of the *Century*. I shall retain it for a while for *possible* corrections, though it is now ready for press. It is 10,000 words.

I enclose a memorandum of the only illustrations for it that occur to me. I think that some additional illustrations, dramatic in effect, would be desirable; but that I must leave to the management of the Magazine.

I do not know what development, beyond my own articles, you have given to Miss Seawell's suggestion.[2] It has occurred to me as possible—for myself—to write some others than those now in hand, with a view to collecting them ultimately into a book; to which I could contribute also a Preface as to the necessity of contemplating battles, not as isolated incidents, but as resulting from certain causes and conducing to certain results. These antecedents and consequents redeem them from the appearance of aimless bloodshed, and give a certain philosophy to the record. I had begun such a preamble, of general application, to the Battle of St. Vincent; but cut it off as unduly increasing the length of the article. If you have time to read that and the Nile you will observe that I do so treat them.

This suggestion is now only tentative—for it will be some time before I can act upon it, but you might consider it. I may mention the Athenian expedition against Syracuse as an instance.

I should say that while these studies (articles) will greatly help my *Life of Nelson*, I do not think (as I did) that they will pass into it nearly verbatim. They are more battle and less Nelson—therefore could be adapted to an independent work.

To Hilary A. Herbert

Slumberside, Quogue, Long Island, October 28, 1895 [NA]

Sir: I respectfully request the Department's permission to change my residence to New York City, where my address will be 10 East 10th Street.[1]

---

1. "Nelson at the Battle of the Nile," *Century Magazine* (January 1897).
2. *See* Mahan to Johnson, March 6, 1896.
1. An apartment hotel. *See* Mahan to Herbert, November 18, 1895.

[Memorandum]

Slumberside, Quogue, Long Island, October 31, 1895 [LC]

In this I have placed all the letters in my case,[1] except the copy of Kirkland's first to Dept. (which the latter sent back) and which I cant now (Oct. 31/95) find.[2]

To Hilary A. Herbert

New York, November 18, 1895 [NA]

Sir: I respectfully report that I have changed my residence in New York City to 489 West End Avenue.[1]

To James R. Thursfield

489 West End Avenue, New York, November 21, 1895 [LC]

My dear Mr. Thursfield: Your letter of the 7th was received two days ago. I am somewhat at a loss for the material which you ask for, because I doubt whether very much of a systematic character has really been done.[1] Our navy being so small, and still but partially developed, it is in practice very difficult to keep the few ships of our home squadron together long enough for maneuvers. Just as we expect them to begin, a bobbery starts up in Central or South America, or Haiti, or elsewhere, and away go one or two ships. They would not be missed from your Channel Fleet, but they radically affect our hopes. I know this has been the case some summers, and I think it was so in the past.[2] I will however see what I can get.

---

1. Concerning Henry Erben's critical fitness report.
2. On February 28, 1895, Rear Admiral William Kirkland wrote the Department disclosing that Erben had left him a memorandum containing a set of accusations against Mahan. These he refuted, and praised Mahan highly for his personal and professional conduct. The Department in return instructed him to confine his comments to the usual record report.

1. Loaned to the Mahans by the architect who was building their new townhouse at 160 West 86th Street. The family moved into the 86th Street property during the second week in February 1896.

1. *See* Mahan to Thursfield, December 2, 1895.
2. In July, seamen and Marines were twice landed in Bluefields, Nicaragua, from the USS *Columbia* and the USS *Marblehead* to protect American lives and property during a period of unrest in the area.

Nelson gets on much less rapidly than I could wish. I have much trouble to keep my hands clear for dealing with it, and I find biography, according to my aims and aspirations, far harder work than philosophizing over history.

Please make my regards to Mrs. Thursfield who I hope has not quite forgotten me.

To Augustus T. Gillender

489 West End Avenue, New York, November 23, 1895 [HUL]

Dear Mr. Gillender: I thank you for your letter of yesterday with particulars about the policies, and I will attend to the getting of the necessary consent—that is informally. When obtained, I suppose you will have to get it put in formal shape for us.

Dennis[1] sent me the enclosed letter (copy) yesterday.[2] He wants to know if I will consent to sell, provided we can get $100,000 for the property.[3] My own idea has been simply to hold on, on the general principle that we are more likely to do well later—and I dont now feel pressed; but I suppose as he wants to be doing something I should do no harm to say I will consent to sell at the figure. If he gets a less offer, but good, then I can consult you again upon it, as something definite.

Will you let me hear your opinion.

[P.S.]   Please return enclosure.

To Hilary A. Herbert

489 West End Avenue, New York, November 23, 1895 [NA]

Dear Mr. Herbert: I have received a letter from a Mr. Thursfield, one of the principal writers upon naval matters for the London *Times*. He wishes to have such information as I can obtain for him on the subject of

1. Dennis Hart Mahan, Jr.
2. Enclosure not found.
3. Property near Tenafly, New Jersey, left Alfred, Dennis, and Frederick Mahan by Jane Leigh Okill Swift. It fronted on the Hudson River at the Palisades.

our naval manoeuvres, for an article in Brassey's next *Naval Annual*. I have concluded that it would be most fitting to refer first to you, whether you would approve, and if so, as to what sources I should go to for information—whether, e.g., to the admiral commanding the North Atlantic Squadron, or to the Intelligence Office. I met Mr. Thursfield more than once in England, and am sure he is a gentleman well fitted to deal properly with material given him. He accompanies a British Squadron, I believe, every summer on manoeuvres.

My own impression has been that the frequency of interruptions, from calls elsewhere, especially to our revolutionary neighbors to the southward, had prevented any very instructive development to our manoeuvres; but I may here be under a misapprehension.

To Robert U. Johnson

489 West End Avenue, New York, November 30, 1895 [NYPL]

Dear Mr. Johnson: I enclose herewith manuscript of the Battle of the Nile. As a good deal of my correcting has been done in lead pencil it may need more careful handling by printer.

Mr. Fraser has had from me suggestions for illustrations. I have noted on margin places where I thought these would suit; but as I have said before these are merely suggestions, not even wishes.

Has the *Century* any relations direct or indirect with Copenhagen by which I might perhaps get some data concerning that battle from Danish standpoint?

To James R. Thursfield

489 West End Avenue, New York, December 2, 1895 [LC]

Dear Mr. Thursfield: I thought it better to go at once to headquarters for information about the operation of our home squadron during the past summer, so I wrote to the Secretary of the Navy. In reply he tells me, as I had thought, that nothing had been attempted beyond certain tactical exercises of a purely evolutionary character, such as are common to all navies.

I am sorry we have nothing more to show you, but with a small navy and such uneasy neighbors it is difficult to keep squadrons together.

To Robert U. Johnson

489 West End Avenue, New York, December 7, 1895 [NYPL]

Dear Mr. Johnson: I have practically entirely recast the first two pages,[1] and shortened to an extent which I hope may meet your wishes; and I have besides omitted even a single mention of the obnoxious name Bonaparte.

I hope that, if occasion ever arises again, you will give me a little more time, for this has occasioned me a good deal of trouble, glad as I am to meet your views in your difficult duties.

To Frederick A. Mahan

489 West End Avenue, New York, December 15, 1895 [NWC]

My dear Fred: I went to see Gillender this week, partly because Dennis wished me to, partly because I wanted myself to find out how things stood as far as G. knows. I learn from him that Dennis has had all but—about —six hundred dollars of Aunty's[1] legacy to him. The precise state of Dennis' affairs I dont understand.

2) G. thinks it would be wisest to divide the Palisade property as soon as possible. He says that Dennis (1) if he must raise money, can do so more advantageously on his third after division, than upon his third part in the joint property. Further, he says, as I think truly, (2) that Dennis, wanting money and being what he is, may, or rather might, go raising money outside on his undivided third, which in the hands of some creditors might much embarrass us as part owners.

3) I think Dennis is already inclined to a division. I am going to write him, and when I do shall state (1) (above) as a reason important to him to weigh. (2) of course I shall not mention. Let that be between *us*.

4) Now, assuming division made, there are certain considerations for you and me to weigh. *First*, Dennis is our brother, and though he can act independent of us, and may very probably act with folly, we cant ignore the duties of blood. We must try, as quietly and unobtrusively as we can, to keep him safe in his business matters, for the sake of himself and his family. *Second*, There are strong reasons of policy to compel us to the same course.

5) Dennis' pay and family conditions—invalid wife and female child— we know. His prospects of increased pay by promotion are slim and dis-

---

1. Of the manuscript of "Nelson at the Battle of the Nile," published in *Century Magazine*, in January 1897.

1. Jane Leigh Okill Swift. *See* Mahan to Gillender, November 23, 1895.

tant. The only increase of income possible and the only provision for wife & child in case he dies, is the Palisade property. If he could at *once* get $25,000 for it, I should hope that even he might exert control enough to live on the interest. What I fear greatly is that, current income not meeting expenses, he may raise a little today, and a little next year, using the loans up in current expenses until the whole disappears.

6) There is, I fear, little chance of getting even $20,000 now, and what I also fear, and gather from his letters is that he has some thousands—say $3,000—indebtedness now, the interest on which would still more embarrass his small income. I may be mistaken in this, but I must reason in the belief.

7) It occurred to me therefore, as a possible solution of the present difficulty that if his present debt—to an extent not exceeding $3,000—could be placed on his share of the land, when divided, you and I might assume the interest of that sum for a period, say, of five years, upon the condition that no more money should be borrowed upon it (or by him) without our knowledge and consent. This would clear him of debt, and although we *might* not be able to make the condition legally binding, we should be giving him freedom from debt, *and* an annual payment of interest of near $200, which we could discontinue if the conditions were broken.

8) This might tend to relieve his present embarrassment, and keep him within bounds until the property might be sold to advantage.

9) As a matter of mere policy, we must remember that if he dies we must support his wife and child—for there is for them no possible provision except this land and our pockets. The same catastrophe, only worse, might ensue, if worry got him back drinking and drunkenness got him out of the navy. The Navy today is keen to make vacancies, and he has had one or two narrow shaves already.[2] Worry might readily upset again a temperament of so little stability.

10) If you will turn this over, and write me what you think, we may get matters en train by the time you come north. If you will, write your reply with reference to Gillender seeing it; for what we do must have all legal sanction & binding force it can.

As I think we had best keep this quiet to ourselves, I send no message to May,[3] but if you think best to consult her give her my love.

[P.S.] I shall of course say nothing to Dennis about all this, except to recommend immediate division.

---

2. Dennis's career did not reflect his brother's apprehensions. Like everyone else in his class, he was caught in the "Hump," but was commissioned Commander in 1901 and retired as a Commodore in 1909. He returned to active duty during World War I.
3. Probably a reference to Mary Morris Mahan, Frederick's wife.

To Augustus T. Gillender

489 West End Avenue, New York, December 26, 1895 [HUL]

Dear Mr. Gillender: I enclose a letter of mine to Fred[1] and his reply, concerning which I intend coming to see you shortly. I cannot fix a day, owing to the *Defender* Committee business.[2] You will observe that Fred has numbered my letter in heads, to which he replies seriatim.

Both Dennis & Fred have expressed their consent, and wish, to proceed as soon as possible to a division of the property.[3]

Jennie[4] and Dennis have both agreed to release the insurance—i.e. to transfer the $2000 policy in Mrs. A. T. Mahan's favor. Dennis's I enclose that you may see if it be sufficient. Jennie's is simply expressed currently in a letter. Perhaps, when you write her, you might enclose for her signature just what you want. To Fred I wrote later and have not yet his reply.

Jennie says in her letter, "Will you please impress on Mr. Gillender that I would like all the business papers, which I shall have to sign in regard to your policy, and also the setting up of Aunty's[5] estate, sent to me *before I leave Paris, January 15.* As after that time we will be moving about a good deal, it will not be so convenient to find a Consul to swear before as here."

Please keep my letter enclosed carefully as Fred wants it returned.

[P.S.]   We must try and keep peace between Fred and Dennis. The latter is trying at times & Fred's patience is small.

To John M. Brown

489 West End Avenue, New York, December 26, 1895 [LC]

Dear Mr. Brown: I have before me a book, published in 1843 by C. C. Little and James Brown, entitled *Nelsonian Reminiscences.* They are the reproduction of articles published in the *Metropolitan* magazine 1837–40, or about forty years after the occurrences they narrate. The author was a Lieut. G. S. Parsons, R.N.

There are in it some few matters that might be useful could I depend upon them. My opinion is that they are actual recollections, told in good faith, by an eye witness, but marred by the errors of memory that creep in after a long time.

1. *See* Mahan to F. A. Mahan, December 15, 1895. Reply not found.
2. *See* Mahan to Luce, December 5, 1896, Footnote 2.
3. *See* Mahan to Gillender, November 23, 1895, and March 1, 1896.
4. Jane Leigh Mahan.
5. Jane Leigh Okill Swift.

Have you any knowledge of the author from the files of your house; and was the *Metropolitan* an American magazine?[1]

There are trival verifiable incidents mentioned, and mangled—but the man *was* promoted just at the date that he says [he] was "by the influence of Lady Hamilton on Lord Nelson."

To James R. Thursfield

489 West End Avenue, New York, January 10, 1896 [LC]

My dear Mr. Thursfield: I shall always be glad to hear from you, but your last letter was particularly welcome, for my literary chariot wheels have been dragging so heavily lately that I had begun to think my right hand had lost its cunning. I was very glad to hear that you had not thought so of what you have seen. I have in the aggregate written a great deal, for me, since my return, but it has for the most part been fragmentary, and the *Life of Nelson*, which has the nearest pull upon me has had to wait. I find that difficulty greater than I had thought—writing biography, I mean—the due presentation of the "milieu" as well as of the man, yet preserving their due relation, so that the importance of the events may not obscure the personality of the man; the handling of an immense amount of detail, by the accumulation of which alone, (in my judgment), and by its proper sorting and adjustment, can a life-like portrait be presented—all this greatly taxes me, for my strength has been, as far as I can judge, rather in singling out the great outlines of events, and concentrating attention upon them, than in the management of details. However, perhaps the harder the work the better the result. I have been fortunate enough to see the notice of *Ironclads in Action*[1] in the *Times* of Dec. 17, and also a letter dealing with my article for the *R.U.S.I.*,[2] in that of the 24th, but unluckily did not see the number of Nov. 18 which I understood had an editorial on the latter.

As regards the other part of your letter, as an officer I of course express no opinion upon the justice of our cause or the course of our government.[3] In case of war it would remain to me only to do the duty for which I have been brought up. But as a matter of personal feeling and even more of personal conviction I am absolutely with you in the belief that no greater evil can possibly happen to either nation or to the world than such a war. My

---

1. *Metropolitan Magazine*, London, 1–58, 1831–1850. An American edition was published in New York, 1–13, 1836–1842.

1. Herbert Wrigley Wilson, *Ironclads in Action, 1855–1895* . . . with an Introduction by Capt. A. T. Mahan. London: S. Low, Marston and Company, 1896.
2. "Blockade in Relation to Naval Strategy," Royal United Service Institution *Journal* (November 1895). Published also in U.S. Naval Institute *Proceedings* (December 1895).
3. In the Venezuela crisis of 1895–1896.

[441]

own belief has long since passed—before I began to write my books—from faith in, and ambition for my country alone, to the same for the Anglo-Saxon race. The former first of course, but a sort of *primus inter pares* (not of course as a fact, but in my own interest). All my reading, both French and English, the only languages of which I am master, have left upon my mind a profound conviction of the reliability and integrity of your statesmen as a class. You have in your national career done things which cannot be justified, but one must be blind not to see that in the main, righteousness and good faith have been the leading motives. In the greatest career that has been open to you—in your Indian statesmen—this has been dazzlingly exemplified.

I have great hopes from the Commission.[4] It will of course have no binding force on you—nor necessarily even on us; but it is composed of men of high reputation here, and of a character that will guarantee the integrity of their work. If they can establish a certainty, I feel sure that neither people will sustain opposition to the result in face of facts. If the result be undermined, I shall fear.

There is one point of view from which I think Englishmen might view with satisfaction the general course of our government, and the underlying idea, however much they repel our stand in the particular incident. It indicates, as I believe and hope, the awakening of our countrymen to the fact that we must come out of an isolation, which a hundred years ago was wise and imperative, and take our share in the turmoil of the world. The arguments in favor of pursuing the former policy, now adduced, are substantially of a simply sordid character—our ease, our wealth, our safety. The leading N. Y. paper that represents this idea has even gone so far as to rejoice that you should do the "grabbing," because *we benefit* by it. "A British conquest is substantially an American conquest, *without the expense and worry.*" Can you imagine anything much more ignoble, or that it tends to carry tranquil, even-balanced minds, by revulsion, over to the war party? My own belief is that nations can no more justly consult their own ease and safety, by refusing to concern themselves about the outside world, than a good citizen can confine his interests to his own property. Whether the United States is right or wrong in the Venezuelan controversy, she is at least showing fidelity to an idea, which, in its inception and development, had a lofty aim;[5] and I trust that this regrettable difference will arouse our people to the knowledge that for valid action there is needed, not merely strength potential, or even actual, but strength *organized.*

[P.S.]   Kind remembrance to Mrs. Thursfield.

---

4. Appointed by Congress in December 1895 to study the disputed boundary between Venezuela and British Guiana and to recommend a location for it agreeable to Venezuela.

5. The Monroe Doctrine.

To Bouverie F. Clark

489 West End Avenue, New York, January 17, 1896 [LC]

My dear Clark: Your very kind letter and Christmas remembrance were received by me in due course, and right glad I was to hear from you and of you again, and to know that you are both well. Let me, in passing, say that the address you used, 160 W. 86th, was quite right. We have been kept out of our house by one of those experiences common to all who expect to have goods delivered on time. The house has not been finished, and very uncomfortable have we been in consequence—but there is good hope we shall be in by the middle of next month. Our winter, which was singularly mild up to New Year, has had a zero turn, occasioning the usual amount of inconvenience. This house, very much exposed and flimsily built, has suffered particularly—water pipes freezing & bursting etc. I have been rather envying you the Devonshire climate. I quite appreciate your uncertainties as to where to settle when your time at Devonshire is up, for we had a mild phase of the same, although New York was for us pretty clearly indicated. What I know of London I like exceedingly, and if I were entirely free from all predisposing causes (which no one is) would, I think, choose it in preference to any place I know for a steady residence; but it is very hard to choose when you are perfectly free to suit yourself, and a boon to have some decisive circumstance which impels, or compels, you to some particular choice. I notice our millionaires are as uneasy as a parched pea—they can do anything they want & they dont know what they want. I fancy that officers of all governments find as you find that if [a] naval officer makes a miss he hears from it—P.D.Q. but if the upper fellows do the same there is no one to set them straight, and particularly a Board. I am awfully sorry for this trouble that has sprung up between our two countries,[1] and the more so because it seems to me that, while it will be hard to straighten out the particular incident, there is not probably at bottom any broad difference of principle. Your people, looking from *your* point of view, must try to make allowance for one fact. The United States started with the idea of having as few external entanglements as possible. That was all right fifty or a hundred years ago, but the time has come, in my opinion, when we should and must count for something in the affairs of the world at large—and naturally America is our sphere. Our people are waking up to this fact, & very likely in their efforts to find their place, may tread unduly on other peoples' toes. If they do, of course, they must take the consequences. It is only six months since our President resisted firmly—and in my opinion most properly—considerable popular clamor to interfere in

---

1. The boundary dispute between Venezuela and British Guiana. *See* Mahan to Thursfield, January 10, 1896.

[443]

your difficulty with Nicaragua.² I dont expect *you* to think him right now, but I think you might remember the other fact, and make allowance for a dictatorial, self-willed man, unused to diplomatic phrasing, expressing himself more strongly that he realized, or perhaps even now understands. Upon the right or wrong of the particular contention I express no opinion; but it seems to me clear that, although Great Britain is so great and long established a power here, it is impossible to say that her interests in the questions of this continent can possibly be as vital to her as ours to us. I am thankful at least for one thing—that we spat before the German Emperor & did not seem to jump on you when you had another affair on hand.³ I will not believe war possible—if it comes, and I am in it, I think I shall have to request the admiralty to hoist on your ships some other flag than the British—for, save our own, there is none other on which I should be so reluctant to fire. Kindest regards to Mrs. Clark.

To Clarence C. Buel¹

489 West End Avenue, New York, January 22, 1896 [NYPL]

Dear Mr. Buel: I have received your letter and the accompanying translation. The latter I have not yet had time to read, but, with what I have, shall doubtless be in possession of the essential facts from the Danish side.² Thanking you for the prompt attention you gave the matter.

To Augustus T. Gillender

489 West End Avenue, New York, February 4, 1896 [HUL]

My dear Mr. Gillender: I have yours of the 3d and will come down tomorrow risking the chance of seeing you. If you cant be in at about 2.30 to 3 please have an appointment for the earliest day you can. Personally, I am in no hurry, but I want to see Dennis fixed off as soon as possible. I believe it better for his interest to expedite matters, & therefore for ours also. I enclose a letter and chart from him, which explain themselves.¹

---

2. Anglo-Nicaraguan tension centering on Nicaraguan insistence that Britain's protectorate over the Mosquito Reserve area of eastern Nicaragua be ended.
3. Tension with Germany related to the Kruger Telegram crisis in South Africa in January 1896.

1. Editor of *Century Magazine*, and, with Robert Underwood Johnson, co-editor of *Battles and Leaders of the Civil War*.
2. *See* Mahan to Johnson, November 30, 1895.

1. Enclosure not found.

To Augustus Lowell

160 West 86th Street, New York, February 13, 1896 [HUL]

Dear Sir: Since our correspondence of last year,[1] I have completed a course of lectures for use before the Naval College at Newport—the general subject being Bonaparte's Italian campaign of 1796. They were delivered there last summer, and will be this, to very small audiences, among whom, however, were quite a number of Newport residents.

The subject cannot be called novel—you will know whether it has been treated before the Institute. From the expressions of satisfaction made to me, I am led to hope that the manner of presentation made more than usually clear the way in which campaigns were fought and won. It would be therefore upon my success as a teller, rather than upon any novelty, that their availability would depend.

In justice to other work I can make no new engagements. That which I had in hand a year ago has dragged far beyond my hopes. If you will kindly let me know if the general subject would be acceptable, or not, I will look up my manuscripts with a view to the special use, and give you an immediate reply.

To J. B. Sterling

160 West 86th Street, New York, February 13, 1896 [LC]

Dear Colonel Sterling: I was very much gratified to receive your letter of January 26. I hope I may in some degree deserve the credit for wisdom which you kindly give me, for I have just had to reply to the letters of two very wise and somewhat prominent men asking me to take part in a great meeting in Philadelphia to advocate the Establishment of a Permanent Tribunal of Arbitration between Great Britain and the U. S. I could reply at once, for my mind I believe is fixed. I said: "In my honor, reverence, and affection, Great Britain stands only second to my own country. As the head of the English-speaking race outside our borders, I feel for her what Mr. Balfour has not ineptly called race patriotism." But I continued—I no longer quote—questions such as should come before such a Tribunal would often involve national convictions of right and wrong. Such should be questions of conscience, and I do not believe in a nation, or an individual, entrusting its conscience with any other keeping than its own. Many cases,—perhaps most—of international dispute, involve interest only. These are often—

---

1. *See* Mahan to Lowell, April 1 and May 9, 1895.

not always—fit subjects for arbitration; our generation for instance must be wary how it sacrifices the interests of its successors.

I write you this because upon the whole I prefer that friends in England as well as here should know where I stand. Personally I think that while peace throughout the world is to be prayed for, I consider no greater misfortune could well happen than that civilized nations should abandon their preparations for war and take to arbitration. The outside barbarians are many. They will readily assimilate our material advance, but how long will it take them to reach the general spirit which it has taken Christianity two thousand years to put into us? What then will protect us?

But in all cases believe me I should deplore any serious difficulty between *us* two peoples. My personal opinions and affections are matters of no great moment, but I am unwilling to be misunderstood on this side or on yours, and when any one is good enough to write me as you have done I try to speak clearly.

[P.S.]   I read the letter you sent me in print[1]—as much as I could, but I think such blatherskite more humiliating to me as written by an American than it could be to you.

To Augustus Lowell

160 West 86th Street, New York, February 21, 1896 [HUL]

Dear Sir: I have carefully considered your letter of the 15th. My postion is this. I am engaged on a *Life of Nelson*, which has now dragged so long that I am making everything yield to it. I will undertake to write the lectures you ask, provided I can finish the *Life* in time to allow me to do so. I have very little doubt that I can finish it, and be prepared with the lectures by the time you indicate—before April 1st, 1897.[1] I will therefore engage to do so, provided it shall not be considered a breach of faith on my part if finishing the *Life* prevents me.

I presume the property in the lectures remains with me after their being first delivered at the Institute, and that I shall afterwards be at liberty to deliver them elsewhere or to publish them at my discretion—but I would like to be so assured.

---

1. Enclosure not found.

1. Mahan delivered ten lectures, on consecutive Wednesdays and Saturdays, commencing March 24 and concluding on April 24, 1897. They dealt generally with tactical and ship-design problems treated in his *Influence* books.

To Augustus T. Gillender

160 West 86th Street, New York, February 21, 1896 [HUL]

My dear Mr. Gillender: I have heard from Fred who is satisfied with Winterburn's plan of division.

A letter from Dennis says he will be on here on Tuesday next.

I hope you wont forget about Mrs. Okill's[1] will and that I may soon have the whole of this bothersome matter so far settled as to free my hands for my writing.

I very much enjoyed your company and Mrs. Gillender's last night.

To Robert U. Johnson

160 West 86th Street, New York, February 27, 1896 [NYPL]

Dear Mr. Johnson: I send herewith the manuscript *Battle of Copenhagen*. It is I believe the most thorough analysis of that battle ever published—I have seen nothing that attempts it and had not myself so treated it before.

Trafalgar is written and will be sent in shortly. Your Art Department tells me they like to get text as early as possible, and I shall be glad to put it in your hands also.

I would like to say here that I shall be quite satisfied and rather better suited if the articles are so spaced in time, as to bring *Trafalgar* towards the end of the year, say November.[1] The intrinsic interest grandeur and pathos of that closing scene can scarcely fail to benefit my *Life of Nelson* which I hope may appear not long afterwards.

I will ask your attention to the note I make to the title, and also remind you that it will be convenient to have *two* galley proofs.[2]

To Augustus Lowell

160 West 86th Street, New York, February 28, 1896 [HUL]

Dear Sir: Yours of the 25th being addressed West 6th Street, only reached me last evening. We will consider the matter arranged on the

---

1. Mary Jay Okill.

1. "Nelson at Trafalgar" was published in *Century Magazine* in March 1897. "The Battle of Copenhagen" appeared in the February 1897 issue.
2. In the margin of this letter Johnson wrote: "C.C.B[uel] How is this?" Buel responded: "$300."

[447]

understanding of my last letter, which you kindly accept, and I will take care to warn you betimes if I find myself prevented. I think that can only arise from circumstances not now apparent.

To Augustus T. Gillender

160 West 86th Street, New York, March 1, 1896 [HUL]

My dear Mr. Gillender: I have today for the first time looked over the copy of portion of Mrs. Okill's[1] will which you were kind enough to send me. I observe that the concluding words direct that in case either of her daughters die without issue, her portion of the Palisade property goes to the other. Had Mrs. Swift[2] predeceased Mrs. Mahan,[3] she would, I apprehend have had no power to devise it to any third party, failing issue to herself.

This of course is tantamount to what I said, *so far as the Palisade property is concerned* viz: that Aunty had no testamentary power over it, if she predeceased mother. I am rather pleased to see there was some foundation in fact for what my memory told me.

As she outlived mother this question did not arise, and if the will contain nothing more on the subject, I see nothing negativing the entire right of either Mrs. Swift or mother to dispose as they pleased of what they held at the time of their respective deaths. Our title, from them, would therefore be indefeasible.

Having but little experience of wills, I should consider the extract you send me muddleheaded in expression to the last degree. The land is first directed divided; and then to be sold and proceeds divided.

Had not some steps better be taken relative to James Okill's[4] portion— as Dennis suggested. The latter has not been able to come on for several reasons—among others his child has measles. Fred should be in Washington today & I hope will soon be here.

[P.S.] I believe I wrote you Fred & Dennis agree to Winterburn's scheme. The survey must of course wait for weather.

---

1. Mary Jay Okill.
2. Jane Leigh Okill Swift.
3. Mrs. Dennis Hart Mahan, Sr.
4. Mary Jay Okill's brother-in-law.

To Robert U. Johnson

161 West 86th Street, New York, March 6, 1896 [NYPL]

Dear Mr. Johnson: With reference to the proofs of the *Nile* will you let me remind you I would like to have them in duplicate?

I will of course endeavor to meet your wishes in reducing the first part of the article. In the *Copenhagen* I endeavored to meet your wishes, and am glad to know I have done so; but, if your original intention was to have the battles without the antecedent and accompanying history, it was unfortunate you should have allowed to pass, without qualification, that part of Miss Seawell's suggestion which proposed Creasy's *Fifteen Battles*[1] as a type of what was wanted.[2] It was under that impression the first two articles were written; and I confess to my mind battles are unintelligible massacres when their place in history is not indicated.

You understand I am all the same ready to meet the exigencies of the Magazine, which is your chief care.

To Seth Low[1]

160 West 86th Street, New York, March 10, 1896 [CUL]

Dear Mr. Low: Pardon my addressing you, which I have no claim to do; but it appears to me that the proposed solution of the Police Board trouble is one most clearly iniquitous, and that you occupy the very strongest position of any man in the city for a pronouncement against it. It is iniquitous, because it involves the righteous and the unrighteous in a common condemnation; and you are especially the man to right it, so far as protest goes, because you have given such conspicuous illustration of how far you are willing to go, in the sacrifice even of your well-matured opinions, for the furtherance of what you believe to be the greater common good.

The issue in the Police Board, as I see it, is so drawn, that all questions of tact, or error of judgment, disappear before the very simple and pronounced contrast between the well doer and the evil doer. Were the new appointment left in the hands of the Mayor, he could reappoint the well doers.

---

1. Sir Edward Shepherd Creasy, *Fifteen Decisive Battles of the World, from Marathon to Waterloo*. New York: S. W. Green's Son, 1882, and other editions.
2. *See* Mahan to Johnson, October 23, 1895.

1. President of Columbia University, a delegate to the First Hague Conference in 1899, and Mayor of New York, 1901–1903.

[449]

If this be so, with such a measure imminent in our midst, how comparatively trivial at such a moment must seem, to one who stops to think, a great meeting of our citizens to endorse arbitration with a country with which the experience of fifty years and a dozen quarrels has taught danger of war is just so great as that of a man's being run over in Broadway—just barely possible.[2]

If you saw your way to saying that a point has been reached at which you could no longer keep silence, I feel sure the city would be stirred to its depths, and Albany too would feel it.

I conclude by admitting that I have no claim upon your attention, but this letter is short and you have only to destroy it.

To Robert U. Johnson

160 West 86th Street, New York, March 11, 1896 [NYPL]

Dear Mr. Johnson: I return the galley proofs of the *Nile*. I have cut out practically all the history, & reduced the article over two thousand words.

To an Unidentified Addressee

New York, March 28, 1896 [NDL]

My Dear Sir: In accordance with your request I send you a sentiment which found favour with so strong a man as Von Moltke.

God's strength is made perfect in weakness.

To John M. Brown

160 West 86th Street, New York, April 11, 1896 [LC]

Dear Mr. Brown: I have to thank your firm for forwarding me a package from [illegible], which was duly recd. I suppose the charge for .75 can be made against my account, if you will be good enough.

I write to you personally instead of to the firm because I want to speak of my *Life of Nelson*. Distractions have been many, but I finished ten

---

2. This agitation led eventually to the signing of an Anglo-American general arbitration treaty on January 11, 1897, a treaty the U.S. Senate refused to ratify. *See* Mahan to Low, March 12, 1897.

days ago what I think the first of the two volumes. I reckon it to have between 100,000 and 105,000 words. The second volume I expect to be about 110,000. My chief reason for mentioning this now is that you may, if you think best, consider what size of page and character of type will be best for the sale of the book—what its general get up.

My hope has been to have it ready to go on the market by Christmas; but, although I have cleared my way of obstacles which have so much delayed me, but little hope is left of that. I console myself by saying perhaps it would interfere with my other books in the Christmas season. What do you think about that? When upon the whole & for the best results all along the line, would be the best time for it to appear?

The work has been one of extreme difficulty, and although I am in the main satisfied with its quality, the expenditure of labor has been much greater than on the same amount of product in other books; from which I reason that biography is not an economical use of brain power for me.

[P.S.]   By June 1 I ought to have some idea of the end.

To J. B. Sterling

160 West 86th Street, New York, April 17, 1896 [LC]

My dear Colonel Sterling: It has been very remiss in me to have delayed so long in answering your kind and more than appreciative letter. Your countrymen have been so good to me, and have shown for my opinions a respect and an interest which my own do not; but I fear that if I am to adopt the practice of committing my opinions on matters of current and *common* interest to your papers, instead of to our own, (although the latter don't want them) I should alienate the confidence of our people at a moment when I might possibly use it to advantage. Alongside of a desirable and growing appreciation of the sterling qualities of your nation, and of the great part you have played and are playing in the development of civilization and righteousness throughout the world—which you know to be my feeling—there is an unworthy, almost contemptible, longing on the part of many of our, in no ways admirable, rich people, for the gewgaws of social distinction which English social development and titles give. These artificial concomitants of your society are to me, as to you, indifferent and accidental, to be neither worshipped nor despised; but there is no doubt that the evident craving for them on the part of some of our people who have no claim to distinction here except that due to gross wealth, so far from conciliating our people generally tends to alienate; and a man even like Mr. Phelps,[1] lately our Minister to your country, runs the risk of being confounded with the mere runners after the "aristocratic" side of London society, if he openly express his admiration or concurrence with your polity or action, contrary to momentary impressions of our public opinions.

This of course is not in the least a reason for holding one's peace—quite the contrary, but it is a reason for so speaking only through our media of communication with the public. Mr. Phelps recently delivered an address on the Venezuelan matter and Cuba, which I regret I did not send you; and you will find in the *North American Review* for April an article by a Mr. D. A. Wells,[2] a very prominent financial writer, which I have not myself read, but which will show you, I doubt not—that pens and voices on this side are working for the rapprochement that I am sure will come. I think not improbable Wells takes a purely dollars and cents view of national policy, which I detest, but which has its useful side. The enclosed clipping I can vouch for.[3] It is from one of our best dailies—the *Tribune*, for which Smalley[4] was so long London correspondent. It appreciates the noble side of the world wide mission that has been entrusted to England, and that by a paper intensely American in tone; nor is it all of the same tendency that has appeared in its columns.

I am at times troubled with doubts as to whether I should not write and think upon contemporary events more than I do. Many thoughts throng through my mind, and for a moment cry for utterance. and the question sometimes arises "ought you not to give these, which die in the utterance, but in dying perhaps give life to the future, to take precedence over work such as you are now doing, from which you hope your own increase of reputation, but which may add little to the general welfare." It is hard to know—one cannot always tell where one's powers lie. Of one thing I feel certain—that God's providence is moving the nations strongly now, and I seem at times to see so clearly the general drift of the future that it conveys to me an idea of what prophetic inspiration may have been; but the feeling, on the other hand, may be only the unbalanced one-sided conviction of semi-lunacy. Inspiration and frenzy were with the ancients not far apart.

---

1. Edward John Phelps addressed the Brooklyn Institute of Arts and Sciences on March 30, 1896. His lecture, essentially an arraignment of the U.S. course in the Venezuelan boundary affair and the Cuban situation, stated that the Monroe Doctrine had brought the United States to the verge of war with Great Britain, and had caused huge economic losses.
2. David Ames Wells, "Great Britain and the United States, Their True Relations," *North American Review* (April 1896).
3. Enclosure not found.
4. G. W. Smalley.

To Robert U. Johnson

160 West 86th Street, New York, April 26, 1896 [NYPL]

Dear Mr. Johnson: I have received a request from Messrs. Longmans, Green & Co. to use the plans of the Battle of St. Vincent which appeared in my book on Sea Power. I have replied that I should have no objection to their using those which appeared in my *Century* article,[1] provided they could make the arrangement with you. The first two figures in the article are substantially the same as those in the *Life of Nelson*, but there are two slight changes in the 2d figure which I found necessary to introduce.

To Augustus T. Gillender

160 West 86th Street, New York, May 3, 1896 [HUL]

Dear Mr. Gillender: I have here in the house the duplicate copies of the book I am now preparing for publication, as far as written.[1] They ought to be in separate places, as a precaution against accident fire or otherwise. Could you receive one of them? All that is required is to put the package— which will be duly marked—somewhere you could find it if required, and that I should know in a general way where it is.

To Robert U. Johnson

Slumberside, Quogue, Long Island, June 9, 1896 [NYPL]

My dear Mr. Johnson: Would you be good enough to note that my address till Oct. 1. will be Quogue, N.Y.

I have been able to progress so rapidly with my *Life of Nelson* lately, that I hope to be able to get it out by Christmas—I may yet fail, but the chances are very good. It is in fact imperative I should finish it during the summer, in order to complete in time the work promised on a twelvemonth to come. I mention it more particularly because you may prefer to get my articles for the *Century* out beforehand. With the exception of about 4 hundred words from *Copenhagen*, I have not used them for the *Life*, but of course there is certain raw material which has to be worked in every case e.g. Nelson's own words on leaving Merton and just before Trafalgar.

---

1. "Nelson at Cape St. Vincent," *Century Magazine* (February 1896).
1. *Life of Nelson.*

As I told you, however, there is a distinct difference of treatment: the *Century* articles being Battles as Battles, Nelson incidental, whereas in the *Life* I enlarge on Nelson and drop incidents foreign to him.

Little and Brown would like to have the book out in November, but the thing is still uncertain.

To Robert U. Johnson

Slumberside, Quogue, Long Island, June 13, 1896 [NYPL]

My dear Mr. Johnson: I think, if you have preserved the letter I wrote you, you will find that its purpose was simply to indicate that my preference was to have the *Trafalgar* article printed in November or December, because I then felt that the *Life of Nelson* could not be produced at Christmas, as my hope had before been it might. It never entered my head that the other articles were to be postponed so indefinitely, a view that was confirmed by the *Nile* galleys when they came to me being marked "May" and then "June." I went to buy two or three extra numbers of the latter for friends in absolute certainty I should find the article. Of course, I recognize, that the time for its appearance is absolutely at your discretion, as it belongs to you, with but a single reservation as to my use of it—which I believe I have not made.

At the same time as I have given you the impression, and in fact wrote you, that the publication of the book could not be until midwinter, it is just that I should not involve you in the consequences of a misunderstanding. I have not had time to communicate with Little & Brown, but I think they will undoubtedly accede to the proposition that I shall make them that the book should not appear till after February 14th. I hope you will try to meet this by getting the articles, if possible at all, in the October, December and February numbers. To crowd them into successive numbers is almost as bad (I should think) as leaving the great interval by which *St. Vincent* is separated from the others, by which it contributes nothing to the impact.[1]

I may add that although the ultimate result to me, financially, will probably be the same there is an immediate inconvenience in standing out of the Christmas receipts—which induced my diligence when I found the spirit of rapid writing once more on me. This does not, however, alter the fact

1. The four articles on Nelson's battles appeared in *Century Magazine* as follows: Cape St. Vincent (February 1896), Nile (January 1897), Copenhagen (February 1897), and Trafalgar (March 1897).

that I owe consideration to your misunderstanding so far as it is due to myself.

[P.S.] If you can send me word at once, I would rather postpone writing Little and Brown, till I can put a clear proposition before them.

To Helen Evans Mahan

Slumberside, Quogue, Long Island, June 14, 1896 [NWC]

Read when at leisure

My darling Helen: I have meant to take advantage of one of these Sundays that we are separated,[1] to say to you one or two things that are better said by letter, because better weighed and more easily referred to. You are now in every way independent of us, except so far as persons living in one house must conform to the general house rules, and I want to make some suggestions to you, based upon my observation of your character, and my experience of my own, for we are both much alike.

It is my wish and hope to make you, though in a small way, independent so far as your personal expenses are concerned, (if I am not disappointed in what seem to me reasonable hopes of a fairly fixed income), by making you an allowance. I am deterred as yet simply from reluctance to take a step from which I may have to recede; and this years expenses have been heavy. I trust we may soon so settle as to enable me to do this.

This, however, is by the way; I mention it only that you may understand my wish to have you your own mistress. But when you are so, your answerability for the ordering of your life is increased, not diminished. Instead of being immediately responsible to us, as when a child, your relations are direct with your own conscience and with God. I do not say this to burden an over scrupulous conscience—rather, I hope, to give relief, where I at your age failed to find it. But you do owe to consider what part you are to bear in the family, and especially towards your mother. You need caution on this side, because you will be, I think, prone to error from the very care and conscientiousness you bestow on your own work. Like all strong characters, for I think yours is strong, you are liable to be *over*-impressed with the importance of your own duties or occupations, and to grudge interruptions in order to attend to other people's duties, or wishes. It is a little difficult to point out the mistake in such cases; for, unless there be the fixedness of purpose, the concentration, that does not willingly yield to distraction, it is impossible to effect much; yet unless, along with that fixedness, there goes

---

1. Helen was visiting at Bar Harbor, Maine.

a readiness to yield for the sake of others, one easily degenerates into self-centredness, which will become selfish.

I have heard mamma say that she dislikes to ask you to do things, because your reply is so apt to be that you have this, that, or the other, to do. I should do harm, and not good, if I failed to see—as she does—that in many cases this is true, and that in all the setness to do your work has its good side. Yet we cannot walk in this life as though our own work was all; things are never so simple as that; and the side-calls, the interruptions, are just as much God's plan for us as is the work itself.

You should study this question, and seek to find your duty in the house. But here I must put in the other caution, drawn from observation, and from my experience of my own very similar disposition. Beware of thinking that the end I am recommending to you, the family duty, and helpfulness, is to be attained chiefly by diligent self-discipline. That is the error that the Bible ever warns us against—the error old as human nature—the error of the Jew, who "had a zeal for God, but not according to knowledge; for being ignorant of God's righteousness and going about to establish their own righteousness," they failed to attain to righteousness. Why? "Because they sought it by the works of the law, not by simple faith"; that is by simply looking to receive it. The blessed paradox runs all through the Bible; and until it is mastered, the preaching of the Cross is foolishness, as paradox ever seems. You must labor and strive, yet ever realize that your labor and strife, of themselves, end only in themselves. Suppose, by the most diligent pains, you could make every outward act perfect, what have you gained, unless the inward man of the heart is renewed also? a bare outward semblance, the whited sepulchre, full of *dead* mens bones. The hypocrite denounced by our Lord was not, essentially, one who pretended to be what he was not; but one who thought that the outward act was the essential, rather than the inward spirit. Many an honest Christian falls unconsciously into the same error; but such a result is a semblance of life, a corpse beautified and jewelled, but lifeless, and here you begin to see the divine philosophy of Christianity which preaches "the new creature." The end I would have you aim at, the unselfishness, is not to be attained by striving, but by the work of the Holy Ghost. *The new creature*; that you are already, by your baptism, and your union therein with Christ; but the new creature, like all creatures, begins weak and must grow; and is it marvelous that he whose life is everlasting, should grow but slowly, but little in the fleeting years of this human life? that in this brief span of an endless existence it should advance little beyond infancy? In this thought, if you embrace the purpose I commend to you, of going more out of yourself into the lives of others, you will find comfort. When you fail, as you often will, you will recognize that failure is to be expected, and will not be discouraged; but you will in the end realize, unless my own experience is utterly misleading, that the Holy Ghost is working, that you are getting better—you know not how (St. Mark IV 20–26). And, in that condition, the beauty and grace is that the outward improvement is not a mere external condition, your own painful accomplishment, *Works*, but the simple, inevitable *fruit* of an inward change, a new life, which you could no more effect yourself than you could bid a mountain remove from its seat and be cast into the sea.

Somehow I am not afraid to say these things even to so young a Christian as yourself. You have the intellectual grasp to understand that although your *works* can do nothing, they are the necessary outcome of a will yielded to God; and unless your will is given Him, the Holy Ghost can do nothing. I do not therefore fear that you will reach the absurd conclusion of those who, because works cannot save, lapse into neglect. And I feel that to one of your conscientious—often morbid—scrupulousness, there will be an immense gain when, after a fall, you recognize that such things are to be expected of you, and that for perseverance, there is no need for discouragement, as the Holy Spirit will not stop working.

Turn therefore your mind to the fact that in the house where once you were a child—under obedience—you are now a grown woman, independent; but that, at the same time, it is your home, the scene of your primary duties, until God gives you another. Seek to see what you should do, and where you fall short; but alike in seeking and in doing, alike in perplexity and in failure, put away anxiety. Light as well as growth are from God only—the work of the Holy Ghost. Therefore they are *sure* to come, however long the waiting—dont trouble—have faith. The process by its very slowness will make clearer to you the reality of the Power that worketh in you. Words fail to express the thoughts—that unutterable reality—that comes to one who has learned—however imperfectly—to realize his own powerlessness and the truth of the inward working. Like some great tree, destined to centuries of existence, the growth from year to year may be imperceptible, the fruit scanty almost to nothingness, yet the fact of growth is to the Christian attested by the consciousness within. I cannot place you at twenty-three where I am at fifty-five, nor can any man's experience be transferred as experience. Each must gain his own. But I can call back to you, from the further stage to which I have reached, that those things are true which our fathers told us—that amid all human failures and impotence there is a Power which works within us, and that the solution of all difficulties is to be found—not indeed in relaxing our efforts, but in recognizing our powerlessness, and in looking ever to Him for light and growth. Once hold that, and doubt and discouragement are at an end. This is what St. Paul and St. John meant in their exaltation of Faith; and when St. James seems to oppose Faith to Works, I have never been able to stumble; for it is to me clear as the sun that he saw in works, not the saving but the *sign* of the inward work—the inward life. Life must result in fruit—in works; but neither fruit nor works *are life.*

I cannot and ought not to write to you often in this way; but I will commend to you the book which more than any other has affected my spiritual life—Goulburn's *Thoughts on Personal Religion.*[2] Years have passed since I opened it, and many others have helped me; but as far as I can tell, it lies unseen among the foundations of my best thought. Of course, if it dont meet your case, I would not have you persist. God will provide.

To John M. Brown

Slumberside, Quogue, Long Island, June 19, 1896 [LC]

My dear Mr. Brown: I have had a disappointment about *Nelson.* The work is well forward and I think can be ready—complete—to go to the printer by the last of July. My trouble is with the *Century.* Four months ago, when I sent them the last of four articles, *Trafalgar,* which I have written on Nelson's Battles, I said I should personally be pleased that it appeared late in the year, November or December, as I thought it would draw attention to the book, which I then expected (and said) would be ready in the winter or spring. Unfortunately, they construed my words to apply to the series, and being weighted down by the *Life of Napoleon* and other historical articles, have dropped mine out in their numbers, which are made up three months in advance. When I found myself working rapidly, which for many months I could not, I wrote them, as I did you, that I hoped to get the book out by Christmas, and mentioned your suggestion of November. Then this misunderstanding appeared, and they remonstrated against the book anticipating the articles. I replied, as above, but said that, as I had certainly mentioned some time after Christmas as the probable time of appearance, I felt partly responsible for the mistake, and would recommend to your firm that the book should not appear before February 14. I enclose their reply, and recommend that we accept their suggestion—the more so that, although, as far as I go, I am sure I could push it through, it is probable the greater time will insure greater accuracy.

I can, I think, safely undertake the delivery of the manuscript by the 31st July, and even if the end be not then reached, fully 4/5 will be, nay is now done. The sooner it then begins to come in as proof the better for

---

2. Edward Meyrick Goulburn, *Thoughts on Personal Religion, being a Treatise on the Christian Life in its Two Elements, Devotion and Grace.* First American from the Fifth London Edition. With a prefatory note by George H. Houghton. New York: D. Appleton & Co., 1865. There were subsequent English and American editions.

me, as things sometimes look different in print and the galleys may give reason to strike out in places. The subject is most difficult, and with so great a favorite of the English—probably our best market—much care is needed.

May I ask you to send me a reply on this subject as soon as possible. My address next week will be Naval War College Newport R.I.[1] I return here Saturday evening June 27.

[P.S.] Would you kindly have my address noted as "Quogue N.Y." until October 1st.
Please return enclosure.

To John M. Brown

Slumberside, Quogue, Long Island, June 19, 1896 [LC]

My dear Mr. Brown: I have for some time been purposing to write you with reference to the *Life of Nelson*, on the subject of my royalty on it. As you know, I have always felt my indebtedness to you for taking up the work of an unknown author on a doubtful subject and have been entirely satisfied in all our business relations. I feel, however, now, that I am no longer unknown, and that both reputation and the subject give this book a fair promise; as far as I can judge, also, it runs smoothly and gives a treatment which is not likely to have a rival speedily. Under the circumstances, therefore, I have decided to propose to you that our agreement for it stand as for the other books, but with the additional stipulation that after two thousand copies are sold, I shall receive twenty-five per cent royalty instead of fifteen.

The question of course is simply what is fair to each of us, under the present conditions; but, although outside of the direct question, I may say I am strongly moved by the wish to avoid the necessity of "pot-boiling" such as I am now pledged to for the coming twelvemonth; and this desirable end can only be reached by obtaining the utmost that I fairly can on the work I do. Fortunately I have been able so to arrange the occasional work for next year that it all hangs together; each part helping the other, and it is work, too, that it becomes me to do; but I do wish to feel when I am ready to take up 1812 and, possibly, as I have been urged, the Rebellion not merely as a naval war but as a whole, that I am not fettered by considerations of income, or the thought that I can make more by occasional papers.

---

1. Mahan's lectures in 1896 were concerned with the subject of the annual war problem, the Caribbean, and the Gulf.

To John M. Brown

Dear Mr. Brown: Your letter was received this morning. I shall not attempt to do more than acknowledge it at the moment, for my time is so much occupied with my lectures and I am besides very much under the weather, head very dull; but we seem at one on the general principle, and I have no doubt therefore will agree as to the details. I will attend to mastering your idea just as soon as I can. I leave here Saturday night for Quogue by the N.Y. boat. I should be delighted to see you personally but I question very much whether I could find time to talk business. The postponement of publishing is a great disappointment to me, the more so as it is my own blunder originally, but I fear it must be. On the other hand, the book will benefit. When I return to Quogue I will submit to you my views as to illustrations, which I presume ought soon to be taken in hand.

To John M. Brown

Slumberside, Quogue, Long Island, June 29, 1896 [LC]

My dear Mr. Brown: I returned here yesterday. As I wrote you from Newport, I was too busy there with my work, and the unavoidable social entanglement which gathers round a short stay in a place where one has been well known, to permit of my making a business appointment. In making my proposition to you, I acted of course on general impressions; and having considered now the more particular information you give me, I shall accept the arrangement you propose which I understand to be: a royalty of twenty per cent from the start on copies sold in this country and of fifteen per cent on copies sold abroad. I confess I am sorry that the trade conditions of which you tell me do not admit more, for I am desirous of obtaining for myself more complete independence in writing—to free myself from the tendency to haste, and producing much, to the injury of producing well.

It would I think be well to consider what price the book could be made to bear. This is a matter of which you are a better judge than I can be.

While in London Mr. Marston once said to me quite casually, that he had at times feared that there was a possible loophole through which the copyright might be evaded. I did not clearly understand him; it was in fact before the time that I at all expected any considerable return from the Sea Power books, and so did not attend. If the *Nelson* succeeds at all, it ought to have a good deal of success and if there be any possible step by which it can be protected against cheap piracies abroad it will be well for us all to see it taken. The English must be our best market.

I hope I have not misled you unintentionally as to the immediate resumption of the Sea Power series. I have committed myself to pot-boilers that will very possibly employ me fully for a twelvemonth hence—after *Nelson* goes to you. I hope the latter & Sea Power with my other income will thenceforth free me from the necessity of job-work.

In the course of this week I hope to send you a list of illustrations.

To Augustus T. Gillender

Slumberside, Quogue, Long Island, July 1, 1896 [HUL]

My dear Mr. Gillender: When I arrived home on Sunday last Mrs. Mahan gave me your note to her of June 24. I am glad to know that the survey of the Palisade property is approaching completion, so that we may each have our individual property. Mrs. Mahan has doubtless explained to you that, since you have been so kind as to allow us time, we had decided to wait the returns from my publishers, due about the middle of this month, before drawing out of the savings bank what may be necessary to square all our accounts.

With regard to writing to the Committee of the Century Club, I shall be very glad to do so, but it will be well to postpone it till fall, when some of the rawness of my membership will be off—the more so, that the Committee, I understand, holds no meetings during the summer. I was told—in reference to my own case—that no candidate was considered till three months after proposed. This, it was said, would carry me past June, and as no further action would take place till autumn, I need not look for election till then. I wish I had not been, for I obtain the privilege of paying the semi-annual dues for the first half of the year, without the least benefit; but so the rule runs.

With kind remembrance to the family.

To John M. Brown

Slumberside, Quogue, Long Island, July 7, 1896 [LC]

My dear Mr. Brown: I want to ask a favor for the *Life of Nelson*. If there be in the Boston Public Library (or other) the Memoirs of Wm.

Beckford[1] (author of *Vathek*[2]), I should like to have someone look it up, and see whether, in the months Novr. 1800–Jan. 1801, there is an account of a visit paid him at Fonthill, his country seat, by Nelson and the Hamiltons; in which occurs the incident that being on a drive in a four-in-hand, the horses becoming restive, Nelson got down and walked home confessing he felt too uneasy to remain. If such there be, a copy would be useful. He also mentions his opinion of Lady H.; to the general effect that he found her coarse, underbred &c.

I dont think the two extracts would be 200 words. I am positive of the general fact, but cannot use it by any information within my reach. The quotation will hang well with another I wish to introduce.

[P.S.]   It is possible I am mistaken in the book or its particular title, trusting, as I do, to a long-gone memory.

To Robert U. Johnson

Slumberside, Quogue, Long Island, July 7, 1896 [NYPL]

My dear Mr. Johnson: I have arranged with Little and Brown, according to your wish, that my *Life of Nelson* shall not appear before March 1, 1897. I hope you will give me the advantage of the articles appearing by that date, for as an advertisement they may help the book.

To John M. Brown

Slumberside, Quogue, Long Island, July 10, 1896 [LC]

Dear Mr. Brown: I wish to thank you for the volume of Beckford's memoirs, which was received this morning, and as I am doing so will at the same time acknowledge the cheque, the receipt for which I enclose. I will make the necessary extract from the book and return it soon.

We may congratulate ourselves upon the returns for the books continuing so good, and I am specially pleased that the demand for the first keeps ahead; for I trust, as times improve that those who have the first will want the second.

---

1. Cyrus Redding, *Memoirs of William Beckford of Fonthill*. London: C. J. Skeet, 1859.
2. William Beckford, *The History of the Caliph Vathek*. 8th ed. New York: W. L. Allison, 1868?, and J. W. Lovell Company, 1868?. *Vathek* was first written in French, in 1782.

I received a letter from a gentleman in England yesterday that he had a photo from a portrait of Lady Nelson the admiral's wife. He will send it when he gets my address. Unfortunately it is taken when well on in middle life, but I hope may prove available.

The work is getting on pretty rapidly, and I hope I shall not fall far behind my last expectations as to readiness viz: Aug 1—a good Nelsonian day, the Battle of the Nile.

To John M. Brown

Slumberside, Quogue, Long Island, July 13, 1896 [LC]

My dear Mr. Brown: I have returned to day by Registered Mail the *Memoirs of Beckford*, which you were kind enough to send me and for which please accept my thanks.

To Augustus T. Gillender

Slumberside, Quogue, Long Island, July 15, 1896 [HUL]

My dear Mr. Gillender: I had a letter yesterday from Dennis that he expects to leave for China about the middle of September.[1] From what you wrote Mrs. Mahan, I presume the survey will by then be completed—indeed long before, and I hope all papers etc may be settled necessary to the final division and settlement of the property. It is of course most desirable that nothing be unfinished when he leaves for what will probably be a three years absence. He asked me, if I saw you, to mention that "it will be *absolutely* necessary for him to have the extra $2000 for which the mortgage was made out." His wife will follow him next spring—meantime he wishes the money to fix her comfortably. I believe I never told you why I did not send the manuscript of which I spoke to you. It was because Mrs. Mahan and myself thought it best to compare the two, as there is a great deal of quotation to be verified; so I brought it here. Very likely I may yet trouble you.

We are all well and very damp. The smudging you may see on the paper is because blotting paper will not absorb nor dry under present conditions.

Mrs. Mahan joins me in kind regards.

[P.S.]   Whom will you vote for in November?

---

1. Dennis joined the *Machias* in October 1896.

To Augustus T. Gillender

Slumberside, Quogue, Long Island, July 28, 1896 [HUL]

Dear Mr. Gillender: Is it possible that I did not acknowledge the receipt of the blue print? I fully meant to, but, if I did not, you could scarcely know it.

I have a letter from Dennis today signifying his willingness to take the exterior lots, A,F,I, L. This I believe was Fred's suggestion and I suppose I shall hear from him in a day or two. I am willing, and I suppose it will end in my having C, D, and two others, but I dont know Fred's wishes as to that.

I am afraid you are catching heat both in N.Y. and Knollwood today.

[P.S.]   I am writing manuscript all morning, hence any neglects in letters.

To Augustus T. Gillender

Slumberside, Quogue, Long Island, August 5, 1896 [HUL]

My dear Mr. Gillender: I have letters from both Fred and Dennis, who I hope have themselves signified to you the plots they will take; but, lest they may not, I will copy from their letters. Dennis says he will take the sections (outside) A, F, I, L. This will leave Fred and me who have no present thought of selling, together. Fred says he will take E, D, J, K, which are northeast and contiguous lots. This leaves for me B, C, H, G; also contiguous.

I hope this will be enough for you to go upon to have the deeds made out. I have copied and compared with their letters to me; but if you want to hear from them direct you can reach them a day sooner than I can. I believe I told you that Dennis is to leave the East by the middle of Sept. en route for China.

We are all well and sorry to think how hot it must be in N.Y.

To Augustus T. Gillender

Slumberside, Quogue, Long Island, August 19, 1896 [HUL]

Dear Mr. Gillender: Fred's wife's name is Mary Morris, and Dennis' Jeannette Katharine (or Katherine) Murat. This latter, Mrs. Mahan tells me, signs herself Jeannette K. M. Mahan.

My Mrs. Mahan's name is Ellen Lyle.

I rejoice in the cool weather for every one, though I was mean not to be sorry it was made hot for Bryan.[1] Even here it was bad. The last day floored me—too much exercise mental and physical. I am just beginning to feel right again.

To Augustus T. Gillender

Slumberside, Quogue, Long Island, August 24, 1896 [HUL]

Dear Mr. Gillender: The deeds go to Fred by this P.M. mail.

I notice Jeannette's name is spelled with one "n"—Jeanette. I dont know whether that matters.

To John M. Brown

Slumberside, Quogue, Long Island, August 31, 1896 [LC]

My dear Mr. Brown: It must be now near two months since I wrote you my hope that I should finish *Nelson* by the beginning of August; and now on its last day I have to confess that something still remains to be done. I have him, however, on board the *Victory* about to leave England for Trafalgar—so that practically the concluding chapter only remains. That I have not been idle will appear from the fact that I have written 70,000 words since June 1st; without speaking of the attendant reading, and the extreme difficult [*sic*] of the mosaic work, which most accurately defines my attempt; mosaic, because built up of innumerable minute fragments, difficult, because necessary so to blend them as not to show the joints nor make the differences of shading conspicuous.

Being so near completion, it seems expedient to reach an understanding as to when to go to press. I fancy, that March is a desirable time for the book to appear. The *Century* writes me that my articles on the Nile, Copenhagen & Trafalgar will appear in the Jany., Feb. and March numbers. If they are as good as the *Centy.* and myself think them, they will be something of an advertisement; and I would suggest for your consideration that a formal and somewhat conspicuous advertisement in those numbers might be politic. This is one reason for the book appearing in March, to which I add that as England is probably our best market, that no time (except Xmas) seems to me more propitious than the month or so preceding the

---

1. William Jennings Bryan, Democratic nominee for the presidency.

Easter Recess and opening of the London season. Of this you and Marston will be better judges than myself, but so it seems to me.

I feel the need of a momentary rest from the pressure of composition, and I am obliged to spend ten days, at least, at Newport in September, besides some more in preparation. The question is, if you take March as the month, when do you wish to begin to print?

I have given so much time to elaboration that, although I do not propose to send the manuscript without one more reading, I look upon it as practically ready now—& type-written. If I can send it to you before Nov. I ready for printer will that do? and will you be willing to begin with the Trafalgar chapter unfinished—say 15,000 to 20,000 words. That chapter ought to be a brilliant peroration, and I should come to it less jaded than I now am; but I am quite competent to re-read as soon as I return from Newport—say Sept. 25—and feed the printer—beginning at Oct 15.

The words actually written I calculate by count at about 255,000. Allowing 20,000 for Trafalgar makes a total of 275,000. *Sea Power in French Revolution* is by my count 270,000. It is not too much for *Nelson*.

To John M. Brown

Slumberside, Quogue, Long Island, August 31, 1896 [LC]

Dear Mr. Brown: I had intended to put all I had to say today under one letter, but a separate subject had best go separate. We are all, I imagine, getting our umbrellas ready to put up, if Bryan is elected; and I should like to have an understanding with you that (in the general upset of values that I suppose would follow on books sold *in England*) my royalty should be on the selling price *there*, which will I imagine be more than equivalent to what you could sell at here. That is, a book now which sells here at $4.00 may be in England 18s; but I suppose if we get on a silver basis, the price abroad would remain as it now is, but you could scarcely raise your price here in proportion to the depreciation of the currency. On sales *here*, I am of course prepared to accept the conditions that will weigh on you and me alike, and must leave to your business judgment what charge is discreet to make; but as a salaried government officer I shall be among the hardest hit, if the change comes, and I want to secure myself on the foreign sales—the gold sales.

If this terrible catastrophe befalls the country, I shall probably consider seriously the wisdom of turning my attention to book work for the English market, which seems my best hold.

I hope for the best, and upon the whole expect it, but one must look out for squalls.

To Augustus T. Gillender

Slumberside, Quogue, Long Island, September 1, 1896 [HUL]

My dear Mr. Gillender: I enclose herewith cheque for $139.84 the third of $419.50—my share of the appraisers and engineers bill—and thank you very much for your trouble in the matter.[1]

We are all well. I was myself somewhat flattened out by the heat, and have to spare myself in head work for the present—much to my discontent, for it means dollars of which I have not too many.

Mrs. Mahan joins me in kind regards.

To John M. Brown

Slumberside, Quogue, Long Island, September 8, 1896 [LC]

My dear Mr. Brown: I shall send you to morrow by registered mail, addressed to the firm, a list of illustrations complete as far as I now know.

Mr. Marston, who has interested himself very much in getting me material, wrote about a year ago that he could get blocks from celebrated pictures of Nelson's career made very reasonably at the British Museum. He added that such would help the book in England.

This is in my eyes purely a business consideration—as affecting the sales; and I leave it to you to settle, but I should be glad if you would exchange views with him. I only hope that such illustrations, if adopted, may be full page. I should not like to see the text broken up by many small plates. It derogates, I think, from the character of a solid book, and gives the impression that the text is subordinate.

I should be satisfied to receive my royalty on English sales in gold upon the selling price of the book here—a price, that is, fixed upon our present gold basis. If we go to silver, I suppose the price of books will go up like other things; but I hardly see how books like mine can be raised to a nominal price equal to that at which they now sell—E.G. that the first *Sea Power* could be raised from $4 to nearly $8. If you now fix *Nelson* at $6 or more —it would scarcely sell at $12 in silver. I feel that my general line of work would be little sought for here, in that case, as compared with England.

I go to Newport from the 16th to the 25th and shall try to see you, if I can hit it off.

---

1. *See* Mahan to Gillender, July 1, 1896.

To John M. Brown

My dear Mr. Brown: Will it be at all convenient for you to do as you suggested in June last—to run down and see me here about any matters that require attention about the book. I am staying with Mr. Samuel Powel in Gibbs Avenue, and Mrs. Powel desires me to say to you that she would be very glad to see you any day of my stay at lunch—between one and two. My last lecture is on Friday the 25th; and if I have seen you before that it will obviate my going to Boston, and enable me to begin *Nelson* again on Monday. I lecture every day except the coming Saturday, and I need that day for rest as I am still somewhat below par.

I have no lunch engagement except Friday the 18th, and will keep all my afternoons free until I hear definitely from you whether you will come or not.

[P.S.]   I am at the College every day—*except Saturday* from 10 to 1. Lecture from 11.30 to 12.30.

To John M. Brown

Lynnfield, Massachusetts,[1] October 4, 1896 [LC]

Dear Mr. Brown: I received the book duly and in good order. It was what I wanted, though it does not seem to contain the additional matter I inferred from Nicolas.[2] I will be careful about returning it. I have at present no thought of going to Boston especially, but shall try to see you as I pass through towards the end of the week. I put in good work last week until Friday, but have since suffered from neuralgia. With a quiet month, I see no doubt the manuscript will be ready by Nov.

To John M. Brown

160 West 86th Street, New York, October 13, 1896 [LC]

Dear Mr. Brown: I arrived home yesterday, I hope for the winter in quiet—and shall send you to day, by express or registered mail, both the

---

1. Mahan was visiting Mrs. Henry Saltonstall.
2. Sir Nicholas Harris Nicolas, ed., *The Dispatches and Letters of Vice-Admiral Lord Viscount Nelson.* 7 vols. London: H. Colburn, 1844–1846. This was an annotated edition.

Memoirs of Lady H[1] and Beatty's *Death of Nelson*.[2] There is nothing new that I think of since I had the pleasure of seeing you on Friday. I am just now a good deal under the weather, but trust it may not delay my work.

To J. Franklin Jameson

160 West 86th Street, New York, October 20, 1896 [LC]

Dear Sir: I will write the notice you ask of Barnes's *Naval Actions*,[1] but cannot *promise* it before the end of November.[2] Please let me know the maximum of words allowed.

To Robert U. Johnson

160 West 86th Street, New York, October 31, 1896 [NYPL]

Dear Mr. Johnson: Unless there has been a further change in the programme, I suppose the proofs of *Copenhagen* will be coming along soon. Will you kindly *send* my manuscript with them, for, after so long an interval, I may feel doubt whether a statement in proof corresponds with manuscript. Of *Trafalgar* I have still my own rough draft.

To John M. Brown

160 West 86th Street, New York, October 31, 1896 [LC]

Dear Mr. Brown: I enclose herewith sketches of some battle plans I require for *Nelson*. Though carefully thought out, I have not elaborated all the *drawing* myself, but think that with the explanation given in writing that the draughtsman can readily do the work; as well, in fact, as if I had drawn all, being a poor draughtsman & having no conveniences here.

I now only think of one other battle plan, possible; and that I cannot do till the proof comes in. It is in the first fourth of the work so that, if I find it necessary, there will be ample time.

---

1. Anon., *Memoirs of Lady Hamilton*, London, 1815; new ed., 1891.
2. Sir William Beatty, *Authentic Narrative of the Death of Lord Nelson*. 3d ed. London: W. Mason, 1825. The first edition was titled *Narrative of Nelson's Last Hours*.

1. James Barnes, *Naval Actions of the War of 1812* . . . New York: Harper & Bros., 1896.
2. *See* Mahan to Jameson, December 12, 1896.

I regret all extra trouble, but am moved continually by Southey's words: "the nation expected and was entitled to expect that while cities vied with each other in consecrating statues in marble and brass to the memory of our Nelson, a literary monument would be erected, which should record his deeds &c." It has not yet been done, and I too may fail—why not. All the same there is more attempted in this than any other I know of.

[P.S.]   The proofs of enclosed of course will come to me.

To Samuel A. Ashe

160 West 86th Street, New York, November 7, 1896 [DUL]

My dear Ashe: I had intended to write to you on the 21st of September, which in my recollection is your birthday, but I was then in Newport lecturing; and to own the truth I do so much writing now-a-days, that I am a most wretched procrastinator in even important letters. But besides hearing of your present conditions, I want now to ask you, as familiar with the feelings of your own part of the country, your views as to the principal conditions which have produced the present political status down your way. To my mind this has been the most important—even critical—election the country has ever passed through in my time; I dont except the war. I imagine you and I have been on opposite sides; for which my only reason is my recollection of what I have heard you say in times past. I believe the Chicago platform to have been in the main wrong and even revolutionary; and I confess that I have not found in the *speeches* of Mr. Bryan the proof that he is both intelligent and honest. He may be the one or the other, I cant find it in his speeches that he is both. But I quite believe that among his supporters there are many men both honest and intelligent, and who have embraced his cause because they believe that it will best further certain objects they think righteous and necessary. It is these objects, and the reasoning of these men, with which you are doubtless familiar from living among them, which I would like to get at; for I am satisfied that quiet can only be obtained by the meeting just claims whether on one side or the other. My earnest prayer has been that righteousness might triumph in this matter, not by the mere trampling of a majority upon a minority by votes, but by the persuasion of men's hearts through the manifestation of truth. In no other way can a satisfactory peace be reached. I am writing by this same mail the same questions to a friend long resident in Colorado.

For my private history there is not a very great deal to say. I wrote you three years ago from Genoa, immediately after meeting Hall there. If you replied the letter never reached me. It is now 18 months since I returned from that cruise, and I have made my home in N.Y. We have bought this house and I hope it will remain our home. My family are all well—much smaller one than yours. I think it probable that I shall ere long avail myself of the privilege of retirement which the law allows after forty years. Can you realize it is forty years since I entered the class? I shrink from further separation from home, and have a number of literary projects in view, to follow out which I need a certainty of non-interference, to which I have no claim unless I retire. I have just finished and sent to the publisher a long and elaborate *Life of Nelson*. It is a work for which there is still room, for although many lives have been written, there is none that "fills the bill." The attempts so far have been like the knights in our story books that went out to slay the dragon. Whether I shall have better luck than my predecessors remains to be seen. If I do it should pay me well. There is at present, mainly in England, a very great interest in naval matters, which has taken such hold on all minds that it promises to endure. My own name is closely associated with it, giving me fair prospects there, and I forecast a similar interest here ere long—although as yet my books here dont pay me for the time and trouble. I have here however an opening for magazine writing; and I own to a wish to run the remainder of my course as a literary man, taking an active interest in the State, Church, and social movement about me, leaving the active pursuit of the sea and its new naval monsters to younger men. I cannot move at once, until some public matters are settled but hope that may not be long.

To John M. Brown

160 West 86th Street, New York, November 9, 1896 [LC]

Dear Mr. Brown: Two years ago, in England, a British army officer told me that Lord Wolseley (Sir Garnet) had said that he would like to review *Nelson*, if he could have advance sheets; and he added you will hear more directly of this. I never did, however, and do not to this day know whether it was a feeler, from Wolseley, or a mere passing remark, forgotten as soon as made.

I have thought of writing the officer in question; for if his remark was made with Wolseley's cognizance, I should be disposed to recommend to you to embrace the offer. Would you see any inconveniences in the way of giving him such advance sheets if it should appear that he meant to make such a proposition.

You may not perhaps know that he is now Commdr. in Chief of the British army in succession to the Duke of Cambridge.

To John M. Brown

160 West 86th Street, New York, November 13, 1896 [LC]

My dear Mr. Brown: I have been a good deal pressed lately, and put off looking at the agreements until yesterday. It occurred to me whether the words "retail price" were sufficiently definite as regards books sold in England, and also whether witnesses & other formalities are necessary to make the document legally valid, looking to the distant future. As between you and myself I am quite satisfied, but my hopes (perhaps undue) look to a future beyond our probable span of life, for the benefit of my children in my copyrights & I want therefore to have all papers connected with my books put in form concerning which no question is likely to arise between our successors. I return one copy signed, but will ask you to let me know whether anything further is required for complete legal precision and obligation.

You will be interested to know that I sent in my application for retirement day before yesterday, immediately on the reasonable certainty that the Venezuela business was out of the way. I have no reply as yet, but have never known a case of such application refused. The President's approval is formally necessary & I anticipate involves some delay.

The battle-plans are ready for returning to you corrected, & will probably go forward tomorrow.

To Augustus Lowell

160 West 86th Street, New York, November 29, 1896 [HUL]

My dear Sir: In the slips recently sent me by Dr. Cotting, I notice that it is expected that every Lowell Institute Lecture should be a new one. I had never expected that my own should be otherwise, but within the last two days it has occurred to me that two lectures, which I have used before the Naval War College at Newport—embracing a "Study of the Strategic Features of the Caribbean Sea and Gulf of Mexico," would afford a useful illustration of the methods by which a strategist proceeds to the solution of his problems.

Having been delivered before audiences small in number, and limited almost wholly to professional hearers, these are practically as new as if they had never been delivered; while the strongly expressed approval of military men, who have heard them is a fair guarantee of their probable value, beyond what an untried lecture can have.

In view of the requirement quoted, however, I have felt that I should ask you whether, if I should continue to think it desirable to use them, I would be at liberty to do so.

To John M. Brown

160 West 86th Street, New York, November 30, 1896 [LC]

Dear Mr. Brown: I enclose a letter from the *Forum*, to which I shall reply tomorrow, giving your name & that of Sampson Low as the publishers. It occurred to me that this matter of advance sheets might require consideration as a matter of precedent—whether other periodicals or papers would have just cause of offence, if conceded to one & not to all; and where you would draw the line. I suppose the *Forum* will write you shortly. How about the London *Times*, for example?

I have written the English officer who mentioned Lord Wolseley's words to me. There has not yet been time enough for a reply. Wolseley is a man of such exceptional distinction, however that he would not constitute a precedent.

I must have the judgment of your experience of such matters—and beg you to advise me. The Washington correspondent of the London *Chronicle* has requested an interview on "Nelson & the British Navy." I replied that I would see him, but did not wish to give away the book beforehand, nor run the risk of partial expressions liable to be misunderstood. He replies as enclosed. I shall appoint him Friday evening next, and would be glad of any suggestions from you in the matter.

In reading the *page* proof I have fancied the type impressions more defective, imperfect, than formerly. This may be imagination only, due to quality of paper, but I mention it.

Marston wrote me that he hopes to get a portrait of Nelson's child from his descendants. If he can *as a child* it will be a valuable addition.

Will you state whether insertions in the galleys cause much trouble or expense. I have several addenda, chiefly whole paragraphs, but occasionally insertions in the body of a paragraph—not over a dozen.

To Stephen B. Luce

160 West 86th Street, New York, December 5, 1896 [LC]

My dear Admiral: Your letter of the 1st was duly received, but I waited until after the dinner to reply.

The history of the dinner, as far as known to me, is this. The day after my retirement appeared in the papers Mr. Whitney sent me a note, asking me to name a day (in the now current week) in which I could meet some gentlemen at dinner with him. I named the 3d., and the dinner so came off.[1] It was much larger than I at all expected, or than Whitney himself first intended—I imagine; and as I was alluded to by the speaker as "the guest of the evening," it was, I think intended as a demonstration of good will [to] me at a very momentous instant of my life. Mr. Whitney made no allusion to the College—to me, or in my hearing. I fancy he regards his action in regard to it as purely official, nor am I disposed myself to regard it otherwise, although there were incidents that annoyed me at the time, and I fear that, like others, some personal feeling mingled with official opposition. I do not think, however, that he ever did anything to me that could possibly justify me in maintaining an attitude of personal hostility. As you know he and I were thrown together a good deal last winter in the Dunraven episode[2] and our relations then were extremely pleasant. In the present instance, of course I cannot but feel that he has extended one of those courtesies which signify a great deal & which I very much appreciate.

Kind remembrances to the ladies & believe me, my dear Admiral [etc.].

To John M. Brown

160 West 86th Street, New York, December 9, 1896 [LC]

My dear Mr. Brown: The ten maps were received to day. They are however almost exclusively battle plans—the map of Northern Italy and the Medn. were not among them; nor yet the Atlantic nor Baltic &c.

With regard to the small Sta. Cruz sketch (Vol. II, Nicolas) the galleys

---

1. *The New York Times* reported a dinner at the house of W. C. Whitney, probably in celebration of Captain Mahan's retirement the previous month. Among those present were Governor Morton, Mayor Strong, H. A. Herbert, B. F. Tracy, General Schofield, Admiral Porter, M. Sicard, Silas Weir Mitchell, C. F. Adams, Henry White, R. D. Evans, and Elihu Root.
2. A reference to the America Cup races, September 7, 10, and 12, 1895, between *Valkyrie III*, belonging to the Earl of Dunraven, and the *Defender*, owned by C. Oliver Iselin, E. D. Morgan, and William K. Vanderbilt of New York. Lord Dunraven's charges concerning the displacement of the *Defender* were made public in a pamphlet and a speech. The New York Yacht Club Committee, consisting of J. Pierpont Morgan, W. C. Whitney, and G. L. Rives, invited Mahan and Edward J. Phelps to join in an official inquiry. Dunraven's charges were dismissed and the Club later presented Mahan and Phelps handsome silver cups in appreciation of their services. Details are in *The New York Times*, January 21, 1896.

in which it must be noted have come in. I will hold them, therefore, till I receive the sketch. I think the galleys now represent full ⅓ of the work. I will return them as rapidly as I can, but can scarcely do efficiently more than ten full galleys per day—about thirty pages of text. The page proof is little trouble.

The battle plans received seem on cursory inspection to be all right—I will look at them again more closely. They will need titles, which I will supply, as there are no detailed references to them in the text.

With regard to the books you mention, it would be well for me to see them on the general principle of seeing everything. If the Paget book be *Paradoxes & Puzzles*[1] by an author of the same name, I have it. I should like to see Laughton's book.[2]

To John M. Brown

160 West 86th Street, New York, December 10, 1896 [LC]

Dear Mr. Brown: I have today a letter from Marston saying he is sending me Laughton's *Nelson Memorial*. If this be *Nelson & His Companions*, as I think likely, dont duplicate it.

Can I be informed at what rate proof need be read, having regard to progress now made, in order to have book out before March 31. I wish to cause no delay, but also not to be unnecessarily hurried, as that injures my work; & besides I have additions to make—not to speak of outside labors.

The proof reader in the same 30 pages has allowed extrordinary to pass, and a hyphen omitted at the end of a line. While I read very carefully, and the galleys always twice, I rather look to him, or her, to correct such inaccuracies and in grammar. These are not the first, though there have not been many. For everything connected with style punctuation &c I hold myself accountable, though very glad to receive suggestions.

[P.S.] The galleys for Santa Cruz sketch are here, and corrected.

---

1. John Paget, *Paradoxes and Puzzles, Historical, Judicial, and Literary*. London: W. Blackwood and Sons, 1874. Paget succeeded Sir William Hamilton as British Ambassador at Naples. Contents of the *Paradoxes* are: The New "Examen": An Inquiry into the Evidence Relating to Certain Passages in Lord Macaulay's History; and Vindications: I. Nelson and Caracciolo. II. Lady Hamilton.
2. Laughton wrote a *Nelson* for the *English Men of Action* series (1895), and also *The Nelson Memorial, Nelson and his Companions in Arms*. London: George Allen, 1896.

To J. Franklin Jameson

160 West 86th Street, New York, December 12, 1896 [LC]

My dear Sir: I send your herewith a Review of Barnes's book.[1] It is not, in my opinion, the kind of work that is entitled to encumber your pages with any thing pretending to serious criticism. I supposed it written by the author's father, who was once a seaman, and is a man of ability. The style is turgid and pretentious.

There is, however, no necessity for saying anything more than I here do—nor shall I feel dissatisfied if you exclude the notice entirely. It is not serious history, as you and I naturally anticipated it would be.

I am sorry to say I have absolutely no time for such writing as you kindly ask.

To John M. Brown

160 West 86th Street, New York, December 15, 1896 [LC]

My dear Mr. Brown: I have returned by today's mail Fraser's *Hic et Ubique.*[1] It is an amusing book, but, if he is not more accurate in other things than in naval reminiscences, it has no great value. Falconer was not lost finally on the scene of the "shipwreck" but somewhere between the Cape of Good Hope & Madagascar, & there is I think another similar blunder which I forget. I have Paget's *Paradoxes and Puzzles.* He is upon the whole right, though much more is known than when he wrote thirty years ago.

Speaking of the Vienna bust it has occurred to me that, *if* you wanted an illustration on the cover, like the ships in *Sea Power,* it might be a good one. This is mere suggestion.

I have looked at the pictures of Horatia,[2] and agree with you that the young lady one is best. My first idea was to have the child that Nelson had seen, and owned as his; but children are so much alike it would probably convey little to readers.

I have just been glancing over the *Nelson Memorial* to see whether Laughton had unearthed a letter upon which I hit in the vast bulk of the Morrison Collection.[3] I dont find it, but confound him he has whipped off

---

1. *See* Mahan to Jameson, October 20, 1896.

1. Sir William Augustus Fraser, *Hic et Ubique.* London: S. Low, Marston & Co., 1893. Scribner's published an American edition.
2. Horatia Nelson Thompson, illegitimate child of Lord Nelson and Lady Hamilton.
3. In 1880, Alfred Morrison discovered the documents on which Pettigrew's *Life* was based, and printed a full transcript. J. C. Jeaffreson used it in his *Lady Hamilton*

some other cream—in the way of rarely quoted material. However, I trust I still have a good deal yet unpublished & more that has drifted out of memory; and I also hope my original contribution of criticism & comment may be found valuable. I am glad, however, that there is a prospect of the book being out, before Nelson is torn to pieces by those who are rushing in.

To J. Franklin Jameson

160 West 86th Street, New York, December 16, 1896 [LC]

Dear Sir: I shall be very pleased to review Oppenheim's book[1] provided you will not press me for time; and I may say that, time permitting, I should not be sorry to bind myself to that careful examination which reviewing requires in the case of any naval historical literature.

As regards Laughton's book I feel some hesitancy—delicacy—as I myself have going through press a work on the same subject—a *Life of Nelson*. I incline to think Laughton's book is a sketchy—possibly hasty—book by a man widely read and thoroughly posted on his subject—but I question whether he has had the time or space to do justice to his knowledge. I have the book but have only glanced at it hastily.

[P.S.] Please enclose slip of what you want in reviews. I have lost the one I had.

To John M. Brown

160 West 86th Street, New York, December 17, 1896 [LC]

Dear Mr. Brown: I return herewith the portraits of Horatia and strongly favor the insertion of the one at 22 years of age.

When you have collected all portraits that are to go in, if you will send

---

and *Lord Nelson* (London: Hurst and Blackett, 1888), and in his 1889 *Queen of Naples and Lord Nelson*, and so apparently did Laughton in his 1895 and 1896 books on Nelson.

1. M. Oppenheim, *History of the Administration of the Royal Navy and of Merchant Shipping in Relation to the Navy, 1509–1660*; with an introduction treating of the earlier period. London: J. Lane, 1896. In that year Oppenheim also edited the first volume of *Naval Accounts and Inventories of the Reign of Henry VII*, for the Navy Records Society.

me a list of them, and copies of plans and maps (not already sent) as they are ready, I will designate just where they are to go, and the titles of plans &c I will write on the face of them. The latter—titles—is a matter of some importance.

I would like your opinion on a certain matter. If you will look at p. 178, *Nelson Memorial*, you will find Lady Hamilton's account of Lady Nelson's conduct. I rather wonder at Laughton's inserting it. I never looked at Harrison's *Life of Nelson*,[1] believing it, as L. says, to be untrustworthy; hence I never saw this, but, had I, I should not have inserted it. The question arises, this being republished, should I insert it *and with it* the account in the *Memoirs of Lady H.* (which you sent me in Newport) of Nelson's conduct towards his wife & especially that nasty episode of Lady N. holding the basin &c when Lady H. was sick, while Nelson was abusing her for heartlessness. Though without partisanship, I have been careful to bring out Lady N's side—but the scene alluded to I never intended to bring in. Now, Laughton has revised Harrison's story, shall I let it go, or shall I apply the corrective? i.e. shall I give both. I would like your opinion, or that of any one you would like to ask; though I confess it is far from improbable I shall decide for myself. Still your opinion will weigh. The incident, in *Lady H's Memoir*, was between Nov. 1800 and January 1801.

Although called *Lady H's Memoirs*, the book is in the interest of the wife.

[P.S.]   Laughton has taken some of my cream, but not all. Of course, my *own* treatment remains my own—the personal equation.

If you recommend to insert—please send me the *Lady H Memoirs*.

To John M. Brown

160 West 86th Street, New York, December 18, 1896 [LC]

Dear Mr. Brown: Marston sends me today a card, that he has unearthed a copy of Brackenridge,[1] Balto 1818, in London. As he seems to have wanted it for my use, it will be needless to trouble you farther, as there are two or three copies in the Astor & Lenox Libraries.

---

1. The *Dictionary of National Biography* describes James Harrison, whose *Life of Nelson* appeared in 1814, as "an obscure writer engaged by Lady Hamilton to exalt her claims on the government."

1. Henry Marie Brackenridge, *Voyage to South America, Performed by Order of the American Government, in the Years 1817 and 1818, in the Frigate Congress*. By H.M.B. . . . Secretary to the Mission. Baltimore: John D. Toy, printer, 1819.

To Alfred Ernest Keet[1]

160 West 86th Street, New York, December 21, 1896 [LC]

My dear Sir: I ought sooner to have answered your letter of the 10th, but it is write, write, all the time, and my pen kicks sometimes at letter writing. As I told you before, I cannot now commit myself to engagements, but I can say that in the matter of the subject suggested in yours of the 8th I will reserve the *formal* treatment for the *Forum*, subject to our future agreement in the matter. You will appreciate that in articles already promised there may be incidental remarks of the bearing of that fact on the U. S. Navy: but for systematic treatment I shall consider the *Forum* "has a lien" as you express it.[2]

To John M. Brown

160 West 86th Street, New York, December 28, 1896 [LC]

My dear Mr. Brown: I have received this morning a letter from Judge W. O'Connor Morris whose address is "Gartnamona, Tullamore, Ireland," asking that he may have advance sheets of *Nelson*, as he thinks he will certainly review it. I very strongly recommend that advance sheets be sent him just as soon and as rapidly as to any other person whatsoever—"most favored nation." He will give as good a notice as he conscientiously can, and is a practiced and capable military writer. He reviewed the other books in the *Academy*,[1] and we have since exchanged courtesies.

What would you think of the enclosed as a Cover and Title page title for the book. It need not affect the page headings. It results from a suggestion of Marston's, coming from Mr. Stuart J. Reid, one of their company, who furnished me a Nelsonian story. They said, what is very true, that there are so many "Lives of Nelson"; and it might be beneficial to catch this on to the Sea Power series, whence it originated.

I was very sorry not to have seen more of you yesterday, but the regret is only personal for, as far as I know, no business *required* talk.

---

1. The original of this letter does not show the addressee, but it seems probable that it is Keet, who was editor of the *Forum* from 1895 to 1897.
2. Mahan did not publish in the *Forum* after the departure of its distinguished editor, Walter Hines Page, in 1895.

1. A journal published in London. After 1902, it was titled *Academy and Literature*. Morris reviewed Mahan's *Nelson* in the June 1, 1897, issue of *Fortnightly Review*.

[Enclosure]

The
Exaltation
of
British Sea Power
in the
Career of Nelson
(Life)
by &c

The
Fulfilment
of
British Sea Power
in the
Career of Nelson

The
Demonstration
in the
Importance of Sea Power
In the
Life of Nelson

N.B.   One of these three, or any combination or modification of them.

To Robert U. Johnson

160 West 86th Street, New York, December 31, 1896 [NYPL]

Dear Mr. Johnson: If in the *Trafalgar* article is used the likeness of Nelson, taken in Sept. 1805, in possession of Sir W. Parker, I hope it may be possible to insert somewhere the certificate to its origin, by the artist, which is on the back of the picture. Sir W. Parker laid some stress upon it, and it is interesting as establishing the date of this, probably the last ever painted.[1]

I am sorry that in the plan of Aboukir Bay, this number, it is not stated to be of 1799—contemporary. The bottom also changes in alluvial waters. It will be so stated in my *Life of Nelson*.

---

1. *See* Mahan to Brown, December 31, 1896, and January 6, 1897.

To John M. Brown

160 West 86th Street, New York, December 31, 1896 [LC]

Dear Mr. Brown: If among the portraits of Nelson, you have obtained that from Sir Wm. Parker, taken in Aug–Sept, 1805, it is desirable that there appear the artist's certificate in the book attesting the authenticity and date. Can you judge now whether they can appear *under* the portrait or shall I introduce a footnote, giving it opposite the page of insertion? The former seems to me best in every way; but if the latter, I should know speedily, as the galleys will soon be in my hand. In this case also please send me the certificate. I told Parker I would endeavor to see this inserted; and with his name as possessor it should be.

To John M. Brown

160 West 86th Street, New York, January 1, 1897 [LC]

My dear Mr. Brown: Your letter was recd. today. I wrote to Major Trench (about Lord Wolseley) on the 25th November. Not knowing his address, I enclosed to Marston to forward. Marston took the matter in hand, but as yet I have heard no more. Marston seemed to think that Wolseley might antagonize the Navy with which he is not popular, but there is nothing to prevent representatives of the Navy having an equal show in advance sheets, and so I wrote him—that I expected he on that side and you on this would see what was needful in the matter done. I have the *Remains of Mrs. Trench*[1] and have quoted freely from them, though I unfortunately forgot to notice her favorable opinion of the intelligence &c shown in his letters to Lady H.,[2] published in 1814—an opinion which shows the fairness and independence of her mind, for the letters were then considered vulgar & damaging. I have spelt Marseilles without the final s because the latter is a causeless English addition to the French; but have retained the s in Nelson's letters. I admit that to be consistent I should spell Lyons Lyon but the Gulf of Lyons is such an extraordinary Anglicized misnomer for Golfe du Lion, that one is at liberty almost to do as one

---

1. *The Remains of the Late Mrs. Richard Trench, being Selections from Her Journals, Letters, and Other Papers,* edited by her son, the Dean of Westminster. 2d edition, revised, London: Parker, Son, and Brown, 1862.
2. Horatio Nelson, *The Letters of Lord Nelson to Lady Hamilton; with a Supplement of Interesting Letters, by Distinguished Characters.* London: T. Lovewell and Company, 1814. The book was edited under the direction of Emma Hamilton.

pleases. If you like, I have no particular objection to Marseilles, but it would be scarcely worthwhile to change now. I like your suggestion for title, but the matter can bide a while. I am a little afraid I have not divided the volumes equally enough. Will you look into that? There are 398 pp. in Vol I—the first two chapters of II are 20 and 30 pages respectively and III has to take the index. Vol I will have the preface but that will not run beyond 4 pages. I do not wish a change, if it can be avoided. The stopping place of I is good.

To Samuel A. Ashe

160 West 86th Street, New York, January 3, 1897 [DUL]

My dear Ashe: I have taken a very long time to acknowledge your letter, much longer than I ought to have waited in expressing my sympathy with the trials I learned for the first time, and my indignation at the shabby treatment you have undergone. I dont wonder you lost heart for the time, but you are not the sort of man that will suffer long from want of pluck.

You will have seen that I carried out my purpose of retiring about the time your letter was received. I had in truth only been waiting for an official announcement that the Venezuela business was settled. Despite the rumors in the press, I could not myself see that matters had changed since the President's message of a year ago, and I shrank from the appearance of retiring while possible trouble from an overt source remained. The day after the Marquis of Salisbury's announcement, I sent in my application being satisfied that he would not have said what he did, if any doubts remained. The step introduces no change in my recent manner of life. It only frees me from the possibility of interruption by the Dept. I lose future promotion and increase of pay, and have taken the chance that I may more than make good the loss by writing. Like all other moves there is a risk of failure, but I think the chances are good. The pay of literature is not great—except in fiction—not at all proportionate, in my case, to the labor I put into it; but upon the whole I like it, and at present there seems a sufficiently fair prospect of demand. But New York is an expensive place, and I cannot for a year or two know just how I stand to win or lose.

I remember your sister whom you name very well indeed, although I think she was scarcely more than a girl when I visited you in Wilmington. Please remember me to her very kindly and thank her for her invitation, which, however, it would be quite impossible for us to accept. The question of expense aside, my occupations for the next six months leave me not a day to spare; I am, in fact, in fear lest I may fail to meet some of my promises—

a bad start in a new career. It is indeed this pressure for time that has delayed my writing—that and the fact that with pen so constantly in hand for business, I procrastinate shockingly taking it up for other work.

I have read, and today re-read, what you say on the silver question. My knowledge is so superficial that I hesitate to call my way of looking "an opinion." So far as I go, it is impossible for me to see in the expression "double standard" anything but a contradiction in terms, and historically, it appears to me that while we have used both metals, and established at one time a legal ratio between them, that notion has been too hard for us. Its ratio has varied despite us, and consequently we have practically been on a single basis always; that basis being the metal, which, at our arbitrary ratio, was the least valuable. The fractional currency I believe is preserved in circulation, by being debased. Having less silver in it than its face value, it did not disappear in the [illegible] days of silver, as the whole dollar did. It is over late in life for me to turn political economist, or to affect anything more than a belief in the broad proposition I advance—just as, on the tariff, I dont pretend to any mastery of detail, but am satisfied, as an economical question, that the government had better leave people to protect themselves and raise only revenue by customs. I detest governmental meddling, and for the same reason incline to the view now advocated by some journals here, that government retire from the banking business by withdrawing its promissory notes. I have little hope of it. The swing of the pendulum seems to me toward Socialism in the sense of the Government taking more and more into its hands—to me the insidious growth of a new slavery. I shall not live to see it, probably, but I grieve for my children and my children's children. As none of mine are either married or engaged, this is perhaps over-careful.

I can entirely appreciate and sympathize, as far as one who has not the same experience can, with the feelings of your people under the distress of which you tell me. The reasons for the failure of prosperity antecedent to the bad times of 90–93 you do not mention; but from my own ignorance of economical matters, I can realize the perplexity of those who see they have lost, for [illegible] both causes. I can understand, too, the feeling that any change may be welcomed in faith, on the mere chance of betterment—but I cannot go so far as to say that my intellect is convinced that the point is reached when it is best to leap without looking.

Altogether the horizon is not yet bright, but things have gone on so since ere the world was, and upon the whole men seem to be really better off than they were a hundred years ago—and God reigns. The last is the point to which I always come back—though I must humbly admit that my faith has not undergone the severe trials from which some have emerged triumphantly.

To John M. Brown

160 West 86th Street, New York, January 6, 1897 [LC]

My dear Mr. Brown: I have taken my time over the portraits, but believe I can answer fully and positively now. The Abbott[1] *with* the hat I dont want, the one without it, I want for the reason I gave. I have made notes on the margin of each. Blackwood I am also willing to give up. If Sir Hyde Parker[2]—the real man—cannot be had, that would make three off; but I hope it may be possible yet to get him. It is vexatious that James[3] should have misled me.

I should be disposed to yield either Sir *Peter* Parker, or Captain Locker[4] if we can get Hyde Parker, and I would put the choice on your art man. Both are early patrons, Locker one of his closest friends. Let the finest face and portrait be chosen and give up the other. I prefer Locker.

The Rigaud[5] portrait we ought to retain as the only one of Nelson in youth. I would give all the other plates.

I note what you say about having no printed matter on the portraits themselves. I am rather sorry for this, but suppose there are decisive reasons. I would suggest, however, that the Abbott portrait be called in the list "Nelson in 1798" the Whichelo,[6] "Nelson in 1805." I intend to place them respectively at the head of the chapters dealing with the Nile and Trafalgar. The Rigaud might similarly be named "Nelson in 1781," and I will place it suitably. If Hoppner's[7] and Beechey's[8] can be dated it would be well enough but less important.

I believe I suggested that Horatia's should be entitled simply Horatia at 22, but you can judge of that better.

I will return at once all the proofs and prints also the plans and maps lately received which I have examined and corrected. Please bear with any marks of haste, especially in over-wordiness. I am really awfully busy.

The alterations for Chaps. XII and XIV were mailed today to the firm and I hope will be found satisfactory.

[P.S.] On the back of the Whichelo portrait is written as follows "This

---

1. Francis Lemuel Abbott, who painted Nelson's portrait in 1798.
2. Commander of the fleet sent to the Baltic in 1801.
3. William James, English naval historian, author of *Naval History of Great Britain from the Declaration of War by France in 1793 to the Accession of George IV*. 5 vols., London, 1822–1824; later editions in 1826, 1837, 1888.
4. Admiral Parker was an early patron of Nelson; and William Locker was a teacher and friend of Nelson.
5. John Francis Rigaud's portrait was done in 1781 for Captain Locker.
6. C. John M. Whichelo.
7. John Hoppner painted a full-length portrait of Nelson.
8. Sir William Beechey.

head was sketched from the Hero during his short stay at Merton the beginning of September 1805 by me. John Whichelo"

Can this be inserted in the list, along with the fact that the original is in the possession of Sir W. B. Parker, Bart., of Blackbrook House, Fareham, Hants?

If it can be, I need make no entry in notes. In speaking to me Parker rather held to this. As I remember, the artist gave it to his father, who was the last to survive of Nelson's captains.

To J. Franklin Jameson

160 West 86th Street, New York, January 9, 1897 [LC]

My dear Sir: I am afraid I cannot undertake the review of James' *Journal*[1] at present. I have it, being a subscriber to the Navy Records Society. Oppenheim's book is not yet recd.[2] I trust I shall have shaken myself a little clear ere it does.

To John M. Brown

160 West 86th Street, New York, January 11, 1897 [LC]

Dear Mr. Brown: It is to be regretted that the enclosed was not sooner sent, but Col. Esdaile, probably, Marston possibly, overlooked it. I recd. it today from the latter. The particular thing Mrs. Eccles requests could scarcely have been done, even had time been given, but I will write to Marston and suggest that if Mrs. Eccles will send particulars of coloring eyes, hair, &c I will see if we can get it inserted, either in List of illustrations, or at the end of Chapter XV, where (on p. 115 old numbering) there is room enough. Which would be best? Oddly enough I received a letter by the same mail from a man in Demerara, who knew an old lady who always spoke of Lady Nelson as the brunette, of whom the blonde, Lady H. got the better. The old lady knew Lady Nelson well.

Please let me know just how the volumes are to be divided, as there are references to pages in Vol II, which I cannot insert rightly till I know.

I expect to get off the last of the galleys this week. The only probable delay being hesitation over letting the last chapter go out of my hands. I finish the next to the last today.

---

1. *Journal of Rear-Admiral Bartholomew James, 1752–1828.* Edited by Laughton and Sullivan. London: Navy Records Society, 1896.
2. *See* Mahan to Jameson, December 16, 1896.

To John M. Brown

160 West 86th Street, New York, January 13, 1897 [LC]

My dear Mr. Brown: Yours of the 11th was recd. yesterday. I note that Vol. 2 begins with Chapter XIV. It is a better division than XIII would have been.

I am puzzled about the "originals" of the two plans sent, to which you allude and ask them to be sent you. I have no recollection of such originals, other than the plans themselves now sent me. That of the "Second Stage of the Nile" is identical—absolutely—with that which appears in the *Century* for January. I have made several additions, to make it more complete than was necessary in the other, and the *Leander* is shown as firing from her bow as no ship could. I cant think how that happened. The other, Copenhagen, is identical with what will be in Feb. *Century*. The only change I have noted on it is the wind arrow, and that the references from the same plan in *Sea Power*, Vol 2. p. 44 should be entered.

I am delighted with the Whichelo Nelson and thank you very much for it. Lady Nelson, I trust will look her sweetest—poor woman, let posterity take to her. Now, as regards questions, please ask all you like. We are both seeking the success of the book. I cannot say why the *Century* spells Trou*b*ridge[1] Trow*b*ridge. They have their own canons and do as they please. I have an autograph letter of his which gives Trou. Mrs. Mahan who typewrites for me almost always puts w, and I may have failed to correct. As regards mar*line*spike, the only dictionaries I have here, *Worcester* & the *Imperial*[2] give it the preference, but they also give marlingspike. If you think it would be better changed I shall have no objection. I am glad to know the proof reading has interested you. It is a new departure for me, handling so much detail. I have tried to keep interest before me as my aim, and I am satisfied it can only be attained in biography by ample room—which I have taken. I have got all the anecdote I could and woven it in to the best of my ability.

I have been all through my desk, but find no copies of the plans nor does my memory recall any. I will hold them for a moment till I hear from you. Tomorrow I go to Phila. to return Saturday. I finish the galley reading tonight, but will hold last chapter till my return—forwarding probably Tuesday. All the rest has gone. I have kept back page proof for Phila, as it is easy work. It is complete through p. 253 (first numbering). The enclosed[3] speaks for itself—dont trouble to return.

---

1. Sir Thomas Troubridge, who served under Sir John Jervis at Cape St. Vincent, and was with Nelson in the operations on the Italian coast in 1799.
2. *The Imperial Dictionary and Cyclopedia.* Robert Hunter, ed. Toronto: J. T. Ford and Company. No information on a *Worcester Dictionary* has been found.
3. Enclosure not found.

To John M. Brown

Dear Mr. Brown: I shall return to-morrow the likenesses of Trou-bridge and Lady Nelson, also two plans: one of Copenhagen the other Second Phase of Nile. As regards the two last they were sent to me exactly as I had sent them corrected—not a change of any sort in accordance with my notes. I now have made the Nile one a little clearer, by drawing in figures myself, which I do exceedingly badly, and by adding names so as to show where they are wanted. I think, however, that as first sent, with a little pains by draughtsman, this trouble might have been avoided. As re-gards Troubridge's likeness, I prefer to leave the final decision in your hands. I am an indifferent judge in such matters, and there is no gainsaying your words that the original should be adhered to. The last of the galleys has been read and marked. I kept the last chapter some time, and the more because I was hunting in vain for an incident I had in it the source of which had escaped me. As page proof is comparatively easy the text is nearly done. The preface I have in pretty good shape already. I think we may con-gratulate ourselves on the returns of the last half year, considering the times.

To John M. Brown

My dear Mr. Brown: I received yesterday proofs with the corrected numbering of the pages affected by the transfer of chapters XII & XIII. Curiosity leading me to see how a certain passage would look in the book I find a bracket missing, which is needed and which *is in* the duplicate page proof now in my hands. I enclose a memorandum. As compared with my other books, the proof reading has seemed to me indifferently done.

I have finished the preface—a short 1,000 words, and nearly finished the "Contents"; hope to send them about the middle of the week. There will then remain the Index, the fixing of the place of the illustrations and battle plans, and drawing up a table of these; also final form for Title and title-page. As regards the illustrations (portraits) I attach importance to putting in the list, along with the Whichelo portrait, the inscription on the back, which I believe I sent you. So much, that is, as certifies authenticity. This I wish because the owner wished it—Sir W. Parker; I think his name as owner with the inscription should appear. Marston writes me with reference to the portrait of Lady Nelson that I would be best to mention "from a photo by E. Kelly photographer of Plymouth"; because by their law he has a copyright in the plate.

I see Vol II comes a little short. I will make the Index copious, & I suppose you will consider whether a little larger type than usual would materially fill out deficiency. I dont know how much it matters, after all.

To John M. Brown

160 West 86th Street, New York, January 26, 1897 [LC]

Dear Mr. Brown: I shall send tomorrow addressed to the firm, the "Contents" for both volumes, and the Preface. I would be glad if you can find time to look over the latter in case of any suggestions.

How do you like the enclosed Title page. I have thought of "Realization," and of "Fulfilment," in place of "Embodiment." All three express the same idea, that Nelson is the highest expression of the capabilities and influence of British Sea Power. While hunting through the Dictionary I found under embodiment this quotation from Macaulay: "Doctrines must be embodied before they can excite strong public feeling." This is just my idea: Nelson embodies, and so gives tangible shape to the idea of British Sea Power. You will find the idea *expressed* in the opening words of the book and of the third chapter.

I have an idea upon which I want your opinion. I have purposely omitted any attempt to summarize Nelson's character &c, thinking it more artistic to aim at producing the impression I seek by the gradual evolution of the book itself. I am thinking now, however, of writing an article on the "Salient Characteristics of Nelson's Genius," with the idea of publishing it [in] about a June number of some magazine. If the book takes well, it will be in demand (the article) and may also react favorably on the book. I will not attempt it unless I can get a very good price, nor unless I can command time, but before taking any step I would like to ask if you see any objection to my doing this.[1]

[Enclosure]

The
Life of Nelson
The
Embodiment
of the
Sea Power of Great Britain
by
Captain A. T. Mahan, D.C.L., L.L.D.
United States Navy

---

1. Mahan did not write such an article.

Author of the *Influence of Sea Power upon History 1660–1783*; of the *Influence of Sea Power upon the French Revolution and Empire*; and of a *Life of Admiral Farragut.*

To John M. Brown

160 West 86th Street, New York, January 31, 1897 [LC]

Dear Mr. Brown: I am entirely satisfied to have Marseilles spelled with an "s." As for Latouche Tréville[1] I have taken this spelling "La*t*ouche," from the only French naval work immediately at hand, and if it occurs differently in my own text, it has been through oversight. Nelson spelled it La Touche, and I have been very careful to preserve his spelling and grammar, the latter of which is often very faulty, as part of himself.

As regards the abrupt termination of the book, I will try and consider the matter; but I own to a very strong feeling that to follow up the death scene at Trafalgar by *anything* else would be of the nature of an anti-climax; and that the obtrusion of my own analysis of his character, however quiet, and however firmly drawn, would be like a post-mortem, and in the contrast would approach bathos. The dying moments as depicted, and drawn from the several accounts of eye-witnesses, have nothing of myself except the arrangement; but it tells the story of his character with absolutely [*sic*] fidelity. His death is an epitome of his life. I prefer at least to await the verdict of the reviewers and I could doubtless arrange with any Review, if I publish such an article, for permission to add it to future editions (with proper acknowledgement) in case the general tendency of criticism should demand it.

It has occurred to me that possibly an acknowledgment should be made, in the preface, of the trouble Marston has taken. I did not forget this, but at the moment thought that, as one of the parties directly interested in the work, it would be as beside the matter as an acknowledgment to myself or to you.

[P.S.]   I should be glad of your opinion in the matter & if you think it should be made, is his name Richard or Robert? I intend to give him a presentation copy, as he has in many ways aided me.

---

1. Admiral Louis René Madeleine Le Vassor, comte de Latouche-Tréville, who captured Port-au-Prince in 1802.

To John M. Brown

160 West 86th Street, New York, February 2, 1897 [LC]

Dear Mr. Brown: I return the queries sent me by you, with my replies. I am very much indebted for the suggestions, though I have not adopted all. I am glad to infer that you think well of the book, and I trust we shall not be disappointed in the result.

To John M. Brown

160 West 86th Street, New York, February 8, 1897 [LC]

My dear Mr. Brown: You will find in the enclosed list of illustrations, and their places, that I have made some unimportant changes in the position of Nelson's own portraits by Hoppner & Whichelo. I have very carefully considered the place for every illustration. There is one point to which I will ask your attention, viz: that the Baltic, as well as Atlantic, may show clear of the paging, just as the Atlantic does in the Sea Power books.

I will also mention, what I believe has been attended to in the *recent* Sea Power Fr. Revn. Editions, viz: that the group I of Spanish ships, in Fig *2*, should be heading in a direction opposite to that shown in the first edition. This was unimportant in *Sea Power*, but essential in *Nelson*. You will recall our correspondence on this matter.

I am sending by this mail to Wilson the Preface, with Marston lines and the Contents. I shall give the rest of this week to the Index.

I am greatly encouraged to hear that you are so favorably impressed with the book. Marston has mentioned in a letter to me that he would be able to increase his first order, he thought, if he had a prospectus to work on—or to issue. Would you like me to prepare one? or could you have one prepared? The *Critic*[1] has been teasing me for information, but I reply I am not anxious to give the book away too soon—that they shall have it as soon as any one. I should welcome any suggestions from you in this matter.

I have been really so driven latterly that I cannot write as thoughtful and coherent a letter as at other times. Fortunately, I believe, as far as *Nelson* is concerned, nothing now remains but the question of policy in increasing the sales—which is yours more than mine.

Dont forget O'Connor Morris; and could you contrive that Roosevelt be asked to write a *full* review.[2]

---

1. *Critic, an Illustrated Monthly Review of Literature, Art, and Life.* New York: 1881–1906.
2. Roosevelt apparently did not review *Nelson*.

To John M. Brown

160 West 86th Street, New York, February 9, 1897 [LC]

Dear Mr. Brown: I had closed and mailed my letter last night before I noticed that Sir P. Parker was not on your list, & that I omitted the ships. For the former I dont care very much. The ships had better face p. 235, Vol II. I was a little disappointed that we did not get the *Agamemnon* and *Victory* separately; for to me a ship has an individuality and I dont think the plate we have makes clear which is the *Agamemnon*. Perhaps, if we have the success we hope for, a future edition, fifth or 6th may justify the two ships separately and Parker; the work would gain in completeness thereby.

To John M. Brown

160 West 86th Street, New York, February 10, 1897 [LC]

Dear Mr. Brown: A few nights ago at a dinner, Dr. Weir Mitchell[1] came to me on behalf of the Century Company with the proposition that I should write something for them on the War of 1812—or the Revolution—to appear serially. When completed they would be willing that it should be published by some other company, or firm, although they like to publish in book form, themselves, what has appeared in the Magazine. I suppose the proposition came from my fighting off a previous proposal, because conflicting with my purpose to write *1812*, as the conclusion of Sea Power, and to publish through you. The arrangement, as conveyed through Dr. Mitchell, would be that they publish serially, and you afterwards in book form; and it came about, I presume from his present novel passing through their hands under the same conditions, and from his visiting the office the same day he was to dine with me. I replied simply that I would take the matter into careful consideration. I should of course like to make the most out of my work, while I feel at the same time that I owe much regard to *our* past relations. My object in writing now therefore is to ask whether you think such an arrangement could be made, to my advantage, without injuring you. I should like to be in full possession of your views before I call upon the Century, which I have promised to do some time this month.

Do you think it would be possible to insert the enclosed at the end of paragraph first, on page 208 Vol I of *Nelson*. Page 200 ends the chapter & has abundant room. My sympathies are greatly enlisted on behalf of Lady Nelson, and I would like to tone down what I have said, the more so as there

---

1. Silas Weir Mitchell, physician, poet, and novelist. His *Hugh Wynne, Free Quaker* was appearing in serial form in *Century Magazine*.

are one or two things I have accidentally omitted, and cannot now insert till a future revision. This must go now or not at all.

[P.S.] Mitchell's book is now actually in print, and held back—the company having paid him $5,000 for the serial publication.

To John M. Brown

160 West 86th Street, New York, February 15, 1897 [LC]

Dear Mr. Brown: I have recast the opening of the Preface with an idea which occurred to me two days ago, and which brings it more in line with the title. I send it for your examination, but chiefly on account of a different point, which you will understand from the enclosed letters sent me by Marston. Shall Mr. Esdaile be called "Mr" or "Lieutenant Colonel?" Personally, I am willing to call him anything that may please him, but I dont want to commit an absurdity in print. Have you not among your friends, somebody who can give us advice in the matter?

I have written to the firm to day, and advised publication as soon after March 15 as possible. I will add to you that I want to get it beyond my power to alter any more. I cannot tell you what a satisfaction your favorable opinion has been to me. In making the Index I have had to realize that with my mind set on Nelson, I have omitted many trivial details—historical &c. A curious instance is that I cannot find a single mention by name of his brother William, though others are often quoted as to his brother. The fault is on the right side. I enclose a memorandum of the only mistake, as distinguished from omission, that I have discovered in this minute overhauling.

Mrs. Eccles' note gives Lady Nelson's coloring, if you see fit to insert it in the List of Portraits. On this subject Marston wrote me (and should have written you) that "our law is that the photographer has the copyright in his particular negative, so it may be wise to mention the portrait is from a photo by him of the original." The photographer alluded to, of Lady Nelson's portrait is Mr. E. Kelly, of Plymouth.

You did not answer my question about the prospectus. With reference to the Century matter, I will keep in view all you say and shall be obliged to you at all times to put all aspects of a case frankly before me. I think I begin to see my way to a satisfactory arrangement for all parties. It was from the first my purpose to make *1812* largely a philosophical study of the causes, course and results of the war in its broader aspects, and only under pressure did I accept the idea of treating the single ship fights. Now it is the latter—the pictorial—the Century wants. I dont say that that will be outcome, but I think something like that. As an author, I should seriously object to a thoughtful work being broken up by impertinent illustrations of fancy battle scenes, medallions and the deuce knows what all, like Sloane's *Napoleon*. If I could arrange with the Century for something of that character, mingled fights and character sketches &c, the two books would be complemental.

[P.S.] The Revolution is part of the Century's suggestion—and dont touch our series.

To Roy B. Marston

New York, February 19, 1897[1]

I have for some time had before me your letter of the 25th ult. asking material for a biographical sketch. I have for the most part succeeded in shunting the interviewers, but I will jot down a few notes of an unsuccessful life—beyond the literary success of the past half-dozen years.

I was born in September, 1840, and am therefore now in my fifty-seventh year. My naval career has been marked by no incidents of special interest beyond the very cordial and distinguished reception given me by your countrymen three years ago, which I attribute to the desire to recognize the just tribute I had paid to the influence of Great Britain upon the world through her sea power.

The manner in which I was led to take up and develop my "life's work," which I suppose may be said so far to consist in the *Sea Power* books, is sufficiently stated in the preface to the French Revolution book. I was at the time attached to a ship on the Pacific station—her commander—in 1884 when the proposition to develop a course of naval history was made to me. Casting around for the method of treatment I reached the solution stated in the preface.

It may be of interest to know it was when reading Mommsen's *History of Rome* in the English Club at Lima that I was struck by the non-recognition of the vital influence of sea power upon Hannibal's career.

The incident is to myself interesting because I attribute any success not to any breadth or thoroughness of historical knowledge but a certain aptitude to seize on salient features of an era—salient either by action or non-action, by presence or absence.

It may be interesting also to know that not only the general idea but the full leading outline of the whole story, from 1660–1812, was written down by me for Admiral Luce before I put pen to paper on the works themselves—before, in fact, I had acquired the knowledge necessary to the full

---

1. Published in R. B. Marston, "Captain Mahan and Our Navy," *The Sphere*, XVII (June 11, 1904), p. 250.

treatment of the subject. This illustrates, I think, the fact that my strength lies not in abundance of minute knowledge but in quick perception and broad grasp of a matter. I am, however, extremely painstaking as to the accuracy of what I insert, though less careful as to what I omit. The three last chapters of *Sea Power in the French Revolution* have, I think, received the most solid recognition of all my work. The idea was perfectly developed in my mind before—two years before—I studied up the matter. I was, of course, prepared to abandon my views if they proved erroneous, but I believe they are accepted.

Finally, I may say the term "sea power," which now has such vogue, was deliberately adopted by me to compel attention and, I hoped, to receive currency. Purists, I said to myself, may criticise me for marrying a Teutonic word to one of Latin origin, but I deliberately discarded the adjective, "maritime," being too smooth to arrest men's attention or stick in their minds. I do not know how far this is usually the case with phrases that obtain currency; my impression is that the originator is himself generally surprised at their taking hold.

I was not surprised in that sense. The effect produced was that which I fully purposed; but I *was* surprised at the extent of my success.

"Sea Power," in English at least, seems to have come to stay in the sense I used it. "The sea Powers" were often spoken of before, but in an entirely different manner—not to express, as I meant to, at once an abstract conception and a concrete fact.

It may seem odd to you, but I do not to this day understand my success. I had done what I intended to; I recognize that people have attributed to me a great success and have given me abundant recognition. I enjoy it and am grateful; but for the most part I do not myself appreciate the work up to the measure expressed by others.

As regards the work of the past year—*The Life of Nelson*—I do not care to reveal my hopes or fears to the public before it has passed its verdict upon it. Let it come to the work with open mind, incurious as yet as to the author's purpose. Some day, if the book succeed, I may tell the story of the strong purpose, the ideal, which I have had before me through its progress.

To James R. Thursfield

160 West 86th Street, New York, February 22, 1897 [LC]

My dear Mr. Thursfield: I had the pleasure of receiving a few days ago a copy of the *Navy and the Nation*, "from the Authors,"[1] the acknowl-

---

1. George Sydenham Clarke and James R. Thursfield, *The Navy and the Nation*. London: J. Murray, 1897.

edging of which, with my hearty thanks, affords me also an opportunity of expressing the gratification that has been caused me by your more than kind notices of my books in the columns of the *Times*. Although I supposed you to be the writer, I could not say anything while you were concealed behind the impersonality of a Journal; but I have nevertheless deeply felt it, and am glad of this chance to say so.

My next venture—*The Life of Nelson*—is even now impending over the market and over myself. It is of a different character from my other books, and has demanded different treatment with perhaps greater care. I am glad to say the publishers express themselves as very sanguine, and as their money is embarked I suppose they are fairly sensible of demerits; nevertheless I shall await the result, with anxiety. The proofs are all read & completed except parts of the Index.

I hope to get a letter off to Clarke in a day or two. With kind remembrance to Mrs. Thursfield, believe me [etc.].

To John M. Brown

160 West 86th Street, New York, March 1, 1897 [LC]

My dear Mr. Brown: I enclose a letter &c received this morning from Marston, for I hope the book can now get out before the portrait of Lady Nelson is "given away" by any one. The last galley proofs of the Index were received by me Saturday, and mailed back to Wilson yesterday, so that the portrait is of course but an incident of the work—nevertheless one I would like to preserve fresh. I am actuated also by an uneasy fear of war in Europe, which would affect sales, and certainly divert from the book attention, which if favorable, is the most important factor to success. Things look to me nasty about Greece.

To John M. Brown

160 West 86th Street, New York, March 8, 1897 [LC]

My dear Mr. Brown: I was more than sorry to have missed seeing you on Saturday, for I was in; but I have found necessary to protect myself from interviewers and other wasters of time. Had I had the least idea of your calling I would have removed the interdict, which our woman has not the judgment to permit discretion given her. I ran out at once hoping to catch you, but you had disappeared.

I enclose two letters from the Editor of *Harper's Magazine*. My reply to the first was that I would write the article for[1] $50 per thousand up to eight thousand words—beyond that no charge; in short for $400. I retain the right to republish after a reasonable period, which I fixed by next Christmas. Number two is their reply. I have a headache and generally under the weather today, and tomorrow have to be out of town. I shall not reply therefore before Wednesday and would be glad to have any suggestions from you, as my purpose was to put the publication in your hands. *Harper* has already published two articles from me—one in Oct 1895— the other this month.[2] I should add that I was on the verge of writing to Mr. Alden[3] to suggest the article he asks, when his note came. I particularly wish to write the article, as a contribution of my own thought to current history and indications of the future. I shall have to tell Alden that the other articles I wanted to embody in a book are out of my control, one in the *Forum* of March 1893, another in the *Atlantic* of Oct. 1893.[4]

Aside from these I have four British Admiral articles in the *Atlantic* for March, May, July 1893, and January 1894. These Scudder declined to recommend them (H.M. & Co)[5] to publish in book form, but told me they would make no objection to my putting them in other hands. My idea would be to enlarge them—possibly; or else, as they stand, to add two more and publish with portraits under the title: Some (or Six) British Admirals.[6] You might look them up and see what you think of the project. It would be incongruous to include them with the other set.

When do you expect to ship *Nelson* to England? and am I right in understanding that you send in sheets, they binding on the other side?

Please return the enclosures.

---

1. "Strategic Features of the Caribbean Sea and the Gulf of Mexico," *Harpers New Monthly Magazine* (October 1897).
2. "The Future in Relation to American Sea Power" and "Preparedness for a Naval War," both in *Harpers New Monthly Magazine*.
3. Henry Mills Alden, editor of *Harpers New Monthly Magazine*.
4. "Hawaii and Our Future Sea-Power" and "The Isthmus and Sea Power." The book of reprinted articles Mahan had in mind was *The Interest of America in Sea Power, Present and Future*. Boston: Little, Brown and Company, 1897.
5. Houghton Mifflin & Co.
6. These articles, together with other materials, appeared in *Types of Naval Officers*. Boston: Little, Brown and Company, 1901.

To J. Franklin Jameson

160 West 86th Street, New York, March 8, 1897 [LC]

My dear Sir: I will undertake the review of Corbett's book.[1] Oppenheim has not yet reached me, somewhat to my surprise, as I have seen mention of it as out in English papers. I rather regret the delay as after March 20 I shall be much in Boston for over a month, giving a set of lectures.

To John M. Brown

160 West 86th Street, New York, March 8, 1897 [LC]

My dear Mr. Brown: My letter to you this morning was accidentally sealed before I meant it to be. I continue: Marston asked me lately to say to you that the writers of his projected History of the British Navy[1] are capable men. I think they are as far as I know them; my experience with the *Life of Farragut*, the quality of which has been attested to me by several capable witnesses, inclines me to think that our people do not yet care for naval matters.

The Century matter hangs fire.[2] I saw them, and if they were eager in the matter they kept it in very well; and I myself have so much work projected, and practically accepted that I am not over anxious to tie myself up with long engagements. I still think that the probable best solution is to continue my serious Sea Power books on the same general lines through 1812–15—and to make a separate picturesque work of the naval battles of single ships, privateers &c.

To John M. Brown

160 West 86th Street, New York, March 11, 1897 [LC]

My dear Mr. Brown: I have so many letters to write that I can now reply only partly to your last. I shall write this evening or tomorrow to

1. Julian Stafford Corbett, *Drake and the Tudor Navy*. New York: Longmans, Green & Co., 1898. For various issues of the *American Historical Review* during this period Mahan reviewed Barnes's *Naval Actions of the War of 1812* (April 1897), Oppenheim's *History of the Administration of the Royal Navy* (July 1897), and J. R. Spear's *History of Our Navy from Its Origins to the Present Day* (October 1897–January 1898). No Corbett book was reviewed.
1. *See* Mahan to Wingate, May 23, 1897.
2. *See* Mahan to Brown, February 10, 1897.

Harpers, renewing my acceptance of the request to write the articles, on the terms before mentioned by me, conditionally upon my being allowed to republish not earlier than Dec. 1. next.[1] If these terms be accepted, it is my purpose to put the publishing in your hands. I do not at present think it at all possible for me to get the *Admirals* ready for publication for Xmas; at all events the matter must lie over for the present. It appears to me that the six sketches should aggregate near 100,000 words—say 15,000 apiece, which means considerable enlarging, as well as two new lives. I hope to get to you by Monday a first set of instructions for drawings for the lectures.[2] As regards the last, you may depend that if they give me any complimentary tickets—you shall have one—or some, according to number. I received the sheets and illustrations you sent me and am greatly pleased with them, as well as with the good news you give me of prospective sales, and of Marston's favorable impressions. I hope the future will give us much cause for mutual congratulation upon our venture.

To Seth Low

160 West 86th Street, New York, March 12, 1897 [CUL]

My dear Mr. Low: If the ground of argument you mention deserves the term "specious" which you employ, cadit quaestio. No one really doubts the animus of the move, nor its practical unrighteousness. Within a week, action may be taken, which, if unresisted, may—will—entail a *moral* disaster from which we shall not recover in twenty years.[1] It matters comparatively little whether resistance such as I suggested fail at the moment; but acquiescence in it is a moral catastrophe. You have a position of advantage, and time passes. The great master of my own profession has told us that War is not made without running risks, and the need of promptness is clear. I would not, indeed, press you not to give due consideration; only, if the balance of *right* is as clear as I think, and you seem to think, dont give too much consideration to questions of expediency. Run the risk. This matter is not going to be turned by argument, but by the intentions of justice, if the latter be appealed to.

This is my last on this subject, for with it I exhaust all my claims on your patience.

1. *See* Mahan to Brown, March 8, 1897.
2. Lowell Institute lecture series. *See* Mahan to Lowell, February 21, 1896.

1. The reference is to the Anglo-American general arbitration treaty, signed on January 11, 1897, which the Senate was then debating, and which it rejected in May 1897.

To the Editor of The New York Times

160 West 86th Street, New York, March 16, 1897[1]

I see in your columns this morning the word "preparedness" is spoken of as of Capt. Mahan's. It will be found in *Worcester*, with a quotation, and also in the *Imperial Dictionary*, an English work bearing the imprint of the Century Company of this city. I did not originate it, therefore, but it may be said that had it not existed already, it would have to be coined.

To Augustus T. Gillender

160 West 86th Street, New York, N.D. Probably, March 16, 1897 [HUL]

Dear Mr. Gillender: Thank you very much for your letter. Can you not at the same time extend your inquires to any other builders or occupiers on our joint lands. Also, could not the direct question be put to Dennis's squatters by what authority they are there.

I go to Boston on Monday or Tuesday next to be absent four or five weeks, though I may be back once or twice for a day.

To Charles E. L. Wingate[1]

160 West 86th Street, New York, March 17, 1897 [HUL]

Dear Sir: I regret to say that I have no photographs of myself, but I believe Messrs. Hollinger and Rockey, 518 Fifth Avenue, N.Y. have several positions and I daresay you may obtain one from them.

To John M. Brown

160 West 86th Street, New York, March 19, 1897 [LC]

Dear Mr. Brown: I enclose two tickets from those sent me for my course at the Lowell. They are end seats of the row; and there is still one between them and the seat of a friend if you wish a third.

---

1. From *The New York Times*, March 17, 1897.

1. Editor with the *Boston Journal*, of which he became managing editor in 1898.

It has been on my mind to ask you whether it would not be right to send complimentary copies of the book to a half dozen people who have aided us. I mean specifically: Mr. Stuart J. Reid, Mr. Edgar Goble, Mr. B. F. Stevens, Col. Esdaile, Mr. Nelson Ward, & Mrs. Eccles—perhaps also Sir Wm. Parker. If you approved, I intended to propose that the firm and myself should divide this matter. The remaining persons mentioned in the preface, Lords Nelson, Radstock & Saumarez; Laughton, [illegible], Marston and Morrison,[1] I feel under personal obligations to & shall myself send copies to them. I shall, I fancy have to order half a dozen copies beyond the ten in our agreement. By the way I suppose there is no chance of those being sent me before I come to Boston; but if there is, *dont* send. I expect to go on Tuesday & hope to see you Wednesday.

[P.S.]   I had a most glowing letter from Marston this morning.

To John M. Brown

160 West 86th Street, New York, March 21, 1897 [LC]

My dear Mr. Brown: This has been a distressingly occupied Sunday & I have no more than time to say how much I appreciate the kindness of your letter, recd. today, placing 20 copies of *Nelson* at my disposal, as well as your other courtesies towards my approaching stay in Boston.

I send the enclosed that you may be ready to discuss the project with me when I can have a little time for talk in Boston.

The N.Y. *Sun* reviews the book at length today. Is that premature?

To John M. Brown

160 West 86th Street, New York, March 22, 1897 [LC]

Dear Mr. Brown: I was so much hurried yesterday in all I did, that it was not till today that I took in your invitation to stay with you while in Boston; pray pardon the oversight in not more explicitly acknowledging your kindness and replying to it. It has been arranged for some time that I should stay with Mrs. Henry Saltonstall at 26 Commonwealth Ave.— an old friend of Mrs. Mahan's family—and I am not without hopes that Mrs. Mahan may be able to join me there during the last week of my stay. Though Belmont is certainly not far it may be more advantageous for me

---

1. Alfred Morrison.

to be in town, as I shall be pretty busy in various ways; but I hope and expect that I shall have the pleasure of often seeing you. My future work, after next summer, must be discussed and, if possible, now decided.

I shall leave to-morrow by the Limited. By the way, Mr. E. L. Godkin of the *Evening Post*, asked if an advance copy of the *Nelson* could be sent him. He wants to read it on the way across, as he sails for Europe on Saturday next. If you think right to send it him, I should be obliged. His address is 36 West 10th St.

To John M. Brown

26 Commonwealth Avenue, Boston, March 29, 1897 [LC]

My dear Mr. Brown: I should have written sooner to express my great regret for the uncomfortable accident that you underwent last Thursday evening; but I was about to go to Groton & I thought I would also wait till you could better see how you would get on before making the following proposition. You were good enough to say you would like me to see a little more of the house and especially of the library than when I was last there, and I wanted also to pay my compliments to Mrs. Brown at some convenient season. How would it suit, having special reference to your convalescence, for me to come out on the 1.10 train next Sunday, and remain over the Monday—April 4 & 5? This will give me time for my Sunday Church before leaving town, for I dont feel up to much after the Saturday evg. lecture, & I ought to get back to my work early Tuesday.

Take your time about answering, for I am well satisfied with an excuse for reserving Sunday and Monday against any possible invitations.

I sincerely trust you are recovering rapidly. I have not been down to the [illegible] today, being busy over lecture work; but I sat w[ith] Norman[1] at 11.

Pray present my compliments to Mrs. Brown.

To Robert U. Johnson

160 West 86th Street, New York, April 5, 1897 [NYPL]

My dear Mr. Johnson: Permit me to introduce to you Mrs. Duncan Kennedy, the wife of an officer in the Navy, who wishes to present certain material for your consideration.

I have known both Mr. and Mrs. Kennedy for many years, and you can rely implicitly upon any statements or assurances either of them may make.

1. Not identified.

To J. Franklin Jameson

26 Commonwealth Avenue, Boston, April 11, 1897 [LC]

My dear Sir: Oppenheim was forwarded to me here from N.Y. by my orders. I find in it one of the most curious conditions that ever came under my notice in a book. The last printed page is 272. It ends with the half word "truthful—," and is followed by full two hundred perfectly blank pages, many of which are uncut. As the termination of the work, by title, is 1660 and the text ends in the time of Charles I, who died in 1649, it is evident there is some queer omission, by accident. If you can, have a full copy sent me to this address, within this week. I shall be here yet a fortnight.

To J. Franklin Jameson

26 Commonwealth Avenue, Boston, April 17, 1897 [LC]

Dear Sir: A perfect copy of Oppenheim has been recd., and the imperfect returns today, by express unpaid, to address given.

I regret that it will not be possible for me to accept your invitation to visit Providence on this occasion.

To John M. Brown

26 Commonwealth Avenue, Boston, April 22, 1897 [LC]

My dear Mr. Brown: I send you some clippings from English papers, which please return to my N.Y. address when you have finished. The *St. James Gazette* you see attacks Troubridge's portrait as maligning "the original." I suggested to McIntyre[1] and Bailey[2] today that it might be well to set this right through Marston; but it is a matter for your judgment and mine, as to whether it is worthwhile.

[P.S.] The *Sat. Review* has a very nice notice by Adm. Colomb.[3]

---

1. James W. McIntyre was on the staff of Little, Brown and Company.
2. Mr. Bailey was also on the staff of Little, Brown and Company.
3. P. H. Colomb, Review of Mahan's *Life of Nelson*, *Saturday Review*, LXXXIII, p. 363.

To James Ford Rhodes[1]

160 West 86th Street, New York, April 26, 1897 [MHS]

Dear Mr. Rhodes: I am very sorry that I should not have been at home when you called last week, but shall look forward hopefully to the renewal of our acquaintance at a future day.

On Saturday evening I closed my long visit to Boston by giving the last lecture of my course; upon which followed a very pleasant evening at the University Club, which you know was in contemplation. Yesterday I returned home.

I suppose my popularity in Great Britian, as an author profoundly in sympathy with their past history, and with the great part that they (in the main) are still playing in redeeming the world from barbarism to civilization, from lawlessness to order, will always ensure me a hearing with them. You may be sure that I desire ever to use such influence—if I have it—to promote our mutual affection. I own, however, to thinking that so long as their ideal is world-wide effort, and ours is isolation, either under the idea of Protection, or of non-interference, that there will be lacking that substantial identity of aims without which cordial esteem is unlikely. In this I doubt if you will agree with me.

To John M. Brown

160 West 86th Street, New York, April 26, 1897 [LC]

My dear Mr. Brown: English friends and an American have drawn my attention to one or two typographical blunders in *Nelson*.

1. Vol. II. p. 1. Chapter heading August 1790 should be 1799.

2. p. 30. sixth line from bottom "west coast of Sicily" should be *east* coast.

3. Vol. II, p. 87, eighth line from bottom, "east side of middle ground" should be *west* side.

4. Laughton, in the *Athenaeum* says Freemantle should be Fremantle. I hardly know whether the expense makes worth while—you must judge. The Index shows when the name occurs.

5. In Vol. I. p. 167, the last three lines would read better thus, after "—north—":

---

1. Author of *History of the United States from the Compromise of 1850* and other historical works. President of the American Historical Association in 1898, he was continuously associated with Mahan on various government committees.

"of the enemy's line, which was quite in his power, and so covering his endangered ships, he allowed the latter to be cut off, thus."

Would this be an expensive change? the number of letters is within one of the same. Tis my slip.

Laughton also says that Vol. II. 223 note, 1894 should be 1886 but in this I think he is mistaken. I will consult a file of the *Times*.

I suppose you can see the *Athenaeum* (Apl. 17).[1] If not I will send it you. It is *very* favorable.

To J. B. Sterling

160 West 86th Street, New York, April 27, 1897 [LC]

My dear Colonel Sterling: Many thanks for your letter of appreciation for my *Life of Nelson* and for the memo. of errata, of which I have notified the publishers. I fear the fault cannot be laid to the printers, as I diligently read all the first proofs *twice*, and the finals once; but it is impossible to eliminate a certain mechanical element in the closest attention, which acts automatically—not intelligently.

The fleet in being controversy may revive; but discussion can only result in a nearer approximation to truth. I suppose you have reasons for expecting to see it appear in the *Quarterly*.

I agree with you in regretting the apparent failure of the treaty of arbitration, though I care little for the formal document. I should have liked to see the demand for it, on our side, rest upon an intelligent appreciation of the great future open to the English-speaking races, and a sympathy with the great part your nation has played and is playing in the advance of humanity. This sympathy, mixed with great admiration, you know I have. But the strength of the movement here lay not in such sympathy and appreciation. It was based upon a somewhat maudlin sentimentality on the subject of war in general, and yet more upon the horrors of unsettled values and Stock Exchange derangement. Upon such a rotten basis I place no reliance for the stability of a paper convention. The solid foundation of mutual regard, and a certain noble outlook to the future, in which the two nations might recognize their power for good, and be prepared, not only to work, but to fight for it, if need be, would have had my glad [?] confidence and rendered treaties needless. I shall not cease to hope for this; till it come I don't worry much over a few columns of words going into the

---

1. *Nelson* was reviewed in *Athenaeum* (April 17, 1897); Laughton reviewed it in *Edinburgh Review* (July 1897), and Thursfield in the *Quarterly Review* (January 1898).

waste paper basket. I cannot but regret, from this point of view, though I do not criticize, the adhesion of Great Britain to the "Concert." Could she have seen her way to insist that the Turkish troops left Crete with the Greeks, a wave of emotion would have swept over our country that would have been worth a dozen treaties. It might have passed away, but it would have left us much nearer you, for we are feeling deeply for Crete and for Greece, and the attitude of the Concert is to us unreasonable and inexplicable.

To Horace E. Scudder

160 West 86th Street, New York, April 28, 1897 [HUL]

Dear Mr. Scudder: I fully meant to get in to see you before leaving Boston, but my time seemed to fritter itself away between keeping my lectures in shape and attending to social duties. A call, however, could not have resulted in any undertaking on my part of an article such as you suggested, for my time is already preoccupied for a long time to come, and my attention now mainly directed to clearing myself so far as to concentrate upon my next serious work.

I dont find much time for magazine reading now-a-days, but I pick up the *Atlantic* often enough to see with pleasure that it increases instead of losing in interest. I read with special interest some of Higginson's reminiscences,[1] and some papers on Days in Greece, or a title like that; the name of the author has slipped me.[2]

With remembrances to Mr. Page,[3] believe me [etc.].

To Theodore Roosevelt

160 West 86th Street, New York, May 1, 1897 [LC]

PERSONAL & PRIVATE

My dear Roosevelt: You will I hope allow me at times to write to you on service matters, without thinking that I am doing more than throw out ideas for consideration. I had occasion to look over a file of the London

1. Thomas Wentworth Higginson, *Cheerful Yesterdays*. Boston: Houghton Mifflin & Co., 1898. It was serialized in the *Atlantic Monthly* from November 1896 to June 1897.
2. B. L. Gildersleeve, "My Sixty Days in Greece," *Atlantic Monthly* (February; March; May 1897).
3. Walter Hines Page left the *Forum* in 1895 to become editor of the *Atlantic Monthly* (1896–1899).

Times yesterday, April 12–17, & there found a statement of the naval programme of Japan, which I think would be important to you to keep in mind. It is to be complete only in 1906, but you need not be told that one has to look far ahead now in building ships. That there is danger of trouble with her towards Hawaii, I think beyond doubt; if this administration is not able to put those islands under our wing, Mr. Cleveland's name will be immortalized a century hence by one thing only, that he refused them when he could have had them. Closely related to this is the need of strengthening our Pacific squadron. In my opinion, rendered decisive by the Venezuela affair, we have much more likelihood of trouble on that side than in the Atlantic. I don't know whether the battle ships we have can make the voyage—their coal endurance is small. Corollary: in building war ships, build on the Pacific side. Also, your best Admiral needs to be in the Pacific. Much more initiative *may* be thrown on him than *can* on the Atlantic man. I would suggest also, as bearing upon the general policy of the Administration, that the real significance of the Nicaragua canal now is that it advances our Atlantic frontier by so much to the Pacific, & that in Asia, not in Europe, is now the greatest danger to our proximate interests. It may be observed that it would suit Russia to see us in trouble with Japan, who is her own most knotty problem at present.

Of course Japan is a small and a poor state, as compared to ourselves; but the question is are we going to allow her to dominate the future of those most important islands because of our lethargy. It may very well happen, if we shut our eyes. I do not know your chief,[1] but I fancy that at his age & having lived his life in what a clever Boston woman styled to me the "backwater" of Boston society, he regards the annexation of the islands, if offered, as an insoluable political problem. To this, in my mind, the only reply is: Do nothing unrighteous; but as regards the problem, take them first and solve afterwards. Had Cleveland taken the islands, we would not be threatened with the present mess. There is, in the same file of the *Times*, a long letter, three or four columns, on Japan, Russia & Corea. In it (I think) occurs the remark that the Japanese are devotedly friendly to the U.S. I am quite willing to hope it, & if so it will much facilitate diplomacy; but withal there should be the most courteous firmness in intimating that the propinquity of Hawaii makes it our supreme concern. I remember when the Chilians would have torn out their eyes for us—in 1866.

You will, I am sure, take this letter as it is meant, as a mere bundle of thoughts.

[P.S.] I shall not mention my writing.

---

1. Roosevelt was at this time Assistant Secretary of the Navy under John D. Long. It was rumored that Lodge had maneuvered the appointment to annoy Long.

To Theodore Roosevelt

160 West 86th Street, New York, May 6, 1897 [LC]

My dear Roosevelt: Your letter has been read and destroyed. You will believe that when I write to you it is only to suggest thoughts, or give information, not with any wish otherwise to influence action, or to ask information. I have known myself too long not to know that I am the man of thought, not the man of action. Such an one may beneficially throw out ideas, the practical effect of which can rest only, and be duly shaped only, by practical men. The comparison may seem vain but it may be questioned whether Adam Smith could have realised upon his own ideas as Pitt did.

With reference to Barker, you have an admirable man—few more so. He is extremely conscientious, and in such a case—and for officials generally—it is necessary that instructions be perfectly clear on the views of the government. All other conscientious scruples in a military mind disappear before the fundamental duty of obedience; but government must speak clearly, without ifs and buts. Even Nelson asked this (Vol. 11, p. 253). Miller is the same.[1]

There are two things that may be interesting to you to recall now. One—personal to myself—is that my article in the *Forum* on Hawaii, four years ago, was elicited by a previous letter of mine to the *N.Y. Times*, pointing out that the question of the future of Hawaii was rather Mongolian than European. Page, seeing this, asked for the magazine article. The circumstance is of interest only as showing the crass blindness of the last administration, to which we now owe a very real present danger of war, easily foreseen then. The second thing to recall is the anxiety we all felt at the time of the Chili trouble over the progress of the *Prat*[2] we not then having any battleship. Today the same situation recurs; shall two Japanese battle ships appear when we have but one and a Monitor? Armaments do not in this day exist primarily to fight, but to avert war. Preparedness deters the foe, and right by show of superior force without use of violence. It is lamentable to have to insist on such commonplaces—more applications of the situation to which I call your attention may reinforce your argument; but at times I despair of our country arousing until too late to avert prolonged and disastrous conflict. In my last lecture to the Lowell Institute I said "The decision not to bring under the authority of one's own government some external position, when just occasion offers, may by future generations be bewailed in tears of blood." God forbid.

---

1. Merrill Miller, class of 1863.
2. *See* Mahan to Luce, January 10, 1892, Footnote 1.

To James Julius Chambers[1]

160 West 86th Street, New York, May 8, 1897 [NWC]

Dear Sir: It is my turn to be surprised, for I thought, from what you said, that you fully understood that my exception was taken distinctly to the *Journal*,[2] the newspaper, of which Mr. Hearst is proprietor. I so entirely dislike and disapprove its method and conduct, that I do not choose to associate my name with it, directly or indirectly, by contribution or interview. This I said sometime ago to a Mr. Townshend (if I rightly recall the name) who came to me from Mr. Hearst. Since then it is that so many clubs, moved I suppose by similar views, have excluded the *Journal* from their tables.

Toward Mr. Hearst, whom I have never met, nor even seen, I can have, and have, no personal feeling, except so far as I cannot but condemn the man who, I presume, is responsible for the results I have seen. For a very long time now I have ceased to look at the *Journal*; but I have never heard any suggestion that its methods have been changed.

Not reading the paper, I was unaware of its advocacy of any claim for me as a literary man. It is a favor I neither asked, desired, nor even imagined; and it cannot in any way enter into a question which rests upon my views of public ethics, and of my own obligations to my own sense of right.

To Silas McBee[1]

160 West 86th Street, New York, May 12, 1897 [UNC]

Dear Sir: I shall be at home on Friday evening, and shall be very glad to see you any time after 8 o'clock, if you should wish to call. I must, however, forewarn you that I have nothing whatever to communicate on the subject of foreign missions. I have never been thrown into close contact with them. Thirty years ago in China I saw a little—a very little—of a few missionaries during a fortnight I spent in Shanghai; but the time was too short to form any estimate of their work that would justify an expression. During two years on the station, I was at no other time at a missionary port. Since that time my service has been on the coasts of S. America and Europe, where I have met no missionaries of the Church, and on only one day passed a few hours with some of a dissenting denomination.

1. Managing editor of the *New York World* until 1891, when he retired and devoted his time to travel and literary work.
2. *The Morning Journal*, New York, of which William Randolph Hearst was owner.
1. Editor (1896–1912) of *The Churchman*, a journal edited and published by Episcopalians in New York. It was not an official Church publication.

To James R. Thursfield

160 West 86th Street, New York, May 21, 1897 [LC]

Dear Mr. Thursfield: I read with great interest the notice of *Nelson* in the *Times*, and am greatly pleased to know that you can subscribe to all the kind things that were there said. As regards the fleet in being, there is always the chance that people may exaggerate their meaning on the one hand, or see opposite sides of a truth on the other; and discussion, in good temper, under such circumstances, however it may fail of convincing either disputant, enlightens public opinion and so insures correct conclusions. In the particular instance of Torrington, I have always felt that, with Tourville's fleet drawn across the Channel, the French crossing could have gone on with no risk greater than war justifies and demands.

We shall be very glad to see your son if his service brings him in our neighborhood. I could wish that it might be during our summer months which, from June 1 to Oct 1, we spend at Quogue, N.Y.—a little place on the south shore of Long Island, about 80 miles from the city. New York at other times provides interest enough for a stranger of itself, but a refuge from [it] is pleasant after June 15. At any rate, if he comes at that time he will know my address.

With kind remembrance to Mrs. Thursfield [etc.].

To William H. Henderson

160 West 86th Street, New York, May 21, 1897 [NMM]

My dear Henderson: I dont find my usual memorandum of a letter that should have been sent you near a month ago, so fear I have overlooked replying to your kind congratulations. The success of the *Nelson* has been most gratifying to me, & not least when it is the means of bringing to me a message from an old friend and correspondent like yourself. I hope never to stop working, but I worked upon *Nelson* as the apogee of my literary career, after which no subject at all equal in varied interest and opportunity can offer. I awaited the result therefore with anxiety and am duly grateful for the success.

Your letter was the first I knew of your return to England. I am glad to know that you have found a congenial billet.[1] Stockton is still in China. He is a man who under a somewhat heavy exterior carries a great deal

---

1. Henderson, after commanding HMS *Devastation* and HMS *Nile* was assigned to the command of the Fleet Reserve, Devonport.

of information & more than usual breadth and acuteness of intellect. As to my visiting England again, everything is as yet uncertain—complicated by family conditions.

To Charles E. L. Wingate

160 West 86th Street, New York, May 23, 1897 [HUL]

Dear Sir: I expect in the autumn to take up the history of the War of 1812,[1] which was part of the original plan of my works on Sea Power. I have during the summer to prepare a treatment of the larger naval operations of the War of 1778 to be a chapter in the *History of the British Navy* now publishing by Sampson, Low of London.[2] Whether I shall ever take up a history of the American Navy at large depends very much upon the interest of the American public in the matter. As far as I can at present observe that interest is not very great. There is no use of a man writing what he has no reason to believe the many will read.

To Augustus T. Gillender

University Club, New York, May 26, 1897 [HUL]

Dear Mr. Gillender: I got your letter this morning & after chewing over it on my way down, write.

---

1. *The Influence of Sea Power in its Relation to the War of 1812* was not published until 1905.
2. Sir William Laird Clowes, *The Royal Navy, a History from the Earliest Times to The Present* ... assisted by Sir Clements Markham ... Captain A. T. Mahan, U.S.N., H. W. Wilson, Theodore Roosevelt, E. Fraser, etc. 7 vols. Boston: Little, Brown and Company; London: S. Low, Marston and Company, Ltd., 1897–1903. Mahan contributed "Major Operations of the Royal Navy, 1762–1783," Chapter XXXI in Volume 3. Clowes, apologizing for the delay in publication, wrote in the Introduction: ". . . [Mahan] was employed in the service of his country at Washington during the late conflict, and was thus prevented for a time from devoting his attention to other matters. So much of the delay as has been caused by his preoccupation will, I am sure, be readily forgiven, seeing that he has now been able to revise proofs, etc. which must otherwise have been sent to press without his final imprimatur." An insert, dated December 12, 1898, states: "Captain A. F. [*sic*] Mahan's Critical Narrative of the Major Operations of the War of the American Revolution, which fills about a third of the present volume, was all written twelve months ago, and was all passed by him in proof before he sailed for Europe last spring. I think it right to mention this, as although the delay in publication enabled Captain Mahan to make some little further revision in his proofs, it was not caused by him in any way, as might be inferred from my remarks on this point in the Introduction, which was written under a misapprehension." This study was revised, expanded, and published separately by Little, Brown and Company in 1913 under the title, *The Major Operations of the Navies in the War of American Independence.*

It appears to me essential to know, as soon as possible, how long the squatters have been there, and who they are. I would suggest your writing at once to Youmans stating that the Mahan heirs find that this wharf and factory is on their property, and asking him if he can give you the names and addresses of the party. If you think proper, you could add that we see that an unintentional mistake has been made in locating the establishment; and that our wish is simply to guard our rights from infringement, and to reach an arrangement equitable to all parties. If he refuse the information, we must then get to work some other way. I could write this myself, but it will probably look more business like coming from a lawyer. If only I could get the thing settled, and off my mind.

Wont you write today?

To Edward L. Burlingame[1]

160 West 86th Street, New York, May 27, 1897 [PUL]

Dear Sir: I have to be at the Astor Library tomorrow, so will not give you trouble of a trip here. I will call upon you at 1 p.m. I cannot stay over twenty minutes, having an engagement at 1.30.

To John M. Brown

10 East 10th Street, New York, May 31, 1897 [LC]

My dear Mr. Brown: I received the enclosed[1] this morning. You will note it has no signature, and the date April 1, is far back. Have you any correspondent in Japan who could investigate the matter? The accounts are very flattering, but several thousands in a day or two seems to me a little fishy. They must have had great confidence in their market to stock it so heavily.

My address till Saturday is 10 East 10th St. After that Quogue N. Y. for the summer.

Hoping the book is still doing well, I am [etc.].

---

1. Editor of *Scribner's Magazine* 1886–1914.

1. Letter from the Oriental Association of Tokyo informing Mahan that the Club of Naval Officers (of Japan) had translated *The Influence of Sea Power upon History* into Japanese and that "to tell the truth, several thousand volumes were sold in a day or two." *See* Taylor, *Life of Admiral Mahan*, pp. 114–116; and Mahan to Brown, June 5, 1897.

[P.S.] Neither Sir F. Jeune nor Alfred Morrison have ever acknowledged the copies sent them. I suppose they must have gone forward. I only heard from O'Connor Morris last week.

To J. B. Sterling

University Club, New York, May 31, 1897 [LC]

My dear Col. Sterling: You will believe that it is not pleasant to me to send, even by cable, a short "No" to your very kind and touching suggestion;[1] and though I do not accept, you will believe that even in declining I fully appreciate and return the "spirit of genuine friendship and of interest in my career"—to use your own words—which has prompted your letter and proposal, if I may use so strong a word. I do not think that the step, if taken, would increase such standing and influence as I may now possess with thoughtful men, or in public opinion, of our two nations; and it might even diminish them—I cannot tell. Certainly, if any such were initiated on your side, and our government, whose consent and approval are pre-requisite, did not approve, the knowledge that I had consented beforehand would injure—not me, for that is a trifle—but my reputation at home, which would be a loss to me indeed. As you know my great desire is to promote a unity of feeling, and a sense of common interest in the two states, and especially in my own; not by way of treaties of permanent arbitration or formal alliances, in which I have little faith, but by quietly showing how much of good and how much in common there is in each. The most grateful and unique tribute *Nelson* has brought me is from a distinguished jurist on your side.[2] "It is," he wrote "worth a ship load of arbitration treaties." I felt then that, die when I may, I have not lived wholly for naught. Believe me, and say so to the others to whom you allude as cognizant of your letter that I feel the idea which they have broached to be a tribute of like character, and one that will be gratefully and always remembered.

[P.S.] Needless to say the substance of your letter remains profoundly *secret*.

---

1. A proposal that Mahan accept an honorary rank in the Royal Navy. Puleston, *Mahan*, p. 180.
2. William O'C. Morris.

To J. Franklin Jameson

University Club, New York, June 1, 1897 [LC]

My dear Sir: My relations of literary intimacy & business association with Mr. Marston & Mr. Laird Clowes are such that I would prefer not to review a book with which they are concerned.[1] I have no doubt but that I should find only good to say of it, but at the same time I prefer to leave the task to some other.

To John M. Brown

University Club, New York, June 5, 1897 [LC]

My dear Mr. Brown: Since I enclosed you the letter from my Jap friend, I have received the book in two volumes.[1] Naturally, I could make more out of it, if it were in Greek; but the plates are there. It is an odd business. When you are finished with the letter return it to me, I must make acknowledgment.

I go to Quogue this afternoon, I trust for the summer.

To John M. Brown

Slumberside, Quogue, Long Island, June 6, 1897 [LC]

Dear Mr. Brown: I have done up a volume of the Japanese translation which I will send you tomorrow. Please put my name in it *in pencil*, and return at your leisure. It begins hind part before as you can see by the illustrations. I found yours of the 3d waiting my arrival here. I am surprised to hear what you tell me of the condition of the naval history. Bad policy, I should think, however regarded. Fortunately, *Nelson* will not be open to adverse criticism on the get up. I have heard today from Sir Francis Jeune. Morrison is now I believe the only delinquent. I will let you know about my work as soon as I can be definitely sure myself. I got Marston to insert the enclosed because I did not want to find any *friend* in my path on the same way—to preempt the ground against those whom I might be unwilling to traverse. As regards others, I should have been willing to stand on my own bottom.

1. *See* Mahan to Wingate, May 23, 1897.
1. *See* Mahan to Brown, May 31, 1897.

[513]

To Robert U. Johnson

Slumberside, Quogue, Long Island, June 9, 1897 [NYPL]

Dear Mr. Johnson: I have read twice Dr. Hanson's[1] comments on Copenhagen. Of the tone you can judge for yourself. As to accuracy: In the result of the battle, Niebuhr,[2] the historian, a Dane, was then residing in the city. He wrote: "We cannot deny it; we are quite beaten. Our line of defence is destroyed. We cannot do much injury to the enemy, as long as he contents himself with bombarding the city, docks, and fleet." This was all the British proposed to do. So their success was complete, and Niebuhr has more to the same effect. As regards Kronborg and Elsinore firing, Nelson wrote to Lady Hamilton: "More powder and shot I believe were never thrown away, for not one shot struck a single ship of the British fleet. The *Elephant* (his ship) made no reply. I hope to keep them (ammut.) for a better occasion." There was no object for this eye witness to falsify. Again the British ultimatum had been presented and rejected (Dr. H. says not). The distinct record is that the envoy went ahead, presented his ultimatum, returned with alarming accounts of Danish preparations etc. *Then* the fleet passed Kronborg, March 30; the envoy having returned on the 23d.—the delay was caused by winds. You will I am sure excuse my going more at length into other mistakes. I will add that I had before me two Danish accounts, one by Allen, a Dane, which was translated for my use by a Dane who is one of the leading subordinates in the Astor Library, and who assured me Allen's reputation was excellent. It was he who furnished the incident of flags shot away and not rehoisted. The author of the other Danish account was at one time employed in the *Century*.[3] I cant remember his name, Frazer [*sic*] may.

I dont think Hanson's paper of the slightest importance, except as an exhibition of untested Danish impressions derived from his grandparents. Now for the Armada paper[4] I will keep it a day or two with your consent, though after one reading I see little I can say. I am so extremely busy, that

---

1. Dr. James Christian Meinich Hanson, historian and librarian, chief of the catalogue department at the Library of Congress. In a footnote to his article on the Copenhagen action (*Century Magazine*, February 1897, p. 525), Mahan says that he used "besides various English narratives, two Danish accounts, one of which appeared in the *Cornhill Magazine* a few years ago. Quotations have also been made from the article 'Battle of Copenhagen' in *Macmillan* for June 1895." The *Cornhill* article was by Peter Toft, reprinted in the *United Service Magazine* for January 1893. The author of the *Macmillan*'s article was William Salter Millard, a midshipman in HMS *Monarch*.
2. Barthold Georg Niebuhr, noted for his contributions to the scientific method of historical criticism.
3. *See* Mahan to Johnson, November 30, 1895, and to Buel, January 22, 1896.
4. W. F. Tilton, "Spanish Armada," *Century Magazine* (June 1898), with an introduction by Mahan.

I should have to make time, for it is not the mere writing words but getting ideas. I should have to ask you $50 to make it worth my while, & I fancy you would think that too much.

To Jane Leigh Mahan

Slumberside, Quogue, Long Island, June 10, 1897 [LC]

My dear Jennie: A stroke of lightning could not have been more unexpected, though certainly less appreciated, than your silver wedding present to us today received. Like all presents worth having, the thought is even more than the gift, although the latter leaves nothing to be desired in the point of simple beauty, and has been impartially admired by the whole family. I thank you too, affectionately, for your congratulations and good wishes. It is certainly something, not unparalleled but I fear rare, not only to have had twenty five years of happiness, but to feel that the end is better than the beginning; that although youth is gone, at no time have things been so entirely well with us. For myself at least the indisposition to live my life over again is not from dissatisfaction with the past, but from firm enjoyment of the present. I should be inclined from my experience to say it is quite logical to put the golden wedding last—the golden age *is* last.

As Elly has written you, I suppose she has told you what little news there is. Do you know that I am to be LLD'd by Yale on the 30th. I understand I will be asked by Prof Marsh[1] or Prof Farnam[2] to stay with them, but I dont want to leave here before the 29th.

To Augustus T. Gillender

Slumberside, Quogue, Long Island, June 12, 1897 [HUL]

Dear Mr. Gillender: I am exceedingly glad to get the information you send about the occupation of Dennis's land, and shall be still more so when I hear that you have had confirmation of the facts from Youmans. I can trust you to represent without offense to him, and to the occupant, that there is no wish on our part to make things unpleasant to any one; but that Dennis is entitled to a fair remuneration for his property. I would suggest that any arrangement that can be reached be submitted to Mrs. Dennis, and a written reply from her requested; and that the arrangement should

---

1. Othniel Charles Marsh, professor of paleontology.
2. Henry Walcott Farnam, professor of economics.

not be for more than three years (if possible); for by that [time] Dennis will be back. I shall not write to Jeannette yet, hoping I may soon have something definite, & not wishing to raise her hopes unduly; but as any sum of rent is important to them I hope you will anticipate the possibility of Youman's getting it again.

[P.S.] We are all very well but till now no summer weather since I came down. Mrs. Mahan joins in kind remembrance.

Certainly *no* ejectment proceedings, nor any other, without explicit instructions from Dennis. I have no wish for anything but to guard against loss to him.

To Augustus T. Gillender

Slumberside, Quogue, Long Island, June 28, 1897 [HUL]

Dear Mr. Gillender: Have you any further news about the fellow & his wharf on Dennis's property? I have not yet written to his wife what you last wrote me, because I fear they may at once jump from a chance to a certainty of getting a better bargain than the event may justify, but I must write soon.

We are going to New Haven tomorrow for Wednesday when I am to be made another L.L.D. by Yale. My law knowledge will soon be immense.

To Henry Villard[1]

Slumberside, Quogue, Long Island, July 2, 1897 [HUL]

Dear Sir: I have gone over the list of retired naval officers, and although I have no doubt there are many competent men, I do not find among them any one whose abilities are so well known to me as to justify my recommending them to you for the place suggested.

I recall with pleasure meeting you at Knollwood.

To John M. Brown

Slumberside, Quogue, Long Island, July 2, 1897 [LC]

Dear Mr. Brown: Your letter of the 28th reached here while I was in New Haven where they have been giving me an L.L.D. As regards the

---

1. Owner of the *New York Evening Post.*

life of Cushing[1] it is quite impossible for me to reply affirmatively at present. I can say *definitely* that until I have completed the 1812 book and after that the text book on Sea Power (Marston's suggestion) my determination is to take up no other work—except occasional papers. I expect those books to take *at least* two years. My hope is that when they are on the market, they will, with those now out, insure me the not excessive income at which I aim, and which would leave me independent to work as I wish and as deliberately as I wish.

If that were secured, I should be inclined to take up Cushing but it would be absurd to bind either them or me to so distant a contingency. My experience with the *Life of Farragut* is so discouraging that I should not now have much hope of pecuniary success from any other naval life. I dont know how the material in Mrs. Cushing's hands is now ordered. It would be desirable, if she has time, to arrange it in order, and where necessary for private reasons to withhold any parts, to have that done, copying what she is willing to give a biographer. The latter, however, ought to receive the confidence of seeing all except those intimate parts of a correspondence which are unnecessary to his depicting of character; nor would I consent to act in such capacity, unless it were understood that the correspondence given me was full barring those parts which only impertinent curiosity would want to see. The great defect in my *Farragut* was that I had no data with which to depict the man.

All this is of course very vague—except that I will not entertain the idea until the other books are complete.

I should think that 60 to 80,000 words should be ample to cover the ground. Cushing's career, though brilliant, was short and in a minor sphere.

To John S. Billings[1]

Slumberside, Quogue, Long Island, July 5, 1897 [NYPL]

Dear Dr. Billings: I have recd. the enclosed through my English publishers.[2] The collection of newspapers is beyond what I care to pay for, and beyond their probable utility to me. Beatson[3] is not—but I can generally

---

1. William B. Cushing, whose most famous exploit was torpedoing the ram *Albemarle* while he was on duty with the North Atlantic Blockading Squadron. Mahan seriously considered writing a biography of him, but never did.

1. Director of the New York Public Library, and of the Astor, Lenox, and Tilden Foundations, and Chairman of the Board of the Carnegie Institution from 1905 until his death in 1913.
2. Enclosure not found.
3. Robert Beatson, *Naval and Military Memoirs of Great Britain from 1727 to 1783*. London: Longman, Hurst, Rees and Orme, 1804. There are two other Beatson titles, but this one seems the most likely.

command a copy, and it is a book which in my opinion is a very useful reference—subject to caution as all references are. If you dont care to obtain either will you return to me here.

To Edward L. Burlingame

Slumberside, Quogue, Long Island, July 5, 1897 [PUL]

Dear Mr. Burlingame: The case stands thus: I am much disposed to accept your offer, but at present I *know* only two episodes which would lend themselves to magazine treatment with much interest. One is the somewhat familiar *Bonhomme Richard* & Paul Jones,[1] the other the comparatively unknown & in my judgment unappreciated naval campaign on Lake Champlain in 1776. For the latter I have some curious data.

The difficulty is that I have to treat both in a contribution I am preparing for *The History of the British Navy*, now publishing by Sampson Low, —Editor Laird Clowes. If you have seen the first volume, which is published, you will recognize that few of your readers will own the book; and I think Marston may feel that a magazine article treating either will not hurt the book.

I am not proposing to give you both the same article. I should write for one without referring to what I had written for the other; and I believe that I can treat both subjects so as to make them as different, almost, as if written by different men.

Nevertheless, it would not be fair to do this without a clear understanding by both Marston and you. If you will be satisfied to take the articles from me I will write to him; and if he consents will say yes to you.

You may wonder that I cannot take something else of the Revolutionary period. The reason is that our naval activity then was confined to privateering & single ship fights. Neither have interested me greatly, and I cannot tell whether there is material in them without an expenditure of research for which I have not the time.

I should add I have written Clowes that the *Bonhomme Richard ought* to be treated by some one else.

---

1. Published in two parts under title "John Paul Jones in the Revolution," *Scribner's Magazine* (July; August 1898).

To Edward L. Burlingame

Slumberside, Quogue, Long Island, July 11, 1897 [PUL]

Dear Mr. Burlingame: Not having heard from you concerning my letter of Monday last, it has occurred to me there may be a misunderstanding —that you understood I would write to the publishers of the *British Naval History*, about the two articles, *without* hearing from you. I have been waiting to hear whether the step I proposed would be acceptable to *you* before writing them.

Meanwhile I have heard from the Editor that he has assigned the Paul Jones episode to another hand. This leaves that clear for me, & I imagine I can arrange the Lake Champlain matter, if my proposition has your approval.

To Edward L. Burlingame

Slumberside, Quogue, Long Island, July 14, 1897 [PUL]

Dear Mr. Burlingame: I write by this mail to Mr. Marston, and ask him to cable his reply. I have asked his permission to publish the article nearly as it stands, attributing it to their forthcoming *History of the Royal Navy*, to which I presume there can be no objection on your part, and will probably be more acceptable to him.

To John M. Brown

Slumberside, Quogue, Long Island, July 14, 1897 [LC]

Dear Mr. Brown: It is needless to say, I suppose, how delighted I was to receive so large a sum as my share in our joint labors of the past year. I begin to think there is more to be said for literature as a substantial pursuit than people are sometimes willing to confess. I trust it may continue.

Marston sent me an advertisement he got out on the day after the Naval Review, in which he said that 5,000 copies[1] had then (June 28) been sold in England. Does this include the new order you say has been received this month? Do they sell in advance there?

---

1. Mahan's *Life of Nelson*.

We have had it here hot, but not unendurable. I trust you have not suffered materially. I have been working hard, wanting to complete my quota for Marston's *Naval History*, and if possible, some 8,000 words long promised the N.Y. *Sun*[2] before I go to town. I want my hands free for *1812* after Oct. 1.

To Walter Hines Page

Slumberside, Quogue, Long Island, July 23, 1897 [HUL]

Dear Mr. Page: I took a day to consider your letter, & regret very much that I could not accept, the more so as I am shortly to get to work on the War of 1812, and the subject would be in the line of that work. I have, however, 50,000 words yet unwritten, to be turned in by the end of September—*promised*—and my knowledge of the Constitution, & the data, is too general for me to estimate the work involved. My mania for accuracy makes everything involving fact extremely laborious to me.

[P.S.]   By the way, does my memory serve me right, that you were led to ask me for that Hawaii article in the *Forum*,[1] by seeing a letter from me to the *N.Y. Times*,[2] pointing out that the question was more Asiatic than English?

To Edward L. Burlingame

Slumberside, Quogue, Long Island, July 26, 1897 [PUL]

Dear Mr. Burlingame: I have received a cable from Sampson Low, Marston & Co., consenting to the publication of the Champlain campaign,[1] as suggested in my letter to them of the 14th inst. and to you of the same date.

---

2. *See* Mahan to Mitchell, December 4, 1897.

1. "Hawaii and Our Future Sea Power."

2. "Sandwich Islands Annexation by U. S. as Barrier against Chinese Invasion," *The New York Times*, February 1, 1893, p. 5.

1. *Scribner's Magazine* published Mahan's "The Naval Campaign of 1776 on Lake Champlain" in its February 1898 issue.

To Edward L. Burlingame

Slumberside, Quogue, New York, July 31, 1897 [PUL]

Dear Mr. Burlingame: Your first letter was received; but I thought that, as I had written you the tenor of my letter to Marston, his reply by cable was all that you needed, to decide upon your course.

I felt, and feel, that Marston has a first right to consideration with regard to any subject that I was writing for him by prior contract, even though written *de novo*; and it did not occur to me that you would feel it a drawback to a magazine article—in most cases an ephemeral thing, to interest readers at the moment—to allow that it was subsequently to appear, substantially as it stood, in permanent form, in the midst of a large five-volume book, the composite work of a number of authors. While thus corresponding with you I have had a request from a leading magazine to allow, in the same way, articles to appear from a work I have in hand; and I believe it is not uncommon so to do. Of course you are the judge in your own case.

No difficulty now exists in giving you the article substantially as it stands, about 6,000 words, modified merely to withdraw it from its context. It remains only for you to say what it is worth to you, and for us to reach an agreement as to terms. As regards time of publication, I understand that the Volume of *Naval History*[1] will not appear till April next; this I have asked Marston to tell me, and I will let you know. In that case, would the January number be time enough for you? The manuscript can be delivered to you any time after September first next.

To Walter Hines Page

Slumberside, Quogue, Long Island, August 2, 1897 [HUL]

Dear Mr. Page: The only person whom I now think of, who I believe would satisfactorily write for you on the present maritime international problems, would be Commd. C. H. Stockton, who ought soon to be back in the U.S. from China. His precise whereabouts I dont know, but a letter addressed Navy Department would reach him.

With regard to your suggestion that some of my *War of 1812* would lend itself to articles for the *Atlantic*,[1] I cannot as yet foresee certainly, but

---

1. Clowes, *The Royal Navy: A History . . .*, Vol. III. *See* Mahan to Burlingame, July 5, 1897.

1. The book was serialized in *Scribner's Magazine*, January 1904 to January 1905.

think it very possible that it may be so. My mind at present is so frightfully preoccupied in working off the burden in hand that I cannot give the subject proper consideration. I will therefore only say that I think probably something can be arranged, and in that case I will communicate with you. I must warn you however that my terms have gone up since I gave you the Hawaii article. I hope I am not unduly mercenary, but I must begin to do less work & more pay, or I shall break down.

To Edward L. Burlingame

Slumberside, Quogue, Long Island, August 3, 1897 [PUL]

Dear Sir: Under the conditions of the case I accept the terms you suggest—$400—for the article in question.[1] I have written Mr. Marston to know the date of the publication of the *History*.

I quote from a letter from him just recd. "The matter is easier for us, because we publish *Scribner's Magazine* over here, & you will have an arrangement with Scribner's by which they protect the copyright, by enabling us to publish a few copies here of your articles *simultaneously* with their publication."

I suppose that you appreciate the point involved and that this arrangement can be made for their house.

To Augustus T. Gillender

Slumberside, Quogue, Long Island, August 9, 1897 [HUL]

Dear Mr. Gillender: I have examined Mr. Berg's specifications and drawings. Of the mechanical fitness to the end in view I dont care to express an opinion, not having any mechanical ability. I think however that the idea is a good one. Instances still occur not infrequently of vessels not being heard from, and breakage is frequently passed which in many cases may belong to such a vessel, but is not susceptible of identification. Such a device might very probably secure evidence of loss which would be invaluable.

As regards the photographs for Mr. and Mrs. Van Schaick, I will be very glad to send them, but I must first send for some as I have not any on hand—never have. When I can get some I will send them through you.

We have had no mosquitoes to trouble here on the south shore. Do you hear anything more of Dennis's tenants?

---

1. "John Paul Jones in the Revolution."

To John M. Brown

Slumberside, Quogue, Long Island, August 17, 1897 [LC]

Dear Mr. Brown: I have to lecture in Newport between Aug 30 and Sept 6. Going or coming I will try to stop in New York and get the numbers of articles that are there. The seventh appears in the Sept. *Harper*[1] and will be equally available by the 15th. The 8th[2] will be also last in the book[3] and is to be in *Harper* Oct.

Have you seen the enclosed[4] or heard anything of it? I infer that Beresford means to be controversial, but upon what point I have no clue. The disagreements about which the two authors make no bones are unknown to me.

[P.S.] Thanks for Mr. Hearne's letter, herewith returned.

To Edward L. Burlingame

Slumberside, Quogue, Long Island, August 23, 1897 [PUL]

Dear Mr. Burlingame: I received the enclosed from Mr. Marston yesterday,[1] having had two days before a postal, saying "Feel sure we shall not publish Vol III before next April." I dont myself believe they can get it out before the end of April, but I suppose with this intimation you will wish the article[2] for the January number. Will you let me know when you wish the manuscript, naming the latest date convenient. Except to make a fair type written copy it is ready now; but I like to hold on to the last moment with a view to the utmost polishing etc.

---

1. "A Twentieth Century Outlook."
2. "Strategic Features of the Carribbean Sea and the Gulf of Mexico."
3. *The Interest of America in Sea Power, Present and Future.* Boston: Little, Brown & Company, 1897.
4. An article in *The Court Journal* (London), dated July 31, 1897, which speculates that Lord Charles Beresford might collaborate with H. W. Wilson on a new biography of Nelson. It says that the book, a "risky adventure," might well attract readers not reached by Mahan's *Nelson*, and adds: "No doubt Lord Charles' Nelson will nearer approach the ideal which has always existed in the minds of Englishmen." The Beresford version of Nelson's career would also point up "the disagreements which the two authors make no bones about."

1. In which Marston noted that Vol. III of Clowes, *The Royal Navy: A History* . . . would likely be published in March 1898. Roy B. Marston to Mahan, London, August 13, 1897, in Princeton University Library.
2. "The Naval Campaign of 1776 on Lake Champlain," *Scribner's Magazine* (February 1898).

To Edward L. Burlingame

Slumberside, Quogue, Long Island, September 6, 1897 [PUL]

Dear Mr. Burlingame: Yours of the 2nd came during my absence. Barring indisposition on my part you can have the article within a week. I wish merely to change the opening words to suit an article. Otherwise it is typewritten and ready.

[P.S.]   *Paul Jones* is not forgotten.

To Walter Hines Page

Slumberside, Quogue, Long Island, September 10, 1897 [HUL]

Dear Mr. Page: Do you recognize the enclosed letter, and if so, do you recall, as my memory does, that the reading it suggested to you to ask for the Hawaii article in the *Forum*.[1]

If you do not yourself remember the fact, would you feel it objectionable for me to preface the article in my proposed published collection with the words—more or less—that the article was requested by the Editor of the *Forum*, upon reading this letter. The statement would rest solely upon my authority and recollection, the latter being quite distinct. I did not see you, I think, till after the article was written; but in any event I remember your saying to me, that the enclosed letter suggested your request to *me*. Doubtless, in the commotion you would have had an article on the question from some one.

[P.S.]   Please return enclosed, as it is my sole copy.

To Edward L. Burlingame

Slumberside, Quogue, Long Island, September 11, 1897 [PUL]

Dear Mr. Burlingame: I enclose the copy for the Lake Campaign—or Campaign on Lake Champlain of 1776, and also a map of the Lake I have had prepared for the *Naval History* of Messrs. Sampson & Low, which I will ask you to return. With reference to this latter, I will suggest for your consideration whether it would not be well to continue St. Lawrence River so as to show Quebec and Montreal.

---

1. *See* Mahan to Page, July 23, 1897.

I have mentioned that the wreck of the *Royal Savage* is still visible at low water of Lake Champlain. This is low water month, I believe. Have you means to verify this statement, which was taken from a work dated about 30 years ago? Unless I can verify, I must strike it out.

To Gaston Fournier[1]

Slumberside, Quogue, Long Island, September 13, 1897 [LC]

Dear Sir: I received yesterday your letter of the 11th, containing also a copy of yours of the same date to Mr. Brown. I am satisfied with the latter and accept your proposition namely: That you shall have the exclusive right to translate and publish the *Life of Nelson* in France, upon the same terms as you propose for the books upon Sea Power, that is ten per cent royalty to me upon each copy sold, except those supplied to the press. *Provided* that, if the translation is not made within one year after the publication of *Sea Power in the French Revolution*, the right of translation reverts to me.

There is one matter as regards the *Sea Power* books that must not be overlooked: that M. Boisse and M. de Diesbach had my authority to make the translations they have made. Nothing, therefore, must be done to injure their right as translators received from me, but I have no reason to doubt they will gladly accept from you the usual terms of translators.

There is no right to translate the *Life of Nelson* except that now conceded to you.

I am glad you should have met Mrs. Powel who is valued friend of Mrs. Mahan and myself. Wishing you a continued pleasant tour and voyage home I am [etc.].

To Robert U. Johnson

Slumberside, Quogue, Long Island, September 26, 1897 [NYPL]

My dear Mr. Johnson: I have been asked by Commander McCalla of the U.S.S. *Marblehead* to introduce the enclosed paper to the notice of the *Century*.[1] It gives me much pleasure to do so, as he expresses a high opinion of the author, and the region described is one as yet untrodden. By my count there are about 6,500 words—not long to read.

---

1. Of Georges Fournier, a publishing house in Paris.

1. Enclosure not found.

I do not express any opinion as to its probable interest to your readers, for that is your province; but I might suggest that naval officers, if capable, are worth encouraging, as they get to out of the way places.

[P.S.] A map doubtless could be supplied.

To Edward L. Burlingame

Slumberside, Quogue, Long Island, September 27, 1897 [PUL]

Dear Mr. Burlingame: I return herewith the corrected galleys of the Lake Champlain article. I have attached thereto, at the beginning the draft of a foot-note, mentioning the relation of the article to the *Hist.* of Sampson Low. This I would like inserted in accordance with the understanding with that firm when they consented to my publishing.

I enclose also the map proof, corrected. Marston was anxious that there should be no failure to produce the particular number of the magazine *on the same day* in England & here for sake of copyright there. This I believe I told you.

To Stephen B. Luce

Slumberside, Quogue, Long Island, September 30, 1897 [LC]

My dear Admiral: I have not sooner replied to Little's[1] letter, because of some hesitancy what to say, and because I am too busy, too preoccupied, to give questions due consideration. I should say that if the College will dispense with my lecturing, I would be willing to have a limited number of copies struck off, such steps being taken as my publishers may think necessary to protect my copyright. I should not relish the idea of reading lectures already printed. I entertain the idea of some day printing my lectures, worked over with some other matter; but this project is still far in the future, and I think it very probable that whatever good the lectures may be, will be greater to a student than to a mere hearer.

No man, however, can expect to improve himself greatly, who will not be content to do as I did; read Jomini, Hamley, the Archduke Charles*[2] &c &c atlas in hand, and with painstaking care.

* Napoleon's Commentaries[3] &c &c

---

1. W. McC. Little.
2. Karl Ludwig, Archduke of Austria. His several studies of war included *Grundsätze der Kriegskunst für die Generäle* (1806); *Grundsätze der Strategie erläutert durch die Darstellung des Feldzugs 1796* (1814); and *Gesch. des Feldzugs von 1799* (1819).
3. *Correspondance de Napoléon I.* 32 vols. Paris, 1858–1869.

To Edward L. Burlingame

Slumberside, Quogue, Long Island, September 30, 1897 [PUL]

Dear Mr. Burlingame: Overhauling my papers yesterday for return to town, I found a memorandum of some trivial matters connected with Champlain, which would add to the fullness of the article, & in so far to its correctness. If you will send me the galleys at once to 10 East 10th St., I will make the necessary changes & return speedily. Or, after Wednesday next, I shall be in my own house 160 West 86th.

The matter is one of a few lines and a few rewrites.

To J. M. Hays[1]

New York, October 19, 1897[2] [APS]

Sir: I have the honor to acknowledge your letter of the 15th inst, informing me that I have been elected a member of the American Philosophical Society. It will give me great pleasure to accept this flattering compliment at the hands of the Society, provided it entails upon me no duties or expenditures, for I have neither the time nor the means to add to those I already bear. Expressing my thanks for the honor conferred I am &c.

To James Ford Rhodes

160 West 86th Street, New York, October 26, 1897 [MHS]

Dear Mr. Rhodes: I cannot give you any information as to the route followed by supplies after they reached Matamoros. That was a detail outside of my special subject, which I did not have occasion to verify, though I see the difficulty now you speak of it. I have not, either, the local knowledge to surmise the solution. There were I remember, numerous steamers in Sabine Pass when I blockaded there in 1863, as there were at Galveston, and the extensive lagoon and river navigation that the maps show had doubtless boats of a type to use them. Texas, when I have passed through it by the Southern Pacific, struck me as an easy wagoning region. The gen-

---

1. Secretary of the American Philosophical Society.
2. Published with permission of the American Philosophical Society.

eral fact, I take it, is certain, but I cannot give you details. Lest you may have overlooked them I will refer you to Porter's letter to Farragut (*Life*, p. 223–4)[1] mentioning ammunition "*all*" coming by Red River, and to my mention of Matamoros again, p. 241. Soley, *Blockade & Cruisers*[2] p. 37, also mentions it.

I was extremely sorry to hear of Mr. Winsor's[3] death, which I had had no reason to expect. He will be a great loss. I remember that he sat next me when I had the pleasure of dining with you last April.

To the Editor of The New York Times

160 West 86th Street, New York, October 28, 1897[1]

In your issue of this morning, referring to the report of the Engineer-in-Chief of the Navy,[2] you not only say that no "reasonable" reply has ever been made to his statements—which may pass as opinion—but that no denials of these statements have ever been so much as attempted, by the "stolid" "foes of reform."

As one who is, substantially, entirely at odds with Mr. Melville's conclusions, I beg to point out that this assertion of yours is wholly erroneous. Many counter-arguments have been presented, but a discussion of the whole subject, from the point of view of the opposition to Mr. Melville's proposals, was published in *The North American Review* of December last:[3] The line officers of the navy who contributed these papers will be accepted, I am sure, by other members of their corps as fairly representing them in this matter, and I personally was assured by two civilians, shortly after the publication, of the convincing character of one of the articles.[4]

---

1. Mahan, *Admiral Farragut*. New York: D. Appleton & Co., 1892.
2. James R. Soley, *The Blockade and the Cruisers*. New York: Charles Scribner's Sons, 1883.
3. Justin Winsor, American historian.

1. From *The New York Times*, October 29, 1897, p. 6.
2. George Wallace Melville.
3. Rear Admiral John G. Walker, Captain A. T. Mahan, Captain R. D. Evans, and Lieutenant S. A. Staunton, "The Engineer in Naval Warfare," *North American Review* (December 1896).
4. On October 30 the Editor of the *Times* replied: ". . . we are more than willing to admit that the line officers have defended their privileges in print, and since Capt. Mahan is with them, that there must be something to be said on their side of the question. . . ."

To James R. Thursfield

160 West 86th Street, New York, December 1, 1897 [LC]

My dear Mr. Thursfield: I purpose sending you next week a little book of mine,[1] to be published on the 8th both here and in England, which is simply a compilation of magazine articles written by me during the past seven years. At the first, I had no purpose of subsequent collection, but the subject has developed without premeditation at my hands; in fact, with the exception of the very last one, each has been written in reply to a definite particular request of the magazine editor. You, I am sure, will expect to find me write as an American, and substantially from the American stand point; but I hope and believe you will recognize that my aim has been throughout to bring before my countrymen's minds the general integrity and beneficence of the expansion of Great Britain. It is not by directly forcing this thought down their throats (a rather mixed metaphor, by the way) but by a frequent recurrence to it in various connections that I seek this aim, tending always in imagination to bring about a better mutual understanding; based upon what I believe to be a substantial identity of interests and political characteristics.

This is a longish preamble to my chief object which is this: I conceive that at this present time Germany rather than France represents the probable element of future trouble for us, and perhaps for you. This depends much upon the Emperor it is true, but I conceive he voices fairly the tendencies and aspirations of the German people. Be that as it may, I wish, and one of my editors wishes to turn an eye upon what Germany has done, is doing, and is likely yet to do, in the way of colonial and commercial expansion abroad—the general tendency of her policy. My idea is that she is likely soon to give us something to think about seriously on this side of the water, where the Monroe Doctrine—define it how you may—has the people unquestionably at its back. There is nothing, I believe, for which our people would be more ready to fight at a moment's notice than any actual attempt at a European political expansion here; and I think your statesmen recognize the substantial justice of the position, however much they may condemn some manners of its manifestation. If our people get roused as to Germany, it would naturally draw their attention not only *from* the traditional jealousy of Great Britain, unhappily not yet at an end, but *towards* a better appreciation of your truly great work in India & Egypt, & of the fact that on this side and in the Pacific we are natural allies, from conditions of interest on which I need not here enlarge. I don't wish to arouse feeling, if no just cause exists, but I do aim to understand and point out actual conditions, and the actual temper of German policy all over the world, Africa,

---

1. *The Interest of America in Sea Power, Present and Future.*

[529]

etc., leaving others to form conclusions. Can you help me to information, either yourself or through your colleagues, by pointing out sources of information not only of the past, but in the current events of the present and future. Most of your magazines I see at my clubs, but for newspapers I am at a loss and even how to frame a query to a cutting bureau. Can you give me any suggestions?

I shall send the book to George Clarke, and you may show this letter to him if you like, for I dont know whether I can find time just now to write. With remembrance to Mrs. Thursfield [etc.].

To Edward P. Mitchell[1]

160 West 86th Street, New York, December 4, 1897 [NYHS]

Dear Sir: I beg to acknowledge the receipt of your letter of yesterday, and at the same time of a cheque for $500 in payment for the article.[2]

I thank you also for the explanation you have been kind enough to give, and which accounts for a delay I could not understand at the time.

To Augustus Lowell

160 West 86th Street, New York, December 9, 1897 [HUL]

My dear Mr. Lowell: You will by this time, I hope, have received a copy of a book I have lately brought out, and which I have asked the publishers to send you. I shall not expect you to agree with me on all points, perhaps on but few; but I trust you will take it as it is, and as a token of the pleasant recollection I have of the Lowell lecture room, and of your kindness to me while in Boston.

Please make my compliments to Miss Lowell.

---

1. A member of the editorial staff of the *New York Sun*, of which he became editor in 1903.
2. The $500 may have been in payment for Mahan's "Distinguishing Qualities of Ships of War," which the Scripps-McRae Newspaper League published in November 1898 and which was included in Mahan's *Lessons of the War with Spain and Other Articles*.

To James Ford Rhodes

160 West 86th Street, New York, December 9, 1897 [MHS]

My dear Mr. Rhodes: You will by this, I hope, have received a copy of my little book, *The Interest of America in Sea Power*, which I have asked the publishers to send you. I imagine you differ from me in many points, but I think you will recognize that in the main I have sought rather to put forward suggestions for thought, than to advocate directly particular modes of action. My métier is that of the naval writer, not of the statesman; and if I by chance slip over the line at times, I none the less recognize that as a rule I should limit myself to stating facts—as I see them—and pointing out their military bearings.

To Roy B. Marston

160 West 86th Street, New York, December 9, 1897 [BPL]

My dear Mr. Marston: I returned the enclosed, of which I have taken a copy, but cannot use for the *Naval History*. In my original suggestion I contemplated an allusion at some length to commerce destroyed as a strategic factor; but the work as you know grew to such proportions that it would have been impossible. I note in the course of my reading quite a number of data which might have been worked up in an interesting way; but space then, and now time, forbids. I should think that if Clowes should see fit to mention somewhere incidentally that "Lloyd's Lists show" such & such loss, Br. & enemy, it might be well to have the information in such accessible form for future use. Lloyd's lists I found imperfect for wars of Fr. Revolution & Empire, but I fancy that for 1776–83 they are the best, if not only, to be had, and will indicate fairly the proportionate gains & losses of the belligerents.

[P.S.] Whatever omissions Clowes makes from my manuscript please have the omitted pages returned to me as they would for the most part be very essential if the matter appear in a separate book.

To John M. Brown

160 West 86th Street, New York, December 13, 1897 [LC]

My dear Mr. Brown: If you have not seen the enclosed[1] it will interest you. It is not in the *N. Y. Times*, but then the latter is not booming any one who favors the annexation of Hawaii. You will recall that the *London News* is of Bryce's party from away back.

It appears to me quite on the cards that a mere trifle might start a run on the book, as dealing with matters of pressing present interest; and I would suggest your considering this with reference to placing advertisements where popular feeling may be strong for Hawaii or Cuba. I have written a letter in hopes of bringing it under the attention of Congress. Use might be made of the attention it seems to have attracted in England.

I consider the failure to annex Hawaii, if it so turn out, a national misfortune amounting to a national humiliation; for our grandchildren I am sure will revile the names of those who allow it to pass into foreign hands. For this in my judgement annexation is the only remedy.

To John M. Brown

160 West 86th Street, New York, December 26, 1897 [LC]

My dear Mr. Brown: Marston has sent me copies of the London *Times*, *News*, & *Chronicle*. I observe in the *News*, cutting from which I enclose,[1] no allusion to Mr. Bryce, such as stated in the *Sun* clipping which I sent you, & you quoted in subsequent advertisement. I have not found it in any other part of the paper. There is I suppose no need of rectifying a mistake for which we had authority; but equally we dont want to repeat it.

Do you send to the *Army & Navy Journal*, of New York, either advertisement or book for review? It seems to me it would be well to do so. My query is prompted by the fact that I see no mention of the book, & I believe of *Nelson*, in it. Army and Navy officers cannot be great book buyers; but it may injure my works if the impression should obtain that I hold aloof

---

1. An article in *The Sun*, New York, December 13, 1897, datelined London, December 12, calling attention to favorable British reviews of Mahan's *The Interest of America in Sea Power, Present and Future*. It noted that the London *Daily News* had contrasted Mahan's book with James Bryce's recent paper on the same subject in the *Forum* and concluded that "the weight of reasoning is rather with the strategist than the statesman."

1. Enclosure not found.

from them. The *A & N* is the best of the service journals—no great shakes but the best, & I believe has a clientèle in the Volunteers of N. Y. State.

I would suggest also sending a copy of the book to the Secretary of U. S. Naval Institute, Annapolis Md, & to the Editor of the *Journal of U.S. Artillery*, Fortress Monroe, Va; in both cases for the general reason given above.

With best wishes of the season to Mrs. Brown & yourself [etc.].

To John M. Brown

160 West 86th Street, New York, December 27, 1897 [LC]

My dear Mr. Brown: After mailing you my letter yesterday, I found the enclosed, which was in a bundle of cuttings, which had been misplaced while I was away from the house. So it was all right about Mr. Bryce &c.

To J. Franklin Jameson

160 West 86th Street, New York, December 27, 1897 [LC]

My dear Sir: I will undertake to review Spears' *History of the Navy*,[1] if you will be easy with me as to the time. Clark Russell[2] I do not wish to; he is in a degree a competitor of mine, and one of whom my opinion is well formed and unfavorable, as to his critical capacity & his style. Another might approach the work with less pre-judgment.

To John C. Ropes

160 West 86th Street, New York, January 5, 1898 [UML]

Dear Mr. Ropes: With reference to your kind request to me to indicate the names of gentlemen to meet me at dinner on the Monday and Tuesday, I would like Mr. Frank H. Appleton,[1] & the Commandant of the

---

1. John Randolph Spears, *History of Our Navy from its Origin to the Present Day*, *1775–1897*. 5 vols. New York: Charles Scribner's Sons, 1897–1899.
2. A writer of popular sea stories, whose only two serious works before this date were *Horatio Nelson and the Naval Supremacy of England* (New York, 1890), and *William Dampier* (London, 1889).
1. Francis Henry Appleton, Massachusetts legislator.

Navy Yard (if agreeable to you) asked on Monday. I do not know who the Commandant is now,[2] so it would be well to make clear to him that he is to meet me. I should prefer that Mr. John M. Brown and Mr. Jas Ford Rhodes should be asked on the less formal occasion on Tuesday. Besides these, as I can now recall, Governor Wolcott,[3] Mr. Chas S. Sargent,[4] and Mr. Augustus Lowell showed me particular attention while in Boston. I will leave it to your judgment, however, to make up the party without expressing a wish in these instances. Do ladies attend the lectures? If they do I will ask of you one or two complimentary tickets.

It has occurred to me with regard to the map of the coast, that if an extension of 50 to 100 miles to the westward be given the courses of the opposing fleets could be laid down—prior to the engagement. Though not vital, this is of interest.

I shall write to the Navy Department tonight for a chart.

To James Ford Rhodes

160 West 86th Street, New York, January 9, 1898 [MHS]

My dear Mr. Rhodes: I cannot lay my hand on your letter, containing your kind wish to have me dine with you in Boston. With reference to it, the case stands thus. It was understood from last spring that I was to stay with Mr. Ropes when I went to lecture.[1] That being arranged, he wrote me at the end of December that he wished me to dine with him Monday, Jan 31, to meet a company. To this as my host's wish, as well as because pleasant to myself, I of course acceded. Tuesday being the night of the lecture, dining out is of course impossible. On Thursday I must return to keep an engagement in N.Y. Now, on Wednesday Mr. Ropes has expressed a wish that I should stay over to attend the Wednesday Evening Century Club at his house. I probably should have stayed over in any event, but you will see it is scarcely possible for me to make any dinner engagement under all the conditions, especially of my obligations to the hospitality of Mr. Ropes. I am sorry that things cannot arrange themselves better, but I dont see how they can. I should have enjoyed greatly such another evening as I had at your house last spring.

2. H. L. Howison.
3. Roger Wolcott, Republican governor of Massachusetts.
4. Professor of arboriculture at Harvard, author, and conservationist.

1. Mahan was to deliver a paper on February 1 at the meeting of the Military Historical Society of Massachusetts, of which J. C. Ropes was the moving spirit. Mahan had joined the Society in 1891. The paper he read on this occasion was "The Battle of Trafalgar," which was printed in the Society's *Proceedings*, I, (1898).

To John C. Ropes

160 West 86th Street, New York, January 9, 1898 [HSP][1]

My dear Mr. Ropes: Mr. John M. Brown is head of the firm Little, Brown & Co, who publish my books. A letter addressed to him to the firm, or to the Somerset Club, will reach him. I am not sure of his house address in the country. I have heard from Captain Robins about the map &c & will communicate with him.

I saw Michie[2] at the Century last evg, looking better than I had dared to hope; quite his old self, but his grog is stopped.

To Robert U. Johnson

160 West 86th Street, New York, January 17, 1898 [NYPL]

Dear Mr. Johnson: I ought, I suppose, to have expected your letter, but somehow I didn't. I think I had rather fallen into the belief that the *Century* was out of concert, not of my articles particularly, but of the subject, and that it would go by default. I am therefore somewhat perplexed to give you a definite answer as to what I can do. There are one or two pending engagements that cannot be postponed, and I am a little complicated by a possibility of going to Europe for the spring & summer—not yet settled. I think I can get up for you Lepanto and the Athenian Expedition against Syracuse; by which I mean I think I have the material in such shape that the effort would be comparatively slight. If not in themselves absolutely decisive, they were at least conspicuous turning points in the tide of history. I should incline to think that Beachy Head (1690) and La Hogue (1692) would be in the list, but whether for one or two articles I cant certainly tell. The others to be given I should say would be (possibly) the action off the Chesapeake in 1781—a poor affair in itself but momentous in its consequences—and Salamis. Of the latter in detail I know practically nothing.

I believe that our agreement as to terms covered only the Nelson articles, undertaken in 1895 for 1896. It will be well to reach, now as then, a conclusion beforehand, and you will be prepared for my expecting a higher rate than formerly as my work grows in demand. In justice to myself I should ask now $500 for each article, ranging above 6,000 words to such

---

1. Published with permission of the Historical Society of Pennsylvania.
2. Possibly, Peter S. Michie, professor at the U.S. Military Academy.

limit, not exceeding 10,000, as you may indicate as a maximum. The question also of my royalty in the book, when produced, had best also be arranged beforehand.[1]

To John M. Brown

160 West 86th Street, New York, January 18, 1898 [LC]

My dear Mr. Brown: I returned at once the receipt for the amount of my semi-annual account, but neglected to acknowledge at the same time the kind letter with which you accompanied the cheque. I am extremely gratified with the result—and trust we may soon again strike something at least nearly as good as *Nelson*. As I hope soon to see you, I will enter no further into business matters.

To James R. Thursfield

160 West 86th Street, New York, January 25, 1898 [LC]

Dear Mr. Thursfield: I am much indebted to yourself and to Sir Donald Wallace[1] for the letters received under your cover a week ago;[2] and I beg you to thank him for me when fit opportunity offers. The exact trend of the Emperor's thought cannot be seen, but it seems to me somewhat like this. He cannot pretend to cope with Great Britian on the seas —except by alliance or by your being handicapped otherwise; the latter being a condition not unapt to arise. But while he cannot meet you, he may well be able to meet us singly, or to counteract you either directly or indirectly in cooperation with others. I presume this Kiao Chau business,[3] which has come up lately is an instance in point. In any event he wants a navy, for Great Britain with her immense colonial occupancy, and we with our Monroe doctrine, threaten to stand in the way of his very natural (and very proper) ambition, which I conceive to be this: that as Germans by blood are becoming too numerous for the old land to hold them, they

---

1. Nothing immediately came of Johnson's inquiry and Mahan's proposal. Mahan did not publish again in the *Century Magazine* until June 1911. But *see* Mahan to Johnson, February 14, 1898, and March 25, 1898.

1. Director of the foreign department of the London *Times* (1891–1906).
2. *See* Mahan to Thursfield, December 1, 1897.
3. The Germans had seized Kiaochow, China, in November 1897.

should migrate not to foreign lands, but to regions which can be brought and kept in political conjunction with home. Your Jubilee of last year[4] must have fired the imagination of one already possessed with this idea, particularly a man like the Emperor possessed of ability, imagination and strength of character. It is really a very respectable, not to say great, ideal; the difficulty I fancy is that the German emigrant like his antecessors the Dutch have not political characteristics that favor independent local development. They are admirable grafts, as we find here; I doubt whether they be the kind of slip which can take root alone in the soil, and acquire independent life. This remark is somewhat common here, where our German fellow citizens are most highly esteemed and identify themselves with us; but it is said they do so likewise in Central America, and in Brazil. As regards the latter country this is confirmed to me by an American resident there many years, in the Southern states. I question therefore whether the individuality of the German emigrant, or the somewhat inelastic form of the German government, is at all suited for that local political development upon which alone a strong colonial system can be based. Of course your proposed colonial system labors under the weakness of all federations, especially when the numbers are widely scattered; divergent interests will prompt divergent action. But you have made an immense stride in advance in the prestige you have gained, and in the growing sense of common interest. The recent action of Germany & Russia[5] will only enhance this sense; and indeed in our country that action has promoted a certain sense of solidarity with you.

I shall read your article in the *Quarterly*[6] with interest, until I see it I cant tell how wide our difference is on the points you mention.

To Robert U. Johnson

160 West 86th Street, New York, January 27, 1898 [NYPL]

Dear Mr. Johnson: Your note just recd. I am going to Boston tomorrow[1] & shall not be in town again until Thursday evening of next week (Feb. 3). I shall have to ask you therefore to make me another appointment.

My address in Boston is Care of J. C. Ropes, 99 Mt. Vernon St.

---

4. Queen Victoria's Diamond Jubilee.
5. The Russians were also engaged in the seizure of leaseholds from China.
6. James R. Thursfield, "Nelson," *Quarterly Review* (January 1898).

1. To lecture the Military Historical Society of Massachusetts on "The Battle of Trafalgar."

To Robert U. Johnson

99 Mount Vernon Street, Boston, February 1, 1898 [NYPL]

Dear Mr. Johnson: Unless something very unforeseen occur I will call on Friday between 3 and 4. I gave your message as desired to Mr. Ropes.

To James H. Kyle[1]

160 West 86th Street, New York, February 4, 1898[2]

Your letter of the third is at hand. You appreciate, doubtless, that to give a categorical reply to questions such as you propose is very like giving a quotation apart from the context in which it stands. I shall try, however, to present such replies and their reasons as summarily as possible.

1. From a military point of view the possession of Hawaii will strengthen the United States. Of course, as is constantly argued, every addition of territory is an additional exposed point; but Hawaii is now exposed to pass under foreign domination—notably Japan—by a peaceful process of over-running and assimilation. This will inevitably involve its possession by a foreign power–a grave military danger to us–against which preoccupation by the United States is, in my judgment, the only security.

2. In replying to the second question, I must guard myself from being understood to think our present Pacific fleet great enough for possible contingencies. With this reservation a greater navy would not be needed for the defense of the Pacific coast than would be required with the islands unannexed. If we have the islands, and in the Pacific a fleet of proper force, the presence of the latter, or of an adequate detachment from it, at the Hawaiian Islands, will materially weaken, if not wholly cripple any attempted invasion of the Pacific coast (except from British Columbia), and consequently will proportionately strengthen us. With a fleet of the same size and Hawaii unoccupied by either party, the enemy would at least be in a better position to attack us; while if he succeeded in establishing himself in any of our coast anchorages, he would be far better off. For, in the latter case, the islands would not menace his communications with

---

1. Senator Kyle, of South Dakota, wrote Mahan on February 3, 1898, posing four specific questions on the strategic features of Hawaii: 1. Would the possession of Hawaii strengthen or weaken the United States from a military standpoint? 2. In case of war, would it take a larger navy to defend the Pacific coast with or without the possession of Hawaii? 3. Is it practicable for any Pacific country to attack the Pacific coast without occupying Hawaii as a base? 4. Could such attack be made by transporting coal in colliers and transferring coal at sea?

2. From 55th Cong., 2d Sess., Senate Report No. 681, p. 99.

home; which they would if in our possession, because Hawaii flanks the communications.

It is obvious also, that if we do not hold the islands ourselves we can not expect the neutrals in the war to prevent the other belligerent from occupying them; nor can the inhabitants themselves prevent such occupation. The commercial value is not great enough to provoke neutral interposition. In short, in war we should need a larger navy to defend the Pacific coast, because we should have not only to defend our own coast, but to prevent, by naval force, an enemy from occupying the islands; whereas, if we had preoccupied them, fortifications could preserve them to us.

3. In my opinion, it is not practicable for any trans-Pacific country to invade our Pacific coast without occupying Hawaii as a base.

4. Coal can be transported in colliers, but as yet it can not be transshipped at sea with either rapidity or certainty. Even if it be occasionally practicable to coal at sea, the process is slow and uncertain. Reliance upon such means only is, in my judgment, impossible. A base must be had, and, except the ports of our own coast, there is none to be named alongside of Hawaii.

To John C. Ropes

160 West 86th Street, New York, February 6, 1898 [HSP] [1]

My dear Mr. Ropes: I found such an accumulation of mail, as well as other matter, awaiting me on arrival, that I have postponed till to day thanking you for your hospitality during my enjoyable visit to Boston. Lecturing is never to me a pleasure, but I am bound to admit that the conditions of the last week were very mitigating.

I trust that the milder weather we now have may help you to get rid of some of your superfluity of snow. It was beautiful, but I think troublesome. We are dissolving, though not fast enough; & the streets are pretty bad. I did not get to the Century meeting last night, much to my regret. The Round Table was but slightly attended, for which I was sorry, as I think it will be my last till next fall.

To Edward L. Burlingame

160 West 86th Street, New York, February 9, 1898 [PUL]

Dear Mr. Burlingame: I find, apparently, in the matter of Paul Jones that there is more than I originally thought, not being closely familiar

---

1. Published with permission of the Historical Society of Pennsylvania.

with the subject. It will be possible, I now think, either to treat the cruise of the *Bonhomme Richard*, with its precedents and consequents in brief, as, say, "Paul Jones and the B. H. R." in a single article; or it would be possible to make two articles of about 7,500 words each under the title of "Paul Jones and his Career in the Revolution."[1]

Antecedently the latter would be more to my taste, as I find more, in the character of his *career*, and in the character of the *man himself*, than I anticipated; and I like to philosophize upon such matters & to expound them, after the manner of my books; but our agreement was only for two articles, of which Champlain was one,[2] and I write therefore to ask whether you would care to have a third on the same terms as the former two, or whether I shall narrow down to the European episode under the American flag.

I have only recently reached this conclusion. The study and the writing has been among the most exasperating I have ever undertaken. The two principal authorities, whence others chiefly draw, have a jumble of arrangement, strictly disregardful of chronology, which wastes untold time in hunting up references, and confuses even one's own notes. Amid all these perplexities, I am kept in constant dread of the pitfalls of error.

To Joseph E. Craig[1]

160 West 86th Street, New York, February 11, 1898 [NA]

My dear Craig: I am writing an account of the fight between the *Serapis* and *Bonhomme Richard*,[2] and in connection with it want one or two items of consequence that your office can furnish me. It is essential to know, *1*, the hour of moon-rise on Sept. *23*, 1779; and, *2* the direction in which the tidal current was setting, off Flamborough Head, east coast of England, between *8* and *10* P.M. of that same day. The first, of course, I could calculate; but I have no tables and throw myself on your good nature. For the second, I presume tidal conditions are practically the same now as then; at any rate I will be satisfied so to take them, from the present establishment of the nearest place indicated, and the modern charts. I enclose the lunar elements taken from a nautical almanac of 1779.

---

1. *See* Mahan to Burlingame, July 5, 1897, Footnote 1.
2. "The Naval Campaign of 1776 on Lake Champlain."

1. Commander Craig, class of 1865, was Hydrographer, an office at that time in the Bureau of Equipment.
2. "John Paul Jones in the Revolution," *Scribner's Magazine* (July and August 1898).

Thursday Sept. 23. 1779

$\mathbb{D}$'s Age   15 Days
$\mathbb{D}$'s Meridian Passage   10h 53m
$\mathbb{D}$'s R.A. noon   338h 42m
         " midnight   344   30
$\mathbb{D}$'s Decln. noon   14   24   s
         " midnight   12   03   "
Equation of Time   7.42

I forget to note Eq.T. increasing or diminishing, but the amount of Eq.T. is really immaterial.

To Edward L. Burlingame

160 West 86th Street, New York, February 13, 1898 [PUL]

Dear Mr. Burlingame: Your letter has been received, and I will prepare the two articles on the plan as now understood between us—i.e. Paul Jones in and through the Revolution, which will allow of course a brief résumé of his career before and after to his death. There will be no difficulty in my communicating to your illustrators the information you ask within the next fortnight. I will mention that I expect to sail for Europe March 26, for a six months absence.. My aim therefore is to put this manuscript into your hands as soon as possible, that I may correct proofs of plans & diagrams before leaving.

I do not know Mrs. Maudslay, but if any letters such as you mention are to be had, I would gladly look over them.[1] Before moving in the matter, however, I would suggest your glancing over the quotations in Morris[2] relative to Jones, by means of the Index. Possibly there may be no others in the unpublished letters. I have already quoted the interview at Paris between Jones and the son of Lord Selkirk.

---

1. On February 11 Burlingame had sent Mahan information about the Paul Jones material in the Gouverneur Morris papers, the whole file of which he had seen when the edited version was given to Scribner's for publication.
2. *Autobiography of Commodore Charles Morris.*

To Robert U. Johnson

160 West 86th Street, New York, February 14, 1898 [NYPL]

My dear Mr. Johnson: I should sooner have written about my interview with yourself and the other gentleman,[1] but I do get so weary writing continually. I want chiefly to say that I purpose writing the articles of which we spoke, and that they will soon be first in order among the *magazine* work that I shall undertake; but I do not want to feel too much tied down by anything like a promise, the non-fulfillment of which would be a reproach to me. I will keep the matter in mind, and will endeavor to send you one or two in time for next year's announcements, but I am beginning to feel the pressure of undone work, with which you doubtless, as a literary and a busy man are familiar, and can understand my reluctance to bind myself too closely.[2]

To Endicott Peabody

160 West 86th Street, New York, February 18, 1898 [HUL]

Dear Mr. Peabody: Our affairs have so straightened out, that I am able to say definitely that Lyle will not return after the Easter vacation. I should be glad, however, to think that in case I should be detained in the country by the Navy Dept. (whose permission to go abroad I now have) that he could return to Groton, rather than pass two months in idleness.

I will not allow this occasion to pass without expressing to you my entire satisfaction with the growth and development of Lyle's character and moral turn, as apparent to us, during his stay at the school. His standards of action and habits of thought, as I see and hear them, and by which I judge, are the guarantee of the wholesome influence exerted by yourself and your associates. That he at times may fall short of best ideals is an infirmity common to man, & in no way imputable to others.

Wishing that Groton may continue to enjoy the prosperity and high esteem which it now has, and with kind remembrances to Mrs. Peabody, and all the Faculty, believe me [etc.].

---

1. Richard Watson Gilder, editor-in-chief of *The Century*, 1881–1909.
2. *See* Mahan to Johnson, January 17, 1898, and May 19, 1902.

To George Sydenham Clarke

160 West 86th Street, New York, February 22, 1898 [LC]

My dear Clarke: Don't mention it. Of course, I expect criticism unfavorable as well as favorable, according to the impressions of my critic; and while I cannot concede the justice of much of your comment, and do not preceive that you have at all recognized my dominant ideas in my writing, I do not find that you have transgressed towards me either as a reviewer or as a friend.[1]

I am sorry to infer that you are less hopeful as the years go on. Don't you think really that the fair lessons of experience, broadly viewed, give more ground for hope as years go by; not necessarily for our particular ideals but for the general progress and welfare. I don't know where you stand theologically, but it seems to me that the old reproach to the Israelites, that though they saw the *works* they did not know the *ways* after forty years, has its lesson for us today; and that too whether we accept a personal Providence, as I do, or whether not. Surely things get better rather than worse.

It is on the cards that I may have the pleasure of seeing you and Lady Clarke this summer. We intend to sail from New York March 26 for Naples and shall work slowly north through Italy and France. I shall not reach England before July 1st, possibly not before July 15th. It will be all new to my girls and I shall take things leisurely, as we will not return till late September.

With remembrances to Lady Clarke [etc.].

To John M. Brown

160 West 86th Street, New York, February 25, 1898 [LC]

Dear Mr. Brown: I have recd today galleys through 49.[1] By one of the curiosities of the mail 32–49 came before 22–31.

There is room for trouble on the question of Capital Letters. Clowes is acting on a plan of his own, and the only safe plan is to follow the "copy"

---

1. *See* George Sydenham Clarke, "Captain Mahan's Counsels to the United States," *Nineteenth Century* (February 1898), a highly critical review of Mahan's *The Interest of America in Sea Power, Present and Future.*

1. "Major Operations of the Royal Navy, 1762–1783," for Clowes, *The Royal Navy: A History*. . . .

as corrected by him. E.G. D'Estaing & D'Orviller, he corrects to a small d: d'Estaing. De Grasse he puts *De Grasse*. The proofreaders are kicking against the former, but subordination is the only rule here. If a mistake, it is not ours. There are other instances. Will you have them instructed?

An anxious time—yes; but will you say to yourselves and friends how absurd that the U.S. should be anxious about Spain.[2] We might and should have had a navy, in which our only anxiety would have been to do right; and Spain's only anxiety would be to do the same because if not she would be hopelessly gone.

To Edward L. Burlingame

160 West 86th Street, New York, February 28, 1898 [PUL]

Dear Mr. Burlingame: You wished to know something about the Paul Jones' papers with reference to illustrations. I can say only this, prior to sending in the paper viz: that for my own part I will submit a diagram probably very simple of the engagement of the *Bonhomme Richard* showing also the course of the *Alliance* when she fired impartially into the two combatants. I should recommend a map outline also, the *southern* line of which should include Ile Groix & the mouth of the Loire on the coast of France; the *western* line about a degree west of Ireland; *northern* line just include Shetland Ils.; *eastern* line to take in all the Texel. If such a map will be sent to me, I will enter the course of the *Ranger* & the *Bonhomme Richard*, and indicate names absolutely necessary to insert.

For the rest, the *Ranger* & Whitehaven episodes are in the first paper; the *Bonhomme Richard* fight in the second. I can give the illustrators no points on this, except to caution them that when the vessels lay together, their starboard sides touched, they were riding by the anchor of the *Serapis*, the latter vessel heading about south, the *Richard* therefore north, and the wind southwest.

The paper is finished, but I need to satisfy myself a little more certainly about the manoeuvres & the crew of the *Richard*. For the former I have written to England, for the latter I hope to see some of Barnes's papers.[1]

---

2. The USS *Maine* exploded and sank in Havana Harbor on February 15, with a loss of 260 officers and men.

1. James Barnes, who worked for Scribner's, and then became assistant editor of *Harper's Weekly*. He was the author of *Naval Actions of the War of 1812*, and various naval biographies.

To J. B. Sterling

160 West 86th Street, New York, March 4, 1898 [LC]

My dear Colonel Sterling: Thank you very much for your messages of sympathy concerning the loss of *Maine*. Nothing can reconcile our wills to the loss of the fine fellows who perished in this sorrowful manner, nor is the loss of the ship a small matter to so small a navy at a time that may prove critical; but I am glad to believe that it will in its way, by the exchange of kindly feelings, tend to draw Great Britian and our country a step nearer. The thought of treachery is not admissible until proved, and I do not myself see any indication of it as yet; though under the conditions, and with a certain inherited distrust the Anglo-Saxon has of the Latin, a moment of suspicion was perhaps inevitable. I am satisfied myself that the tendency is for our two countries to draw together, but the process is inevitably slow, and particularly with a huge, and as yet not homogeneous, body politic as ours here, it takes a long time for a sentiment to permeate the mass. As you say France seems in a parlous state; but then again our English tradition makes impossible to understand a Frenchman. Heaven help them!

I am cherishing the hope of turning up in England sometime in July —expecting now to sail for Naples on the 26th inst.

To Edward L. Burlingame

160 West 86th Street, New York, March 4, 1898 [PUL]

Dear Mr. Burlingame: I enclose the manuscript of "Paul Jones in the Revolution." The second of the two articles is somewhat longer than even I anticipated; but I have marked in red crayon passages that may well be omitted at your discretion—especially from page 32 to the end of the *second* article.

I still expect from England the evidence in the trial of Pearson;[1] but in view of my expected sailing on March 26, and that I really do not look for anything materially changing my views—am only taking this last precaution —I would suggest having this be set up at once, and sent to me in galley form, so that I may be able to return it to you, entirely ready for the final publication, before I leave. If your judgment coincides with this, may I

---

1. Sir Richard Pearson, Captain of HMS *Serapis* when she was defeated by Jones in the *Bonhomme Richard* on September 23, 1779. He was honorably acquitted by court-martial in 1780.

hope the galleys may be hastened back to me; for I have much proof-reading, and many other chores, besides this.

With regard to the diagram of the action,[2] I have with me a rough draft of the text to guide my drawing, and I want to lose no time now, in forwarding enclosed.

In case you reject note on p. *11 Second* Article, may I ask you to clip it off, and return to me, for memorandum.

The whole involved more, and more interesting, historical study than I had anticipated.

To William H. Henderson

160 West 86th Street, New York, March 7, 1898 [NMM]

My dear Henderson: I am much gratified by your letter received today. The official expression of sorrow, and the generally—universally—sympathetic manner in which the English press have spoken of our sad calamity have been greatly valued, but I think there is something even more grateful in the spontaneous utterances of individuals, writing like yourself now, without any possible necessity so to do, except that which springs from professional and national good feeling. I have letters of similar turn to yours from Col. Sterling and Sir George Clarke, & also from an officer of the R.M.A., named Hill, stationed at Portsmouth. I cannot recall him, though we may be acquaintances. I hope and believe that these are but indications of a wide spread good will in your country, & one that equally exists, though I fear less universal, in our own. I think, however, it is distinctly growing here.

I hope you will like Jamaica. I have never been there, but think it the most important single position in the West Indies.[1] I must be sorry you go out so soon, for I am expecting now to be in England in July. Still, if you come home our way I shall see you then.

To J. Franklin Jameson

160 West 86th Street, New York, March 10, 1898 [LC]

My dear Sir: I enclose my promised Review of Spears' *Naval History*.[1]

I expect to sail for Europe March 26, but I think you will scarcely need my help for proof reading.

---

2. The *Bonhomme Richard* versus the *Serapis*.

1. Henderson had been appointed Commodore at Jamaica.

1. *See* Mahan to Johnson, December 27, 1897.

To Edward L. Burlingame

160 West 86th Street, New York, March 16, 1898 [PUL]

Dear Mr. Burlingame: I send you back the corrected proofs of the first of the Paul Jones' papers. The corrections in one place are more than they would have been, had I not received from Laughton the testimony in the *Drake* Court Martial[1] since I sent you the copy. I have also received the evidence in the trial of Captain Pearson of the *Serapis*. There is in it, however, little cause for modification.

I have been disappointed not to receive so far today the proofs of the 2d paper. As the time of sailing is so near, I am anxious to finish, and to get my hands clear for preparations for sea.

To Edward L. Burlingame

160 West 86th Street, New York, March 21, 1898 [PUL]

My dear Mr. Burlingame: I enclose herewith a plan of the action between *Bonhomme Richard* & *Serapis*. The galleys returned today have the necessary references interpolated in them (Galleys 11, 13, 14). I have but one caution, and that is that the *wind* be drawn in *possibly*, as per specimen pinned on; that is, when yards are braced up, that the wind strikes their rear side. The relative length of the three yards is sufficiently shown also in the specimen, as also their distance apart. When the yards are squared, the wind strikes in front of them to push ship back.

Let the two ships, *Serapis* and *Richard* be of the same size; A, C, P, a little smaller. With these cautions follow my drawing, which is rough, for I have to rely on draughtsmen for finishing. There is time enough to send me a proof of this, which of course is desirable.

[P.S.] I sail Saturday.

To John M. Brown

160 West 86th Street, New York, March 21, 1898 [LC]

My dear Mr. Brown: I am very glad you are going to have a holiday, and trust that your going abroad proceeds from nothing of an unpleasant

---

1. The Admiralty inquiry into the loss of the sloop-of-war *Drake* to Jones in the *Ranger*. The *Drake* was the first Royal Navy vessel to be taken as an American prize.

character. I am afraid, however, that unless your stay in France is more prolonged we shall hardly meet. We sail Saturday and are due in Naples April 7. From there we go north somewhat deliberately, stopping along, and our itinerary calls for our being in London about, but not before July 10.

I cannot give you any assurances about the *Admirals*.[1] The first part of the year up to the present has been given, a little to *1812*, but chiefly to completing magazine engagements; the latter somewhat with a view to providing the wherewithal for our trip, but still more to clear off my slate of promises. The year 1898 therefore seems to me now doomed to unproduction; possibly the respite may restore my working powers, for though I dont feel tired out, I feel near it. The quantity of my work seems up to mark, but the consciousness of work undone ahead wears on me. It would I think be well if in discussing with Marston you could reach a conclusion as to whether I had best—for pecuniary results, take up on my return the text book on 1812. You represent opposite points of view I think, and so discussion would be fruitful.

To Edward L. Burlingame

160 West 86th Street, New York, March 24, 1898 [PUL]

Dear Mr. Burlingame: My address while abroad will be Morgan, Harjes & Co., Paris, till July 10; afterwards J. S. Morgan & Co., London. We are due back in N. Y. Oct. 4.[1]

To Robert U. Johnson

160 West 86th Street, New York, March 25, 1898 [NYPL]

My dear Mr. Johnson: As we are sailing tomorrow, I write you with reference to the projected series of articles, ultimately to become a book.[1] My address abroad will be Morgan, Harjes and Co., Paris.

I will undertake to supply the articles as by schedule submitted to you, and will give two of them for the year 1899. I cannot engage for anything

---

1. *See* Mahan to Brown, March 11, 1897.
1. On March 22, 1898, Secretary of the Navy John D. Long appointed Mahan Honorary Representative of the United States at a celebration to be held in Florence in honor of Amerigo Vespucci and Paolo dal Pozzo Toscanelli, the cosmographer who advised Columbus.
1. *See* Mahan to Johnson, January 17, 1898, and February 14, 1898.

this year. The two for next year will be Salamis and the Athenian Expedition against Syracuse. The treatment will be on the general lines of my *Influence of Sea Power*: a statement of general historical conditions, sufficient to understand the setting of the special incident in the mosaic of history; the sequences of cause and effect as I understand them. The incident will be treated chiefly from its military and naval point of view, technically and scientifically, as an illustration of the art of war, either by its merits or defects, or both. I shall keep prominently in mind the investing the narrative with the glamour and brilliance of war, the interest of anecdote, etc. For this I have to dig again into the original authorities Thucydides, Plutarch etc.

The length of each article to be not less than 6,000 nor (except by your consent) more than 10,000 words; the payment $500 per article, irrespective of length, within the above limits.

The question of royalty on the book was not settled. I should consider 15 per cent fair.

I shall attach especial importance to so tracing events that no one shall be able to say—with Caspar—"What they fought each other for, I cannot well make out."[2] In fact, I started the first of the articles already published with those words, but cut them out to save space.

We are due back in New York October 4th.[3]

To Edward L. Burlingame

160 West 86th Street, New York, March 25, 1898 [PUL]

Dear Mr. Burlingame: In looking over my letters from Marston, I find that he asks that there be a clear understanding that the *Champlain* article is not to be published otherwise than in the magazine. I have understood that such was the status—unless at some future day his firm should give permission—but I think it best before sailing to write so definitely to you.

Goodbye, until the fall.

To Augustus T. Gillender

Rome, Italy, April 20, 1898 [HUL]

Dear Mr. Gillender: I enclose cheque for $2,000, with which I will ask you to buy me *four* drafts on J. S. Morgan & Co. of London, of about

---

2. From Robert Southey's "The Battle of Blenheim."
3. Johnson wrote on this letter: " 'Lepanto' preferable if practicable."

£100 each, and to forward to me by separate covers, Care of Morgan, Harjes & Co., Paris. My object is to get my money on this side, in case the value of money is affected seriously by present troubles. Therefore please buy speedily, and forward by different mails. Kind regards from us both.

N. B. Drafts to *order of Ellen L. Mahan.*

To the Secretary of the Navy League of Great Britain

N.P., N.D.   Probably, April 1898[1]

. . . I am extremely glad to note that the League "attaches still greater importance to the growth of a good feeling and most cordial relationship between Great Britain and the United States." This is certainly a matter of much more consequence than the personal compliment to myself, greatly as I appreciate this; and, while I feel the propriety of keeping myself from suggestions to the League, I shall see with great satisfaction the prominence given to the idea of good fellowship between the two countries. It has been my endeavour, on this side, to keep the utility and the grandeur of this idea before my countrymen, measuring my words, however, very carefully, in order to avoid any hold for an imputation that my own country's interests are not with me supreme. Any utterance that seems to ignore this first loyalty of a citizen does harm instead of good; and a disposition of such gush on this side, by well-meaning persons, has done harm. I believe you yourselves have men with whom, as they say, "Everyone is right but England herself . . . ."

To J. Franklin Jameson

Rome, April 21, 1898 [LC]

My dear Sir: With reference to the *Life of Admiral Duncan*[1] I do not care to make engagements for future work, prior to my return, when my hands will be very full compensating for lost time.

---

1. From *The Times*, London, April 21, 1898, under the heading "Capt. Mahan on Anglo-American Relations." *The Times* noted: "The following is an extract from a letter from Captain A. T. Mahan, U.S.N., to the secretary of the Navy League, in answer to a communication respecting an invitation to dine with the League. The letter was not primarily written with a view to publication, but in reply to a request for permission to give it publicity a cordial assent was granted."

1. Robert Adam Philips Haldane Duncan, Earl of Camperdown, *Admiral Duncan*. London: Longmans, Green & Co., 1898. Mahan was asked to review the book.

To William R. Day[1]

Telegram   Paris, France, April 29, 1898 [NWC]

Captain Mahan offers following suggestions:[2]

FIRST. If two or three enemy's battleships enter Porto Rico, or elsewhere, they should at once be blocked by a force superior to any combination possible by the enemy at the moment.

SECOND. In such case and in existing conditions it seems probable that Havana could be left to light vessels, swift enough to escape if unfortunately surprised by superior force.

THIRD. It is improbable enemy fleet would seek to enter Havana adding to the burden of food subsistence, unless meaning to fight, which of course we wish.

FOURTH. M. does not think any enemy large ship would venture to enter any of our Atlantic ports. Torpedo vessels might, but they can be handled.

FIFTH. M. heartily approves naval strategy up to date especially refusing to oppose ships to the Havana forts. He would not favor any dispersal of battle ships as he is reported to have done to guard ports against attack.

SIXTH. M. requests secrecy as to his movements till his return.

To John D. Long

Naval War Board, Washington, D.C., May 10, 1898[1] [MHS]

Sir: I respectfully recommend that the "Board of War" be abolished, and that in place of it, to perform the functions with which it is now entrusted, there be appointed a single officer, to be known by such title as may seem convenient to designate his duties.

2. To this officer there would be appointed such assistants as shall be expedient, with whom he can consult at his pleasure, individually or collectively, directing their special study of the general situation, or of particular features, and inviting suggestions; but, in the end, the opinions officially submitted will be his own, for which he alone will be responsible, and for whose success he alone would receive credit.

---

1. The Secretary of State from April 26 to September 16, 1898.
2. This telegram, which conveys Mahan's initial views on the naval strategy of the Spanish-American War, was transmitted through Horace Porter, U.S. Ambassador to France.

1. Recalled from Europe on the outbreak of the Spanish-American War, Mahan reported for duty in Washington on May 9, 1898.

3. The change suggested is from a Council of War, which the Board virtually is, with corporate responsibility and without individual responsibility, to the single, individual responsibility, which alone achieves results in war.

4. I do not forget that the Secretary himself exercises such single responsibility. But, with the varied and onerous duties resting upon him, it is inevitable that, in such highly technical matters as the conduct of war, he must depend largely upon the technical familiarity with the subject that only seamen, and military seamen, can possess. Professional opinion should come to him, not as the result of a majority vote, but with the far weightier sanction of a single competent man, acting under the high sense of high personal responsibility.

5. I offer the suggestion at once, before any difference with my colleagues has arisen, or could arise. Resting, as my opinion does, upon a wide study of military history, it is not liable to change, and at present it has the advantage of absolute impersonality.

To Robert U. Johnson

Naval War Board, Washington, D.C., May 17, 1898 [NYPL]

My dear Mr. Johnson: Your various notes have been received, but not until I arrived here, (and some days later) a week ago. As regards the matter of writing about the war, I had already promised McClure,[1] who first approached me, that *if* I wrote an article, or series of articles, he should have the first chance to buy them, at my price. You come second in order of application to me, and there is a third now. Of course I am forced to know now a good deal of what goes on, and am making my mental comments on the operations, as illustrative of the theory & practice of war. I should be very glad to see you when you come to Washington, and think that about 3 p.m. Sunday would be a good hour. If this conflict with your arrangements I will gladly meet you at another hour, though I must reserve a little time to square up my visiting. I shall then be at 1810 N St.

---

1. S. S. McClure, editor and publisher of the monthly *McClure's Magazine*. Mahan wrote five articles on the Spanish-American War for *McClure's* which were published December 1898 through April 1899. They were reprinted in Mahan's *Lessons of the War With Spain, and Other Articles*. Boston: Little, Brown and Company, 1899.

To Montgomery Sicard[1]

Naval War Board, Washington, D.C., May 19, 1898 [NA]

I submit to you herewith a skeleton plan of operations for our fleet in West Indian waters, which I request may be laid before the Board for such consideration as it may desire and entered upon the record.

With the assembling of our entire force of battle ships and armored vessels—except the *Oregon*[2]—in Cuban waters, and with the orders for its distribution now issued by the Department, a new phase of the naval campaign opens.

The position and plans of the Spanish squadrons remain unknown; yet upon them our plans must depend. My own inference is, that the Cape Verde fleet has communicated with Cienfuegos—or will before our division gets there—and has introduced such supplies as it may have convoyed. Though important, such succor is scarcely yet decisive in character.

Having done so much, I infer that it must proceed to Porto Rico; and I reason further that it will there be joined by the division from Cadiz, reported to have sailed, or to be about to sail. I do not believe that that division, with its transports, is bound to the Philippines. If it be, we cannot know the fact for certain till it has advanced far towards Varz, and must accept the more probable destination of Porto Rico. A very large sum of money should be offered to secret agents, payable after the event has shown the correctness of their information. It will be valuable, and may be invaluable, to us.

Accepting Porto Rico as the enemy's point of juncture, a division of at least four swift cruisers, not more than one of which would be less than wholly armed, should be kept before that port. The Cape Verde division may attempt a diversion by proceeding towards, or even as far as, our Atlantic coast. Personally, I believe we should accept whatever damage it can thereafter, or ever do, rather than loosen our grip on Havana or Cienfuegos; if the Spanish division can play on our fears like a musician on a piano, good bye success. The only thing that can justify our leaving those two ports, would be a fair expectation of striking their navy. Such opportunity can best be secured by the division of four cruisers (E. G. *New Orleans, Minneapolis, Columbia*—or *Newark*—and *St. Paul*),[3] before the

---

1. President of the Naval War Board.
2. A 10,288-ton, 351-foot battleship commissioned in 1896. A twin-screw vessel capable of 16 knots, she mounted (in 1898) four 13-inch, eight 8-inch, four 6-inch guns and three 18-inch deck torpedo tubes.
3. The *New Orleans*: a 3,769-ton, 354-foot, 20-knot cruiser commissioned in 1898 and mounting six 6-inch, four 4.7-inch guns and three 18-inch torpedo tubes. The *Minneapolis*: a sister ship of the *Columbia*: *See* Mahan to Ellen Kuhn Mahan, November 27, 1894, Footnote 4. The *Newark*: a 4,083-ton, 328-foot, 19–knot cruiser

port of San Juan, watching and following every movement of the division within, and reporting the same according to judgment of the Senior Officer.

Should it prove that the Cadiz division is coming this way, it very probably will bring troops to Porto Rico, which I gather is inadequately garrisoned. If so, measures should be taken to worry it enroute; but these can wait. Assuming the worst; that it gains San Juan, our whole battle navy should be instantly gathered off the port. To do this with the least delay, clear and comprehensive instructions should be issued beforehand, *by letters, marked "most secret,"* to the Commanding Officers off Havana and Cienfuegos, of the following general tenor:

The vessels are to be kept coaled; not necessarily full, but upon such lines as shall give best speed and fighting immersion, while leaving a reasonable supply when San Juan is reached. They shall be ready to start the instant (not a few hours later) that the order reaches them, proceeding to a point of junction about a hundred miles from San Juan, whence they will go on together. It is unnecessary to insist upon the necessity for pressing speed, with vessels so slow as ours. Time will be needed by the Spaniards in San Juan to make all arrangements, but we shall have none to spare.

In order that the Cienfuegos division may receive news most speedily, two of the (American line) auxiliary steamers, having the greatest speed, should be kept coaled, not full, but at highest steaming immersion—moving slowly all the time to insure perfect engine conditions and least foul bottom, and ready to start at full speed, at a moment's notice, for Cienfuegos. The distance—300 miles—they should cover in little more than 24 hours. Two should go in case of accident to one; and the one arriving should accompany the fleet off San Juan. In case of coming off Cienfuegos at night, a very clear night signal indicating immediate departure should be prearranged.

Though we do not certainly know, I have no doubt we have lost the first move in the game, through the flying squadron being kept in the Chesapeake, instead of Cuban waters. This was perhaps inevitable, owing to popular nervousness; and the result, though mortifying, is not vital. But if the enemy succeed, not only in entering Porto Rico, but quitting it, coaled and ready, with the Cape Verde and Cadiz division united, our perplexity will become extreme, and may lead to a vital misstep. The enemy would be stronger than either of our divisions, and either Cienfuegos or Havana must be unblockaded, which means free access to Blanco;[4] while, if either division of ours be met singly and badly beaten, they will have control of the sea till we get new ships out.

commissioned in 1891 and mounting twelve 6-inch guns. The *St. Paul*: a 16,275-ton, 544-foot, 22-knot merchantman converted to auxiliary cruiser; built in 1895, chartered in 1898, she mounted six 5-inch guns. All were twin-screw vessels save the *Minneapolis* and *Columbia*, which were triple-screw.
4. Ramon Blanco y Erenas, Captain-General of Cuba.

For the latter reason I urge, finally, that work be concentrated on the two new battle ships nearest completion, in order that they may take the sea at the earliest moment.

To John D. Long

Endorsement   Naval War Board, Washington, D.C., May 20, 1898 [NA]

SUBJECT: Scrymser, James A., Pres., Pacific Cable Co.
Further information, particularly in regard to cable between Hong Kong and Manila. Respectfully returned to the Secretary of the Navy, contents noted.

2. The Board recommend that no action be taken at present. There is no question that the cable if laid would be of benefit for naval operations, while we are holding the Philippines, but the Board has not at present the time to consider the expediency of the project.[1]

To John D. Long

Endorsement   Naval War Board, Washington, D.C., May 20, 1898 [NA]

SUBJECT: Scrymser, James A., Pres., Pacific Cable Co.
Telegrams to Admiral Irwin[1] relative to cable between Hong Kong and Manila.
Respectfully returned to the Secretary of the Navy; contents noted.
2. It is recommended that no action be taken in this matter at present.

To Robert U. Johnson

N.P., N.D.   Probably, Washington, D.C., May 22, 1898 [NYPL]

Dear Mr. Johnson: I have just received a summons to a meeting of the "War Board" at 3, and as I do not know the cause I cant tell how long it will last.

---

1. This and other communications to Long were signed by Mahan in his capacity as Acting President of the Naval War Board in the absence of Sicard.
1. John Irwin.

To George Sydenham Clarke

My dear Clarke: I much appreciated your letter expressing your sympathy with our cause in this war. Personally, I believe that it not only is a just war, but that the feelings of our "democracy," as a whole, in entering upon it have been free from base alloy. What the final outcome it is useless to predict. At present there is a noticeable, a more than noticeable, a most emphatic change in the point of view. One of our leading magazine editors was speaking of it to me only yesterday.[1] The extension of the influence of the United States, territorial expansion, colonies, etc, are so accepted as to be almost a commonplace of thought by papers heretofore steadily opposed thereto. The ground taken by you among the first, and by me afterwards, a mere vision six weeks [ago], rapidly takes on an appearance at least of solidity. Men who could only see that our Constitution provided no way for developing colonies, are now persuaded, as we were, that where there is a will the Americans can find a way. This and the attitude of the Continent in general and of France in particular is rapidly driving the people of the United States to that other pet hope of you and me, the entente with Great Britain. I trust at least that our people will awake from the absurd illusion that France helped us in our Revolution for unselfish reasons. As you may probably know, I was brought home to be a member of a naval "War Board" to advise the Secretary as to naval operations. I put myself on record at once that a Board was an absurd institution for directing military movements, and then settled to work. We are, of course, the most unpopular and ridiculed body of men in the country. Cervera's[2] Squadron first appeared at Martinique ten to twelve days ago and has since amused itself "evading." That it has not already been caught and demolished is to the "public" preposterous. So far this does not move me for I conceive my well established reputation to be that of a writer and have no ambition to be considered a great general officer, or man of action, for I know I am not either. I trust my nonchalance, thus based, may continue, for I can conceive few more pitiful sensations than that of fretting about what the public thinks. The public is an honest and in the main well meaning fellow, but in current questions of the day a good deal of a fool.

Please make my compliments to Lady Clarke.

---

1. Probably, R. V. Johnson of *Century Magazine*.
2. Admiral Pascual Cervera y Topete, commander of Spain's hastily formed Cuba Squadron.

To Willard H. Brownson[1]

Washington, D.C., May 26, 1898[2]

My dear Brownson: I congratulate you upon being ordered to the South. A telegram from the squadron has informed us of difficulty of coaling when a swell is on. During the former war, blockading off Sabine Pass, we frequently coaled in the open, and with considerable swell, without injury. The collier lay at anchor, heading to wind or tide. The *Seminole*,[3] our ship, dropped her anchor on the (say, starboard) bow of the collier, so that, by veering a long range of cable, she would ride about a hundred feet on collier's starboard beam. A spring from starboard quarter led to anchor ring. As the cable was veered the *Seminole* hauled alongside nearly, the distance between the two being 15 to 20 feet. The *Seminole* was thus held in a bridle from clashing with the collier, and my memory is that rolling 10° or 15°, we coaled (yard & stay) without trouble. I distinctly recall having to watch my chance to pass from the one to the other.

This far from elegant drawing will doubtless convey the idea. You might suggest it to your senior officers.

I may without breach of confidence say to you, confidentially, that your personal official qualities have influenced your present orders.

To an Unidentified Addressee

Washington, D.C., May 29, 1898 [NDL]

My dear Sir: Your letter of the 25th was duly received and I must begin by thanking you for the appreciative mention you make of my books. As regards the rest of the subject matter, however, I am not in agreement with you. I believe that the United States has duties to the world outside, as well as to herself—that in a general way the extension of "Anglo-Saxon" control

1. Commanding officer of the auxiliary cruiser *Yankee* from March to September 1898.
2. This letter was made available through the courtesy of Mrs. Thomas C. Hart, Sharon, Connecticut.
3. A 1,235-ton, 188-foot, single-screw, bark-rigged sloop capable of 11 knots. Commissioned in 1860, she mounted eight guns of various calibres.

is a distinct benefit to the world—and, although naturally conservative, I do not think that the policy of 50 or 100 years ago is proved suitable for today, by simply calling it our tradition. Traditions wax old and useless, like other things. You will see therefore that I can not adopt the course you suggest. Thanking you much for your letter, I am [etc.].

To John S. Barnes

Washington, D.C., May 30, 1898 [NYHS]

My dear Captain Barnes: Thank you very much for your letter and the clipping. I have too little spare time to answer your letter properly, but I may say that in my own judgment San Juan was the proper destination of the Spanish fleet; Cienfuegos a probable one, for reasons said to exist; but Santiago I should not at all have expected. The evidence that it was there, however, was too strong to be disregarded, and the movements of the vessels & squadrons for near a fortnight past were based upon that assumption, which is now shown to have been correct. I trust our impatient countrymen will not be wholly dissatisfied with the results up to date. They have abused us heartily enough, heaven knows.

To John D. Long

Naval War Board, Washington, D.C., June 3, 1898 [NA]

A telegram received today from Commodore Schley, off Santiago, lays stress upon his great need of light draft vessels for picket duty. The War Board recognizes the urgent necessity of vessels of that class, for the purpose specified, and it recommends that five of the ten light draft steamers or yachts, of the *Dorothea* and *Restless* class, originally purchased expressly for the naval service, and afterwards diverted to the Auxiliary Defence fleet, should be at once dispatched to reinforce Admiral Sampson, for use on picket line. It is meant, of course, that those which are to be sent, should be taken from those which are now ready, and not from those in course of preparation, as there is no reason to apprehend for the present an attack upon United States harbors; whereas, the decisive center of the war, at present, is off Santiago.

To John D. Long

Naval War Board, Washington, D.C., June 3, 1898 [NA]

Commodore Schley's telegram received today recommends that a large number of coal bags, to hold about 51 pounds each, be sent to the vessels off Santiago, for coaling ship. In view of the difficulties necessarily experienced by those vessels in coaling, the Board recommends that the Bureau of Equipment be directed to send immediately a large number of such bags for that purpose, as requested by the officer on that station.

To John D. Long

Naval War Board, Washington, D.C., June 3, 1898 [NA]

It is learned that the Hospital ship *Solace* has gone to New York, from Key West.

As soon as practicable, after her arrival, the Board recommends that she be sent to Admiral Sampson, off Santiago, as she has been asked for by Commodore Schley, the present senior officer on the blockade of that place.

From an interview with the Surgeon General of the Navy, it is learned that it is the intention of the Bureau of Medicine etc., to send the *Solace* to Santiago.

To Robert U. Johnson

Washington, D.C., June 5, 1898 [NYPL]

My dear Mr. Johnson: You quite misunderstood my meaning.[1] I am not pledged to McClure that I will write at all, but I am pledged that if I *do* write he shall have the refusal of the article on my terms. I have, at present at least, a great repugnance to writing *at all* upon the present war. This may pass away, under more congenial surroundings; though in any event I shall be loath to postpone work on my intended books.

At present I hold myself under no pledge to anybody that I will write upon this war.

1. *See* Mahan to Johnson, May 17, 1898.

To Edward L. Burlingame

Navy Department, Washington, D.C. June 16, 1898 [PUL]

Dear Mr. Burlingame: I have had several propositions made to me to write about the current war, and have promised that *if* I write, two, if not three, magazines shall have the refusal in order of their applying to me. I do not think that I shall do more for any one than give a brief narrative summary of events—particularly in the West Indies—pointing out what I conceive to be the lessons involved. So doing, I think I may be of service to the country, by making laymen perceive, through a concrete example, what some of the determining conditions of naval warfare are, as well as, among professional men & those already interested, to throw the weight of my opinion and arguments, whatever that may be, against what I conceive to be some *professional* fallacies on naval matters. Beyond this somewhat philosophical treatment I feel myself much indisposed to touch the present war at all; but then in Washington heat I am indisposed to do anything. What a place to carry on the public business of a great state!

To Endicott Peabody

1810 N Street, Washington, D.C., June 20, 1898 [HUL]

Dear Mr. Peabody: You will scarcely expect any of the Mahan family on the 27th inst.,[1] but as your kind remembrance bore R.S.V.P., I drop a line to express my regret and theirs. My last letters from them are from Pau,[2] where they arrived on the 3d. By this I suppose them to be in Paris. I am glad to say that they appear to have enjoyed their trip across southern France. The weather most fortunately was not hot, and my favorite places, Avignon, Arles, Nimes & Carcassonne fulfilled entirely their utmost expectations.

I want at this time to ask you whether the return to me of $308, by the Treasurer at your request, was entirely according to rule and custom.[3] I have heard with regret that you have had scarlet fever, and broken up the school for a time. Whether this is true or not I dont know—I hope not; but I would like to know whether this return was a usual thing, or in any way special to us.

With kind remembrance to Mrs. Peabody [etc.].

---

1. Lyle Mahan's class was to graduate from Groton School on that date.
2. When Mahan hurried home from Rome, his wife and daughters went to Pau to visit Rosalie Evans, who had married Dr. Francis Leonard Brown of that city.
3. Refund of second-term room, board, and tuition charges for Lyle, who had accompanied his parents to Europe in March.

To John M. Brown

1810 N Street, Washington, D.C., June 21, 1898 [LC]

My dear Mr. Brown: I have latterly been inclining to revise my determination to write *1812* at once, and to undertake instead the Text Book on Sea Power for English schools. My reason is chiefly pecuniary, believing that the latter will most quickly and certainly give me the assured income, which I desire to secure; and also that it will be more remunerative. Also, *1812* can wait; it will be as good two years hence as now, whereas the Text Book is urgently needed, and another may get the field while I wait.

I shall sacrifice practically nothing by the change of plan, my preparation for *1812* being but little in advance of what I have written, which is just one chapter—no more. I have frankly no faith in the paying quality of *1812*.

Let me know what you think. I know your previous opinion, of course. I may add I am not in the least concerned about reputation, or the trilogy, believing that *1812* will not add to my reputation, though I trust it wont detract.

I have had a letter from O'Connor Morris about certain plans he wishes to use. I am content to let him have them, full credit being given; subject to your approval.

To Willard H. Brownson

Navy Department, Washington, D.C., July 7, 1898[1]

My dear Brownson: You may rely upon it that, as far as my voice goes, you will accompany Watson's squadron.[2] I am speaking of course of present conditions, not engaging myself irrevocably for the *unforeseen* future; but as far as I can at all foresee now, I shall advocate your going, believing you to be very markedly a man for the work.

As far as known to me there is no feeling in any member of the Board likely to thwart your wishes.

---

1. This letter was made available through the courtesy of Mrs. Thomas C. Hart, Sharon, Connecticut.
2. Commodore John Crittenden Watson was in command of a division of the North Atlantic Squadron. A plan to send his force to bombard Spain coastal cities and to prevent the departure of Spanish naval units in home waters was being considered.

To John S. Barnes

Navy Department, Washington, D.C., July 9, 1898 [NYHS]

My dear Mr. Barnes: Your letter was duly recd. & I intended to reply sooner. The navy has generally, I think, and the Dept certainly has held the same view that you express, that the attack of the army should have been, [as viewed] by this Dept., to seize the heights at the entrance[1] & to allow the ships then to remove the mine fields and advance into the harbor. It is to be remembered, however, that our knowledge of the topography is somewhat imperfect, and that reconnaissances *may* have developed reasons to the contrary; moreover the army may naturally have wished to cut off reinforcements & supplies, as far as possible. The *great* trouble has been that the army was late and not big enough.

It is to be regretted that New Yorkers are not looking out for their man— Sampson—in the way, or rather in a more becoming way, than Maryland, her Govr. and the press hereabouts are "booming" Schley.[2] The latter is a gallant man and a good officer; but Sampson has borne the burden and the responsibility of the long watch before Santiago, and was unquestionably responsible for the disposition of the ships. The shame would have been his had Cervera escaped from bad dispositions.[3] I have of course had to watch the general course of events pretty closely, and I have no hesitation in saying that in my judgment, from first to last, nothing has happened to deprive Sampson of the just claim of a commander in chief to priority of consideration—not even to *lessen* his claim. You are at liberty to say so, not of course for the press, but in conversation if you choose, as my deliberate opinion.

[P.S.] The talk, in some papers, of the Dept or the War Board, holding Schley's coattails to prevent his rushing into Santiago, and Sampson being sent to prevent such rashness, is not merely pure moonshine, but absolutely contrary to truth.

To Henry Cabot Lodge

Navy Department, Washington, D.C., July 12, 1898 [MHS]

My dear Mr. Lodge: I handed your letter to the Secretary[1] yesterday and left it with him. He sent it back to me later in the day, without com-

---

1. To Santiago, Cuba.
2. Mahan's first reference to what would soon become the heated Sampson-Schley controversy.
3. Cervera's squadron had been defeated at the Battle of Santiago Bay, July 3, 1898.
1. John D. Long.

ment; but I know that he is fully alive to the changes in the general situation due to Cervera's defeat and to Cámara's[2] return, & I have no doubt the final dispositions taken will take full account of them.[3]

I will not close my letter without expressing my sense of the kind attention shown to me by yourself and Mrs. Lodge, while in town,[4] and I beg you to remember me most kindly to her.

To Edith Kermit Carow Roosevelt

Washington, D.C., July 17, 1898 [LC]

Dear Mrs. Roosevelt: The enclosed[1] can scarcely fail to please you, and may lie outside your newspaper circle.

It may interest Mr. Roosevelt to know that, in conversation with Comdr. Brownson two days ago, the latter held that to the dispositions of Adm. Sampson before Santiago is to be attributed the successful detention of Cervera's squadron in port for so long, and equally the ease with which its destruction was effected when it attempted to get away. Brownson was not present at the fight, but he knew of the dispositions; and the spontaneous opinion of an officer of his exceptional merit should silence the shameful attempts of the Maryland Press & people to disparage Sampson's merits in the attempt—I trust vain—to exalt Schley.

Dont answer this.

To the Naval War Board

Naval War Board, Washington, D.C. July 18, 1898 [NA]

The conditions of things now under deliberation may be summarized thus:

The United States, having definitely established naval preponderance over the enemy, and with it the control of the sea, in the military sense, wishes to do two things:

---

2. Admiral Cámara, commanding a small Spanish naval force, returned to Cadiz when Spain learned of American plans to bombard the Spanish coast.

3. On July 23 Lodge replied that the Secretary had assured him of his intention to strengthen the fleet.

4. Mahan apparently visited the Lodges on several occasions during the "hot and anxious days" of June and July 1898.

1. Enclosure not found.

1. Proceed against Porto Rico, including therein the capture of the Capital, San Juan.

2. Send a reinforcement, of at least two battleships, to Dewey at Manila.

This second object, however, is more properly stated in the terms of its principal difficulty, thus: The United States wishes to send a Division of two battleships through the Straits of Gibraltar, the place where such naval strength as remains to Spain can be most effectively concentrated.

The true strategy of the Spanish Navy, under the apprehension now entertained of bombardment of coast cities, would be as follows:

The most important of exposed cities, Cadiz, Malaga and Barcelona, are within, or close to the Straits of Gibraltar; consequently the best defense for those cities would be to concentrate the entire available navy at Cadiz; whence, with proper scouting, it could be thrown against our force in the straits, or at the least follow it so closely as to bring it to action before harm could be done.

It matters not the least that the Spanish fleet, by pursuing this course may be beaten. It is its proper course, which it cannot refuse without shame.

Now, if the enemy should penetrate our ultimate design of sending these ships to Manila, the same course is incumbent—concentration at Cadiz, and attack in the Straits, is his proper course.

We may believe that our Division, increased as proposed to three, by the addition of the *Brooklyn*,[1] would emerge victorious from such attack; but we have no right to assume that at least one ship would not be seriously injured. Two shells struck the *Iowa*[2] on July 3rd, and several the *Brooklyn*.

I submit that the crucial feature of the whole situation, military and diplomatic, at present, is the control of the sea; and that while we unquestionably possess it, as against Spain, we have no such margin as justifies a risk without adequate gain. No other battleship is promised before eight months, and such promises are rarely fulfilled as to date.

Per contra, reverting to the first object of the United States, what role are the battleships, as distinguished from monitors, to perform at Porto Rico?

To my mind, none. There is an evident hint, in more quarters than one, that they are to engage the sea coast batteries of San Juan. To any such course, I record my emphatic dissent. The teaching of the war, so far, is that such attacks are useless; and if we persist, we will get the further teaching that they are dangerous to ships far beyond the point of any possible gain from them.

---

1. A 9,215-ton, 400-foot, twin-screw armored cruiser commissioned in 1896. She mounted eight 8-inch, twelve 5-inch guns and four 18-inch torpedo tubes.
2. An 11,410-ton, 362-foot, twin-screw battleship commissioned in 1897. Capable of 17 knots, she mounted four 12-inch, eight 8-inch, six 4-inch guns and four 14-inch torpedo tubes.

By doing this, as well as by sending a Division of three through the Straits of Gibraltar, we run a needless risk of injury to battleships, for which injury there is no prospective compensation. Disable your battleships, and you will soon find a change in your diplomacy. I have no objection to risk them against enemy's ships, for there you seek an adequate gain.

The operations against Porto Rico, including San Juan, are distinctly land in character; the part of the navy is only to control the sea and cover the landing, a part minor, but indispensable, to which the battleships are not necessary. When the army approaches San Juan, it takes it in the rear where the guns of the ships are not likely to be effective. If the bombardment of the sea front is wanted, send in the monitors. They are as useless to the control of the sea, as any armored vessel that floats can be; and no particular harm will be done if one or more is knocked out.

The true solution of our present doubt, in my judgment, is this; either send the six armored ships together, seeing Watson[3] through the Straits, or else postpone sending Watson and concentrate on Porto Rico. For the reasons set forth above, I do not consider our force justifies the contemplated division of it. However beneficial the effect upon our diplomacy to reinforce Dewey, it is by no means equal to the injury to our diplomacy caused by a couple of armored ships being disabled.

To this I would add, that the approach of the hurricane season would, by itself alone, require the removal of the battleships from West Indian waters, which the proposed expedition to the Spanish coast insures. The whole turns upon the efficiency of the armored fleet; upon the same, turns the negotiations for peace, and the possible interference of foreign powers. The Spanish navy, concentrated at Cadiz, will not, in my opinion, dare to attack six armored ships. If they fail to attack two or three, with their present force, in their own waters, they are utterly disgraced.

In order to leave no important possibility unconsidered, I mention the contingency that Spain may send some of her armored ships against our coast, or try to disturb our operations in the West Indies, during the absence of our fleet. Without denying a certain plausibility to such a move, it is to be remembered that Spain now scarcely has more than two armored vessels capable of a long voyage, viz, the *Pelayo* and the *Carlos V*; that of these two, the former carries little coal; that they dare not depart till sure that our fleet is really crossing; that our fleet will soon be on the way back; that the presence of the monitors and the *Texas*[4] at Fajardo or San Juan, will protect the army base and communications; that, consequently, the breaking of the Cuban blockade, or some interruption to our coasting trade, would be the extent of the injury open to their ships before the return of our fleet would shut them up in port.

---

3. *See* Mahan to Brownson, July 7, 1898, Footnote 2.
4. A 6,315-ton, 308-foot twin-screw, 17-knot battleship commissioned in 1895. She mounted two 12-inch, six 6-inch guns and two 14-inch torpedo tubes.

Personally, I do not believe they will venture to send important vessels so far from home, when their own coast is threatened with attack. Their best chance against us is always in the Straits of Gibraltar. So evident is this, that we surely would never dream of sending our fleet there, except to help Dewey.

It is further to be considered that, if the three ships, *Massachusetts*,[5] *Oregon*, and *Brooklyn*, should reach Dewey without injury—which is certainly possible—the armored force left in the Atlantic, viz., the *Iowa*, *Indiana*,[6] *Texas* and *New York*,[7] will be less than is desirable in case of complications with a third Power, which is the chief reason for now reinforcing Dewey. The *Brooklyn* is better placed here.

To John S. Barnes

Washington, D.C., July 21, 1898 [NYHS]

My dear Mr. Barnes: I read with much interest your views on the military and political situation. Personally, I have not yet become wholly adjusted to the new point of view opened to us by Dewey's victory at Manila. It has opened a vista of possibilities which were not by me in the least foreseen, though the intimate contact of the East with the West, and a probable imminent conflict (not necessarily war-like) between the two civilizations had long been a part of my thought. As it is, I look with a kind of awe upon the passage of events in which the will of man seems to count for little. Justice Brown,[1] I see in this morning's paper, says not one representative in four in January last would have voted for the acquisition of the Philippines. In a month ten thousand American troops will be there, and Dewey's fleet reinforced by two double-turreted monitors.[2] I see the Justice also says that the Monroe Doctrine excludes us from the Philippines, because it is an assurance to European powers that, while we resist their

---

5. A 10,288-ton, 351-foot, twin-screw, 16-knot battleship commissioned in 1896. She mounted four 13-inch, eight 8-inch, four 6-inch guns and three 18-inch torpedo tubes.
6. A sister ship of the USS *Massachusetts* commissioned in 1895.
7. An 8,150-ton, 384-foot, twin-screw, 21-knot armored cruiser commissioned in 1893. She mounted six 8-inch, twelve 4-inch guns and two 14-inch torpedo tubes.
1. Henry Billings Brown, Associate Justice of the Supreme Court.
2. The *Monterey* and *Monadnock*. The latter was a 3,990-ton, 262-foot, twin-screw, 12-knot vessel launched in 1883 and commissioned in 1896. She mounted four 10-inch, and two 4-inch guns. The *Monterey* was a 4,084-ton, 261-foot, twin-screw, 13.5-knot vessel, commissioned in 1893. She mounted two 12-inch and two 10-inch guns.

intrusion here, we will not intrude on "their continent." But how is China, or the Philippines [a] European continent, i.e. geographically. The Justice concedes a great deal.

I am greatly indebted to you for your kind invitation to visit you at Lenox; but I fear from present indications I shall not be much absent from Washington.

To John D. Long

N.P., N.D. Probably, Washington, D.C. July 23, 1898 [MHS]

Dear Mr. Long: It has occurred to me that, as Germany might possibly think our reinforcement to Dewey too plainly intended to provide against her action, that it might be convenient to Mr. Day to say (what is perfectly, though secondarily, true) that we are obliged now to restore the equilibrium of our naval force between the Pacific and Atlantic coasts; that the treacherous destruction of the *Maine* had compelled us to bring the *Oregon* round, to insure a force in Cuba, the expected seat of war, equal to that, nominally at least, possessed by Spain; that the absence of the *Oregon* had compelled us to send to Dewey's aid the two monitors, never intended for such a mission, (and that the world knows by how narrow a margin we got them out, owing to their slowness, if Camara had had nerve to continue); that even in the Philippines they are of less use owing to their slowness at sea; but that in any event now that the naval war in the West Indies is demonstrably over, by Cervera's destruction, we feel the necessity of at once reinforcing the Pacific fleet upon which the Asiatic fleet depends; and that finally (this I would emphasize) we feel free to do it, because in six months we shall have two new battleships to take the place of those dispatched hence. This puts Manila as only a secondary object with Watson.

Mr. Day seemed to me a little worried about the effect of our action in this respect upon other Powers. The above, as a train of *military* reasoning appears to me correct; and when the movement becomes apparent it may serve for *diplomatic* explanations. Of course, there is no reason the ships should *hurry* from Manila.

[P.S.][1] *Instead* of saying, as Mr. Day seemed to think advisable, what our object in sending a force to Spain really is, why not, without at all disclosing our object, (which no one has a right to know), why not state

---

1. It is not clear that this addendum accompanied the main body of Mahan's letter to Long, July 23, 1898. It may have been an afterthought or a draft rejected as part of the letter.

perfectly clearly that this Country has no purpose of any territory of Spain in either Europe or Africa (I would include Canaries); and, further, that for the present at least we do not propose to bombard *mercantile* ports, unless forced to do by some action of Spain, as for instance if our fleet in its operations were annoyed by torpedo boats. (Torpedo boats of course are legitimate warfare, but we want to choke them off, by a tit for tat.) That, of course, we must reserve bombardment as a final measure of coercion, if Spain resist beyond reasonable limit, but that we are most averse to it.

I quite feel, with Mr. Day, that it may be *politic* to assure European Powers upon our purposes, in a *negative* way; but, as a military man, I cannot conceive that they are entitled to know more than that we do not propose certain things, reasonably distasteful to them. That they should be informed of our *positive* plans seems to me erroneous, for what they know the enemy also will know; and in any case it is none of their business.

To John M. Brown

Washington, D.C., July 24, 1898 [LC]

Dear Mr. Brown: With regard to Cushing's life, the anxiety of Mrs. Cushing is natural and pardonable; but I think your memory will bear me out in saying that I never gave any hope of taking it up until *1812* & the Text Book were disposed of. I suggested also that the material should be sorted & arranged, according to its kind, and its chronological sequence; in such wise, at any rate, as to relieve me of dealing with a heterogeneous mass. If this has been done, I would now suggest the papers being sent to me whole or in part, that I may by exm judge what I can make of it, & whether I can deal with it at all, *shortly*. As regards the cost, do you know anything of Mrs. C's circumstances? A magazine article is worth to me $500. I suppose this life would run to five mag. arts—in extent. Of course, it will never begin to yield any such amount. *Farragut* has not, in six years, brought me $500. I suppose the only thing for me to propose would be a share in the royalty, calculating the latter on my usual terms. If Mrs. C. feels it proper, in view of my delay, to place the work in other hands, pray encourage her to do so. I say this, not in annoyance, but that she may feel quite easy as to my feeling.

Of course the semi-annuals are very satisfactory; but I own after the sky rockets of last year I hoped for more. With regard to immediate work, I must mention that my duty at the Dept and the heat incapacitate me at present for much more.

To Henry Cabot Lodge

Washington, D.C., July 27, 1898 [MHS]

Dear Mr. Lodge: You are my only point of contact with the Legislative Body, with which indeed I have rarely need to communicate; but it is in that connection that I wish to mention to you that Brownson, for whose capacity as an officer I have the highest value, told me, when here rather less than a fortnight ago, that he attributed our success over Cervera chiefly to Sampson's excellent and sustained dispositions of the fleet before the port. This expression was entirely unasked by me—quite spontaneous; but I own it was very grateful, for the attacks of the press upon Sampson either virulently or by constant sly innuendo, have kept my blood boiling. It it my belief that the closeness of the watch at night largely induced the sortie by day—unwise as that was.

In connection with the negotiations for peace, although all I have seen of the President has tended to give me a higher opinion of his decisiveness of character than I had before entertained, I suppose he certainly is a man more disposed to follow public opinion that to lead, or even guide, it. Public opinion I assume will insist that Spain quit America for ever. But feeling as to the Philippines is much more doubtful. I myself, though rather an expansionist, have not fully adjusted myself to the idea of taking them, from our own standpoint of advantage. It does seem to me, however, that the heavy force, army and navy, we have put into Luzon has encouraged the revolutionists to an extent for which we are responsible. Can we ignore the responsibility & give them back to Spain? I think not. Spain cannot observe a pledge to govern justly, because she neither knows what good govt. is, nor could she practise it if she knew. As to an agreement with other Powers, I hope no entangling alliances for us. But we have done nothing in the other islands of the group. Might it not be a wise compromise to take only the Ladrones & Luzon; yielding to the "honor" & exigencies of Spain the Carolines and the rest of the Philippines.

To John D. Long

Washington, D.C., July 28, 1898 [MHS]

Dear Mr. Long: I venture to put my oar in again, because I think I have an idea which will scarcely occur to any one else. I assume that the published news of Spain asking our terms of peace is true. It is not improbable that she will ask an armistice, which I trust will not be granted; but whether she asks or not, the agitation of the question of peace puts a new view upon our proposed expedition to the Straits of Gibraltar etc. It is said that the expected approach of Watson's squadron stirred up the war spirit; and a recent confidential dispatch of our secret service at Madrid, through our attaché at Paris, said (I quote from memory) that the postponement of Watson's sailing strengthened Sagasta's[1] hands—i.e. for peace. Now what I have to suggest is this: While a *general* armistice could work us nothing but injury and expense, *local* armistices are not uncommon. Whether Spain ask an armistice or not, it would be open to us to say that we had a large expedition just ready to start for the coast of Spain, but, understanding that the effect of such a step upon the susceptibilities of the Spanish people would be unfavorable to the attainment of peace, (which we most heartily desire), we will consent to postpone the sailing of the fleet for a reasonable space to permit the conclusion of negotiations, and will accept an armistice for the European possessions of Spain, including her European trade and the Canaries; *provided*, that Spain on her part engages not to molest our two battleships and our crusiers and colliers, which were to have gone to the east under cover of the operations, nor to object to their coaling (from their own colliers?) in neutral Mediterranean ports. I should insist that those ships must go forward without delay, because we must increase our force in the Pacific; and that unless they accept this condition the fleet will sail as first proposed.

It is evident this step would relieve us from an onerous undertaking, and it seems to me also evident that it will tend to facilitate peace. We *should* undertake that the two ships would not appear in sight of the coast of Spain except as unavoidable in passing through the Straits.[2]

To John D. Long

Navy Department, Washington, D.C., July 29, 1898 [MHS]

Dear Mr. Long: Not to trouble you with an interview, may I add to yesterday's letter, that if any such advance come from our side, it should not be till as nearly as possible when our expedition is ready to start; and if from theirs, that the reply from us should be delayed as far as propriety admits for a similar time; and that they should not be allowed over 48 hours for a reply, Yes or No; in the latter event we to start at once.

What I mean is, that the risk of our move, which against a valid enemy would be appreciable, should be minimized by giving the enemy the least possible time to *prepare his mind* what to do against our coming.

---

1. Spanish Premier Práxedes Mateo Sagasta.
2. Under date of July 28, 1898, President McKinley wrote: "Dear Mr. Secy—There are some good suggestions in the foregoing. Think of them."

To Henry Cabot Lodge

Navy Department, Washington, D.C. July 29, 1898 [MHS]

Dear Mr. Lodge: I have before me a translation of a letter from the paymaster of the Spanish *Maria Teresa*, giving an account of the transactions in Santiago, including the battle of the 3d. Concerning the last he says: "At this time, (after July 1) telegrams began to come from Madrid & Havana for the squadron to leave immediately. The Admiral did not wish to leave as he saw it was impossible, there being 20 war ships waiting for us outside. Nevertheless, other telegrams came ordering the squadron out at no matter what cost. In view of this, [illegible phrase] same first day, all the landing men were embarked, and the sortie time determined on. *It was thought to make this at dusk on this day* but we desisted *because the enemy's ships were then at the very mouth of the harbor*, and it was decided to delay the sortie until 8 or 9 a.m. of the next day."

This confirms what Brownson said to me—that Sampson kept a battle ship at night a mile from the harbor's mouth, with search lights turned on. The Spaniard says in another place: "At night they also fired. *Then* the large ships would come very near the coast and turn on their electric search lights, which illuminated the mouth of the harbor, as though the sun was shining, the purpose being to prevent us from coming out under cover of darkness."

In view of the scandalous attacks still daily kept up here upon Sampson, this evidence clearly shows that the admirable dispositions of our admiral forced the enemy to come out *in daylight* (for which he has been utterly condemned by the British service papers) and therefore contributed more than any other one cause to the entire destruction of the hostile fleet; a victory of which may be said, as Nelson said of the Nile, Victory is not the word for such a scene as I have witnessed.

To John M. Brown

[Navy Department, Washington, D.C.], August 2, 1898 [LC]

Dear Mr. Brown: After closing my last letter it occurred to me to remind you, with reference to Cushing, that what I said was that I would not think of attempting till I had completed *1812* and Marston's suggested text book. When I mentioned two years, it was merely that I thought that the *minimum* I needed; but if it takes longer, those books must first be finished.

I am awfully pressed at present, feel pressed to a degree.

The enclosed[1] was sent me from Ireland the other day, for extra illustration. I am not doing anything of that sort, so I send it, in case you possibly would like it.

To Henry Cabot Lodge

Navy Department, Washington, D.C. August 4, 1898 [MHS]

Dear Mr. Lodge: Assuming, as seems pretty certain, that the U.S. is to acquire Porto Rico, may I suggest the advisability, as a corollary to this step, *after peace is signed*, the purchase of St. Thomas. I never favored the acquisition of that small and very distant island, when it was to be an isolated possession. The case to my mind is different, when we hold Porto Rico. The group would form a compact strategic entity, yielding mutual support. Sta. Cruz is immaterial, though it might have to be accepted, but the harbor of St. Thomas is very fine.

In the beginning of the present war the local authorities at St. Thomas extended to us a very benevolent and useful neutrality; but latterly the natives have been very much tighter as to coaling—to practice exclusion, as near as I can gather. The question is no longer very material as we have the coaling question well in hand; but I should consider the port of St. Thomas, reasonably fortified, a distinct addition to the military strength of Porto Rico, considered as a naval base.

To John D. Long

N.P.   Probably, Washington, D.C., August 5, 1898 [MHS]

Dear Mr. Long: Every one in general and Mr. Day in particular knows the procrastination and prevarication of the Spaniard. Of this, therefore, I say nothing; but from the point of view of Sampson's and Watson's sailing, one thing must be clearly remembered. It has been expected that the ships must coal somewhere near Straits of Gibraltar, whether within or without Medn. This is a step vital to their existence; and in its recommendations to the Dept., the Board have counted upon the probability of weather, good enough for coaling *outside*, to the end of August. There is an old saying —June, July, August and Port Mahon are the only good harbors in the Mediterranean. It is needless to observe that by the time the fleet reaches the

---

1. Enclosure not found.

other side, *now*, the last of the three good months will be declining. In this respect, and in the advance of the hurricane season, Spanish delays, however convenient to their mental habits, are most embarrassing, and may be most injurious, even fatal, to our naval efficiency.

May I remind you again, what each day increasingly shows, that upon the armored fleet depends *entirely* the present imposing position of the U.S. The demoralization of the army in Cuba seems to be complete. Miles's[1] line of operations in Porto Rico, I have viewed from the first with great distrust, & the news is not calculated to justify his course in choosing the farthest point, almost, he could find from San Juan to land.

To the Editor of the New York Sun

Washington, D.C., August 5, 1898[1]

In your issue of July 29 a correspondent asks: "Why did Nelson, second in command, receive the credit for Copenhagen, if Schley is not to have it for Santiago?"

A better knowledge of history would have shown the essential differences between the two cases, and have saved the question. At Copenhagen, Nelson did not merely do the fighting. The entire conception of the method of attack was his, and by him was *forced*—the word is not too strong—upon a reluctant commander-in-chief. When the latter had yielded his consent, the separate and decisive attack was made by Nelson, commanding a detachment from the main fleet, all the movements of which detachment, including the positions in the order of battle, were prescribed by him. With the preliminary dispositions and subsequent conduct of this detachment his commander-in-chief, Parker, had nothing to do, although within signal distance, beyond making the since historic signal to "withdraw from action," which Nelson refused to obey. It is to be added that, although Parker was not formally censured—as far, at least, as I know—he was recalled to England as soon as the accounts of the battle were received there, Nelson being left in command in his place. A stronger implied censure than the recall of a commander-in-chief after such a victory is difficult to imagine.

At Santiago all the dispositions prior to action, and for over a month before, were made by the commander-in-chief. A number of orders, issued from time to time by him, for the enforcement of the close watch of the harbor's mouth, were published in the *Washington Post* of July 27, and I presume by other journals as well. There is very strong ground for believing

---

1. Major General Nelson A. Miles, USA, commander of Army forces in Puerto Rico.

1. From the New York *Sun*, August 7, 1898, p. 6.

that Cervera's attempt to escape by day instead of by night—the incident of his conduct which has been most widely censured and is most inexplicable—was due to the fact that the United States ships kept so close to the harbor mouth at night that a dash like his, desperate at best, had a better chance when the ships were at day distance. This was so stated, substantially, to Admiral Sampson by the Captain of the *Colon*. If so, the merit of this, forcing the enemy to action under disadvantageous conditions—and it is one of the highest achievements of military art—belongs to the commander-in-chief. *It was the great decisive feature of the campaign, from start to finish.* Few naval authorities, I imagine, will dispute this statement.

It will be noted also, by comparing the report of Admiral Sampson, stating the disposition of the ships, with the [report] of Capt. Cook,[2] commanding the *Brooklyn*, Commodore Schley's flagship, that the United States ships chased and fought in the order, from left to right, established by Sampson. There is in this no particular merit for the latter, beyond that, in placing the two fastest ships, *Brooklyn* and *New York*, on the two flanks, he had made the best provision for heading off the enemy, which the *Brooklyn* so handsomely effected. But the fact that the ships chased as they stood shows that it was unnecessary for Schley to make a signal; and in truth, from first to last, the second in command needed to make no signal of a tactical character, and made none, so far as is shown by his own report, or that of the Captain of the ship. That is, the second in command exercised no special directive function of a flag or general officer while the fighting lasted. In this there was no fault, for there was no need for signals; but the fact utterly does away with any claim to particular merit as second in command, without the least impairing the Commodore's credit for conduct in all respects gallant and officerlike. So far as plan is concerned, the battle was fought on Sampson's lines; and to quote Collingwood before Trafalgar, "I wish Nelson would stop signalling, for we all know what we have to do." The second in command and the Captains before Santiago all knew what they had to do, and right nobly they all did it.

But the distinctive merit of the series of events which issued in the naval battle of Santiago is that so far as appears, Cervera was forced to fight as he did on account of the unrelenting watch, through more than a whole moon, including its dark nights, maintained by Admiral Sampson. The writer has been told by a naval officer[3] whose name he has not authority to mention, but who would be recognized as one of the most efficient of his mature years, and who had been off Santiago during part of the eventful month, that he regarded Sampson's watch of the harbor as the decisive feature in the great result. This neither ignores the merits of the Captains nor of the "man behind the gun." But Captains and the men behind the

2. Francis A. Cook.
3. W. H. Brownson.

guns may be of the best, the Colonels of the regiments and the privates of land warfare the same, but vain are their valor and their skill if the commander-in-chief be wanting in either. "Better an army of stags led by a lion than an army of lions led by a stag."

The phrase of the *Washington Post*, meant for a sneer, "Admiral Sampson wishes the American people to believe that . . . things could not have happened otherwise, even if Admiral Sampson had been seventy instead of seven miles away," expresses an exact truth. With the wise and straight methods laid down and enforced by the Admiral, it would not in the least have mattered, as things happened, with such ships and such Captains, had the commander-in-chief and the second in command, either or both, been seventy miles away. It is exactly with the fleet as with the single ships. The merit of each Captain was not only, nor chiefly, that he handled and fought his ship admirably on the day of the battle. His greatest merit was that, when he took his ship into action, she was so organized and trained that, had he himself been absent or struck dead by the first shot, the ship would none the less have played her full part efficiently in the fight, under her second in command.

Few things in the observation of the writer have been more painful than the attempt of a portion of the press and of the public to rob Sampson of his just and painfully won dues. During the night hours of July 2–3, when there is strong reason to believe that Cervera, despite the full moon, wished to come out, the commander-in-chief with the whole of his force lay close to the harbor's mouth, and the Spanish attempt was deferred till day, when it might be supposed from their usual practice that the besieging vessels would be more distant, and perhaps off their guard. At 4 A.M., when day began to break, the *Massachusetts*, commanded by one of the most spirited officers in the service,[4] silently withdrew, to coal at Guantanamo, forty miles away. Half an hour before the enemy was discovered coming out, the flagship *New York* also proceeded west. In doing this the commander-in-chief, Admiral Sampson, was obeying a specific and direct order of the Navy Department, to confer personally with the commander-in-chief of the army. To this was owing that, to use the words of Sampson's despatch, the flagship "was not at any time within range of the heavy Spanish ships." Upon this circumstance, mortifying as a mere disappointment, that the ship, though pushed to her utmost speed, could not retrieve her original disadvantage of position–incurred in obedience to the Navy Department– has been raised the shameful outcry, designed to deprive an eminent officer of the just reward of his toils.

The injustice is with many doubtless unintentional and unwitting. The same excuse can scarcely be made for the charge that the Admiral has grudged praise to his subordinates. Some Washington papers have in this

4. Francis J. Higginson.

matter been particularly vicious, and the *Post* of that city, in an editorial of July 31 to that effect, is guilty, in quoting from one paragraph of Sampson's despatch, of suppressing these following words in the succeeding paragraph: "The commanding officers merit the greatest praise for the perfect manner in which they entered into this plan [of blockade] and put it into execution. The *Massachusetts*, which, according to routine, was sent that morning to coal at Guantanamo, like the others had spent many weary nights upon this work, and deserved a better fate than to be absent that morning." Again, as regards the action: "When all the work was done so well, it is difficult to discriminate. The object of the blockade of Cervera's squadron was fully accomplished, and each individual bore well his part in it—the Commodore in command of the Second Division, the Captains of ships, their officers and men. The fire of the battleships was powerful and destructive, and the resistance of the Spanish squadron was, in great part, broken almost before they had got beyond the range of their own forts." If higher praise is expected, the only reply that can be made is that it is, historically, rarely given. When individual men are named, unless some conspicuous and unusual deed compels it, those passed over feel slighted; while, if each who has done his duty is individually named, all distinctive effect is lost. Those who doubt may examine the despatches of men like Nelson and Farragut.

It would be improper to conclude without saying that there is not the slightest proof that Commodore Schley is in the least responsible for the malicious attempts made to depress Admiral Sampson with a view to exalt the second in command. On the contrary, when they came to his ears he telegraphed to the Navy Department (on July 10) his "mortification" at the fact, handsomely attributing the victory to the force under the command of the commander-in-chief of the North Atlantic station: "to him the honor is due." More than this there is no occasion for him to say, nor need he have said anything but for the obligation forced upon him by the indiscreet and ungenerous clamor of those posing as his friends, from whom he might well pray to be saved.

So far as precedents may properly influence opinion in a matter of this kind, it is interesting as well as instructive to notice two other instances in the career of Nelson, for he was usually a second in command and was prone to come to the front, as at Copenhagen, not by the absence of his superior, but by his own initiative. At Cape St. Vincent, Nelson—not being second, but third or fourth—of his own motion, without orders, took a step during the course of the battle which was a leading cause of its success, and threw upon his own ship the largest single share in the whole fighting. Nevertheless, although for this he received ample recognition, official as well as public, the greater reward by far was rightly adjudged to his chief, whose ship was much less exposed, but to whose previous dispositions and action it was owing that Nelson had the opportunity he so well improved.

At the Nile, Nelson, in seniority of flag rank upon the station, was again only third or fourth, but he was in sole command of a large detachment, 2,000 miles away from his nearest superior. The battle therefore was fought solely "off his own bat"; the decision to fight, the methods, and the actual fighting, were all his own. Nevertheless, although the commander-in-chief was absent in a very full sense of the word, the fact that Nelson was not a commander-in-chief was held, unjustly I think, to diminish his claim to reward. The reward, quite inadequate to the achievement, was "the highest," wrote the First Lord of the Admiralty, "that has ever been conferred upon an officer of your standing who was not a commander-in-chief." This decision, therefore, was based on precedent, and throws light on British practice and opinion–and in naval matters no nation has had a wider experience –as to the relative responsibilities and claims of commanders-in-chief and flag officers junior to them.

To John D. Long

N.P. Probably, Washington, D.C., August 7, 1898 [MHS]

Dear Mr. Long: Sampson's telegram, which you showed me yesterday, shows evidently the unrest and relaxation of temper which naturally follows upon a prolonged tension, when that is succeeded by a period of inactivity. He reflects, doubtless, the feelings of officers and men; many of the former not improbably have been urging the claims of the crews to some indulgence. Yesterday also Captn. Bartlett[1] told me that the Govr. of Michigan[2] had telegraphed that, now the war was over, he would like the Michigan reserves, on board the *Yosemite*,[3] let go; and Bartlett was replacing them with R.I. reserves. As the *Yosemite* is detailed to convoy the colliers for Sampson, I begged him to see no delay was thus caused.

All these incidents show incipient demoralization, which will increase in geometrical progression as unemployed days go by; and, coupled with the expiring of enlistments, of which I spoke to you yesterday, may seriously cripple the fleet for an appreciable time.

The cause is the absurd delay of Spain. Why should not the President send for M. Cambon,[4] and civilly tell him the brute truth, viz: that we

1. John Russell Bartlett, class of 1863, who had retired in 1897 but returned to active duty for the war.
2. Hazen S. Pingree.
3. A 6,179-ton, 405-foot, single-screw auxiliary cruiser mounting ten 5-inch guns and capable of 14.5 knots. Formerly the merchantman *El Sud*, she was purchased by the Navy in April 1898.
4. Jules Cambon, French Ambassador to the United States, who represented Spain in preliminary peace negotiations.

thoroughly understand that Spain is powerless before us owing to our relative naval supremacy; that she would still be so, did every man in our armies die tomorrow; that she is unable to replace her navy; that delay is for many reasons inconvenient to us; that our terms are a minimum, & therefore an ultimatum; and for these reasons the offer of them, if not accepted, will be withdrawn at noon of next Wednesday (Washington time).

I *believe* this peremptory dealing would strengthen the Spanish ministry in accepting the terms. I *know*, that a prolongation of this uncertainty will produce restlessness, discontent and disorganization which is the worst thing that can befall us. Settled Peace, or renewed War, will avoid this. Let it be known that war is again on, and start Sampson's armored ships, whether towards Europe as proposed, or north, (*not for relaxation* but for refit) and officers and men will all be contented—even happy.

[P.S.]   I cannot exaggerate my sense of the importance of this matter.

To John S. Barnes

Washington, D.C., August 10, 1898 [NYHS]

Dear Mr. Barnes: Thank you very much for your letter.[1] I dont think people quite appreciate how much good they do the cause of public morals by expressing a timely approval of the step taken by another man. Outside the navy, my step was scarcely popular, and involved a certain amount of trouble. I certainly grudged neither, for I was so worked up that the writing was rather a relief. Nevertheless, backing is good and comfortable, and when it comes from a man of your standing, & knowledge of the navy, outweighs the snarling of a hundred yellow journals.

As far as the talk of the squadron goes, and you know how such things travel from ear to ear, it is all pro-Sampson if not anti-Schley; and the same is true in naval circles here, as far as it comes to me. There will, however, be no scandal, unless indiscreet friends of Schley (or of seniority) provoke it. Of this I have some fear but will use my influence against it as far as I can; unless, of course, the abuse of Sampson becomes intolerable. A very decent & intelligent press man told me today that he was satisfied the talk was largely fomented by men in the service who have not forgiven the selection of Sampson for his command & acting rank.

---

1. Barnes to Mahan, August 9, 1898, in Charles C. Taylor, *Life of Admiral Mahan*, p. 92. In this letter Barnes praised Mahan for his letter of August 5 to the editor of the New York *Sun*.

To George Sydenham Clarke

My dear Clarke: Thank you very much for your two last letters received in rapid succession, and for their expression of your well tried interest in our cause and future. After some deliberation, I took the second,
with your suggestions as to the administrative control of the Philippines, to
Mr. Moore, our First Assistant Secretary of State (for Foreign Affairs).[1]
He is one of the leading authorities on International Law and related matters in our country, being professor of the same at one of our leading universities and going there from our State Department, when his reputation
was already established. It is understood that his chief only consented to
take office on condition of his acceptance, and that he only accepted on
condition that his term was temporary—till the war was over. It is said, I
believe with truth, that he is to go to Paris as legal adviser to our Commission. I felt the suggestion would be better in such special hands, in close confidential relations with our leading Peace Commissioners, than given to the
President, who has a hundred other matters to think of, and will be likely
to accept, though not inconsiderately, the views Moore's chief puts before
him.

I have had occasion to see the President somewhat from the inside, in
the occasional consultations on Army and Navy matters, and have been
very favorably impressed with his force and firmness, which I had been
inclined to doubt. He waits on popular opinion which is wise, but I think
he has nevertheless influence because he dont force things. He does not
resist, but deflects; which is much the same as saying that he attempts the
possible, not the impossible. For the rest, the national tendency upon the
whole is I think in the right direction. The present of course is formative,
opinion on some points still fluid; but the *mere* opportunist, the *mere* dollar and cents view, the *mere* appeal to comfort and well being as distinct
from righteousness and foresight, in a word *mere* selfishness and regard
for present ease, are being rapidly dropped behind, and nobler, if somewhat
crude and even vain glorious, feelings are taking possession of the people.
For after all, if the love of mere glory is selfish it is not quite as low as the
love of mere comfort. To the latter the so-called respectable and intellectual
class have unfortunately made themselves the mouth piece. I think, however, the islands will be forced upon us by the refractoriness of the insur-
gents themselves. As in Cuba, so in Luzon, long before the Commissioners
at Paris can act, our nation will be forced to feel that we cannot abandon to
any other the task of maintaining order in the land in which we have been

---

1. John Bassett Moore.

led to interpose. "Chance" said Frederick the Great. "Deus vult" say I. It was the cry of the Crusader and the Puritan, and I doubt if man ever utters a nobler.

To Joseph H. Choate[1]

Washington, D.C., August 19, 1898 [LC]

Dear Mr. Choate: I have read in this morning's paper, with great satisfaction your words before the Bar Association: "Nothing can be more certain than that we should have incurred real national dishonor" &c.[2]

As this expresses exactly my own position, as one unlearned, you can believe it was a great pleasure to see it so clearly stated, by an eminent citizen of a somewhat legal turn of mind. Our friend Godkin (so I see) attributes the War to the yellow journals; which seems to me a fair rival to some explanations of the origin of the milk in the cocoanut.

One of these days I hope you will direct your brilliant wit against the present use of the term Jingo, and show a portion of our community that a vague sneer is not an argument. To the *Post* you are yourself henceforth a Jingo, as you know.

Not knowing your exact address, I must let this take its chance, like the letter addressed Horatio Nelson, Italy. The writer explained that there was but one Horatio Nelson.

To Graeme Mercer Adam[1]

Slumberside, Quogue, Long Island, August 31, 1898 [UML]

Dear Sir: Your letter of the 25th has just reached me. In reply I regret to say that my time for the immediate future is so occupied that I am unable to make any further engagements.

1. A lawyer and diplomat who served as U.S. Ambassador to Great Britain from 1899 to 1905 and as a U.S. representative at the Second Hague Conference in 1907.
2. *See* Mahan to Brown, October 26, 1898, Footnote 1.

1. Author of books chiefly on Canada.

To John D. Long

Naval War Board, Washington, D.C., [August 15–20], 1898 [OANHD]

Sir:

1. The Naval Committee of the Senate having requested of this Board to consider and report to the Department what coaling stations should be acquired by the United States, outside their own territorial limits, the following report is submitted:

2. Such coaling stations in order to be of any considerable utility to the nation, must be available to the Navy in time of war. During peace, the ordinary commercial coaling facilities of the world will meet all ordinary requirements.

3. The question at once arises whether, if such coaling station be granted during peace by a neutral nation, and coal be there stored, the said neutral during war will, or without violation of its neutrality can, permit unrestricted use of coal; that is, allow a single ship, or a fleet, to coal at such times, and as frequently, as we may desire; and whether, also the enemy of the United States would, under such conditions, respect the neutrality of the port and refrain from destroying the coal. This question although raised by this Board, is evidently beyond its competency to answer positively.

4. It is obvious, however, that the United States does require coaling stations outside its own territory, from which coal can be freely and certainly obtained during war. Such stations therefore should now be obtained, and under such conditions, either of use or cession, as shall enable us to assure their safety and free use in time of war. As conductive to this, and also in order to avoid any possible conflict of municipal or civil jurisdiction with the adjacent territory of the ceding nation, it will be always desirable that the station ceded be an island, whose boundaries are defined by the surrounding water. To this should be added, when possible, the power of unaided self-defense, uncommanded by adjacent points of the mainland, or of other islands.

Such stations divide naturally with two classes:

5. A. Those which will be useful to our navy merely in process of transit from one point of the globe to another, passing through regions which are not then the scene of hostilities. The recent voyage of the *Oregon* is an instance in point; that ship having skirted nearly the entire coast of South America, a territory which was not then and is extremely unlikely at any time to be, involved with war with the United States. If, on the other hand, we were at war in that region, as the ally of any one of those states, its ports would be open for our coal supply. Under this first class fall also all coaling stations on the route to the Far East by the Mediterranean and the Suez

Canal, for it also passes through regions in which the United States is very unlikely to engage in war.

6. B. The second class of coaling stations, outside of our own territory, would be those situated in regions, which, owing to unsettled political conditions, and our having great political and commercial interests in them, are liable to become scenes of war. In which we may be engaged, directly or indirectly.

7. The two principal regions answering to this description, are the Pacific Ocean—notably the northern Pacific—and the Caribbean Sea. It is true that the continent of Africa is largely in a formless state of political development; but its territory has been preempted by European countries, and our own indisposition to meddle in its political development has been so clearly manifested, that it may be considered to belong wholly to the European system of polity. We are not likely to be drawn into hostilities concerning it, nor in case of war, to carry out operations there.

8. For the reasons advanced, the Board is of the opinion that the United States does not need to acquire permanent coaling stations, except in the Pacific Ocean and Caribbean Sea. It is also of the opinion that, if at all possible, any stations that may be acquired should become wholly the property of the United States, with so much of the surrounding land and water as may be needed to establish adequate protection against an enemy.

9. In the Pacific Ocean, the notorious changes that are taking place in the political relations of China, the intrusion of European control upon her territory, and the consequent effect upon her trade relations, make the future of China the most interesting commercial question of the Pacific to us at the present moment.

10. The port of Manila is very centrally situated, as regards the whole sweep of the eastern coast of Asia. From it as a centre with a radius of 2,000 miles, very easy steaming distance,—there is embraced Pekin on the north and the Islands of Sumatra and Java on the south, and that of Guajan, or Guam, on the east. Hong Kong and Canton are but 600 miles distant, and Shanghai but 1,000. The bay and port are suitable to the purpose, and although the dimensions of the former make it rather difficult of defense, it is realized that in case of our ultimate retention of the place, the position must in any event be adequately defended on account of the political and commercial importance of Manila, and therefore the naval station might as well be situated there and share in the defense provided. It must however be admitted that Manila Bay is not nearly so strong naturally as Subic Bay, Port Matalvi, Port Masinglock, Dazol Bay and many others. These last are really very fine positions in a military sense.

11. The Island of Guam, before mentioned, one of the Ladrone Islands, is comparatively small, being about thirty miles in length, with an excellent harbor, a little less than 1500 miles from Manila, and 3,500 miles from

Hawaii. The latter distance is somewhat greater than desirable; but it may be observed that the use of Guam would not primarily be to serve as a base of operations, as Manila, and in a less degree, Hawaii, would be, but to facilitate transit from America to Asia. As it is observed that by the protocol lately signed between the United States and Spain, the former is to "select" one of the Ladrones, and as the Board is not fully informed as to the precise character of the harbors in the other islands of the group, it is recommended that before a "selection" is made, one of our cruisers should be sent to the Ladrones to examine the different harbors and to recommend the most suitable one.

12. The ports above mentioned have been Spanish possessions up to the present war. In the opinion of the Board, they would, as regards position and other advantages, be satisfactory as coaling or naval stations, and the cession of one on Luzon and one in the Ladrones for that object might be considered in the treaty of peace. In the Board's opinion, they, with Hawaii, would largely meet the needs of the United States for naval stations, both for transit to China, and for operations of war, if need be, in Eastern Asiatic waters; for naval stations, being points for attack and defense, should not be multiplied beyond the strictly necessary. Notwithstanding the foregoing remark, the Board is impressed with the advisability of acquiring a coaling station nearer to central China than is Manila, and for this purpose recommends one of the harbors embraced among the Islands of the Chusan Archipelago, near the mouth of the Yangtze Kiang, for example Chang Tau harbor or that of Tai Shei Shan. These are about 1,000 miles north of Manila and 1,600 miles north westerly of the Ladrones.

13. The advantages of Hawaii have been so widely discussed of late that it is unnecessary here to recapitulate them. In the opinion of the Board, possession of these islands, which happily we now own, is militarily essential, both to our transit to Asia, and to the defense of our Pacific coast.

14. In the southern Pacific, the station of Pago-Pago, in the Samoa group, already at the disposal of the United States as a coaling station, is so central, and otherwise so suitable in case of operations in that quarter, that it is recommended to be retained. If possible, political possession of the whole island in which the port is, or at least of ground sufficient for fortifications, is desirable. Pago-Pago is about 2,100 miles from Honolulu and from the east coast of Australia, and therefore a convenient half way station between the two.

15. Between the Pacific Ocean and the Caribbean Sea, lies the Isthmus of Panama, the interest of which to the United States is admitted.

16. In the Pacific, San Francisco, which is the nearest United States port suitable for naval purposes, is distant from Panama about 3,200 miles, and from Brito, Nicaragua, about 2,700 miles. The former distance though long is not too great for modern men-of-war, but in the distribution of coal-

ing stations should not be exceeded and both distances are longer than desirable. It would seem desirable therefore that a coaling station should be secured, if practicable, near the entrance of the proposed Nicaragua Canal, and preferably a little north (towards the United States); for the military significance of the Canal, to us, is rapid communication between our Atlantic and Pacific coasts.

17. In the Pacific Ocean, two such ports seem to have many advantages, viz: Port Culebra and the southern port of Port La Union just off the west shore of Punta Sacate Island, in the Gulf of Fonseca. The former belongs to Costa Rica, and is about sixty miles south of Brito, the proposed terminus of the Nicaragua Canal. The latter is about one hundred and fifty miles north of Brito, and belongs to Salvador. Both these places are north of Panama, and distant from it, Culebra, a little over five hundred miles, and Sacate Island seven hundred miles. It may be properly remarked that Port Elena, one hundred and twenty seven miles south of Brito, or Salinas Bay within a few miles of Elena, are either of them suitable for the particular purpose in view, being more land locked than Culebra and quite susceptible of defense. With reference to the distances of all these harbors, it may be observed, (if thought too far from a possible Panama Canal, though very favorably situated for a Nicaragua Canal), that the positions recommended by the Board in the Caribbean will, if accepted, insure a station as near as can possibly be desired to the Atlantic terminus of either Canal.

18. The Caribbean Sea is one of the most interesting and vital regions in the world to the United States, considered from the point of view of commerce and of war; not that most of our commerce passes there, or ever will pass there, but because there our interests may be most seriously interrupted, by hostile navies, in time of war. The land-girt character of the sea, and the fact that there are in it and in the Gulf of Mexico, only two or three positions of surpassing commercial and naval importance, give particular facilities for enforcing control or inflicting injury.

19. The Board is of the opinion that two kinds of positions are needed in the Caribbean, viz: 1: Upon the circumference or entrance to the sea; 2: In the neighborhood of the Isthmian Canal.

20. For the former Porto Rico is advantageously situated and the harbor of San Juan would be the one apparently best adapted for the purposes of a coaling station. As regards San Juan, it appears that at the entrance to the harbor, there is a bar, exposed to the sea, and the water on it is not more than sufficient for our present large ships. Within the bar the water is rather scant, but it is presumed that a reasonable amount of dredging would improve the harbor sufficiently. It is perhaps doubtful whether much dredging could be done on the bar. The position does not lend itself very readily to defense against modern naval ordnance. The base of the peninsula upon which the city stands consists of comparatively low land, and the inner

harbor would therefore be exposed to the fire of hostile ships lying to the eastward of the town. Furthermore the danger range for hostile ships cannot be made much more formidable by the use of stationary mines, for 200 fathoms of water are found only three miles from the city. This condition of affairs must be met by the erection of shore batteries at the proper points: along the coast to the eastward and westward; as San Juan is commercially the most important and most populous city on the island, and probably the best port regarded simply as an anchorage, no doubt our government will expect to give its harbor adequate gun and mine protection, in which naval coaling stations, if placed there, would share.

21. With reference to the position of the United States in the Caribbean Sea, assuming the Island of Porto Rico to belong to us, it is the opinion of the Board that the further acquisition of a strong neighboring position would substantially strengthen the general military control conferred by Porto Rico, for the following reasons:

It is a general truth that any base of military, and still more of naval, operations is decisively stronger with two strong positions than it is with one; the reason being that when there is but one the enemy can interpose before it, without dividing his force. That which is true of any coast line which serves as a base of naval operations, is very especially true when such base is essentially an advanced and somewhat isolated post, as Porto Rico must be; for it is 1200 miles from the Capes of the Chesapeake, and 1400 from New York, a line of communication that can only be maintained by a superior navy. Porto Rico in fact, occupies a position analogous to that of Key West, communication with both being entirely by water. It is recognized by sound naval opinion, in which the Board concurs, that the value of Key West would be greatly enhanced by a fortified coaling station at Dry Tortugas. In a precisely similar way a second and near strong postion would add to the value of Porto Rico. Our ships operating in those waters would have two fortified bases, upon which to fall back by various routes, from both of which the enemy could not exclude them, unless so greatly superior as to appear before both in as great force as our total fleet. This reason may be called strategic, having reference to the general plan of campaign. There are, however, certain specific reasons of a local character which dictate that the principal station should not be San Juan, Porto Rico, on account of its commercial primacy, and its comparatively weak position in a military sense, as set forth in paragraph 20. Therefore, in looking for the second port above mentioned, we should endeavor to choose a naturally strong position, though not too far from San Juan.

22. There are a couple of points in the vicinity, either of which would appear to answer as the second and stronger of the fortified positions referred to above; they are the Island of St. Thomas and the Bay of Samana, and it is observed that owing, as before remarked, to the commercial im-

portance and military weakness of San Juan, it would be desirable to draw the enemy's principal attention to the second strong point rather than to San Juan itself, because in the latter, did we fix our chief naval station, we should be much more vulnerable commercially and militarily.

23. St. Thomas or rather Charlotte Amalie, its chief harbor, is of much less importance commercially than San Juan, and at the same time much more susceptible of defense; the projection of Water Island, terminating on a hill 230 feet high, called Flamingo Point, of steep but not precipitous incline, enables the outer defenses of the harbor to be pushed two miles to seaward, and adds thereby that distance to the range at which hostile ships could otherwise be kept by the inner defenses permitted by the contour of the land near the harbor's mouth. Nor is this projecting point liable to the weakness commonly to be noted in salients; for the batteries on the main island could be so located that any attempt to surround Flamingo Point by a converging fire, would bring the hostile ships under a close or closer range of some of the defenses on the main island as they would be of Flamingo Point itself. Assuming that a hostile fleet would be willing to lie within three miles of batteries, they must retire to five miles from the anchorage at St. Thomas. It may be added that Flamingo Point appears to offer reasonable facilities for guns at the sea level, as well as on the hill top; giving thus the double advantage of horizontal and of plunging fire. This question is of course, technically one of engineering; but it is believed that the foregoing remarks will be borne out by examination.

24. The harbor of St. Thomas has the disadvantage of being open to the south, so that ships lying within would be in sight of hostile vessels outside, and therefore, if the enemy were willing to lie within five miles of the batteries on Flamingo Point, he could throw shells into the harbor or town of St. Thomas, at a range of not over six miles. He would, however, then be a little over three miles from the batteries of Long Point. Our ships could, however, if too much exposed in St. Thomas harbor, steam round Cowell Point and anchor north of and near to Water Island where behind Banana Point they would apparently be better sheltered from hostile fire.

25. With regard to defense by torpedo mines, the Island of St. Thomas rises from a bank of soundings, upon which more or less practicable torpedo ground extends between five and ten miles from the principal anchorage, and for a sweep of five miles, could be under cover of the guns of the place, but exposed to the sea.

26. Without Porto Rico, St. Thomas is too small and too distant from United States territory, but with Porto Rico, the group of islands would form a territory susceptible of defense and valuable for military and commercial control.

27. It is supposed that St. Thomas could not probably be acquired without purchasing the rest of the Danish Islands. One of the important ad-

vantages of acquiring these islands would be to prevent some foreign power from purchasing them and thus acquiring a strong position near our new possessions in the West Indies. This of course is an important consideration, and if Congress thinks that such foreign ownership would be disadvantageous to us, it will depend upon that body to determine whether the disadvantages would be sufficiently great to induce the purchase of St. Thomas rather than Samana.

28. The other port that might be considered, alternatively to St. Thomas, as the strong place from which San Juan, Porto Rico, should derive support, is the Bay of Samana in the Island of San Domingo. It is about 180 miles west from San Juan, a very suitable distance, and as it is very much larger in area than the harbor of St. Thomas, our ships could lie where they would not be seen by an enemy from outside, and the bay could probably be made nearly as secure against an enemy's attack as could St. Thomas, though doubtless with greater expense for fortifications. It is true that the entrance is considerably wider than desirable, but about three quarters of its area is most seriously obstructed with very dangerous shoals, and while there are channels between these shoals that might be navigated by the use of proper running marks, in time of peace, they would be so difficult to traverse in war, under the fire of our shore batteries, obstructed with mines and threatened by our ships and torpedo boats, that an enemy would be very unlikely to attempt such an adventure. There is also an area of soundings less than 25 fathoms with a radius of five miles from Point Balandra, but like that off St. Thomas it is exposed to the sea. Furthermore, Samana Bay ought to cost very much less money than would the Danish Islands. If, then, the Bay of Samana would answer properly as the second fortified port, aforementioned, it would seem that the only remaining reason inducing the acquisition of the Danish Islands instead, would be to prevent some foreign power from purchasing them as before remarked.

Prior to arriving at a conclusion on the relative merits of St. Thomas and Samana Bay, it would be well for Congress to have the opinion of the proper authorities of the War Department as to the relative natural strength of the two positions and the cost of adequately fortifying each. The best position for the coaling station in Samana Bay would seem to be St. Lorenzo Point.

29. The Board has just heard of another position that might perhaps be useful as the second strong place instead of St. Thomas or Samana Bay. It is called "Great Harbor," in the island of Culebra, 55 miles easterly from San Juan, Porto Rico, and 23 miles to the westward of St. Thomas. The harbor is not large, but it appears to be defensible and runs in such a way as probable to conceal ships, lying well within the port, from the view of a hostile fleet outside. A vessel of the North Atlantic Squadron has been directed to examine this place and report upon its capabilities. If found

suitable it might be used, as it probably belongs to Spain, and if so will be ceded to us. Such an arrangement, however, does not dispose of the question of the possible acquisition of the Danish Islands by a foreign power. To sum up, therefore, any naturally strong position, not too far removed, would, in relation to Porto Rico, supply when properly fortified, a defensible anchorage stronger than any in Porto Rico, and based upon which a smaller fleet, or even a few swift cruisers, were we brought so low, could operate with embarrassing effect upon the communications of a fleet carrying on extensive operations against Porto Rico. In itself, apart from Porto Rico, either of the stations aforementioned is too isolated to be held independent of the control of the sea; but resting upon Porto Rico, the two together present elements of strength which would materially protract, and perhaps determine the issue, in a struggle where the opposing fleets approached equality. No positions can confer control where great naval inferiority is a permanent condition.

30. But, besides these places, it must be remembered that the Windward Passage, between Cuba and Haiti, is the great direct commercial route between the whole North Atlantic coast and the Isthmus. No solution of the problem of coaling and naval stations can be considered satisfactory, which does not provide for military safety upon that route. The two most available ports for that purpose are Santiago and Guantanamo on the south shore of Cuba; to those may be added the Bay of Nipe on the north. When Cuba becomes independent, the United States should acquire, as a naval measure, one of these ports, with a portion of adjacent territory; following for example, the line traced in the treaty of surrender negotiated between General Shafter and General Toral. Santiago or Guantanamo is preferable in strategic position to Nipe; but investigation may develop sanitary or other reasons preferring the northern port. As between the two places on the south side, Santiago is the more land locked and defensible harbor, but the entrance is narrow, the least width between 30 ft. depths on each side of the channel being 330 feet, whereas similar width at Guantanamo is about 2,557 feet. This greater width, however, has the disadvantage of not leaving the harbor as well sheltered as Santiago from storms or from the view of an enemy outside, or for the purposes of defense by mines; therefore Santiago would appear preferable were it not that the narrow entrance seems to make it so less accessible in all weathers for very long ships. Furthermore, it has the reputation of being a very unhealthy location. As the Board finds it very difficult to choose between these two ports, it suggests that before a decision is reached the advice of officers experienced in entering and using both harbors be taken.

31. At or near the Isthmus, the surpassing hydrographic advantages presented by the Chiriqui Lagoon have long been recognized. It lies midway between the Caribbean outlets of the proposed Panama and Nicaragua

canals, being about 120 miles from each. The Board considers that it would be desirable to acquire from the Columbian Government, Almirante Bay, together with the islands it contains, and those within which it is embraced, together with a strip of the mainland skirting the bay. This fine sheet of water contains a number of very excellent harbors, of which Shepard's Harbor, Palos Lagoon and Poerras Lagoon are the chief. Either of them would be suitable, with Shepard Harbor preferred, but it must be borne in mind that whichever is taken, the surrounding islands and sufficient of the main to meet the needs of military defense must also be acquired, and these would seem to include Christobal Island, Columbus Island and Careenage Cay and Provision Island also Popa Island and the peninsula containing Saddle Hill, the various entrances to Almirante Bay. If a strip of the mainland skirting the bay could be obtained, it should be stipulated that Colombia should not grant any other nation any rights, of erecting fortifications etc., at least commanding that division of the Lagoon known as Almirante Bay. For, if the right so to fortify were granted to another maritime power, our use of either of the harbors could be checkmated, by works erected even in time of peace, and by a nation from whose naval strength we might otherwise have nothing to fear.

32. Further than this, the United States does not, in the opinion of the Board, need naval or coaling stations in the Caribbean. As before observed, every such station, while affording facilities for naval operations, on the other hand imposes upon the fleet a burden of support and communication. The just balance, between too few and too many, should therefore be carefully struck.

33. And for this latter reason, the Board doubts the expediency of acquiring coaling stations in the Mediterranean, or on the route by the Cape of Good Hope to the East. The true alternative to any such plan is to recognize the implicit obligation of the Monroe Doctrine to keep our hands off Europe and all regions fairly included within the exclusively European polity, as we require European hands kept off the two Americas. Consequent upon these reciprocal obligations, there follows directly the national necessity to *dig the Nicaragua Canal*. The accomplishment of this work, under due guarantees of its use to us, in peace and in war, and the providing of a navy of suitable strength will take the place of, and wholly obviate the necessity for coaling stations in the Mediterranean or in Africa. The usefulness,—nay, the necessity—of the Nicaragua Canal, has been painfully forced upon the Navy Department during the current war, by the difficulties encountered in organizing a reinforcement of battleships for Admiral Dewey, to proceed by the Suez Canal. The need of providing coal, which neutral ports would not supply, and the exposure of a small detachment to attack at the two points, the Straits of Gibraltar and the neighborhood of the Suez Canal, by which it was certain that it would have to pass,

constituted a military—or naval—problem of a very difficult character. It is not necessary here to enter into all the intricacies of detail and danger offered by that problem. It will suffice to say that with the nominal force of the two navies, had that of our enemy been efficient, the problem might have been well nigh insoluble, even after Cervera's defeat. Had the Nicaragua Canal existed, there would have been no problem.

34. Before any harbors that may be selected as naval stations are permanently acquired, each should be visited, carefully examined and reported upon fully by competent naval officers sent for this purpose in one of our cruisers.

35. As a final summing up: The Board recommends the following stations, outside of the present territory of the United States to be acquired, if possible, and to be occupied as coaling or naval stations; and the Board sees no necessity for recommending any others. The stations are eight in number and divide into three principal groups as follows: (The stations are not arranged in the order of relative merit.)

Group A. In the Pacific Ocean, 4 stations.
Group B. Near the Isthmus of Central America, 2 stations.
Group C. In the Caribbean Sea, 2 stations.

  A. In the Pacific Ocean:
    1. One of the Ladrone Islands—probably Guam.
    2. The city and bay of Manila, or Subic Bay; if all Luzon Island be not ceded.
    3. One of the Chusan group of islands, belonging to China, near the mouth of Yang-tze Kiang.
    4. The island of Pago-Pago, Samoan group.
  B. Near the Isthmus of Central America:
    5. On the west coast: either (a) the Island called Punta Sacate, in the Gulf of Fonseca, belonging to the Republic of Salvador; or (b) Port Elena or Salinas, coast of Costa Rica; or (c) Port Culebra also on the coast of Costa Rica.
    6. On the east coast of the Isthmus of Almirante Bay and the islands that embrace it or are contained in it also if practicable, a strip of the main shore skirting the bay. With this position especially, but generally with all, the right of fortification should be acquired upon cession or purchase.
  C. In the Caribbean Sea: (or one of the bays mentioned at close of tenth paragraph)
    7. The east end of Cuba, embracing Santiago or Guantanamo Bays, and preferably including the Bay of Nipe (on north coast).
    8. Either (a) the Island of St. Thomas, or (b) Samana Bay, or (c) possibly Culebra Island.

36. Beyond these eight positions the Board is not prepared to recommend acquisitions.

37. Where alternates are mentioned, as they are in several cases, the Board recommends a speedy examination by naval vessels, in order to determine which possesses the most decided local advantages as a naval or coaling station; for charts cannot be considered to give sufficient data for such determination. In fact, as before remarked, all stations should be examined before being acquired; also the War Dept. should report upon the relative military strength of alternate positions and the cost of fortifying them.[1]

To Stephen B. Luce

Quogue, Long Island, August 31, 1898 [LC]

CONFIDENTIAL

My dear Admiral: Your letter followed me here and was not received until Monday. As regards its suggestion I am of course wholly in accord with the need of some embodiment of the military idea, now lamentably wanting. The most amusing concrete illustration—object lesson—of the condition of affairs in this *War* Institution called a Navy Dept. was that when it had constituted its *War Board*, it had absolutely no place to put it; and when I arrived we were under the eaves of the Dept. Building in a room with one window, which theretofore had been used as a lumber room for books no longer needed for the Library. As the Board was supposed to furnish the Dept. with brains for the trivial & secondary purpose of carrying on the operations of the war, the high eligibility of this pasture for broken down books "turned out to grass" was immediately clear, and the forcing process of a Washington summer under such conditions upon our mental faculties was evident also. However, war being actually on, and a wholesome fear of the enemy existent, it was conceded that possibly a naval organization existed for some other purpose than to administer, and we recd. regard enough at last to give us two rooms from the Library. The incident, nevertheless aptly shows the place preparation for war occupied in the mind of the Dept; and after all we must recognize that like Popes and Czars, Secretaries pass away, but the Papacy, & the Czardom, & the Navy Dept. remain. It is with an institution, not a person, chiefly that we have to deal.

I own, I question the utility of my interfering with Mr. Long. A man

---

1. While Admiral Sicard and Captain Arent S. Crowninshield were also signatories to this letter, its style, organization, and thought are indubitably Mahan's. Crowninshield, class of 1864, a member of the Naval War Board, was also at this time Chief of the Bureau of Navigation.

who values Sicard so highly as to frame the last sentence of that letter addressed [to] Sicard personally—"member" not members—cant value me much; I mean in the particular capacity of the War Board. Sicard is a clear headed man for Bureau work, but very second or third rate for what we had to do—in my judgment; and the Secretary knows this, for I told him so several times. Notwithstanding, he goes out of his way, according to the copy of the letter sent me here, to laud him beyond fault. Long of course knows nothing about these matters himself, being a peace man; but he had the sound sense to see that he was being well served by a number of capable men, in the Board and the Bureaus, and to allow them scope.

I do not wholly refuse to do what you suggest, but I own to a certain hopelessness which is not conducive to doing. As far as a *Board* is concerned, I dont believe in it at all; and less than ever since I served on this. I told the Secy so as soon as I arrived, and repeated it more than once. One man—a chief and subordinates—is needed; but I fear we cant get him because the service and the Dept. dont want him. During my whole time on the Board, historical parallels to our positions were continually occurring to me. How many men in the Navy, do you suppose, know naval history, or think of naval operations, in that way; or how many, if they read this, would fail to vote me an egotistic, superannuated ass! Yet unless there can be found in the Navy a reasonable body of opinion to recognize that war may be regarded that way, I dont see how any demand for a General Staff is to arise, beyond a mere desire to get the better of the Staff by a side wind. But such a motive will effect nothing.

I believe that a series of articles for a magazine[1] I am just beginning will afford a better lever to move public opinion, & naval opinion than a letter to the Secy. The instant a man leaves the room, or a letter is pigeon holed it is forgotten. The last thing the Board did—I wrote the letter—was to implore the Dept to get the battle-ships at once in first class order, and to have no parades & celebrations & traveling from port to port. When we left the dispositions seemed excellent, but to day I see the *Massachusetts* is going to Boston, & I suppose some to Newport &c.

The Navy—in my opinion—wants to stop grubbing in machine shops and to get up somewhere were it can take a bird's eye view of military truths, and see them in their relations & proportions. I dont believe this can be done by letters to the Secy; certainly not to one who sees in the President of the War Board a grand war horse. If I believed it would do good, I would feel bound to write; but I have written & talked and stormed for three months before the Board, the Secy, & the President, and I feel now very much like the teacher who after laborious explanations, receives from one of his boys one of those answers we see in the funny columns of a newspaper.

---

1. *McClure's Magazine.*

To John M. Brown

Slumberside, Quogue, Long Island, September 4, 1898 [LC]

Dear Mr. Brown: If you keep letters, not strictly of business, and if you have the one I wrote you first, relative to the proposition to write a sketch of Cushing's life, can you let me see it, in order that I may inform myself as to exactly what I then undertook to do.

I recd. yesterday a letter from Mrs. Cushing, from which I infer that she has a very exaggerated idea as to the proper scale of the work, its interest to the public, and its paying value. She asks several questions about correspondence existing &c. I am now sorry I did not at the first say No decidedly; but by whatever I did say I must now stand.

I am satisfied that the work will not much more than pay for the cost of bringing it out—that is, I so infer from my returns from the *Life of Farragut*, a far more interesting subject.

To John M. Brown

Slumberside, Quogue, Long Island, September 10, 1898 [LC]

My dear Mr. Brown: If entirely convenient to you I would be glad to know what Swan understood, for you probably read him my letter. If I have given fair reason to believe that I had promised to undertake the work, I will do it in due time. My recollection is that I said I would do it in two or three years from the time of writing, which was probably about a year ago. Mrs. Cushing *seems* to me to have an exaggerated idea of the length the book should be and probably is over-hopeful as to profits. As regards length, that depends of course on matter; but my *Farragut* is within 100,000 words, & I should think 50 to 60,000 ought to be ample for Cushing. On this point I can be positive, subject only to the suggestions of your business experience. There will be very little money in it judging by *Farragut*. It is natural that a woman should be impressed with her husband's interest to the public, but we must look at facts.

I enclose two letters, to neither of which will I reply till I hear from you. As regards Mr. Taylor's I should be glad if you would give him the information, as far as you have it. I will write him about Japan & Russia, concerning the latter of which I dont think we have any facts. As to France, this, & M. de Diesbach's letter, suggest the question, have you heard anything from our friend M. Gaston Fournier, of last year. If, for example, he did not accept de Diesbach's translation, perhaps that was ill done. I do not propose a history of the late war, neither now nor later; but I am writing for *McClure's Mag.* a kind of running commentary upon it, which will reach 30,000 words more or less.[1] I have written not over 5,000 as yet, having lost the last week through indisposition, caused by the extreme heat. After weathering Wash. so well, it was disheartening to knock up at Quogue, but I was brain powerless for a whole week, & miserable all over. Pretty nearly all right now.

I am sorry *Nelson* is not doing better, but it was a book that went with a rush at first, & I suppose there had to be a pause. The London *Times's* "Literature" took a whack at it on the score of my not having consulted the letters recently sold to the Br. Museum by Lord Bridport.[2] Nothing of much consequence was adduced, and nothing at all that modified the portrayal of Nelson; but possibly some undefinable harm may have been done. I am sorry to say that there is lately manifested a clear disposition to jealousy of my work, by a class—doubtless very small—of writers on naval history— David Hannay[3] &c. No naval men are mixed up in it, but I have to expect sneers from these chaps, who write for magazines as well as in books, with, I fancy, no startling success. We shall probably see their hand again when the next vol. of Marston's *Nav. Histy* appears.[4]

To John D. Long

Slumberside, Quogue, Long Island, September 14, 1898 [MHS]

CONFIDENTIAL

Dear Mr. Long: I learn that Captain Taylor,[1] doubtless after due consideration, and I am led to infer after having satisfied himself as to the attitude of the Bureau of Navigation towards the War College, has decided finally that he would not be willing to accept again the headship of that institution. He might justly anticipate, and I myself presume, that it would be given him by the Dept., if he so wished, as its friends have wished.

As my chief anxiety, with reference to the Navy, is that my nominal retirement may become actual and complete—final, it is with regret I yield

1. Mahan's writings on the Spanish War, later incorporated in *Lessons of the War with Spain and Other Articles* (Boston: Little, Brown and Company, 1899) appeared in *McClure's Magazine* from December 1898 through April 1899.
2. Alexander N. Hood, Viscount Bridport, the son of Nelson's niece, sold a group of Nelson's papers to the British Museum in 1895, and a second miscellaneous collection in 1908.
3. David Hannay, author of lives of Marryat, Smollett and Rodney, and of *A Short History of the Royal Navy*, of which only two volumes were published.
4. Clowes's *The Royal Navy: A History.* . . .

1. H. C. Taylor.

to the conviction that I ought to write you on this matter. Briefly, what I have to say is this, with all the weight that can be attached to my opinion, that the College stands for, and tends to supply, that in which the Navy is beyond all things deficient (in my judgment): a knowledge, ingrained, of the principles and methods involved in the correct Conduct of War; a thing quite distinct from all questions of seamanship, of technology, and of administration, though doubtless affected by each of these. My observation of officers in general, and of the Board as well, satisfied me how much this is needed.

To correct this is needed: *1* the introduction into the course of the Naval Academy of an elementary course of naval history (not confined to American) with an analysis of great naval operations, in which, until recently (Farragut), our Navy had little share; *2* the fostering of the War College on its general lines heretofore observed—i.e. since 1886.

I do not undertake to criticize the steady, quiet, opposition to the College of the Bureau of Navigation since Adm. Walker's[2] day; it doubtless has had reasons that seemed to it adequate; nor do I know Crowninshield's[3] position. There is one plausible argument against which I would guard you, viz: that the work of the College, mainly intellectual and studious, can be supplanted by problems worked practically by the N.A. squadron. This cannot be done, for experience has shown it; and moreover Strategy, as Jomini says, is an affair of the closet, & as Napoleon said, it is the fruit of *study*, pre-eminently of history.

Wishing to be drawn into no controversy, nor further action of any kind on this subject—wishing in fact that this letter may prove my last will and testament in relation to the active affairs of the Navy, I have marked it confidential. Its intention is simply to put you in possession of my views on a subject matter, to which I owe *all* the acquirements that have underlain the reputation I have gained. Granting any natural capacity you may attribute, the fact remains that all my usefulness this summer depended upon my studies at the College, which illuminated to me every step I advocated to you.

Unless you are willing to let the College drop, I would suggest your sending for Taylor, and learning from him, personally and thoroughly, just the difficulties he sees. If you decide that the College may die, so well. If you decide otherwise, it will probably be necessary for you to say decisively to the opponents, or advocates of change, whether at the Dept. or the Commdt. at Newport, that the thing *must* be heartily supported; that they suppress all indications of opposition, whatever their opinions. This practically Herbert did, who from the bitterest enemy became a warm and stubborn friend.

---

2. J. G. Walker.
3. A. S. Crowninshield.

To John M. Brown

Slumberside, Quogue, Long Island, September 16, 1898 [LC]

Dear Mr. Brown: You have given me only the sales of the first *Sea Power* for Mr. Taylor. Will you not send me also those of the second in English? I will write him and refer him to Marston for information concerning Germany & France—and Russia, if he knows, which I question. I will also mention Japan to Mr. Taylor. The recovery of those two letters bearing on the Cushing matter were a great relief to me. I have now written to her saying I cannot possibly begin the work before the summer of 1900, that I do not think it can be a great pecuniary success &c. I will retain the letters till her reply and then return them to you.

Marston tells me that you can give me advance sheets, and plans, of the chapter or chapters, in the forthcoming volume (III) of their *Histy of Royal Navy*, which contains my contribution to it.[1] I wish you would do so; for I have found, as I wrote you, a disposition to the nasty on the part of some English writers on naval subjects, and I want to supply him with an answer to faultfinders, when I can foresee their comments.

To Joseph E. Craig

160 West 86th Street, New York, September 30, 1898 [NA]

My dear Craig: We had before us in the War Board a coloured map of Cuba, compiled by the office, from data of War Dept and our own charts, of which I would much like to have a copy. I especially want the railway system.[1] Can you send me this addressed as above?

To John M. Brown

Rockwood, Lynnfield, Massachusetts, September 30, 1898 [LC]

My dear Mr. Brown: I have been staying here a week with Mrs. Henry Saltonstall, and on Monday will be passing through Boston on my way to N.Y., to meet there my family, who are due to arrive on the 5th. I intend to call at your office about 11—intending to take the Air Line train at 1

---

1. "Major Operations of the Royal Navy, 1762–1783."

1. This information was used in Mahan's *Lessons of the War With Spain and Other Articles*.

P.M. I have really no business of importance to talk about—unless it be to indicate some errors in diagrams—maps—in Marston's *Nav. Histy*, in case these still admit of correction; which should be made as the mistakes in two or three instances are rather gross, yet not hard of correction. I shall bring the proof with me, intending to leave it with you.

As the business is of no more importance dont make a point of awaiting me, in case of other engagements.

To John D. Long

160 West 86th Street, New York, October 6, 1898 [MHS]

My dear Mr. Long: When I first learned the unfortunate incident on the U.S.S. *Badger*,[1] in which my brother, Lieut. Mahan, was concerned, I took the liberty of speaking to you on the subject. Being then in ignorance of the full facts of the case—that he was weakened by illness, and had been given an opiate by the surgeon—I am sure I did my brother an injustice and probably prejudiced his case in your mind.

After the Department ordered him before the Board for examination for promotion, I wholly refrained from any further reference to the case, feeling that all the facts would be fully brought before three of the most competent and honorable officers of the Navy, perfectly capable of fully weighing all the circumstances, whose just judgment in the case I hoped would be satisfactory both to the Department and to the country. I learn, however, that he may yet be ordered for trial by Court Martial.

Now that the decision of the Board of Examiners has been rendered, and my brother has been found mentally, morally, and professionally fit to perform all the duties of the grade to which he is to be promoted, I venture to ask that he may not be subjected to this second trying ordeal.

He has, of course, suffered already greatly from the mental strain, and from the sore disappointment and chagrin of losing the one opportunity of his life to do battle for his country. These things affect him physically, & may yet prevent his entire restoration to health before the physical examination yet to be passed.

The prospect of a Court Martial, with its unpleasant notoriety, and the dragging of my name and that of the family before a curious and unsympathetic public give me great concern. I am satisfied that one of the carrion

---

1. Whatever the "unfortunate incident" was, it did not reach the press or the *Army and Navy Journal*. The *Badger* (ex-*Yumuri*) was a 4,784-ton, 329 foot, single-screw, converted auxiliary cruiser capable of 16 knots. Purchased by the Navy in April 1898, she mounted six 5-inch guns. She was later (April 1900) transferred to the Army and became the troop transport *Lawton*.

sheets[2] of this city, for which I have refused frequently to write, even when urged at a dollar a word, because I would not associate my name with it, will be only too happy to strike me, through an opportunity for which I am not responsible. Will you wish to make me dread hereafter to spurn such men?

My father was long in the service of the country, and was the instructor of many of the bravest and best of its soldiers. Every one of his sons has belonged to one or the other of the strong arms of the Government, and all their days have stood ready to render faithful service. Our name is not unknown in the Army and Navy of the United States; and it is within your knowledge that in this generation it has become familiar to foreign navies, not to its own credit only, but also to that of the service with which it has been associated. As it came to us untarnished from our father, so we would all wish above every other thing to transmit it to our children. It is for this reason chiefly that I now write.

No one of the name has ever asked much of the Government; and if, through the long years that cover the lives of two generations, the Country, its Army, or its Navy, is indebted to us for any service rendered, I trust that this, standing to our credit, may now serve to shield and protect the good name our father bore and gave to his children.

To John M. Brown

160 West 86th Street, New York, October 7, 1898 [LC]

My dear Mr. Brown: I have just come across the enclosed letter from Marston.[1] I suppose you have from him instructions to the same effect as the passage marked, or possibly others of later date; but to avoid error I send this, which there is no need to return.

I must tell you how much I enjoyed your company *and* your lunch on Monday. It is to the disparagement of neither to say that I enjoyed *both* extremely, and both were due to you.

My family arrived on schedule time Wednesday. We are shaking down, & as the weather becomes more favorable I trust I may soon do a normal days work.

---

2. Hearst's New York *Journal.*

1. Enclosure not found.

To John D. Long

160 West 86th Street, New York, October 10, 1898 [MHS]

My dear Mr. Long: Your letter was received by this morning's mail. Before expressing my deep sense of personal obligation and gratitude for your action,[1] I wish to say that I have from the first, as far as is possible to an interested party, and with a certain official instinct, put myself in your place. I have no difficulty in admitting the entire justice of your position—and I have so written my brother—that the case on its mere merits, antecedent, required the sifting of regular legal method.

I have believed, however, that the circumstances, as learned by me upon closer inquiry than was at the first possible, were such as could scarcely fail to obtain for him Executive clemency after the trial, if the Court failed to clear him. The discretion of Courts as to extenuating circumstances is very limited in the Navy. If technical fault exists it must be found in the verdict, and mitigating circumstances left wholly to the Executive. This being so, I have felt that the action you would almost certainly feel to be just after trial—if the verdict were against him—would be justified in the eyes of reasonable men by the considerations external to the case which I put before you. Such antecedent interference of the Executive, to stop proceedings, is of course not unprecedented; and in this case it can undergo no suspicion of motives less than worthy, for we have had no power either to benefit or to injure you in any way.

I look upon your action, therefore, as proceeding from an unwillingness to drag a name honorably connected with the Navy, through the mire of publicity, in which men never stop to really weigh the facts; and I believe men not interested as I am will so think also. Nevertheless, when all this has been said in favor of the substantial justice of your action, the fact of its mercifulness and kindness remains. You not only need not have done what you have, but you would probably have received greater credit for greater sternness. I hope I appreciate all this, and I think that I do. Certainly I thank you with my whole heart for this relief from apprehension and anxiety.

To an Unidentified Addressee

160 West 86th Street, New York, October 12, 1898 [NYPL]

Dear Sir: Your letter of the 30th September was received about a week ago when I returned home. I do not care at the present time to go into the

---

1. *See* Mahan to Long, October 6, 1898.

matter which you suggest. I have expressed to the Secy and Asst. Secy my opinion of the utility of the War College in terms as strong as I think necessary to use, and I feel that now I have fairly earned my retirement from the contentions of the service. Any expression of opinion as to the effect of the College in the war would be chiefly as to its utility to myself. This I have already said to the Dept.,[1] and further shall express in a series of articles I am now writing,[2] if it seems expedient to do so.

To an Unidentified Addressee

New York, October 12, 1898 [LC]

Dear Madam: The reports received of the gallantry of our soldiers and seamen during the recent hostilities with Spain give us just cause for pride and for confidence in the future of our country.

To Henry Cabot Lodge

160 West 86th Street, New York, October 18, 1898 [MHS]

Dear Mr. Lodge: There have been other attacks at anchor, but I do not now recall—after some effort made—any at all celebrated engagement under those conditions, save the ones you mention—Aboukir and Copenhagen.

It will give me much pleasure to look over the proofs as [you] suggest. It is perhaps right I should tell you I have promised the *Century* papers on Cavite and Santiago, though I cannot foresee just when I can take them up. I have been loath to do them, for though in a strict sense decisive battles—much more so than most naval actions of the past, they seem to give little scope for my usual treatment.[1] At present I am writing for McClure a sort of commentary on the lessons of the war.

---

1. *See* Mahan to Long, September 14, 1898.
2. For *McClure's Magazine*.

1. The papers in question were never written.

To the Comptroller of the Treasury

Draft   160 West 86th Street, New York, October 18, 1898 [LC]

Sir: My claim for traveling expenses,[1] incurred in returning from Rome, Italy, to New York, in obedience to the Navy Department's order of April 25th, 1898, has been disallowed by the Comptroller of the Treasury. I beg, therefore, to submit to you the following statement of my case, with a review of the opinion in the case of Captain Chadwick; a reference to which is the only explanation given for the rejection of my own claim. I trust, that a consideration of my argument may lead to a reversal of this Decision, upon which my own claim is refused.

I have before me a copy in full of the opinion rendered in Captain Chadwick's case,[2] as well as a volume of Comptroller's Decisions. I shall quote only so much of either as is essential to the presentation of my rejoinder.

The circumstances in my case are: that on March 26th, 1898, I left the United States for Europe, in virtue of a six-month's leave of absence for that purpose granted me by the Department; that on April 25th, at Rome, I received an order directing me to report at the Department; that on April 27th, I left Rome in obedience to that order; on May 7th I reached New York, and on May 9th I reported in Washington. Mileage from New York to Washington was allowed, and forms no part of the present contention.

To obviate the necessity of referring to the law governing travel *abroad*, it is here quoted in full:

"And officers of the Navy, travelling abroad *under orders* hereafter issued, shall travel by the most direct route, the occasion and necessity of such order to be certified by the officer issuing the same; and shall receive, in lieu of the mileage now allowed by law, only their actual and reasonable expenses, certified under their own signature, and approved by the Secretary of the Navy."
Act of August 5, 1882, Paragraph 5.

To the law here quoted, the Decision, here under review, applies a further condition, not to be found in that law, that the travel must be "upon public business." This is taken from another and distinct Act, viz: that of June 30, 1876, governing mileage for travel *within* the United States. The latter Act reads thus:

"So much of the (previous) Act which "provides that only actual traveling expenses shall be allowed to any person holding employment

---

1. *See* Memorandum of Actual Expenses Incurred . . . [May 10, 1898].
2. The Chadwick decision has not been found.

[601]

or appointment under the United States, *while engaged on public business*, as is applicable to officers of the Navy so engaged, is hereby repealed; and the sum of eight cents per mile shall be allowed such officers, while so engaged, in lieu of their actual expenses."

To the use of the words underlined [italicized] there could be no particular objection, were it not that after having interpolated them in the letter of the law governing travel abroad, where they do not exist, the Decision next builds upon them, considered as a definition, a distinction between "travel under orders" and "travel upon public business." The Decision in the Chadwick case reads thus:

"The leave being granted for the benefit of the officer, . . . *such travel, although performed under orders, would not be travel upon public business*, and in order to entitle one to traveling allowances, the travel must not only be performed under orders, or by lawful authority, but it must be upon public business."

It is upon the ground of this distinction that these claims are denied. I believe that upon closer examination the distinction will be found untenable.

It is obvious that, in both enactments, Congress intended to confine the payment of officers to cases when the travel was performed for the service of the government; and that these two phrases, which I have underlined [italicized], and which alone, in the respective enactments, define the character of the travel, were, in the apprehension of the law-making body, not contradictory, but identical in meaning.

The words underlined [italicized]—in the one Act "traveling abroad *under orders*," in the other "while engaged *on public business*"—are, in the respective enactments, the only phrase that expresses and characterizes the *public* nature of the employment, under which alone traveling expenses, either actual or by mileage, can be paid. "Under orders," and "on public business," are evidently interchangeable phrases in the consciousness of the law-makers. Yet the Decision, rendered in Chadwick's case, overrides the plain wording of the Act, allowing actual expenses for travel abroad *under orders*, and not only imports into it words not to be found there, viz: "upon public business"—but, having so imported them, affirms that "such travel, (as Captain Chadwick's), although performed *under orders*, would not be travel *upon public business*."

This Decision, therefore, does not follow the strict letter of the law which governs the particular case. After due consideration, I forbear to analyze at length the course of reasoning by which it is attempted to show that the Decision is in accordance with equity; for all the special pleading upon which the Decision rests, about the benefit of the officer and the injustice to the United States, is simply a plea in equity.

[602]

The whole question, in equity and in law, turns in my own case upon one simple point. On the 26th day of April, before I had begun to obey the Department's order, I was unquestionably on leave. On the 27th of April, when, by beginning my journey, I began to obey the order, was I under orders or on leave? There is no middle term. I was undoubtedly under orders, and an officer acting under orders is undoubtedly engaged in public business. It is common sense to begin with; and, besides, the legislature uses the two expressions as equivalents.

The erroneous premise, advanced in the Decision, practically amounts to this: that an officer, leaving his station, or usual residence, on formal leave, continues on leave, constructively, till he gets back to it, even though the leave be interrupted by the Government. The Decision in Captain Chadwick's case so states:

> "The theory ... is that an officer granted leave of absence is supposed to return to the place where he was stationed, when the leave was granted, *at its expiration* without expense to the government."

"At its expiration," doubtless; every officer returns to his station when his leave *expires* at his own expense; but that is not the case in point. The argument begs the issue, as the Chadwick decision does throughout. The Department's act, in giving orders, does not operate, according to this decision, till the officer has returned to his station, even though the Department orders him back. The fact is, that the Department's act in giving him orders destroys the existing status of leave, and substitutes for it that of "under orders," with all the benefits as well as all the drawbacks connected therewith. The benefits and the hardships alike, whether they affect the officer or the United States, are mere incidents of the status, and have absolutely no bearing upon the case. Yet it is upon them, that the argument in support of the Decision—the plea in equity—rests. The "rule," and "the principle," and "the theory," "that an officer granted leave of absence is *supposed* to return to the place where he was stationed when the leave was granted, at its expiration, without expense to the Government" are, *when thus applied to a leave interrupted by the Government*, wholly irrelevant.

These assumptions—(for such, despite their plausible names, they are)—have no standing ground whatever under existing law. It would of course be competent for the law-making power—for Congress—to impose such a restriction; but that it did not do so, having entire knowledge that such cases might arise, must be assumed to show that it did not intend to do so and it is beyond the competence of a ministerial officer thus to import into the law a qualification which the law-makers did not impose.

I will offer a further illustration which, though supererogatory, will tend, I think, to show clearly that this Decision is not really in accordance with equity. If, instead of being ordered to return home, I had been ordered to report for duty as attache to our Ambassador at Rome—a perfectly possible case—would I, when I so reported, have been on duty, and, in my duty, attending to public business? Was I then less on duty the same day, when I was actually traveling in obedience to orders, and for the public service, which required me in Washington?

The Government, in this supposed case, would have reaped the benefits of the officer's travel to Europe, and certainly an officer should not claim payment for the travel that took him there. The Comptroller, in a case of that character, has ruled, rightly I think, that no claim would lie. But when the boot gets on the other foot, the rule is found to work both ways. Inasmuch as the officer will then reap, not benefit, but mere compensation, for money actually spent for the Government's use, the business ceases to be public. "Though performed under orders, it is not public business." (Decision in Chadwick's case). It appears therefore, that a man may be *ordered* to travel upon *private* business. In Mathematics, this would be the reductio ad absurdum that proves a case.[3]

To John C. Ropes

160 West 86th Street, New York, October 19, 1898 [HSP][1]

Dear Mr. Ropes: I dont see how I can manage a lecture,[2] much as I should enjoy repeating my last year experience of Boston—a city where I always enjoy myself. I have already engaged to write a good deal upon the subject, which it would scarcely be fair to the parties concerned to publish beforehand; and besides, my work before planned is greatly in arrears owing to the interruption in it caused by the war & its sequences.

---

3. *See* Mahan to Long, October 26, 1898, requesting that this letter be forwarded to the Comptroller of the Treasury with Navy Department endorsement.

1. Published with permission of the Historical Society of Pennsylvania.
2. Ropes had probably invited Mahan to read another paper for the Military Historical Society of Massachusetts.

To Daniel C. Gilman[1]

160 West 86th Street, New York, October 23, 1898 [JHU]

My dear Sir: I have just been reading your sane, judicious and well balanced speech at Princeton last evening.[2] It is a real refreshment, in these wildly partisan times, to recognize a healthy optimism, which does not ignore nor affect to undervalue the difficulties awaiting us, but which is able, all the same, to accept as duties the responsibilities thrust upon the country, with a cheerful confidence that if honestly met they will be victoriously surmounted. Do you remember Genl. Grant's "superstition": that he feared to assume any burden upon which he thrust himself, but quite otherwise as to one thrust upon him.

I was glad, too, to see the country reminded that our shibboleths of self government, and the consent of the governed, are not of universal application. Races, like men, have a childhood in which they are not fit for one or the other.

If the strong conservative forces, of which Carl Schurz and the *Nation* are our N.Y. representatives, would stop bewailing the past, and address themselves like men to guiding the future, they might effect the good at which their confessed integrity aims. But men whose main argument is to shout "Jingo," with variations, can do nothing.

Your utterance deserves a more careful comment, which I have no time to write; but I hold that when a man has spoken profound wisdom, it behoves one whom he has impressed to say God-speed, and to be so far partaker of his good deeds.

To John D. Long

160 West 86th Street, New York, October 24, 1898 [MHS]

Dear Mr. Long: This morning's papers announce that advance proofs of Sampson's report of his operations, up to and including the destruction of Cervera's squadron, have been made public by the Department.[1] Assuming this to be so, I write to ask if you will permit your secretary to send me a

---

1. President of Johns Hopkins University, 1875–1901, and first President of the Carnegie Institution, 1901–1904. He had been a member of the U.S. Commission in the Venezuela dispute, 1896–1897.

2. Gilman was guest of honor at the exercises marking the 152nd anniversary of Princeton. Although not an expansionist, he advised that the United States use its now-powerful position for the good of mankind. The entire text of his address "Books and Politics" is in *The New York Times*, October 23, 1898, p. 4.

1. *Annual Report of the Navy Department*, 1897/98. Vol. 2, "Appendix to the Report of the Chief of the Bureau of Navigation."

copy. I am writing not so much a narrative of the war, as a discussion of the lessons, I think, deducible from it. The proofs in question will be useful to me, not for purposes of quotation, but to keep my idea exact as to the sequence of events, and what actually happened.

I may add that the first of the papers in the series—which will probably run to five—appears on December 1st in *McClure's Magazine*; so that any reference to the proofs I now ask would not appear before January 1st, by which time I presume they will be in the hands of the public in full.

To Molly Elliot Seawell

160 West 86th Street, New York, October 25, 1898 [DUL]

Dear Miss Seawell: The book you have been kind enough to send me[1] arrived only today; having been delayed in the Quogue P.O. owing to formalities of the red-tape order. I assure you that I prize very highly this thought of me, and very much more the assurance of regard you have entered on the book itself.

I have had the pleasure of seeing very flattering notices of this and other works of yours in the English papers, and confidently expect from their tone some agreeable hours from the reading of it.

To John M. Brown

160 West 86th Street, New York, October 26, [1898?] [LC]

My dear Mr. Brown: I do not know whether the Boston papers will have reproduced the enclosed as fully; and remembering our conversation two weeks ago about Lopez's intended publication, I thought I would send you this. It is not the argument chiefly, though by one of our very first N.Y. lawyers, but the *facts* he gives; nowhere so collected and summarized as in this speech, so far as my reading goes.[1]

We are beyond question right, in my opinion, in our general course in the Philippines, but this is the most complete demonstration I have seen.

---

1. Miss Seawell might have sent him *Twelve Naval Captains* (1897), or her latest publication, *The Loves of Lady Arabella*. London: 1898.

1. Enclosure not found. If the lawyer was Joseph Choate, the speech referred to was one delivered before the American Bar Association in August 1898. Entitled "On Trial by Jury," it had an opening section devoted to the making of the peace, and the proper aims of the nation's foreign policy; the remainder was legal argument in the great tradition. *See* Mahan to Choate, August 19, 1898.

To John D. Long

Draft   N.P., N.D.   Probably, New York, October 26, 1898 [LC]

Sir: Referring to the Department's letter No. 7414–98, of October 24, 1898, I enclose herewith a letter to the Comptroller of the Treasury.[1]

If the Department shall approve, and forward, this letter, it will I trust be accompanied by a reasonably strong expression of its conviction of the solidity of the argument presented; for it appears to me not too much to say that an official who could adopt as his own such reasoning as appears in the Chadwick Decision, is not to be moved by reasoning, but only by a weight of authority—which will not attach to the letter of a private naval officer, however unanswerable in itself.

To Daniel C. Gilman

160 West 86th Street, New York, October 27, 1898 [JHU]

My dear Sir: In thanking you for the copy of your address, which I have read with care and increased interest, I do not write for the purpose of further encomium, which, considering your reputation, might be going beyond what our relative positions justify. I may however be permitted to remark the *healthy* optimism which does not ignore the greatness of our task, nor our national defects; but yet takes courage from equally obvious national virtues, & especially from the fact that, the past being past, the burden cannot be honorably refused. O si sic omnes! expansionists and non-expansionists alike.

My object in writing, however, is purely practical: to suggest to you, who may be in a position to carry out, by another, this suggestion; that the origins and history of the British Government of India—whence by direct succession has derived the wonderful administration of Egypt—be studied, as to whether they justify the assertion of the anti-Jingo, that, Great Britain has original aptitudes for such work which we do not and cannot possess. To my mind no such noble *group* of administrators exists as the men who have made British India what it is—but are they not a result, as well as a cause? What was British rule at the beginning? What the history of its amelioration? What the condition of the mother country, in internal order, in political purity, when British rule in India began? Is, in general, the great result we see now due to original developed fitness, or to germs of fitness, which have developed gradually into their present ripe efficiency, by steady use at the call of duty.

---

1. *See* Mahan to Comptroller of the Treasury, October 18, 1898.

I believe that the responsibility for India, acting on men of a nation in which the sense of personal, individual, responsibility had developed *conscience*, both national and personal—that the sense of responsibility, I say, has not merely benefited India, and regenerated its officials, but has reacted for good on Great Britain itself. But my knowledge is imperfect, nor do I feel called upon to turn from work to which I am competent, to engage in prolonged labor whose results I cant foresee. It occurred to me that you, as an educator, might know some younger men, to whom such a study might be attractive. Certainly, if the fact be as I imagine, its exposition to our people at this turning point could not but be advantageous.

You will forgive a certain incoherence in one part of the letter, due to the fact that my thought outran my pen. The main idea of the letter I think I see already existing in your mind, and shown in your address. If so, you will understand me easily, without further words.

It will give me great pleasure to accept your invitation, if an opportunity offers, and I thank you for it.

To Reuben G. Thwaites[1]

160 West 86th Street, New York, November 1, 1898 [SHSW]

My dear Sir: I beg to acknowledge the receipt of your letter of Oct. 28. I am very sensible of the honor done me by the invitation of the Society, and beg to express my thanks; but I regret that the pressing nature of my engagements prevent my acceptance.

To J. Franklin Jameson

160 West 86th Street, New York, November 1, 1898 [LC]

Dear Mr. Jameson: Although I postponed, I did not mean to allow so long a time to pass before answering yours of Oct. 18. I cannot think that the *Life of Esek Hopkins*[1] falls within my special lines. His connection with the navy of the Revn. was brought to a sudden violent end whether justly or unjustly. In either case it scarcely touches naval history—and I

---

1. Secretary of the State Historical Society of Wisconsin, and editor of *Jesuit Relations and Allied Documents* (1896–1901), and of the *Original Journals of the Lewis and Clark Expeditions* (1904–1905).

1. Edward Field, *Esek Hopkins, Commander-in-Chief of the Continental Navy, 1775–1778*. Providence, R.I.: Preston and Rounds Company, 1898.

should think for satisfactory review had better go to a historic student interested in the period. It may be that it resembles the *Life* of one of the Biddles published in Phila. for private circulation,[2] in which case its interest would be considerable.

I received two months ago a book called *Russia's Sea Power*, by a friend of mine Col. Sir. G. Clarke[3]—and he intimated he would like me to review it—a rather unreasonable request *from* an *author*. If I can review, would you give it room, & how much? It has about 80,000 words—by rough estimate.

I thank you sincerely for your very kind expressions as to the share of our Board in the management of the naval war. Appreciation is always pleasant.

To John D. Long

160 West 86th Street, New York, November 7, 1898 [MHS]

Dear Mr. Long: I have to thank you for your letter of the 4th, and for the proofs.[1] The latter are but this moment received.

I shall observe carefully the conditions you prescribe, and, to make assurance surer, will not allow any quotations to leave my own care before December 1st.

To John D. Long

160 West 86th Street, New York, November 10, 1898 [MHS]

Dear Mr. Long: I find, upon looking over the advance sheets you were good enough to send me, that they are almost entirely deficient in the very point I most need in order to treat my present subject in the method employed in my previous works. The telegrams framed in the War Board scarcely appear at all, except so far as quoted by the officers to whom sent; which presents of course only a partial, irregular and disconnected series. It is very important to me, in order to present an instructive commentary on

---

2. James E. Biddle, ed., *Autobiography of Charles Biddle, Vice President of the Supreme Executive Council of Pennsylvania, 1745–1821.* Philadelphia: Privately printed by E. Claxton & Co., 1883.
3. Sir George Sydenham Clarke, *Russia's Sea-Power, Past and Present, or, The Rise of the Russian Navy.* London: J. Murray, 1898.
1. *See* Mahan to Long, October 24, 1898.

the operations, to refer to the telegrams; and if you can have sent me the series, *after* the present need of the Department for them has passed, it will greatly facilitate the work.

Permit me to congratulate yourself and the Administration upon the result of the elections. It can fairly be construed as an endorsement; but, what I doubt not you will value more, it shows that under your conduct the country has been reverting to the paths of integrity, has gained in prosperity, and has placed in the hands of the Administration the means of further progress.

To John M. Brown

160 West 86th Street, New York, November 10, 1898 [LC]

My dear Mr. Brown: At the request of Judge O'Connor Morris, I enclose a letter which explains itself.[1] I will add only that from considerable correspondence, and our long interviews, with the Judge, I am satisfied that he is not the least the kind of man willingly to withhold full credit. In fact, in view of Blackie's letter,[2] I fail to see why the publishers are not chiefly at fault. If you think proper, their letter might be sent to Marston with thanks for his interference in the matter, which was prompt. I am equally obliged to your firm for the explicit instructions which guarded my rights beyond argument. Morris explicitly does not wish its return.

I want to send, for Christmas, to a person in England who showed much attention to Mrs. Mahan while there, a copy of *Nelson* bound in calf—handsomely. Could you have the binding done for me—first letting me know the cost? and will it be feasible also to let me have a fly leaf, on which to write his name &c &c, prior to binding; in order that you may send the books direct? I ask this complicated arrangement because the making up of books for mail or express is to me so difficult. If, however, the fly leaf business is impossible, the books will have to come here.

To the Editor of The New York Times

New York, November 15, 1898[1]

The movement of the Chamber of Commerce which receives the editorial endorsement of *The Times* this morning, "to promote the freedom from

---

1. Enclosure not found. *See* Mahan to Brown, June 21, 1898.
2. Blackie & Son, Ltd., a Glasgow publishing house.

1. From *The New York Times*, November 17, 1898.

seizure on the sea of private property in time of war," is on the surface plausible, but demands careful examination rather than an off-handed acceptance based upon superficial impression. The idea is undoubtedly one of long standing and has had in times past the backing of the United States Government but there is in it a certain amount of fallacy and a failure to recognize the true influence of commerce upon war.

There is fallacy, for the term private property is misleading. Goods embarked for the purpose of trade are undoubtedly the property of individuals, and in so far, private property; but in a very important sense they differ from private property which is not being used for purposes of exchange. The exchange of goods, commerce, is the financial life of a nation, and it is now a commonplace that money is the sinews of war. Commerce, therefore, and especially maritime commerce, bears to the military life of a nation at large just the relation that the communications of an army in campaign bear to the efficiency of the army. Break the communications of an army with its base, and the army is, as a rule, paralyzed. Destroy the commerce of a nation and its military life is so far sapped as to reduce its powers of resistance and so to hasten peace. Is is against commerce only that the present practice of seizing the merchant ships and cargoes of an enemy is directed. The strictly private property of the individuals on board them for purposes of trade is inviolate, and when an instance to the contrary occurs it is recognized on all hands as an abuse.

A still more important point which is overlooked is the deterrent effect exercised by commercial interests upon threatening warfare in these days. It is to the increase and extension of commercial bonds, and their intricate blendings, whereby so many communities are affected financially by an outbreak of war, that we owe more than to any other one influence, the comparative rarity of war now. Few would say that the combative instincts of European and American nations are less than they once were. Assure the nations and the commercial community that their financial interests will suffer no more than the additional tax for maintaining active hostilities; that the operations of maritime commerce, foreign and coastwise, will undergo no hindrance, and you will have removed one of the most efficient preventatives of war.

Up to forty years ago, when this matter was last agitated at the time of the Treaty of Paris, American diplomacy was, from the National point of view, perfectly sagacious in seeking this immunity for commerce. It was much to our interest, for then we had an immense merchant shipping and almost no navy. Now that our long-voyage merchant shipping is almost naught (though we have a great coasting trade) and that our new transmarine responsibilities will entail necessarily a considerable navy, we are rather interested to hold over the heads of a possible enemy the chance of serious injury befalling him by stopping his maritime commerce.

The tendency of the present rule, therefore, is to deter from war; while if war unhappily comes, and commerce is immune, the effort must be to destroy men's lives, to kill and wound them, instead of the more humane and scientific process of exhausting the resources of the nation and so compelling peace.

To John D. Long

160 West 86th Street, New York, November 16, 1898 [MHS]

PERSONAL

My dear Mr. Long: Now that the opening of Congress is near, I beg your permission to suggest to you two considerations, not as urging you to act upon them, but because they may not have occurred to you yourself.

First: As to the rewards to our admirals. The Administration has awarded promotion to three, and so far made a final decision for which I have neither criticism nor quarrel. There remains the question of a Vote of thanks. This carries with it, when given *individually*, ten years additional on the active list. In my judgment it is not desirable to give Schley ten years on the active list. Personally, if again called upon for the duty I performed this summer, I should strongly protest against any responsibility for operations intrusted to him as commander-in-chief, on the ground of what he did while acting as such. It appears to me that the well-earned vote of thanks to Dewey and to Sampson should not go below them, *by individual mention* unless for *special* services; nor, in the nature of things, is there necessity for going below the one man responsible.

Second: *Assuming* that Dewey be brought forward for promotion to Vice-Admiral, should it be tolerated that there should be hooked on to this richly earned recompense a measure to promote Miles to Lieut-General? I dont propose to resist the latter measure, standing by itself, but I do suggest that it should stand upon its own merits—or Miles's own—and not that the Army should have because the Navy receives. Dewey has made proof of very eminent qualities, both at and after Cavite. If promoted, as I hope he will be, I trust that the praise will not be watered down by coupling in the same measure a man who is undoubtedly a very gallant soldier, but who has done nothing conspicuous this war. You and I know that to the President's tenacity was chiefly due that the Santiago garrison was not permitted to retire to Holguín with the honors of War, as Miles recommended. Miles may have been right, but if so, our achievement at Santiago would have been far from brilliant. The Porto Rico landing I once said to you, at Guánica, and the initiation of operations there, appears to me a military stupidity so great, that I can account only by a kind of obsession of vanity, to do a singular & unexpected thing. This opinion I *may* modify after closer study; but I still retain it after reading his letter to Higginson.[1] It seems to me, however, perfectly clear that to build upon Dewey's advancement a claim for the same reward to Miles, to equalize the two services would materially detract from the compliment and reward due to the former, implying that their achievements were equal—or their merits.

I have been more argumentative than I intended; but, while submitting cordially to your final decision, there seems no impropriety in suggesting these views and their reasons. It is for you only to take action—positive or negative; and it would not be becoming in me to do anything of myself, beyond writing to you. The two questions concern, one the interests, the other the credit, of the Navy, and are therefore especially in your hands & those of the President. My own views upon them may be wrong, & I recognize also that policy as well as strict right has to be considered, in many cases.

To the Editor of The New York Times

New York, November 21, 1898[1]

In your editorial of Saturday, commenting on my first letter to you[2] on the subject of the proposed immunity of commerce in war, you adduce the abandonment of the right to seize "private" property on sea or land belonging to the one belligerent which at the outbreak of the war happens to be within the territory of the other, as indicating a tendency to the modification of the principle advocated by me, which principle, as you accurately enough state, "is that injury to commerce is an expedient mode of waging war, and sound method of hindering war." You adduce also, and to the same end, the relinquishment of the practice of cancelling debts to the enemy contracted prior to the war.

It appears to me that these departures from a former practice are not due chiefly to a disposition to diminish the hardships to individuals involved in the embarrassment of commerce; although, if this were true, it would not be a reply to my contention that such modifications are not really in the direction of general greater humanity. The relinquishment of these rights has been due to the recognition that, although legalized by precedent, they were not equitable, and therefore were morally indefensible. The property of the individuals, now become enemies, entered the national territory

---

1. Francis J. Higginson, who commanded the *Massachusetts* during the War with Spain.

1. From *The New York Times*, November 23, 1898.
2. *See* Mahan to the Editor of *The New York Times*, November 15, 1898.

under the guarantee of the national good faith, and while, undoubtedly, the reserved right of confiscation in case of war did exist implicity, because sanctioned by precedent, nevertheless there was a breach of hospitality, of natural justice, in thus taking advantage of the trust reposed. As regards debts between individuals, the same feeling of honor and honesty is repugnant to their repudiation. They were contracted in good faith, in peace; and indeed it may be fairly claimed that the enforcement of either of these rights by the mutual distrust that would accompany commercial transactions in peace, would be injurious to the commerce of both belligerents in peace, as well as the one who gained, in a particular instance, as of the one who suffered loss. Either practice attacks the commerce of peace rather than the commerce of war; consequently it is contrary to sound policy. The limited and trivial gain in war implies a loss in peace which would doubtless be much greater, though it cannot be exactly estimated.

The relinquishment of these legal rights, in short, proceeds upon the same general ground that, in the case of a blockade, permits neutrals already in the port to complete their ladings. It conduces to the security, upon which prosperity of commerce, in peace, so largely depends, that transactions begun in good faith, in peace, should be allowed to proceed undisturbed to completion. But new transactions of the same sort cannot be begun. To permit an enemy's ships or property in your port to leave unharmed, or even to guarantee its safety, until it has regained its own ports, is evidently a very different thing from guaranteeing it the same immunity when it again puts forth, on commercial venture, in open war. Whatever other arguments may be advanced, such permission alone does not shake the general position "that injury to commerce in war is an expedient mode of waging war, and a sound method of hindering war."

To John M. Brown

160 West 86th Street, New York, November 21, 1898 [LC]

Dear Mr. Brown: Many thanks for the copies of the Major Operations.[1] I will observe your caution about letting them leave my hands before the day of publication.

Thank you also for attending to the Fournier matter. He seemed so interested last year that I have been surprised not to hear from him.

---

1. "Major Operations of the Royal Navy, 1762–1783," in Clowes, ed., *The Royal Navy: A History.* . . . Little, Brown and Company published the American edition.

To John M. Brown

160 West 86th Street, New York, November 24, 1898 [LC]

My dear Mr. Brown: I wrote to one of the McClure firm a week ago suggesting that when the first of my articles on the War appeared (Dec 1) copies should be sent to two men in England, whom I named. In reply,[1] they said they would of course do so, but that they had made arrangements to publish in the London *Times* and this morning I see notice of publication, yesterday, I presume, and of a eulogistic notice.

This step was taken without prior consultation with me, and notwithstanding that my letter stating terms stipulated that I should retain the right to republication, when three months had expired from the appearance of the papers. There is no formal agreement, for I have never yet had occasion for any as to magazine articles. As regards the first paper the harm is done, there is not even simultaneous publication on the two sides to protect me. I have been paid for this article. The second is printed, proof revised, and is due to appear Jany 1. I have not yet been paid for it. The 3d & 4th are nearly completed and are still in my hands. I hope a 5th will close the series.

Of course I shall try to arrange the matter pleasantly, but I would be glad of your opinion as to my rights, and my best future action.

The McClures have twice approached me, once by interview, and again by letter, which I have, to publish in book form. My reply has been that my relations with your firm were such that I preferred to publish through you, though I gave them no decisive answer. I have, however, never had any other intention. I have entertained, though unformulated as yet, the project of combining my yet unpublished lectures on Naval Strategy (with possibly the Lowell lectures) & the Spanish War papers in one series or book. I think today I shall write McClure my dissatisfaction; pleasantly, but a sort of caveat.

To John M. Brown

160 West 86th Street, New York, November 27, 1898 [LC]

My dear Mr. Brown: I enclose to you a letter from Mr. McClure's partner[1]—as I understand with whom much of my correspondence has been done. It appears to me satisfactory, inasmuch as parts of each article being

---

1. August F. Jaccaci to Mahan, Copy, New York, N.Y., November 16, 1898, in the Library of Congress.

1. John S. Phillips, general manager and supervising editor. Enclosure not found.

simultaneously published, it would avail little to reproduce the disconnected fragments, if the latter are not protected; but I would be glad of your opinion.

I am glad to learn of Marston's telegram. I infer that he has found possible to obtain for me copies of certain papers, rather voluminous, concerning Nelson, about which I wrote him fully three weeks ago, and have also mentioned to you. I made clear, I think that they were essential to revision, and that without revision I was unwilling to bring out a wholly new edition.[2] If this expectation is realized, I find myself pretty favorably placed for beginning the work of correction. I have finished all the "copy" I have to give McClure before Feb. 1, and have nothing else pressing. I hope therefore to give the month of December almost wholly to revision, if Marston can send on the data alluded to. As soon as I am informed on this point I will write you again. Meantime, will you consider when you *must* begin printing—the latest I mean. Unfortunately, most of the correction I now anticipate falls in volume I of the present edition, which is bad for the page proof and I dont know whether galleys will be needed in this case. I suppose you can send me on short notice sheets of the present edition; it may facilitate preparation for the printer.

P.S.   I have found Jaccaci's letter to me, which I feared I had destroyed. It puts you in possession of all the facts.

By the way, the manner in which my chapter is bound in Clowes book and *covered* &c suggests the question whether there is any present intention of publishing separately.

To Silas McBee

160 West 86th Street, New York, November 27, 1898 [UNC]

My dear Sir: I wish to express to you my satisfaction and admiration for the editorial paragraphs in your issue[1] of the 19th, which for some reason reached me only yesterday. I refer to those beginning with "The Nation's Duty," and so on. The plane of thought on which they move, and the tone of them, are Christian and lofty. The refutation of that "indictment against the whole nation"—to use Burke's phrase—because of the undeniable wrongs and shortcomings in the case of the negro and the Indian, seem to me quite conclusive for the space occupied; and I should think further development of the facts—many of which were new to me—would be

---

2. *The Life of Nelson, the Embodiment of the Sea Power of Great Britain.* 2d ed., revised. Boston: Little, Brown and Company, 1899.

1. *The Churchman.*

beneficial. May I suggest to you that the argument, that our declaration of purpose before the war binds us in iron fetters for all time, the absurdity of which you well show, applies with far greater force to the British occupation of Egypt. The British Govt. there is bound by promise, not by mere general declaration, yet what civilized Christian would desire to see her observe now the letter of the promise under the changed conditions. The *Guardian* in its leader for Nov 16 affirms the English position in this, as it has often before. I entirely agree; but why then cast in our teeth our inequality of citizenship as compared with Great Britain? See also Sir E. Grey's speech, *Guardian*, p. 1769.

You will have observed that even the *Evening Post*, which publishes Bp. Potter's[2] tirade but refuses Bp. Doane's[3] address, has been forced to give place to the more hopeful augury of Mr. Booker Washington.[4] I lately had a visit from a colored presbyter of Richmond, Rev. J. W. Johnson, who spoke similarly hopefully of the upward progress of his race, while not concealing his keen sense of the inequality of treatment he and his brethren still receive in our Church South. The truth is that under our civilization the negro *is* advancing; the movement is upward.

I have written because I feel that appreciation is due to the writing that may so strongly help the nation at a critical moment. I will add only that the thought of churchmen might with benefit be directed to earnest prayer for the descent and influence of the Holy Ghost upon our land and people in this hour of decision. After comparing your editorial with Bp. Potter's utterances, and with the extraordinary distortions to which so able a man as Dr. Huntington[5] is driven in his Thanksgiving sermon, I am satisfied the weight of argument is overwhelmingly with you—but after all it is the office of the Holy Spirit to *convince*.

[P.S.] Do Churchmen, even Bishops and Priests, practically consider the gift of the Holy Ghost, and the powers of the world to come to be potential factors in a nation's politics and welfare?

To Silas McBee

160 West 86th Street, New York, December 9, 1898 [UNC]

My dear Sir: In response to your letter of last week I send the enclosed communication.[1] If you see fit to accept it I have only one condition to

---

2. Henry Codman Potter, Protestant Episcopal Bishop of New York.
3. William Croswell Doane, Bishop of the Protestant Episcopal Diocese of Albany.
4. Booker Taliaferro Washington, Negro educator, head of Tuskegee Institute.
5. William Reed Huntington, rector of Grace Episcopal Church in New York (1883).
1. Enclosure not found.

make—in view of its length—and that is that it appear as it stands, & in one issue; not divided. Its length may make it impracticable to do this, in which case I will ask you to return it.

I may add that after writing I have had the advantage of the advice of a very distinguished clerical friend, who approved it as it now stands, having suggested a few changes of detail. The blue line on last page was a reference to him.[2]

To Silas McBee

160 West 86th Street, New York, December 17, 1898 [UNC]

Dear Sir: Do you not think that the word "fate" as used in 2d. paragraph, Chronicle & Comment, is somewhat objectionable from the Christian stand point; not only from old heathen associations, but from those with "fatalism" of modern times.

I enclose my subscription for 1899.

To John M. Brown

160 West 86th Street, New York, December 20, 1898 [LC]

My dear Mr. Brown: I return Marston's letter, and Fournier's, for which many thanks. As regards the map, I have today written Marston that it presents no difficulty, if confined to the period when he [Nelson] was a lieutenant & captain & after; prior to 1778, it would be difficult to accomplish unless certain logs I named, but which I doubt can be found, are accessible. I would of course prefer to do it myself—and when we hear from him [Marston] I will write you. How would it do now to prepare a sheet showing from the Equator to 62° N, and from the *east* end of Medn. to include *west* shore of Gulf of Mexico? This covers all his great career; leaving open the question of extending it to take in Greenland & East Indies which he visited as midshipman.

I have looked up the question of revision[1] and apprehend no trouble in beginning to print Jan. 15, provided Marston and Stevens send me betimes data I have asked them for. As near as I can judge, there need be little change, except the last 30 pages of vol. I which I shall recast; but I am extremely

---

2. Probably, S. DeLancey Townsend, rector of All Angels Episcopal Church, Mahan's place of worship at this time.

1. Of his Nelson biography.

anxious to get the material for which I have asked them, and to make a job that will last. Nothing has turned up that affects the *Life* as a *portrait*; and the errors of fact are entirely unimportant. The pages above, so far as I now see, require altering not because erroneous, but in order to meet an ill-founded attack.[2] You will, I suppose, keep in view the changing of the first and more expensive edition, as soon as possible after revision.

I would like your opinion on the enclosed,[3] which came to me from the London *Times*, through McClure, from Berger Levrault. As they want to publish "en volume" it cannot be done till the last article is out, which will not be till April 1, possibly May 1. What should we do as regards Fournier? Should he be consulted? and would I do well to ask either Frenchman to employ M. de Diesbach, who translated *Fr. Revn.*? The latter has expressed a wish to translate anything I write, but I am in no wise bound to him.

[P.S.]   I congratulate you indeed upon the success of your work on the *Naval Histy*. It looks extremely well in the pamphlet shape.

To J. B. Sterling

160 West 86th Street, New York, December 23, 1898 [LC]

My dear Col. Sterling: I was very glad to receive your letter. Few things will do more, in a quiet way, to promote and sustain the good feeling we all wish to see between our two countries, than those who know and esteem each other should at times exchange ideas and good wishes.

We have, as you say, passed through an extraordinary year in this country, and the outcome is certainly one of the most unforseen. That Cuba should one day be free, and possibly under our control, was within the scope of our vision; but I confess the Philippines, with all they mean, had not risen above my mental horizon. As you know, I am one of those who looked with anxious speculation toward the Chinese hive; but I never dreamed that in my day I should see the U.S. planted at the doors of China, advancing her outposts and pledging her future, virtually to meeting the East much more than half way. To Dewey's victory, apparently, is due that we annexed Hawaii.

2. By F. P. Badham in *The Saturday Review*, May 15, 1897, and November 3, 1897; and in *English Historical Review*, April 1898. Badham charged that Mahan had handled Nelson's erratic political and personal behavior in Naples in June 1799 much too gently. Mahan responded to this attack in the revised edition of *Nelson*, in *The Athenaeum* (July 8; July 22, 1899), and in *English Historical Review* (July 1899; October 1900).
3. Enclosure not found.

We have undoubtedly a difficult road before us. I look at it with no light heart but as a believer in a Divine Providence. I do not lack confidence that we shall be able to walk in the path in which, as it seems to me, our feet are set for us.

Your episodes with France[1] I have watched with great interest; but I believe that she was so absurdly in the wrong that she got no sympathy even from her great ally Russia. I heard nowhere here, and read nowhere, any approval of her course. Who was it said there are two kinds of nature—human nature and French nature?

To Augustus T. Gillender

160 West 86th Street, New York, December 27, 1898 [HUL]

Dear Mr. Gillender: I recd. the enclosed this evening, and will ask you what you think of it; not of the proposition, for of course I have no money to put in such apparent wildcatting, nor has Dennis, but of the calm assumption that the factory is not on Dennis's property.[1] As the latter is still much under the weather, I think it best not to bother him yet.

It appears from this that Youmans is the owner. He enclosed with it his business card, with which I dont trouble you.

I dont think I have been in Wall St since the family arrived, and scarcely below Eighth. I am so busy that I cannot keep up at all. I have heard from the Colonial Club, and accepted, though the date suggested is most inconvenient; but it will be no little thing that will absent me from honoring Sampson. I declined the Lotos Club's invitation to honor Schley, considering that he had done *nothing* to merit distinction, I did not think necessary to say this in full, but I gave no reason & expressed no regrets.

To John D. Long

160 West 86th Street, New York, December 28, 1898 [MHS]

My dear Mr. Long: I noticed in General Miles's testimony a week or so ago, a statement, or at the least an implication, that the Navy had in some way failed to meet its engagements to provide facilities for landing the army at Santiago. I presume there was not wanting some one to remind you—if *you* forgot—that the Dept. at the suggestion of the War Board

1. Anglo-French rivalry in the Sudan.
1. *See* Mahan to Gillender, May 26, 1897.

wrote to the War Dept., to know if such aid were wanted; and that the reply was that they would do their own landing, asking of us only safe convoy to the spot.

I wish also to say to you that an opinion attributed to Senator Hanna[1] by the papers, that the conditions of naval war-ship construction are so unsettled, that we should postpone further increase of the navy, and should await the results of other nations' experiments, is wholly without *practical* foundation; by which I mean that there is nothing so far in sight, indicating such radical change, that it is expedient for us to postpone by a day such naval development as our political conditions demand, and our financial conditions permit. On political & financial considerations I do not undertake to speak; but on the military question I submit the above as my professional opinion.

To John M. Brown

160 West 86th Street, New York, December 30, 1898 [LC]

My dear Mr. Brown: With regard to the map that Marston desired for the new *Nelson*, I have written him today advising to omit the Arctic & E. Indies, and specifying, in case he wants them, what he must get in the way of data.

Meanwhile, it would be well to start the map here now, as far as I *do* recommend, and for that I must ask your head of such matters—Mr. Bailey, is it not?—to have the outline drawn for me. For me to do it personally would be waste of time. What is wanted is shown clearly enough in the map of North Atlantic, (*Nelson*, II, p. 318). This needs to be extended so that its boundaries may be: N. parallel of 60°–61° would be better. S. parallel of 5° N. E Longitude 36° E from Greenwich W Longitude 95° W from Greenwich. This embraces the Medn., the West Indies, and the Baltic, with every important place mentioned in Nelson's career. There is already in *Nelson* the Baltic—vol 2, and in all the books the Medn.; but of course these and Atlantic, being separate, are not on the same scale.

The map had best be drawn on a pretty large scale for me—I suppose it can be reduced afterwards in photo. Send it to me, and I will then undertake to enter the lines of voyages & cruisings. The final size, and whether it had best be bound in, or placed in a pocket, can be settled as we go on.

I have progressed so far that I feel quite sure of being able to begin printing Jan. 15 and to go straight on *provided* I receive in time the papers for which I have written to Marston & Stevens. The pace is heavy but I think

1. Mark Hanna, Republican of Ohio.

I can do. I wrote Fournier as you suggested. Did I tell you I have an application from a German offr. concerning same for a military journal. As Marston hitherto has attended to the German business I have referred to him; telling him to insure my copyright for *book* form.

[P.S.] When the revised cheaper edition is out, what will you do about the present more expensive ones? I want to get these revised also, and propose to do so, in case of *additions*, of which there may be a very few, by appending a note to the proper chapter. There are some erroneous statements. These I shall try to recast in such wise as not to alter the paging. The value of the book, as a biography, is not, in my judgment in the least affected by these errors. They dont touch the *man*, and for the most part dont even concern him. All the same they *are* errors & must be changed.

It would be as well to send me at once the unbound sheets of which we spoke.

To J. Franklin Jameson

160 West 86th Street, New York, January 3, 1899 [LC]

Dear Prof. Jameson: I have sent back Hopkins' *Life* by express.[1] I could not give time to read it thoroughly, but from the glance I gave it did not appear to me to possess particular naval interest. How could it, in fact? He was something of an accident, was barely a year in a most irregular navy, and then removed. Whether the dismissal was unjust or just may be a matter of personal or local interest, but there appears to me nothing *naval* in it.

To James R. Thursfield

160 West 86th Street, New York, January 12, 1899 [LC]

My dear Mr. Thursfield: I am delighted that you are visiting this country, though for so short a time, and greatly envy you the escape to Bermuda from our bitter and changeable weather.

Will you not dine with us on Monday, at 7:30 quite en famille, unless

1. *See* Mahan to Jameson, November 1, 1898.

I can get one of our Santiago captains, whom I have asked to meet you.[1] Also on Sunday we lunch at 1:30, and at 7 have a cold supper; at either or both of which, or at 5 o'clock tea, we shall be delighted to see you. I presume that Mrs. Thursfield does not come with you as you speak only of yourself.

I enclose a card for our University Club, corner of Madison Ave and 26th St., a very central and convenient locality, where you will find comfortable reading rooms and a good restaurant.

I shall of course endeavor to get down to see you Saturday if your arrival is known to me in time; but everything is arriving shockingly late just now.

[P.S.] A long standing engagement prevented my naming Tuesday evening instead of Monday. I could do nothing about the Customs, because of a recent change of regulations. Made the attempt.

To John S. Barnes

160 West 86th Street, New York, January 13, 1899 [NYHS]

My dear Mr. Barnes: It will give me much pleasure to dine with you, and to meet your distinguished guests, on Friday, January 20, at 7:30 o'clock, at the Metropolitan Club.

To John M. Brown

160 West 86th Street, New York, January 13, 1899 [LC]

My dear Mr. Brown: We are but two days from the 15th, when you wished to begin printing for the new *Nelson*. A letter from Marston of Dec. 28 says, "I think we shall have to give you more time." I dont know whether he wrote the same to you, but the reason is he had felt sure that the letters to Lady N., upon which the attack in *Literature*[1] was based, were in the Bridport Collection, in Br. Museum; while now he is satisfied

---

1. The only one of the captains who was stationed ashore in the area was John W. Philip, class of 1861, who was Commandant of the New York Navy Yard. During the Spanish-American War he commanded the *Texas*, and was famous for his admonition, "Don't cheer, boys, the poor devils are dying," and for the accuracy of his fire.

1. Between February and April 1898, this London weekly had published some newly found Nelson letters and the corrected text of parts of his diary.

they are not and was taking measures to get them, by corresponding with *Literature* or otherwise. Personally, I regret to delay because I am sure my critic put forward at once the best foot against me; and if he has nothing more in reserve he cant begin to prove his case, or to shake mine on the particular point. It will, however, probably be best to await at least his next letter, which I hope may arrive on the *St. Louis* due tomorrow.

Meanwhile, I think, and am fully persuaded that you will be able to print page proof at once if you wish as far as Vol I, p. 295; without the interposition of galleys. After that, probably, there will be some slight interpolations to alter the pagination; because Chap IX runs to the bottom of p. 316. This fact however may induce me to omit the details I have for insertion, so far as the larger book is concerned.

The last chapter of Vol I will, I think, receive about 4000 additional words —say 10 pages. I do not know how you will regard this, with reference to the size of the two volumes—No 1 being already the more voluminous. I cannot speak positively on this point however till I receive the material which Marston writes me is on the way, and until I know what he may hope for additional.

So far as yet indicated the changes in Vol 2 will be slight, but just what their effect may be as regards the pagination of the bigger book I cannot tell.

My idea is when we decide to begin that I can keep well ahead of you because of the start of nearly 300 pages, which require practically no change. I should like you to entertain the idea of sparing me proof reading on such smooth ground. The distinctly new matter of course I should want to read both in galley and page.

Upon the whole my present feeling is we had better wait to hear further from Marston; for, although I am convinced nothing will change materially the first 280 pages, it is just possible something might. I have told you all I know, if you think it expedient to begin type setting now, I can send at once 120 pages, and the remainder of the 300 by a week hence.

To John D. Long

160 West 86th Street, New York, January 16, 1899 [MHS]

Dear Mr. Long: While you were good enough to dispense me from replying to your letter of the 1st, you will believe that I should not have availed myself of such permission had not a combination, of press of work and indisposition, prevented my doing so promptly.

After looking the matter up in the appending to Bu. Navn. report,[1] I

---

1. Appendix to the Report of the Chief of the Bureau of Navigation, 1898.

find that the navy convoy was reported ready to proceed Sat. evening, June 4. My *recollection* is very clear that on the morning of June 8, when Southerland's[2] report of a Spanish squadron was recd., our anxiety was increased by the fact that we had gone home the evening before expecting the transports to sail on the morning of the 8th. Whether they would have got away I dont know, but they were stopped. The rest of the record, however, is clear. When the naval vessels returned from scouring the place where the suspicious sails were reported, they had to coal, and the result was (p. 675) that they left Key West for the rendezvous the same day, June 14, that the transports sailed from Tampa (Remey's and Hunker's[3] telegrams, p. 675). The delay in the final sailing was from the 8th to at least the 14th, unless I am wrong as to the army's readiness on the 8th; and was due to Southerland's report, and the action taken on it.

As regards the panic, I was speaking more from the popular point of view, as represented in the press and in general conversation. Since your letter, I have had three occasions to observe the impressions of other men, at dinner tables, in conversation, not originated by me. The coincidence was singular, as I had your letter in my mind; and I find that all those present agreed in the fact that very exaggerated apprehensions were felt, and precautions taken by the seaboard populations. Writing as I was for the public as well as for the navy, hoping to convey ideas useful for the future, if a similar future should arise, I felt justified in pointing pretty sharply the baseless nature of much of the fears, as well as the proper means of securing us against the recurrence of the same.

With regard to the function of the Flying Squadron, I think there is no real difference between us. Its object I apprehend to be as you say; to attack the Spanish fleet if it came north. That, however, in a military sense, is coast protection; the offense-defensive, as some call it. My point was that proper fortification of the coast, would have released that squadron, for offensive operations on the Cuban coast. I develop this further in succeeding papers.

I feel much indebted to you for your trouble in criticizing the papers.[4] Even when a man thinks himself substantially right, it is helpful to see that his words may require modification, either by softening, or retrenchment, or amplification.

---

2. William Henry Hudson Southerland, class of 1872, was commanding officer of the converted yacht *Eagle* in 1898.
3. Commodore George C. Remey, who commanded a division of the North Atlantic Squadron in 1898; and John Jacob Hunker, class of 1866, commanding officer of the gunboat *Annapolis*.
4. "The War on the Sea and Its Lessons. Part I. How the Motive of the War Gave Direction to Its Earliest Movements," *McClure's Magazine* (December 1898); Part II. "The Effect of Deficient Coast Defense on the Movement of the Navy," *ibid.* (January 1899).

If you should ever happen to have the curiosity to look at the telegram I sent from Paris, April 29th,[5] to State Department you will recognize the relation my present papers bear to the general ideas with which I approached the subject. The telegram seemingly never got on the Navy Dept. files, and I had to recover it, for myself, through the State Dept.

To John M. Brown

160 West 86th Street, New York, January 18, 1899 [LC]

My dear Mr. Brown: I was very glad to see from the cheque recd. yesterday that the old books are still doing well.

A letter from Marston tells me that there is no chance of getting access to the Lady Nelson letters—that it has in fact been refused. This being settled, I shall proceed tomorrow to read *again* the articles in *Literature*, so as to be sure that no change in the text will be needed before a certain place. Assured on that point I will forward the pages as fast as read, beginning I hope tomorrow certainly on Friday. Meanwhile, from my accounts from the other side, from both Marston and Stevens, I hope the data I want will soon be here, in time not to involve any great delay. The table of contents will of course have to wait till pagination is advanced.

My idea is to write another preface for this edition, additional to the other, and referring to it. In the second I propose to notice my critics, sufficiently to point out the triviality, or the mistakes of their criticism; avoiding, as far as possible that offensively magisterial manner which critics affect. There is nothing, I fully believe, in what has been said, to shake in the least whatever value the work ever possessed.

To John D. Long

160 West 86th Street, New York, January 19, 1899 [MHS]

Dear Mr. Long: Dining out last night I found myself close to Genl. (Wallace) Randolph, who was, I believe, Chief of Artillery with Shafter's[1] corps. I asked him whether it was true that the expedition was ready, when held up by the report of a Spanish division. He replied yes, that four transports had already gone down the bay; and that in the intervening time water had been used to such an extent on board some vessels as to require

---

5. *See* Mahan to Day, April 29, 1898.

1. Major General William R. Shafter, commanding Army forces in Cuba, 1898.

rewatering before another start, involving a fresh delay. One man's memory of course is not final demonstration; but it shows the need of establishing the point decisively, for such recollections find their way through society and become part of the stock of belief as commonly held.

To John S. Barnes

160 West 86th Street, New York, January 21, 1899 [NYHS]

My dear Mr. Barnes: I scarcely understand how, even amid the many miscellaneous adieus of last evening, I managed to leave without expressing to my host the pleasure I had received from his hospitality; and you can imagine my confusion of face when I realized I had not done so. At least, however, it gives me the occasion to write you, and not only to say that I enjoyed the evening extremely myself, but to congratulate you upon the success of the gathering in all its features.

Wishing you a pleasant stay in Madison, and hoping that I may be fortunate enough to find you at home some time after your return, believe me [etc.].

To Henry Cabot Lodge

160 West 86th Street, New York, February 7, 1899 [MHS]

My dear Mr. Lodge: I shall allow myself the pleasure of congratulating you upon the ratification of the treaty.[1] We have a long row to hoe yet, but I believe that, having no two-thirds yoke left on our neck, the country is now fairly embarked on a career which will be beneficent to the world and honorable to ourselves in the community of nations.

I try to respect, but cannot, the men who utter the shibboleth of self government, and cloud therewith their own intelligence, by applying it to people in the childhood stage of race development.

Pray make my compliments to Mrs. Lodge, who I know shares to the full the satisfaction of yourself and of us all.

---

1. The Treaty of Paris, signed on December 10, 1898.

To William H. Rideing[1]

160 West 86th Street, New York, February 18, 1899 [YUL]

Dear Sir: I dont quite understand from yours of yesterday whether you *want* an article on Farragut's youth such as I said I could give. As regards any other subject, I dont now think of such, neither can I afford the time to ransack my store of information, such as it is, to find a theme which, when found, might not suit your magazine. The Farragut, as I described it, I could do without serious encroachment upon my existing promises of work.

To John D. Long

160 West 86th Street, New York, February 26, 1899 [MHS]

Dear Mr. Long: I have to thank you for the copy of Hunker's letter to Southerland.[1]

I have read it twice attentively. It is clear that the expedition, so far as the army was concerned, could not have started on the day which we were at the time given to understand; i.e. June 8th. It seems equally clear that much delay was occasioned by the telegram of Southerland's report, which was the point I desired to emphasize. The delay was improved—or more properly was beneficial—in permitting a larger number of troops to go; but I should say from Hunker's letter there can be no question that delay there was. This in no way reflected upon the navy at large, and if any expression of mine seems to imply it, I will to the utmost of my power correct it. No such impression has ever been in my mind; but I thought then, and think now, that the precipitancy with which the report was brought—or, it may be more accurate to say, the failure to wait till daylight to test an appearance antecedently most improbable—was a grave fault on the part of the officer. I dont suppose there was a man on our Board who believed the report to be well-founded; but when sent by an officer of Southerland's intelligence, we thought then, and I think now, it would have been culpable to disregard it. Had that convoy been seriously injured, we had *no* army to replace the one it carried.

---

1. Editor of *Youth's Companion* and *North American Review*. He probably wanted the article for the former. Over the years Mahan's articles for the former publication included: "An Old Time Frigate" (September 22, 1898), an account of his cruise in the *Congress*; "The Youth of Admiral Farragut" (June 28, 1900); "The Personal Factor in Naval History" (October 29, 1907), Part V of a series written by Woodrow Wilson, James Bryce, and others; and "The Seaman" (November 6, 1913), Part VI of a series "The Making of Successful Men."

1. *See* Mahan to Long, January 16, 1899.

The precipitation to carry the report, when waiting a few hours for daylight would have tested the matter, is one of those lessons which the service should take to heart.

I shall of course be at pains to bring my paper[2] into strict accordance with the facts, as now shown to me. I fear it may be too late to make the change in my final paper, due to appear April 1. What I say, however, is entirely general, no names mentioned, and the whole incident treated merely as a military lesson. It is mentioned, also, wholly incidentally. The date June 8 is really the only thing out.

To James Ford Rhodes

160 West 86th Street, New York, March 26, 1899 [MHS]

My dear Mr. Rhodes: Your note with its interesting quotations reached me but a very short time before I left Boston, and it has not been easy for me to acknowledge it since. The line between controlling events and being controlled by them, would, I imagine, be difficult to draw; and, as in most matters, truth is best secured by holding both sides of the proposition—men both control events and are controlled by them. A mighty movement cannot be withstood, but may be guided, or deflected. Between events and man's will there is a resultant of forces.

I should in any event have written you to express the pleasure I received from last Monday's dinner. A well selected company of four to six of the same sex, or not exceeding eight of the two sexes, gives I fancy the maximum of social pleasure that the table affords. Conversation can be general and not so engrossing as to prevent enjoying the courses. You were certainly successful on that occasion.

To Joseph E. Craig

160 West 86th Street, New York, March 28, 1899 [NA]

My dear Craig: Would you be good enough to send me the course which a sailing vessel would most profitably follow from Madeira to Barbados, profiting by the trade winds—a *general* reply.

---

2. "The War on the Sea and Its Lessons. Part V. The Guard Set Over Cervera and the Watch Kept on Camara," *McClure's Magazine* (April 1899).

To Francis V. Greene[1]

160 West 86th Street, New York, April 5, 1899 [LC]

My dear Greene: I have not yet had time to read Sampson's article,[2] nor shall have for some days. The publishers wish to get out a cheap edition of *Nelson*, & the English publisher is clamorous for speedy delivery, as this is their best season; but I have not been willing to let it go out without some revision, necessitated by certain criticisms & by some new matter I have found. The result is I have sworn off all other mental exercise until this is completed.

In a general way, my view was, and is, that our center of operations was Havana, with Cienfuegos, and that, until definite news was had, that our squadrons should remain at the center, and do no guess work as to probable movements of the enemy. The trip to San Juan began some days before I reported, and as soon as I had time to recognize, which I did not for a day or two, the excentric character of the movement, I was anxious that the fleets should regain their positions and be held in readiness there for instant action. The *Indiana*[3] was hopelessly slow—though not so bad as the monitors.

To John M. Brown

160 West 86th Street, New York, April 7, 1899 [LC]

My dear Mr. Brown: I enclose my proposed preface to Second Edition. I would be glad if you would scrutinize it carefully, either, or both, personally, and by any one in whom you have confidence, to see if anything jars upon your feeling of taste, or of discretion. I think such judgment best passed upon it when in print, & I should be glad to receive back *as soon* as *possible* proofs for correction, and your own opinion upon the matter. The passage marked with blue brackets in enclosed, I had some idea of putting foot note, referring to the magazine where it may appear, but I fear time will not allow this.

My aim has been to answer, without seeming to attach needless importance to, the criticisms of Badham in the *Eng. Hist. Mag*,[1] and those of

---

1. Major General Greene, USMA class of 1870, took part in the second assault on Manila.
2. W. T. Sampson, "The Atlantic Fleet in the Spanish War," *Century Magazine* (April 1899).
3. A 10,288-ton battleship commissioned in 1895 and capable of making 15.55 knots. Sister ship of the *Massachusetts* and the *Oregon*.

1. F. P. Badham, "Nelson and the Neapolitan Republicans," *English Historical Review* (April 1898).

Literature—at the same time not naming them. I have felt obliged to credit *Literature*, *in loco*, when I have availed myself of its little grains of new matter.

You have seen my appointment to the Hague.[2]

To Ralph Pulitzer

Draft Telegram   N.P., N.D. Probably, New York, April 8, 1889 [LC]

Accept *World*'s offer[1] as per your letter of April 7 conditioned only by mine mailed today by special delivery which you should receive by 8 p.m.

To J. Franklin Jameson

160 West 86th Street, New York, April 8, 1899 [LC]

My dear Sir: Replying to yours of the 28. ult, my going on the Peace Commission of course prevents my undertaking the review of La Roncières' book.[1] Otherwise I should have accepted it if you felt at liberty to give me plenty of time. If you choose to take the chance upon my return, I will probably be able to do it.

I should not wish to review Barnes's book.[2]

To Robert U. Johnson

160 West 86th Street, New York, April 8, 1899 [NYPL]

Dear Mr. Johnson: I cannot at this moment lay my hand on your letter, which I had before me yesterday. I think, however, you judge rightly in believing the public a little weary of papers on the late war. If I write at

---

2. Mahan had been appointed to serve on the American delegation to the First Hague Peace Conference.

1. Possibly, to report his impressions of the First Hague Conference for the *New York World*. He seems to have published nothing in the *World*, however.

1. Charles de la Roncière, *Histoire de la marine française*. Paris: E. Plon, Nourrit et cie., 1899–   .

2. James Barnes, *David G. Farragut*. Boston: Small, Maynard and Company, 1899. Or perhaps Jameson offered Mahan Barnes's other publication of the same year, *Drake and His Yeomen* New York: Macmillan, 1899.

all, it would be better some months after the appearance of your now current articles. I have ideas on the Santiago fight which I have not seen enounced elsewhere. If no one else strikes them, they may be valuable. The matter had therefore better stand open, as you suggest, neither the *Century* nor I committed, for future decision. Of course the Peace Commission temporarily arrests all my work. Fortunately, I am at a good halting place.

To John M. Brown

160 West 86th Street, New York, April 15, 1899 [LC]

Dear Mr. Brown: I have not been able before to reply to yours of the 11th. I am sorry Marston is in any way dissatisfied. I wrote him again yesterday that until I got Ruffa's letters I had to hold the printing beyond p. 375; that I read them last Monday, and on Wednesday notified you that revision was completed & that you could print as fast as you chose. This a.m. I recd. from printers the re-set pages 376–80 which are now in the mail, approved. The proofs of chaps XIV–XVIII have all been corrected also, and mailed back last night—the day I got them. The map is sealed for mailing, with crosses in red indicated, and I shall mail it with this. As regards the "get up" of the cheap Ed.,[1] I have left it in your hands, as I do all technical matters. It is evident that in a one vol book you must have either bulk, or fine print. Personally I should prefer the former, as I think you have done.

Upon the *McClure* papers I can do no work before departure, probably not before return. I will bear in mind what you say about welding them together. For title, when I can get time to think, I may find one. I have done nothing but work at *Nelson*, and the mag. article on him.[2] Both are now finished, I rejoice, but I have one more mag article promised months ago.

Marston has certainly done everything I have asked of him, although I was not wholly satisfied with the judgment of one man he employed in the Br. Museum Mss. I then went, as I should have done at first to Stevens, who has very great experience in such matters; but to him I gave comprehensive orders, which I had not to Marston. The result is I got all I wanted, and a bill of near £20. The latter was perfectly fair, even moderate, but it shows M. was not to blame in being cautious.

---

1. In 1899 Little, Brown and Company published a single-volume, 764-page *Life of Nelson*.
2. "The Neapolitan Republicans and Nelson's Accusers," *English Historical Review* (July 1899).

To John M. Brown

160 West 86th Street, New York, April 16, 1899 [LC]

My dear Mr. Brown: Before I went to Europe last year, you were kind enough to offer to advance me some money if needed. It was not then necessary, but it may be convenient to me this year, in view of the wholly unexpected occasion of my being sent to the Hague, & Mrs. Mahan possibly accompanying me. I write to ask therefore whether if I find it necessary, you could advance me a thousand dollars by May 1; and possibly later, by July 1, five hundred more. The sum will be perfectly covered, if, as I understand, Marston takes 5,000 copies of the Revised *Nelson* independent of any sales of other [of] my books.

I hate to trouble you, but I do not know in what way the Govt. proposes to reimburse my expenditures.[1] It often refuses payment until *after* the expense is incurred, taking no regard of current expenses.

[P.S.] I will send by express tomorrow the two books requested by the Library and the others will follow very soon.

To James Ford Rhodes

160 West 86th Street, New York, April 28, 1899 [MHS]

Dear Mr. Rhodes: Thank you very much for your letter of the 25th, which reached me only yesterday. I shall be very glad to meet you again at the Hague. The Secretary to the Comm.[1] writes me that rooms have been taken for us at the Hotel Vieux Doelen, or at a house connected with it, I dont clearly understand which. I trust the Conference may realize whatever the time is ripe for; what that is is not immediately clear to my mind.[2]

---

1. On April 18, 1899, George Frederick William Holls, Secretary of the U. S. Commission, wrote to Mahan concerning financial arrangements for the trip to the Hague. Mahan was to be paid $500.00, and to be provided a "best" double stateroom for the voyage. So that the delegates should not be personally out of pocket for expenses, the Commission was to be accompanied by a disbursing officer. Holls had reserved two rooms for the Mahans on the *St. Louis*, but the Government would only pay for one of them. The cost of the second was $325.00. Mrs. Mahan stayed at home.
1. G. F. W. Holls, who was an internationally famous New York lawyer, with strong German affiliations. He desired the close friendship of Germany, England, and the United States, and advocated that all three should work in harmony with Russia.
2. For a witty and well-documented account of The Hague Conference, *see* Calvin DeArmond Davis, *The United States and the First Hague Conference*. Ithaca, New York: Cornell University Press, 1962.

To John D. Long

My dear Mr. Long: As I see the *Evening Post* of this city is trying to pick to pieces your speech before the Essex Club,[1] I borrow a moment from the hurry of packing to say to you how much solid common sense I found in it. Of course I am of your way of thinking, but common sense, like good taste, is the final verdict of the great mass of sensible people, and that I am persuaded you have with you. The trivialities to which the *Post* is driven, and the calm logic of a respectable Democratic paper like the *Times*, alike endorse the course of the Administration.

To John M. Brown

Hotel Vieux Doelen, The Hague, May 26, 1899 [LC]

My dear Mr. Brown: I have not wholly lost sight of the title for the next small book, but I have not struck any which I would wish to commit myself to as a finality. Would not something like that adopted by McClure, "Lessons from the Spanish War" answer temporarily for notices? To this might be added "and other Papers." The first, however, embraces so large a proportion of the proposed book that it is entitled to the leading place, in both title page and cover. Personally, I should prefer "A Study of the War between the U.S. & Spain," study being a less presumptuous word than lessons. My mind has been excessively dull since I stopped working a month ago, and rouses only under the influence of something more immediately stimulating than the search for a title.

I have been here now ten days. We have just got really to work & it is impossible yet to foresee the duration of our session. I suppose however that we will get through by the 1st July more or less. If so, I intend taking a fortnight or so on this side, hoping to reach home about August 1st. This country has interest but the weather has been detestably cold, raw & gloomy. Our fine wind, westerly, is their abomination & prevails.

---

1. Long had addressed the guests at the Dewey Day dinner at Young's Hotel, Boston, at which the speakers were introduced by George von L. Meyer, Secretary of the Essex Club. Long's speech was a tribute to Dewey and the Navy, and a defense of the administration's expansionist policy, especially with regard to the Philippines.

To John D. Long

My dear Mr. Long: This morning's papers tell us that the question of maintaining offensive operations in the Philippines has been under consideration by our Govt.; and one, the *Manchester Guardian*, states that they were to be suspended. This, however, is contradicted by the *Standard*, which I believe & hope is better informed.

I feel it to be somewhat presumptuous to intrude my opinion, unasked; but the trust with which you honored me last year leads me to hope I may be forgiven for saying, that, from the point of view of *general* military principle and experience, in dealing with enemies of this character, the decision would be disastrous, and if in the *particular* case the commander on the spot favors continuance in offensive movement, all reasons would combine to adopt his view.

The effect of inaction upon our own troops would be demoralizing, especially as they are largely new to the habits of disciplined endurance; while relaxation would not only encourage the immediate enemy, but its influence would not unlikely be felt among the ill-disposed in Cuba & Porto Rico.

I doubt if our public at all realize under what odds we have been contending in Luzon. I do not refer to numerical shortness, though that there has unavoidably been, but to the comparative rawness of our troops, a condition which must still last some time; for our new regulars, though admirable material, (I am here quoting the opinion of Col. Lee, the British attaché), are still only recruits. This difficulty is the inevitable result of a large task thrown upon a nation that has heretofore maintained a very small army. It will diminish with every month, and when our men are "aguerri," to use the expressive French word, they will handle the business decisively.

I have never seen any reason for discouragement in the military conditions; while, as regards the political considerations inseparable from a popular form of government, I am satisfied that steady persistence in aggressive advance will most surely lead to the success which people too impatiently desire.

It may interest you to know that, meeting Mr. Low[1] casually this morning, he remarked "I dont like the news from the Philippines." He had seen the *Guardian* which is regularly sent to each of us. I then told him what the *Standard* said, at which he expressed himself relieved, and upon my saying I *thought* of writing to either you or Mr. Hay,[2] he said he hoped I

---

1. Seth Low.
2. John Hay had succeeded Day as Secretary of State in September 1898.

[635]

would, & to my inquiry replied he had no objection to being quoted. The opinion of this eminent civilian, joined to my own, is I hope but one of many the President is receiving.

I have written with the view that you show this letter to the President, if you thought proper. May I add that in case serious doubt arises, I hope that Genl. Francis V. Greene, who was last year in Luzon, may be consulted. He is a man who to great brilliancy of intellect, and military acquirement, adds unusual energy and sound judgment.

[P.S.] Army officers used to say that our Western Indians began to be thoroughly overcome only when our troops gave up the habit of winter quarters, & followed the savages through the bitter winters of the plains.

To John D. Long

International Conference at The Hague, June 7, 1899 [MHS]

My dear Mr. Long: I have received an application from a Russian officer for detailed information concerning the course at the War College in its development and present condition. I replied that this could best be shown by successive reports of the Presidents of the College, and at his request I undertook to ask that copies should be sent him for the last ten years if possible. They are included in the yearly reports of the Bureau of Navigation, until the College was transferred to the Asst. Secretary.

Would you give directions that they be sent as far as possible, from & including 1886. The officer's rank & name is—*Lieutenant de Vaissian Ovtchinnikow*, and I would suggest sending through the Russian Embassy at Washington.

[P.S.] If there should seem any irregularity in sending through the Embassy data, for which the request had not come through the Embassy, the package addressed to Lt. Ovtchinnikow at the Department of Marine, St. Petersburg would doubtless reach him.

They wish to establish a College of their own, with which this officer is to be associated.

To James Ford Rhodes

Vieux Doelen, The Hague, June 10, 1899 [MHS]

Dear Mr. Rhodes: Will not Mrs. Rhodes and yourself give me the pleasure of dining with me at Scheveningen, or at this hotel, as may best please you, to-morrow, Sunday, at 7.30.

I should have said Scheveningen solely, but for the weather, which takes something of the color out of a summer sea-side. If you decide for it I will call for you myself with a carriage.

To James R. Thursfield

International Conference at The Hague, June 17, 1899 [LC]

My dear Mr. Thursfield: I fear I shall not be able to accept the very flattering offer you make me from Sir Donald Wallace. Since my *Life of Nelson* was completed, near two and a half years ago, I have been entirely stopped from serious book work by occasional articles, and the necessity of limiting myself very strictly in that direction has been more and more forced upon my mind. I have two books which I have been *intending* to write for two years, and I must not postpone undertaking them farther than my return home.

May I suggest that, if my memory serves me, there is no article on Impressment in the *Encyclopedia?*

I have asked Prof. Gardiner[1] to send you the July number of the *Eng. Hist. Mag.*, in which I am to have an article "The Neapolitan Republicans & Nelson's Accusers." This was forced from me, and has given me more trouble than any equal amount of result I have ever produced. The Revised *Life* will doubtless come into your hands in the way of review. The principal modifications are indicated in the preface.[2]

I will be greatly obliged to you if at a convenient moment you will express to Sir Donald my sense of the compliment paid by his request.

With kind remembrance to Mrs. Thursfield [etc.].

To the Comité d'Examen

The Hague, N.D.   Probably, June 20, 1899 [LC]

1. In maritime wars of the future, it will be frequent occurrence that merchant steamers, yachts, vessels of news agencies, and others will be present at the scene of a naval engagement. In many such cases they will be under a neutral flag, and it is at least difficult to say how far the admiral

---

1. Samuel Rawson Gardiner, historian of the English Civil War.
2. The revision enlarged mainly upon Nelson's activities at Naples and modified earlier less critical judgments. The new material was also published in the *English Historical Review* article to which Mahan refers.

of a belligerent fleet has power to keep them distant, they being on the common ground of the open sea.

2. In case of a serious accident, whether in a fleet battle, or in a duel between single ships, whereby men, whether many or few, belonging to either belligerent are overboard and in danger of drowning, it would be, to say the least, an act of humanity, in strict accord with the objects of the Geneva Convention, for such neutrals to save struggling men, when possible.

3. But, as such men are but *hors de combat* by the incidents of the fight they may be considered justly as part of the results of the fight; part of the gain, very probably, to the victor. This is the more evident, because now that there are no men aloft, their being in the water will probably be the result of a great catastrophe, such as the sinking of a ship. While such sinking may be the result of collision with a friend, it seems more likely and simpler, in formulating a rule, to attribute it to the act of the enemy.

4. Victors, however willing to use every means accident may place in their power to save life, in the cause of humanity, will certainly object strongly to see the spoils of battle carried from them under cover of a neutral flag.

5. I propose, therefore, for consideration, amendment and adoption the following proposition:

a. In case of neutral merchant vessels, yachts, boats, or neutral vessels of any kind, being on the scene of a naval engagement, which may as an act of humanity, save wounded men or men in danger of drowning, such neutral vessels shall not be considered as having violated their neutrality by that fact alone. They will, in so doing, however, act at their own risk and peril.

b. Men thus rescued shall not be considered under the protection of the neutral flag, in case a demand for their surrender is made by a ship of war of either belligerent. If such demand is made, the men so rescued shall be given up.

c. In case no such demand is made, the men so rescued, having been delivered from the consequences of the fight by neutral interposition, are to be considered as prisoners of war to the other party, not to serve again during the war until duly exchanged. The Contracting Governments engage to prevent as far as possible, such persons from serving without exchange.[1]

I will observe, in concluding, that neutral vessels, in the case supposed, not acting under direct commissioning nor supervision by their own governments, cannot be practicably subjected to such guarantees as are the hospital ships contemplated by the other articles proposed. Experience shows that ships, not so guaranteed, are capable of many irregularities. It is not only

---

1. Section 5, parts a, b, and c, appear in a revised form in James Brown Scott, ed., *Instructions to the American Delegates to the Hague Peace Conferences and Their Official Reports.* (New York: Oxford University Press, 1916), p. 43, as a section of the "Paper read by Captain Mahan before the Second Committee of the Peace Conference on June 20, 1899." *See* Mahan to Fisher, June 21, 1899.

supposable, but very possible, that, having been permitted to save life, they may arrogate to themselves the privilege, by virtue of superior speed, or of other accident, to carry off the men they have picked up. Unless this difficulty is obviated, belligerents may strenuously prevent their interposition, though in the cause of humanity. All navies are short of seamen, and still more of trained officers. The escape of such, under the conditions, and their return to active service, cannot be viewed with indifference.

To John A. Fisher[1]

The Hague, June 21, 1899 [LC]

Copy. Suggestion for Final Form sent Fisher June 21:

In case any of the vessels mentioned in Articles 1, 2, 3 and 6,[2] shall upon the scene of a naval battle take on board, for any reason, combatants belonging to either belligerent, such combatants shall not be considered under the cover of the neutral flag, while on board, but shall be liable to capture, or re-capture. In case a demand for them shall be made by a national ship of war, they must be given up, and shall then have the same status as though they had not been under a neutral flag.

If no such demand is made, and the said combatants are carried into a port, whether neutral or belligerent, they shall not be free to serve again during the war, unless exchanged. The Contracting Governments undertake that, when belligerents, they will as far as possible prevent such persons from serving, until exchanged.

It is known to the members of the Sub-committee, by which these articles were accepted, that I stated there was an important omission, to rectify which I desired an additional article or articles. The omission was to provide against the case of a neutral vessel, such as is mentioned in Article 6, picking up *naufragés* on the scene of a naval battle, and carrying them away, either accidentally or intentionally. What, I asked, is the status of such *combattants naufragés?*

My attention being absorbed by the case of vessels under Article 6, it was not until last night that I noticed that there was equally an omission to provide for the status of *combattants naufragés*, picked up by hospital ships. In order that nonprofessional men, men not naval officers, may certainly comprehend this point, allow me to develop it.

---

1. Admiral Fisher, 1st Baron Fisher of Kilverstone, First Sea Lord, 1904–1910 and 1914–1915, was a member of the British delegation at the First Hague Conference, where he was appointed Chairman of the Comité de Rédaction. *See* Mahan to Fisher, July 18, 1899.
2. *See* Mahan to U.S. Commission to the Peace Conference, July 26, 1899.

On a field of naval battle, the ships are constantly in movement; not merely the movement of a land battle, but a movement of progress, of translation from place to place, more or less rapid. The scene is here one moment; a half hour later it may be five miles distant. In such a battle it happens that a ship sinks; her crew become *naufragés*; the place of action shifts; it is no longer where these men are struggling for life; the light cruisers of their own side come to help, but they are not enough; the hospital ships with neutral flag come to help; neutral ships other than hospital ships also arrive; a certain number of *combattants naufragés* are saved on board neutral ships. To which belligerent do these men belong? It may happen that the neutral vessel, hospital or otherwise, has been with the fleet opposed to the sunken ship. After fulfilling her work of mercy, she naturally rejoins that fleet. The *naufragés combattants* fall into the power of the enemy, although it is quite possible that the fleet to which they belong may have had the advantage.

I maintain that unless some provision is made to meet this difficulty, much recrimination will arise. A few private seamen, more or less, a few sub-officers, may not matter, but it is possible that a distinguished general officer, or valuable officers of lower grade may be affected. This will tend to bring into discredit the whole system proposed for hospital ships; but further, while hospital ships, being regularly commissioned by their own government, may be supposed to act with perfect impartiality, such pre-supposition is not permissible in the case of vessels named in Article 6. Unless the status of *naufragés combattants* saved by them is defined, the grossest irregularities may be expected—the notoriety of which will fully repay the class of men who would perpetuate them.

As many cases may arise, all of which it is impossible to meet specifically, I propose the following additional articles based upon the single general principle, that *combattants naufragés*, being ipso facto *combattants hors de combat*, are incapable of serving again during the war, unless recaptured or until duly exchanged:

1. In the case of neutral vessels of any kind, hospital ships or others, being on the scene of a naval engagement, which may, as an act of humanity, save men in peril of drowning from the results of the engagement, such neutral vessels shall not be considered as having violated their neutrality by that fact alone. They will, however, in so doing act at their own risk and peril.

2. Men thus rescued shall not be considered under the cover of the neutral flag, in case a demand for their surrender is made by a ship of war of either belligerent. They are open thus to capture, or to recapture. If such demand is made, the men so rescued must be given up, and shall then have the same status as though they had not been under a neutral flag.

3. In case no such demand is made by a belligerent ship, the men so

rescued, having been delivered from the consequences of the fight by neutral interposition, are to be considered *hors de combat*, not to serve for the rest of the war, unless duly exchanged. The contracting Governments engage to prevent, as far as possible, such persons from serving until exchanged.

To John M. Brown

My dear Mr. Brown: In the new Ed. of *Nelson*, of which Marston has sent me a copy, I have found two misprints. The most important is on p. 444, line 13, "on *my* account" should be "on *any* account." The other on p. 590, line 4, "where they had been *seen*" should be "where they had been *sent*." The latter is self evident.

I am glad to hear that your spring business in general, and my books with it, has been doing so well. May I ask of you to do as you have done before, send to Mrs. Mahan at Quogue, N.Y. a cheque for the July settlement. I hope to be at home by August 10th, but though probable this is not quite certain, & there are some matters which I have asked her to attend to, if feasible.

I have no news of any interest to you. Upon my return I hope to take up at once the proposed Text Book, and to edit the Spanish War series for book form. I have declined a request to write an article on Sea Power for the *Encyclopedia Britannica*, because hindering my work.

[*Memorandum*][1]

The Hague, July 17, 1899 [LC]

Ayant été absent de la Haye, ce n'était qu'hier que j'ai lu le projet de rapport qui est maintenant devant la Commn.

Ayant considéré, anterieurement, que les conclusions de la 1e. Commn. étaient deja fixés, j'ai été surpris de trouver quelques choses tout-à-fait

---

1. These remarks were intended for discussion of a *Projet de Rapport* introduced by A. Raffalovich, a Russian delegate.

nouvelles: c'est à dire tout à fait à dehors de ce qui s'est passé, selon ma recollection, ou dans la Commn., ou dans la Sous-Commn., de laquelle j'étais membre.

Je dois supposer que c'était dans la compétence du rapporteur d'insérer, de cette manière, les deux stipulations proposées, c'est à dire de renouveler la Decln. de S. Petersbourg, et de consentir, à l'unanimité, à deux propositions qui avaient été rejetées par la Delgn. des E.U., en y fixant une limitation de cinq ans.

Quant à la première de ces deux, je ne puis, ni parler, ni voter, ne l'ayant pas discutée avec notre Delgn., par manque de temps. Je regrette beaucoup un délai à des procédés déjà très prolongés, mais la matière est nouvelle, et je ne puis pas faire autrement.

Quant aux propositions nombrées 2 et 3 il faut remarquer que les objections qui ont determiné le vote des Etats-Unis ne disparaissent pas par une limitation de 5 ans.

Il est possible que quelques uns, parmi nos collègues d'autres pays, ont pensé que nous, la Délégn. des E.U., avons agi par motifs pas assez bien considérés, dans nos votes précédents.

Je dois, donc, expliquer que, en refusant d'accepter la prohibition d'obus à gas asphyxiants, la Délégn. des Etats Unis croit que cette prohibition n'est ni logique, ni dans la voie d'humanité, ayant égard des autres moyens de destruction qui restent permis. Pour l'unanimité nous ferions beaucoup; mais nous ne pouvons pas nier nos convictions, ni admettre comme vérité ce que nous croyons contraire à la raison. C'est mieux, selon nous, avoir raison, seuls, que d'avoir tort a l'unanimité.

Quant à l'emploi des balles qui s'épanouissent, etc, quoique cela appartient plus exclusivement à mon associé, Capte. Crozier,[2] je désire l'appuyer, en disant que, selon mes propres convictions, la définition adoptée par la Commn. manque de précision; qu'elle se mêle de details, au lieu d'adopter un principe, tel que celui qui a été proposé par le Capte. Crozier; c'est à dire de prohiber les projectiles dont l'effet aille au delà de ce qui soit nécessaire pour mettre un homme, a l'instant même, hors du combat.

J'ai cru qu'il est du à notre Delgn., à moi même, et à la Conférence, d'expliquer franchement et nettement, pourquoi nous ne pouvons pas changer nos votes sur ces deux propositions, et je demande que ces explications entrent, in extenso, dans le procès verbal d'aujourd'hui.

Quant à renouveler la Decln. de S. Petersbourg, si la Commn. désire, je demanderai les instructions de la Delegn. des E.U. Je ne puis pas voter au moment.

---

2. William Crozier, U.S. Army, member of the U.S. Commission.

To John A. Fisher

The Hague, July 18, 1899 [LC]

My dear Sir John: I intend to forward by the first mail the articles concerning the Geneva Cross agreed upon by our Sub. Com. In doing so I propose to indicate the omission which, as you know, I consider has been made viz: to provide against the case of a neutral vessel, which has picked up men in danger of drowning from the scene of a naval battle, and has attempted to carry them off.[1] Not only in fairness to those who have differed with me but in order to avoid any disappointing delays on the part of my govt., I wish to be quite sure of the accuracy with which I state the argument of the Comité d'Examen as well as my own. Will you be good enough to cast your eye over the enclosed and see if in any way I err, either by excess or defect, as regards the views of the Comité.

I am instructed by the Delegation of the United States to say, with reference to the three additional articles proposed by them, and now withdrawn, that they are withdrawn not because of any change of opinion as to the necessity to provide for the cases they were intended to meet, and which are very likely to arise, but in order to facilitate the conclusion of the work of the Conference.

The Delegation wishes it to be distinctly understood that, finding the ten articles materially defective, in not providing for the cases indicated, they accept them only provisionally, subject to the subsequent approval of their government, to which they reserve entire liberty of action; and, moreover, that it will be necessary for them to communicate to their government, in the fullest manner, the doubts they feel, with such recommendations as they may hereafter find necessary.

Acting under instructions (on the part of the Government of the United States), I ask the Committee's permission to abstain from voting on, or even discussing, the articles fixing the size of navies, and the expenditures for naval purposes, proposed by the representative of the Imperial Russian Navy; and for the following reasons:

Having regard to the population of the United States, and to the extent of their coastline, the naval force maintained has been heretofore, and still continues to be, far smaller, in proportion, than that of other great naval states.

Furthermore, the conditions which constitute the necessity for a navy, and control its development, have within the past year changed for the United States, so markedly, that it is impossible yet to foresee, with certainty, what degree of naval strength may be needed to meet them.

---

1. *See* Mahan to Fisher, June 21, 1899.

Under such circumstances, engagements of the definite character proposed by the Russian representative cannot be contracted with prudence; nor can even the precedent discussion be conducted with the precision, which is due to international proposals of so serious a nature.

[Enclosure]

Captain Mahan brought up for consideration, as requiring special provision, the case of a neutral vessel which, happening to be on the scene of a naval engagement, should save from drowning men who were exposed to that fate, in consequence of incidents of the combat. Capt. M. submitted to the Comité, a paper explanatory of his views, in which were embodied three propositions, tentative only so far, to cover the case in *all* its aspects.

Of the three propositions, the first, defining the immunity of the neutral for her act, did not differ essentially from the views of the Comité. The second was by the Comité considered to be met by the words of the report, on page 9, beginning with the words, "La situation à faire" etc. If the neutral vessel is met on the same, or on any subsequent day, with those men on board, by an enemy's cruiser, they become, on demand, prisoners of war, with whose destination the captor is at liberty to deal as he sees fit. It was considered also by the Comité that the men thus rescued fall under the words of Art 9—"qui tombent au pouvoir de l'autre belligérant."

Captain Mahan contended that there was still no adequate provision for the case of a neutral, which, having rescued men as stated, should seek, by means of superior speed, or through temporary inability of the victor to board her, to carry the men off. He cited the well-known case of the *Deerhound* taking off the *Alabama*'s men, by which they entirely escaped capture. The third proposition (c) submitted by him was intended to obviate the difficulty; and he rested it upon the ground of humanity, in that a victor would be less disposed to allow such humane intervention, if he was thereby to lose prisoners, among whom might be some of great importance.

The Comité saw no way to meet the case, or considered it already met by other provisions, either in the Article, or in the accompanying report. In this view Captain Mahan was unable to concur; nor did it seem to him that the report, valuable as it is as a commentary, elucidating the full meaning of the articles, could have the same binding force as the latter. It is unlikely that contracting nations, accepting the ten articles, will also pledge themselves to all the reasonings by which they are preceded.

Captain Mahan suggested, as a possible solution, the modifying of Article 10, in such sense that men thus rescued and landed on a neutral deck should be considered in the same light as if landed in a neutral port; a neutral deck being but the extension of the neutral territory, but this was not accepted.

To John A. Fisher

The Hague, July 18, 1899 [LC]

My dear Admiral: I have the honour to inform you that, having in view the difficulties which impede the adoption of the three additional articles proposed by me,[1] and referred to the *Comité de rédaction* of which you are president, and in order to facilitate the conclusion of the labors of the Conference, the Delegation of the United States withdraws those articles.

I beg you therefore to notify this withdrawal to the President of the Second Commission, in order that he may communicate it to the Conference, it being clearly understood that the communication will be made at a full meeting of the Conference, in order that opportunity may be allowed to this Delegation, to give such explanation of its reasons for the withdrawal as may seem to it necessary.

To John A. Fisher

The Hague, July 18, 1899 [LC]

My dear Fisher: Possibly because I am a pig-headed cuss, I am not wholly satisfied with Renault's form—I say nothing of his French, for I know nothing.[1] Moreover, I see no reason why I should not write to you in English. I wish particularly, however, to assure myself the opportunity for speech in the Conference, for which I look primarily to you; and I would suggest that your letter make perfectly clear to Martens,[2] that the withdrawal is to be formally announced by the Prest. of Second Commn. in full Conference. Otherwise, we may find that a communication to Dr. Staal,[3] privately, is considered to settle the matter, and it will never come before the Conference at all.

---

1. *See* Mahan to Fisher, June 21, 1899.

1. Enclosed in this letter was Mahan's translation into English (undated, but circa July 18, 1899) of a letter from Louis Renault, a French expert on international law and member of the Comité de Rédaction, to Fisher, which Fisher had forwarded to Mahan for information. In his letter, Renault listed the various objections of members of the Comité d'examen to Mahan's three proposals relating to the legal role of neutral and hospital ships that rescued survivors of naval engagements. (*See* Mahan to Fisher, June 21, 1899.)

2. Feodor de Martens was the second Russian delegate, and head of the Second Commission.

3. Baron de Staal was Russian Ambassador in London, and President of the Peace Conference of 1899.

To the U.S. Commission to the Peace Conference

I have the honor to submit to the Commission the following report, which I believe to be in sufficient detail, of the general proceedings, and of the conclusions, reached by the Second Committee of the Conference in relation to Articles 5 and 6 of the Russian Circular Letter of December 30, 1898.

In the original distribution of labor of the Conference, Articles 5, 6, and 7, of the said letter, were attributed to the Second Committee. The latter was sub-divided into two Sub-Committees, to one of which was assigned the articles 5 and 6, as both related to naval matters. Of this Sub-Committee I was a member, and it has fallen to me especially among the United States delegates, to follow the fortunes of the two articles named in their progress through the Sub-Committee, and through the Full Committee; but not through the smaller special Committee, the Comité de Rédaction, to which the Sub-Committee entrusted the formation of its views. Of that Comité de Rédaction I was not a member.

These two articles are as follows:

"5. Adaptation to naval wars of the stipulations of the Geneva Convention of 1864, on the base of the Additional Articles of 1868.

"6. Neutralization, for the same reason, of boats or launches employed in the rescue of the shipwrecked during or after naval battles."

The general desirability of giving to hospital vessels the utmost immunity, consistent with the vigorous prosecution of war, was generally conceded and met, in fact, with no opposition; but it was justly remarked at the outset, that measures must be taken to put under efficient control of the belligerents all hospital ships fitted out by private benevolence, or by neutrals, whether associations or individuals. It is evident that unless such control is explicitly affirmed, and unless the various cases that may arise, in which it may be needed, are, as far as possible, foreseen and provided for, incidents may well occur which will bring into inevitable discredit the whole system of neutral vessels, hospital or other, devoted to the benevolent assistance of the sufferers in war.

The first suggestion, offered almost immediately, was that the simplest method of avoiding such inconvenience would be for the said neutral vessels, being engaged in service identical with that of belligerent hospital vessels, to which it was proposed to extend the utmost possible immunity, should frankly enter the belligerent service by hoisting the flag of the belligerent to which it offered its services. This being permitted by general consent, and for purposes purely humanitarian, would constitute no breach

---

1. Published in Scott, *op. cit. See* Mahan to Comité d'Examen, June 20, 1899, Footnote 1.

of neutrality; which the control of either belligerent, when in presence, could be exercised, without raising those vexed questions of neutral rights, which the experience of maritime warfare shows to be among the most difficult and delicate problems that belligerents have to encounter.

This proposition was supported by me, as being the simplest and surest mode of avoiding difficulties easy to be foreseen, and which in my judgment are wholly unprovided for by the articles adopted by the Conference. The neutral ship is, by common consent, permitted to identify itself with the belligerent and his operations for certain laudable purposes, why not for the moment assume the belligerent's flag? The reasoning of the opposition was that such vessels should be considered in the same light as national vessels and that to require them to hoist a foreign flag would be derogatory (porterait atteinte) to the sovereignty of the state to which they belonged. This view prevailed.

The first three meetings of the Sub-Committee, May 25th, 30th and June 1st, were occupied in a general discussion of the Additional Articles of 1868, suggested by the Russian Letter of December 30, 1898, as the basis for the adaptation to naval wars of the Geneva Convention of 1864. In this discussion was also embraced Article 6 of the Russian letter, relating to the neutralization of boats engaged in rescuing the shipwrecked ((naufragés); that is, men overboard for any cause) during or after naval battles.

At the close of the second meeting it was decided that the president of the Sub-Committee should appoint the Comité de Rédaction, before mentioned. As finally constituted, this Comité de Rédaction contained a representative from Great Britain, from Germany, from Russia and from France. At the close of its third session the Sub-Committee was adjourned to await the report of the Comité de Rédaction. It again assembled and received the report on June 13th, this being the fourth meeting of the Sub-Committee.

The Comité de Rédaction embodied in ten Articles the conclusions of the Sub-Committee. The articles were preceded by a lucid and comprehensive report, the work chiefly of M. Renault, the French member of the Comité de Rédaction. This report embraces the reasoning upon which the adoption of the articles is supported. A copy of the report and of the articles (marked A) accompanies this letter.

Upon receiving the report and the articles, I pointed out to one of the members of the Comité de Rédaction, that no adequate provision was made to meet the case of men, who by accident connected with a naval engagement, such for instance, as the sinking of their ship, were picked up by a neutral vessel. The omission was one likely to occur to an American, old enough to remember the very concrete and pertinent instance of the British yacht *Deerhound* saving the men of the *Alabama*, including her captain, who were then held to be under the protection of the neutral flag. It requires no flight of imagination to realize that a hostile commander-in-chief, whom it has always been a chief object of naval warfare to capture, as well as other valuable officers, might thus escape the hands of a victor.

At the meeting of the Sub-Committee June 13th, I drew attention to this omission when the vote was reached on Article 6, which provides that neutral vessels of various classes, carrying sick, wounded or shipwrecked (*naufragés*) belligerents, cannot be captured for the mere fact of this transportation; but that they do remain exposed to capture for violations of neutrality which they may have committed. I had then—unaccountably now to myself—overlooked the fact that there was an equal lack of satisfactory provision in the case of the hospital ships under neutral flags, whose presence on a scene of naval warfare is contemplated and authorized by Article 5. It was agreed that I should appear before the Comité de Rédaction, prior to their final revision of the report and articles. This I did but after two hours, more or less, of discussion, I failed to obtain any modification in the report or the articles. When, therefore, on the 15th of June, the matter came before the full Second Commission, I contented myself,— as the articles were voted only ad referendum—subject to the approval of the governments—with registering our regret that no suitable provision of the kind advocated, had been made.

The matter was yet to come before the full Conference.[2] Before it did so, I had recognized that the difficulty I had noted concerning neutral vessels other than hospital ships, might arise equally as regards the latter, the presence of which was contemplated and authorized, whereas that of other neutral ships might very well be merely accidental. I accordingly drew up and submitted to the U.S. Commission three additional articles, preceding these with a brief summary of the conditions which might readily occasion the contingency against which I sought to provide. This paper (annexed and marked B) having received the approval of the Delegation, was read and the articles submitted to the Second Commission in a full session, held June 20, immediately prior to the session of the Conference at 4 P.M. the same day to ratify the work of the Committee. The three additional articles were referred to the Comité de Rédaction with instructions to report to the full Committee. The ten articles were then reported to the Conference and passed without opposition, under the reserve that the articles submitted by the United States Delegation were still to be considered.

Here matters rested for some time, owing, as I understand, to certain doubtful points arising in connection with the three proposed articles, which necessitated reference to the home governments by one or more of the delegations. Finally, I was informed that not only was there no possibility of a favorable report, nor, consequently of the three proposed ar-

2. Scott, *op. cit.*, p. 41, uses the word *committee*, rather than *Conference*.

ticles passing, but also that, if pressed to a full discussion, there could scarcely fail to be developed such differences of opinion upon the construction of the ten articles already adopted, as would imperil the unanimity with which they had before been received. This information was conveyed by me to the U.S. Commission, and after full consideration I was by it instructed to withdraw the articles. This was accordingly done immediately by letter, on July 18th, to Vice-Admiral Sir John Fisher, Chairman of the Comité de Rédaction, and through him to the President of the Second Commission.

At the subsequent meeting of the Full Conference, July 20th, the withdrawal being communicated by the President of the Second Committee, it was explained that this Commission, while accepting the ten articles and withdrawing its own suggested additions, must be understood to do so, not because of any change of opinion as to the necessity of the latter, but in order to facilitate the conclusion of the labors of the Conference; that the Commission were so seriously impressed with the defects of the ten articles, in the respects indicated, that it could sign them only with the most explicit understanding, that the doubts expressed before the Second Committee would be fully conveyed to the United States government, and the liberty of action of the latter wholly reserved, as to accepting the ten articles.

By this course the ten articles, which else might ultimately have failed of unanimous adoption, have been preserved intact, with several valuable stipulations embodied in them. But while there is much that is valuable, it seems necessary to point out to the Commission that to the hospital ships under neutral flags, mentioned in Article 3, and to neutral vessels in certain employments, under Article 6, are conceded a status and immunities hitherto unknown. While this is the case, there is not, in my opinion, in the articles, any clear and adequate provision to meet such cases as were meant to be met by the three articles proposed by the Commission, and which are perfectly conceivable and possible. Upon reflection, I am satisfied that no necessity exists for the authorization of hospital vessels under a neutral flag upon the scene of naval war, and that the adhesion of our government to such a scheme may be withheld without injury to any one. As regards Article 6, conceding immunities heretofore not allowed to neutral vessels—for the transport of belligerents has heretofore been a violation of neutrality, without reservation in favor of the sick and wounded—it appears to me objectionable and premature unless accompanied by reservations, in favor of the belligerent rights of capture and re-capture. These the articles fail to provide explicitly. For these reasons it is my personal opinion that Articles 3 and 6 should not be accepted by the Government of the United States. If the Delegation concur in this view, I recommend that such opinion be expressed in the general report.

To the U.S. Commission to the Peace Conference

N.P., N.D.   Probably, The Hague, late July, 1899 [HUL][1]

Gentlemen: I beg to make the following report concerning the deliberations and conclusions of the Peace Conference on the questions of disarmament, and of the limitations to be placed upon the development of the weapons of war, so far as navies are concerned.

These questions were embraced in the first four articles of the Russian Letter of December 30, 1898, and were by the Conference referred to a Committee, known as the First Committee. The latter was divided into two Sub-committees, which dealt with articles 2, 3, and 4, as they touched naval or military subjects, respectively. The general drift of these three articles was to suggest limitations, present and prospective, upon the development of the material of war, either by increase of power, and of consequent destructive effect, in weapons now existing, or by new inventions. Article 1, which proposed to place limits upon the augmentation of numbers in the personnel of armed forces, and upon increase of expenditure in the budgets, was reserved for the subsequent consideration of the full Committee.

As regards the development of material, in the direction of power to inflict injury, there was unanimous assent to the proposition that injury should not be in excess of that clearly required to produce decisive results; but in the attempt to specify limitations in detail, insurmountable obstacles were encountered. This was due, partly to the inherent difficulties of the questions themselves, partly to an apparent failure, beforehand, to give to the problem submitted that "étude préalable technique," a wish for which, expressed by the Conference to the governments represented, was almost the only tangible result of the deliberations.

Three propositions were, however, adopted; one, unanimously, forbidding during a term of five years the throwing of projectiles, or explosives, from balloons, or by other analagous methods. Of the two others, one, forbidding the use of projectiles the sole purpose of which was, on bursting, to spread asphyxiating or deleterious gases, was discussed mainly in the naval sub-committee. It received in that, and afterwards in the full Committee, the negative vote of the United States naval delegate alone, although of the affirmative votes several were given subject to unanimity of acceptance. In the final reference to the Conference, in full session, of the question of *recommending* the adoption of such a prohibition, the Delegation of Great Britain voted No, as did that of the United States.

As a certain disposition has been observed to attach odium to the view adopted by this Commission in this matter, it seems proper to state, fully and

---

1. Published in Scott, *op. cit. See* Mahan to Comité d'Examen, June 20, 1899, Footnote 1.

explicitly, for the information of the Government, that on the first occasion of the subject arising in Sub-Committee, and subsequently at various times in full Committee, and before the Conference, the United States naval delegate did not cast his vote silently, but gave the reasons, which at his demand were inserted in the reports of the day's proceedings. These reasons were, briefly: 1, that no shell emitting such gases is as yet, in practical use, or has undergone adequate experiment; consequently, a vote taken now would be taken in ignorance of the facts, as to whether the results would be of a decisive character, or whether injury in excess of that necessary to attain the end of warfare, the immediate disabling of the enemy, would be inflicted. 2, that the reproach of cruelty and perfidy, addressed against these supposed shells, was equally uttered formerly against fire-arms and torpedoes, both of which are now employed without scruple. Until we knew the effects of such asphyxiating shells, there was no saying whether they would be more or less merciful than missiles now permitted. 3, that it was illogical and not demonstrably humane, to be tender about asphyxiating men with gas, when all were prepared to admit that it was allowable to blow the bottom out of an iron-clad at midnight, throwing four or five hundred into the sea, to be choked by water, with scarcely the remotest chance of escape. If, and when, a shell emitting asphyxiating gases alone has been successfully produced, then, and not before, men will be able to vote intelligently on the subject.

The question of limiting armaments and budgets, military and naval, likewise resulted in failure to reach an agreement, owing to the extensive and complicated considerations involved. A general wish was emitted that the subject in its various relations might in the future receive an attentive study, on the part of the various governments; and there was adopted without dissent a resolution proposed in the First Committee, in full session, by M. Bourgeois, the First Delegate of France, as follows: "The Committee consider that the limitation of the military expenditures which now weigh upon the world is greatly to be desired, for the increase of the moral and material welfare of humanity." This sentiment received the assent of the Conference also.

The military and naval delegates of the United States Commission bore a part in all the proceedings in Sub- and Full Committee; but, while joining freely in the discussion of questions relating to the development of material, reserve was maintained in treating the subject of disarmament and of limitation of budgets, as being more properly of European concern alone. To avoid the possibility of misapprehension of the position of the United States on this matter, the following statement, drawn up by the Commission, was read at the final meeting of the First Committee, July 17, when the report to be presented to the Conference was under consideration:

"The Delegation of the United States of America have concurred in the conclusions upon the first clause of the Russian letter, of December 30th, 1898, presented to the Conference by the First Commission; namely, that the proposals of the Russian representatives, for fixing the amounts of effective forces and of budgets, military and naval, for periods of five and three years, cannot now be accepted, and that a more profound study upon the part of each state concerned is to be desired. But, while thus supporting what seemed to be the only practicable solution of a question submitted to the Conference by the Russian letter, the Delegation wishes to place upon the Record that the United States, in so doing, does not express any opinion as to the course to be taken by the States of Europe."

This declaration is not meant to indicate mere indifference to a difficult problem, because it does not affect the United States immediately, but expresses a determination to refrain from enunciating opinions upon matters, into which, as concerning Europe alone, the United States has no claim to enter. The words drawn up by M. Bourgeois, and adopted by the First Commission, received also the hearty concurrence of this Delegation because, in so doing, it expresses the cordial interest and sympathy with which the United States, while carefully abstaining from anything that might resemble interference, regards all movements that are thought to tend to the welfare of Europe. The military and naval armaments of the United States are at present so small, relatively to the extent of territory and to the number of the population, as well as in comparison with those of other nations, that their size can entail no additional burden of expense upon the latter, nor can even form a subject for profitable mutual discussion.

To William H. Rideing

Draft   N.P., N.D.   Probably, Quogue, Long Island, August 20, 1899 [LC]

Dear Sir: While at the Hague Mr. Leveson Gower[1] proposed to me, on your behalf, to write for the *North American* an article of some 5,000 words, more or less, derived from my experience at the Peace Conference, for which the payment of £100 was offered.[2]

I had no time, nor did I think it fitting, to submit such a paper before the end of the Conference. The subject, however, occupied my mind both then and afterwards, and during my passage home I have thrown the matter into such shape that I think I can give you an article by Sept. 1st. I ask, however, that I may not be too narrowly restricted to 5,000 words, and also to be

---

1. Leveson Gower cannot be identified with certainty. He may have been a son of George Leveson-Gower, 2nd Earl Granville.
2. "The Peace Conference and the Moral Aspect of War," *North American Review* (October 1899).

permitted the latest date possible for sending in the manuscript, as I find by experience that every day ripens thought or expression.

Presuming that my date of sending in will permit publication in the October number, I wish to stipulate not only that I have the right to republish hereafter in permanent form, but that I may do so in a book on the Spanish-American War, which I hope to publish about—but not before—November 15.[3] This reservation is essential to me, because I believe in the importance to the nation of what I have to say; and, while I fully recognize the very great value of the *North American* as a medium of communicating with our people at large, I wish also to put my ideas into more permanent form, and in connection with that war—a connection which I imagine is not only of sequence but of con-sequence. The Conference was to the war not only *post* but *propter*.

To John D. Long

Slumberside, Quogue, Long Island, August 21, 1899 [MHS]

My dear Mr. Long: My recollection of the incident is as follows:

General Shafter had telegraphed that the Spanish commander[1] offered to surrender Santiago, upon the condition that the garrison should be at liberty to march out and go where it chose. Both Shafter and Miles approved, under the conditions existing, and their telegrams to that effect were before the council, whom the President had called—among whom were several members of the Cabinet, yourself among them, our Board & some army men. I favored the proposition myself, considering that the place was what we then needed chiefly, and also because of Miles' and Shafter's opinion, who were on the spot, and I understood most of those present to hold the same view; but the President was very emphatically opposed to it—indeed *vehemently*, and in speaking of the surrender I have for that reason always said since that it was owing to the President—primarily, & to no one else—that the Spanish demand was rejected. I think, however, that he was going to yield, not because of his own change of mind but in acquiescence with the weight of professional opinion, when it occurred to me, and I suggested, that to surrender and to return to Spain would meet all our requirements, & perhaps be acceptable to them. The matter was settled, and the telegram to our General drawn up (if not sent) before we broke up, so there is no possibility of its having originated outside. As regards my part in it, I began to suspect my own memory, and wishing to reinforce it, I went to you a very few days after, and asked, "Do you recall who it was in

3. *Lessons of the War with Spain and Other Articles.*
1. General José Toral.

[653]

the Council suggested the Santiago garrison be allowed to return to Spain?" You replied at once and without hesitation, "Yes, it was you." This was before you left Washington, and you did not return until after I left. As I said, I have had no desire to have the facts made public, but I do object to the credit, if such there be, being attributed to another by the public & in history.

The telegrams would very probably establish the sequence of action, and the time of sending them. I suppose they are on record with their dates.

This seems a fitting time to suggest to you, that the Navy Dept. should insist upon the Rules for adapting the Geneva Convention to Maritime War, passed by the Peace Conference, should undergo the scrutiny of its law officers. I formulated certain objections to them, & proposed amendments, for which I could obtain no support; but I am quite sure I was right, and I should regret to think that our government should accept this work (formulated in 10 articles) without careful consideration of the articles themselves, & of my comments upon them. Our Delegation left them unsigned, pending the decision of our Govt. upon them.

To Silas McBee

Slumberside, Quogue, Long Island, August 27, 1899 [UNC]

Dear Sir: I think I can promise you a few words of comment on Dr. Parkin's[1] article, but I cannot certainly undertake that you shall have them before going to press for this week's issue.[2]

To Silas McBee

Slumberside, Quogue, Long Island, September 8, 1899 [UNC]

Dear Sir: A year or so ago there was an excellent editorial in the *Churchman* on a Man's Right to Grow. If I were to allow myself to speak whenever

---

1. Sir George Robert Parkin, educator and imperialist. At this time he was principal of Upper Canada College in Toronto. The article mentioned was Parkin's Review of David Starr Jordan, *Imperial Democracy* (New York: D. Appleton & Co., 1899), in *The Churchman*, September 9, 1899.
2. McBee carried on a three-way correspondence with Parkin, Talcott Williams, and Mahan, about each other's works, reviews, and comments. A strong expansionist, he apparently wished to have these powerful and sympathetic names appear often in the pages of the *Churchman*. The letters may be seen in the Southern Historical Collection of the University of North Carolina Library. The Mahan to McBee correspondence for 1899 has been misdated 1898 on the manuscripts in this collection.

asked, on religious subjects, or even to write, I should have no time to grow in my special line, which is sufficiently known. As far as indications go, to treat a certain range of secular subjects, imparting to them, when it can be done without straining, a coloring consistent with religious thought, is the line marked out for me by Providence. What I do outside that line must be charily limited.

I write this with reference to Mr. Wood's letter, to which I send a similar reply.

To John M. Brown

Slumberside, Quogue, Long Island, September 8, 1899 [LC]

My dear Mr. Brown: I had noted with regret the falling off in the Sea Power sales, by the last settlement. Since my return, three weeks ago, I have been occupied mainly with an article for the *North Amn. Review*, concerning which I have stipulated for the right to republish in the book *Lessons of Spanish Am. War* on Nov. 15. If you think that date too late for publication, I daresay they would permit Nov. 1.; or it may be omitted, though that I should regret. The article is between six & seven thousand words.

I have made a beginning—no more—on that which we have heretofore called the Text Book—Marston's suggestion. I do not quite understand to what you refer as the "Sea Power of To-day," my understanding being that the only publn. contemplated this fall was the Spanish Amn. War, with which were to go two or three casual articles, the whole about 50,000 words. I have before me the *printed* text of the War Articles, which I will take up tomorrow; and as I intend little or no change I should be able to send it you by the 20th, perhaps before. It is 37,000 words about. The other articles will equally receive little change, and all should be in your hands about Oct 1.

I hope to make an effective book of the Text Book, for which our title "The Present Interest of the English Speaking Communities in Sea Power" —whether adopted or not, expresses my main scope. It is my intention to devote myself exclusively to it after sending you the copy for the "Spanish War" though I am of course liable to be called off by a magazine article, especially if my book income drops too much. There are reasons why I think the Text Book will be at more advantage next year than this—but in any event it is impossible for this.

[P.S.]   The letter of Countess Stanhope has been duly acknowledged.

To Silas McBee

Slumberside, Quogue, Long Island, September 15, 1899 [UNC]

Dear Sir: I return Dr. Parkin's letter[1] with many thanks to you for allowing me to see it.

To William McKinley

Slumberside, Quogue, Long Island, September 18, 1899 [LC]

Captain Mahan has the honor to acknowledge and to accept the invitation of the President to dinner, to meet Admiral Dewey, on Tuesday, October 3d at 8 o'clock.

To Augustus T. Gillender

Slumberside, Quogue, Long Island, September 22, 1899 [HUL]

Dear Mr. Gillender: Would you be good enough to ascertain the street address of enclosed, and send it for me?[1]

I am delighted to learn through Jennie, who is with us, that you have benefited so much by your holiday.

Mrs. Mahan joins me in kind regards.

To Silas McBee

Slumberside, Quogue, Long Island, September 23, 1899 [UNC]

Dear Sir: I was much interested in your—the *Churchman*'s—account of the points in dispute in the Transvaal. Seeing the truculent and positive tone in which some of our papers are condemning Great Britain, I hope that the *Churchman* will keep an eye on the facts, and help to keep the opinion of Churchmen right. If Great Britain is wrong, by all means let us have the truth, but the disposition seems to be to prejudge, & to *assume* that the cause of essential justice is that of the Boers. My own paper—the *Times*

---

1. A letter to McBee, September 9, 1899, praising the clarity of Mahan's thought and the elegance of his style.

1. Enclosure not found.

—especially seems so; & from its action in the Sampson-Schley matter, which I flatter myself I *do* understand, I am satisfied it cannot be trusted for justice and yet is capable of doing much harm. The statement that G. B. demands suffrage for the foreigners in the Transvaal, without loss of original citizenship, appears to me probably distorted. It seems that she claims this only for British subjects, and for them on the ground that they are constructively in British dominions, when residing in the Transvaal, a vassal state. I am, however, painfully ignorant of the details of the matter; and it may be that my strong desire to see drawn closer our ties to the one power that stood by us 18 months ago may prejudice me.

To John M. Brown

Slumberside, Quogue, Long Island, September 23, 1899 [LC]

My dear Mr. Brown: I enclose a galley slip of an article coming out in the *North Amn.* for October,[1] which I also propose to introduce into our next book. I am a little uncertain about the Latin line I have quoted, and want to ask you if you have some scholarly friend, who could express a competent opinion as to its signification justifying the paragraph which I have hung upon it. You will observe that it is in no way essential, only a convenient peg, or text, for what follows. A friend here whom I have asked, a Latin teacher, pointed out that it is a hexameter, that "justitia" therefore is ablative. He questioned whether it might not be justitiae—genitive. If ablative, it would translate, "By justice violence yields to the sword of Mars," or "By justice the violence of Mars yields to the sword." If genitive, it would be "The violence of Mars yields to the sword of justice." In any event, justice & the sword put an end to violence. As regards justit*ia* and justit*iae*, I copied the inscription myself, and am therefore fairly certain I made no mistake. I have ransacked all the hexameters of Virgil and Horace to find the line, but have not. Though a little shaky, I considered that the general sense permitted me to risk it in a magazine; but for the more permanent book form I should like to be certain, and if you can help me I wish you would. Time is of importance as I propose this article to follow the one from *McClure*—the first.[2]

---

1. "The Peace Conference and the Moral Aspect of War."

2. *Lessons of the War with Spain and Other Articles* contained, in order: "Lessons of the War with Spain, 1898," "The Peace Conference and the Moral Aspect of War," "The Relations of the United States to Their New Dependencies," "Distinguishing Qualities of Ships of War," and "Current Fallacies upon Naval Subjects."

To Samuel A. Ashe

Slumberside, Quogue, Long Island, September 23, 1899 [DUL]

My dear Ashe: You will probably be somewhat interested to know that this summer, at the Hague, I met a Col. A'Court[1] of the British army. I remembered to have heard you say, in the far past at Annapolis, that the Ashe a'Courts in England were connected with your family so I took occasion one day to say to him that I had had an intimate friend, a'Court Ashe. He replied that it was interesting to hear, for that Ashe was one of his own family names—so I suppose that in the far away back you and his ancestry would strike. He is a man I should think now verging on forty, a fresh complexioned Englishman but rather darker than the average. He was, I believe, with Kitchener[2] in the Soudan campaign, and at present is military attaché to Brussels & the Hague. He was attached to their delegation at the Peace Conference, after we met, I believe because of his knowledge of French, to help the British naval delegate[3] whose acquaintance with the language was indifferent. I did not see very much of him, but what I did I liked.

The Conference itself was very well for a time, and interesting in a way; but ten weeks of it was rather too much. What the results will be remains to be seen. Personally, I am satisfied that Russia has not the slightest intention either of reducing her armaments, or even discontinuing the programme for their increase. Neither does she intend to change her forward policy; nor do I think any other state differs from her. The one most generally abused, Great Britain, did offer to stop two battle ships, if Russia would do the same; but the latter took no notice of the proposal. This I was told by the first Lord of the Admiralty himself. My own persuasion is that the immediate cause of Russia calling for the Conference was the shock of our late war, resulting in the rapprochement of the U.S. and Great Britain and our sudden appearance in Asia, as the result of a successful war. In peace, Russia's aggressive advance moves over the inert Asiatics like a steam-roller; but the prospect of America and England, side by side, demanding that China be left open for trade, means either a change in her policy, or war. Hence she wishes peace—by pledge.

I have an article in the next *North American*, in which I develop the general views I have long held on the subject of arbitration. In summary, these are that arbitration should always be a nation's first thought, but that it should never pledge itself, by treaty or otherwise, to arbitrate before it knows what the subject of dispute is. Needless to say, I have no sympathy with those who hold that war is never imperative.

---

1. Charles A'Court.
2. General Horatio H. Kitchener.
3. John A. Fisher.

To John D. Long

My dear Mr. Long: I received yesterday a letter from Mr. Low, in which he says that he told the President last week that, while he did not "Venture to differ from me, as to the technical aspects of the Geneva Cross Convention," as adapted to Maritime Warfare, in the "Ten Articles" recommended by the Hague Conference, he "thought it had a public and non-technical aspect which demanded careful consideration, and would lead me (him) to sign it."

Personally, I care little about the matter, although I have recommended nonconcurrence. I wish chiefly to have no more bother; but I suppose I ought, in view of this act of Mr. Low's, to write something to you.

The Ten Articles have two principal bearings: 1, upon hospital ships belonging to belligerent powers, and flying their national flag; 2, upon vessels of the same kind belonging to neutral states, and flying the flags of the latter, but benevolently attending belligerent fleets. The articles contain, besides, provisions to meet the case of neutral vessels carrying sick or wounded belligerents, or picking them up.

To the provisions concerning the first class I had, and made, no objection. Concerning the others I formulated very carefully certain objections, which appear to me incontestable, and of which the *Deerhound* and *Alabama* incident gave a very concrete illustration.

As all this is fully set forth in my reports to the Commission,[1] and in papers submitted by the latter, there is no need for me to repeat here. I have already recommended to you that the international legal aspect be reviewed by the legal authorities of the Department. I venture now to suggest to you that the views of the latter, and possibly my own report etc. to the Commission—in short the general subject of the neutral flag *authorized* on a scene of naval warfare—be submitted to Dewey and Sampson, with another flag officer or senior captain.

The United States will never need neutral hospital ships. Their presence will certainly incommode rather than benefit *us*; and as regards other neutral vessels, I would have such a Board consider the embarrassment of neutral press-boats, which are going to be more troublesome even than war correspondents on shore, because it is so much more difficult to define the limits of belligerent naval local control than it is of military.

I dont believe our people will care a rap how our government decides upon this question of *neutral hospital ships* on a field of battle. Where not wholly cranky, (you should have heard some of the ideas), it is largely academic. It is most unlikely that there ever will be such neutral hospital

---

1. *See* Mahan to the U.S. Commission . . . , July 26, 1899.

ships; but there will be other neutral intermeddling, which, unless controlled by previous definitions, will do more harm than good.

I cant quite understand Low's point of view, but I have little congenital aptitude for getting into line. "Be sure you're right, then go ahead," is a motto not only simple, but on the whole most apt to win—even with the populace. There are, I conceive, grave military inconveniences, and consequent international difficulties between neutrals and belligerents,—possibly most embarrassing to the latter,—to be apprehended, unless further definitions be adopted, in the sense of the recommendations we tried to carry in the Conference. You yourself must remember that during the late hostilities the action of neutral powers, and the avoidance of occasion of offense to them, had to be constantly in our minds. Is it wise, is it just, to lay up additional causes for such anxieties for the future, in order to avoid in the present a possible grumble among our people? I personally do not believe discontent can arise on such a subject; there is more fight than compromise just now in the air; but in any event, the opinion of officers recently in responsible chief command, which they have borne with conspicuous ability, cannot fail to contribute valuable light to the Government in forming its decisions upon this question of extending neutral immunities, in a manner likely to cause hereafter international friction.

To Edward K. Rawson[1]

Slumberside, Quogue, Long Island, September 29, 1899 [NA]

Dear Prof. Rawson: Thank you for your letter of the 27th. I do not care for the photo you mention, and if the Library would like it will be glad to give it you. There is also somewhere a photo of the Church in which he [Nelson] was married at Nevis & of the ruins of the house where he courted his wife. All which, if found, are herewith presented.

---

1. A Congregationalist minister who had served as a chaplain in the Navy, taught Ethics at the Academy, and, at this time, was Superintendent of the Office of Naval Records and Library, Washington, D.C. His *Twenty Famous Naval Battles* was published in 1899.

To the Editor of The Churchman

N.P., N.D.   Probably, Quogue, Long Island, September, 1899[1]

To respond adequately to your request, for comment upon Dr. Parkin's review of President Jordan's book, would require a reading of the latter, for which both time and opportunity are wanting to me. Accepting Dr. Parkin's evidently candid presentation as an accurate, even if—necessarily—an incomplete account of the argument of the book, the following considerations occur to me immediately, because part of my steady habit of thought; the results, as I hope, of reflection constantly maintained upon the contemporary events in question. I may add that my general thought, and this present writing, depend upon my convictions as a Christian and a Churchman—the strongest convictions that I entertain; for to me the Church is a greater fact than any State, and Christianity is more than any political creed.

The argument to withhold our hand from external action, as in accepting our new dependencies, because "at home Americans have on hand, and still unsolved, the greatest political and social problems of the world," is to me simply the repetition of the old cry as to missions: "Why carry Christianity to the distant heathen, when we have so many practical heathens at home?" To this we have, fortunately, the answer of our Lord's own charge to us; and, while it may be admitted that we have no similar specific instruction for the State, it is to be remembered that both State and Church are God's own children—"powers ordained by God"—sisters, each with its proper sphere of action. Constituted by the same supreme authority, it is not unreasonable to believe that the duty of external activity rests upon the one as well as upon the other, coincident in both cases with internal obligations still unfulfilled, and which probably never can be wholly fulfilled. At the present day the home calls upon the Church of Christ are continually outstripping the power of the Church to meet them. Must missions then be abandoned? Belief in the exterior mission of the State is reinforced by the clear charge to the individual man as to his neighbor, which runs throughout the New Testament and is summarized in the parable of the Good Samaritan. Where an explicit duty is laid upon the Church and upon the individual, it is not a strained implication to infer the same for the State.

The argument that the United States is not prepared at present for the duty of governing dependencies, is as far as it goes, a repetition of the homely fallacy, "not to go into the water till you know how to swim." That we at this moment are less fitted than is Great Britain, after over a century of experience, to grapple with the complicated practical difficulties of a

---

1. Printed as an addendum to George Parkin's review of David Starr Jordan's *Imperial Democracy* (New York: D. Appleton & Co., 1899) in *The Churchman* (September 9, 1899), p. 292. Jordan was President of Leland Stanford University. *See* Mahan to McBee, August 27, 1899.

colonial system, is antecedently most probable. But the argument based upon this fact—if fact it be—involves a double begging of the question. First, it assumes that we have less natural aptitude than Englishmen for dealing with novel political problems; and secondly it ignores the corruption and scandals attendant upon the early days of England in India—the days when she was learning to swim. In fact, in a somewhat warm controversy between the writer and an American statesman of national reputation, it was upon the very scandals and iniquities of those early days that my opponent based his arguments against our attempting colonial rule.[2] England has so recuperated from the evil of that time that the blessings of her sway are universally admitted. Why should Americans despair of themselves?

Doubtless we shall have to consider—and to reconsider—some of our political commonplaces, and to recognize their limitations. "Government depends upon the consent of the governed." As a principle, doubtless; but does the government of children, of imbeciles, of the mentally incompetent, of criminals, so depend? Were the States that held to the Union, a generation ago, justified in imposing upon the seceding States a government which the latter resisted by arms, at the loss of thousands of lives, and until they could fight no longer? Clearly, the axiom has its exceptions. Where, then, do these exceptions begin, and where end? "Taxation without representation is tyranny." Doubtless a fundamental constitutional principle in any free government; but what constitutes representation? Is the power to express personal will, by a vote, essential to it? Why, then, are women and minors taxed? Are representation and universal suffrage equivalent terms?

The generalizations, that "the great political service of England is to teach respect for law," of the United States "respect for the individual man," with all deductions proceeding from them, are essentially unsound, as guides to conduct, in this respect: Divine Providence does not permit men, or nations, thus to formulate their destinies in phrases. He does not permit to either thus to see "the distant scene," in the light of a fire of their own kindling. To teach, "one step's enough." It is the wisdom of men, and of nations, to address themselves to the duty of the day, or the hour, to see in each event the calling of God, not always clear at first, but sure to be made clear to honest search—the Christian will add, to earnest prayer. Events such as those of the past year are to a nation a call. I do not say that they constitute a call to expansion, although, to use the slang of the day, I am an "expansionist." I say only that the devolution upon a nation of such a question as the future of several peoples, heretofore unused to, and probably not yet fit for, self-government, is not to be solved, Christianly, by washing our hands and sending them about their business. The complicated political questions involved are sufficiently familiar to all readers of secular papers; there is neither space nor reason to discuss them here.

---

2. *See* Mahan to Gilman, October 23 and 27, 1898.

When a priest is called by constituted authority to be a bishop, there is a presumption—though by no means a certainty—that the call is from above. When a nation finds thrust upon it a number of communities, probably for the moment politically helpless, there is a presumption—though by no means a certainty—that God means it to do something for them. I do not for one moment claim that my view of what is required is hereby demonstrated; but I feel reasonably sure that the true course is to be found by a devout recognition of the divine hand in all this and a prayerful effort to see what is right to do in the light of actual conditions; not in the light of stock phrases, applicable to conditions of a different time and to communities of a different character.

In conclusion, while there is seeming good ground for President Jordan's assertion that the present is a crisis in the history of the nation comparable only to that of the formation of the Constitution, and to the maintenance of the Union in 1861—a view in which I am inclined to coincide—it is to be remembered, as a ground of quietness and confidence, that, from the Christian standpoint, differences of smaller or greater, in conditions, entail no difference in the attitude of men or nations to their doubts and their duties. To do what is right at the moment, as shown by a conscience illuminated by the Holy Spirit in response to prayer, is the one course of safety in matters great and in matters small. To the man or the nation thus seeking guidance, perplexity is no occasion for discouragement; nor does difficulty, or supposed danger, indicated by political proverbs, justify a refusal to follow the light.

To J. Franklin Jameson

Slumberside, Quogue, Long Island, October 2, 1899 [LC]

Dear Prof. Jameson: Replying to yours of the 28th, I ought to say No at once, and would have to do so were not the book[1] one into which I ought to look. If you are willing to send me it at once, addressed "Care Mrs. H. Saltonstall, Lynnfield, Essex Co., Mass." I will look over it and see if it deserves such careful reading as would enable me to review it.

I have returned from the Conference distinctly below par for work, and as I have much to do I must refuse everything not directly contributive to that actually in hand.

[P.S.] I cannot take the *Logs of Sea Fights*—which I have.[2]

---

1. La Roncière, *Histoire de la marine française*, previously declined in Mahan to Jameson, April 8, 1899.
2. T. S. Jackson, ed., *Logs of the Great Sea Fights, 1794–1805*. London: Navy Records Society, 1899.

To Silas McBee

Lynnfield, Massachusetts, October 13, 1899 [UNC]

Dear Sir: The attempt made by Bourke Cockran,[1] and others of his type, to use the Transvaal matter to stir up our people and Govt. against Great Britain, may prove a matter of very serious moment. If G. B. be wrong, by all means let us know it, but not by means of denunciation & *mere* outcry. Let us have calm, measured, unimpassioned statements of facts. Measured by myself, the ignorance of our people of the true state of the case must be colossal. I enclose a slip, the author of which I understand is a prominent Unitarian clergyman of Boston, able and candid. The importance of good-feeling between G. B. and U. S. is so great, and her service to us two years since so marked, that misdirected abuse by us will be most regrettable and ungrateful. By all means let us have truth—clearly and positively stated; but let us be sure it is truth, and unexaggerated.

To James R. Thursfield

160 West 86th Street, New York, October 28, 1899 [LC]

My dear Mr. Thursfield: I must permit myself to express to some one of my British friends the profound interest and sympathy which I feel for your present struggle in the Transvaal. On broad general principles I am satisfied of the right and duty of great Powers, when occasion offers, to put an end to gross evils at their doors, and while I can see two sides to the present question, I think upon the whole your interference justified—nay, imperative—upon grounds much the same as our own in Cuba. Taxation without representation is not as bad as starvation by reconcentration, but the principle is the same. My only fear has been lest, by the Conventions of 1881 and 1884—the text of which I have not been able to obtain yet—you might have pledged away the rights which under international law are yours as they are of every state, to interfere by force where necessity requires—of which requirement it is the sole judge.

Be this yea, or nay, I cannot but think the incident most fortunate, as a warning to states—immediately after the Hague Conference—not to sign away their right to maintain justice by war, by entering into a pledge beforehand to arbitrate, *except* on questions most strictly limited and defined.

---

1. William Bourke Cockran, a Tammany man whose speeches at this period were sponsored by the New England Anti-Imperialist League. They were addressed to pro-Boer or anti-imperialist groups and to his anti-British Irish-American constituency.

In fact, I myself agree entirely with the position of the German Emperor, to constitute a Tribunal, so as to facilitate arbitration, but not to promise, before the case arises, that any subject whatever (not even a postal treaty) will be referred to it. I have an article to that effect in the *North American Review* for Oct., in which I argue the moral aspect of war.

I have had some fear that a noisy section of our people might so conduct themselves as to produce an impression on your public that we were against you, and had already forgotten your good offices during our late war. Meetings were called by the Irish element, and by some who pander to it, notably Democrats (party name) with Dutch names, with a view to bring pressure upon the public, & ultimately upon the Administration. The attempt I think has failed, despite the usual political fear about votes—and the Irish vote here is no small matter, being not only numerous but cohesive. The meetings, when held, evoked considerable dissent in the audience, and I have good reason to know that the Admn. has no intention to proffer mediation. I enclose some cuttings from two of our most reputable dailies— the *N.Y. Times* and *Tribune*, the latter marked blue. The *Times* at first was somewhat pronounced against you, admitting the anachronism & injustice of the Boer polity, but questioning strenuously the right and the wisdom of your interference. I read it daily, and am struck by a much greater moderation, due I think to a dawning recognition of how much is to be said on the other side. The advocacy of neither paper toward you is warm—though the bias of the *Tribune* is evident; but it is far better so. The great end of checking and thwarting a factious attempt, here, to raise sympathy for "the weaker party," irrespective of justice, an attempt directed ultimately against the growing accord between the English speaking states, will be rather hindered than furthered by evident partisanship. These two papers, both advocates of expansion for ourselves, though of differing political tone otherwise, will do much to guide our opinion; for expansion carries the day here.

It is I hope needless to say that next to duty to my own country—and indeed among those duties—the maintenance of the present cordial understanding with yours is among the first of my interests. I watch the papers with interest scarcely less than during our trouble, and singularly enough with livelier agitation, due probably to ignorance of conditions. Though in a responsible position, I never worried then—now I do. Remember me to Sterling, Clarke & other friends, and say to them how much I feel in the matter. I was so sorry to see Colomb's death.[1]

---

1. Admiral P. H. Colomb died on October 13.

To Joseph E. Craig

160 West 86th Street, New York, October 30, 1899 [NA]

My dear Craig: Have you any sailing directions of the Yangtze, which would tell me how far up the river is navigable for vessels of—say—two classes viz: about 20 and 25 feet?[1]

I dont want charts; not, at least, at present.

To James Ford Rhodes

160 West 86th Street, New York, October 30, 1899 [MHS]

My dear Mr. Rhodes: For my delay in replying to your kind letter and invitation I am wholly without excuse, except that of extreme indecision. I have disliked to decline, and yet have shrunk from committing myself to any engagement for a time so far away. But above all, speaking to any serious effect (I dont much mind after dinner trifles) becomes to me increasingly troublesome—almost painful—and I much doubt my usefulness in that function. Besides all this I expect the renewal of a request, which I declined last year, to make an address; and I may feel obliged to accede, if now repeated.[1]

For these reasons I have finally concluded that I had better not add, to the load of work already upon me, the obligation of an address which with me would require much preparation.

It is possible that when the time comes I may be able to run on to Boston for a few days and be allowed to attend some of your meetings as a listener. My old friend, Mrs. Saltonstall, has a kind of mortgage upon me for my occasional vacations in Boston, and as in the course of nature her time cannot be very long I dont like to disappoint her. She does not however grudge to me any amount of time out, if my headquarters are there. I cannot, however, decide anything now.

My compliments to Mrs. Rhodes.

[P.S.] What a sad loss we have had in Ropes.

---

1. Mahan wanted this information for his series of articles "The Problem of Asia," which ran in *Harper's Monthly* (March, April, and May 1900) and was included in his *The Problem of Asia and Its Effects Upon International Policies*. Boston: Little, Brown and Company, 1900.

1. Because of the death of J. C. Ropes, on October 28, 1899, Mahan felt that if the Military Historical Society of Massachusetts were to invite him again, he would not be able to refuse. There is no evidence that he was again invited.

To James Ford Rhodes

160 West 86th Street, New York, November 1, 1899 [MHS]

Dear Mr. Rhodes: I had intended before closing my letter day before
yesterday to thank you for Vol. IV of your *History of the U.S.*,[1] which I
had found awaiting me upon my return home last week for the first time
since the Hague. I already had the previous volumes, and was intending to
buy this as soon as I knew of its coming out, but I very much value the
compliment & the possession of a volume from the author. I have never found
time to read all, but I have parts, and assure you that I have found it in-
terestingly and lucidly told as well as most instructive. I can honestly and
heartily congratulate you upon it.

To the Editor of The New York Times

160 West 86th Street, November 1, 1899[1]

I wish to express through your columns my obligations to Mr. Everett
P. Wheeler for his letter in your issue of the 30th inst. Mr. Wheeler's
party affiliations on National questions, as well as his personal reputation,
give especial value to his suggestion on the Assembly contest in the Nineteenth District. To me it is a matter of surprise that clear-headed men in
this district should fail to recognize, not only that Tammany is using the
Citizens' Union candidate to punish Mr. Mazet[2] for his part in the recent
investigations, but that the one supreme conclusion which the general public
will form, if Mr. Mazet be defeated, will be that it is not safe for a public
man to make himself obnoxious to Tammany.

In a fight of any kind, it is a good rule to fasten on the main issue, the key
of the position. For the above reason, which I think the decisive point in this
struggle, I shall vote for Mr. Mazet, as two years ago I voted for Mr. Stewart.
It is, I fear, too late to hope that the Citizens' Union may withdraw a
candidate whose success will be attributed, by the impressionable mass of
the community, not to his personal merits, but to the ubiquitous power of
Tammany; but I do trust that my fellow-readers of *The Times* in this district

1. James Ford Rhodes, *History of the United States from the Compromise of 1850.*
   New York: Harper, 1893–1899. 9 vols., of which Harper published the first four, and
   Macmillan the remainder, 1900–1928. Volume IV covers the period 1862–1864.

1. From *The New York Times*, November 2, 1899, p. 3.

2. Robert Mazet was chairman of the committee investigating the government of New
   York City.

will consider the effect of their votes, as for and against Tammany, in this contest, in which there has been accomplished for the first time, to use Mr. Wheeler's words, "the union of one of the great party organizations with the independent organizations upon a non-partisan basis in municipal matters." The predominant effect of Mr. Mazet's defeat will be municipal, not partisan; for whatever else it shows, the victory of Tammany will over-shadow all other impressions in the popular mind.

I do not understand Mr. Wheeler to advocate Mr. Mazet's candidacy, but I do understand him to deprecate, as I do, the ignoring of his services actually rendered, and the untimely and unjustified insistence upon his alleged partiality in the recent investigation as reasons for defeating him for the next Assembly. Taken in connection with Mr. Root's letter in your issue of the same day, upon the Astoria Gas bill, and with the Governor's[3] advocacy of Mr. Mazet's election, we have here a combination of three of the names most respected in our municipality, well worthy of the consideration of voters.

To J. Franklin Jameson

160 West 86th Street, New York, November 2, 1899 [LC]

Dear Mr. Jameson: While at Lynnfield I read quite a little of La Roncière's *Hist. de la Marine Française.* The period covered by this first volume is one with which I am entirely unfamiliar, and into which I have not, nor expect to have any occasion to enter. To review adequately would require something very like hard study of a matter for which I should have no other use. Its interest appears to be chiefly archaeological, & that not of a character likely to throw useful light on present or general problems; although of this also I cannot speak certainly without further study.

The truth is my head is too full and my time too much occupied to afford time for serious attention to matters out of my own line.

I return the book by mail regretting that in this instance I am not able to help you.

---

3. Theodore Roosevelt.

To the Editor of The New York Times

New York, November 15, 1899[1]

In common with some other of your readers who have at intervals made known their dissatisfaction, I have watched with silent regret many utterances of *The Times* in what, for want of a better name, may be called the Sampson-Schley controversy. It is no more than just to the two admirals to say that, so far as appears, they have had no personal share in this unofficial discussion, which apparently does not possess the power of stopping itself, unless, and until, some authoritative solution is reached.

Regrettable as I have thought much that *The Times* has before said, it appears to me that in its editorial of Monday, Nov. 13–"The Enemies of Schley"–it passed beyond the limits of fair, not to say sane, discussion. In the first place, while stigmatizing a letter of Secretary Long's in terms made only more objectionable by the worn device of an ostentatious disclaimer of intentional severity, it has not given the text of the letter alluded to, which apparently is one published in *The New York Sun* of Nov. 11, purporting to be translated from a German paper in the West. I am led to believe that this letter is the one to which *The Times* refers, because it is described as "warning the President not to be won over to the Schley party by the blandishment of a delegation of Maryland Republicans." This characterization of the letter–unless supported by something approaching demonstration–is grossly unfair; but it indicates the occasion of its writing sufficiently for identification.

Assuming this to be the letter, the weakness and unfairness of *The Times* editorial consist, first, in attributing the Secretary's letter to the inspiration of naval officers, and not to natural self-defence–against an odious charge of unworthy persecution–or to duty, as an adviser to the President in the special matter. I am entirely ignorant of what moved the Secretary to act, as I was of the letter itself, until it was published in *The Sun*; but, while *The Times* has a right to believe, and I suppose to say, what it pleases, it is evident that this is assumption without accompanying probable proof. It is therefore weak; yet, as the average reader does not analyze, it is an injurious insinuation.

Secondly, the statement that the Secretary's letter is "impertinent" is not only wanton but demonstrably incorrect. There is no "impertinence" in the common though secondary usage of the word in a man in charge of a department in any organization–or Government–making suggestions concerning it to the head of the organization. In the stricter sense of "non

---

1. From *The New York Times*, November 18, 1899, p. 6, followed by a two-column editorial rebuttal.

pertinent," *The Times* is even more in error. The Secretary's letter, which I read carefully, in whatever it may err, is perfectly pertinent to the matter in hand, and exactly such a brief as a superior, about to receive a statement on the opposite side of a question, needs to have. The editorial of *The Times* itself is more justly open to the charge of impertinence—in applying the epithets "disgraceful and impertinent" to the Secretary's letter—and of non-pertinence, for, while the Secretary's letter is a statement of alleged facts, susceptible of refutation by counter-proof, if such there be, *The Times* does not adduce proof, but simply indulges in abuse.

I have certainly no intention to enter, uncalled, into this deplorable dispute as to the merits or demerits of Admiral Schley; but the sneering declaration in your editorial that "the awkward circumstance that Sampson was not in the fight at Santiago . . . has made it inconvenient to use his name as a rallying cry," justifies me in repeating what I have only once before— fifteen months ago—written for publication, that, in my opinion, the first credit of the battle, as of the campaign, belongs to the man whose dispositions prevailed in both—to Admiral Sampson. This is, indeed, not a rallying cry, nor meant to be, or an attack on such credit as Admiral Schley may be justly entitled to; it is merely my personal opinion, given as a student for many years of naval history, and measuring the Santiago campaign, of which I have adequate knowledge, by the many other naval campaigns it has been my business to study. I speak for no one else and am authorized to speak for no one; but I am satisfied from what I do know, that the professional opinion of those who served in the West Indies will, if tested, support my estimate of the facts, as here stated. That such was the opinion of the men upon whom the responsibility of the naval war fell—of the President and of the Secretary of the Navy—the men who, had failure come, would have borne the chief burden of blame, is evident from the nomination of Sampson for the senior promotion. To it, having been honored during the war with the position of a responsible adviser to them, I wish, after fifteen months of reflection, to add my deliberate assent.

To Seth Low

160 West 86th Street, New York, November 18, 1899 [CUL]

My dear Mr. Low: I replied last evening to the invitation of the Universal Peace Union, that as far as I had casually followed its course, and, specifically, in the matter of urging the President to offer mediation in the Transvaal business, unasked by Great Britain, I thought that so far from representing the conservative spirit of our delegation, and of the Conference generally, it was directly contrary to our reticent caution, in asserting the

U.S. adherence to her traditional policy, of non intervention in matters that did not concern us. For this reason I felt compelled to decline the invitation, lest my presence, as a delegate, should be thought to imply my adhesion to Mr. Love's[1] statement—in his letter—that their pressure on the President was in the line of our action.

I did not think necessary to answer a late letter of yours, but take this opportunity to say that, so far from feeling uneasiness, I was very glad to have your endorsement in the Mazet matter. Though the immediate result was unfavorable, I trust that the two names will make the *hot heads* of the Citizens Union feel a little more careful about handling Tammany pitch hereafter.

To Silas McBee

160 West 86th Street, New York, November 19, 1899 [UNC]

Dear Sir: I have sent you two copies of an address I made to the Church Club—in Boston, thinking that you might possibly like to see it yourself, and would be good enough to send one to Dr. Parkyn [*sic*] whose address I dont know.[1]

Do not trouble to acknowledge.[2]

To Robert U. Johnson

160 West 86th Street, New York, December 3, 1899 [NYPL]

Dear Mr. Johnson: With reference to the distance maintained by Schley prior to Sampson's arrival, I have looked up in App. to Report of

---

1. Alfred Henry Love, editor of *The Bond of Peace*, *The Voice of Peace*, and other pacifist publications; president of the Universal Peace Union, and a leader in various feminist, abolitionist, and prison-reform movements.

1. On November 22, McBee did mail Parkin a copy of Mahan's paper, "The Relations of the Church to the State," given before the Episcopal Club of Massachusetts, in mid-October 1899.

2. The Mahan-McBee correspondence ceased at this point. After Mahan's death in December 1914, McBee, on January 25, 1915, wrote to Roosevelt praising his obituary article on Mahan in the *Outlook*, and made this comment: "The Admiral knew the history of sea power, but he did not know the philosophy of history, or perhaps I should say, he did not show in his writings that he had a philosophy of history." He continued with a criticism of a *N.Y. Evening Post* interview with Mahan on August 3, 1914, expressing shock over Mahan's lack of ethics. McBee Collection, University of North Carolina Library.

Bu. of Navn. pp. 404–428.[1] Upon cursory exn., it appears that on May 28, 4.05 pm, Schley signaled (p. 422) "general meeting place 25 miles S. of Santiago." This probably accounts for the particular figure. Schley (404) states distance, night of 28th, 4 to 5 miles out. McCalla,[2] same night, p. 426 states distance 8 p.m., 10 miles. The *Marblehead*[3] was 2 miles inshore of squadron. I find no other precise statements, so conclude Schley plucked up courage to remain nearer than 25 miles, but, in view of Muller's[4] & Mc-Calla's statements probably deceived himself in imagining he was only 4 to 5.

A similar liability to self deception appears in the estimate of ranges during reconnaisance of May 31. Schley gives it 7000 yards (pp 427–428). Higginson[5] 7,500 to 9,500, after which turned to the southward, farther off, and fired, "good line shots range generally *short*." (p. 417) Evans[6] (419) says "range at which our guns fired 8,500 yards but shots fell short. Range during this run gradually increased to 9,000 (2,000 yards=1 mile). During second passage sights set first at 9,500 gradually increased to 11,000 yards."

To Robert U. Johnson

160 West 86th Street, New York, December 11, 1899 [NYPL]

Dear Mr. Johnson: The enclosed may interest you,[1] but is of course not for use in any way. After reading, please destroy it. You will notice that C's[2] conclusions from the logs are not materially different from mine from the reports.

---

1. Appendix to the Report of the Chief of the Bureau of Navigation, 1898.
2. Commander B. H. McCalla.
3. A 2,072-ton, 269-foot, unarmored cruiser, mounting (in 1897) ten 5-inch guns and two 18-inch torpedo tubes. Commissioned in 1894, her twin screws drove her at 18.5 knots.
4. Lieutenant Muller, of the Spanish Navy.
5. Captain F. J. Higginson.
6. Captain Robley D. Evans.

1. Enclosure not found.
2. Probably, F. E. Chadwick, who commanded the *New York* at Santiago and who later wrote *The Relations of the United States and Spain: Diplomacy* (New York, 1910); *The Relations of the United States and Spain: The Spanish-American War*. 2 vols. (New York, 1911); and *The New American Navy* (New York, 1915).

To John D. Long

160 West 86th Street, New York, December 12, 1899 [MHS]

My dear Mr. Long: I have received a letter from Chadwick, in which he mentions a letter addressed by him to the President, through the Department, protesting against Schley's advancement until he shall have been cleared of heavy charges affecting his professional character, made as these are not by irresponsible persons, but by very responsible ones.

I have no difficulty in saying that, be these charges true or erroneous, there would be to me something monstrous, and to military experience unheard of, (as far as I know), in advancement under such conditions. In leaving the Dewey dinner, Sampson told me he had been consulted by Senator Chandler[1] as to a bill making him and Schley vice-admirals, and asked my opinion. I replied that I thought he ought to be a vice-admiral, but to make Schley one, under known conditions, would be a disgrace to the Navy; and I authorized him to say I so said, if necessary.

Personally, I have upon most of these charges no opinion to which I am committed. As to their truth I hold opinion in suspense; but as regards the impropriety of promoting an officer who lies under such charges, and seeks no inquiry, these is no room, in my judgment for differing opinions.

But, *personally*, I consider that Schley's utter unfitness for command is conclusively demonstrated, over his own signature, by two facts. One is the well-known telegram announcing his purpose to return to Key West; the other is the statement, in his letter of May 30, that the speed of the squadron was reduced, from 7.5 to 8.5 knots, to 4 or 5, going from Cienfuegos to Santiago, to allow the *Eagle* to keep up. The man who, under all the circumstances, could do those two things, is demonstrably unfit for command; and I have always purposed, in case my opinion were asked, to rest it on these two statements. In my judgment as a student of military history, there is no escape from this conclusion.

To James R. Thursfield

160 West 86th Street, New York, December 15, 1899 [LC]

My dear Mr. Thursfield: I have duly received the book you were kind enough to send me, and a couple of evenings ago put myself through the educational discipline of reading Mr. Bryce's introduction, Karl Blind's

---

1. W. E. Chandler, Republican from New Hampshire, who had been Secretary of the Navy from 1881 to 1885.

article in the *Fortnightly*[1] and Mr. Balfour's speech at Dewsbury.[2] I had already read Bryce's book in the first edition,[3] with principal reference to the historical question. I find my conclusions, or bias, whichever it be, but little affected, except as regards the policy of temporizing—by which I mean allowing the Boer system to die of its own moribund political conditions, instead of putting it to death. The hard work you are having suggests doubt in either direction. Had you waited longer they might have been militarily stronger, or they might have died of their own injustice and unfitness to modern conditions. Who can tell? I am satisfied you had just cause for intervention, I incline to think sound policy demanded it, and in your present reverses you are, in my opinion, reaping the reward not of present injustice but of past weak indulgence, beginning with Gladstone, who at about the same moment sacrificed Gordon.[4]

I cannot express with what deep sorrow and anxiety your checks affect me. In themselves they seem to me little, but of course in your wide empire there is always danger of other trouble at an embarrassing moment. But I cannot believe God will permit so beneficent a government to be permanently disabled; you may need chastening, but the hopes of the world rest upon you largely. From Bryce's book I draw one conclusion: that Africa has little promise of permanent intrinsic value. It would be a gain for you I believe to lose it, and to be forced to concentrate your energies on Egypt and the Levant, without the alternative of the Cape route. But I dont want you beaten.

To J. Franklin Jameson

160 West 86th Street, New York, December 24, 1899 [LC]

My dear Mr. Jameson: I fear I cannot help you in this matter. I have both books, Rawson having sent me his,[1] and I being a subscriber to the N.R.S.[2] The former struck me as poor, but I should not wish to say so,

1. Karl Blind, "Transvaal Independence and England's Future," *Fortnightly Review* (November 1899).
2. On November 28 Balfour addressed the National Union of Conservative Associations on foreign criticism of the Boer War, the negotiations. the refusal of the Boers to extend the franchise, and government policy after Majuba.
3. James Bryce, *Impressions of South Africa*. New York: Century Company, 1897. The 3d edition, published in London by Macmillan in 1899, had a timely section on the Boer War.
4. General Charles G. ("Chinese") Gordon, soldier of fortune, killed in the Egyptian service at Khartoum in 1885.

1. Edward Kirk Rawson, *Twenty Famous Naval Battles: Salamis to Santiago*. 2 vols. New York: Crowell, 1899. There is no evidence that Mahan reviewed Rawson's book.
2. Navy Records Society.

being under obligation to Rawson, both for kindnesses and in friendship. As regards the *Logs*[3] I shall probably have to go through them some day, & for that very reason do not care to do so now—it would be time and labor lost when I shall have to go over it again. I may add that the *Logs* are only undigested material—most valuable as such but scarcely a work for criticism. Doubtless, in reading one may strike a curious item here and there, but logs are dreary reading except to the initiated & half rations for them.

To Mr. Dodge[1]

160 West 86th Street, New York, January 4, 1900 [LC]

My dear Mr. Dodge: At the time of my last writing the promised re-publication of *Review* articles[2] had not been received. They came yesterday. I note that you have reproduced those of Mr. Low and M. Martens; also one by the distinguished Mr. Holls; but that you do not give circulation to my own on the Moral Aspect of War, which appeared in the same magazine as Mr. Low's and M. Martens'.

I presume that you will not suspect me of any petty jealousy as to my own writing—especially as my reputation is made in another field—and will believe that I especially note here the relegation to an inferior position of the moral side of the question. Such an attitude toward this moral side is doubtless wholly unconscious on the part of the advocates of arbitration. The shocking evils of war have so impressed their imagination, that they fail to recognize its moral character. Yet worse things can happen to a man —far worse—than to be mangled by a shell, or to a nation than to be scourged by war. It profits neither to gain the world and to lose his soul.

I do not presume to read the actions of Providence, but I see not how it can fail to strike you that at the moment the very sound Arbitration so fills men's ears that they can listen to nothing else, their device is returned in mockery on their hands by two wars, just if ever war was just, and into which one of the parties in either case could not have refused to enter, except at the cost of dereliction to conscience. And it seems as if there were even a chance that our country would have been thus derelict, had not the inexplicable catastrophe of the *Maine* swept our people into the decisive action, to which no such stimulus should have been needed.

Candidly, do you think your efforts for Arbitration can be blessed—I dont say successful—while you fail to accompany them with an attempt to edu-

---

3. *See* Mahan to Jameson, October 2, 1899.

1. No further identification has been found.

2. A series of articles in the *North American Review* in 1899 on the Peace Conference at The Hague.

cate people on the other side, viz: that there are contingencies which do not admit arbitration, duties which a nation must discharge even at the cost of war and suffering? Unless you and your associates do so you may effect arbitration, but I do not believe you will have scored a step in the nation's advance. You may have made material prosperity more secure, but if the countervailing truth is not preached, understood, and accepted, it will have been better for the nation that it had never been born.

To John M. Brown

160 West 86th Street, New York, January 16, 1900 [LC]

My dear Mr. Brown: Thank you very much for your letter and accompanying cheque. The latter is better than I had feared from the way you spoke when I saw you, and shows I am not quite gone under yet—nor *Sea Power* either, which is of more consequence. This return, with my triple article for *Harpers*,[1] now nearly finished, puts me quite at ease for this year and will enable me, I hope, to give undivided attention to the Text Book.

I heartily wish, indeed, that you may find yourself fully restored by my next coming to Boston.

To Theodore Roosevelt

160 West 86th Street, New York, January 18, 1900 [LC]

My dear Governor: I shall look forward with pleasure to meeting you at Mr. Robinson's on Saturday. I infer from the papers you have a very difficult task in the Payn matter,[1] but I am also confident that if you decide it in utter disregard of the effect on your *own* future—which I am sure you will—you will be guided aright. You wont mind my saying that I hope the power of the Spirit may rest upon you in this.

I almost never see the *Independent*, but shall look up your article[2] at the Club.

1. "The Problem of Asia," (*Harpers Monthly*, March; April; May 1900).

1. As Governor of New York, Roosevelt displaced Louis F. Payn, Superintendent of Insurance, a lifelong political friend of Republican boss Thomas C. Platt.
2. Theodore Roosevelt, "Expansion and Peace," *The Independent* (December 21, 1899).

To the Editor of The New York Times

New York, January 20, 1900[1]

Mr Shearman's excellent letter in your issue of the 17th inst. upon the merits of the controversy between the Transvaal and Great Britain, which has issued in the present war, does not mention one point of considerable importance in itself, but still more as illustrative of the Boers' ideas of justice.

When the population now known as the Uitlanders were encouraged by the Boer Government to enter the Transvaal and to develop the gold fields, the period of naturalization, fixed by the law of 1882, was five years; but before the time came that the new-comers could avail themselves of this right, the law was, in 1890, changed, the period being extended to fourteen years, with further restrictions of method which made the franchise still more illusory. Whether this was strictly ex post facto legislation I am not lawyer enough to know, but it is clearly a violation of fair dealing and is wholly characteristic.

May I suggest to our citizens generally, and to the Boer sympathizers especially, the inadvisability of public meetings on this question. There are very many among us, myself certainly one, who feel as strongly in favor of Great Britain as others do of her opponents. Let us all be careful not to provoke one another by immoderate expressions of opinion, to which public meetings tend. Those on one side provoke retaliation on the other, nay they make it necessary, for, in the problems of the near future good understanding with Great Britain is too important for us to permit the impression that we are all against her here, and we may find ourselves in the unseemly state of party divisions for and against foreign States, as in the beginning of this century between the French and British parties. I avail myself of this opportunity to say that, in my judgment, not only is the cause of Great Britain just, but to have failed to uphold it would have been to fail in national honor.

To the Editor of The New York Times

New York, January 25, 1900[1]

When one man uses the letter of another as a peg on which to hang an argument, the least he can do is to quote with reasonable accuracy. Your correspondent of this morning, Mr. H. R. Ostrom, says Capt. Mahan "confesses he does not know the facts of the Boer war as a lawyer." I said nothing

---

1. From *The New York Times*, January 22, 1900, p. 6.
1. From *The New York Times*, January 26, 1900, p. 6.

of the kind; nothing in the least like it. I made the statement that when the Boer Government encouraged the Uitlanders to enter the country and to institute improvements, which raised its revenue from less than $1,000,000 to $20,000,000, the term for attaining full franchise stood at five years; and that, before the new-comers as a class could avail themselves of this privilege, the term was extended to fourteen years, accompanied with other conditions, which made the franchise still more illusory. Concerning this particular action, which is but one incident, and not in the least directly connected with the war, I said I was not lawyer enough to know if it was strictly—i. e., technically—ex post facto; but that it was evidently unjust, and, in my opinion, illustrative of the general characteristics of the Boer Government.

In view of the failure in so many quarters to appreciate the real origin of this war, it may be desirable to emphasize the fact that Great Britain did not demand the franchise for the Uitlanders. Sir Alfred Milner, her representative at the Bloemfontein conference, last June, admitted implicitly that the franchise was a matter of the internal affairs of the Transvaal, control of which Great Britain had formally renounced. He said only that, in view of the many complaints of injustice made by British subjects there resident, and concerning which Great Britain had to make representations—as she would in like conditions to the United States—it was suggested that an extension of the franchise would of itself constitute a remedy, which would silence most complaints, and so remove causes of friction between the two countries. Krüger[2] objected that, as the Uitlanders much exceeded the Boers in number—a significant fact little regarded by American sympathizers with so-called republics—the granting of suffrage to all would swamp the older inhabitants. This, Milner at once admitted, was too much to be expected; he said only that some representation, a possibility of returning one-fourth of the principal house—the first Volksraad, which practically controls legislation—would enable them to make their voices heard on the floor of the representation of the State, and to influence legislation, which it is needless to say they could not have controlled with such a proportion. Under the pressure of the situation, the Transvaal Government proposed eventually to submit to the Legislature terms of franchise similar to those indicated by Milner, but with the offer they coupled conditions irrelevant to franchise, which the British Government refused to accept; whereupon the offer was withdrawn. It appears, therefore, that the willingness to allow a reasonable representation to the population which produced nineteen-twentieths of the revenue, did not exist, independent of external urgency, such as that exercised by Great Britain on behalf of the Uitlanders, most of whom were her subjects, but among them many citizens of other nationalities, none of

---

2. Stephanus Johannes Paulus Kruger, President of the Republic of Transvaal and Boer leader against Great Britain.

whom, of course, were willing to renounce their native citizenship so long as they could not, simultaneously with its relinquishment, obtain the privileges of Transvaal citizens, which under the law they could not.

Persons who will look carefully into this matter will find that the Boers doubtless are in their own opinion fighting to preserve their own liberty, but they have been brought into this dilemma because national liberty was in Mr. Krüger's mind inseparably associated with the right of a dominant minority, sole possessors of political power—in other words, an oligarchy—to oppress a majority, to tax it heavily, and to refuse it representation. The cause of the Uitlanders is in principle identical with that of the American Revolutionists; and when Mr. Ostrom says "the war is one of gold" he may be correct as regards Krüger's motives, but as regards the rights of the Uitlanders he takes the position of those—and there are some—who say our forefathers of 1776 fought, not for the principle, but to save their pockets.

To Edward K. Rawson

160 West 86th Street, New York, January 26, 1900 [NA]

Dear Mr. Rawson: Can you lend me Sir Wm. Monson's *Naval Tracts?*[1] I am making a new book,[2] complementary of my Sea Power books, and shall probably want to trouble your kindness much this year.

To James Ford Rhodes

160 West 86th Street, New York, January 30, 1900 [MHS]

My dear Mr. Rhodes: I thank you very much for your letter. My own[1] has made more stir than I at all anticipated. Some one, Smalley I suppose, telegraphed the substance to England where it was welcomed; and, besides letters in the press, I have had a dozen or so from various parts of the country; mostly thanking me, two or three abusive.

The pro-Boer movement is, I think, chiefly—not solely—anti English, and naturally very much Irish. To call the Transvaal a Republic is a bull too delicious for the Irish to miss. The native American opposition will be

---

1. Sir William Monson, *Naval Tracts. In Six Books.* In Awnsham Churchill, comp., *A Collection of Voyages and Travels.* London, 1704; and 1732.
2. *The Influence of Sea Power in its Relation to the War of 1812.* Boston: Little, Brown and Company, 1905.
1. His letter to *The New York Times*, which appeared January 22.

found to be largely anti-Imperialist; a funny name, but one that will serve its turn for the present. I had all ready a paper, elicited by the Boer meeting in Boston and by Senator Hoar's[2] letter, analyzing the one principle which I believe underlies the opposition to our Philippine policy and to the British action, and showing its substantial fallacy—as I think it. The paper is to appear in this week's *Independent*.[3]

I neglected to secure any copies of my first letter, but I have some cuttings of a second, elicited by a reply to mine, which covers the same ground but more fully. Perhaps this may interest Mr. Ashley,[4] but I would be glad if he would return it, as I have further need of it.

[P.S.]   Last night's pro-Boer meeting here was beneath contempt in intellectual or moral weight. Of course in a city that gives Tammany 250,000 votes it is never difficult to fill an auditorium of 10,000 with people who hate England.[5]

To John D. Long

160 West 86th Street, New York, January 31, 1900 [MHS]

My dear Mr. Long: It is hard to keep my excellent intentions of withdrawing wholly from discussions of to-day's naval matters. The report I see, that the Construction Board has decided upon battle-ships of 14,000 tons, prompts me now to offer a suggestion which I had in fact drawn up while in Washington during the late war.

The various difficulties inherent in the problem of a battle-ship are peculiarly felt by each Bureau, from which the Construction Board is drawn. A ready way to get what each, and all, want, is to increase size. It is, however, a strictly momentary expedient, analogous to meeting household difficulties, not by management but by increased expenditure. Logically, the process may lead to ships of 25,000 tons, if harbors will admit them.[1]

---

2. George F. Hoar, Republican, of Massachusetts, and prominent anti-imperialist.

3. "The Transvaal and the Philippine Islands," *The Independent* (February 1, 1900).

4. Possibly, Roscoe Lewis Ashley, author of textbooks in American history.

5. Rhodes sent this letter to Secretary of State John M. Hay with the notation: "Dear Colonel Hay. When you have read this please return it to 392 Beacon St. Boston. I do not enclose the newspaper clipping."

1. As early as June 25, 1890, the dispute concerning the size of ships elicited this sarcastic comment from W. E. Chandler to B. F. Tracy: "I regret to learn that Acting Rear Admiral Walker's Squadron draws so much water that the Atlantic Ocean is too shallow for the vessels to visit the Argentine Republic. This shows very clearly the necessity of building no more large ships. By all means, let us have some small ships, and some small admirals, so that they can go to Buenos Ayres."

The difficulty is that, from its constitution, the Construction Board necessarily tends to view the question rather from the technological than from the military side. Unless the country—and Congress—is prepared for practically unlimited expenditure, bigger ships means fewer ships. Now there are strong military reasons why numbers of ships are wanted; and in view of the steady increase in size, due to increasing demands of each technical factor in the battle-ship, the time has arrived when the military experts should be called in, and directed to consider what the limits of size should be. This would take two forms, viz: what is the best normal tonnage for the bulk of the battle-fleet—for the *mean* battle-ship? and, further, what *exceptional* battle-ships should be built, in number and in individual size, for the tactical purpose of strengthening certain parts of an order of battle? This is the old question of the two-decker and three-decker, of Nelson and his times.

The military question by no means excludes consideration of technical details, but it should dominate them. If I were submitting it to a special Board, I should pose the question before them somewhat thus:

"Having in view, on the one hand, the advisability of concentrating in the single battle-ship the highest offensive power, combined with adequate armor protection, and such coal endurance as our national strategic conditions require, together with a high and sustained, but not extreme, sea speed; and, considering on the other hand, the necessity of having numerous ships, in order to meet the various demands of a war, which require facility of combining and of distributing the aggregate tonnage of the fleet, as well as the maintenance of relief ships in reserve, in order that, through frequent exchanges, the efficiency of the vessels can be maintained, it is desirable to establish a standard size of battle-ships. The Board is directed to consider and report within what limits of size, maximum and minimum, the average medium battle-ship, the type of the fleet in general, should be kept. The Board will also report if, for tactical reasons, occasional heavier battle-ships are desirable; and, if so, their size, and their numerical proportion to the fleet as a whole."

An excellent Board, in my judgment, for this purpose, would be Dewey, Sampson, and Harry Taylor; the first two for obvious reasons, and Taylor as being one of the most maturely informed officers in the service, on military considerations as opposed to those which are chiefly technical.

I would like to add, for your personal information, that in my recent book, *Lessons of the War with Spain*, pp. 30–42, and in the Article, "Distinguishing Qualities of Ships of War," pp. 257–273,[2] I have expressed these views at a length not suited to this letter. I would like only to add that the serious defect of all navies, except possibly Germany, is that all these

2. Originally published by the *Scripps-McRae Newspaper League* in November 1898. Reprinted in *Lessons of the War with Spain*.

decisions are made by the technologist rather than by the military expert. The military reasons for which navies exist are not given the primacy they should have.

To John D. Long

160 West 86th Street, New York, February 15, 1900 [MHS]

My dear Mr. Long: I fear I must have expressed myself badly, for you have misapprehended my meaning in two particulars.

I did not intend to advocate a permanent Board of three, although I think that the distinctly military element is inadequately represented by a Board of Bureau Chiefs. What I hoped was that a decision might now be reached, through a Board such as suggested, as to how the battle ship tonnage of the Navy was to be allotted: to very big ships, or to a determined medium size, which would allow a greater number.

Again, I certainly meant to criticize the decision to build ships of 14,000 tons, because, in my opinion, they are larger than needed, and likely to result in too few ships. I believe that I know that one Bureau wants increased size, to attain a speed which I consider extravagant; and that another wants size, in order to [insure] a coal endurance which I believe unnecessary; and that both, for these ends, are willing to increase size without commensurate gain in offensive power. Both I consider distinctly contrary to sound military principle. The Navy does not exist for ships, but ships for the navy; and correct conclusions cannot be *secured* unless you call in those who think *first* what does the Navy need for war, and next what kind of ships fulfill those needs. The technologist & Bureau man necessarily thinks first of his own specialty.

If such a Board as I suggested affirm in the main the decisions of the Construction Board—well; if not, a serious error may be timely averted, before the country be seized with a parsimonious fit, & we be left with a few monsters, instead of a number adequate to our varied requirements.

To Seth Low

160 West 86th Street, New York, February 15, 1900 [CUL]

My dear Mr. Low: The *Navy Regulations* with some propriety direct that officers are not to discuss in public measures of the Administration that are pending. This does not prevent me from answering your questions, but it has prevented my paying much attention to the Treaty;[1] for why trouble myself about that which I could not affect? Consequently, till your letter came I had not read it attentively.

It seems to me that the effects flowing from the treaty are so far from being easily obvious, that a somewhat prolonged consideration is desirable. I cant myself feel that I see all round it, and through it, now. At first I objected strenuously to a seeming joint guarantee on the part of other Powers; for the undertaking to guarantee might plausibly be made—by Germany, for instance—the ground for needing a naval station near by, on which to base her force. *The Sun*, Feb. 9, makes much of the joint "guarantee," but I cannot find either the word or its equivalent. The "invitation to the other Powers to *adhere*" (Art III) asks them only to pledge, by treaty, that they will not violate the neutrality of the canal, in any of the points specified under Art. 2.

As regards fortifications at the Canal itself, I have always regarded unfavorably the idea of safeguarding the Canal, militarily, by a land force. Nevertheless, if we had a navy sufficient to predominate in the Caribbean, the Canal, unfortified, would be to the fleet something like what our undefended ports were in 1898—a source of distraction, apprehension and a divided navy. Let us suppose the navy absent, for any military reason, some hostile ships might pass the canal, being entirely free to do so by this treaty. On the other hand, unless San Francisco and Puget Sound are miserably undefended, it is difficult to see why they should go for them, and leave unnoticed the far more important Atlantic centres; not to speak of removing their fleets so much farther from their great centres of interest, in Europe, and the Mediterranean.

Upon the whole, I am inclined to favor the treaty, upon one condition, viz: that the country adopt a decisive policy of keeping our navy equal at least to that of Germany. Who however can insure that? Even did we undertake the guarantee, and the fortifications, by ourselves alone, would we provide, betimes, either the forts or the necessary navy? I doubt it much. Like Great Britain, we are not forehanded.

I think the Administration has made a mistake, if it has concluded this treaty without careful consultation with, and between, some capable officers of army & navy. On the face of it, military considerations are, if not supreme, of very great importance. There is no indication that the opinion of any military or naval man has been asked. It is not only a mistake in itself,

---

1. The first Hay-Pauncefote Treaty of February 1900 which, in effect, abrogated the Clayton-Bulwer Treaty of 1850 to the extent that Britain would permit the United States unilaterally to own, construct, and neutralize an Isthmian canal, but under no conditions to fortify such a waterway. The Senate refused to accept the non-fortification clause and the treaty died in March, 1901.

but a grave political blunder in tactics; for the statement that (e.g.) Miles and Dewey approved would have immense weight with the public. As it is, they have no expert backing to meet the inevitable assault. It is so like politicians.

The analogy implied between this Canal and Suez is, I think, overstrained. In one way, Suez is far more important than Panama, and will long remain so; but no European Power except Great Britain (in India) is so exposed by Suez, as our Pacific coast will be by Panama. Besides Great Britain had nothing to do with the making of Suez. We are about to open a way to our Pacific towns etc, and the question of the effect upon them demands a more mature consideration *by qualified men* than seems to have been given.

My mind is yet open. If you have at hand a copy of my *Interest of America in Sea Power*, you can find on pp. 13 and 22 my opinions on this thing ten years ago. In a series of articles about to appear in *Harpers*, "The Problem of Asia," I regard Panama and its approaches as entirely our concern. I am not sure however that this treaty conflicts with that position.

To William Peterson[1]

160 West 86th Street, New York, February 28, 1900 [MCGUA][2]

It gives me much pleasure to accept the offer you have made me, of proposing my name for the honorary degree of Doctor of Laws from McGill University. I shall much appreciate the distinction.

I am very glad to know that any utterance of mine has given satisfaction to the people of Canada. At this period of the world's history whatever tends to draw closer the ties of kinship between the United States and the British Empire, whether in its whole or in its parts, is a matter of congratulation. The result of cordial mutual understanding is sure to be reached, provided those of us who realize the importance can have the patience to bear with the extravagances of opponents on one side or the other.

I am glad that my reply has been delayed long enough to enable me to congratulate you upon the distinguished share of the Canadian troops in the recent successful operations in South Africa.

---

1. Principal of McGill University 1895–1919; an imperialist who desired a continued and closer connection between Canada and Great Britain.
2. From the *Montreal Gazette*, March 22, 1900.

To William Peterson

160 West 86th Street, New York, March 9, 1900[1] [MCGUA]

I meant my last letter to be understood that I would come to Montreal for the proceedings of April 30.

I have received and read with pleasure your pamphlet, with which it is needless to say I am in general agreement. I do not greatly value arbitration, except in deciding pure matters of fact. As regards the relations of the two peoples, you do not dwell upon what to my mind is the crucial necessity, viz., patience on the part of those who think as we do, with the volatile, prejudiced, unthinking or malevolent parts of the community. In a way Great Britain needs this more than we, because your comparatively homogeneous people find hard to understand the violent utterances and professions of a nation which has not yet reached the stage even of being composite, but is simply heterogeneous, with prejudices often akin to the soil. In this the Irish are conspicuous, but even the Germans do not wholly escape, although as Americans they have a higher and more intelligent patriotism. But if it is hard for Great Britain to bear, what is it to those of us who see the righteousness and policy of the state endangered by such folly and malevolence as has been shown here lately. There is but one thing—patience, faith that as the elements of future understanding between the English-speaking peoples exist, so they will progress to perfection if only we are patient in action and in endurance.

To Seth Low

160 West 86th Street, New York, March 28, 1900 [CUL]

My dear Mr. Low: I have written Mr. Whitehouse[1] a letter with a good send off for the Doctor.

Have you any formal ideas as to the best way of reaching the public ear through the press? To reach, that is, the class that thinks understandingly, and most shapes that formless thing we call public opinion. Are weeklies like the *Independent* better than the good dailies? The country, and I think the Administration, is floundering a good deal at present on some subjects—notably S. African mediation.

---

1. From the *Montreal Gazette*, March 22, 1900.
1. H. R. Whitehouse.

To William Peterson

... A cordial understanding between Great Britain and the United States is sure to be reached, provided that those of us who are aware of its importance have the patience to bear with the volatile, prejudiced or malevolent parts of our community. Great Britain needs patience more than we do, because your homogeneous people find it difficult to understand the violent utterances of our nation, which is not yet even composite, but simply heterogeneous. In this connection the Irish are conspicuous, but the Germans are not blameless. But if this is hard for Great Britain to bear, what is it for those of us who see the righteousness and policy of the State endangered by such folly and malevolence as have lately been shown here? ....[2]

To John M. Brown

160 West 86th Street, New York, April 9, 1900 [LC]

My dear Mr. Brown: The frank and cordial relations that have always been between us, lead me to let you know at once that I have consented to write a text, of about fifty thousand words, for an illustrated book on the Boer War, which the Collier Weekly Co. are going to produce.[1] I was led to comply, while deeply regretting the temporary abandonment of the Text Book, by their offering me an extremely high commission. This is of course confidential to you, as being partly their business as well as mine. I do not expect to retain any rights in the work, which I am to finish by July 15.

I do not think I could have completed the Text Book, on the lines in my

---

1. From *The Times*, London, March 24, 1900, under the heading, "Captain Mahan on Anglo-American Relations." *The Times* noted: "Captain Mahan concludes his letter with an admonition to both sides to act patiently and endure, so that out of the existing elements the entente may finally be perfected."
2. Cf. Mahan to Peterson, March 9, 1900. The differences are slight but interesting.

1. *The War in South Africa; a Narrative of the Anglo-Boer War from the Beginning of Hostilities to the Fall of Pretoria*. With an Introduction by Sir John G. Bourinot. New York: P. F. Collier & Son, 1900. Also, *The Story of the War in South Africa 1899–1900*. With Map and Portrait of the Author. 2d ed. London: S. Low, Marston and Co., Ltd., 1900.

mind, in time for the fall season. In the meanwhile, I calculate, if you approve, to publish the three articles now appearing in series in *Harper*, under the title of *The Problem of Asia*.[2] I expect to add to it a fourth, on the Development of the Navy necessitated by expansion, which *Harper* has agreed to take for the Nov. number,[3] leaving me free to publish in book form on Dec. 1. With the fourth article the whole would run about 40,000 words; and the subject I think one likely to be timely, perhaps even to become suddenly timely. In the latter event, I would publish it on the moment without No. 4.

I think I can in due time make of the Text Book an interesting and thoroughly individualized work—and the Collier commission will make me very much at my ease, barring exceptional circumstances.

To George R. Carpenter[1]

160 West 86th Street, New York, April 11, 1900 [CUL]

Dear Prof Carpenter: Your note with enclosures did not reach me till Monday evening. I am extremely indebted to you for the trouble you have taken. The average opinion is perhaps less enthusiastic than the fond parent would desire, but I personally am not disposed greatly to trouble myself about the immaturity and shortcomings of a lad[2]—he is scarcely more yet—of whose general conscientiousness and right mindedness I have constant observation.

If his purpose holds as to career, I suppose he will have to begin to specialize a little next year; but I want him not to let go the classics and English any more than is absolutely necessary.

---

2. *The Problem of Asia and its Effect upon International Policies*. Boston: Little, Brown and Company, 1900.
3. Mahan did not have an article in *Harper's Monthly* for November. He did, however, publish "Effect of Asiatic Conditions upon World Policies" in the November 1900 issue of *North American Review*.

1. Professor of Rhetoric at Columbia University.
2. Lyle Evans Mahan, who was graduated from Columbia in 1902.

To Robert U. Johnson

160 West 86th Street, New York, April 11, 1900 [NYPL]

Dear Mr. Johnson: I find that my copy of the Report of Bu. of Navn.—advanced sheets—has the *report* of the Wainwright Board[1] but not the *plans*. You see I am so far an un*pre*judiced person as regards the *battle* though pretty well settled as to the campaign.

To John M. Brown

160 West 86th Street, New York, April 15, 1900 [LC]

My dear Mr. Brown: There can I think be no doubt that the title, *Problem of Asia* will stand. If, as I think most probable, I produce the further article upon necessary naval development, it can be covered on title page by a sub-title. I am to finish the Collier work by July 15—a probably close call; upon which I purpose immediately taking up the article, and that completed to revert to the Text Book and finish it. It is probable that for a year to come England will be more absorbed in the S. African War than in anything relating to Sea Power; but the Problem of Asia is looming largely, if vaguely, upon the future and may be precipitated at a moment. There was an article this week in the *N.Y. Coml. Advr.* from a London correspondent, which I might have thought written after a talk with me.

I note what you say about magazine articles.

To John Bassett Moore

160 West 86th Street, New York, May 7, 1900 [LC]

My dear Mr. Moore: Can you tell me whether Portugal bases her action, in permitting British troops to land at Beira and pass through her territory to Rhodesia, upon any treaty stipulation; and, if so, what is the character of that stipulation, in a general way?

Personally, I cannot see that there is in this any breach of neutrality,

---

1. The Board of Navigation convened for the purpose of plotting and reporting upon the positions of the Spanish vessels and the vessels of our own fleet at the beginning of and during the Battle of Santiago, on July 3, 1898. Admiral Richard Wainwright class of 1868, was senior member for the latter portion of the Board's existence. His testimony is in *Record of Proceedings of a Court of Inquiry in the Case of R. Adm. Winfield S. Schley, U.S. Navy*, Vol. 1, p. 670 ff.

though it may very probably be highly inconvenient to the Boers. I may, however, overlook some element in the case; & I have inferred, from casual mention that Great Britain has in the past acquired some privilege in the nature of a right of way.

To John Bassett Moore

160 West 86th Street, New York, May 11, 1900 [LC]

My dear Mr. Moore: Thank you very much for the enclosed,[1] which arrived after I mailed my first—a sad warning against undue punctuality. There is clearly no doubt as to the ground of action of the Portuguese, or as to the treaty rights.

To John Bassett Moore

160 West 86th Street, New York, May 11, 1900 [LC]

Dear Mr. Moore: I am extremely obliged to you for your clear and comprehensive reply to my inquiry. I think I can, without risk of more than a small contention, retain my statement that Great Britain has by treaty "a right of military way" through the Portuguese territory.

To Seth Low

160 West 86th Street, New York, May 29, 1900 [CUL]

My dear Mr. Low: I am now able to say positively that I can attend the ceremonies of Columbia on June 13, according to the kind offer tendered to me.[1] You will doubtless let me know in due time just when and where I am to present myself. I am leaving town in a few days but will be no farther off than Quogue, Long Island, at the time appointed.

As tomorrow is a holiday I send this to your house instead of to the University.

---

1. A note on the back of the enclosure reads: "This refers to a clipping from the London *Standard* of April 27, 1900, under the headlines—'The Powers and the War—The Boer Peace Mission—Portugal and the Beira Route.' I saw it almost immediately after sending to Capt. Mahan my letter of the 9th of May, 1900, and enclosed it to him with a request for its return. J.B.M."

1. To receive an honorary LL.D. degree.

To Edward K. Rawson

University Club, New York, May 31, 1900 [NA]

My dear Mr. Rawson: I have today returned by registered mail the 3d Volume, Nicolas's *Nelson*.[1] Many thanks.

Do you keep the English *Army & Navy Gazette*? If so would it be possible to lend me the file from January 1? I dont think I shall ask it, but may, if you are willing to let it go. I am writing a brief outline of the Boer War. Address 160 W. 86 as usual.

To John Bassett Moore

Slumberside, Quogue, Long Island, June 14, 1900 [LC]

My dear Mr. Moore: I want to say, what I had not opportunity for yesterday, how much I appreciated your well weighed and interesting words in presenting Lord Pauncefote.[1] The just mean which separates well merited eulogium from mere flattery was admirably preserved, and the synopsis of his career was so clearly and adequately given as to convey to the audience the evidence of his distinction without wearying them. I congratulate you heartily.

To Seth Low

Slumberside, Quogue, Long Island, June 28, 1900 [CUL]

My dear Mr. Low: I wish I could feel sure that it was right to authorize the public use of that incident,[1] but I am not. I dont know how far the general obligation of silence as to what occurs in such meetings would apply here, and so, although I have not on occasion hesitated to say to others what I did to you, it is different to give publicity. If you think it would at

---

1. *See* Mahan to Brown, October 4, 1896.

1. Pauncefote also received an honorary LL.D. degree from Columbia University on June 13, 1900.

1. A meeting at the White House on July 13, 1898, attended by President McKinley, Secretary of War Russell A. Alger, Secretary of the Navy John D. Long, Mahan, and others. It was called to deal, in part, with a renewed request by General Shafter to Admiral Sampson to bring about the surrender of Santiago substantially by naval action. *See* Walter Millis, *The Martial Spirit* (New York: The Literary Guild of America, 1931), p. 322; and Margaret Leech, *In the Days of McKinley* (New York: Harper & Brothers, 1959), pp. 266–267.

all tend to the same end, I should have no objection to your saying, at any time, that I had frequently occasion to see the President at moments of anxiety and perplexity, and that I was particularly struck by his equability, composure, and rational firmness and decision under such circumstances. I was inspired with a feeling of great confidence in his resolution of purpose, which has since always remained with me.

I suppose I told you that the consequence of the President's determination was that I suggested the alternative, ultimately adopted—that the surrender of the Spaniards at Santiago be accepted conditional upon their quitting Cuba for Spain.[2] About this I said nothing, until last summer, while we were at the Hague, I saw in the press that Alger was claiming this to his credit. I then wrote Long (Sec. Navy)[3] asking whether under the circumstances he ought not to make known that the credit, such as it was, was due me and the Navy. He replied that when he returned to Washington in the fall he would give a correct statement to the Press. (It happened that about ten days after the incident I had asked Long if he remembered who made the suggestion, and he replied, 'Yes, you did.') He never did, however, nor have I reminded him. Whether this was because he thought the transactions confidential, or whether he simply forgot, I dont know.

To the Duke of Cambridge

Quogue, Long Island, July 10, 1900[1]

Sir: I have the honour to acknowledge the receipt of your letter of 31st May, transmitting to me the Chesney Gold Medal, with the gratifying notification that the Council of the Royal United Service Institution have awarded it to me in recognition of the bearing of my works—*The Influence of Sea Power* and *The Life of Nelson*—upon the welfare of the British Empire.

In expressing my thanks, it seems scarcely necessary to say how deeply I feel the personal honour of this distinction, conferred by the unanimous wish of a professional organisation of the high standing of this, over which your Royal Highness presides. May I be permitted to add that I value even more highly, if that be possible, the assurance that in such competent judgment, my works have contributed in some degree to the welfare of the British Empire, the strength of which is so essential to the cause of our English-speaking race, and of mankind in general.

---

2. Surrender terms for the Spanish garrison at Santiago also were discussed at the meeting. *See* Mahan to Low, August 7, 1900, Footnote 3.
3. *See* Mahan to Long, August 21, 1899.
1. From the Royal United Service Institution *Journal* (October 1900), p. 1098.

To Seth Low

Slumberside, Quogue, Long Island, August 7, 1900 [CUL]

Dear Mr. Low: Thank you for your letter of the 3d. The President, I think is right as regards a formal reference to the War Board.[1] My recollection is that we were summoned to the White House, and there met, whether by intention, or coincidence, a number of other persons, chiefly members of the Cabinet, and two or three Army officers—Corbin[2] I think among them; in all 12 or 15 persons. In the discussion the members of our Board took part as members, not as a Board supporting a view reach(ed) collectively; for we knew nothing of the telegram[3] until we entered the room. This has been my recollection all along, and if it appear otherwise in my letter to you—if you still have it—it is through inadvertence.

I daresay it would be unwise to open the matter *now*, but if Alger over a year ago claimed the credit of the suggestion, I fail to see why it could not have been corrected last September, when I suggested. The telegram is of course a matter of record. The Administration has been too cautious in such matters. To me the injury is too trivial for mention, and is negative; but lack of boldness in tackling a situation has resulted in Sampson's case in injury positive, grave and lasting his life, I fear. History doubtless will do justice.

To Francis V. Greene

Slumberside, Quogue, Long Island, August 12, 1900 [LC]

My dear General: May I ask you whether the enclosed[1] deserves my attention, from the names of the signers. I purpose of course to contribute to the Campaign funds,[2] and, in the present uncertainty as to the nominees for Governor, prefer to help in the legislative districts—Congressional and State—to the general State ticket. I infer from recent utterances of Mr. Platt that he is again on the "Rule or Ruin" path that gave us a Tammany

---

1. *See* Mahan to Low, June 28, 1900, and Footnotes.
2. Henry C. Corbin, Adjutant General in the War Department.
3. From General Miles in Santiago, July 13, 1898, stating that yellow fever had broken out in the American Army and recommending easy surrender terms for the Spanish garrison. These terms were granted.

1. Enclosure not found.
2. Greene, a staunch supporter of Roosevelt, spearheaded the anti-Bryan campaign in New York.

City Govt. two years ago. Organization and centralization of effort is absolutely necessary—no military man can doubt that; but when supreme control of the organization falls into such hands the term "machine" is due, in its most opprobrious sense. Organization then has the danger of a standing army in reckless hands.

To William McKinley

Quogue, Long Island, September 2, 1900 [LC]

Dear Mr. McKinley: There is evident presumption in a man in my position addressing one in yours, unasked; but the Government's Instructions of August 29[1] have caused me such consternation, that I trust my rashness may be forgiven.

That the Government of the United States should follow its own judgment, even if clearly mistaken, is one thing; but that in an enterprise, heretofore joint, the Government should abandon its own judgment because one of five or six other Powers proposes to separate its action from the others, can scarcely fail to have a most injurious effect upon the reputation and standing, not of the Government only, but of the nation.

That the Power which thus controls our action is Russia will be thought worst of all. I presume that no one who has followed Russia's course about the Hague Conference, and about China, will doubt that in this step she is not only playing her own game—all states do that—but playing it with the unscrupulous craft of the Asiatic.

Do you know that the Russian Minister in China, last May, in a private interview with the British Minister, said that "there were only two countries with serious interests in China—England and Russia" (Parl. Paper 'China' No. 3, 1900). To what end, then, does she now seek the cooperation of the U.S.? Clearly in order to break up the Concert, not by a general disagreement but by the principle that the withdrawal of one neutralizes all.[2]

---

1. Instructions to withdraw American forces from the joint Western military intervention in the Boxer Rebellion at Peking. The Russians had signified their intention to withdraw their forces and legation to Tientsin, the better to make a separate and more desirable arrangement with the Chinese Government on reparations for the Boxer outrages during the siege of Peking.
2. Receipt of this letter was acknowledged by George Cortelyou, Secretary to the President, on September 5, 1900.

To an Unidentified Addressee

Slumberside, Quogue, Long Island, September 15, 1900 [YUL]

Dear Sir: I have the honor to acknowledge your letter of the 8th, and to thank you for the offer to give me James *Naval Occurrences*.[1] If you are quite sure you may not yourself need it, I will with many thanks accept it; but I should tell you that, although I am not familiar with it, I believe it was the precursor only of his well known *Naval History*,[2] and that the latter embodies all of value in the former. As I have ready access to the later work, the former would be to me only a convenience & a possible loss to you.

My project of writing the *War of 1812* has remained in suspense, although fairly begun. Present day interests have diverted me continuously from the seclusion proper to historical writing. I hope I may continue it & conclude; for I believe I have that to say which will scarcely occur to any one else.

To Francis V. Greene

Slumberside, Quogue, Long Island, September 17, 1900 [LC]

My dear General: I enclose cheque for $200 for the campaign fund. I leave it entirely in the hands of the Committee, expressing, however, a preference that if practicable—or desirable—half should go to my own Congressional District.

I do not feel the alarm this year that I did four years ago; not because I share the prevailing assurance of Republican victory, but because I think I can read between the lines of current happenings that even defeat would not be the overwhelming disaster it would then have been. A disaster yes; and very real—but not irretrievable. Neither on the silver question, nor on imperialism, will Bryan if victorious have behind him a party sufficiently united to revolutionize.

Nevertheless, in a political sense he is a bad man, a *very* bad man; all the worse if he be as honest as reported. He stands, personally, for essential

---

1. William James, *A Full and Correct Account of the Chief Naval Occurrences of the Late War between Great Britain and the United States of America. . . .* London: T. Egerton, 1817.
2. William James, *The Naval History of Great Britain, from the Declaration of War by France in 1793, to the Accession of George IV. . . .* A new edition. . . . London: R. Bentley, 1847.

revolution, and reversal of certain well initiated advances—towards the gold standard & expansion not to speak of the still worse attitude towards riot & the Courts. In my conception, if he is elected the country will still progress towards them; but not with the steady onward movement now and lately, but with the bewildered staggering of a man who has "come a cropper" and has a slight concussed brain. Accordingly, I send my money and shall be careful to vote.

Has it struck you in the late dealing with the China question that there has been a wobbling view recollective of the dealing with silver twenty years ago?

[P.S.]   I leave here today. Address in town though I shall not be there.

To John Bassett Moore

160 West 86th Street, New York, October 25, 1900 [LC]

My dear Mr. Moore: As my pamphlet mail is not forwarded during my summer absences, it was only on my return yesterday that I have your paper—A Hundred Years of American Diplomacy[1]—for which I beg to thank you very heartily.

To John S. Billings

160 West 86th Street, New York, October 26, 1900 [NYPL]

My dear Dr. Billings: This will introduce to you Captn. Chas. H. Stockton of the Navy, who has some work to do in connection with the service in the field of International Law. For this purpose he wishes as free access to the Library shelves as it may be possible to extend him, analogous to the former alcove privilege.

You can entirely depend upon Captn. Stockton, who is long known to me, not only not in any way to abuse your courtesy, but also to use his privileges in a manner really conducive to the good of the Navy.

---

1. John Bassett Moore, "A Hundred Years of American Diplomacy." A Paper Read at Saratoga Springs [to the American Bar Association], August 30, 1900. N.P., N.D. [New York, 1900].

To Charles S. Fairchild

160 West 86th Street, New York, October 28, 1900 [NYHS][1]

My dear Mr. Fairchild: I wish to express to you the great pleasure and admiration with which I read your powerful speech at the Roosevelt reception.[2]

Men in your position of strong and lifelong Democratic antecedents, have been advantageously placed above all others for exercising a decisive influence in the rejection of the man who has usurped your title; but I have known of none, of equally conspicuous standing, who has spoken as opportunely and courageously as you have on this particular occasion.

To J. Franklin Jameson

160 West 86th Street, New York, November 6, 1900 [LC]

My dear Mr. Jameson: Your letter has reached me at an unfortunate moment for your request, for I have had forced upon me of late the recognition, and determination, that if I am to accomplish anything further in life I must resolutely exclude all side issues in which I have no special interest.

Three busy years have now passed in which I have done only occasional work. Unless I resolutely practice exclusiveness of purpose, my short remaining time will be frittered in like trivialities.

[P.S.] Have you ever tried Capt. C. H. Stockton of the Navy?

To James Ford Rhodes

160 West 86th Street, New York, November 9, 1900 [MHS]

My dear Mr. Rhodes: It gives me much pleasure to renew my acceptance of your invitation for the 28th, at 7.30 at the Century.

I will say to you what I say to my other correspondents since the election, let us congratulate one another.

---

1. Courtesy of the New York Historical Society, New York City.
2. A rally at Madison Square Garden, October 26, of which General F. V. Greene was chairman. Roosevelt spoke against Bryan. Among the other speakers was Fairchild, representing the Gold Democrats.

Poor Mr. Schurz![1] Three years ago he told me with deep feeling what he had undergone in having to support Greeley in 1872. What would he have then felt to know he would live to support Bryan.

To George F. W. Holls

160 West 86th Street, New York, November 13, 1900 [HUL]

Dear Mr. Holls: Upon returning from a short absence last night I found awaiting me the copy of the *Peace Conference at the Hague*,[1] which you have been kind enough to present me, and for which I beg to express my sincere thanks.

To Charles Scribner's Sons

160 West 86th Street, New York, November 22, 1900 [PUL]

Gentlemen: I beg to acknowledge the receipt of, and to thank you for, the copy of Buell's *Paul Jones*,[1] with which you have been so kind as to favor me.

To the Authors' Club of New York

160 West 86th Street, New York, December 1, 1900 [CUL]

Captain Mahan has much pleasure in accepting the invitation of the Authors' Club to the reception to be given to Mr. Edmund Clarence Stedman on Dec. 5.[1]

---

1. Carl Schurz, editor, reformer, and scholar.
1. George Frederick William Holls, *The Peace Conference at the Hague and its Bearings on International Law and Policy*. New York: The Macmillan Company, 1900.
1. Augustus C. Buell, *Paul Jones, Founder of the American Navy; a History*. 2 vols. New York: Charles Scribner's Sons, 1900.
1. The reception marked the completion of Stedman's *American Anthology*.

To Henry Cabot Lodge

160 West 86th Street, New York, December 8, 1900 [MHS]

My dear Mr. Lodge: If you are spared to your full span of life, as I earnestly hope you may be, the position you have already earned by distinguished public service makes sure that you are to be one of the determining factors in our country's future. I am rejoiced, consequently, to know that your opinion coincides in general outline with my own, concerning the community of interest between ourselves & Great Britain in some of the great questions of the future.

While, however, I recognize much imperfection in the quality of her recent action in Africa, I do not share your inference as to her practical decadence. Financially, of course, I am wholly inexpert; nor is politics greatly in my line. So far as England may be said to have gone to war with the Transvaal, it was not for the franchise, as I understand the matter; but the good government and fair dealing towards her citizens there domiciled, and because of the pressure by her subjects in the other adjacent colonies. The franchise was not demanded, but indicated as a means to good government; as such means, discussion turned upon it. As usual, the cause of the war differs from the occasion, and men's opinions will differ as to both. The cause, in my apprehension, was the purpose, evident though possibly not formulated, of the Dutch race to impose supremacy in South Africa. This the British both at home & abroad, were determined not to have—their purpose possibly equally not formulated. From such a condition war is bound to follow; but it is the object of both parties, especially in these days when the world sits in judgment day by day, to throw the onus on the other. Partly from the sense that odium would attach to war with a weaker party, partly to unite her own people, Great Britain was compelled not to assemble the force sufficient to repel aggression, until past the moment of reasonable safety. That mistakes of detail should occur was inevitable. In the main I think her policy, as policy, justified. The indisposition of the Boer govt. to grant fair terms, *except coupled* with impossible conditions, was demonstrated to many minds besides my own—notably to the colonies; & the Transvaal declared war because of the dispatch of troops not in excess of the numbers at the disposal of the two Boer states. To my mind Great Britain won the diplomatic game.

As regards the military operations, these, being on land, are not my specialty; but I have given a running commentary upon them in my book on the S. African war. In summary, there are grave errors of incapacity in some quarters—Buller[1] notably; but there has been to my mind quite a suf-

---

1. General R. H. Buller, Commander-in-Chief in South Africa until relieved by Lord Roberts.

ficient showing of great capacity and good fighting quality to relieve any fear of decadence. Consider McClellan and Pope in our civil war—Bull Run, Chancellorsville, Fredericksburg—could decadence be inferred from them? Burnside & Hooker were not only gallant gentlemen, but trained soldiers, graduates of one of the best military schools in the world. McClellan was not only all this, but a man of exceptional military accomplishment, and his capacity as an organizer—which is also Buller's strong point—was evidenced; yet he failed hopelessly. In his first decision, to divide his advance—upon Ladysmith and Kimberley—Buller was under sore trial, and merely failed to rise to a strength few soldiers have; but I own to thinking that his advance upon Ladysmith showed a most singular facility for choosing the wrong road whenever a choice was open to him.

To Mary Edith Powel

160 West 86th Street, New York, December 16, 1900[1]

My dear Mrs. Powel: I am sending to you tomorrow a copy of my *Story of the Boer War*—one published in England, not in this country, & for which I have had to send as not being on the American market. It has the advantage—in the author's opinion—of not having the text cut up by numerous illustrations, mostly irrelevant to the page on which they stand. For the reader the lightness—in avoirdupois—is a commendation; and if you do me the honor to read it, I trust you may find its mental calibre rather solid than heavy. In any event, it is short—only 55,000 words.

I beg you will accept it as a passing incident and recollection of our pleasant friendship, now extending over quite many years. By the way, we parted yesterday with a companion whose life just measured the span of my acquaintance with you—our old bull terrier Jomini. He was over twelve, but seemed well and jolly till he broke down all of a sudden. We tried for a week to prolong his health, but then finding that hopeless, chloroform put an end to his suffering.

Mrs. Mahan joins with me in love to Mr. Powel and yourself.

To Bouverie F. Clark

160 West 86th, Street, New York, December 19, 1900 [LC]

My dear Clark: It was a very small matter to send you an advanced copy of the *Boer War*, after your invaluable help in giving me data for

---

1. Letter courtesy of Mr. Stephen Adamson, Stoughton, Massachusetts.

one of the most interesting—to me—& useful chapters in it.[1] I wanted to lay it on to you a little thicker than I did, for I know well enough that the smoother & more efficiently a machine runs, the less credit does the driver get with the outside world. But I was afraid my intention by being too obvious might defeat itself; and I trusted that the unqualified praise I gave to the work itself, and coupling your name immediately with it, as the person most directly responsible, would get you your due with thinking men. Upon the whole, my book has recd as good treatment from the press as I could have expected. In my own judgment, it is the *sort* of thing the man in the street needs; whether it is a good thing of the sort is another question.

China is a pretty muddle isn't it? I take no stock in "Concerts"; and therefore while I not only desire but continually insinuate in my writings cordial understanding between you and us, I have no use for an alliance. Tell each people the truth about our common interests & mutual traditions & influence—keep on telling & repeating until the thing takes hold, and be patient till it has time to grip; but no paper ties, if you please. As regards the Chinese, I found out something in my experience with my children. When they have done wrong, if you insist on their doing something, they sometimes curtly *will* to do it. Consequently, after some disastrous failures, I adopted this plan which always worked. I required no amends at the moment, no promise for the future. I just gave them a good whaling & let them go. The same thing rarely occurred again. Of course I see we have difficulty at reaching the Chinese culprits but I think they could be made to feel fear for the future . . . [remainder of letter lost].

To an Unidentified Addressee

160 West 86th Street, New York, December 19, 1900 [LC]

My dear Sir: It will give me much pleasure to endorse your candidacy. I shall, of course, in undertaking to do this be obliged to verify my impressions of your eligibility by some particular inquiry, for one is not justified, in my opinion, in endorsing without something more positive than mere general impression—but in your case there can be little difficulty in my obtaining the necessary assurance.

---

1. Clark was Director of Transports during the War. On p. 86 of *The Story of the War in South Africa* (the second, English edition, which Mahan preferred), Mahan gave Clark credit for the successful conduct of the war. This chapter, "The Colonies and the Transports," presented statistics which he no doubt received from Clark.

To James Ford Rhodes

University Club, New York, January 3, 1901 [MHS]

My dear Mr. Rhodes: I shall be more than grateful to you, in case I proceed on to the Presidency,[1] to be relieved of the detail duties of administration. Administration has at all times been distasteful to me, but of late years I have found myself more and more obliged to cut away ruthlessly all side issues that may interfere with what I regard as my proper work. You see I am now sixty, and it seems to me that I have already, clearly in view and well defined, work enough to last me the remainder of my three score & ten. I have besides been diverted, as you know, by ephemeral work connected with the passing issues of the last few years in national policy. These seem to me to have passed now beyond my probable or necessary influence, & I wish now to resume, without distraction, my self-prescribed work.

Your offer therefore is more than acceptable, more than welcome to me & I thank you for it very sincerely.

To Albert B. Hart

160 West 86th Street, New York, January 5, 1901 [NYPL]

My dear Professor Hart: I am very much indebted to you for the copy of your book[1] which has been safely received. It is needless to tell you that I am much interested in the subject always, and I look forward with anticipation to adding to my stock of facts and of ideas from what you have written.

I cannot pass without notice the compliment with which you have doubled the pleasure of your gift. I am always a little surprised to find I have done anything for history, but such recognition as you flatter me with, is very much valued.

---

1. Of the American Historical Association. Mahan became vice president of the Association in 1901, president in 1902, and from 1903 to 1914 served as a councilor. He served also on the Association's Federal Documentary History Committee in 1910, and on its Committee on the Federal Archives Building in 1911.

1. Albert Bushnell Hart, *Foundations of American Foreign Policy*. New York: Macmillan, 1901. Of the three books published by Hart in 1901, this seems the most likely gift to Mahan.

To Edward K. Rawson

160 West 86th Street, New York, January 8, 1901 [NA]

Dear Mr. Rawson: I return Monson[1] by registered mail. I regret that I did not know it was in demand, for I supposed in these go-ahead days only potterers in the past like myself would trouble about him, & I was holding the book for further consultation besides the very copious notes already made.

Thanking you very much for the use of it I am [etc.].

To J. Franklin Jameson

160 West 86th Street, New York, January 18, N.D.   Probably, 1901 [LC]

My dear Prof. Jameson: I am not willing to undertake any work outside of my present professional engagements for at least six months to come. I find in my life, what I continually teach as a student of war, that if a man wants to accomplish any principal object he must refuse to entangle himself with minor—to him—matters; & my attitude toward the myriad of activities that thrust their claims upon me is rapidly passing from wonder, through lack of sympathy, to something like antagonism. I cannot find it possible to believe, and my recollection of the days when I was unknown disproves, that such dissemination of effort is as fruitful of result as concentration is. I dont believe in the spirit of the age, as thus manifested, and I intend not to be led captive by it at its will, now that I have recognized the tendency.

To John M. Brown

160 West 86th Street, New York, January 22, 1901 [LC]

My dear Mr. Brown: I have been wondering whether it might not be expedient for me to have addressed to M. Gaston Fournier a question, as to whether there are yet any proceeds from the sale of the French translations. He kindly sent me some half dozen copies before I left the Hague, a year ago last July. I have usually preferred to transact such business through the publishers rather than personally, & if you think well I should be glad to have your firm make the inquiry, as you dealt with him. Todays

---

1. *Naval Tracts.*

mail brings me a request for permission to do *The Problem of Asia* into German. This I will refer to Marston as he has heretofore undertaken the European countries except France.

You may be interested incidentally to know that a German officer has also asked to translate the *Boer War*.

At present I am reading with a view to the text book, but as the subject & the treatment I would wish to give grow on my mind, I find myself compelled to master much which will bear to the result the unseen relation which foundations bear to a building. They must have breadth and depth, which means time & digging.

[P.S.]   I have never had any returns from M. Fournier.

To Henry Cabot Lodge

160 West 86th Street, New York, February 19, 1901 [MHS]

My dear Mr. Lodge: I observe the introduction of the bill for making two Vice Admirals.

When in Washington eighteen months ago, at the dinner given by the President to Dewey, Sampson waited for me in the lower hall as we were leaving, & told me that this compromise had been suggested to him by a Senator. He asked my opinion. I replied that, in my judgment, he (Sampson) had eminently deserved the honor; that its bestowal was due to the Navy as well as to himself, for he represented all the Navy had done before Santiago; but that even this justice would be too dearly purchased by the implied recognition of merit in a man in whom the Navy, as a corps, saw nothing but discredit. I understood Sampson to coincide with this view, but I know nothing of his subsequent action.

I am in no sense authorized to speak for the Navy, but I have had considerable intercourse, direct and indirect, with officers from before Santiago, and I believe the view I express agrees substantially with theirs. It is now but three days that I was speaking in the club with an officer—a retired rear-admiral, whose name perhaps stands highest among such in naval estimation—and he said, "It should never be tolerated that a man should be thus promoted, whom nine-tenths of the Navy look upon as they do." I forbear the epithet he used.

As regards Sampson, I may quote Erben—no friend of mine—who spoke to me spontaneously in the Club within the week. "I hope," he said, "that Sampson will get his promotion now. I have been abroad since the war, and have heard the opinion of foreign officers—men of the stamp you and I knew there," (there were none higher in repute), "and they understand & value most highly the *operations as a whole*, conducted by Sampson. They recognize what *he* did. The battle was creditable to our people. They did everything that was open to them to do, and did it thoroughly; but in itself, merely as a battle, it has no extraordinary merit among several other battles; but taken with the antecedent operations, the whole was a very fine piece of work." These I understood to be the sentiments of the foreigners which Erben quoted. I dont answer for his own. They certainly, however, express *my* opinion.

On the other hand, speaking as a student of naval history, I do not think Schley's reputation can possibly survive the "return to Key West" telegram; and, with less certainty, because I have not so clearly known the facts, I believe the story of Santiago likely still further to discredit him.

Can the Senate afford to go on record, as placing him in a list with which so far are associated only the names of Farragut, Porter, Rowan, & (constructively) Dewey; for the latter passed through the rank. It must be remembered that history has yet to speak in this matter. There can be no question what her verdict will be, or that it will be plainly spoken. The mere fact that under such grave imputations Schley did not ask for a court, not even after Dewey's return made it possible for him to preside, will receive—can receive—but one interpretation. He dared not.

Words fail to express the pathos and outrage of Sampson's situation. Byng[1] has long stood as the type of national & governmental injustice; but, despite the extreme penalty, there was nothing even approaching the injustice done Sampson by the press & the people. I have found it hard to believe that, if it came to a vote, the majority of the Senate would refuse to endorse his eminent services; but to promote Schley along with him will be not to endorse, but to depreciate.

To George F. W. Holls

160 West 86th Street, New York, March 11–13,[1] 1901 [HUL]

Dear Mr. Holls: My attention has been called to the account given by you, in your book on the Peace Conference, (pp. 268–270), touching the origin of the reservation made by our Delegation, in signing the "Convention pour le Réglement Pacifique etc." I find this acount so irreconcilable

---

1. Admiral John Byng, RN.

1. *See* Memorandum, circa March 14, 1901.

with the facts that my memory recalls, that I have thought proper to write to you in the matter.

My recollection of the events leading to that reservation is as follows:

Two days, or so, subsequent to the adoption of Article 27 by the Full Third Committee, my eye was caught by an editorial in the *Manchester Guardian*, rejoicing over the extreme results insured by that adoption. I then went to the printed minutes, supplied to delegates, and read the Article; which I had not before done, not being on the Committee immediately concerned. After brief reflection, I became satisfied that it was compromising, as then worded, to our settled national policy, and I decided to bring the subject at once before our Delegation at the meeting which was to be held that forenoon, by appointment. This I did, and an animated discussion followed; all the members being present, and all accepting my views almost immediately. Mr. White,[2] I especially remember, was particularly impressed with the urgent necessity of rectifying the matter. You, however, argued against my contention, and stood out for some time against the admission that the article, for the acceptance of which you among us were primarily responsible, would in operation have the practical effect that I alleged. The matter, indeed, had gone inconveniently far; it was extremely awkward for us, the Conference then nearing its close, to ask to revise, or to dissent from, an article to which our consent had been given, not only in sub-committee but in full committee as well. If, however, you had mentioned to us this reservation, of which your book speaks, our path would have been clear and simple; our retreat would have been kept open. No such mention was made to me then, or at any subsequent time; nor did I ever hear any allusion, by any member of the delegation, to such reservation by you, at that time or afterwards.

The discussion in our delegation resulted in a decision to gather several of our principal foreign associates at a breakfast, to discuss the way out of our dilemma. It is not necessary to pursue farther the history of the reservation, as finally framed, for it is with its origin only that I am here concerned.

If the facts be as I state above—and my memory of them is very clear—, it is hard to reconcile them with either the general coloring of your account, or with your specific assertion that you qualified your approval in sub-committee by "reserving the right to make a declaration * * * after consultation with your colleagues." At our meeting when I brought up the matter, no one present mentioned any previous consultation by you on the matter, and I certainly had not been consulted; although, if the importance of the matter had been realized, as your account implies, I was certainly entitled, as a délégué plénipotentiaire, to be consulted. And at no

---

2. Andrew D. White, chairman of the U.S. delegation to the First Hague Conference.

subsequent stage of the proceedings, at the breakfast, or elsewhere, did I ever hear any mention of this antecedent reservation, or of any antecedent consultation.[3]

To Theodore Roosevelt

University Club, New York, March 12, 1901 [LC]

My dear Vice President: It has been my purpose, somewhat vague I fear, to write you at any time since election, congratulating you on the event; but I have been busy, & I knew you had many to preform to you that function of felicitation, & moreover I did not so wholly congratulate myself upon the concomitant result of your removal from the Governorship here. Truth to say, it seems to me I need not deny myself the deplorable satisfaction of feeling that my premonitions were correct. So far as I can understand matters, it seems to me that your successor is showing far less than the sound judgment & discretion which you, despite a temper impetuous & not overcautious, appeared to me to display in your general course.

I do, however, rejoice in one thing; and that is that you are withdrawn perforce, & not by your own volition, for a prolonged rest from the

3. All of Mahan's contentions in his dispute with Holls are substantiated by a letter from Stanford Newel, U.S. Minister to The Netherlands, to John Hay, dated January 12, 1901:

Capt. Mahan has written calling my attention to pages 269–271 of Holls' book *The Peace Conference at the Hague*—Holls did not make our reservation in the 'Comité d'Examen' and when the Committee reported the plan of arbitration to the Commission . . . Holls, against the advice of Seth Low made a speech in favor of Article 27, and in the official report it is summarized as follows: 'Mr. Holls a fait ressortir à son tour l'importance de l'affirmation d'un devoir moral des États comme corollaire de la solidarité qui unit les peuples.'

The sole credit is due to Capt. Mahan. Without him we would have permitted the adoption of that article without any reservation. At his suggestion the delegation met and after his vigorous and unanswerable statement it was agreed that we should offer a reservation which was then actually drawn by Andrew D. White, and modified to suit Mahan—Holls was crestfallen at that meeting & then we followed it up by inquiring the next day how he came to be a member of the 'Comité d'examen' anyway, not being a delegate; which was never explained by Holls or White to our satisfaction. We then had Seth Low put on the committee which prepared the final Procès Verbal.

You will remember in connection with the present made to Jarousse de Sillac, that I wrote you of a conversation in which he told me, he had received a letter from Mr. Holls who wished inserted in the Procès Verbal a reservation which he had omitted or forgotten to have a minute made of at the time.

I have no words to properly express my opinion of that degree of pure cheek, unleavened. . . .

responsibilities and cares of office. . . . Idle it is not in you to be; but work is a very different thing from the grinding friction of executive office on a large scale. A very sagacious clergyman once remarked to me on the providential ordering in the life of St. Paul—whose career, I think, you will agree was at the least strenuous—by which in midcourse he was arrested, and spent two years of enforced inactivity under Felix in Judaea, followed by two more in the Roman captivity. The total, four, as you will observe, is just a Vice Presidential term; & I trust this period may be to you, as it was to him, a period of professional rest coupled with great intellectual advance and ripening.

As you were in Washington on the 3d., I propose to send you the number of the *Sun* for that day, which has my paper on the development of naval material during the century.[1] It is not amiss to observe that it was sent in before the Spanish War, & never revised beyond proofreading. I was satisfied to let my conclusions of 1897 stand.

I hope you may read—but I dont ask to know whether you do—my *Problem of Asia*. It ought to be, & I intend it shall be, my swan's song on contemporary politics. I become continually more and more convinced that the average man can't tell—as years advance—when he has really got out of touch with the times, & becomes a mere "wind-jammer"—to use a naval expression for useless talk. Look at the eminently respectable Mr. Howe,[2] and I fear Mr. Harrison also. If his present illness prove fatal, what a pity it will seem that he did not get out, or be silent, before he wrote his recent articles.[3] I haven't read them, but have gathered their drift. I trust it may not be so with us, but I feel—itself perhaps an indication that I am dropping behind—that neither we nor Great Britain, separate or combined, can adequately check Russia by main force in Northern China; and that therefore naval power always at hand & available in the Yangtze valley—the heart of China in every sense of the word—is the true counter-check. It will work in two ways; (1) it will at once humanize & strengthen China, the surest element of resistance to Russian mastery, & to consequent brutalizing of Chinese development; & (2) its pressure will operate by force of moral assurance to Russia, that, trespass as she will in our quarter, a solid core of resistance, invincible, is building up in the decisive field & will be perfected before she can have strength to reach so far. If the Sea Powers, to reach [?]

---

1. "The Past Century: Its Progress in Great Subjects. A Set of Remarkable Articles. Eleventh Paper of the Series, by Captain Mahan. 'Naval Ships.'" This article appeared in the New York *Sun* Sunday Supplement, March 3, 1901. It occupied nine columns, and consisted mainly of a history of ordnance and armor.
2. Probably, Frederic C. Howe, journalist, author, pacifist, and reformer.
3. Benjamin Harrison, "Musings upon Current Topics," *North American* (February–March 1901); "Status of Annexed Territory and its Inhabitants," *ibid.* (January 1901); and *Views of an Ex-President.* . . . Compiled by Mary Lord Harrison. Indianapolis: Bowen-Merrill Company, 1901.

physical and moral support in the Yang Tse, will require of China simple, but entire, liberty of entrance for European *thought*, as well as European commerce, China will in my judgment be saved, or rather, & better, will save herself.

Such I say, & hope, is my swan song. After sixty, one cant tell how soon behindedness will be his lot; but I cannot but hope that this idea may enter, for whatever it is worth, into the grasp of one who by years has still much of activity & growth before him, & by achievement & promise the reasonable prospect of affecting, for good or ill, the future course of a great Christian State.

To Theodore Roosevelt

160 West 86th Street, New York, March 12, 1901 [LC]

My dear Mr. Roosevelt: It has occurred to me that the enclosed[1] might interest you as bearing on very current foreign politics. The writer is the Missionary Bishop of the Episcopal Church in the Yangtze valley—at Shanghai—and is very highly esteemed by all who know him. I have never met him. Dont trouble to return the letter.

[*Memorandum*]

160 West 86th Street, New York, March 14, 1901 [LC]

Memorandum as to the date of letter to Holls. The letter was first typewritten by Mrs. Mahan March 11th & therefore so dated.[1] It was not mailed until Wednesday March 13, because I had not yet decided whether to send a copy to the other Delegates,[2] and in case I did so send I wished my letter to reach White as soon as any from Holls could do so, because I believed

---

1. The enclosure consisted of a shorthand passage with the following words in longhand: "Asiatic problems," "Yangtze Kiang," "Millard," "Chaffee and Wilson," "punitive." Thomas F. Millard, author and "Old China Hand"; General Adna R. Chaffee, commander of the American contingent in the relief of Peking; James Wilson, at this time McKinley's Secretary of Agriculture. All favored the establishment of an American commercial and ecclesiastical presence in China and to that end supported the Hay Open Door policy.

1. *See* Mahan to Holls, March 11–13, 1901. The draft dated March 11 is also in the Library of Congress. It contains the penned changes to which Mahan refers at the end of this memorandum. The corrections are minor and do not alter the meaning of the version dated March 13.

2. A. D. White, Stanford Newel, S. Low, and Captain William Crozier.

that Holls could persuade him of anything he chose unless counter arguments were already before him. As Holls would receive his letter on the 13th probably (it being mailed at W³ before 10 A.M.) he had to Friday evening, 15th, to write to White; perfectly even with me.

As Mrs. Mahan had copied by mistake certain phrases I wished omitted, she typewrote the letter to Holls again on the 12th, I preserving the first as my copy; from this were made the copies for the other delegates but as the date—11th, which she copied might mislead them as to the time Holls received I changed it myself, with pen, to 13th, the date it was mailed to him.

To Andrew D. White

160 West 86th Street, New York, March 15, 1901 [CorUL]

My dear Mr. White: I have thought it expedient to address to Mr. Holls a letter, a copy of which I enclose,[1] and the contents of which sufficiently explain themselves. Before writing, I have of course been at pains to verify my recollections by such tests as satisfied me of their substantial accuracy.

I am mailing a copy of my letter to each member of our Delegation.

My compliments to Mrs. White.

To George F. W. Holls

160 West 86th Street, New York, March 25, 1901 [HUL]

Dear Mr. Holls: In commenting upon your letter of March 15, let me first disabuse you of the impression that I find fault with your omission of my personal part in the action of our Delegation touching Article 27. Had you confined your statement to the bare fact that the Delegation considered that the Article could not by it be accepted without a declaratory reservation, such as was made, you would never have heard from me a word of comment, for I should have required nothing more.

I find fault, not with the omission of credit to me, but with the assumption of credit to yourself, by the clear implication that there was a connection between your reservation and the action of the Delegation in deciding to make a qualifying declaration. This you again affirm, explicitly in your letter to me, (p. 7): "None the less it (the Declaration) covered the point which I had in mind on July 3d, and hence, from the point of view of a

---

3. Washington, D.C.

1. Mahan to Holls, March 11–13, 1901.

[709]

history of the Conference, it was *the*" (your underlining [italicization]) "declaration for which I had made a reservation."

There can be, I think, no question that upon a general reader, not otherwise informed of the true state of the case, the narrative of your book will produce the impression that you had foreseen, and provided against, the abandonment of the Monroe Doctrine, involved in the acceptance of Article 27 by the United States, as now so forcibly stated by you on page 270. This is what I mean by the coloring of your narrative; it is so arranged and developed as to produce this effect, which I hold is inaccurate. Granting that a complete account of what you style the "res gestae" required the first mention (book, p. 269)—viz: "the American representative qualifying his approval by reserving, etc,"—the demands of the "res gestae" were by this amply fulfilled. But when, on the same page, you repeat and expand this statement, into these words, "*The declaration* for which *Mr. Holls* made a reservation in the Comité d' Examen, and *which* was afterwards carefully formulated," (my underlining) you do that which not only is wholly superfluous, but which can scarcely be understood otherwise than as intimating a connection between your reservation and the declaration, of a character meritorious to you, as expressed in the words immediately succeeding the above. In them you say that this declaration, for which *you* made a reservation, "is for the U.S. by no means the least important part of the entire convention." To this credit you must excuse my saying, I do not find you entitled. In my opinion, this connection does not exist, judged by the facts, either as I recollect them, or as your letter of the 15th reveals them.

Your letter itself presents here a marked contradiction. In your book, (p.269, 4th line from bottom), you state that you made a reservation in the Comité d' Examen for the Declaration afterwards formulated; whereas in your letter to me you say (p.5), "That reservation * * * had no other effect beyond enabling me, *in that Committee*," (your underlining), "to recur to the point without being out of order or raising a new issue." This was all, and it appears that in the Comité d'Examen you did not further use this reservation. As you do not claim, nor does the record show, that you ever revived it, but on the contrary gave the Article *unreserved* approval at the time when the action of the Comité d'Examen was discussed and adopted by the Full Third Committee, July 20, I fail to see how you can make the claim your book intimates, that for the Declaration there had been made by you any reservation, valid in effect.

That your reservation, such as it was, was dead, if not formally buried, at the time of the meeting of the Full Third Committee, July 20, is further shown by the fact that M. Descamps, in his report to the Conference, July 25, while he mentions the dissent of the Balkan States, and the subsequent discussion on Article 27, including your own speech, entirely omits so important a fact as that the United States might only sign subject to a declaration safeguarding the Monroe Doctrine. He states a unanimous vote in favor, and properly; for, though he knew of our purposed declaration, it was not formally before him in the records on which he based his report.

If, as I consider, the effect of your narrative, pp.268–270, is not only to gloss what I conceive, and I believe most persons would think, a serious error on your part as a negotiator, but further to intimate, not indistinctly, that your reservation was the originating source of our Declaration,—a matter quite to your credit as a negotiator,—you will see that the above inferences raise a very serious doubt as to the correctness of your work. How far my conclusions are sustained, I must leave to the judgment of my colleagues, to whom this letter will be sent.

I might here leave the matter, but it will be better to pursue to the end—so far as the end now appears—the proof of my contention. The question at issue is not whether you in the Comité d'Examen made a reservation of some sort, upon which by your own showing you took no further action. The question is whether your reservation had any effect whatever upon the Delegation in deciding to make its Declaration; whether, indeed, the Delegation even knew that you had made such reservation.

It must be supposed that you did not comprehend the far-reaching tendency of Article 27, when it was adopted by the Comité d'Examen on July 3. No other supposition could in the least justify your failure, at any time between July 3 and July 22, when my intervention occurred, to draw the attention of the Delegation to such tendency. A casual mention such as you allege in your letter to me, (pp.1,2), by no means fulfilled your duty to us, your principals, to keep us fully alive to all possibilities. The various motives and persuasions to delay on the part of foreign members of the Comité d'Examen, mentioned by you, and yielded to by you, (pp.2,3) had of course no weight compared with your obligations to the representatives of your own nation, for whom you were acting. In this state of non-comprehension you remained until July 22; for on that day, in the meeting of our Delegation, your letter states that, in reply to my challenge, you said you "did not consider" Article 27, "in itself a very serious, fundamental and important provision." (p.3). Under this imperfect apprehension, you so wholly failed to convey to the Delegation the importance of the Article, or your reservation, that I do not remember ever to have heard of the one or the other; and from the speech and action of the various members when I brought up the matter, I am persuaded none of them had ever heard of your reservation, between which and this Declaration your book asserts a connection.

Their unconsciousness of the facts lasted thus to July 22, when my intervention occurred; consequent upon which was initiated the course of action which issued in their Declaration. So far as anywhere appears,—and this also I leave to the recollection of my colleagues—our qualifying action had its origin then and thus, and was pushed to completion by July 25, without any knowledge on our part of any reservation made by you, and without our being in any way influenced by anything you had done. This is the actual history of how the Declaration actually came about, as distinct from the more technical, but perfectly sound, point taken above, that excludes, as inoperative, your reservation, which in point of fact did not enter at all into the matter.

If this be so, the first statement of your book, that in Comité d'Examen you made a reservation,—which your letter of the 15th. explains was simply "personal to me" (p.5), and of which you never availed yourself—might be allowed to pass as a part, though a wholly inoperative part, of the "res gestae"; but the further statement, that you had "made a reservation for the Declaration afterwards formulated" is not consistent with the facts.

In closing, I will say that you are perfectly correct in remembering that I wished no declaration, but did wish the removal, or substantial qualification, of the Article. Had you made us fully alive to its purport, instead of leaving us unconscious from July 3 to July 22, I do not know what action the Delegation might have taken, but there would certainly have been a warm discussion. But thus thrust to the end of the Conference, I submitted, for my part, to what seemed the only way out. I have no claim to credit for the Declaration, and am quite content with the knowledge of my colleagues that I started the movement which led to it.

To Andrew D. White

160 West 86th Street, New York, March 26, 1901 [CorUL]

My dear Mr. White: I enclose to you a copy of a letter addressed by me to Mr. Holls, in reply to one from him of date March 15. As I understand from him that you will have received a copy of this latter no further allusion to it is necessary.

To Jarousse de Sillac[1]

Draft   N.P., N.D.   Probably, New York, circa late March 1901 [LC]

My dear M. de Sillac: Will you kindly permit me to recall myself to your memory, as the naval delegate of the U.S. to the Peace Conference in

1. An attaché of the French Embassy and assistant secretary to the Third Commission (Arbitration) at the First Hague Conference.

1899, and in that capacity allow me to ask of you the favor of some information, which I desire concerning the printed Procès Verbaux of the Conference.

In the Procès Verbaux du Comité d'Examen de la Commission d'Arbitrage, on p. 170, I observe that the words, "M. Holls se reservant le droit, en nom de son Gouvernement. . . . qu'il a formulé plus haut, p. 167," are embraced in a parenthesis.

From an examination of the remainder of the Procés of the Comité d' Examen, the use of the parenthesis, covering in this instance a very important act of reservation by a delegate, is quite exceptional. The parenthesis elsewhere seems to be used only to cover references of no importance except as a convenience to readers *1*. Is there any special reason for the use of the parenthesis in this case? Did the words appear in the first printing, or were they inserted, for convenience of reference, after M. Holls had asked for the insertion on p. 167. (for, the reservation of M. Holls, as here stated, was of grave importance.) *2*. Again, does this reservation, stated p. 170, apply to all the remarks of Mr. Holls's on p. 167? Does the reservation include not only the first three and a half lines, p. 167, but also the words, "En ce qui concerne . . . Américaines." These I understand were inserted at the request of M. Holls when the printing of the Procès Verbaux already was far advanced.

My attention has been very forcibly drawn to this matter from the fact it appears, from the Procès Verbaux, that neither in the Comité d' Examen, nor in the Seances of the full Commission does M. Holls appear to have made any use of this reservation, or to have recurred at all to his remarks, p. 167, or to his reservation, p. 170.

Making my excuses for the trouble which I ask of you believe me to be [etc].

To Seth Low

160 West 86th Street, New York, April 4, 1901 [LC]

My dear Mr. Low: Holls's letters are long and touch much non-essential matter; hence tend to confusion. The point at issue is perfectly clear and simple.

Is is this: In his book pp.268–270 he has given of the origin of the Declaration made by our Delegation an account in terms such that you, when you read it, Newell, when he read it, and Crozier when he read it, all, independently, pronounced to be misleading and inaccurate. My attention was first drawn to the passage by a New York lawyer who had heard me, in private conversation, give the account in which you, Crozier, Newell, and myself are substantially agreed. You three, severally, gave me your account in reply to a letter from me, in which, as I remember, I simply drew your attention to the passage in question, and without other suggestion asked your recollections. Your own words in your letter of Nov. 21 are, "The statement, according to my recollection, is altogether inaccurate." Mr. Rives,[1] after receiving from me the same account, was clearly and vividly impressed with the same discrepancy between our account and that of the book in question.

In the face of such agreement as to the impression conveyed by Holls's book, and of the further fact that that impression is all to create a strong outside opinion in Holls's favor, it is preposterous for him to argue that his narrative has not the effect which five men at least have recognized; nor is his disclaimer in his private letter of March 30 of the slightest consequence, so long as the published statements of the book remain uncorrected. It is elementary that public misstatement needs equally public correction. His anxieties about the Monroe Doctrine, as stated to you, his reservation—if he made it—are nothing to the purpose. The Declaration of the American Delegation was, to the U.S., one of the most important outcomes of the whole Convention. It had a history which we all know; the account given by Holls not only ignores that history, which would be a small matter; it falsifies the history. The *suppressio veri* is bearable; the *suggestio falsi* is clear and intolerable. This, and this only, is the point at issue.

To George F. W. Holls

160 West 86th Street, New York, April 9, 1901 [HUL]

Sir: It appears, from your letters of March 15 & 30, that there is between you and me no substantial difference as to the facts which led to the Declaration by the American Delegation at the Hague Conference.

You maintain, however, (Letter, March 30, p.1), that the account in your book, pages 268–270, does not intimate that your reservation was "the originating source of our Declaration"—the words in quotations being from my letter of the 25th. I assume that you equally deny my other and equivalent assertion in the same letter: "I find fault with the assumption of credit to yourself, by the clear implication" (of your book) "that there was a connection between your reservation and the action of the Delegation in deciding to make a qualifying declaration." You, (March 30, p.1), think me "mistaken in believing that such an impression will be produced upon the general reader by my" (your) "narrative."

---

1. George L. Rives.

The question then stands out perfectly clear, and shorn of all confusing details. Your motives and intentions, your anxieties about the Monroe Doctrine, and the recollections of Dr. Shaw,[1] however interesting collaterally, are nothing to the point. Equally irrelevant are the considerations, to which you invite my historical sense, of your personal and public parts in a Committee, of which general discussion, with a view to consensus, was the principal feature. I had drafted an answer to this suggestion, but will not burden my letter with such an issue, the apartness of which from the matter in hand will be evident to every thoughtful and experienced person. The question is simply this: Does the narrative of your book convey a truthful impression of the occurrences connected with the American Declaration? or does it, as I have alleged, by suppression, combined with arrangement and implication, convey the idea that your course—personal or public—in the Comité d'Examen, led to, or materially contributed to, the Declaration? In short, the Declaration has a history; has your narrative limited itself to the suppression of that history, or has it suggested an alternative history, devoid of foundation?

My first knowledge of your narrative was soon after its publication, through a letter from a New York lawyer,[2] to whom I had some time before given that account of the Declaration, which you admit is substantially accurate. He called my attention to the fact that your account did not tally with mine. I then brought the matter to the attention of four other persons, informed of the state of facts which my letters to you set forth, and which you admit. All agreed that, judged by that standard, your account is wholly inaccurate.

To my mind this is decisive of the general verdict on the question, which after all simply involves the meaning of language. In my letters, I have purposely, and I believe continuously, spoken not of "you", but of "your narrative," or "your book"; intending, while I impugned the latter, to dissociate yourself from it, leaving it open to you to remedy the impression it conveys, which I asserted to be false. I shall wait with interest to the end of the current week, to learn whether you are disposed to rectify this impression, which I maintain results from the tenor of your narrative, which you have given to the public. Failing such an intimation from you, I shall then assume that you identify yourself with this account, maintaining that it conveys a true impression of the history of the Declaration. The facts being in, and admitted,—viz: the transactions within our Delegation, and the account in your book, pp.268–270,—I see no occasion for further discussion; and, barring new facts transpiring, the correspondence on my part here closes.

---

1. Albert Shaw, founder and editor of *Review of Reviews*. He published Mahan's "Relations of the United States to Their New Dependencies" in March 1899, and ran articles on Mahan and Holls in May 1899.
2. George L. Rives.

To Andrew D. White

160 West 86th Street, New York, April 11, 1901 [CorUL]

My dear Mr. White: I enclose to you a copy of my third letter to Mr. Holls, which I hope and believe terminates my correspondence with him and the necessity of further troubling you in the matter.

To Albert B. Hart

160 West 86th Street, April 12, 1901 [NYPL]

My dear Prof. Hart: By all means help yourself, and very welcome. I shall be both pleased and profited by the attention.[1]

To John M. Brown

160 West 86th Street, New York, April 15, 1901 [LC]

My dear Mr. Brown: I received during last week a request from Prof. A. Bushnell Hart, of Harvard, to publish certain passages from the *Lessons of the Spanish War* for a series he is publishing of History told by Contemporary Writers.[1] Without thinking, I gave permission before consulting you, as my rule is; but as I know you incline to liberality in such matters, I trust no harm is done. He promised that extracts should be credited to *publishers* as well as author.

I had also an application from a M. S. Tanaka, a professor of History in a Japanese University at Tokio to translate *The Problem of Asia* into Japanese. This I granted of course; there is no money in the Japanese translations. They publish at half the retail price of the original.

Marston sent me a number of letters, from school masters & others, as to the chances of his suggested text-book. They were far from encouraging —regarded from the text-book point of view; so much so that I shall take time & reconsider the whole subject. As a matter of fact, my aim had gradually been changing to a "History of the English-speaking Communities," centering round the broad idea of Sea Power. Consequently, my winter's reading, thus governed, is in no sense thrown away; the more so as I believe that community of sentiment & action of the English speaking

---

1. *See* Mahan to Brown, April 15, 1901.
1. *American History Told by Contemporaries.* New York: Macmillan, 1898– .

peoples is a coming question just as Sea Power was ten years ago. But I have had to recognize that in my plan for this history, the War of 1812 was a very important factor, & it was already becoming a question with me whether I had not better take it up again, and complete my *special* knowledge which in any event I should need for the *general* mention that would be required in the wider work.

As yet I have decided nothing, but am busying myself to complete the introduction to the Memoir of Admiral Philip,[2] of which my son tells me he has spoken to you. That done I shall consider the other question, and at present think that I shall *first* realize upon the winter's reading, by committing it to paper in form for the History of English-speaking Communities;[3] *next* get the Admiral articles[4] in shape for a Christmas pubn. & *then* tackle *1812.*

This of course is as yet tentative; nothing decided.

To George Dewey

160 West 86th Street, New York, April 18, 1901 [LC]

My dear Dewey: I have been asked to write an introduction to some sketches of Jack Philip that are soon to be published.[1] In the course of so doing I have let my pen run away into the enclosed, concerning the practice cruise of 1857, of which you and I are among the few survivors actually on the Navy list. After writing I became doubtful of recollections now near 44 years old, and an awful fear came over me that some reminiscent cuss might recall that Jack used to French it below on a rainy watch, or some such un-

---

2. J. W. Philip had died very suddenly of a heart attack in 1900. The small volume of letters received by him and, later, by his widow (in the National Archives) contains nothing from Mahan. The work to which Mahan contributed was: Edgar Stanton Maclay, *Life and Adventures of "Jack" Philip, Rear Admiral, U.S.N.* (A Memorial Magazine in Four Numbers, May, June, July and August, 1903) . . . Assisted by Barrett Philip, with Contributory . . . Articles by William McKinley . . . Alfred Thayer Mahan . . . John Davis Long [and others]. New York: The Illustrated Navy, 1903. Mahan's Introduction ran to nine pages, and did not contain the jovial description of Philip as a young man which he sent to Dewey on April 18, 1901.
3. Never written.
4. *Types of Naval Officers Drawn from the History of the British Navy.* Boston: Little, Brown and Company, 1901. Mahan's subjects and their special qualities were Hawke, the spirit; Rodney, the form; Howe, the general officer as tactician; Jervis, the general officer as disciplinarian and strategist; Saumarez, the fleet officer and division commander; and Pellew, the frigate captain and partisan officer.
1. *See* Mahan to Brown, April 15, 1901, Footnote 2.

zealousness. Yet it seems to me, as I recall, he was always one of the forward ones - a natural topman.

Will you tell me if your recollections at all bear out this impression?

You will observe a fine mixture of tar, salt water, & marlinspike in my phraseology, a kind of "D———n your tarry toplight" style, highly characteristic. I fancy people on shore rather like that kind of thing, probably because they know nothing about it but think it sounds all right. Seriously, however, it is at times pleasant to recall that there once were such things as tacks sheets & reef points, and that I actually saw them with my own eyes. Who would think it now?

[Enclosure]

Philip was fortunate in the choice, or chance, of his profession. Whatever in ultimate analysis was the groundwork of his native character, he found himself at once thoroughly at home and at ease in the seaman's calling. I remember that even in that early cruise, when probably he first saw the sea, —for he came from inland,—there was a happy forwardness about him in all the workings of the ship, that showed he was enjoying himself. Whatever was going on, if you remembered anything about it afterwards, you were pretty sure also to remember Philip's face, keen and smiling among the throng. He stood out among others by dint of the constant repetition with which the eye seemed ever involuntarily to light upon him, and simply because he was always there, where the weight of the work fell; at the bunt in furling, at the earing in reefing, and close to the block in a heavy drag. He was not one to be found walking away with the slack, unless conditions justified the indulgence in practical humor, which was not the least developed of his characteristics.

To John D. Long

160 West 86th Street, New York, April 25, 1901 [LC]

My dear Mr. Long: You will perhaps remember my writing you eighteen months ago, toward the end of the summer of 1899,[1] concerning the claims made by General Alger, as stated in the press, to have been the originator of the proposition under which the Spaniards evacuated Santiago. I reminded you that it was *I* who had made the suggestion, and that I had taken the precaution to fix the fact in your memory, by asking you in your

1. *See* Mahan to Long, August 21, 1899.

office, a week after the occurrence, whether you recalled *then* who broached the idea. Your reply then was that I had done it.

In reply to my letter, you expressed your purpose to have the matter put straight on your return to Washington from Hingham. Nothing has been done, nor have I again troubled you; presuming some consideration of expediency intervened. My attention has been again called to the subject, by seeing in the *Army & Navy Register* of last Saturday, April 20, (p. 304) allusion to Gen. Alger as the author of the proposition, which in 1898 received a degree of applause that I confess surprised me.

The credit, such as it is, belongs to me, and yet more than to me, to the Navy, which shares at large in whatever good thing its members do. To you, as head of the Navy, I therefore recall the matter, without, however, fussing you for action. You can scarcely fail to remember the perplexity of that day's council, under the discouraging news from the generals at the front, & their recommendations as to the terms to be granted. The way out was found through this suggestion, & it appears to me monstrous that it should stand to the credit of a man who, as far as I could judge him, was a monument of incapacity.

As head of the Navy, you may also be interested to know that it was to the intervention of a naval officer that was owing the drawing up of the Declaration, attached to the signatures of the U.S. delegates at The Hague; which was the only part of the proceedings of the Conference that the President quoted in his Message of 1899. It was only on July 22—a bare week before final adjournment—that I detected in a proposition, which had then passed the full Committee to whom it belonged, but of which I was not a member, a stipulation which all our members agreed (when pointed out) contravened the Monroe Doctrine. The Declaration was none of my begetting, it was not the way I would have chosen; but that the necessity was recognized and the Declaration framed to meet it, was due wholly to my intervention.

In this case, as in the other instance, I said nothing—save to a very few intimates. I was content the matter should go in to the general results. But here again I find another claiming my work, though it is only just to say that he not only disclaims any such intention, but denies that his language implies such claim. I think, however, that anyone who will read Mr. Holls's— the Secretary to our Delegation—book on *The Peace Conference of The Hague*, pp. 268–71, will agree with me that the natural & primary impression conveyed by his language is that the Declaration was the consequence of a reservation previously made by him. He assures me that a number of persons, whose opinion he has asked, do not so construe his words; but I am satisfied that, whatever secondary sense may be wrung from them, as equivocal, like the old oracles, the impression of the reader will be that Holls did it.

My early acquiescence in silence for over a year after each event will I trust be assurance that I am not over-greedy of credit, but I own that on finding the credit, whatever it be, grasped by others, has stirred a moderate amount of feeling.

To Augustus T. Gillender

160 West 86th Street, New York, April 27, 1901 [HUL]

My dear Mr. Gillender: As regards James Okill's[1] career etc I have some pretty distinct recollections of certain leading incidents communicated to me incidentally by my mother; but they would I think have no value as proof, only as clues to such search as may be profitable to make .

Before troubling you with them, I will write them to Jenny & ask her to verify or add to them, if she can. *His* title in the property[2] depends upon my grandmother's will, which I presume is on file. She died about the middle of December, *1859.*

I had already written Fred before your letter of the beginning of the week reached me.

To John M. Brown

160 West 86th Street, New York, April 29, 1901 [LC]

My dear Mr. Brown: I have received your letter and *Our Naval Heroes.*[1] Curiously enough the same day Saturday came a letter from Marston saying he also had sent the book, which arrived this morning. I have looked over it sufficiently to satisfy myself that the general treatment is entirely different from my own; and even the matter, to a much greater degree than I should have thought possible, dealing with the same careers.

All the same the book will doubtless be a competitor to ours, and as it gives a great deal more (as well as very different) matter, it seems to me desirable to give closer consideration to ours as regards price and get up. In amount I should say 75,000 words would be my limit. As title I have tentatively settled on "Types of Naval Seamen, drawn from the Admirals of the British Navy." It is as types I treated them in the *Atlantic.*[2] Now, I am

---

1. Mahan's maternal great uncle.
2. The so-called Palisades property near Tenafly, New Jersey.
1. George Eden Marindin, *Our Naval Heroes.* London: Dutton, 1901.
2. *Atlantic Monthly* (March, May, July, and October 1893).

put on my metal [*sic*] by the presence of a competitor, and I think it would be well as a business matter if you would give consideration to the same fact; recognizing clearly that for his money, whatever the price, their customer will get a great deal more print than ours. Whether he will get more interesting or better treatment remains to be seen. My idea would be a gift book, commending itself by quality of paper, type, illustrations &c.

Will you kindly send me sheets of *Peter Simple* and *Midshipman Easy*, of your edition of Marryatt.³ I have a daughter who is learning book binding & I have taken a fancy to her binding these.

[P.S.]   Fly leaf alluded to in your prior letter has not yet come—11 a.m.

To John S. Billings

160 West 86th Street, New York, May 1, 1901 [NYPL]

Dear Sir: May I ask to be informed, on the enclosed addressed postal card, whether I can find in the Library the *British* "Army and Navy Gazette," (weekly), for November, *1890*.¹

To Bouverie F. Clark

160 West 86th Street, New York, May 3, 1901 [LC]

My dear Clark: I saw in our house papers ten days ago that you were named for the K.C.B., but one does not like to be premature in congratulation upon such matters, so I have waited till the *Army and Navy Gazette*¹ gave me the assurance yesterday. You will believe that I am heartily glad of it, and feel that you have most worthily earned it by the importance, severity, and success, of your labors during those many anxious months. I congratulate both Lady Clark and yourself most heartily on a well-merited reward.

---

3. For *Peter Simple*, the earliest listed edition is 1850, by R. Bentley of London; for *Mr. Midshipman Easy*, the Appleton edition of 1866. The Library of Congress lists many other editions of these works but not a Little, Brown edition of either.

1. *The Army and Navy Gazette* for November 22, 1890 carried an article by J. K. Laughton, "The Earl of St. Vincent."

1. "To be an Ordinary Member of the Military Division, or Knight Commander of the Most Honorable Order of the Bath:—Rear Admiral B. F. Clark, R. N." *Army and Navy Gazette*, XLII (April 20, 1901), p. 391.

My own life has been singularly uneventful since the date of my last letter— somewhere in January, I think. I have not been writing even, but have given myself wholly to reading with a view to some rather extensive projects of future writing that I have entertained. In no year since my return from Europe in 1895 have I produced so little as this year promises.

On the surface it looks as if we were pretty nearly at the end of our fighting troubles in the Philippines, but I somewhat mistrust those fellows, and hope we shant go to sleep & stop watching them. In any event the difficulties after peace will be as great as before, though differing in character. I believe however that both there and in the Transvaal a short experience of the comforts of peace and good government, coupled with a vivid recollection of the miseries of being ever on the run, will contribute to make both Boers and Filipinos careful about quarreling with their bread and butter—their material prosperity—in the near future. DeWet[2] and his fellows are obstinate Dutchmen, no doubt; but they have not been enjoying themselves lately, and when once they have given in, tasted a quiet schnapps and pipe, and the comfort of a decent night's sleep, I doubt they will hesitate about renewing the rumpus. From this point of view it is not a bad thing that they have had to take such a lot of licking; it will do good in the end, but I hope the end will now soon come.

To Edward K. Rawson

160 West 86th Street, New York, May 8, 1901 [NA]

My dear Mr. Rawson: Can you do me the favor of loaning me the books on the enclosed list. I have not so far found mention of *Sailing and Fighting Instructions* earlier than the enclosed—(1742); but I have not yet completed the process of going through your catalogues, having got only so far as *K*. If your own knowledge [of your] shelves can give me an earlier, I should greatly like to have it so as to institute comparisons.

[P.S.]   The shelf references I quote are from the *Catalogue of Authors* of 1891.

[Enclosure]

1. *Trials of Burrish and others*[1] 1799e.3

---

2. Christian Rudolf DeWet, Boer general and statesman.

1. British Captain George Burrish, commanding officer of the *Dorsetshire*, in the battle of Toulon, 1744, was court-martialed for failing to assist the *Marlborough*, or to bear down on the enemy. Library and Naval War Records apparently had copies of the minutes of the courts-martial of Admiral Thomas Mathews, commanding in the Mediterranean, his second-in-command Richard Lestock, Admiral of the Fleet Sir John Norris, Burrish, and others, which were in the Admiralty Library.

2. *Sailing & Fighting Instructions,*[2] London 1741 0.47:23
3. *Sailing etc. Instructions,* 1782 0.47:3
4. *James II. Memoirs* etc.[3] 0.32:36
5. Hannay's *Life of Rodney*[4] 2165:9

Is there not a Trial of Admiral Matthews as well as of his captains, Burrish etc, for the fiasco of 1744?[5]

To John M. Brown

160 West 86th Street, New York, May 9, 1901 [LC]

My dear Mr. Brown: I do not think the plan of running the memoirs together, in a single narrative, would work well. The title I have suggested, "Types of Naval Officers," is in itself distinctive; but types in order to be recognizable and emphasized require to be treated separately. There is a certain superficial resemblance in *Our Naval Heroes* to my projected work;[1] but the resemblance is purely superficial, though very possibly misleading to a cursory examination. My title suggests and asserts the difference. As for treatment, the English book is rather historical than biographical—gives the matter the man was concerned with, rather than his own personality. Mine aims at the latter, is much more anecdotical and gossipy, while also giving, as I flatter myself, a more discriminating estimate of the man's value, as a personal factor in the Navy, not of his own day only, but in the development of the British navy. I may add that I had sufficient testimony to the interesting character of the articles to Americans, at the time they appeared —1893.

I hope to finish by the middle of June. After that, I have about consented to do a piece of work for a friend of mine, Mr. Wm. Beverley Harison, who has been asking me for four years back to prepare for him a History of the U.S. for a text book for children.[2] He thinks I can make a particular success of it. I am not so sure; but, after long refusal even to entertain the idea, I

---

2. These instructions were originally drawn up by the admirals themselves. The first official ones were based on Admiral Sir George Rooke's. Julian Corbett first published them in 1905 for the Navy Records Society; a later series followed in 1908, and *The Loss of Minorca* in 1913.

3. James II, King of Great Britain, *Memoirs of the English Affairs, Chiefly Naval, from the Year 1660 to 1673* ... London, 1729.

4. David Hannay, *Rodney*. London: Macmillan, 1891.

5. *See* Footnote 1 above. Mathews joined battle at Toulon without support of the rear under Lestock, flew conflicting signals, lost the battle, and retreated. He was tried on charges brought by Lestock, and was dismissed from the service.

1. *See* Mahan to Brown, April 29, 1901.

2. Never written.

have been decided by the fact that it will efficiently serve to develop the idea that had gradually formed in my mind, out of Marston's suggested text book—viz: a History of the English speaking races as connected with and developed through Sea Power.

I believe I have already mentioned to you this idea; but as I have pursued my study it has been borne upon me, more and more, that that History will be more concerned with this Continent than with the Old. Hence, it is, I think, that the book Harison wishes will be a useful first study; just as my previous *Sea Powers* have familiarized me with the History of Great Britain & the Continent, and considerable portions of our Colonial History, and as my present reading for *1812* has forced me to cover much of our own history, but only since the Revolution, but also economical data prior to the Revolution.

I have now a pretty fair understanding of the *War* of 1812 and a very miserable showing it is for our people. Its antecedents require a little more study still, and I must also verify my conclusions by a little more independent research. One other conclusion I have reached, and that is to aim henceforth at the American market rather than the English.

To John M. Brown

160 West 86th Street, New York, May 28, 1901 [LC]

My dear Mr. Brown: Yours of yesterday received. I am much indebted for the proposed list of portraits, although, except by suggestion, I leave these art matters wholly in your hands.

I return the announcement with one or two slight alterations. Involuntarily, almost, I have been led to write some 3,000 words on the subject of naval war at the beginning of the 18th century, and the relations of the two new lives, Hawke & Rodney, to it.[1] Though this will probably in the end form an Introductory chapter[2]—as distinct from a preface—it to a certain extent realizes your idea of a narrative treatment; and at any rate will be a distinct feature of the book that may as well be brought forward.

In the preface, I lead off by remarking that though British officers they all touch America in some degree—either in their naval service or by family connection. Hawke was very nearly related to the Maryland Bladens. Caesar Rodney of Delaware, signer of Decln. of Independence, was of the same family as Rodney. Howe was the friend of Franklin, and was sent on

---

1. For purposes of the book, Mahan added sketches of Hawke and Rodney to those of Jervis, Saumarez, Pellew, and Howe published in 1893 in the *Atlantic Monthly*.
2. To *Types of Naval Officers*.

a mission of reconciliation in 1775, while his brother was the most popular British officer among colonial troops. Pellew served in the Revn. on Lake Champlain, Saumarez at the attack on Fort Moultrie &c.

[P.S.]   I go to Quogue for the summer on June 1st.

To Edward K. Rawson

160 West 86th Street, New York, May 30, 1901 [NA]

My dear Mr. Rawson: I have today returned by registered mail the *Duke of York* book[1] you were good enough to send me. I had hoped at the same time to send most of the others; but I have found the Mathews action too difficult, especially in lack of the testimony of the Admiral himself. I am taking the books with me to "Quogue, N.Y." where I hope to be as usual during the summer; and I am going to ask of you the further favor to lend me there the books named on the opposite page. With them I think I can speedily reach a clearer understanding.

Hoping this will not inconvenience you I am [etc.].

2132:1 Adml. Mathews' charge against Vice Adml. Lestock dissected[2]
1799c:38 Lestock—Defence to the Court Martial etc. etc.[3]

To Edward K. Rawson

Slumberside, Quogue, Long Island, June, 1901 [NA]

My dear Mr. Rawson: I am sending back by registered mail the following, of the books kindly loaned me by you:

1. *Minutes of Court Martial*, (Burrish, etc) *1745*
2. *Sailing and Fighting Instructions, 1741*
3. *Mathews and Lestock* (2132.1)
4. *Lestock's Defence* (1799.38)

The *Memoirs of James II* were returned from N.Y. I hope it may not inconvenience you to let me retain a while longer the "*Sailing etc Instruc-*

---

1. *See* Mahan to Rawson, May 8, 1901, Footnote 3.
2. *Admiral Mathews' Charge against Vice-Admiral Lestock Dissected and Confuted.* By a Kings Letterman. London, 1745. *See* Mahan to Rawson, May 8, 1901, Footnote 5.
3. *Vice-Admiral Lestock's Vindication, as Spoke by Him at the Bar of the Hon. House of Commons.* . . . 8 pp. J. Jingle: at the Nine Muses, on the Sea Shore, 1745.

tions" for 1781–2, which I have, and Hannay's *Life of Rodney*, both which I need for a sketch of Rodney which I am about to write.[1]

It will also help me much if you can lend me, further, a copy of *Byng's Court Martial*,[2] and Granville Penn's *Life of Sir Wm. Penn*.[3]

To Arthur S. Lloyd[1]

Quogue, Long Island, June 15, 1901 [CHS][2]

My dear Dr. Lloyd: I dont know whether I am right in thinking that you came from Norfolk to the Board of Missions; but if so, or in any case, can you give me the name of a Church clergyman there, who would be willing to make some inquiries for me concerning the condition and character of a woman living there, who for a year past has beset me with begging letters?

To Augustus T. Gillender

Slumberside, Quogue, Long Island, June 15, 1901 [HUL]

My dear Mr. Gillender: Thank you very much for the trouble you have taken. There is one point not clear to me, which seems of considerable importance. What is meant by the *"value"* of the property?[1] Is it the present value—today—or the value twenty years hence? by natural increase, or by improvements? Suppose we should sell to some person a few years hence, and he by business arrangements should raise the value to a considerable amount—say $40,000. If an heir then turns up, the owner will have a good title, taken from us, and is not troubled; but will we be responsible for the $40,000?

---

1. "Rodney: the Form," in *Types of Naval Officers.*
2. There were two accounts of Byng's court martial in 1757: the verbatim report taken by his lawyer, Thomas Cook, with letters and reports, and that by Charles Fearne, the Judge Advocate.
3. Granville Penn, *Memorials of the Professional Life and Times of Sir William Penn . . . from 1644 to 1670.* London: J. Duncan, 1833.

1. General Secretary of the Episcopal Foreign and Domestic Missionary Society. He had been rector of St. Luke's Church, Norfolk, before his election to the Missionary Society.
2. By permission of The Church Historical Society, Austin, Texas; a part of "The Domestic and Foreign Missionary Society Papers: Secretary's Papers."

1. *See* Mahan to Gillender, April 27, 1901.

It appears to me, seeing the present small value of the land, and the improbability that, in our hands and our lifetime, it can increase to any large extent, and be worth anything material to us—for these reasons—the transaction would only be advisable if the bond be for the *present value* of the land. Also, in that case, I think the value should be determined by appraisers, officially appointed, and should be stated in the bond in dollars and cents.

I presume, from your letter, that the American Surety Company in New Jersey would guarantee the payment of the bond, in the case of the heir turning up—and that the premium we would annually pay would be to them, upon this insurance. If this is correct, please assure me so.

Finally, is there no *time limit* when all this will end? or can J.O.'s[2] heirs come back on us to the third and fourth generation?

To John D. Long

Quogue, Long Island, June 17, 1901 [LC]

My dear Mr. Long: Circumstances that have occurred since the close of the War with Spain lead me to ask you whether the following statement of certain facts, connected with an incident of the war, agrees with your own recollection.

At the opening of negotiations before Santiago, between the commanders of the contending armies, for the surrender of the place, the Spaniards demanded as their conditions that the garrison should be allowed to march out, not as prisoners of war, and to rejoin their forces elsewhere. Our own generals, both General Shafter and General Miles, in telegraphing these terms, recommended the acceptance of them on account of the existing conditions. These telegrams are doubtless on record, and the fact therefore not dependent on memory. In consequence, the Naval War Board was summoned to the White House, where were met the President and Cabinet, with representatives of the Army; and in this assemblage the Spanish propositions were discussed. I cannot speak positively to the opinion of any one person there, except that of the President and my own; but my impression is that the general sense of those present favored acceptance. I personally did, and said so clearly, on the ground that officers of the position of our generals, on the spot, could judge better of the exigencies of the situation, as regarding the defences of the place and the actual effects of the climate on the health of our troops, than we could. The kernel of the matter—especially from a naval point of view—was to get the harbor and release our ships to other duties; Cervera's squadron having been already destroyed.

---

2. James Okill.

The President, on the other hand, took very strong ground against acceptance, expressing himself not only vigorously but with a certain vehemence very foreign to his usual manner. He argued that the impression at home, and to a certain degree abroad, would be most unfavorable to us, would tend to foreign complications and to prolong the war; for it would be assumed that such terms were extorted only from our sense of weakness. As decision rested absolutely with him, the rest of us being purely advisory, the matter hung thus in suspense for a time, during which there was desultory discussion; and in the course of this the thought occurred to me, and was by me submitted, that our Government should present as its terms the capitulation of the place and of the garrison, and the stipulation that the latter should be carried to Spain, with their arms, at our expense.

That these were, in substance, the terms of the surrender is sufficiently known. I was somewhat surprised to find them so warmly applauded as they were by a portion of our people as a happy solution of a painful and embarrassing situation; but this fact led me to go to your office about a week after the occurrence and ask if you remembered from whom the suggestion came. You reflected for a moment, and then replied, "Yes I do; it was from you."

I had then no idea of publicity; but a year later, while I was a delegate at the Hague Conference, a paragraph went the round of the press that another member of the assemblage at the White House[1] had claimed the credit of originating the proposal. Within the last three months I have seen the claim again asserted for that person.

I will ask, therefore, whether you will favor me with your own recollection of the matter, and whether you will permit me to publish the correspondence, if, in my judgment, due occasion arises.

To Augustus T. Gillender

Quogue, Long Island, July 16, 1901 [HUL]

Dear Mr. Gillender: It is perhaps unnecessary for me to say that in telling you the plots marked by red-cross on plan are *mine*, I give only my recollection, which would need verification. The marks were for my own convenience in case of reference, and I have no memorandum further.

I presume, of course, that in such transfer the lawyers verify the titles from public records. Where are such records kept in this case? Mrs. Mahan tells me that my title to my share by the final partition is in her safe deposit.

---

1. Russell A. Alger, Secretary of War from 1897 to 1899.

To John M. Brown

My dear Mr. Brown: If among your many affairs you have thought at all upon *Types of Naval Officers*, you must have speculated why I was so far behind my expected time. I wont weary you with the causes; but as I have written full 50,000 words since May 1st, you will see I have not been idle.

The present status of the text is that I have finished the Introductory Chapter "Remarks on Conditions of Naval Warfare in early 18th Century"; also the Life of Hawke, and about two-thirds that of Rodney. When the latter is finished all the new part of the book—probably 9/10 of the whole labor—will be done. I hope thus to complete (i.e. Rodney) by a fortnight from to-day. I may add I have also written the Preface, though I always consider that open to amendment to the last moment.

Would it be expedient to begin printing about August 1, with the material then in hand? My anticipation is that, of the four remaining lives, Exmouth & Saumarez will be very little changed. Howe and St. Vincent more so, but rather by insertions than by revision of the text. I think therefore I should probably keep ahead of the printer.

I have single copies of each of the *Atlantic*s in which these articles appear. It would, however, much facilitate my preparation of copy could I obtain duplicates, enabling me to cut out and paste by having both sides of each page. I have purposed asking Houghton & Mifflin if they can give—or sell—me copies; but concluded it would first be well to ask you whether I had better apply to them personally, or through you. The numbers are. *St. Vincent*, March, 1893; *Saumarez*, May 1893; *Pellew*, July, 1893; *Howe*, January 1894.

As Rodney will (with the preceding matter) round up our 50,000 words, I think you can safely estimate the book entire at 100,000, at least, and make price accordingly. It will prove in all respects a more solid piece of work than I at first anticipated. I hope it may prove a good prize book for Marston, who I fear has been disappointed pecuniarily by the revised *Nelson*.

I have this moment recd. a Firm letter—July 19—to which this, as regards text, replies.

To Edward K. Rawson

Slumberside, Quogue, Long Island, July 22, 1901 [NA]

My dear Mr. Rawson: Can you lend me for a few days Drinkwater's *Siege of Gibraltar?*[1]

I am well along with the work depending on the books you have lent me, and hope to return them upon its conclusion towards the end of this month.

To Edward K. Rawson

Slumberside, Quogue, Long Island, July 31, 1901 [NA]

My dear Mr. Rawson: I am returning by today's registered mail Granville's *Life of Penn*, and will get off the other books from the Library tomorrow, or Friday at latest.

It might be well to call your clerk's attention to the fact that the *Trial of Burrish* etc, was returned a month ago—acknowledged by Library letter of June 28.

In returning these I beg to thank you again for the constant courtesy of the Library under your administration. Being yourself an author, you can understand how much I appreciate it.

Could you without inconvenience have verified for me the enclosed memorandum, by reference to Charnock?

[Enclosure]

Memorandum

Charnock's *Biographia Navalis*[1]

Captains of 1758—Robert Carkett

1. Did he enter Royal Navy from before the mast?
2. Was the loss of the *Sterling Castle*, under his command, in 1780, accompanied by the loss of almost all the crew?[2]

If replies to these questions can be sent me briefly, I should be greatly indebted.

I have made a somewhat interesting discovery concerning the *Fighting*

---

1. John Drinkwater, afterwards Bethune, *A History of the Late Siege of Gibraltar, with a Description and Account of that Garrison, from the Earliest Periods*. London, 1785.

1. John Charnock, *Biographia Navalis; or, Impartial Memoirs of the Lives and Characters of Officers of the Navy of Great Britain from the Year 1660 to the Present Time* . . . London: R. Faulder, 1794–1798.

2. Carkett and all on board the *Stirling Castle* were lost in a hurricane off Jamaica in 1780.

Instructions of 1741, which you might perhaps like to note on a fly-leaf. In Article *1* there is a manuscript addition, to which Lestock alludes in a letter to Mathews, on p. 33 of the *second* pamphlet bound in "Mathews and Lestock."[3] From a comparison of the two it seems pretty certain that the Department Copy of 1741 was one issued by Mathews to his fleet, and very probably was actually in use at his battle.

The same Ms. insertion is not to be found in the same Article, in 1782, though otherwise verbatim the same.

To Jarousse de Sillac

Slumberside, Quogue, Long Island, August 20, 1901 [LC]

Dear M.De Sillac: I am much indebted to you for your letter of July 23d., but regret that mine[1] should have reached you when you had not at hand a copy of the Procès.

The members of the Comité D'Examen had of course the right to revise their remarks; but in the case of M. Holls, *p. 167*, there are two clauses; and of these *two*, one, I understand, was inserted, at his request, several months after the adjournment of the Conference; so long after, that you doubted at first whether you could make the insertion, because the printing was so far advanced.

These clauses are:

1. M.Holls "voudrait avoir le temps d'y réfléchir, afin d'être bien certain que les Gouvernements ne pourront pas être *gênés par la suggestion de l'arbitrage.*"

2. (Inserted several months after). "En ce qui concerne spécialement les Etats Unis d'Amérique, il y aura lieu d'examiner avec attention si la proposition ne pourrait pas *porter atteinte* à la distinction établie par la politique traditionelle de ce pays entre les questions purement Européennes ou purement Américaines."

Here are *two distinct ideas*—propositions—not necessarily connected. The first was in the original report of the secretaries to the Committee. The second was not in the minutes of the secretaries, but was added several months later, at the request of Mr. Holls.

What I wanted to know was this: Does the parenthesis on *p.170* ("M. Holls se réservant le droit . . . de faire une déclaration dans le sens de celle qu'il a formulée plus haut") refer to No. 1, or to No. 2? Was the parenthesis a part of the original report? or was it also added, at he time when the

---

3. *See* Mahan to Rawson, June 1901.

1. *See* Mahan to de Sillac, circa late March 1901.

words "En ce qui concerne spécialement," &c. were inserted at Mr. Holls's request?

I beg to congratulate you upon your excursion in Canada and the United States, from which I hope you may receive much pleasure. Should it suit your plans to call upon me in New York, I should have much pleasure in seeing you. My address there is 160 West 86 St., after October 10. But as regards this business, in which you have done me the favor to reply, it would not be necessary to inconvenience yourself, if your time or engagements prevent your doing so easily. I only desire to know whether the parenthesis refers to clause 1, or 2, or both.

To Leopold J. Maxse[1]

Slumberside, Quogue, Long Island, August 23, 1901 [LC]

Dear Sir: The subject indicated in your note to me certainly ought to receive treatment, & as you think me the proper person, for reasons assigned, I shall be very willing to undertake it, even though less convinced than you, of my fitness.

It will have, however, to wait until I can complete a book[2] now preparing for the press, and upon which my publishers count. I hope to complete this by October 1st, after which I can take up the article. As my mind is pretty sure to work on it meanwhile, I should hope to mail it you before Nov. 1.[3]

Though the importance of the subject is distinct, it is not so imminent, in my judgment, as to suffer from the delay of two or three months; but if you think otherwise, please notify me to that effect and I will understand the matter is off.

The honorarium you propose is satisfactory. I will specify only that it be remitted in a draft for $250.00 payable in New York.

To Unidentified Addressee

Slumberside, Quogue, Long Island, August 27, 1901 [LC]

Your letter of the 10th inst has been duly received, & I have earnestly to thank you for having, among so many preoccupations, found time to pay

---

1. Editor of *National Review*.
2. *Types of Naval Officers*.
3. "The Influence of the South African War Upon the Prestige of the British Empire," *National Review* (December 1901). Reprinted in *Retrospect and Prospect, Studies in International Relations, Naval and Political*. Boston: Little, Brown and Company, 1902.

the exhaustive attention that you have to my rather troublesome request. The extracts you send appear to my present judgement to settle the case decisively against Carkett's action,[1] whatever excuses may be made for a *man*, probably nearly sixty, and confronted with ideas wholly novel to his mind.

I cannot say that I find Article XXI saved from marked ambiguity by its own terms; but the clear precept of other articles—the prevailing sense of the whole—that distances should be taken *from the centre*, should have controlled Carkett.

As regards one of your questions, I think you certainly justified in assuming that the Additional Instructions had been given to all captains. Rodney's to Carkett clearly implies it also. At the same time, in excuse for Carkett, it is to be remembered that the battle was fought only three weeks after Rodney's arrival in the West Indies.

My exception to your mention of my note concerning the Additional Instructions was merely that it seemed to make me give an absolute statement instead of a qualified one, for which alone I had any ground. I am usually very careful to qualify, unless absolutely certain of my grounds, & this perhaps disposes me to sensitiveness. Otherwise the matter is unimportant, and I can understand your being misled by misapprehension of my intention.

In accordance with your suggestion, it will give me great pleasure to write Mr. Pritchard[2] personally, thanking him for facilitating my wishes through yourself.

As regards your question concerning the utility and advisability of publishing the Additional [Instructions] of 1779, and in the Navy Records Series, I would say very decidedly that publicity for these very important materials, of which only rare and scattered copies now survive, is of the utmost importance. In a study of the subject—necessarily brief and cursory, from the paucity of materials on this side,—I am led to think that the question of progressive development of naval tactics and signals of the sail period is capable of much fuller, more consecutive, and so to say more philosophical treatment than it has yet received. This can scarcely be satisfactorily done, till something approaching a complete series of the individual Additional Instructions of various admirals becomes accessible. Of these Rodney's must be among the most important.

I would, however, suggest your consulting, at an early period of your undertaking, Prof. Laughton, the Secretary of the Society. Laughton's knowledge of all these matters is very extensive, and he better than any one

---

1. Carkett was accused by Rodney of disobeying orders in the action off Martinique (1780).
2. Probably William Tarn Pritchard, author of *Digest of Admiralty and Maritime Law*, 3d ed., London, 1887, and also of analytical digests of admiralty and prize cases.

I know of can tell you how far your project would fill a known want. His close association with the United Service Institution, and his constant prolonged habit of search among naval documents, has familiarized him beyond most men with the mass of existent but yet unpublished materials for naval history. Unluckily, occupation has prevented his giving to the world much of the knowledge stored away in the recesses of his brain.

If at any time my examination and suggestion can help—as you intimate may be the case—you may rely upon my readiness. Renewing my thanks, believe me [etc.].

To Stephen B. Luce

Slumberside, Quogue, Long Island, September 3, 1901 [LC]

My dear Admiral: There was no constituted Board at the time of the Chilean imbroglio in 1891–2. I was ordered to Washington, and directed to study the military side of the question, to be ready to prepare plans,[1] or to express opinions, as a result of my reflections; but Mr. Tracy kept matters in his own hands, consulted when he wished to consult and acted without consultation as he chose. Nor do I remember that I was ever directed to consult anyone else in the Dept.; certainly very rarely, if ever. At times, I saw War Dept. officials by the Secretary's direction, for a specific purpose.

Mr. Tracy consulted others as he did me—Ramsay, Folger, I know, & doubtless others; but there was no Board known to me.

Occasionally, once or twice, I gave brief written expression to my views; but these were simply memoranda, and I do not think ever went on file.

Mr. Tracy at one time, in 1890, directed Folger and me to draw up outline plans of operations necessary to be undertaken at once in case of war with foreign nations. I drew up two—that I remember—possibly more; in the case of Great Britain & of Spain. I have had an impression that these, in which Folger concurred, found their way to the Bureau of Intelligence; for which also I at some time discussed the general question of Pacific Coast operations. This employment was at the time secret. Whether there would be any objection to its being known now I cant tell.

---

1. It would seem from this passage that Mahan did not draw up a contingency war plan for Chile in 1892, certainly not an extensive or formal one. The editors have not found a Chilean plan. The war plan for Spain advocated the division of the battle fleet—a notion later condemned by Mahan. For Mahan's Contingency Plan of Operations in Case of War With Great Britain, *see* his Paper, December 1890.

Thank you for your kind words about "War from the Christian Stand-point."[2] They convinced myself.

With kind remembrances to Mrs. Luce & your daughters from us both, believe me [etc.].

To Edward K. Rawson

Slumberside, Quogue, Long Island, September 9, 1901 [NA]

My dear Mr. Rawson: Can the Library spare me for a few days Brenton's *Life of St. Vincent*?[1]

To Leopold J. Maxse

160 West 86th Street, New York, November 1, 1901 [LC]

My dear Sir: I am very sorry that my promised article cannot be mailed today, but it is in such shape that it will go by the steamer of Wednesday next, *Nov. 6*. It is now complete, and in process of typewriting; but it is my practice after this last has been done to give a final pruning and polishing. This is the more necessary in this case, as I presume I shall not have the opportunity to read the proofs. It will, from the pages already type-written, be about 6,000 words; rather less, I think, than more.

I am concerned for the delay beyond the date I named, Nov. 1; but I am sure it will be better for the paper and it was inevitable.

To Leopold J. Maxse

160 West 86th Street, New York, November 5, 1901 [LC]

My dear Sir: I have sent you today the promised article by registered mail; but did not have time to enclose this, because today, being an election day, is a general holiday and the P.O. closes at 10.

---

2. "War from the Christian Standpoint," written in November 1900, was not published at this time. It was published in *Some Neglected Aspects of War*, Boston, Little, Brown and Company, 1907; and reprinted in *The Harvest Within*, Boston, Little, Brown and Company, 1909.

1. Edward Pelham Brenton, *Life and Correspondence of John, Earl of St. Vincent*. London: H. Colburn, 1838.

I have in addition only to ask that, as I shall presumably not have the opportunity of proofreading, that you will give me a careful reader of the proofs. I may say also that I should prefer, as you also doubtless will, that the spelling should be made to conform to the English standards. In itself the question is immaterial, but I think readers are often prejudiced by such trifles when they run counter to prepossessions.

To John M. Brown

160 West 86th Street, New York, November 13, 1901 [LC]

My dear Mr. Brown: Thank you for your letter of the 11th, and for the wrapper cover, which is very satisfactory. As I have received a proof copy of the Index[1] there will, I suppose, be no doubt of the sheets going forward as you expected at the end of this week. I have assumed that no action on my part upon the Index was expected, for it would have resulted in nothing but needless delay.

It remains only to hope that the results may be satisfactory to us all.

To Leopold J. Maxse

160 West 86th Street, New York, December 9, 1901 [LC]

My dear Sir: I have to acknowledge the receipt of your letters of Nov. 15 and 29, and today through Messrs. Drummond I have received the draft for $250, for which I beg to thank you.

I am sincerely gratified to know by the cuttings you have been good enough to send me, that the Article[1] has been well received, and that there is a possibility of its exercising a beneficial effect. I realize that a foreign opinion, as presumably unprejudiced, may at particular moments have a special weight of its own, and nothing could give me more pleasure than to believe that I have in any way contributed to the cause of Great Britain in this matter, believing as I do that it is in all essentials entirely just, and also in truth the cause of the English speaking peoples & their common tradition.

As regards any future writing, I shall remember with pleasure your kind

---

1. For *Types of Naval Officers*.

1. "The Influence of the South African War upon the Prestige of the British Empire," *National Review* (December 1901).

offer of the hospitality of the *National Review*, and, if occasion offer, will gladly avail myself of it. I wish, however, to guard myself from any understanding of a *promise*, as I have experienced the inconvenience of such an impression obtaining.

To George F. W. Holls

160 West 86th Street, New York, December 10, 1901 [LC]

Sir:　In our correspondence last spring, in your letter of March 15, on its first page, you state, "I made the reservation (see official record, part 4, pp. 167 and 170) and subject to that, voted for the article."

Again in your letter of March 30, p.5, you say, "I can of course understand that you were greatly astonished when you ascertained for the first time that *the point of your objection* to Article 27 has been previously *covered by my reservation* in the Comité d'Examen, and the same is true of our other colleagues." The words here underscored [italicized] are mine.

The "point of my objection" was, that Article 27, as it stood, laid upon the United States a duty to infringe the Monroe Doctrine, in certain cases: (1) by intermeddling by suggestion with questions purely European; and, (2) by admitting European intermeddling in questions purely American; as was apparently contemplated, if not attempted, by some European governments when hostilities were imminent concerning Cuba in 1898. This point, you wrote, had been covered by "your reservation," previously made, and now appearing as above indicated.

At the time of our correspondence I had reason to think that this, "your reservation," had been amplified in the text of the official record; but I did not know certainly. I am now in a position to say[1] that I have ample reason for certainty, that, at a period much subsequent to the adjournment of the Conference, there were inserted, at your request, on p.167, part 4, the words enclosed in brackets in the following quotation, which embraces all attributed to you on the said page 167.

"M.Holls considère que l'idée qu'elle exprime est très importante: si elle peut être rendue pratique, il en sera sincèrement heureux. Mais il voudrait avoir le temps d'y réfléchir, afin d'être bien certain que les Gouvernements ne pourront pas être gênés par la suggestion de l'arbitrage. [En ce qui concerne spécialement les Etats Unis d'Amérique, il y aura lieu d'examiner avec attention si la proposition ne pourrait pas porter atteinte à la distinction établie par la politique traditionelle de ce pays entre les questions purement Européennes ou purement Américaines.]"

---

1. *See* Mahan to de Sillac, August 20, 1901.

The words bracketed were not, as I have the best ground for believing, part of the original record of those who kept the minutes of the proceedings of the Comité d'Examen. I have also the same reason to believe that they were not added by you during the Conference, in pursuance of the admitted right of every man to amend immediately the report of his words, either by change or addition; but that they were added at a time so far subsequent to the Conference that the printing of the proceedings was already far advanced.

If this be so, it is clear that these words, to which you refer me as authority, as part of the official record,—which in form they are,—owe their presence there to action taken by you long subsequent to my intervention in the matter; which intervention I rested upon the precise ground, taken in those added words, that Article 27 entailed contravention by the United States of its traditional policy.

Again, this argument of mine against the acceptance of the Article was not by you conceded when I advanced it, although at that moment your action in the Comité d'Examen, to which the above quotation applies, was already three weeks old; and not only so, but the Third Committee in full session had also adopted the Article, with your more than approval; with your expressed laudation. Further, nowhere in the Proceedings of the Conference, either in the Comité d'Examen or in the full Committee, do I find any use made by you of this, your "previous" reservation, nor any allusion made to it by any other member.

Nevertheless, it is to these interpolated words, unsupported by any collateral evidence in the records, that you have referred me as proof of your having made the reservation, which, on pages 268–270 of your book, you allege to have been first made by you; and you so referred me without any mention of the fact that the presence of those words was due to your long subsequent action, and not to the compilers of the records, as of their own knowledge.

To John M. Brown

160 West 86th Street, New York, December 13, 1901 [LC]

My dear Mr. Brown: I have sent off before now all the copies of the new book[1] that I wished, except one, so it is scarcely worth while to trouble you about that. I understand of course that the sending them here was one of oversights inevitable from time to time. As regards persons to whom it

---

1. *Types of Naval Officers.*

would be expedient to send copies, I scarcely know of any. I always send one to Prof. Laughton, the chief English authority on naval matters of all kinds, & one has already gone to him.

I am glad to hear such good accounts of sales & notices. From its subject the work is really a supplement to *Nelson*, from the biographical standpoint. In glancing over it in book form, it has seemed to me a better piece of work than I had thought, though I naturally am not the best judge. Still, I hope that its merits will be found sufficient to stimulate purchasers who care for naval biography.

To Hamilton Holt[1]

160 West 86th Street, New York, December 22, 1901 [NDL]

Dear Mr. Holt: I recd. your letter, enclosing Benjamin's review,[2] yesterday morning, just as I was leaving town for the day. I put it in my pocket, and read it in the train, noting the points.

He has entirely neglected the main thesis of the book, and has confined his work to an attack upon a secondary, though certainly very important, point, the distinction I draw between errors of judgment and errors of conduct. This he evidently does in pursuance of the philippic in which he is now engaged in Schley's behalf; justly recognizing that, if the distinction is valid, it bears hardly on his adopted client.

I can, I think, very well afford to allow the thoughtful reader to judge between me and him, and the thoughtless is not easily made to attend. Mr. Benjamin, however, having studied my writings mainly with a view to convict me of inconsistency, has fallen into the error of supposing that the above distinction was first drawn by me in this last book, whereas I had enunciated it distinctly, three years ago, in *Lessons from the Spanish War*. It is certainly true that I had not drawn it in my earlier writings; for circumstances had not then led me to question the common phrase, "error of judgment," which lends itself facilely to confusion of thought and consequent condonement of grave military misdoing.

Whither this confusion tends is clearly shown by an utterance in the *Independent* of Dec. 19, which bears the clear mark of Mr. Benjamin's

---

1. Office editor and managing editor of *The Independent*, a liberal weekly. He was interested in the idea of world federation, and was a founder of the New York Peace Society.
2. Park Benjamin, "A Casuistry in Naval Ethics," *The Independent* (December 19, 1901), a review of Mahan's *Types of Naval Officers*. See Mahan to Long, January 16, 1902.

rhetoric (p. 3032). After quoting Schley's remark, "I did the best I could," etc. the *Independent* is seduced into saying "We submit this is all the American people asks . . . of any public servant." The fallacy is evident, & involves just the difference between error of judgment & error of conduct. The American people, & every nation, or private employer, demands of an employee not merely that he should do his best, but that he should be capable; that his best should reach at least a high average standard of his profession; that an admiral should not only do his own personal best, but should accomplish good admiral's work—up to standard. In other words, there are "standards of action external to the individual," just as there are standards of taste; and this is certainly true, although Mr. Benjamin finds it "not easy to appreciate" what he considers "a somewhat subtle distinction." The distinction is one perfectly familiar, though possibly not formulated, to every practical man.

Mr. Benjamin is equally unfamiliar with my position as to disobedience of orders, which he criticizes. The line of my thought, & the genesis of the above distinction might prove an instructive rejoinder, interesting to thoughtful readers; but before I undertake it in the *Independent* I must have an understanding.

In your issue of the 19th, you give much misleading comment on the decisions of the Court,[3] but specifically you speak of the "majority" and "minority" reports. This may be ignorance, in which case it is excusable, though little creditable to your editorial guidance; but it is so wholly misleading that, unless corrected by a clear statement, I cannot possibly associate my name again with the *Independent*.[4] There was a set of "findings" and of "opinions" of the *Court*; *not* of a *majority*. To this was appended a minority opinion, which qualified the finding of the Court to the extent, and only to the extent of that minority opinion. This is clear, not only from general practice, but from the fact that Dewey had accepted the duty, & taken the oath of member. He therefore could not escape the obligation of pronouncing an opinion upon *all* the points submitted to the Court.

The *Independent*, and the *Times*, by promoting this idea, are deliberately or ignorantly, doing their best to mislead and pervert public opinion already

---

3. Court of Inquiry in the Sampson-Schley controversy. *The Independent* (December 19, 1901), p. 3030, stated: "The rest of the report is the judgment of the majority of the Court concerning the tactics of Rear Admiral Schley during the nine days preceding June 1st, 1898, and at the battle of Santiago. . . . The surprise of the hour is Admiral Dewey's vigorous dissent from the findings of Admirals Benham and Ramsay, for a dissenting opinion is against the usual interpretation of the rules of the Navy, and is without precedent."

4. Mahan had published three articles in *The Independent* in 1900, viz., "The Transvaal and the Philippine Islands" (February 1), "The Philippines and the Future" (March 22), and "The Boer Republic and the Monroe Doctrine" (May 10). He did not publish therein again.

considerably excited on the question at issue, and therefore peculiarly liable to be deceived. From my conversation with lawyers, and observation of the Press, I assume the point is as clear as it is certain. Unless, therefore, the *Independent* sees fit to correct its misstatement in this matter, it will not be possible for me to write for it in this or any other matter.

To George F. W. Holls

160 West 86th Street, New York, December 23, 1901 [HUL]

Sir: Reply to your letter of the 19th has been unavoidably delayed.

In mine of the 10th, I did not revive the issues of last Spring. In so assuming, as you seem to do, you are mistaken, and, I cannot but think, willingly mistaken.

The single issue now presented is the statement that I now have proof, which last spring I had not, to me satisfactory, that a passage in the Proceedings of the Conference, to which you then referred me as evidence of your contention, was not in the minutes of the Secretary to the Comité d'Examen. On the contrary, that it was interpolated by your request, at a period much subsequent to the adjournment of the Conference, and therefore subsequent to my intervention of July 22. I said, "when the printing was already far advanced." I must add that my information is clear that this interpolation was made, not in the first proofs, as I understand yours of the 19th to say, but in the last proofs; so late, indeed, that it was doubted whether room could be made for it.

This statement you do not deny, but decline to discuss on the ground of your confidential relations to the Comité d'Examen; and perhaps others. I greatly doubt if such confidential relations exist as towards the United States Delegates, whom you were there allowed to represent, though you were not one of them; but even granting this, the interpolation, as stated, is long after the dissolution of both Comité and Conference, and so not covered by such confidential relations towards them.

You decline discussion. This is wholly unnecessary. The statement is clear. In its present state it admits of denial or disproof, for which I afford you opportunity; but prior to one or the other, there is no place for discussion. To refuse either may be discreet; of that you are your own judge.

A copy of this letter, and of mine of December 10, will be sent to my colleagues in the late Delegation.

To James Ford Rhodes

160 West 86th Street, New York, December 24, 1901 [MHS]

My dear Mr. Rhodes: With reference to a possible change in the place of meeting,[1] at which you hint for next year,—as such movements are usually preceded by certain pourparlers among those interested, I think it best to say betimes that if Nashville, or any similarly distant city, be the proposed rendezvous, I have the strongest personal objection to any such departure from the traditional routine, which brings the Assn. to an Eastern city for 1902. As President, I must be present from first to last. I have no choice as to whether I attend or not. Of course, if routine had gone against me, I would have accepted what are to me the distasteful inconveniences of a long railway journey in midwinter, & additional expense both of money and of time. But as routine has favored me, I shall not cheerfully accept a transfer to Nashville, or other equally remote western city, in the year of my presidency. I can see no reason why Nashville should not wait another year.

Of course, this may not be the drift of your letter. I may add it seemed to me the great preponderance of voice was in favor of Philadelphia in the Council.

To Leopold J. Maxse

University Club, New York, December 26, 1901 [LC]

My dear Sir: As I write here to day, by accident, it may be well to say that my address, as you already have it, is permanent; as far as permanency holds of things here below.

You should be under bonds as a disturber of the peace—my peace—by advancing such propositions as in your letter of the 6th. With the exception of the disposition of your navy, the subjects you suggest have all a certain attraction for me. Incidentally, I have expressed opinions on most of them in a very general way, especially in my *Problem of Asia*; and I suppose I might enlarge my obiter dicta in the various cases into an article, more detailed, precise, and guarded, as becomes a treatment that is special and direct, instead of fugitive mention.

But, at the same time, I have also in hand a piece of work in the shape of

1. The annual meeting of the American Historical Association.

a text book,[1] the probable paying value of which has been strongly urged upon me; and you can understand that, being well along in years, I look longingly to what may, if realized, simplify somewhat my problems of life. Between the two, while much inclined to do what you ask, I cannot yet bring myself to *promise*, but I shall turn the matter over carefully, hoping for the inspiration that overcomes obstacles.

An idea has occurred to me which I will submit to you. Your terms are satisfactory to me, in being, as I believe, extremely good by your English standards; such, at least, has been my experience. I am not asking for a rise, but I have in view, for your consideration, the possibility of a simultaneous publication here in a magazine as yet little known—*The International Monthly*[2]—which from the titles of its articles seems to aim at solider work than our great illustrated monthlies for the most part favor. I have written quite a little for all these latter, and they pay very high. My precise status with them, now, I dont know; but in fact I have rather defaulted toward them than they toward me—having refused or neglected work proposed to me. If such an arrangement with the *International* were feasible—I see cases of it in light literature—it would much increase my compensation, without, I fancy, injuring you or it. I have never broached this to the other party, who has approached me several times for an article; but I have today written proposing to him a paper on "The Military Rule of Obedience." Will you consider the question. I, from my point of view, do not perhaps possess the imagination to divine yours; but you can readily understand that when I have frequently had £100 for an article, the question naturally arises whether to do work I like for less, or work I dont much fancy for more. The question of time also enters, for the more I have to bestow on a special subject the less I have for my main interest.

There is a subject which my recent reading and thought has powerfully recommended to me. I am at a loss for a title, but the general idea is: What are the substantial reasons, the unifying motive, to keep alive, foster, and strengthen Imperial federation? What the common interest around which sentiment can clasp?[3] What to correspond to "The Union," the almost idolatrous veneration for which, based equally upon interest and sentiment, is one of the reminiscences of my youth which thrills me even now, though long security renders feeling more tame.

---

1. A children's history of the United States, never written; or a textbook on naval history for high-school students, never written.
2. "The Military Rule of Obedience," *National Review* (March 1902) was published simultaneously in *International Monthly* and was reprinted in *Retrospect and Prospect*. *International Monthly*, edited by Frederick A. Richardson, later became *International Quarterly*.
3. This idea took form in the article "Motives to Imperial Federation," *National Review* (May 1902). It was reprinted in *Retrospect and Prospect*.

To Hamilton Holt

160 West 86th Street, New York, December 27, 1901 [NDL]

Dear Mr. Holt: I am on the point of leaving home for three days, & have not an *Independent* of Dec. 19 to refer to. I think, if you will refer to my letter,[1] that I did not speak of your editorial comment, but of your statement of facts, in which, by speaking of the opinion of the *majority* & *minority* of the Court, you left uninstructed readers to infer that Adml. Dewey, with his great *popular* weight, was opposed to undistinguished colleagues. You obscured, if not suppressed, the fact that Dewey agreed with his colleagues, except where he specifically differed, and therefore on the most important points. This, if true, is misstatement, not difference of opinion; and upon this, not upon editorial comment, I based my letter. When I return, I will verify my impression. Meantime, I invite your own rereading of my letter as to the exception took, and suggest you see whether the *Independent* of the 19th has done as I said above. If it has, it owes correction to itself, and to the public. If unwilling to correct frankly, can you wonder at my attitude; considering as I do that I know the facts of the case.

To William Crozier

160 West 86th Street, New York, December 31, 1901 [LC]

My dear Crozier: That the sentence immediately preceding that bracketed *might* involve, by implication, something of a squint toward the Monroe Doctrine, to which the bracketed words explicitly point, is true. That it does not *necessarily* involve any such implication is, however, certified by the fact that the strongest opponents of Art.27 in the Full Third Committee (for they had no representative in the Comité d'Examen) were the Balkan States and Turkey. It may be assumed without stretch of imagination that these were but faintly interested in the Monroe Doctrine.

It would need therefore some collateral proof to show that Holls, in the words admitted to be his, (the first sentence), did anything more than reflect the doubts and hesitations of states other than the U.S. We *know* that scarce any state, but France, liked 27. If, however, he did then think of the Monroe Doctrine, of which the bracketed interpolation is a summary, why

---

1. *See* Mahan to Holt, December 22, 1901.

did he not say so clearly? and if he did say so clearly, how did it escape the Secretaries? But, granting that it might escape them, possibly, even if distinctly enunciated—unlikely though that is,—how account for the fact that he never again referred to so important a reservation? or, again, how account for his attitude of unreserved praise to Art. 27, in the subsequent debate in the Full Committee? or again, how account for his words and actions in our Delegation, when I brought the matter up, all which probably remains in your memory?

I do not say that no account *can* be given; but I think it safe to say no satisfactory account *has* been given of the insertion of the words bracketed. You yourself were witness of the wrath and unwillingness of the French deputies to admit any qualification of Art.27; and Holls's letters to me of last spring admitted explicitly the reluctance asserted by Dr. Staal, to allow any qualifying reservation attached to signatures. In other words, granting that Holls ever thought of the Monroe Doctrine, in connection with 27, matters had gone so far, through his maladroitness, that only a late recognition of conditions and a desperate kick, on our part, saved the situation. Yet, if he had made the reservation, the concession of our demand, the awkwardness of which, coming so late, we all felt, would have been a matter of right; not of grace, as it actually appeared.

I want you to recognize that what I am after is not my own credit, but the demonstration of Holls's character. He is ambitious, pushing, and intriguing. I purpose to get at the bottom facts, if I can, of what so far appears to me a consistent piece of dirty manoeuvring. If Holls's competency as a negotiator, and integrity as a historian, emerge uninjured, so much the better; but if things be as they now appear, I dont intend that he shall, with my acquiescence, impose himself upon men in high office as competent and cleanhanded. That you believe me substantially disinterested, I am sure; but were there otherwise any doubt, my failing to claim credit, until Holls put forth his grab, would prove it.

This far from also, w
convey the idea. You
senior officers

    may without to
you, confidentially, the
qualities have influen